# Dedication

*To Phil, Noah, and Sam for loving and supporting me through multiple editions of this book.*

— K.M.

*To my wife, Carley, for supporting me in all that I do and reminding me of what's important along the way.*

— B.G.

*To the record player on my desk. Thanks for keeping me company through all this. I promise I'll get you a new needle soon.*

— B.P.

*To my dad, David, for teaching me the value of hard work. To my mom, Lisa, for pushing me to always do the right thing.*

— C.S.

# Android Programming
## THE BIG NERD RANCH GUIDE

Kristin Marsicano, Brian Gardner, Bill Phillips & Chris Stewart

**Big Nerd Ranch**

# Android Programming: The Big Nerd Ranch Guide

by Kristin Marsicano, Brian Gardner, Bill Phillips and Chris Stewart

Big Nerd Ranch, LLC.
200 Arizona Ave NE
Atlanta, GA 30307
(770) 817-6373
http://www.bignerdranch.com/
book-comments@bignerdranch.com

The 10-gallon hat logo is a trademark of Big Nerd Ranch, Inc.

Exclusive worldwide distribution of the English edition of this book by

Pearson Technology Group
800 East 96th Street
Indianapolis, IN 46240 USA
http://www.informit.com

ISBN-10 0135245125
ISBN-13 978-0135245125

Fourth edition, second printing, January 2020

# Acknowledgments

With this being our fourth edition, we find ourselves used to saying this. It always needs to be said, though: Books are not created by authors alone. They are shepherded into existence by a community of collaborators, risk-takers, and other supporters, without whom the burden of comprehending and writing all this material would be overwhelming.

- Brian Hardy, who, along with Bill Phillips, had the gusto to bring the very first edition of this book into the world.

- Eric Maxwell, for single-handedly writing the For the More Curious section on dependency injection, for improving our coverage of notification channels, and for addressing numerous editor remarks that touched so many pages of this book.

- David Greenhalgh and Josh Skeen, for lending their expertise as we "Kotlinified" this book and learned how to be Android developers in a Kotlin world.

- Jeremy Sherman for being a surprise Android expert just when we needed him most. Thank you, Jeremy, for your detailed, thoughtful reviews and for letting us use some of your words directly in Loopers, Handlers, and HandlerThread.

- Bryan Lindsey, our resident **LiveData** expert (and expert in so many other Android-related things). Thanks for the special attention you gave to BeatBox and PhotoGallery.

- Andrew Bailey, the most intelligent rubber duck we have ever met. Thank you for offering a listening ear many times over and for helping us talk through some tough conceptual decisions. Also, thank you for adding Oreo updates to our discussion on broadcast intents.

- Jamie Lee, our intern-turned-developer-writer-editor extraordinaire. Thank you for editing slides, reviewing solutions, and addressing remarks. Your attention to detail is unparalleled and greatly appreciated.

- Andrew Marshall, for proactively pushing improvements to the book, for leading one of our classes in a pinch, and for jumping in and finishing up slide edits during crunch time.

- Zack Simon, our fantastically talented and soft-spoken Big Nerd Ranch designer, who beautified the nifty cheat sheet attached to this book. If you enjoy that sheet, you should find Zack and tell him so yourself. But we will also thank Zack right here: Thanks, Zack!

- Jeremy Kliphouse and Lixin Wang for helping us get a second printing out the door with updated screenshots. And Brett McCormick for sneaking in a few tweaks as well.

- Our editor, Elizabeth Holaday. The famous beat author William S. Burroughs sometimes wrote by cutting up his work into little pieces, throwing them in the air, and publishing the rearrangement. Without a strong editor like Liz, our confusion and simpleminded excitement may have caused us to resort to such techniques. We are thankful that she was there to impose focus, precision, and clarity on our drafts.

- Ellie Volckhausen, who designed our cover.

# Acknowledgments

- Anna Bentley, our copyeditor and proofreader. Thank you for sanding away the remaining rough edges of this book.

- Chris Loper at IntelligentEnglish.com, who designed and produced the print and eBook versions of the book. His DocBook toolchain made life much easier, too.

- Thanks to Aaron Hillegass, Stacy Henry, and Emily Herman. As a practical matter, it is not possible to do this work without Big Nerd Ranch, the company Aaron founded and that Stacy (CEO) and Emily (COO) now fearlessly lead. Thank you.

Finally, thanks to our students. There is a feedback loop between us and our students: We teach them out of these materials, and they respond to it. Without that loop, this book could never have existed, nor could it be maintained. If Big Nerd Ranch books are special (and we hope they are), it is that feedback loop that makes them so. Thank you.

# Table of Contents

Learning Android ........................................................................... xvii
   Prerequisites ............................................................................ xvii
   What's New in the Fourth Edition? ...................................... xviii
      Kotlin vs Java ....................................................... xviii
   How to Use This Book ........................................................ xix
   How This Book Is Organized ............................................. xix
      Challenges ............................................................. xx
      Are you more curious? ........................................... xx
   Typographical Conventions ................................................ xx
   Android Versions ................................................................ xx
The Necessary Tools ................................................................... xxi
   Downloading and Installing Android Studio ....................... xxi
   Downloading Earlier SDK Versions .................................... xxi
   A Hardware Device ............................................................ xxii
1. Your First Android Application .............................................. 1
   App Basics ......................................................................... 2
   Creating an Android Project .............................................. 3
   Navigating in Android Studio ............................................ 8
   Laying Out the UI ............................................................. 10
      The view hierarchy ............................................... 15
      Widget attributes .................................................. 16
      Creating string resources ...................................... 17
      Previewing the layout ........................................... 18
   From Layout XML to View Objects ................................... 20
      Resources and resource IDs .................................. 21
   Wiring Up Widgets ............................................................ 25
      Getting references to widgets ................................ 25
      Setting listeners ................................................... 26
   Making Toasts ................................................................... 27
   Running on the Emulator .................................................. 29
   For the More Curious: The Android Build Process ............ 33
      Android build tools .............................................. 34
   Challenges ........................................................................ 35
   Challenge: Customizing the Toast ..................................... 35
2. Android and Model-View-Controller ...................................... 37
   Creating a New Class ........................................................ 38
   Model-View-Controller and Android ................................. 40
      Deciding to use MVC ........................................... 41
   Updating the View Layer ................................................... 42
   Updating the Controller Layer .......................................... 45
   Adding an Icon ................................................................. 49
      Adding resources to a project ............................... 50
      Referencing resources in XML ............................. 52
   Screen Pixel Densities ....................................................... 52
   Running on a Device ......................................................... 54

Challenge: Add a Listener to the TextView ................................................................. 56
Challenge: Add a Previous Button ............................................................................ 56
Challenge: From Button to ImageButton ................................................................... 57
3. The Activity Lifecycle ............................................................................................ 59
Rotating GeoQuiz ..................................................................................................... 59
Activity States and Lifecycle Callbacks ................................................................... 61
Logging the Activity Lifecycle .................................................................................. 63
Making log messages ............................................................................................ 63
Using Logcat ......................................................................................................... 65
Exploring How the Activity Lifecycle Responds to User Actions ............................... 66
Temporarily leaving an activity ............................................................................... 66
Finishing an activity .............................................................................................. 70
Rotating an activity ............................................................................................... 70
Device Configuration Changes and the Activity Lifecycle ......................................... 71
Creating a landscape layout .................................................................................. 71
For the More Curious: UI Updates and Multi-Window Mode .................................... 75
For the More Curious: Log Levels ........................................................................... 76
Challenge: Preventing Repeat Answers ................................................................... 76
Challenge: Graded Quiz ......................................................................................... 76
4. Persisting UI State .................................................................................................. 77
Including the ViewModel Dependency ...................................................................... 78
Adding a ViewModel ................................................................................................ 79
ViewModel lifecycle and ViewModelProvider ......................................................... 81
Add data to your ViewModel .................................................................................. 84
Saving Data Across Process Death .......................................................................... 88
Overriding onSaveInstanceState(Bundle) ............................................................... 89
Saved instance state and activity records ............................................................... 92
ViewModel vs Saved Instance State ......................................................................... 93
For the More Curious: Jetpack, AndroidX, and Architecture Components ................. 95
For the More Curious: Avoiding a Half-Baked Solution ............................................ 96
5. Debugging Android Apps ......................................................................................... 97
Exceptions and Stack Traces .................................................................................... 99
Diagnosing misbehaviors ...................................................................................... 100
Logging stack traces ............................................................................................. 101
Setting breakpoints .............................................................................................. 102
Android-Specific Debugging .................................................................................... 107
Using Android Lint ............................................................................................... 107
Issues with the R class ......................................................................................... 111
Challenge: Exploring the Layout Inspector .............................................................. 112
Challenge: Exploring the Profiler ............................................................................ 112
6. Your Second Activity ............................................................................................... 113
Setting Up a Second Activity ................................................................................... 115
Creating a new activity ......................................................................................... 115
A new activity subclass ........................................................................................ 118
Declaring activities in the manifest ....................................................................... 119
Adding a cheat button to MainActivity .................................................................. 120
Starting an Activity ................................................................................................. 122
Communicating with intents .................................................................................. 122

Passing Data Between Activities ................................................................ 123
    Using intent extras .................................................................... 124
    Getting a result back from a child activity ............................... 127
How Android Sees Your Activities ...................................................... 131
Challenge: Closing Loopholes for Cheaters ...................................... 134
Challenge: Tracking Cheat Status by Question ................................ 134
7. Android SDK Versions and Compatibility ........................................ 135
Android SDK Versions .......................................................................... 135
Compatibility and Android Programming ......................................... 136
    A sane minimum ......................................................................... 136
    Minimum SDK version ............................................................... 138
    Target SDK version ..................................................................... 138
    Compile SDK version ................................................................. 138
    Adding code from later APIs safely ......................................... 139
    Jetpack libraries ......................................................................... 142
Using the Android Developer Documentation ................................. 143
Challenge: Reporting the Device's Android Version ....................... 145
Challenge: Limited Cheats .................................................................. 145
8. UI Fragments and the Fragment Manager ....................................... 147
The Need for UI Flexibility ................................................................ 148
Introducing Fragments ........................................................................ 149
Starting CriminalIntent ....................................................................... 150
    Creating a new project .............................................................. 153
Creating a Data Class ......................................................................... 155
Creating a UI Fragment ...................................................................... 156
    Defining CrimeFragment's layout ............................................ 156
    Creating the CrimeFragment class .......................................... 159
Hosting a UI Fragment ....................................................................... 166
    Defining a container view .......................................................... 166
    Adding a UI fragment to the FragmentManager .................... 168
Application Architecture with Fragments ......................................... 173
    Deciding whether to use fragments ......................................... 174
9. Displaying Lists with RecyclerView ................................................. 175
Adding a New Fragment and ViewModel ......................................... 177
    ViewModel lifecycle with fragments ....................................... 178
Adding a RecyclerView ....................................................................... 180
Creating an Item View Layout ........................................................... 182
Implementing a ViewHolder .............................................................. 183
Implementing an Adapter to Populate the RecyclerView .............. 185
    Setting the RecyclerView's adapter ......................................... 188
Recycling Views ................................................................................... 190
Cleaning Up Binding List Items ........................................................ 191
Responding to Presses ......................................................................... 192
For the More Curious: ListView and GridView ............................... 193
Challenge: RecyclerView ViewTypes ................................................ 193
10. Creating User Interfaces with Layouts and Widgets ...................... 195
Introducing ConstraintLayout ............................................................ 196
Introducing the Graphical Layout Editor ......................................... 197

Using ConstraintLayout ..................................................................... 201
    Making room ...................................................................... 202
    Adding widgets ................................................................... 204
    ConstraintLayout's inner workings ...................................... 208
    Editing properties .............................................................. 209
    Making list items dynamic .................................................. 214
More on Layout Attributes ............................................................... 215
    Styles, themes, and theme attributes ................................... 217
For the More Curious: Margins vs Padding ....................................... 218
For the More Curious: New Developments in ConstraintLayout ........... 219
Challenge: Formatting the Date ........................................................ 220
11. Databases and the Room Library .................................................. 221
Room Architecture Component Library .............................................. 222
Creating a Database ....................................................................... 223
    Defining entities ................................................................ 223
    Creating a database class ................................................... 224
Defining a Data Access Object ......................................................... 226
Accessing the Database Using the Repository Pattern ....................... 227
Testing Queries ............................................................................. 230
    Uploading test data ........................................................... 231
Application Threads ........................................................................ 234
    Background threads ........................................................... 235
Using LiveData .............................................................................. 236
    Observing LiveData ........................................................... 237
Challenge: Addressing the Schema Warning ...................................... 241
For the More Curious: Singletons .................................................... 242
12. Fragment Navigation ................................................................. 243
Single Activity: Fragment Boss ....................................................... 244
    Fragment callback interfaces .............................................. 244
    Replacing a fragment ........................................................ 247
Fragment Arguments ...................................................................... 249
    Attaching arguments to a fragment ..................................... 250
    Retrieving arguments ......................................................... 251
Using LiveData Transformations ...................................................... 252
Updating the Database .................................................................... 256
    Using an executor .............................................................. 257
    Tying database writes to the fragment lifecycle ..................... 258
For the More Curious: Why Use Fragment Arguments? ...................... 259
For the More Curious: Navigation Architecture Component Library ....... 260
Challenge: Efficient RecyclerView Reloading ..................................... 261
13. Dialogs ................................................................................... 263
Creating a DialogFragment .............................................................. 264
    Showing a DialogFragment ................................................. 266
Passing Data Between Two Fragments .............................................. 268
    Passing data to DatePickerFragment ................................... 269
    Returning data to CrimeFragment ....................................... 271
Challenge: More Dialogs ................................................................. 274
14. The App Bar ............................................................................ 275

AppCompat Default App Bar ......................................................... 276
Menus ........................................................................................ 277
    Defining a menu in XML ...................................................... 278
    Creating the menu ............................................................... 280
    Responding to menu selections ............................................. 283
Using the Android Asset Studio .................................................. 285
For the More Curious: App Bar vs Action Bar vs Toolbar ............. 288
For the More Curious: Accessing the AppCompat App Bar ............ 290
Challenge: An Empty View for the RecyclerView ........................ 290
15. Implicit Intents .......................................................................... 291
Adding Buttons .......................................................................... 292
Adding a Suspect to the Model Layer .......................................... 293
Using a Format String ................................................................ 294
Using Implicit Intents ................................................................ 296
    Parts of an implicit intent .................................................... 296
    Sending a crime report ........................................................ 298
    Asking Android for a contact ............................................... 302
    Checking for responding activities ....................................... 307
Challenge: Another Implicit Intent ............................................. 309
16. Taking Pictures with Intents ....................................................... 311
A Place for Your Photo .............................................................. 311
File Storage ............................................................................... 315
    Using FileProvider .............................................................. 316
    Designating a picture location ............................................. 317
Using a Camera Intent ................................................................ 318
    Firing the intent .................................................................. 319
Scaling and Displaying Bitmaps ................................................. 322
Declaring Features ..................................................................... 327
Challenge: Detail Display ........................................................... 328
Challenge: Efficient Thumbnail Load .......................................... 328
17. Localization ............................................................................... 329
Localizing Resources ................................................................. 330
    Default resources ................................................................ 333
    Checking string coverage using the Translations Editor .......... 334
    Targeting a region ............................................................... 335
Configuration Qualifiers ............................................................. 337
    Prioritizing alternative resources ......................................... 338
    Multiple qualifiers .............................................................. 340
    Finding the best-matching resources .................................... 341
Testing Alternative Resources ..................................................... 342
For the More Curious: More on Determining Device Size ............. 343
Challenge: Localizing Dates ....................................................... 343
18. Accessibility .............................................................................. 345
TalkBack ................................................................................... 346
    Explore by Touch ............................................................... 350
    Linear navigation by swiping ............................................... 351
Making Non-Text Elements Readable by TalkBack ...................... 353
    Adding content descriptions ................................................. 353

Making a widget focusable ......................................................................... 356
Creating a Comparable Experience ........................................................... 357
For the More Curious: Using Accessibility Scanner ................................. 359
Challenge: Improving the List .................................................................. 364
Challenge: Providing Enough Context for Data Entry ............................. 364
Challenge: Announcing Events ................................................................. 365
19. Data Binding and MVVM ......................................................................... 367
Different Architectures: Why Bother? ...................................................... 368
MVVM View Models vs Jetpack ViewModels .......................................... 368
Creating BeatBox ..................................................................................... 369
Implementing Simple Data Binding .......................................................... 370
Importing Assets ....................................................................................... 373
Accessing Assets ...................................................................................... 376
Wiring Up Assets for Use ........................................................................ 377
Binding to Data ........................................................................................ 381
Creating a view model ........................................................................ 383
Binding to a view model ..................................................................... 384
Observable data .................................................................................. 386
For the More Curious: More About Data Binding .................................... 389
Lambda expressions ............................................................................ 389
Syntactic sugar .................................................................................... 389
BindingAdapters .................................................................................. 390
For the More Curious: LiveData and Data Binding .................................. 391
20. Unit Testing and Audio Playback ............................................................. 393
Creating a SoundPool .............................................................................. 393
Accessing Assets ...................................................................................... 394
Loading Sounds ........................................................................................ 394
Playing Sounds ......................................................................................... 396
Test Dependencies .................................................................................... 397
Creating a Test Class ............................................................................... 398
Setting Up Your Test ............................................................................... 400
Setting up the test subject .................................................................. 400
Writing Tests ............................................................................................ 401
Testing object interactions .................................................................. 402
Data Binding Callbacks ............................................................................ 406
Unloading Sounds ..................................................................................... 407
For the More Curious: Integration Testing .............................................. 408
For the More Curious: Mocks and Testing .............................................. 409
Challenge: Playback Speed Control ......................................................... 410
Challenge: Play Sound Across Rotation .................................................. 410
21. Styles and Themes ................................................................................... 411
Color Resources ....................................................................................... 412
Styles ........................................................................................................ 412
Style inheritance ................................................................................. 414
Themes ...................................................................................................... 416
Modifying the theme ........................................................................... 416
Adding Theme Colors ............................................................................... 418
Overriding Theme Attributes ................................................................... 419

Theme spelunking .................................................................................. 419
Modifying Button Attributes ................................................................. 423
For the More Curious: More on Style Inheritance ................................ 427
For the More Curious: Accessing Theme Attributes .............................. 428
22. XML Drawables .......................................................................................... 429
Making Uniform Buttons ..................................................................... 430
Shape Drawables ................................................................................. 431
State List Drawables ........................................................................... 433
Layer List Drawables .......................................................................... 435
For the More Curious: Why Bother with XML Drawables? ................... 437
For the More Curious: Mipmap Images ............................................... 438
For the More Curious: 9-Patch Images ................................................ 439
Challenge: Button Themes ................................................................... 446
23. More About Intents and Tasks .................................................................. 447
Setting Up NerdLauncher ................................................................... 448
Resolving an Implicit Intent ............................................................... 449
Creating Explicit Intents at Runtime .................................................. 454
Tasks and the Back Stack ................................................................... 456
Switching between tasks .................................................................. 457
Starting a new task ......................................................................... 458
Using NerdLauncher as a Home Screen ............................................. 462
For the More Curious: Processes vs Tasks ......................................... 464
For the More Curious: Concurrent Documents ................................... 467
Challenge: Icons .................................................................................. 468
24. HTTP and Background Tasks .................................................................... 469
Creating PhotoGallery ........................................................................ 471
Networking Basics with Retrofit ......................................................... 474
Defining an API interface ................................................................ 475
Building the Retrofit object and creating an API instance ............... 476
Executing a web request ................................................................. 478
Asking permission to network ......................................................... 480
Moving toward the repository pattern ............................................. 481
Fetching JSON from Flickr .................................................................. 485
Deserializing JSON text into model objects ..................................... 488
Networking Across Configuration Changes .......................................... 493
Displaying Results in RecyclerView ..................................................... 496
For the More Curious: Alternate Parsers and Data Formats ............... 498
For the More Curious: Canceling Requests .......................................... 499
For the More Curious: Managing Dependencies ................................... 500
Challenge: Adding a Custom Gson Deserializer ................................... 502
Challenge: Paging ................................................................................ 503
Challenge: Dynamically Adjusting the Number of Columns ................ 503
25. Loopers, Handlers, and HandlerThread .................................................... 505
Preparing RecyclerView to Display Images .......................................... 505
Preparing to Download Bytes from a URL ........................................... 508
Downloading Lots of Small Things ...................................................... 509
Assembling a Background Thread ........................................................ 510
Making your thread lifecycle aware .................................................. 511

Starting and stopping a HandlerThread ............................................................ 514
Messages and Message Handlers .................................................................... 516
Message anatomy ..................................................................................... 518
Handler anatomy ...................................................................................... 518
Using handlers ......................................................................................... 519
Passing handlers ...................................................................................... 523
Listening to the View Lifecycle ...................................................................... 527
Retained Fragments ....................................................................................... 531
Rotation and retained fragments ................................................................ 531
Whether to retain .................................................................................... 534
For the More Curious: Solving the Image Downloading Problem ....................... 535
For the More Curious: StrictMode .................................................................. 536
Challenge: Observing View LifecycleOwner LiveData ..................................... 536
Challenge: Improving ThumbnailDownloader's Lifecycle Awareness ............... 537
Challenge: Preloading and Caching ............................................................... 537
26. SearchView and SharedPreferences ..................................................................... 539
Searching Flickr ........................................................................................... 540
Using SearchView ......................................................................................... 544
Responding to SearchView user interactions ................................................ 546
Simple Persistence with SharedPreferences ..................................................... 549
Polishing Your App ....................................................................................... 552
Editing SharedPreferences with Android KTX ................................................... 553
Challenge: Polishing Your App Some More ..................................................... 554
27. WorkManager ................................................................................................. 555
Creating a Worker ......................................................................................... 555
Scheduling Work .......................................................................................... 557
Checking for New Photos ............................................................................... 560
Notifying the User ........................................................................................ 563
Providing User Control over Polling ................................................................ 568
28. Broadcast Intents ............................................................................................ 573
Regular Intents vs Broadcast Intents ............................................................... 573
Filtering Foreground Notifications .................................................................. 574
Sending broadcast intents ......................................................................... 575
Creating and registering a standalone receiver ............................................ 575
Limiting broadcasts to your app using private permissions ........................... 577
Creating and registering a dynamic receiver ............................................... 580
Passing and receiving data with ordered broadcasts .................................... 582
Receivers and Long-Running Tasks ................................................................ 586
For the More Curious: Local Events ............................................................... 587
Using EventBus ....................................................................................... 587
Using RxJava .......................................................................................... 588
For the More Curious: Limitations on Broadcast Receivers ............................. 589
For the More Curious: Detecting the Visibility of Your Fragment ..................... 590
29. Browsing the Web and WebView ....................................................................... 591
One Last Bit of Flickr Data ............................................................................ 592
The Easy Way: Implicit Intents ...................................................................... 594
The Harder Way: WebView ........................................................................... 596
Using WebChromeClient to spruce things up .............................................. 601

Proper Rotation with WebView ................................................................... 604
    Dangers of handling configuration changes ....................................... 604
WebView vs a Custom UI ......................................................................... 605
For the More Curious: Injecting JavaScript Objects ................................ 606
For the More Curious: WebView Updates ................................................. 607
For the More Curious: Chrome Custom Tabs (Another Easy Way) ................. 608
Challenge: Using the Back Button for Browser History ............................. 610
30. Custom Views and Touch Events .......................................................... 611
Setting Up the DragAndDraw Project ....................................................... 612
Creating a Custom View .......................................................................... 612
    Creating BoxDrawingView .................................................................. 613
Handling Touch Events ............................................................................ 614
    Tracking across motion events ........................................................... 616
Rendering Inside onDraw(Canvas) ........................................................... 618
For the More Curious: GestureDetector ................................................... 620
Challenge: Saving State .......................................................................... 620
Challenge: Rotating Boxes ...................................................................... 621
Challenge: Accessibility Support .............................................................. 621
31. Property Animation ............................................................................... 623
Building the Scene .................................................................................. 623
Simple Property Animation ...................................................................... 626
    View transformation properties .......................................................... 629
    Using different interpolators ............................................................... 631
    Color evaluation ................................................................................. 632
Playing Animators Together .................................................................... 634
For the More Curious: Other Animation APIs ........................................... 636
    Legacy animation tools ...................................................................... 636
    Transitions ......................................................................................... 636
Challenges .............................................................................................. 636
32. Afterword ............................................................................................. 637
The Final Challenge ................................................................................ 637
Shameless Plugs ..................................................................................... 637
Thank You ............................................................................................... 638
Index ........................................................................................................ 639

# Learning Android

As a beginning Android programmer, you face a steep learning curve. Learning Android is like moving to a foreign city. Even if you speak the language, it will not feel like home at first. Everyone around you seems to understand things that you are missing. Things you already knew turn out to be dead wrong in this new context.

Android has a culture. That culture speaks Kotlin or Java (or a bit of both), but knowing Kotlin or Java is not enough. Getting your head around Android requires learning many new ideas and techniques. It helps to have a guide through unfamiliar territory.

That's where we come in. At Big Nerd Ranch, we believe that to be an Android programmer, you must:

- *write* Android applications

- *understand* what you are writing

This guide will help you do both. We have trained thousands of professional Android programmers using it. We will lead you through writing several Android applications, introducing concepts and techniques as needed. When there are rough spots, or when some things are tricky or obscure, you will face them head on, and we will do our best to explain why things are the way they are.

This approach allows you to put what you have learned into practice in a working app right away rather than learning a lot of theory and then having to figure out how to apply it all later. You will come away with the experience and understanding you need to get going as an Android developer.

## Prerequisites

To use this book, you need to be familiar with Kotlin, including classes and objects, interfaces, listeners, packages, inner classes, object expressions, and generic classes.

If these concepts do not ring a bell, you will be in the weeds by page 2. Start instead with an introductory Kotlin book and return to this book afterward. There are many excellent introductory books available, so you can choose one based on your programming experience and learning style. May we recommend *Kotlin Programming: The Big Nerd Ranch Guide*?

If you are comfortable with object-oriented programming concepts, but your Kotlin is a little shaky, you will probably be OK. We will provide some brief explanations about Kotlin specifics throughout the book. But keep a Kotlin reference handy in case you need more support as you go through the book.

# What's New in the Fourth Edition?

This edition involved a major overhaul – every chapter was altered. The biggest change in this version is that the apps are written using Kotlin instead of Java. Because of this, our unofficial working name for this edition has been "Android 4K."

Another sweeping change is the inclusion of Android Jetpack component libraries. We now use Jetpack (sometimes called AndroidX) libraries in place of the Support Library. Additionally, we incorporated new Jetpack APIs when applicable. For example, we use **ViewModel** to persist UI state across rotation. We use Room and **LiveData** to implement a database and to query data from it. And we use WorkManager to schedule background work. These are just a few examples; you will find Jetpack components woven into all the projects in this book.

To focus on how modern Android applications are developed, this book now uses third-party libraries instead of just the APIs within the framework or within Jetpack. One example is dropping **HttpURLConnection** and other lower-level networking APIs in favor of using Retrofit and the suite of libraries it depends on. This is a big departure from our previous books, and we believe that this will better prepare you to dive into professional application development after reading our book. The libraries we chose to use are libraries we use in our daily lives as Android developers for our clients.

# Kotlin vs Java

Official support for Kotlin for Android development was announced at Google I/O in 2017. Before that, there was an underground movement of Android developers using Kotlin even though it was not officially supported. Since 2017, Kotlin has become widely adopted, and it is most developer's preferred language for Android development. At Big Nerd Ranch, we use Kotlin for all our app development projects – even legacy projects that are mostly Java.

The tide has continued to turn toward Kotlin in a very big way. The Android framework team has started adding @nullable annotations to legacy platform code. They have also released more and more Kotlin extensions for Android. And, as of this writing, Google is in the process of adding Kotlin examples and support to the official Android documentation.

The Android framework was originally written in Java. This means most of the Android classes you interact with are Java. Luckily, Kotlin is interoperable with Java, so you should not run into any issues.

We have chosen to display API listings in Kotlin, even if they are implemented behind the scenes in Java. You can see the Java API listings by browsing for the class you are interested in at developer.android.com/reference.

Whether you prefer Kotlin or Java, this book teaches you how to write Android apps. The knowledge and experience you gain in developing apps for the Android platform will translate to either language.

# How to Use This Book

This book is not a reference book. Its goal is to get you over the initial hump to where you can get the most out of the reference and recipe books available. It is based on our five-day class at Big Nerd Ranch. As such, it is meant to be worked through from the beginning. Chapters build on each other, and skipping around is unproductive.

In our classes, students work through these materials, but they also benefit from the right environment – a dedicated classroom, good food and comfortable board, a group of motivated peers, and an instructor to answer questions.

As a reader, you want your environment to be similar. That means getting a good night's rest and finding a quiet place to work. These things can help, too:

- Start a reading group with your friends or coworkers.

- Arrange to have blocks of focused time to work on chapters.

- Participate in the forum for this book at `forums.bignerdranch.com`.

- Find someone who knows Android to help you out.

# How This Book Is Organized

As you work through this book, you will write seven Android apps. A couple are very simple and take only a chapter to create. Others are more complex. The longest app spans 11 chapters. All are designed to teach you important concepts and techniques and give you direct experience using them.

| | |
|---|---|
| *GeoQuiz* | In your first app, you will explore the fundamentals of Android projects, activities, layouts, and explicit intents. You will also learn how to handle configuration changes seamlessly. |
| *CriminalIntent* | The largest app in the book, CriminalIntent lets you keep a record of your colleagues' lapses around the office. You will learn to use fragments, list-backed interfaces, databases, menus, the camera, implicit intents, and more. |
| *BeatBox* | Intimidate your foes with this app while you learn about sound playback, MVVM architecture, data binding, testing, themes, and drawables. |
| *NerdLauncher* | Building this custom launcher will give you insight into the intent system, processes, and tasks. |
| *PhotoGallery* | A Flickr client that downloads and displays photos from Flickr's public feed, this app will take you through scheduling background work, multi-threading, accessing web services, and more. |
| *DragAndDraw* | In this simple drawing app, you will learn about handling touch events and creating custom views. |
| *Sunset* | In this toy app, you will create a beautiful representation of a sunset over open water while learning about animations. |

# Challenges

Most chapters have a section at the end with exercises for you to work through. This is your opportunity to use what you have learned, explore the documentation, and do some problem-solving on your own.

We strongly recommend that you do the challenges. Going off the beaten path and finding your way will solidify your learning and give you confidence with your own projects. If you get lost, you can always visit `forums.bignerdranch.com` for some assistance.

# Are you more curious?

Many chapters also have a section at the end labeled "For the More Curious." These sections offer deeper explanations or additional information about topics presented in the chapter. The information in these sections is not absolutely essential, but we hope you will find it interesting and useful.

# Typographical Conventions

To make this book easier to read, certain items appear in certain fonts. Variables, constants, and types appear in a fixed-width font. Class names, interface names, and function names appear in a bold fixed-width font.

All code and XML listings are in a fixed-width font. Code or XML that you need to type in is always bold. Code or XML that should be deleted is struck through. For example, in the following function implementation, you are deleting the call to `Toast.makeText(…).show()` and adding the call to `checkAnswer(true)`.

```
trueButton.setOnClickListener { view: View ->
    Toast.makeText(
        this,
        R.string.correct_toast,
        Toast.LENGTH_SHORT
    )
        .show()
    checkAnswer(true)
}
```

# Android Versions

This book teaches Android development for the versions of Android in wide use at the time of writing. For this edition, that is Android 5.0 (Lollipop, API level 21) - Android 9.0 (Pie, API level 28). While there is still limited use of older versions of Android, we find that for most developers the amount of effort required to support those versions is not worth the reward. If you would like information on supporting versions of Android earlier than 5.0, see earlier editions of this book. The third edition targeted Android 4.4 and up, the second edition targeted Android 4.1 and up, and the first edition targeted Android 2.3 and up.

As new versions of Android and Android Studio are released, the techniques you learn in this book will continue to work, thanks to Android's backward compatibility support (discussed in Chapter 7). We will keep track of changes at `forums.bignerdranch.com` and offer notes on using this book with the latest versions. We may also make minor changes to this book in subsequent printings to account for any changes, such as updating screenshots or button names.

# The Necessary Tools

To get started with this book, you will need Android Studio. Android Studio is an integrated development environment used for Android development that is based on the popular IntelliJ IDEA.

An install of Android Studio includes:

*Android SDK*

> the latest version of the Android SDK

*Android SDK tools and platform tools*

> tools for debugging and testing your apps

*A system image for the Android emulator*

> a tool for creating and testing your apps on different virtual devices

As of this writing, Android Studio is under active development and is frequently updated. Be aware that you may find differences between your version of Android Studio and what you see in this book. Visit forums.bignerdranch.com for help with these differences.

## Downloading and Installing Android Studio

Android Studio is available from Android's developer site at developer.android.com/studio.

If you do not already have it installed, you will also need to install the Java Development Kit (JDK 8), which you can download from www.oracle.com.

If you are having problems, return to developer.android.com/studio for more information.

## Downloading Earlier SDK Versions

Android Studio provides the SDK and the emulator system image from the latest platform. However, you may want to test your apps on earlier versions of Android.

You can get components for each platform using the Android SDK Manager. In Android Studio, select Tools → SDK Manager. (You will only see the Tools menu if you have a project open. If you have not created a project yet, you can instead access the SDK Manager from the Android Welcome dialog. Select Configure → SDK Manager.)

The SDK Manager is shown in Figure 1.

Figure 1  Android SDK Manager

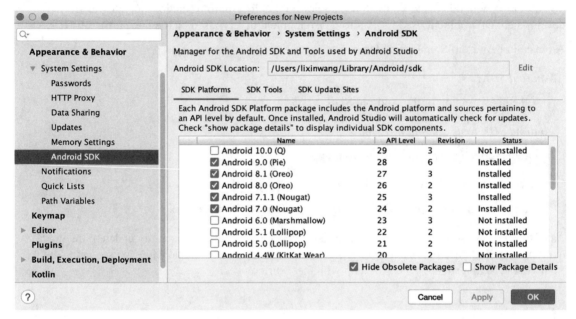

Select and install each version of Android that you want to test with. Note that downloading these components may take a while.

The Android SDK Manager is also how you can get Android's latest releases, like a new platform or an update of the tools.

# A Hardware Device

The emulator is useful for testing apps. However, it is no substitute for an actual Android device when measuring performance. If you have a hardware device, we recommend using it at times when working through this book.

# 1

# Your First Android Application

This first chapter is full of new concepts and moving parts required to build an Android application. It is OK if you do not understand everything by the end of this chapter. You will be revisiting these ideas in greater detail as you proceed through the book.

The application you are going to create is called GeoQuiz. GeoQuiz tests the user's knowledge of geography. The user presses TRUE or FALSE to answer the question onscreen, and GeoQuiz provides instant feedback.

Figure 1.1 shows the result of a user pressing the TRUE button.

Figure 1.1  Do you come from a land down under?

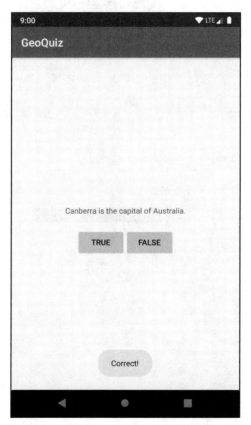

# App Basics

Your GeoQuiz application will consist of an *activity* and a *layout*:

- An activity is an instance of **Activity**, a class in the Android SDK. An activity is responsible for managing user interaction with a screen of information.

  You write subclasses of **Activity** to implement the functionality that your app requires. A simple application may need only one subclass; a complex application can have many.

  GeoQuiz is a simple app and will start off with a single **Activity** subclass named **MainActivity**. **MainActivity** will manage the user interface, or UI, shown in Figure 1.1.

- A layout defines a set of UI objects and the objects' positions on the screen. A layout is made up of definitions written in XML. Each definition is used to create an object that appears onscreen, like a button or some text.

  GeoQuiz will include a layout file named activity_main.xml. The XML in this file will define the UI shown in Figure 1.1.

The relationship between **MainActivity** and activity_main.xml is diagrammed in Figure 1.2.

Figure 1.2 **MainActivity** manages what activity_main.xml defines

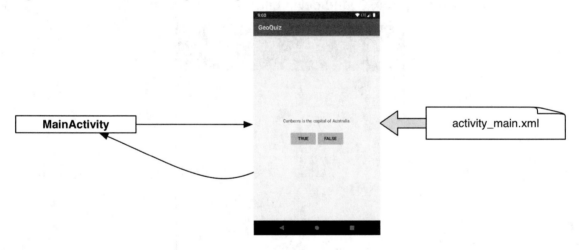

With those ideas in mind, let's build an app.

# Creating an Android Project

The first step is to create an Android *project*. An Android project contains the files that make up an application. To create a new project, first open Android Studio.

If this is your first time running Android Studio, you will see the Welcome dialog, as in Figure 1.3.

Figure 1.3  Welcome to Android Studio

If you are using Android Studio 3.3 or older, before you begin your project you may want to take a moment to turn off a feature that could interfere with your work. Instant Run is designed to streamline development by allowing you to push code changes without building a new APK. Unfortunately, it does not always work as intended, so we recommend that you disable it while working through this book.

At the bottom of the Welcome dialog, click Configure, then choose Preferences. On the lefthand side of the Preferences for New Projects screen (Figure 1.4), expand Build, Execution, Deployment and choose Instant Run. Uncheck the box next to Enable Instant Run to hot swap code/resource changes on deploy (default enabled) and click OK.

(If you have used Android Studio before and do not see the Welcome dialog when you start up, go to Android Studio → Preferences, then expand Build, Execution, Deployment and continue as above.)

Figure 1.4  Preferences for New Projects

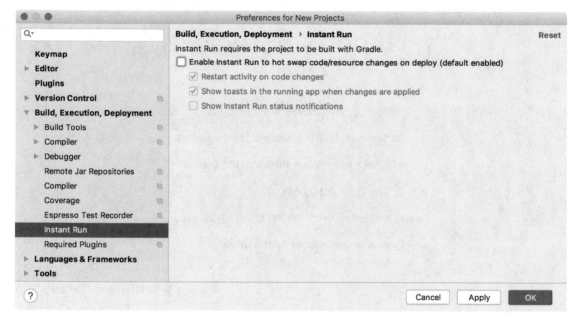

Back at the Welcome dialog, choose Start a new Android Studio project. If you do not see the dialog, choose File → New → New Project....

Welcome to the Create New Project wizard (Figure 1.5). Make sure the Phone and Tablet tab is selected, pick Empty Activity, and click Next.

Figure 1.5  Choosing a project template

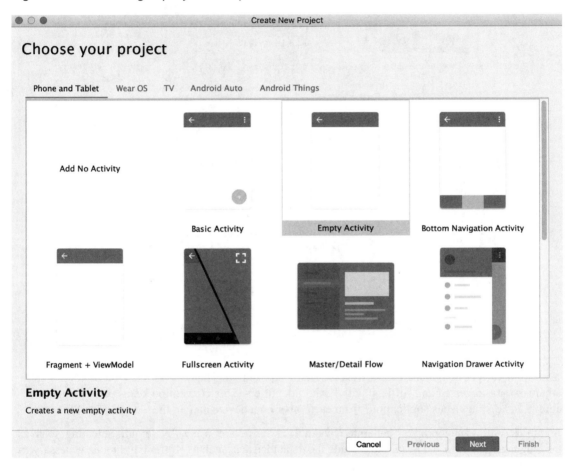

You should now see the Configure your project screen (Figure 1.6). Enter GeoQuiz as the application name. For package name, enter com.bignerdranch.android.geoquiz. For the project location, use any location on your filesystem that you want.

Select Kotlin from the Language drop-down menu. Select a Minimum API level of API 21: Android 5.0 (Lollipop). You will learn about the different versions of Android in Chapter 7. Last, make sure the checkbox next to Use AndroidX artifacts is checked. Your screen should look like Figure 1.6.

Figure 1.6 Configuring your new project

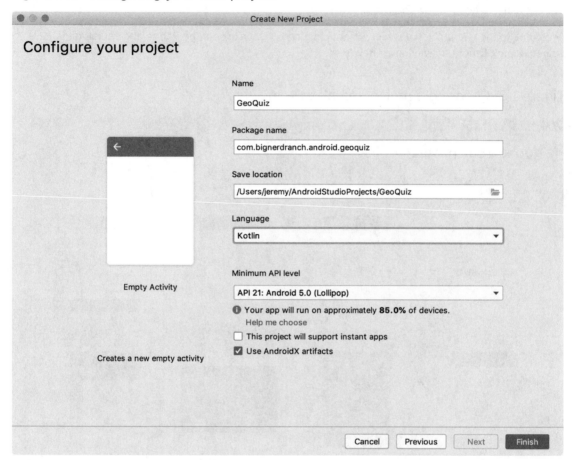

Notice that the package name uses a "reverse DNS" convention: The domain name of your organization is reversed and suffixed with further identifiers. This convention keeps package names unique and distinguishes applications from each other on a device and on the Google Play Store.

As of this writing, new projects generated by Android Studio are in Java by default. Selecting Kotlin as the language tells Android Studio to include the dependencies, such as Kotlin build tools, necessary to write and build Kotlin code for your app.

Java was the only development language officially supported until May 2017, when the Android team announced official support for Kotlin for Android development at Google I/O. These days, Kotlin is preferred by most developers, ourselves included, which is why this book uses Kotlin. But if you choose to use Java in your projects outside of this book, the Android concepts and content you will learn here will still be applicable.

Google used to provide a monolithic "support" library of helpers and compatibility shims. AndroidX explodes this single library into many independently developed and versioned libraries, collectively called "Jetpack." Selecting Use AndroidX artifacts makes your project ready to use these newly independent tools. You will learn more about Jetpack and AndroidX in Chapter 4, and you will use various Jetpack libraries throughout this book.

(Android Studio updates regularly, so your wizard may look slightly different from what we are showing you. This is usually not a problem; the choices should be similar. If your wizard looks very different, then the tools have changed more drastically. Do not panic. Head to this book's forum at forums.bignerdranch.com and we will help you navigate the latest version.)

Click Finish. Android Studio will create and open your new project.

# Navigating in Android Studio

Android Studio opens your project in a window like the one shown in Figure 1.7. If you have launched Android Studio before, your window configuration might look a little different.

Figure 1.7  A fresh project window

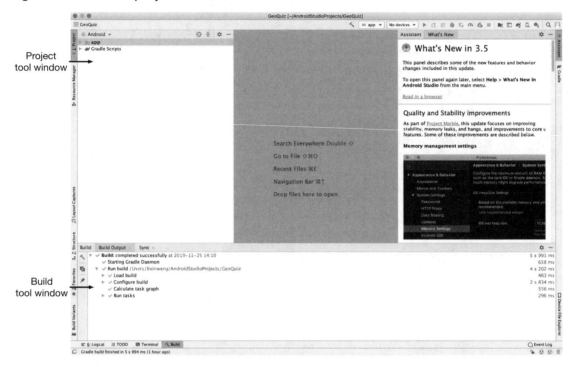

The different panes of the project window are called *tool windows*.

The lefthand view is the *project tool window*. From here, you can view and manage the files associated with your project.

The view across the bottom is the *build tool window*. Here you can view details about the compilation process and the status of the build. When you created the project, Android Studio automatically built it. You should see in the build tool window that the process completed successfully.

In the project tool window, click the disclosure arrow next to app. Android Studio automatically opens the files activity_main.xml and MainActivity.kt in the main view, called the *editor tool window* or just the *editor* (Figure 1.8). If this is not your first time opening Android Studio, the editor tool window may have opened automatically when you created the project.

## Figure 1.8  Editor engaged

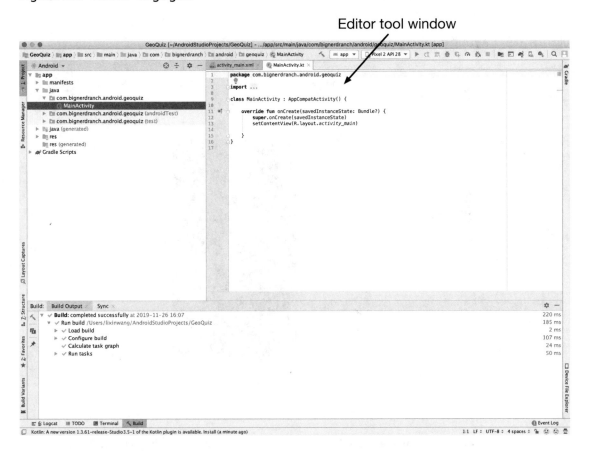

Notice the Activity suffix on the class name. This is not required, but it is an excellent convention to follow.

You can toggle the visibility of the various tool windows by clicking on their names in the strips of tool buttons on the left, right, and bottom of the screen. There are keyboard shortcuts for many of these as well. If you do not see the tool button strips, click the gray square button in the lower-left corner of the main window or choose View → Tool Buttons.

# Laying Out the UI

Click the tab for the layout file, `activity_main.xml`. This will open the layout editor in the editor tool window (Figure 1.9). If you do not see a tab for `activity_main.xml`, do not worry. Expand `app/res/layout/` in the project tool window. Double-click `activity_main.xml` to open the file. If `activity_main.xml` opens but shows XML instead of the layout editor, click the Design tab at the bottom of the editor tool window.

## Figure 1.9  Layout editor

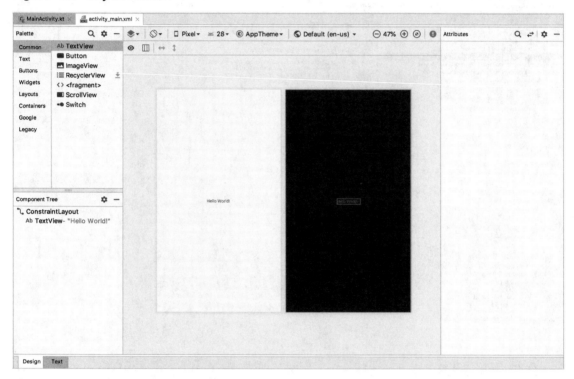

By convention, a layout file is named based on the activity it is associated with: Its name begins with `activity_`, and the rest of the activity name follows in all lowercase, using underscores to separate words (a style called "snake_case"). So, for example, your layout file's name is `activity_main.xml`, and the layout file for an activity called **SplashScreenActivity** would be named `activity_splash_screen`. This naming style is recommended for layouts as well as other resources that you will learn about later.

The layout editor shows a graphical preview of the file. Select the Text tab at the bottom to see the backing XML.

Currently, `activity_main.xml` holds the default activity layout template. The template changes frequently, but the XML will look something like Listing 1.1.

## Listing 1.1 Default activity layout (`res/layout/activity_main.xml`)

```xml
<?xml version="1.0" encoding="utf-8"?>
<androidx.constraintlayout.widget.ConstraintLayout
        xmlns:android="http://schemas.android.com/apk/res/android"
        xmlns:tools="http://schemas.android.com/tools"
        xmlns:app="http://schemas.android.com/apk/res-auto"
        android:layout_width="match_parent"
        android:layout_height="match_parent"
        tools:context=".MainActivity">

    <TextView
            android:layout_width="wrap_content"
            android:layout_height="wrap_content"
            android:text="Hello World!"
            app:layout_constraintBottom_toBottomOf="parent"
            app:layout_constraintLeft_toLeftOf="parent"
            app:layout_constraintRight_toRightOf="parent"
            app:layout_constraintTop_toTopOf="parent"/>

</androidx.constraintlayout.widget.ConstraintLayout>
```

The default activity layout defines two *Views*: a **ConstraintLayout** and a **TextView**.

Views are the building blocks you use to compose a UI. Everything you see on the screen is a view. Views that the user can see or interact with are called *widgets*. Some widgets show text. Some widgets show graphics. Others, like buttons, do things when touched.

The Android SDK includes many widgets that you can configure to get the appearance and behavior you want. Every widget is an instance of the **View** class or one of its subclasses (such as **TextView** or **Button**).

Something has to tell the widgets where they belong onscreen. A **ViewGroup** is a kind of **View** that contains and arranges other views. A **ViewGroup** does not display content itself. Rather, it orchestrates where other views' content is displayed. **ViewGroup**s are often referred to as layouts.

In the default activity layout, **ConstraintLayout** is the **ViewGroup** responsible for laying out its sole child, a **TextView** widget. You will learn more about layouts and widgets and about using **ConstraintLayout** in Chapter 10.

Figure 1.10 shows how the **ConstraintLayout** and **TextView** defined in Listing 1.1 would appear onscreen.

Figure 1.10  Default views as seen onscreen

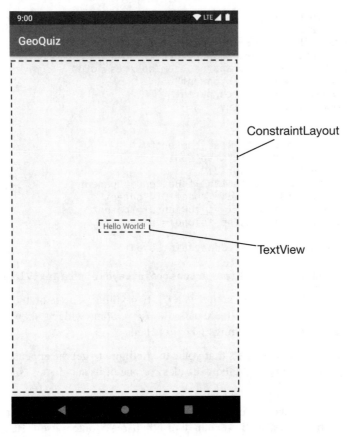

But these are not the widgets you are looking for. The interface for **MainActivity** requires five widgets:

- a vertical **LinearLayout**

- a **TextView**

- a horizontal **LinearLayout**

- two **Button**s

Figure 1.11 shows how these widgets compose **MainActivity**'s interface.

## Figure 1.11  Planned widgets as seen onscreen

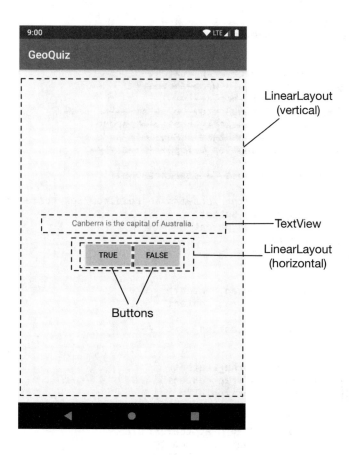

Now you need to define these widgets in your layout XML. Edit the text contents of activity_main.xml to match Listing 1.2. The XML that you need to delete is struck through, and the XML that you need to add is in bold font. This is the pattern we will use throughout this book.

Do not worry about understanding what you are typing; you will learn how it works next. However, do be careful. Layout XML is not validated, and typos will cause problems sooner or later.

You will see errors on the three lines that start with android:text. Ignore these errors for now; you will fix them soon.

## Listing 1.2  Defining widgets in XML (`res/layout/activity_main.xml`)

```
<androidx.constraintlayout.widget.ConstraintLayout
      xmlns:android="http://schemas.android.com/apk/res/android"
      xmlns:tools="http://schemas.android.com/tools"
      xmlns:app="http://schemas.android.com/apk/res-auto"
      android:layout_width="match_parent"
      android:layout_height="match_parent"
      tools:context=".MainActivity">

    <TextView
          android:layout_width="wrap_content"
          android:layout_height="wrap_content"
          android:text="Hello World!"
          app:layout_constraintBottom_toBottomOf="parent"
          app:layout_constraintLeft_toLeftOf="parent"
          app:layout_constraintRight_toRightOf="parent"
          app:layout_constraintTop_toTopOf="parent"/>

</androidx.constraintlayout.widget.ConstraintLayout>

<LinearLayout xmlns:android="http://schemas.android.com/apk/res/android"
    android:layout_width="match_parent"
    android:layout_height="match_parent"
    android:gravity="center"
    android:orientation="vertical">

    <TextView
        android:layout_width="wrap_content"
        android:layout_height="wrap_content"
        android:padding="24dp"
        android:text="@string/question_text" />

    <LinearLayout
        android:layout_width="wrap_content"
        android:layout_height="wrap_content"
        android:orientation="horizontal">

        <Button
            android:layout_width="wrap_content"
            android:layout_height="wrap_content"
            android:text="@string/true_button" />

        <Button
            android:layout_width="wrap_content"
            android:layout_height="wrap_content"
            android:text="@string/false_button" />

    </LinearLayout>

</LinearLayout>
```

Compare your XML with the UI shown in Figure 1.11. Every widget has a corresponding XML element, and the name of the element is the type of the widget.

Each element has a set of XML *attributes*. Each attribute is an instruction about how the widget should be configured.

To understand how the elements and attributes work, it helps to look at the layout from a hierarchical perspective.

## The view hierarchy

Your widgets exist in a hierarchy of **View** objects called the *view hierarchy*. Figure 1.12 shows the view hierarchy that corresponds to the XML in Listing 1.2.

Figure 1.12  Hierarchical layout of widgets and attributes

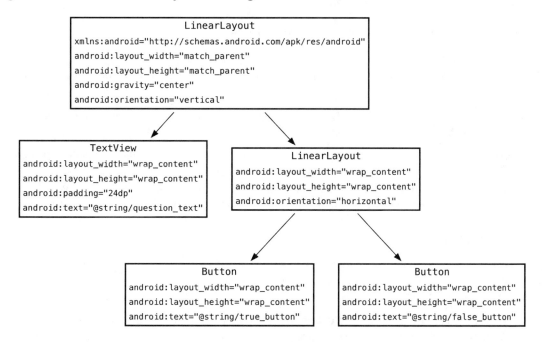

The root element of this layout's view hierarchy is a **LinearLayout**. As the root element, the **LinearLayout** must specify the Android resource XML namespace at http://schemas.android.com/apk/res/android.

**LinearLayout** inherits from **ViewGroup**, which, as we said earlier, is a subclass of **View** that contains and arranges other views. You use a **LinearLayout** when you want views arranged in a single column or row. Other **ViewGroup** subclasses that you will meet later include **ConstraintLayout** and **FrameLayout**.

When a view is contained by a **ViewGroup**, that view is said to be a *child* of the **ViewGroup**. The root **LinearLayout** has two children: a **TextView** and another **LinearLayout**. The child **LinearLayout** has two **Button** children of its own.

# Widget attributes

Let's go over some of the attributes that you have used to configure your widgets.

## android:layout_width and android:layout_height

The `android:layout_width` and `android:layout_height` attributes are required for almost every type of widget. They are typically set to either `match_parent` or `wrap_content`:

| | |
|---|---|
| `match_parent` | view will be as big as its parent |
| `wrap_content` | view will be as big as its contents require |

For the root **LinearLayout**, the value of both the height and width attributes is `match_parent`. The **LinearLayout** is the root element, but it still has a parent – the view that Android provides for your app's view hierarchy to live in.

The other widgets in your layout have their widths and heights set to `wrap_content`. You can see in Figure 1.11 how this determines their sizes.

The **TextView** is slightly larger than the text it contains due to its `android:padding="24dp"` attribute. This attribute tells the widget to add the specified amount of space to its contents when determining its size. You are using it to get a little breathing room between the question and the buttons. (Wondering about the dp units? These are density-independent pixels, which you will learn about in Chapter 10.)

## android:orientation

The `android:orientation` attribute on the two **LinearLayout** widgets determines whether their children will appear vertically or horizontally. The root **LinearLayout** is vertical; its child **LinearLayout** is horizontal.

The order in which children are defined determines the order in which they appear onscreen. In a vertical **LinearLayout**, the first child defined will appear topmost. In a horizontal **LinearLayout**, the first child defined will be leftmost. (Unless the device is set to a language that runs right to left, such as Arabic or Hebrew. In that case, the first child will be rightmost.)

## android:text

The **TextView** and **Button** widgets have `android:text` attributes. This attribute tells the widget what text to display.

Notice that the values of these attributes are not literal strings. They are references to *string resources*, as denoted by the `@string/` syntax.

A string resource is a string that lives in a separate XML file called a *strings file*. You can give a widget a hardcoded string, like `android:text="True"`, but it is usually not a good idea. Placing strings into a separate file and then referencing them is better because it makes localization (which you will learn about in Chapter 17) easy.

The string resources you are referencing in `activity_main.xml` do not exist yet. Let's fix that.

# Creating string resources

Every project includes a default strings file named res/values/strings.xml.

Open res/values/strings.xml. The template has already added one string resource for you. Add the three new strings that your layout requires.

### Listing 1.3  Adding string resources (res/values/strings.xml)

```
<resources>
    <string name="app_name">GeoQuiz</string>
    <string name="question_text">Canberra is the capital of Australia.</string>
    <string name="true_button">True</string>
    <string name="false_button">False</string>
</resources>
```

(Depending on your version of Android Studio, you may have additional strings. Do not delete them. Deleting them could cause cascading errors in other files.)

Now, whenever you refer to @string/false_button in any XML file in the GeoQuiz project, you will get the literal string "False" at runtime.

The errors in activity_main.xml about the missing string resources should now be gone. (If you still have errors, check both files for typos.)

Although the default strings file is named strings.xml, you can name a strings file anything you want. You can also have multiple strings files in a project. As long as the file is located in res/values/, has a resources root element, and contains child string elements, your strings will be found and used.

## Previewing the layout

Your layout is now complete. Switch back to `activity_main.xml` and preview the layout in the Design pane by clicking the tab at the bottom of the editor tool window (Figure 1.13).

Figure 1.13  Previewing `activity_main.xml` in the Design pane

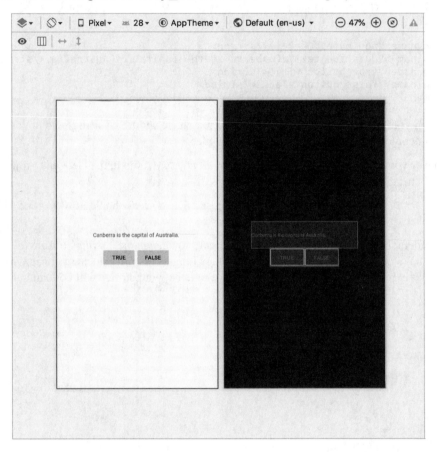

Figure 1.13 shows the two kinds of preview available. You can select from the preview types using a menu that drops down from the blue diamond button leftmost in the top toolbar. You can show either kind of preview individually or both together, as shown here.

The preview on the left is the *Design* preview. This shows how the layout would look on a device, including theming.

The preview on the right is the *Blueprint* preview. This preview focuses on the size of widgets and the relationships between them.

The Design pane also allows you to see how your layout looks on different device configurations. At the top of the pane, you can specify the type of device, the version of Android to simulate, the device theme, and the locale to use when rendering your layout. You can even pretend your current locale uses right-to-left text.

In addition to previewing, you can also build your layouts using the layout editor. On the left there is a palette that contains all of the built-in widgets (Figure 1.14). You can drag these widgets from the palette and drop them into your view. You can also drop them into the component tree in the bottom left to have more control over where the widget is placed.

Figure 1.14 shows the preview with *layout decorations* – the device status bar, app bar with GeoQuiz label, and virtual device button bar. To see these decorations, click the eyeball button in the toolbar just above the preview and select Show Layout Decorations.

## Figure 1.14  Graphical layout editor

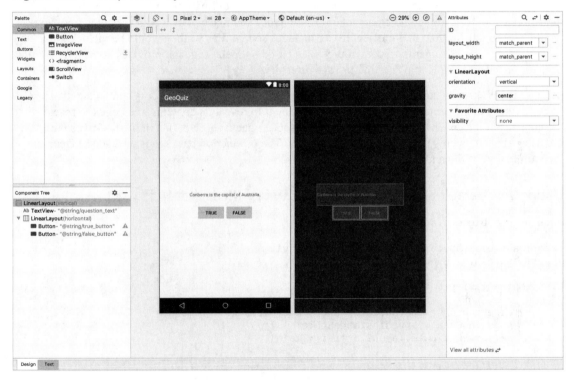

You will find this graphical editor especially valuable when working with `ConstraintLayout`, as you will see for yourself in Chapter 10.

# From Layout XML to View Objects

How do XML elements in `activity_main.xml` become **View** objects? The answer starts in the **MainActivity** class.

When you created the GeoQuiz project, a subclass of **Activity** named **MainActivity** was created for you. The class file for **MainActivity** is in the app/java directory of your project.

A quick aside about the directory name before we get into how layouts become views: This directory is called java because Android originally supported only Java code. In your project, because you configured it to use Kotlin (and Kotlin is fully interoperable with Java), the java directory is where the Kotlin code lives. You could create a kotlin directory and place your Kotlin files there, but you would have to tell Android that the new folder includes source files so they would be included in your project. In most cases, separating your source files based on their language provides no benefit, so most projects just place their Kotlin files in the java directory.

MainActivity.kt may already be open in a tab in the editor tool window. If it is not, locate the app/java directory in the project tool window and click on it to reveal its contents, then click to reveal the contents of the com.bignerdranch.android.geoquiz package. (Not one of the packages with the name shaded green – those are the test packages. The production package is unshaded.) Open the MainActivity.kt file and take a look at its contents.

## Listing 1.4  Default class file for **MainActivity** (MainActivity.kt)

```
package com.bignerdranch.android.geoquiz

import androidx.appcompat.app.AppCompatActivity
import android.os.Bundle

class MainActivity : AppCompatActivity() {

    override fun onCreate(savedInstanceState: Bundle?) {
        super.onCreate(savedInstanceState)
        setContentView(R.layout.activity_main)
    }
}
```

(Wondering what **AppCompatActivity** is? It is a subclass of Android's **Activity** class that provides compatibility support for older versions of Android. You will learn much more about **AppCompatActivity** in Chapter 14.)

If you are not seeing all of the import statements, click the + symbol to the left of the first import statement to reveal the others.

This file has one **Activity** function: **onCreate(Bundle?)**.

The **onCreate(Bundle?)** function is called when an instance of the activity subclass is created. When an activity is created, it needs a UI to manage. To give the activity its UI, you call **Activity.setContentView(layoutResID: Int)**.

This function *inflates* a layout and puts it onscreen. When a layout is inflated, each widget in the layout file is instantiated as defined by its attributes. You specify which layout to inflate by passing in the layout's *resource ID*.

# Resources and resource IDs

A layout is a *resource*. A resource is a piece of your application that is not code – things like image files, audio files, and XML files.

Resources for your project live in a subdirectory of the app/res directory. In the project tool window, you can see that activity_main.xml lives in res/layout/. Your strings file, which contains string resources, lives in res/values/.

To access a resource in code, you use its resource ID. The resource ID for your layout is R.layout.activity_main.

To see the current resource IDs for GeoQuiz, you must bravely explore into the world of auto-generated code – code that the Android build tool writes on your behalf. First, run the build tool by clicking the green hammer icon in the toolbar at the top of the Android Studio window.

By default, Android Studio displays the Android project view in the project tool window. This view hides the true directory structure of your Android project so that you can focus on the files and folders that you need most often. To see the files and folders in your project as they actually are, locate the dropdown at the top of the project tool window and change from the Android view to the Project view (Figure 1.15).

Figure 1.15  Project tool window: Android view vs Project view

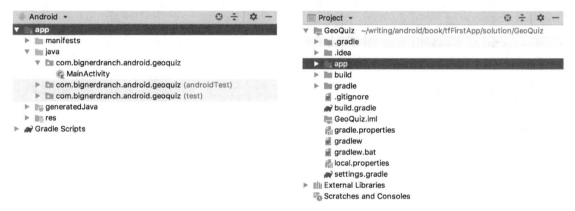

In the Project view, expand the GeoQuiz directory and keep going until you can see the contents of GeoQuiz/app/build/generated/not_namespaced_r_class_sources/debug/ processDebugResources/r/. In this directory, find your project's package name and drill down until you find R.java within that package (Figure 1.16).

## Figure 1.16  Viewing R.java

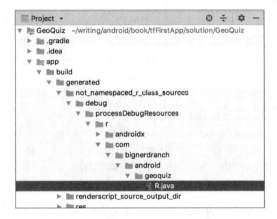

Double-click on the file to open it. Because R.java is generated by the Android build process, you should not change it, as you are subtly warned at the top of the file (Listing 1.5).

## Listing 1.5  Current GeoQuiz resource IDs (R.java)

```
/* AUTO-GENERATED FILE.  DO NOT MODIFY.
 *
 * This class was automatically generated by the
 * aapt tool from the resource data it found.  It
 * should not be modified by hand.
 */

package com.bignerdranch.android.geoquiz;

public final class R {
    public static final class anim {
        ...
    }
    ...
    public static final class id {
        ...
    }
    public static final class layout {
        ...
        public static final Int activity_main=0x7f030017;
    }
    public static final class mipmap {
        public static final Int ic_launcher=0x7f030000;
    }
    public static final class string {
        ...
        public static final Int app_name=0x7f0a0010;
        public static final Int false_button=0x7f0a0012;
        public static final Int question_text=0x7f0a0014;
        public static final Int true_button=0x7f0a0015;
    }
}
```

By the way, you may not see this file instantly update after making a change to your resources. Android Studio maintains a hidden R.java file that your code builds against. The R.java file in Listing 1.5 is the one that is generated for your app just before it is installed on a device or emulator. You will see this file update when you run your app.

The R.java file can be large, and much of this file is omitted from Listing 1.5.

This is where the R.layout.activity_main comes from – it is an integer constant named activity_main within the **layout** inner class of **R**.

Your strings also have resource IDs. You have not yet referred to a string in code, but if you did, it would look like this:

```
setTitle(R.string.app_name)
```

Android generated a resource ID for the entire layout and for each string, but it did not generate resource IDs for the individual widgets in activity_main.xml. Not every widget needs a resource ID. In this chapter, you will only interact with the two buttons in code, so only they need resource IDs.

To generate a resource ID for a widget, you include an android:id attribute in the widget's definition. In activity_main.xml, add an android:id attribute to each button. (You will need to switch to the Text tab to do this.)

## Listing 1.6  Adding IDs to **Button**s (res/layout/activity_main.xml)

```
<LinearLayout ... >

    <TextView
        android:layout_width="wrap_content"
        android:layout_height="wrap_content"
        android:padding="24dp"
        android:text="@string/question_text" />

    <LinearLayout
        android:layout_width="wrap_content"
        android:layout_height="wrap_content"
        android:orientation="horizontal">

        <Button
            android:id="@+id/true_button"
            android:layout_width="wrap_content"
            android:layout_height="wrap_content"
            android:text="@string/true_button" />

        <Button
            android:id="@+id/false_button"
            android:layout_width="wrap_content"
            android:layout_height="wrap_content"
            android:text="@string/false_button" />

    </LinearLayout>

</LinearLayout>
```

Notice that there is a + sign in the values for android:id but not in the values for android:text. This is because you are *creating* the resource IDs and only *referencing* the strings.

Before moving on, change the project tool window from the Project view to the Android view. Throughout this book, the Android view will be used – but feel free to use the Project version if you prefer. Also, close R.java by clicking the x in its editor tab.

# Wiring Up Widgets

You are ready to wire up your button widgets. This is a two-step process:

- get references to the inflated **View** objects

- set listeners on those objects to respond to user actions

## Getting references to widgets

Now that the buttons have resource IDs, you can access them in **MainActivity**. Type the following code into MainActivity.kt (Listing 1.7). (Do not use code completion; type it in yourself.) After you save the file, it will report two errors. You will fix the errors in just a second.

Listing 1.7  Accessing view objects by ID (MainActivity.kt)

```kotlin
class MainActivity : AppCompatActivity() {

    private lateinit var trueButton: Button
    private lateinit var falseButton: Button

    override fun onCreate(savedInstanceState: Bundle?) {
        super.onCreate(savedInstanceState)
        setContentView(R.layout.activity_main)

        trueButton = findViewById(R.id.true_button)
        falseButton = findViewById(R.id.false_button)
    }
}
```

In an activity, you can get a reference to an inflated widget by calling **Activity.findViewById(Int)**. This function returns the corresponding view. Rather than return it as a **View**, it is cast to the expected subtype of **View**. Here, that type is **Button**.

In the code above, you use the resource IDs of your buttons to retrieve the inflated objects and assign them to your view properties. Since the view objects are not inflated into and available in memory until after **setContentView(…)** is called in **onCreate(…)**, you use lateinit on your property declarations to indicate to the compiler that you will provide a non-null **View** value before you attempt to use the contents of the property. Then, in **onCreate(…)**, you look up and assign the view objects the appropriate properties. You will learn more about **onCreate(…)** and the activity lifecycle in Chapter 3.

Now let's get rid of those pesky errors. Mouse over the red error indicators. They both report the same problem: Unresolved reference: Button.

These errors are telling you that you need to import the **android.widget.Button** class into MainActivity.kt. You could type the following import statement at the top of the file:

```kotlin
import android.widget.Button
```

Or you can do it the easy way and let Android Studio do it for you. Just press Option-Return (or Alt-Enter) to let the IntelliJ magic under the hood amaze you. The new import statement now appears with the others at the top of the file. This shortcut is generally useful when something is not correct with your code. Try it often!

This should get rid of the errors. (If you still have errors, check for typos in your code and XML.) Once your code is error free, it is time to make your app interactive.

# Setting listeners

Android applications are typically *event driven*. Unlike command-line programs or scripts, event-driven applications start and then wait for an event, such as the user pressing a button. (Events can also be initiated by the OS or another application, but user-initiated events are the most obvious.)

When your application is waiting for a specific event, we say that it is "listening for" that event. The object that you create to respond to an event is called a *listener*, and the listener implements a *listener interface* for that event.

The Android SDK comes with listener interfaces for various events, so you do not have to write your own. In this case, the event you want to listen for is a button being pressed (or "clicked"), so your listener will implement the **View.OnClickListener** interface.

Start with the TRUE button. In MainActivity.kt, add the following code to **onCreate(Bundle?)** just after the variable assignments.

## Listing 1.8  Setting a listener for the TRUE button (MainActivity.kt)

```
override fun onCreate(savedInstanceState: Bundle?) {
    super.onCreate(savedInstanceState)
    setContentView(R.layout.activity_main)

    trueButton = findViewById(R.id.true_button)
    falseButton = findViewById(R.id.false_button)

    trueButton.setOnClickListener { view: View ->
        // Do something in response to the click here
    }
}
```

(If you have an Unresolved reference: View error, try using Option-Return [Alt-Enter] to import the **View** class.)

In Listing 1.8, you set a listener to inform you when the **Button** known as trueButton has been pressed. The Android framework defines **View.OnClickListener** as a Java interface with a single method, **onClick(View)**. Interfaces with a *single abstract method* are common enough in Java that the pattern has a pet name, *SAM*.

Kotlin has special support for this pattern as part of its Java interoperability layer. It lets you write a function literal, and it takes care of turning that into an object implementing the interface. This behind-the-scenes process is called *SAM conversion*.

Your on-click listener is implemented using a lambda expression. Set a similar listener for the FALSE button.

## Listing 1.9  Setting a listener for the FALSE button (MainActivity.kt)

```
override fun onCreate(savedInstanceState: Bundle?) {
    ...
    trueButton.setOnClickListener { view: View ->
        // Do something in response to the click here
    }

    falseButton.setOnClickListener { view: View ->
        // Do something in response to the click here
    }
}
```

# Making Toasts

Now to make the buttons fully armed and operational. You are going to have a press of each button trigger a pop-up message called a *toast*. A toast is a short message that informs the user of something but does not require any input or action. You are going to make toasts that announce whether the user answered correctly or incorrectly (Figure 1.17).

Figure 1.17  A toast providing feedback

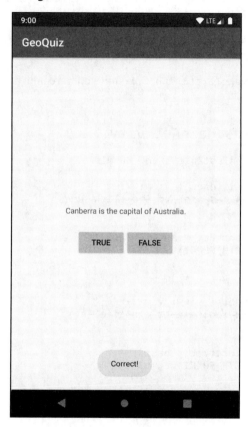

First, return to strings.xml and add the string resources that your toasts will display.

Listing 1.10  Adding toast strings (res/values/strings.xml)

```
<resources>
    <string name="app_name">GeoQuiz</string>
    <string name="question_text">Canberra is the capital of Australia.</string>
    <string name="true_button">True</string>
    <string name="false_button">False</string>
    <string name="correct_toast">Correct!</string>
    <string name="incorrect_toast">Incorrect!</string>
</resources>
```

Next, update your click listeners to create and show a toast. Use code completion to help you fill in the listener code. Code completion can save you a lot of time, so it is good to become familiar with it early.

Start typing the code shown in Listing 1.11 in `MainActivity.kt`. When you get to the period after the **Toast** class, a pop-up window will appear with a list of suggested functions and constants from the **Toast** class.

To choose one of the suggestions, use the up and down arrow keys to select it. (If you wanted to ignore code completion, you could just keep typing. It will not complete anything for you if you do not press the Tab key, press the Return key, or click on the pop-up window.)

From the list of suggestions, select `makeText(context: Context, resId: Int, duration: Int)`. Code completion will add the complete function call for you.

Fill in the parameters for the `makeText(…)` function until you have added the code shown in Listing 1.11.

## Listing 1.11  Making toasts (MainActivity.kt)

```
override fun onCreate(savedInstanceState: Bundle?) {
    ...
    trueButton.setOnClickListener { view: View ->
        // Do something in response to the click here
        Toast.makeText(
                this,
                R.string.correct_toast,
                Toast.LENGTH_SHORT)
                .show()
    }

    false.setOnClickListener { view: View ->
        // Do something in response to the click here
        Toast.makeText(
                this,
                R.string.incorrect_toast,
                Toast.LENGTH_SHORT)
                .show()
    }
}
```

To create a toast, you call the static function **Toast.makeText(Context!, Int, Int)**. This function creates and configures a **Toast** object. The **Context** parameter is typically an instance of **Activity** (and **Activity** is a subclass of **Context**). Here you pass the instance of **MainActivity** as the **Context** argument.

The second parameter is the resource ID of the string that the toast should display. The **Context** is needed by the **Toast** class to be able to find and use the string's resource ID. The third parameter is one of two **Toast** constants that specify how long the toast should be visible.

After you have created a toast, you call **Toast.show()** on it to get it onscreen.

Because you used code completion, you do not have to do anything to import the **Toast** class. When you accept a code completion suggestion, the necessary classes are imported automatically.

Now, let's see your app in action.

# Running on the Emulator

To run an Android application, you need a device – either a hardware device or a *virtual device*. Virtual devices are powered by the Android emulator, which ships with the developer tools.

To create an Android virtual device (or AVD), choose Tools → AVD Manager. When the AVD Manager appears, click the +Create Virtual Device... button in the lower-left corner of the window.

In the dialog that appears, you are offered many options for configuring a virtual device. For your first AVD, choose to emulate a Pixel 2, as shown in Figure 1.18. Click Next.

Figure 1.18  Choosing a virtual device

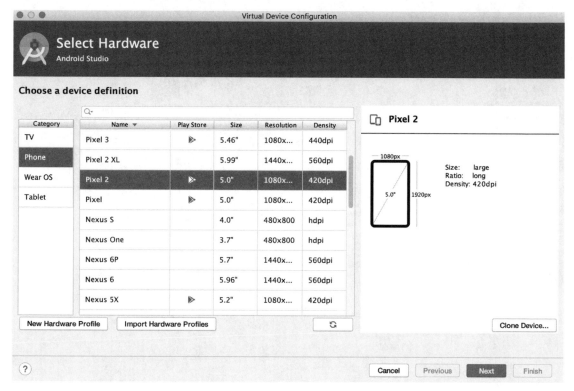

On the next screen, choose a system image for your emulator. For this emulator, select an x86 Pie emulator and select Next (Figure 1.19). (You may need to follow the steps to download the emulator's components before you can click Next.)

Figure 1.19  Choosing a system image

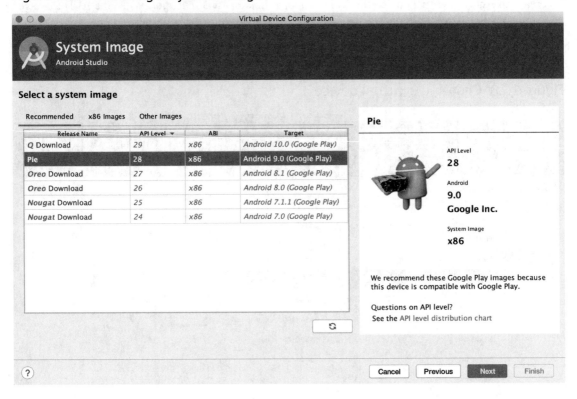

Finally, you can review and tweak properties of the emulator. You can also edit the properties of an existing emulator later. For now, name your emulator something that will help you to identify it later and click Finish (Figure 1.20).

Figure 1.20  Updating emulator properties

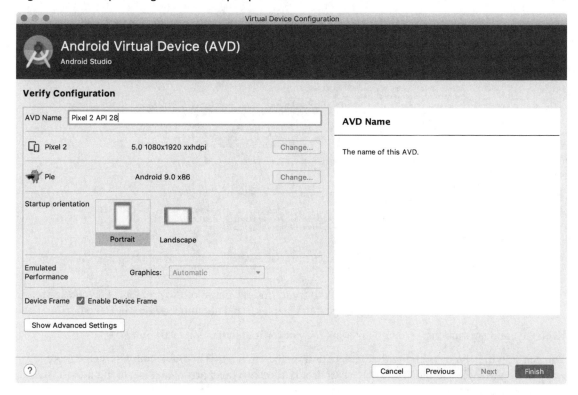

Once you have an AVD, you can run GeoQuiz on it. From the Android Studio toolbar, click the run button (it looks like a green "play" symbol) or press Control-R (Ctrl-R). In the Select Deployment Target box that appears, choose the AVD you just configured and click OK. Android Studio will start your virtual device, install the application package on it, and run the app.

Starting up the emulator can take a while, but eventually your GeoQuiz app will launch on the AVD that you created. Press buttons and admire your toasts.

If GeoQuiz crashes when launching or when you press a button, useful information will appear in the Logcat tool window. (If Logcat did not open automatically when you ran GeoQuiz, you can open it by clicking the Logcat button at the bottom of the Android Studio window.) Type MainActivity into the search box at the top of the Logcat tool window to filter the log messages. Look for exceptions in the log; they will be an eye-catching red color (Figure 1.21).

## Figure 1.21  An example **UninitializedPropertyAccessException**

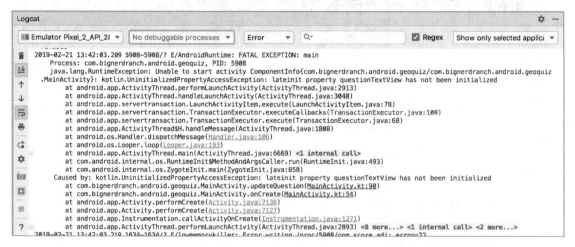

Compare your code with the code in the book to try to find the cause of the problem. Then try running again. (You will learn more about using Logcat in Chapter 3 and about debugging in Chapter 5.)

Keep the emulator running – you do not want to wait for it to launch on every run.

You can stop the app by pressing the Back button on the emulator. The Back button is shaped like a left-pointing triangle (on older versions of Android, it looks like an arrow that is making a U-turn). Then rerun the app from Android Studio to test changes.

The emulator is useful, but testing on a real device gives more accurate results. In Chapter 2, you will run GeoQuiz on a hardware device. You will also give GeoQuiz more geography questions with which to test the user.

# For the More Curious: The Android Build Process

By now, you probably have some burning questions about how the Android build process works. You have already seen that Android Studio builds your project automatically as you modify it, rather than on command. During the build process, the Android tools take your resources, code, and AndroidManifest.xml file (which contains metadata about the application) and turn them into an .apk file. This file is then signed with a debug key, which allows it to run on the emulator. (To distribute your .apk to the masses, you have to sign it with a release key. There is more information about this process in the Android developer documentation at developer.android.com/tools/publishing/preparing.html.)

How do the contents of activity_main.xml turn into **View** objects in an application? As part of the build process, aapt2 (the Android Asset Packaging Tool) compiles layout file resources into a more compact format. These compiled resources are packaged into the .apk file. Then, when **setContentView(…)** is called in **MainActivity**'s **onCreate(Bundle?)** function, **MainActivity** uses the **LayoutInflater** class to instantiate each of the **View** objects as defined in the layout file (Figure 1.22).

Figure 1.22 Inflating activity_main.xml

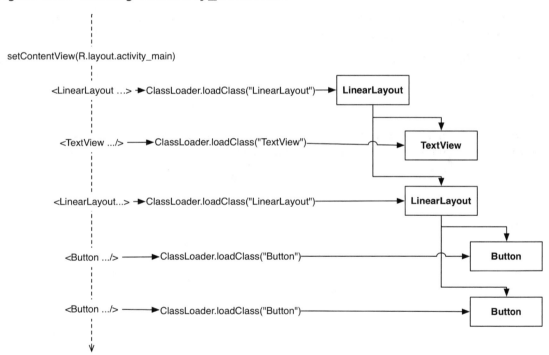

(You can also create your view classes programmatically in the activity instead of defining them in XML. But there are benefits to separating your presentation from the logic of the application. The main one is taking advantage of configuration changes built into the SDK, which you will learn more about in Chapter 3.)

You will learn more details of how the different XML attributes work and how views display themselves on the screen in Chapter 10.

## Android build tools

All of the builds you have seen so far have been executed from within Android Studio. This build is integrated into the IDE – it invokes standard Android build tools like aapt2, but the build process itself is managed by Android Studio.

You may, for your own reasons, want to perform builds from outside of Android Studio. The easiest way to do this is to use a command-line build tool. The Android build system uses a tool called Gradle.

(You will know if this section applies to you. If it does not, feel free to read along but do not be concerned if you are not sure why you might want to do this or if the commands below do not seem to work. Coverage of the ins and outs of using the command line is beyond the scope of this book.)

To use Gradle from the command line, navigate to your project's directory and run the following command:

```
$ ./gradlew tasks
```

On Windows, your command will look a little different:

```
> gradlew.bat tasks
```

This will show you a list of available tasks you can execute. The one you want is called installDebug. Make it so with a command like this:

```
$ ./gradlew installDebug
```

Or, on Windows:

```
> gradlew.bat installDebug
```

This will install your app on whatever device is connected. However, it will not run the app. For that, you will need to pull up the launcher and launch the app by hand.

# Challenges

Challenges are exercises at the end of the chapter for you to do on your own. Some are easy and provide practice doing the same thing you have done in the chapter. Other challenges are harder and require more problem solving.

We cannot encourage you enough to take on these challenges. Tackling them cements what you have learned, builds confidence in your skills, and bridges the gap between us teaching you Android programming and you being able to do Android programming on your own.

If you get stuck while working on a challenge, take a break and come back to try again fresh. If that does not help, check out the forum for this book at forums.bignerdranch.com. In the forum, you can review questions and solutions that other readers have posted as well as ask questions and post solutions of your own.

To protect the integrity of your current project, we recommend you make a copy and work on challenges in the new copy.

In your computer's file explorer, navigate to the root directory of your project. Copy the GeoQuiz folder and paste a new copy next to the original (on macOS, use the Duplicate feature). Rename the new folder GeoQuiz Challenge. Back in Android Studio, select File → Import Project.... Inside the import window, navigate to GeoQuiz Challenge and select OK. The copied project will then appear in a new window ready for work.

# Challenge: Customizing the Toast

For this challenge, customize the toast to show at the top instead of the bottom of the screen. To change how the toast is displayed, use the **Toast** class's **setGravity** function. Use Gravity.TOP for the gravity value. Refer to the developer documentation at developer.android.com/reference/kotlin/android/widget/Toast#setgravity for more details.

# 2

# Android and Model-View-Controller

In this chapter, you are going to upgrade GeoQuiz to present more than one question, as shown in Figure 2.1.

Figure 2.1  Next!

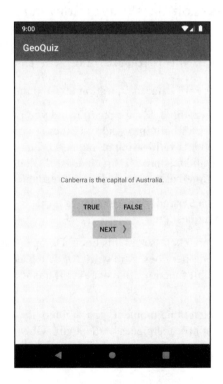

To make this happen, you are going to add a data class named **Question** to the GeoQuiz project. An instance of this class will encapsulate a single true/false question.

Then, you will create a collection of **Question** objects for **MainActivity** to manage.

# Creating a New Class

In the project tool window, right-click the com.bignerdranch.android.geoquiz package and select New → Kotlin File/Class. Enter Question for the name. Select Class from the Kind dropdown. Click OK (Figure 2.2).

Figure 2.2  Creating the **Question** class

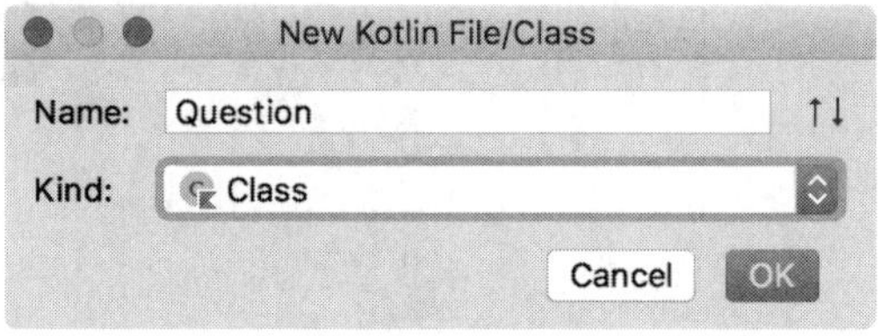

Android Studio will create and open a file called Question.kt. In this file, add two member variables and a constructor.

Listing 2.1  Adding to **Question** class (Question.kt)

```
class Question {
}
data class Question(@StringRes val textResId: Int, val answer: Boolean)
```

The **Question** class holds two pieces of data: the question text and the question answer (true or false).

The @StringRes annotation is not required, but we recommend you include it for two reasons. First, the annotation helps the code inspector built into Android Studio (named Lint) verify at compile time that usages of the constructor provide a valid string resource ID. This prevents runtime crashes where the constructor is used with an invalid resource ID (such as an ID that points to some resource other than a string). Second, the annotation makes your code more readable for other developers.

Why is textResId an Int and not a String? The textResId variable will hold the resource ID (always an Int) of the string resource for a question.

We use the data keyword for all model classes in this book. Doing so clearly indicates that the class is meant to hold data. Also, the compiler does extra work for data classes that makes your life easier, such as automatically defining useful functions like **equals()**, **hashCode()**, and a nicely formatted **toString()**.

Your **Question** class is now complete. In a moment, you will modify **MainActivity** to work with **Question**. First, let's take a look at how the pieces of GeoQuiz will work together.

You are going to have **MainActivity** create a list of **Question** objects. It will then interact with the **TextView** and the three **Button**s to display questions and provide feedback. Figure 2.3 diagrams these relationships.

Figure 2.3  Object diagram for GeoQuiz

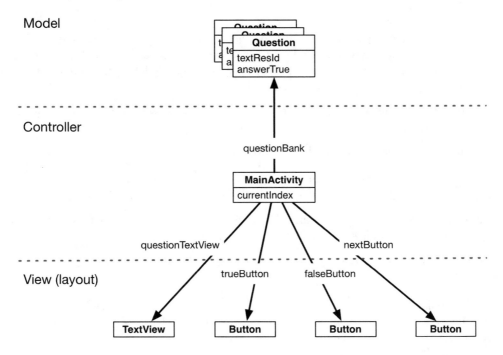

# Model-View-Controller and Android

Notice that the objects in Figure 2.3 are separated into three sections labeled Model, Controller, and View. The Android APIs were originally designed around an architecture called *Model-View-Controller*, or MVC. In MVC, all objects in your application must be a *model object*, a *view object*, or a *controller object*.

- Model objects hold the application's data and "business logic." Model classes are typically designed to *model* the things your app is concerned with, such as a user, a product in a store, a photo on a server, a television show – or a true/false question. Model objects have no knowledge of the UI; their sole purpose is holding and managing data.

  In Android applications, model classes are generally custom classes you create. All of the model objects in your application compose its *model layer*.

  GeoQuiz's model layer consists of the **Question** class.

- View objects know how to draw themselves on the screen and how to respond to user input, like touches. A simple rule of thumb is that if you can see it onscreen, then it is a view.

  Android provides a wealth of configurable view classes. You can also create custom view classes. An application's view objects make up its *view layer*.

  GeoQuiz's view layer consists of the widgets that are inflated from res/layout/ activity_main.xml.

- Controller objects tie the view and model objects together. They contain "application logic." Controllers are designed to respond to various events triggered by view objects and to manage the flow of data to and from model objects and the view layer.

  In Android, a controller is typically a subclass of **Activity** or **Fragment**. (You will learn about fragments in Chapter 8.)

  GeoQuiz's controller layer, at present, consists solely of **MainActivity**.

Figure 2.4 shows the flow of control between objects in response to a user event, like a press of a button. Notice that model and view objects do not talk to each other directly; controllers sit squarely in the middle of everything, receiving messages from some objects and dispatching instructions to others.

Figure 2.4 MVC flow with user input

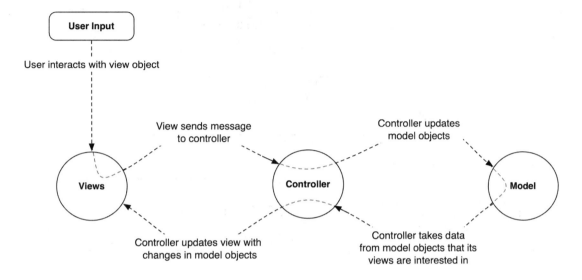

## Deciding to use MVC

An application can accumulate features until it is too complicated to understand. Separating code into classes helps you design and understand the application as a whole; you can think in terms of classes instead of individual variables and functions.

Similarly, separating classes into model, view, and controller layers helps you design and understand an application; you can think in terms of layers instead of individual classes.

Although GeoQuiz is not a complicated app, you can still see the benefits of keeping layers separate. In a moment, you are going to update GeoQuiz's view layer to include a NEXT button. When you do that, you will not need to remember a single thing about the **Question** class you just created.

MVC also makes classes easier to reuse. A class with restricted responsibilities is more reusable than one with its fingers in every pie.

For instance, your model class, **Question**, knows nothing about the widgets used to display a true/false question. This makes it easy to use **Question** throughout your app for different purposes. For example, if you wanted to display a list of all the questions at once, you could use the same object that you use here to display just one question at a time.

MVC works great for small, simple apps like GeoQuiz. In larger, more complicated apps, the controller layer can get very large and complex. In general, you want to keep your activities and other controllers *thin*. Thin activities contain as little business and setup logic as possible. Once MVC no longer lends itself to thin controllers in your app, you should consider alternative patterns, such as Model-View-View Model (which you will learn about in Chapter 19).

# Updating the View Layer

Now that you have been introduced to MVC, you are going to update GeoQuiz's view layer to include a NEXT button.

In Android, objects in the view layer are typically inflated from XML within a layout file. The sole layout in GeoQuiz is defined in activity_main.xml. This layout needs to be updated as shown in Figure 2.5. (Note that to save space we are not showing the attributes of unchanged widgets.)

## Figure 2.5  New button!

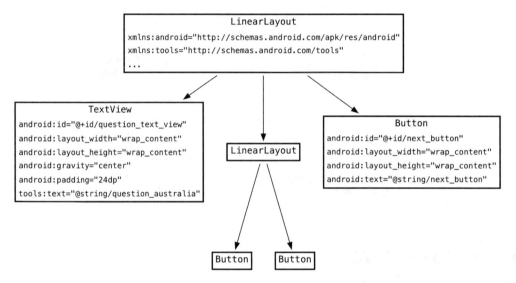

So the changes you need to make to the view layer are:

- Give the **TextView** an android:id attribute. This widget will need a resource ID so that you can set its text in **MainActivity**'s code. Position the **TextView**'s text in the center of the text view by setting gravity to "center".

- Remove the android:text attribute from the **TextView**. You no longer want a hardcoded question to be part of its definition. Instead, you will set the question text dynamically as the user clicks through the questions.

- Specify a default string for the Design tab to display in the **TextView** when rendering a preview of your layout. To do this, add a tools:text attribute to the **TextView** and point it to a string resource representing a question using @string/.

  You will also need to add the tools namespace to the root tag of your layout so that Android Studio can make sense of the tools:text attribute. This namespace allows you to override any attribute on a widget for the purpose of displaying it in the Android Studio preview. The tools attributes are ignored when rendering the widgets on a device at runtime. You could use android:text and just overwrite the value at runtime, but using tools:text instead makes it clear that the value you provide is for preview purposes only.

- Add the new **Button** widget as a child of the root **LinearLayout**.

Return to `activity_main.xml` and make it happen.

## Listing 2.2  New button ... and changes to the text view (res/layout/activity_main.xml)

```xml
<LinearLayout xmlns:android="http://schemas.android.com/apk/res/android"
        xmlns:tools="http://schemas.android.com/tools"
        android:layout_width="match_parent"
        android:layout_height="match_parent"
        ... >

    <TextView
        android:id="@+id/question_text_view"
        android:layout_width="wrap_content"
        android:layout_height="wrap_content"
        android:gravity="center"
        android:padding="24dp"
        android:text="@string/question_text"
        tools:text="@string/question_australia" />

    <LinearLayout ... >
        ...
    </LinearLayout>

    <Button
        android:id="@+id/next_button"
        android:layout_width="wrap_content"
        android:layout_height="wrap_content"
        android:text="@string/next_button" />

</LinearLayout>
```

You will see familiar errors alerting you about missing string resources.

Return to `res/values/strings.xml`. Rename `question_text` and add a string for the new button.

## Listing 2.3  Updating strings (res/values/strings.xml)

```xml
<string name="app_name">GeoQuiz</string>
<string name="question_text">Canberra is the capital of Australia.</string>
<string name="question_australia">Canberra is the capital of Australia.</string>
<string name="true_button">True</string>
<string name="false_button">False</string>
<string name="next_button">Next</string>
...
```

While you have `strings.xml` open, go ahead and add the strings for the rest of the geography questions that will be shown to the user.

## Listing 2.4  Adding question strings (res/values/strings.xml)

```
<string name="question_australia">Canberra is the capital of Australia.</string>
<string name="question_oceans">The Pacific Ocean is larger than
  the Atlantic Ocean.</string>
<string name="question_mideast">The Suez Canal connects the Red Sea
  and the Indian Ocean.</string>
<string name="question_africa">The source of the Nile River is in Egypt.</string>
<string name="question_americas">The Amazon River is the longest river
  in the Americas.</string>
<string name="question_asia">Lake Baikal is the world\'s oldest and deepest
  freshwater lake.</string>
...
```

Notice that you use the escape sequence \' in the last value to get an apostrophe in your string. You can use all the usual escape sequences in your string resources, such as \n for a new line.

Return to `activity_main.xml` and preview your layout changes in the graphical layout tool.

That is all for now for GeoQuiz's view layer. Time to wire everything up in your controller class, **MainActivity**.

# Updating the Controller Layer

In the previous chapter, there was not much happening in GeoQuiz's one controller, **MainActivity**. It displayed the layout defined in activity_main.xml. It set listeners on two buttons and wired them to make toasts.

Now that you have multiple questions to retrieve and display, **MainActivity** will have to work harder to tie GeoQuiz's model and view layers together.

Open MainActivity.kt. Create a list of **Question** objects and an index for the list.

### Listing 2.5  Adding a **Question** list (MainActivity.kt)

```kotlin
class MainActivity : AppCompatActivity() {

    private lateinit var trueButton: Button
    private lateinit var falseButton: Button

    private val questionBank = listOf(
            Question(R.string.question_australia, true),
            Question(R.string.question_oceans, true),
            Question(R.string.question_mideast, false),
            Question(R.string.question_africa, false),
            Question(R.string.question_americas, true),
            Question(R.string.question_asia, true))

    private var currentIndex = 0
    ...
}
```

Here you call the **Question** constructor several times and create a list of **Question** objects.

(In a more complex project, this list would be created and stored elsewhere. In later apps, you will see better options for storing model data. For now, we are keeping it simple and just creating the list within your controller.)

You are going to use questionBank, currentIndex, and the properties in **Question** to get a parade of questions onscreen.

First add properties for the **TextView** and the new **Button**. Then get a reference for the **TextView** and set its text to the question at the current index. While you are at it, get a reference for the new **Button** as well (you will configure the click listener for the NEXT button later).

### Listing 2.6  Wiring up the **TextView** (MainActivity.kt)

```kotlin
class MainActivity : AppCompatActivity() {

    private lateinit var trueButton: Button
    private lateinit var falseButton: Button
    private lateinit var nextButton: Button
    private lateinit var questionTextView: TextView
    ...
    override fun onCreate(savedInstanceState: Bundle?) {
        ...
        trueButton = findViewById(R.id.true_button)
        falseButton = findViewById(R.id.false_button)
        nextButton = findViewById(R.id.next_button)
        questionTextView = findViewById(R.id.question_text_view)

        trueButton.setOnClickListener { view: View ->
            ...
        }

        falseButton.setOnClickListener { view: View ->
            ...
        }

        val questionTextResId = questionBank[currentIndex].textResId
        questionTextView.setText(questionTextResId)
    }
}
```

Save your files and check for any errors. Then run GeoQuiz. You should see the first question in the array appear in the **TextView**.

Now let's make the NEXT button functional. Set a **View.OnClickListener** on it. This listener will increment the index and update the **TextView**'s text.

### Listing 2.7  Wiring up the new button (MainActivity.kt)

```kotlin
override fun onCreate(savedInstanceState: Bundle?) {
    ...
    falseButton.setOnClickListener { view: View ->
        ...
    }

    nextButton.setOnClickListener {
        currentIndex = (currentIndex + 1) % questionBank.size
        val questionTextResId = questionBank[currentIndex].textResId
        questionTextView.setText(questionTextResId)

    }

    val questionTextResId = questionBank[currentIndex].textResId
    questionTextView.setText(questionTextResId)
}
```

You now have the same code in two separate places that updates the text displayed in questionTextView. Take a moment to put this code into a function instead, as shown in Listing 2.8. Then invoke that function in the nextButton's listener and at the end of **onCreate(Bundle?)** to initially set the text in the activity's view.

## Listing 2.8  Encapsulating with a function (MainActivity.kt)

```
class MainActivity : AppCompatActivity() {
    ...
    override fun onCreate(savedInstanceState: Bundle?) {
        ...
        nextButton.setOnClickListener {
            currentIndex = (currentIndex + 1) % questionBank.size
            val questionTextResId = questionBank[currentIndex].textResId
            questionTextView.setText(questionTextResId)
            updateQuestion()
        }

        val questionTextResId = questionBank[currentIndex].textResId
        questionTextView.setText(questionTextResId)
        updateQuestion()
    }

    private fun updateQuestion() {
        val questionTextResId = questionBank[currentIndex].textResId
        questionTextView.setText(questionTextResId)
    }
}
```

Run GeoQuiz and test your new NEXT button.

Now that you have the questions behaving appropriately, it is time to turn to the answers. At the moment, GeoQuiz thinks that the answer to every question is "true." Let's rectify that. You will add a private named function to **MainActivity** to encapsulate code rather than writing similar code in two places:

```
private fun checkAnswer(userAnswer: Boolean)
```

This function will accept a Boolean variable that identifies whether the user pressed TRUE or FALSE. Then, it will check the user's answer against the answer in the current **Question** object. Finally, after determining whether the user answered correctly, it will make a **Toast** that displays the appropriate message to the user.

In `MainActivity.kt`, add the implementation of **checkAnswer(Boolean)** shown in Listing 2.9.

### Listing 2.9  Adding **checkAnswer(Boolean)** (MainActivity.kt)

```kotlin
class MainActivity : AppCompatActivity() {
    ...
    private fun updateQuestion() {
        ...
    }

    private fun checkAnswer(userAnswer: Boolean) {
        val correctAnswer = questionBank[currentIndex].answer

        val messageResId = if (userAnswer == correctAnswer) {
            R.string.correct_toast
        } else {
            R.string.incorrect_toast
        }

        Toast.makeText(this, messageResId, Toast.LENGTH_SHORT)
                .show()
    }
}
```

Within the buttons' listeners, call **checkAnswer(Boolean)**, as shown in Listing 2.10.

### Listing 2.10  Calling **checkAnswer(Boolean)** (MainActivity.kt)

```kotlin
override fun onCreate(savedInstanceState: Bundle?) {
    ...
    trueButton.setOnClickListener { view: View ->
        Toast.makeText(
            this,
            R.string.correct_toast,
            Toast.LENGTH_SHORT
        )
            .show()
        checkAnswer(true)
    }

    falseButton.setOnClickListener { view: View ->
        Toast.makeText(
            this,
            R.string.correct_toast,
            Toast.LENGTH_SHORT
        )
            .show()
        checkAnswer(false)
    }
    ...
}
```

Run GeoQuiz. Verify that the toasts display the right message based on the answer to the current question and the button you press.

# Adding an Icon

GeoQuiz is up and running, but the UI would be spiffier if the NEXT button also displayed a right-pointing arrow icon.

You can find such an arrow in the solutions file for this book, which is a collection of Android Studio projects for each chapter of this book. The solutions are hosted at `www.bignerdranch.com/solutions/AndroidProgramming4e.zip`.

Download the solutions file and open the `02_MVC/GeoQuiz/app/src/main/res` directory. Within this directory, locate the `drawable-hdpi`, `drawable-mdpi`, `drawable-xhdpi`, `drawable-xxhdpi`, and `drawable-xxxhdpi` directories.

The suffixes on these directory names refer to the screen pixel density of a device:

| | |
|---|---|
| `mdpi` | medium-density screens (~160dpi) |
| `hdpi` | high-density screens (~240dpi) |
| `xhdpi` | extra-high-density screens (~320dpi) |
| `xxhdpi` | extra-extra-high-density screens (~480dpi) |
| `xxxhdpi` | extra-extra-extra-high-density screens (~640dpi) |

(There are a few other density categories that are omitted from the solutions, including ldpi and tvdpi.)

Within each directory, you will find two image files – `arrow_right.png` and `arrow_left.png`. These files have been customized for the screen pixel density specified in the directory's name.

You are going to include all the image files from the solutions in GeoQuiz. When the app runs, the OS will choose the best image file for the specific device running the app. Note that by duplicating the images multiple times, you increase the size of your application. In this case, this is not a problem because GeoQuiz is a simple app.

If an app runs on a device that has a screen density not included in any of the application's screen density qualifiers, Android will automatically scale the available image to the appropriate size for the device. Thanks to this feature, it is not necessary to provide images for all of the pixel density buckets. To reduce the size of your application, you can focus on one or a few of the higher-resolution buckets and selectively optimize for lower resolutions when Android's automatic scaling provides an image with artifacts on those lower-resolution devices.

(You will see alternatives to duplicating images at different densities, along with an explanation of the `mipmap` directory, in Chapter 22.)

## Adding resources to a project

The next step is to add the image files to GeoQuiz's resources.

Make sure the project tool window is displaying the Project view. Expand the contents of GeoQuiz/ app/src/main/res, as shown in Figure 2.6. You will see that some folders, such as mipmap-hdpi and mipmap-xhdpi, already exist.

### Figure 2.6  Exploring resources in Project view

Back in the solutions files, select and copy the five directories that you located earlier: drawable-hdpi, drawable-mdpi, drawable-xhdpi, drawable-xxhdpi, and drawable-xxxhdpi. In Android Studio, click on the app/src/main/res directory in the project tool window and paste the copied directories. Click OK in the confirmation pop-up. You should now have five density-qualified drawable directories, each with an arrow_left.png and arrow_right.png file, as shown in Figure 2.7.

Figure 2.7  Arrow icons in GeoQuiz `drawable` directories

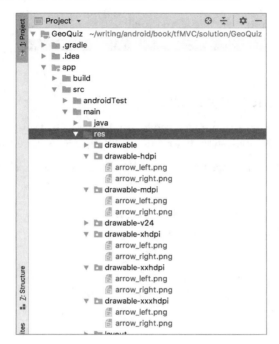

If you switch the project tool window back to the Android view, you will see the newly added drawable files summarized (as shown in Figure 2.8).

Figure 2.8  Summary of arrow icons in GeoQuiz `drawable` directories

Including images in your app is as simple as that. Any `.png`, `.jpg`, or `.gif` file you add to a `res/drawable` folder will be automatically assigned a resource ID. (Note that filenames must be lowercase and have no spaces.)

These resource IDs are not qualified by screen density, so you do not need to determine the device's screen density at runtime. All you have to do is use this resource ID in your code. When the app runs, the OS will determine the appropriate image to display on that particular device.

You will learn more about how the Android resource system works starting in Chapter 3. For now, let's put that right arrow to work.

## Referencing resources in XML

You use resource IDs to reference resources in code. But you want to configure the NEXT button to display the arrow in the layout definition. How do you reference a resource from XML?

Answer: with a slightly different syntax. Open `activity_main.xml` and add two attributes to the **Button** widget definition.

### Listing 2.11  Adding an icon to the NEXT button (res/layout/activity_main.xml)

```
<LinearLayout ... >
    ...
    <LinearLayout ... >
        ...
    </LinearLayout>

    <Button
        android:id="@+id/next_button"
        android:layout_width="wrap_content"
        android:layout_height="wrap_content"
        android:text="@string/next_button"
        android:drawableEnd="@drawable/arrow_right"
        android:drawablePadding="4dp" />

</LinearLayout>
```

In an XML resource, you refer to another resource by its resource type and name. A reference to a string resource begins with `@string/`. A reference to a drawable resource begins with `@drawable/`.

You will learn more about naming resources and working in the `res` directory structure starting in Chapter 3.

Run GeoQuiz and admire your button's new appearance. Then test it to make sure it still works as before.

## Screen Pixel Densities

In `activity_main.xml`, you specified attribute values in terms of `dp` units. Now it is time to learn what they are.

Sometimes you need to specify values for view attributes in terms of specific sizes (usually in pixels, but sometimes points, millimeters, or inches). You see this most commonly with attributes for text size, margins, and padding. Text size is the pixel height of the text on the device's screen. Margins specify the distances between views, and padding specifies the distance between a view's outside edges and its content.

As you saw in the section called Adding an Icon, Android automatically scales images to different screen pixel densities using density-qualified drawable folders (such as `drawable-xhdpi`). But what happens when your images scale, but your margins do not? Or when the user configures a larger-than-default text size?

To solve these problems, Android provides density-independent dimension units that you can use to get the same size on different screen densities. Android translates these units into pixels at runtime, so there is no tricky math for you to do (Figure 2.9).

## Figure 2.9  Dimension units in action on `TextView`

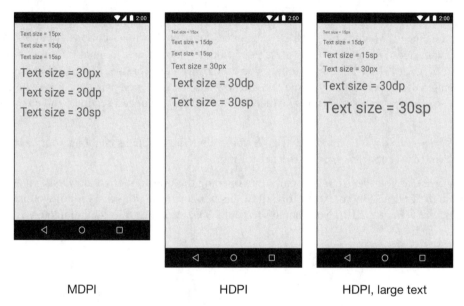

| MDPI | HDPI | HDPI, large text |

| px | Short for *pixel*. One pixel corresponds to one onscreen pixel, no matter what the display density is. Because pixels do not scale appropriately with device display density, their use is not recommended. |
| dp | Short for *density-independent pixel* and usually pronounced "dip." You typically use this for margins, padding, or anything else for which you would otherwise specify size with a pixel value. One `dp` is always 1/160 of an inch on a device's screen. You get the same size regardless of screen density: When your display is a higher density, density-independent pixels will expand to fill a larger number of screen pixels. |
| sp | Short for *scale-independent pixel*. Scale-independent pixels are density-independent pixels that also take into account the user's font size preference. You will almost always use `sp` to set display text size. |
| pt, mm, in | These are scaled units, like `dp`, that allow you to specify interface sizes in points (1/72 of an inch), millimeters, or inches. However, we do not recommend using them: Not all devices are correctly configured for these units to scale correctly. |

In practice and in this book, you will use `dp` and `sp` almost exclusively. Android will translate these values into pixels at runtime.

# Running on a Device

It is fun to interact with your app on an emulator. It is even more fun to interact with your app on a physical Android device. In this section, you will set up your system, device, and application to get GeoQuiz running on your hardware device.

First, plug the device into your computer. If you are developing on a Mac, your system should recognize the device right away. On Windows, you may need to install the adb (Android Debug Bridge) driver. If Windows cannot find the adb driver, then download one from the device manufacturer's website.

Second, enable USB debugging on your Android device. To do this, you need to access the Developer options settings menu, which is not visible by default. To enable developer options, go to Settings → About Tablet/Phone. Scroll down and press Build Number seven times in quick succession. After several presses, you will see a message telling you how many steps (presses of the build number) you are from being a developer. When you see You are now a developer!, you can stop. Then you can return to Settings, see Developer options (you may need to expand the Advanced section), and enable USB debugging.

The options vary considerably across devices. If you are having problems enabling your device, visit developer.android.com/tools/device.html for more help.

Finally, confirm that your device is recognized by opening the Logcat tool window using its button at the bottom of Android Studio. At the top left of this window, you will see a drop-down list of connected devices (Figure 2.10). You should see your AVD, also known as your emulator, and your hardware device listed.

## Figure 2.10  Viewing connected devices

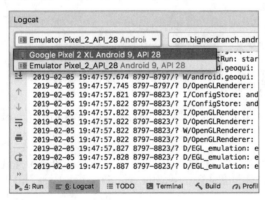

If you are having trouble getting your device recognized, verify that your device is turned on and that the USB debugging option is enabled.

If you are still unable to see your device in the devices view, you can find more help on the Android developers' site. Start at developer.android.com/tools/device.html. You can also visit this book's forum at forums.bignerdranch.com for more troubleshooting help.

Run GeoQuiz as before. Android Studio will offer a choice between running on the virtual device or the hardware device plugged into your system. Select the hardware device and continue. GeoQuiz will launch on your device.

If Android Studio defaults to your emulator without offering a choice of device to run the app on, recheck the steps above and make sure your device is plugged in. Next, if you are running Android Studio 3.5 or later, ensure that the device is selected in the dropdown at the top of the screen. For earlier versions of Android Studio, ensure that your run configuration is correct. To modify the run configuration, select the app drop-down list near the top of the window, as shown in Figure 2.11.

## Figure 2.11  Run configurations

Choose Edit Configurations... and you will be presented with a new window with details about your run configuration (Figure 2.12).

## Figure 2.12  Run configuration properties

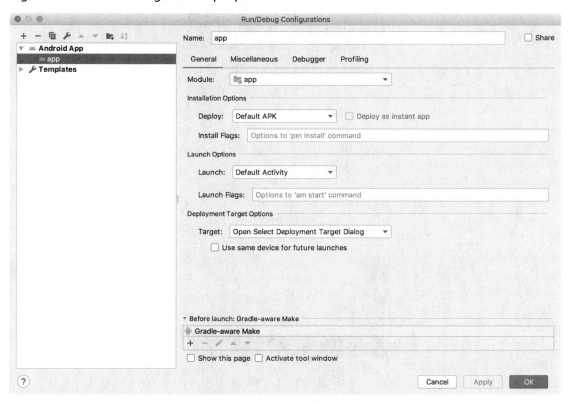

Select app in the left pane and verify that Deployment Target Options is set to Open Select Deployment Target Dialog and that Use same device for future launches is unchecked. Select OK and rerun the app. You should now be presented with a choice of device to launch the app on.

## Challenge: Add a Listener to the TextView

Your NEXT button is nice, but you could also make it so that a user could press the **TextView** itself to see the next question.

Hint: You can use the **View.OnClickListener** listener for the **TextView** that you have used with the **Button**s, because **TextView** also inherits from **View**.

## Challenge: Add a Previous Button

Add a button that the user can press to go back one question. The UI should look something like Figure 2.13.

Figure 2.13  Now with a previous button!

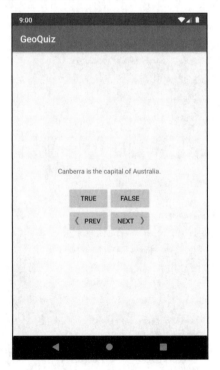

This is a great challenge. It requires you to retrace many of the steps in these two chapters.

# Challenge: From Button to ImageButton

Perhaps the UI would look even better if the next and previous buttons showed *only* icons, as in Figure 2.14.

Figure 2.14  Icon-only buttons

To accomplish this challenge, these two widgets must become **ImageButton**s instead of regular **Button**s.

**ImageButton** is a widget that inherits from **ImageView**. **Button**, on the other hand, inherits from **TextView**. Figure 2.15 shows their different inheritance hierarchies.

## Figure 2.15  Inheritance diagram for **ImageButton** and **Button**

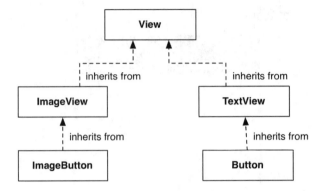

You can replace the text and drawable attributes on the NEXT button with a single **ImageView** attribute:

```
<~~Button~~ ImageButton
    android:id="@+id/next_button"
    android:layout_width="wrap_content"
    android:layout_height="wrap_content"
    android:text="@string/next_button"
    android:drawableEnd="@drawable/arrow_right"
    android:drawablePadding="4dp"
    android:src="@drawable/arrow_right"
    />
```

Of course, you will need to modify **MainActivity** to work with **ImageButton**.

After you have changed the buttons to **ImageButton**s, Android Studio will warn you about a missing android:contentDescription attribute. This attribute supports accessibility for users with vision impairments. You set the value to a string, which is read aloud when users have the appropriate settings applied.

Add an android:contentDescription attribute to each **ImageButton** to complete the challenge.

# 3

# The Activity Lifecycle

In this chapter you will learn the cause of the dreaded – and very common – "rotation problem." You will also learn how to leverage the mechanics underlying the rotation problem to display an alternate layout when the device is in landscape mode (Figure 3.1).

Figure 3.1  GeoQuiz in landscape orientation

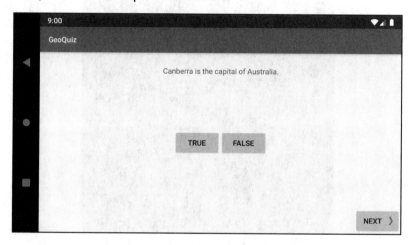

## Rotating GeoQuiz

GeoQuiz works great … until you rotate the device. While the app is running, press the NEXT button to show another question. Then rotate the device. If you are running on the emulator, click the rotate left or rotate right button in the floating toolbar to rotate (Figure 3.2).

Figure 3.2  Control the roll

If the emulator does not rotate after you press one of the rotate buttons, turn auto-rotate on. Swipe down from the top of the screen to open Quick Settings. Press the auto-rotate icon, which is the third icon from the left (Figure 3.3). The icon will change from grayed out to a teal color to indicate that auto-rotate is now on.

Figure 3.3  Quick Setting for auto-rotate

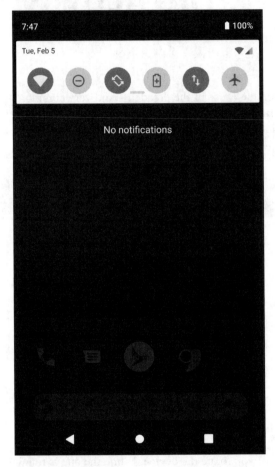

After you rotate, you will see the first question again. How and why did this happen? The answers to these questions have to do with the activity lifecycle.

You will learn how to fix this problem in Chapter 4. But first, it is important to understand the root of the problem so you can avoid related bugs that might creep up.

# Activity States and Lifecycle Callbacks

Every instance of **Activity** has a lifecycle. During this lifecycle, an activity transitions between four states: resumed, paused, stopped, and nonexistent. For each transition, there is an **Activity** function that notifies the activity of the change in its state. Figure 3.4 shows the activity lifecycle, states, and functions.

Figure 3.4  Activity state diagram

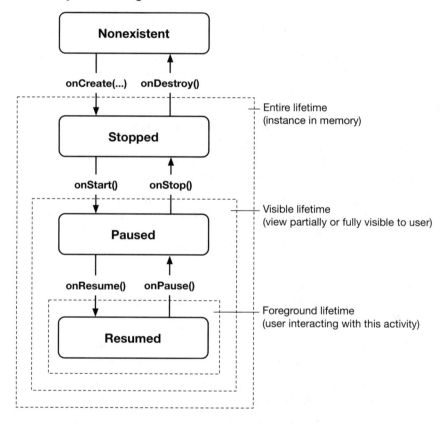

Figure 3.4 indicates for each state whether the activity has an instance in memory, is visible to the user, or is active in the foreground (accepting user input). Table 3.1 summarizes this information.

## Table 3.1  Activity states

| State | In memory? | Visible to user? | In foreground? |
|---|---|---|---|
| nonexistent | no | no | no |
| stopped | yes | no | no |
| paused | yes | yes/partially* | no |
| resumed | yes | yes | yes |

(* Depending on the circumstances, a paused activity may be fully or partially visible.)

*Nonexistent* represents an activity that has not been launched yet or an activity that was just destroyed (by the user pressing the Back button, for example). For that reason, this state is sometimes referred to as the "destroyed" state. There is no instance in memory, and there is no associated view for the user to see or interact with.

*Stopped* represents an activity that has an instance in memory but whose view is not visible on the screen. This state occurs in passing when the activity is first spinning up and re-occurs any time the view is fully occluded (such as when the user launches another full-screen activity to the foreground, presses the Home button, or uses the overview screen to switch tasks).

*Paused* represents an activity that is not active in the foreground but whose view is visible or partially visible. An activity would be partially visible, for example, if the user launched a new dialog-themed or transparent activity on top of it. An activity could also be fully visible but not in the foreground if the user is viewing two activities in multi-window mode (also called "split-screen mode").

*Resumed* represents an activity that is in memory, fully visible, and in the foreground. It is the activity the user is currently interacting with. Only one activity across the entire system can be in the resumed state at any given time. That means that if one activity is moving into the resumed state, another is likely moving out of the resumed state.

Subclasses of **Activity** can take advantage of the functions named in Figure 3.4 to get work done at critical transitions in the activity's lifecycle. These functions are often called *lifecycle callbacks*.

You are already acquainted with one of these lifecycle callback functions – **onCreate(Bundle?)**. The OS calls this function after the activity instance is created but before it is put onscreen.

Typically, an activity overrides **onCreate(Bundle?)** to prepare the specifics of its UI:

- inflating widgets and putting them on screen (in the call to **setContentView(Int)**)

- getting references to inflated widgets

- setting listeners on widgets to handle user interaction

- connecting to external model data

It is important to understand that you never call **onCreate(Bundle?)** or any of the other **Activity** lifecycle functions yourself. You simply override the callbacks in your activity subclass. Then Android calls the lifecycle callbacks at the appropriate time (in relation to what the user is doing and what is happening across the rest of the system) to notify the activity that its state is changing.

# Logging the Activity Lifecycle

In this section, you are going to override lifecycle functions to eavesdrop on **MainActivity**'s lifecycle. Each implementation will simply log a message informing you that the function has been called. This will help you see how **MainActivity**'s state changes at runtime in relation to what the user is doing.

## Making log messages

In Android, the **android.util.Log** class sends log messages to a shared system-level log. **Log** has several functions for logging messages. Here is the one that you will use most often in this book:

```
public static Int d(String tag, String msg)
```

The **d** stands for "debug" and refers to the level of the log message. (There is more about the **Log** levels in the section called For the More Curious: Log Levels near the end of this chapter.) The first parameter identifies the source of the message, and the second is the contents of the message.

The first string is typically a TAG constant with the class name as its value. This makes it easy to determine the source of a particular message.

Open MainActivity.kt and add a TAG constant to **MainActivity**:

Listing 3.1  Adding a TAG constant (MainActivity.kt)

```
import ...

private const val TAG = "MainActivity"

class MainActivity : AppCompatActivity() {
    ...
}
```

Next, in **onCreate(Bundle?)**, call **Log.d(…)** to log a message.

Listing 3.2  Adding a log statement to **onCreate(Bundle?)** (MainActivity.kt)

```
override fun onCreate(savedInstanceState: Bundle?) {
    super.onCreate(savedInstanceState)
    Log.d(TAG, "onCreate(Bundle?) called")
    setContentView(R.layout.activity_main)
    ...
}
```

Now override five more lifecycle functions in **MainActivity** by adding the following after
`onCreate(Bundle?)`:

## Listing 3.3  Overriding more lifecycle functions (`MainActivity.kt`)

```kotlin
class MainActivity : AppCompatActivity() {
    ...
    override fun onCreate(savedInstanceState: Bundle?) {
        ...
    }

    override fun onStart() {
        super.onStart()
        Log.d(TAG, "onStart() called")
    }

    override fun onResume() {
        super.onResume()
        Log.d(TAG, "onResume() called")
    }

    override fun onPause() {
        super.onPause()
        Log.d(TAG, "onPause() called")
    }

    override fun onStop() {
        super.onStop()
        Log.d(TAG, "onStop() called")
    }

    override fun onDestroy() {
        super.onDestroy()
        Log.d(TAG, "onDestroy() called")
    }

    private fun updateQuestion() {
        ...
    }
    ...
}
```

Notice that you call the superclass implementations before you log your messages. These superclass
calls are required. Calling the superclass implementation should be the first line of each callback
function override implementation.

You may have been wondering about the `override` keyword. This asks the compiler to ensure that the
class actually has the function that you want to override. For example, the compiler would be able to
alert you to the following misspelled function name:

```kotlin
override fun onCreat(savedInstanceState: Bundle?) {
    ...
}
```

The parent **AppCompatActivity** class does not have an **onCreat(Bundle?)** function, so the compiler
will complain. This way you can fix the typo now, rather than waiting until you run the app and see
strange behavior to discover the error.

## Using Logcat

Run GeoQuiz and messages will start materializing in the Logcat tool window at the bottom of Android Studio, as shown in Figure 3.5. If Logcat did not open automatically when you ran GeoQuiz, you can open it by clicking the Logcat button at the bottom of the Android Studio window.

### Figure 3.5 Android Studio with Logcat

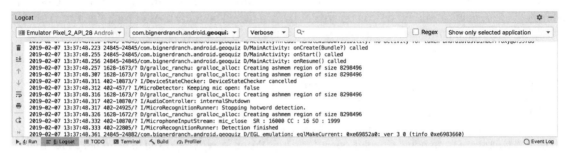

You will see your own messages along with some system output. To make your messages easier to find, you can filter the output using the value you set for the TAG constant. In Logcat, click the dropdown in the top right that reads Show only selected application. This is the filter dropdown, which is currently set to show messages from only your app.

In the filter dropdown, select Edit Filter Configuration to create a new filter. Name the filter MainActivity and enter MainActivity in the Log Tag field (Figure 3.6).

### Figure 3.6 Creating a filter in Logcat

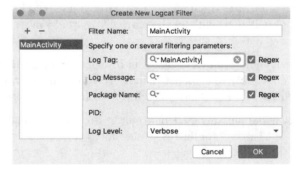

Click OK. Now, only messages tagged "MainActivity" will be visible in Logcat (Figure 3.7).

### Figure 3.7 Launching GeoQuiz creates, starts, and resumes an activity

# Exploring How the Activity Lifecycle Responds to User Actions

Three lifecycle functions were called after GeoQuiz was launched and the initial instance of **MainActivity** was created: **onCreate(Bundle?)**, **onStart()**, and **onResume()** (Figure 3.7). Your **MainActivity** instance is now in the resumed state (in memory, visible, and active in the foreground).

As you continue through the book, you will override the different activity lifecycle functions to do real things for your application. When you do, you will learn more about the uses of each function. For now, have some fun familiarizing yourself with how the lifecycle behaves in common usage scenarios by interacting with your app and checking out the logs in Logcat.

## Temporarily leaving an activity

If GeoQuiz is not already running on your device, run the app from Android Studio. Now press the Home button. The home screen displays, and **MainActivity** moves completely out of view. What state is **MainActivity** in now? Check Logcat for a hint. Your activity received calls to **onPause()** and **onStop()**, but not **onDestroy()** (Figure 3.8).

Figure 3.8  Pressing the Home button stops the activity

By pressing the Home button, the user is telling Android, "I'm going to go look at something else, but I might come back. I'm not really done with this screen yet." Android pauses and ultimately stops the activity.

So after you press the Home button from GeoQuiz, your instance of **MainActivity** hangs out in the stopped state (in memory, not visible, and not active in the foreground). Android does this so it can quickly and easily restart **MainActivity** where you left off when you come back to GeoQuiz later.

(This is not the whole story about pressing the Home button. Stopped applications can be destroyed at the discretion of the OS. See Chapter 4 for the rest of the story.)

Go back to GeoQuiz by selecting the GeoQuiz task card from the *overview screen*. To do this, press the Recents button, which is next to the Home button (Figure 3.9).

Figure 3.9  Back, Home, and Recents buttons

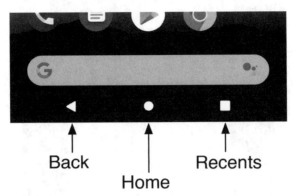

If your device does not have a Recents button, and instead has a single Home button (as shown in Figure 3.10), swipe up from the bottom of the screen to open the overview screen. If neither of these approaches works on your device, consult the device manufacturer's user guide.

Figure 3.10  Single Home button

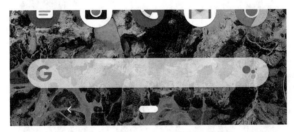

Each card in the overview screen represents an app the user has interacted with in the past (Figure 3.11). (By the way, the overview screen is often called the "Recents screen" or "task manager" by users. We defer to the developer documentation, which calls it the "overview screen.")

Figure 3.11  Overview screen

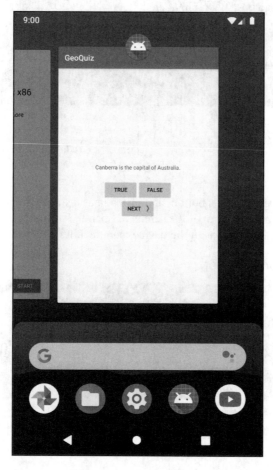

Click on the GeoQuiz task card in the overview screen. **MainActivity** will fill the screen.

A quick look at Logcat shows that your activity got calls to **onStart()** and **onResume()**. Note that **onCreate(…)** was not called. This is because **MainActivity** was in the stopped state after the user pressed the Home button. Because the activity instance was still in memory, it did not need to be created. Instead, the activity only had to be started (moved to the paused/visible state) and then resumed (moved to the resumed/foreground state).

Earlier, we said that it is possible for an activity to hang out in the paused state, either partially visible (such as when a new activity with either a transparent background or a smaller-than-screen size is launched on top) or fully visible (in multi-window mode). Let's see multi-window mode in action.

Multi-window mode is only available on Android 7.0 Nougat and higher, so use an emulator to test it if your device is running an earlier version of Android. Open the overview screen again and long-press the icon at the top of the GeoQuiz card. Select Split screen (shown on the left in Figure 3.12), and a new window appears on the bottom portion of the screen displaying a list of app cards (shown in the center in Figure 3.12). Click on one of the cards to launch the corresponding app.

This launches multi-window mode with GeoQuiz in the top window and the second app you selected in the bottom window (shown on the right in Figure 3.12).

Figure 3.12 Opening two apps in multi-window mode

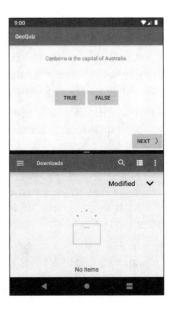

Now, click on the app in the bottom window and look at the logs in Logcat. **onPause()** was called on **MainActivity**, so the activity is now in the paused state. Click on GeoQuiz in the top window. **onResume()** was called on **MainActivity**, so the activity is now in the resumed state.

To exit multi-window mode, swipe the window separator in the middle of the screen down to the bottom of the screen to dismiss the bottom window. (Swiping the separator up dismisses the top window.)

# Finishing an activity

Press the Back button on the device and then check Logcat. Your activity received calls to **onPause()**, **onStop()**, and **onDestroy()** (Figure 3.13). Your **MainActivity** instance is now in the nonexistent state (not in memory and thus not visible – and certainly not active in the foreground).

## Figure 3.13  Pressing the Back button destroys the activity

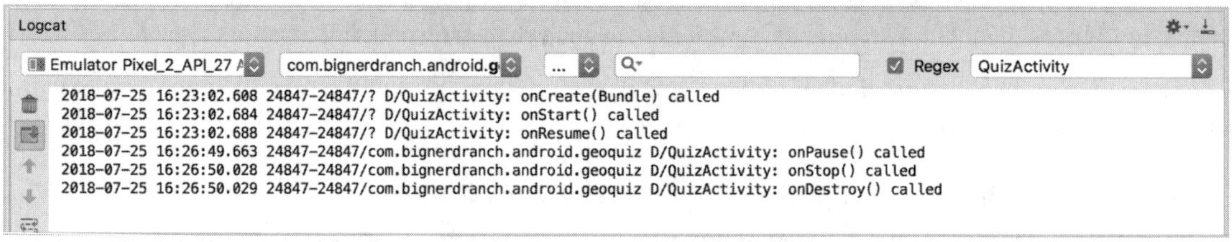

When you pressed the Back button, you as the user of the app *finished* the activity. In other words, you told Android, "I'm done with this activity, and I won't need it anymore." Android then destroyed your activity's view and removed all traces of the activity from memory. This is Android's way of being frugal with your device's limited resources.

Another way the user can finish an activity is to swipe the app's card from the overview screen. As a developer, you can programmatically finish an activity by calling **Activity.finish()**.

# Rotating an activity

Now it is time to get back to the bug you found at the beginning of this chapter. Run GeoQuiz, press the NEXT button to reveal the second question, and then rotate the device. (On the emulator, click the rotation icon in the toolbar.)

After rotating, GeoQuiz will display the first question again. Check Logcat to see what has happened. Your output should look like Figure 3.14.

## Figure 3.14  **MainActivity** is dead. Long live **MainActivity**!

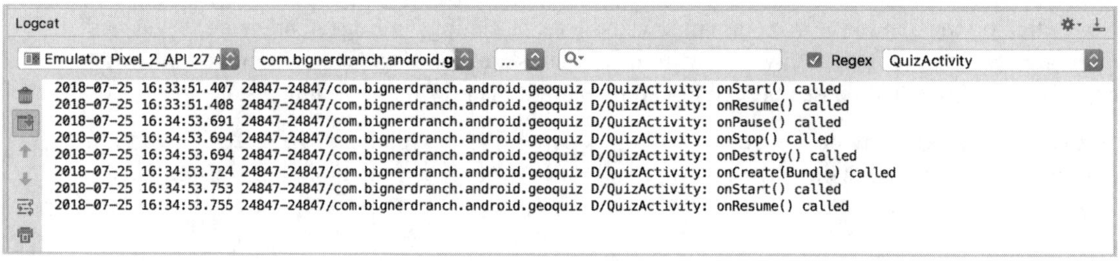

When you rotated the device, the instance of **MainActivity** that you were looking at was destroyed, and a new one was created. Rotate the device again to witness another round of destruction and rebirth.

This is the source of your GeoQuiz bug. Each time you rotate the device, the current **MainActivity** instance is completely destroyed. The value that was stored in currentIndex in that instance is wiped from memory. This means that when you rotate, GeoQuiz forgets which question you were looking at. As rotation finishes, Android creates a new instance of **MainActivity** from scratch. currentIndex is initialized to 0 in **onCreate(Bundle?)**, and the user starts over at the first question.

You will fix this bug in Chapter 4. Before making the fix, take a closer look at why the OS destroys your activity when the user rotates the device.

# Device Configuration Changes and the Activity Lifecycle

Rotating the device changes the *device configuration*. The device configuration is a set of characteristics that describe the current state of an individual device. The characteristics that make up the configuration include screen orientation, screen density, screen size, keyboard type, dock mode, language, and more.

Typically, applications provide alternative resources to match device configurations. You saw an example of this when you added multiple arrow icons to your project for different screen densities.

When a *runtime configuration change* occurs, there may be resources that are a better match for the new configuration. So Android destroys the activity, looks for resources that are the best fit for the new configuration, and then rebuilds a new instance of the activity with those resources. To see this in action, create an alternative resource for Android to find and use when the device's screen orientation changes to landscape.

## Creating a landscape layout

In the project tool window, right-click the res directory and select New → Android Resource File. You should see a window similar to Figure 3.15 that lists the resource types and qualifiers for those types. Type activity_main in the File name field. Select Layout in the Resource type dropdown. Type FrameLayout in the Root element field. Leave the Source set option set to main.

Figure 3.15  Creating a new resource file

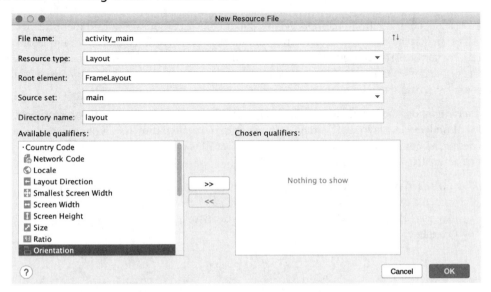

Next, you will choose how the new layout resource will be qualified. Select Orientation in the Available qualifiers list and click the >> button to move Orientation to the Chosen qualifiers section.

Finally, ensure that Landscape is selected in the Screen orientation dropdown, as shown in Figure 3.16. Verify that the Directory name now shows layout-land. While this window looks fancy, its purpose is just to determine the name of the directory where the new resource file will be placed. Click OK.

Figure 3.16  Creating `res/layout-land/activity_main.xml`

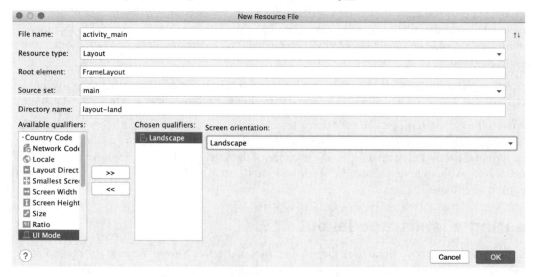

Android Studio will create the `res/layout-land/` folder in your project and place a new layout file named `activity_main.xml` in the new folder. Switch the project tool window to the Project view to see the files and folders in your project as they actually are. Switch back to the Android view to see the summary of the files.

As you have seen, configuration qualifiers on `res` subdirectories are how Android identifies which resources best match the current device configuration. The `-land` suffix is another example of a configuration qualifier. You can find the list of configuration qualifiers that Android recognizes and the aspects of the device configuration that they refer to at `developer.android.com/guide/topics/resources/providing-resources.html`.

You now have a landscape layout and a default layout. When the device is in landscape orientation, Android will find and use layout resources in the `res/layout-land` directory. Otherwise, it will stick with the default in `res/layout/`. Note that the two layout files must have the same filename so that they can be referenced with the same resource ID.

At the moment, `res/layout-land/activity_main.xml` displays an empty screen. To fix this, copy all the contents except the root **LinearLayout** open and closing tags from `res/layout/activity_main.xml`. Paste the code into `res/layout-land/activity_main.xml`, between the open and closing **FrameLayout** tags.

Next, make the changes shown in Listing 3.4 to the landscape layout so that it is different from the default.

## Listing 3.4  Tweaking the landscape layout (res/layout-land/activity_main.xml)

```xml
<FrameLayout xmlns:android="http://schemas.android.com/apk/res/android"
    xmlns:tools="http://schemas.android.com/tools"
    android:layout_width="match_parent"
    android:layout_height="match_parent" >

    <TextView
        android:id="@+id/question_text_view"
        android:layout_width="wrap_content"
        android:layout_height="wrap_content"
        android:gravity="center"
        android:layout_gravity="center_horizontal"
        android:padding="24dp"
        tools:text="@string/question_australia"/>

    <LinearLayout
        android:layout_width="wrap_content"
        android:layout_height="wrap_content"
        android:orientation="horizontal"
        android:layout_gravity="center_vertical|center_horizontal">

        <Button
            .../>

        <Button
            .../>

    </LinearLayout>

    <Button
        android:id="@+id/next_button"
        android:layout_width="wrap_content"
        android:layout_height="wrap_content"
        android:layout_gravity="bottom|right"
        android:text="@string/next_button"
        android:drawableEnd="@drawable/arrow_right"
        android:drawablePadding="4dp"/>

</FrameLayout>
```

**FrameLayout** is the simplest **ViewGroup** and does not arrange its children in any particular manner. In this layout, child views will be arranged according to their android:layout_gravity attributes. This is why you added android:layout_gravity to **TextView**, **LinearLayout**, and **Button** – they are all children of the **FrameLayout**. The **Button** children of the nested **LinearLayout** can stay exactly the same since they are not direct children of the **FrameLayout**.

Run GeoQuiz again. Rotate the device to landscape to see the new layout (Figure 3.17). Of course, this is not just a new layout – it is a new **MainActivity** instance as well.

Figure 3.17 **MainActivity** in landscape orientation

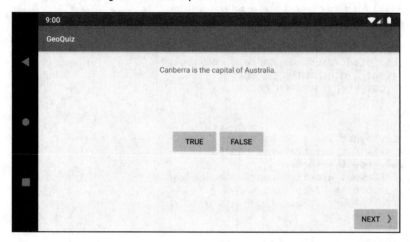

Rotate back to portrait to see the default layout and yet another new **MainActivity**.

What good is an app that resets itself when the user rotates the device, even if it has a lovely landscape-specific layout? In Chapter 4, you will learn how to fix the GeoQuiz bug caused by the rotation problem.

# For the More Curious: UI Updates and Multi-Window Mode

Prior to Android 7.0 Nougat, most activities spent very little time in the paused state. Instead, activities passed through the paused state quickly on their way to either the resumed state or the stopped state. Because of this, many developers assumed they only needed to update their UI when their activity was in the resumed state. It was common practice to use **onResume()** and **onPause()** to start or stop any ongoing updates related to the UI (such as animations or data refreshes).

When multi-window mode was introduced in Nougat, it broke the assumption that resumed activities were the only fully visible activities. This, in turn, broke the intended behavior of many apps. Now, paused activities can be fully visible for extended periods of time when the user is in multi-window mode. And users will expect those paused activities to behave as if they were resumed.

Consider video, for example. Suppose you have a pre-Nougat app that provides simple video playback. You start (or resume) video playback in **onResume()** and pause playback in **onPause()**. Multi-window mode comes along, but your app stops playback when it is paused and users are interacting with another app in the second window. Users start complaining, because they want to watch their videos *while* they send a text message in a separate window.

Luckily, the fix is relatively simple: Move your playback resuming and pausing to **onStart()** and **onStop()**. This goes for any live-updating data, like a photo gallery app that refreshes to show new images as they are pushed to a Flickr stream (as you will see later in this book).

In short, in the post-Nougat world, your activities should update the UI during their entire visible lifecycle, from **onStart()** to **onStop()**.

Unfortunately, not everyone got the memo, and many apps still misbehave in multi-window mode. To fix this, the Android team introduced a spec to support *multi-resume* for multi-window mode in November 2018. Multi-resume means that the fully visible activity in each of the windows will be in the resumed state when the device is in multi-window mode, regardless of which window the user last touched.

You can opt in to using multi-resume mode for your app when it is running on Android 9.0 Pie by adding metadata to your Android manifest: <meta-data android:name="android.allow_multiple_resumed_activities" android:value="true" />. You will learn more about the manifest in Chapter 6.

Even if you opt in, multi-resume will only work on devices whose manufacturer implemented the multi-resume spec. And, as of this writing, no devices on the market implement it. However, there are rumors that the spec will become mandatory in the next version of Android (the yet-to-be-named Android Q).

Until multi-resume becomes a readily available standard across most devices in the marketplace, use your knowledge of the activity lifecycle to reason about where to place UI update code. You will get a lot of practice doing so throughout the course of this book.

# For the More Curious: Log Levels

When you use the **android.util.Log** class to send log messages, you control not only the content of a message but also a *level* that specifies how important the message is. Android supports five log levels, shown in Table 3.2. Each level has a corresponding function in the **Log** class. Sending output to the log is as simple as calling the corresponding **Log** function.

Table 3.2 Log levels and functions

| Log level | Function | Used for |
|-----------|----------|----------|
| ERROR | Log.e(…) | errors |
| WARNING | Log.w(…) | warnings |
| INFO | Log.i(…) | informational messages |
| DEBUG | Log.d(…) | debug output (may be filtered out) |
| VERBOSE | Log.v(…) | development only |

In addition, each of the logging functions has two signatures: one that takes a TAG string and a message string, and a second that takes those two arguments plus an instance of **Throwable**, which makes it easy to log information about a particular exception that your application might throw. Listing 3.5 shows some sample log function signatures.

Listing 3.5 Different ways of logging in Android

```
// Log a message at DEBUG log level
Log.d(TAG, "Current question index: $currentIndex")

try {
    val question = questionBank[currentIndex]
} catch (ex: ArrayIndexOutOfBoundsException) {
    // Log a message at ERROR log level, along with an exception stack trace
    Log.e(TAG, "Index was out of bounds", ex)
}
```

# Challenge: Preventing Repeat Answers

Once a user provides an answer for a particular question, disable the buttons for that question to prevent multiple answers being entered.

# Challenge: Graded Quiz

After the user provides answers for all of the quiz questions, display a **Toast** with a percentage score for the quiz. Good luck!

# 4

# Persisting UI State

Android does a great job of providing alternative resources at the right time. However, destroying and re-creating activities on rotation can cause headaches, such as GeoQuiz's bug of reverting back to the first question when the device is rotated.

To fix this bug, the post-rotation `MainActivity` instance needs to know the old value of `currentIndex`. You need a way to save this data across a runtime configuration change, like rotation.

In this chapter you will fix GeoQuiz's UI state loss on rotation bug by storing its UI data in a `ViewModel`. You will also address a less easily discoverable, but equally problematic, bug – UI state loss on process death – using Android's saved instance state mechanism.

# Including the ViewModel Dependency

In a moment, you are going to add a **ViewModel** class to your project. The **ViewModel** class comes from an Android Jetpack library called lifecycle-extensions, one of many libraries that you will use throughout this book. (You will learn more about Jetpack later in this chapter.) To use the class, you must first include the library in the list of *dependencies* for your project.

Your project's dependencies live in a file called build.gradle (recall that Gradle is the Android build tool). In the project tool window, with the Android view enabled, expand the Gradle scripts section and take a look at the contents. Your project actually comes with two build.gradle files: one for the project as a whole and one for your app module. Open the build.gradle file located in your app module. You should see something similar to Listing 4.1.

## Listing 4.1  Gradle dependencies (app/build.gradle)

```
apply plugin: 'com.android.application'

apply plugin: 'kotlin-android'

apply plugin: 'kotlin-android-extensions'

android {
    ...
}

dependencies {
    implementation fileTree(dir: 'libs', include: ['*.jar'])
    implementation"org.jetbrains.kotlin:kotlin-stdlib-jdk7:$kotlin_version"
    implementation 'androidx.appcompat:appcompat:1.0.0-beta01'
    ...
}
```

The first line in the dependencies section specifies that the project depends on all of the .jar files in its libs directory. The other lines list libraries that were automatically included in your project based on the settings you selected when you created it.

Gradle also allows for the specification of new dependencies. When your app is compiled, Gradle will find, download, and include the dependencies for you. All you have to do is specify an exact string incantation and Gradle will do the rest.

Add the lifecycle-extensions dependency to your app/build.gradle file, as shown in Listing 4.2. Its exact placement in the dependencies section does not matter, but to keep things tidy it is good to put new dependencies under the last existing implementation dependency.

## Listing 4.2  Adding lifecycle-extensions dependency (app/build.gradle)

```
dependencies {
    ...
    implementation 'androidx.constraintlayout:constraintlayout:1.1.2'
    implementation 'androidx.lifecycle:lifecycle-extensions:2.0.0'
    ...
}
```

When you make any change to build.gradle, Android Studio will prompt you to sync the file (Figure 4.1).

## Figure 4.1 Gradle sync prompt

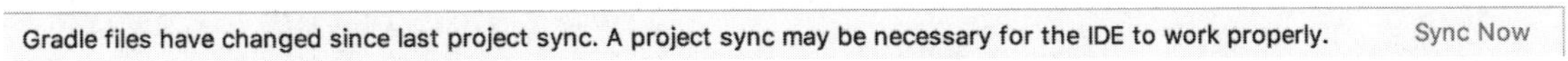

Gradle files have changed since last project sync. A project sync may be necessary for the IDE to work properly.    Sync Now

This sync asks Gradle to update the build based on your changes by either downloading or removing dependencies. To sync, either click Sync Now in the prompt or select File → Sync Project with Gradle Files.

# Adding a ViewModel

Now, back to **ViewModel**. A **ViewModel** is related to one particular screen and is a great place to put logic involved in formatting the data to display on that screen. A **ViewModel** holds on to a model object and "decorates" the model – adding functionality to display onscreen that you might not want in the model itself. Using a **ViewModel** aggregates all the data the screen needs in one place, formats the data, and makes it easy to access the end result.

**ViewModel** is part of the androidx.lifecycle package, which contains lifecycle-related APIs including *lifecycle-aware* components. Lifecycle-aware components observe the lifecycle of some other component, such as an activity, and take the state of that lifecycle into account.

Google created the androidx.lifecycle package and its contents to make dealing with the activity lifecycle (and other lifecycles, which you will learn about later in this book) a little less painful. You will learn about **LiveData**, another lifecycle-aware component, in Chapter 11. And you will learn how to create your own lifecycle-aware components in Chapter 25.

Now you are ready to create your **ViewModel** subclass, **QuizViewModel**. In the project tool window, right-click the com.bignerdranch.android.geoquiz package and select New → Kotlin File/Class. Enter QuizViewModel for the name and select Class from the Kind dropdown.

In QuizViewModel.kt, add an init block and override **onCleared()**. Log the creation and destruction of the **QuizViewModel** instance, as shown in Listing 4.3.

## Listing 4.3 Creating a **ViewModel** class (QuizViewModel.kt)

```kotlin
private const val TAG = "QuizViewModel"

class QuizViewModel : ViewModel() {

    init {
        Log.d(TAG, "ViewModel instance created")
    }

    override fun onCleared() {
        super.onCleared()
        Log.d(TAG, "ViewModel instance about to be destroyed")
    }
}
```

The **onCleared()** function is called just before a **ViewModel** is destroyed. This is a useful place to perform any cleanup, such as un-observing a data source. For now, you simply log the fact that the **ViewModel** is about to be destroyed so that you can explore its lifecycle (the same way you explored the lifecycle of **MainActivity** in Chapter 3).

Now, open `MainActivity.kt` and, in **onCreate(…)**, associate the activity with an instance of **QuizViewModel**.

## Listing 4.4  Accessing the **ViewModel** (MainActivity.kt)

```
class MainActivity : AppCompatActivity() {
    ...
    override fun onCreate(savedInstanceState: Bundle?) {
        ...
        setContentView(R.layout.activity_main)

        val provider: ViewModelProvider = ViewModelProviders.of(this)
        val quizViewModel = provider.get(QuizViewModel::class.java)
        Log.d(TAG, "Got a QuizViewModel: $quizViewModel")

        trueButton = findViewById(R.id.true_button)
        ...
    }
    ...
}
```

The **ViewModelProviders** class (note the plural "Providers") provides instances of the **ViewModelProvider** class. Your call to **ViewModelProviders.of(this)** creates and returns a **ViewModelProvider** associated with the activity.

**ViewModelProvider** (no plural), on the other hand, provides instances of **ViewModel** to the activity. Calling **provider.get(QuizViewModel::class.java)** returns an instance of **QuizViewModel**. You will most often see these functions chained together, like so:

```
ViewModelProviders.of(this).get(QuizViewModel::class.java)
```

The **ViewModelProvider** acts like a registry of **ViewModel**s. When the activity queries for a **QuizViewModel** for the first time, **ViewModelProvider** creates and returns a new **QuizViewModel** instance. When the activity queries for the **QuizViewModel** after a configuration change, the instance that was first created is returned. When the activity is finished (such as when the user presses the Back button), the **ViewModel-Activity** pair is removed from memory.

## ViewModel lifecycle and ViewModelProvider

You learned in Chapter 3 that activities transition between four states: resumed, paused, stopped, and nonexistent. You also learned about different ways an activity can be destroyed: either by the user finishing the activity or by the system destroying it as a result of a configuration change.

When the user finishes an activity, they expect their UI state to be reset. When the user rotates an activity, they expect their UI state to be the same before and after rotation.

You can determine which of these two scenarios is happening by checking the activity's isFinishing property. If isFinishing is true, the activity is being destroyed because the user finished the activity (such as by pressing the Back button or by clearing the app's card from the overview screen). If isFinishing is false, the activity is being destroyed by the system because of a configuration change.

But you do not need to track isFinishing and preserve UI state manually when it is false just to meet your user's expectations. Instead, you can use a **ViewModel** to keep an activity's UI state data in memory across configuration changes. A **ViewModel**'s lifecycle more closely mirrors the user's expectations: It survives configuration changes and is destroyed only when its associated activity is finished.

You associate a **ViewModel** instance with an activity's lifecycle, as you did in Listing 4.4. The **ViewModel** is then said to be *scoped* to that activity's lifecycle. This means the **ViewModel** will remain in memory, regardless of the activity's state, until the activity is finished. Once the activity is finished (such as by the user pressing the Back button), the **ViewModel** instance is destroyed (Figure 4.2).

Figure 4.2 **QuizViewModel** scoped to **MainActivity**

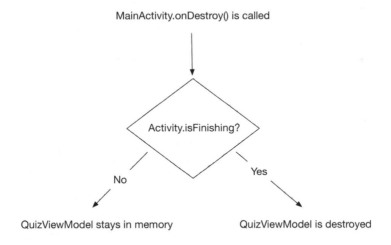

This means that the `ViewModel` stays in memory during a configuration change, such as rotation. During the configuration change, the activity instance is destroyed and re-created, but the `ViewModel`s scoped to the activity stay in memory. This is depicted in Figure 4.3, using `MainActivity` and `QuizViewModel`.

Figure 4.3  **`MainActivity`** and **`QuizViewModel`** across rotation

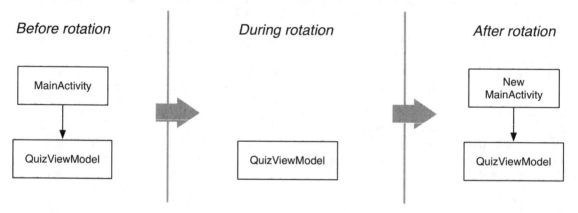

To see this in action, run GeoQuiz. In Logcat, select Edit Filter Configuration in the dropdown to create a new filter. In the Log Tag box, enter QuizViewModel|MainActivity (that is, the two class names with the pipe character | between them) to show only logs tagged with either class name. Name the filter ViewModelAndActivity (or another name that makes sense to you) and click OK (Figure 4.4).

Figure 4.4  Filtering **`QuizViewModel`** and **`MainActivity`** logs

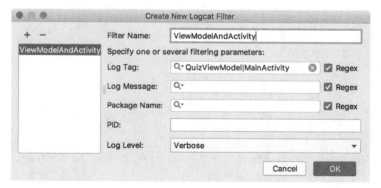

Now look at the logs. When **MainActivity** first launches and queries for the **ViewModel** in **onCreate(…)**, a new **QuizViewModel** instance is created. This is reflected in the logs (Figure 4.5).

Figure 4.5 **QuizViewModel** instance created

Rotate the device. The logs show the activity is destroyed (Figure 4.6). The **QuizViewModel** is not. When the new instance of **MainActivity** is created after rotation, it requests a **QuizViewModel**. Since the original **QuizViewModel** is still in memory, the **ViewModelProvider** returns that instance rather than creating a new one.

Figure 4.6 **MainActivity** is destroyed and re-created; **QuizViewModel** persists

Finally, press the Back button. **QuizViewModel.onCleared()** is called, indicating that the **QuizViewModel** instance is about to be destroyed, as the logs show (Figure 4.7). The **QuizViewModel** is destroyed, along with the **MainActivity** instance.

Figure 4.7 **MainActivity** and **QuizViewModel** destroyed

The relationship between **MainActivity** and **QuizViewModel** is unidirectional. The activity references the **ViewModel**, but the **ViewModel** does not access the activity. Your **ViewModel** should never hold a reference to an activity or a view, otherwise you will introduce a *memory leak*.

A memory leak occurs when one object holds a strong reference to another object that should be destroyed. Holding the strong reference prevents the garbage collector from clearing the object from memory. Memory leaks due to a configuration change are common bugs. The details of strong reference and garbage collection are outside the scope of this book. If you are not sure about these concepts, we recommend reading up on them in a Kotlin or Java reference.

Your **ViewModel** instance stays in memory across rotation, while your original activity instance gets destroyed. If the **ViewModel** held a strong reference to the original activity instance, two problems would occur: First, the original activity instance would not be removed from memory, and thus the activity would be leaked. Second, the **ViewModel** would hold a reference to a stale activity. If the **ViewModel** tried to update the view of the stale activity, it would trigger an **IllegalStateException**.

## Add data to your ViewModel

Now it is finally time to fix GeoQuiz's rotation bug. **QuizViewModel** is not destroyed on rotation the way **MainActivity** is, so you can stash the activity's UI state data in the **QuizViewModel** instance and it, too, will survive rotation.

You are going to copy the question and current index data from your activity to your **ViewModel**, along with all the logic related to them. Begin by cutting the currentIndex and questionBank properties from **MainActivity** (Listing 4.5).

### Listing 4.5  Cutting model data from activity (MainActivity.kt)

```kotlin
class MainActivity : AppCompatActivity() {
    ...
    private val questionBank = listOf(
        Question(R.string.question_australia, true),
        Question(R.string.question_oceans, true),
        Question(R.string.question_mideast, false),
        Question(R.string.question_africa, false),
        Question(R.string.question_americas, true),
        Question(R.string.question_asia, true)
    )

    private var currentIndex = 0
    ...
}
```

Now, paste the `currentIndex` and `questionBank` properties into **QuizViewModel**, as shown in Listing 4.6.

Remove the `private` access modifier from `currentIndex` so the property value can be accessed by external classes, such as **MainActivity**. Leave the `private` access modifier on `questionBank` – **MainActivity** will not interact with the `questionBank` directly. Instead, it will call functions and computed properties you will add to **QuizViewModel**. While you are editing **QuizViewModel**, delete the `init` and `onCleared()` logging, as you will not use them again.

## Listing 4.6  Pasting model data into **QuizViewModel** (QuizViewModel.kt)

```
class QuizViewModel : ViewModel() {

    init {
        Log.d(TAG, "ViewModel instance created")
    }

    override fun onCleared() {
        super.onCleared()
        Log.d(TAG, "ViewModel instance about to be destroyed")
    }

    private var currentIndex = 0

    private val questionBank = listOf(
        Question(R.string.question_australia, true),
        Question(R.string.question_oceans, true),
        Question(R.string.question_mideast, false),
        Question(R.string.question_africa, false),
        Question(R.string.question_americas, true),
        Question(R.string.question_asia, true)
    )
}
```

Next, add a function to **QuizViewModel** to advance to the next question. Also, add computed properties to return the text and answer for the current question.

## Listing 4.7  Adding business logic to **QuizViewModel** (QuizViewModel.kt)

```
class QuizViewModel : ViewModel() {

    var currentIndex = 0

    private val questionBank = listOf(
        ...
    )

    val currentQuestionAnswer: Boolean
        get() = questionBank[currentIndex].answer

    val currentQuestionText: Int
        get() = questionBank[currentIndex].textResId

    fun moveToNext() {
        currentIndex = (currentIndex + 1) % questionBank.size
    }
}
```

Earlier, we said that a **ViewModel** stores all the data that its associated screen needs, formats it, and makes it easy to access. This allows you to remove presentation logic code from the activity, which in turn keeps your activity simpler. And keeping activities as simple as possible is a good thing: Any logic you put in your activity might be unintentionally affected by the activity's lifecycle. Also, it allows the activity to be responsible for handling only what appears on the screen, not the logic behind determining the data to display.

However, you are going to leave the **updateQuestion()** and **checkAnswer(Boolean)** functions in **MainActivity**. You will update these functions shortly to call through to the new **QuizViewModel** computed properties you added. But you will keep them in **MainActivity** to help keep your activity code organized.

Next, add a lazily initialized property to stash the **QuizViewModel** instance associated with the activity.

## Listing 4.8  Lazily initializing **QuizViewModel** (MainActivity.kt)

```
class MainActivity : AppCompatActivity() {
    ...
    private val quizViewModel: QuizViewModel by lazy {
        ViewModelProviders.of(this).get(QuizViewModel::class.java)
    }

    override fun onCreate(savedInstanceState: Bundle?) {
        ...
        val provider: ViewModelProvider = ViewModelProviders.of(this)
        val quizViewModel = provider.get(QuizViewModel::class.java)
        Log.d(TAG, "Got a QuizViewModel: $quizViewModel")
        ...
    }
    ...
}
```

Using by lazy allows you to make the quizViewModel property a val instead of a var. This is great, because you only need (and want) to grab and store the **QuizViewModel** when the activity instance is created – so quizViewModel should only be assigned a value one time.

More importantly, using by lazy means the quizViewModel calculation and assignment will not happen until the first time you access quizViewModel. This is good because you cannot safely access a **ViewModel** until **Activity.onCreate(…)**. If you try to call **ViewModelProviders.of(this).get(QuizViewModel::class.java)** before **Activity.onCreate(…)**, your app will crash with an **IllegalStateException**.

Finally, update **MainActivity** to display content from and interact with your newly updated **QuizViewModel**.

## Listing 4.9  Updating question through **QuizViewModel** (MainActivity.kt)

```
class MainActivity : AppCompatActivity() {
    ...
    override fun onCreate(savedInstanceState: Bundle?) {
        ...
        nextButton.setOnClickListener {
            currentIndex = (currentIndex + 1) % questionBank.size
            quizViewModel.moveToNext()
            updateQuestion()
        }
        ...
    }
    ...
    private fun updateQuestion() {
        val questionTextResId = questionBank[currentIndex].textResId
        val questionTextResId = quizViewModel.currentQuestionText
        questionTextView.setText(questionTextResId)
    }

    private fun checkAnswer(userAnswer: Boolean) {
        val correctAnswer = questionBank[currentIndex].answer
        val correctAnswer = quizViewModel.currentQuestionAnswer
        ...
    }
}
```

Run GeoQuiz, press NEXT, and rotate the device or emulator. No matter how many times you rotate, the newly minted **MainActivity** will "remember" what question you were on. Do a happy dance to celebrate solving the UI state loss on rotation bug.

But do not dance too long. There is another, less-easily-discoverable bug to squash.

# Saving Data Across Process Death

Configuration changes are not the only time the OS can destroy an activity even though the user does not intend it to. Each app gets its own *process* (more specifically, a Linux process) containing a single thread to execute UI-related work on and a piece of memory to store objects in.

An app's process can be destroyed by the OS if the user navigates away for a while and Android needs to reclaim memory. When an app's process is destroyed, all the objects stored in that process's memory are destroyed. (You will learn more about Android application processes in Chapter 23.)

Processes containing resumed or paused activities get higher priority than other processes. When the OS needs to free up resources, it will select lower-priority processes first. Practically speaking, a process containing a visible activity will not be reclaimed by the OS. If a foreground process does get reclaimed, that means something is horribly wrong with the device (and your app being killed is probably the least of the user's concerns).

But stopped activities are fair game to be killed. So, for example, if the user presses the Home button and then goes and watches a video or plays a game, your app's process might be destroyed.

(As of this writing, activities themselves are not individually destroyed in low-memory situations, even though the documentation reads like that is the case. Instead, Android clears an entire app process from memory, taking any of the app's in-memory activities with it.)

When the OS destroys the app's process, any of the app's activities and **ViewModel**s stored in memory will be wiped away. And the OS will not be nice about the destruction. It will not call any of the activity or **ViewModel** lifecycle callback functions.

So how can you save UI state data and use it to reconstruct the activity so that the user never even knows the activity was destroyed? One way to do this is to store data in *saved instance state*. Saved instance state is data the OS temporarily stores outside of the activity. You can add values to saved instance state by overriding **Activity.onSaveInstanceState(Bundle)**.

The OS calls **Activity.onSaveInstanceState(Bundle)** any time an activity that is not finished moves to the stopped state (such as when the user presses the Home button and then launches a different app). This timing is important, because stopped activities are marked as *killable*. If your app process is killed because it is a low-priority background app, then you can rest assured that **Activity.onSaveInstanceState(Bundle)** was already called.

The default implementation of **onSaveInstanceState(Bundle)** directs all of the activity's views to save their state as data in the **Bundle** object. A **Bundle** is a structure that maps string keys to values of certain limited types.

You have seen this **Bundle** before. It is passed into **onCreate(Bundle?)**:

```
override fun onCreate(savedInstanceState: Bundle?) {
    super.onCreate(savedInstanceState)
    ...
}
```

When you override **onCreate(Bundle?)**, you call **onCreate(Bundle?)** on the activity's superclass and pass in the bundle you just received. In the superclass implementation, the saved state of the views is retrieved and used to re-create the activity's view hierarchy.

# Overriding onSaveInstanceState(Bundle)

You can override **onSaveInstanceState(Bundle)** to save additional data to the bundle, which can then be read back in **onCreate(Bundle?)**. This is how you are going to save the value of currentIndex across process death.

First, in MainActivity.kt, add a constant that will be the key for the key-value pair that will be stored in the bundle.

### Listing 4.10  Adding a key for the value (MainActivity.kt)

```
private const val TAG = "MainActivity"
private const val KEY_INDEX = "index"

class MainActivity : AppCompatActivity() {
    ...
}
```

Next, override **onSaveInstanceState(Bundle)** to write the value of currentIndex to the bundle with the constant as its key.

### Listing 4.11  Overriding **onSaveInstanceState(…)** (MainActivity.kt)

```
override fun onPause() {
    ...
}

override fun onSaveInstanceState(savedInstanceState: Bundle) {
    super.onSaveInstanceState(savedInstanceState)
    Log.i(TAG, "onSaveInstanceState")
    savedInstanceState.putInt(KEY_INDEX,  quizViewModel.currentIndex)
}

override fun onStop() {
    ...
}
```

Finally, in **onCreate(Bundle?)**, check for this value. If it exists, assign it to currentIndex. If a value with the key "index" does not exist in the bundle, or if the bundle object is null, set the value to 0.

### Listing 4.12 Checking bundle in **onCreate(Bundle?)** (MainActivity.kt)

```
override fun onCreate(savedInstanceState: Bundle?) {
    super.onCreate(savedInstanceState)
    Log.d(TAG, "onCreate(Bundle?) called")
    setContentView(R.layout.activity_main)

    val currentIndex = savedInstanceState?.getInt(KEY_INDEX, 0) ?: 0
    quizViewModel.currentIndex = currentIndex
    ...
}
```

**onCreate** accepts a nullable bundle as input. This is because there is no state when a new instance of the activity is launched by the user the first time, so in this case the bundle would be null. When the activity is re-created after rotation or process death, the bundle object will be non-null. The non-null bundle will contain any key-value pairs you add in **onSaveInstanceState(Bundle)**. The bundle may also contain additional information added by the framework, such as the contents of an **EditText** or other basic UI widget state.

Rotation is easy to test. And, luckily, so is the low-memory situation. Try it out now to see for yourself.

On your device or emulator, find and click on the Settings icon within the list of applications. You need to access the developer options, which are hidden by default. If you are using a hardware device, you may have enabled the developer options in Chapter 2. If you are using an emulator (or you did not already enable developer options), go to System → About emulated device (or System → About Tablet/Phone). Scroll down and click (press) the Build number seven times in quick succession.

When you see You are now a developer!, use the Back button to return to the system settings. Scroll down to find Developer options (you may need to expand the Advanced section). On the Developer options screen you will see many possible settings. Scroll down to the Apps section and turn on the setting labeled Don't keep activities, as shown in Figure 4.8.

## Figure 4.8  Don't keep activities

Now, run GeoQuiz, press NEXT to move to another question, and press the Home button. Pressing the Home button causes the activity to be paused and stopped, as you know. The logs tell you that the stopped activity has also been destroyed, just as if the Android OS had reclaimed it for its memory. However, as the logs also show, `onSaveInstanceState(Bundle)` was also called – so there is hope.

Restore the app (using the list of apps on the device or emulator) to see whether your state was saved as you expected. Pat yourself on the back when GeoQuiz opens to the question you last saw.

Be sure to turn Don't keep activities off when you are done testing, as it will cause a performance decrease. Remember that pressing the Back button instead of the Home button will always destroy the activity, regardless of whether you have this development setting on. Pressing the Back button tells the OS that the user is done with the activity.

# Saved instance state and activity records

How does the data you stash in **onSaveInstanceState(Bundle)** survive the activity's (and process's) death? When **onSaveInstanceState(Bundle)** is called, the data is saved to the **Bundle** object. That **Bundle** object is then stuffed into your activity's *activity record* by the OS.

To understand the activity record, let's add a *stashed* state to the activity lifecycle (Figure 4.9).

## Figure 4.9  The complete activity lifecycle

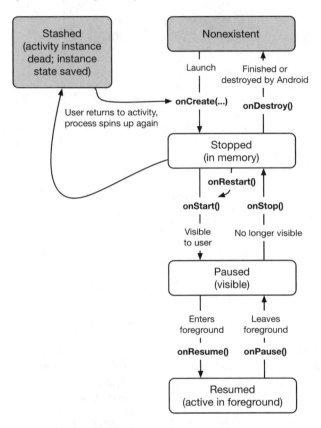

When your activity is stashed, an **Activity** object does not exist, but the activity record object lives on in the OS. The OS can reanimate the activity using the activity record when it needs to.

Note that your activity can pass into the stashed state without **onDestroy()** being called. You can rely on **onStop()** and **onSaveInstanceState(Bundle)** being called (unless something has gone horribly wrong on the device). Typically, you override **onSaveInstanceState(Bundle)** to stash small, transient-state data that belongs to the current activity in your **Bundle**. Override **onStop()** to save any permanent data, such as things the user is editing, because your activity may be killed at any time after this function returns.

So when does the activity record get snuffed? When the activity finishes, it really gets destroyed, once and for all. At that point, your activity record is discarded. Activity records are also discarded on reboot. (For a reminder about what it means for an activity to finish, see the section called Finishing an activity in Chapter 3.)

# ViewModel vs Saved Instance State

While saved instance state stores an activity record across process death, it also stores an activity record across a configuration change. When you first launch the activity, the saved instance state bundle is null. When you rotate the device, the OS calls `onSaveInstanceState(Bundle)` on your activity. The OS then passes the data you stashed in the bundle to `onCreate(Bundle?)`.

If saved instance state protects from both configuration changes and process death, why bother with a `ViewModel` at all? To be fair, GeoQuiz is so simple that you could have gotten away with saved instance state only.

However, most apps do not rely on a small, hardcoded question bank data set like GeoQuiz does. Most apps these days pull dynamic data from a database, from the internet, or from a combination of both. These operations are asynchronous, can be slow, and use precious battery and networking resources. And tying these operations to the activity lifecycle can be very tedious and error prone.

`ViewModel` really shines when you use it to orchestrate dynamic data for the activity, as you will see firsthand in Chapter 11 and Chapter 24. For example, `ViewModel` makes continuing a download operation across a configuration change simple. It also offers an easy way to keep data that was expensive to load in memory across a configuration change. And, as you have seen, `ViewModel` gets cleaned up automatically once the user finishes the activity.

`ViewModel` does not shine in the process death scenario since it gets wiped away from memory along with the process and everything in it. This is where saved instance state takes center stage. But saved instance state has its own limitations. Since saved instance state is serialized to disk, you should avoid stashing any large or complex objects.

As of this writing, the Android team is actively working to improve the developer experience using `ViewModel`s. `lifecycle-viewmodel-savedstate` is a new library that was just released to allow `ViewModel`s to save their state across process death. This should alleviate some of the difficulties of using `ViewModel`s alongside saved instance state from your activities.

So it is not a matter of "which is better, `ViewModel` or saved instance state?" Savvy developers use saved instance state and `ViewModel` in harmony.

Use saved instance state to store the minimal amount of information necessary to re-create the UI state (for example, the current question index). Use `ViewModel` to cache the rich set of data needed to populate the UI in memory across configuration changes for quick and easy access. When the activity is re-created after process death, use the saved instance state information to set up the `ViewModel` as if the `ViewModel` and activity were never destroyed.

As of this writing, there is no easy way to determine whether an activity is being re-created after process death versus a configuration change. Why does this matter? A `ViewModel` stays in memory during a configuration change. So if you use the saved instance state data to update the `ViewModel` after the configuration change, you are making your app do unnecessary work. If the work causes the user to wait or uses their resources (like battery) unnecessarily, this redundant work is problematic.

One way to fix this problem is to make your **ViewModel** a little smarter. When setting a **ViewModel** value might result in more work, first check whether the data is fresh before doing the work to pull in and update the rest of the data:

```
class SomeFancyViewModel : ViewModel() {
    ...
    fun setCurrentIndex(index: Int) {
        if (index != currentIndex) {
            currentIndex = index
            // Load current question from database
        }
    }
}
```

Neither **ViewModel** nor saved instance state is a solution for long-term storage. If your app needs to store data that should live on as long as the app is installed on the device, regardless of your activity's state, use a persistent storage alternative. You will learn about two local persistent storage options in this book: databases, in Chapter 11, and shared preferences, in Chapter 26. Shared preferences is fine for very small, very simple data. A local database is a better option for larger, more complex data. In addition to local storage, you could store data on a remote server somewhere. You will learn how to access data from a web server in Chapter 24.

If GeoQuiz had many more questions, it could make sense to store the questions in a database or on a web server, rather than hardcoding them into the **ViewModel**. Since the questions are constant, it makes sense to persist them independent of activity lifecycle state. But accessing databases is a relatively slow operation, compared to accessing values in memory. So it makes sense to load what you need to display your UI and retain that in memory while the UI is showing using a **ViewModel**.

In this chapter, you squashed GeoQuiz's state-loss bugs by correctly accounting for configuration changes and process death. In the next chapter, you will learn how to use Android Studio's debugging tools to troubleshoot other, more app-specific bugs that might arise.

# For the More Curious: Jetpack, AndroidX, and Architecture Components

The lifecycle-extensions library containing **ViewModel** is part of Android Jetpack Components. Android Jetpack Components, called Jetpack for short, is a set of libraries created by Google to make various aspects of Android development easier. You can see a listing of all the Jetpack libraries at developer.android.com/jetpack. You can include any of these libraries in your project by adding the corresponding dependency to your build.gradle file, as you did in this chapter.

Each of the Jetpack libraries is located in a package that starts with androidx. For this reason, you will sometimes hear the terms "AndroidX" and "Jetpack" used interchangeably.

You may recall that the New Project wizard, as shown in Figure 4.10, has a checkbox for Use AndroidX artifacts. In almost every case, you should enable this option, as you did for GeoQuiz. This will add some initial Jetpack libraries to your project and set your app up to use them by default.

Figure 4.10  Adding Jetpack libraries

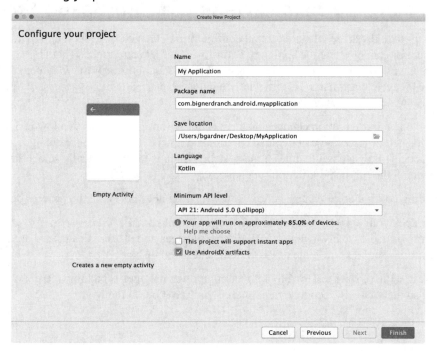

The Jetpack libraries are broken into four categories: foundation, architecture, behavior, and UI. Libraries in Jetpack's architecture category are often referred to as *architecture components*. `ViewModel` is one such architecture component. You will learn about other major architecture components later in this book, including Room (Chapter 11), Data Binding (Chapter 19), and WorkManager (Chapter 27).

You will also learn about some foundation Jetpack libraries, including AppCompat (Chapter 14), Test (Chapter 20), and Android KTX (Chapter 26). You will use Notifications, a behavior Jetpack library, in Chapter 27. And you will also use some UI Jetpack libraries, including Fragment (Chapter 8) and Layouts (Chapter 9 and Chapter 10).

Some of the Jetpack components are entirely new. Others have been around for a while but were previously lumped into a handful of much larger libraries collectively called the Support Library. If you hear or see anything about the Support Library, know that you should now use the Jetpack (AndroidX) version of that library instead.

# For the More Curious: Avoiding a Half-Baked Solution

Some people try to address the UI state loss on configuration change bug in their app by disabling rotation. If the user cannot rotate the app, they never lose their UI state, right? That is true – but, sadly, this approach leaves your app prone to other bugs. While this smooths over the rough edge of rotation, it leaves other lifecycle bugs that users will surely encounter, but that will not necessarily present themselves during development and testing.

First, there are other configuration changes that can occur at runtime, such as window resizing and night mode changes. And yes, you could also capture and ignore or handle those changes. But this is just bad practice – it disables a feature of the system, which is to automatically select the right resources based on the runtime configuration changes.

Second, handling configuration changes or disabling rotation does not solve the process death issue.

If you want to lock your app into portrait or landscape mode *because it makes sense for your app*, you should still program defensively against configuration changes and process death. You are equipped to do so with your newfound knowledge of `ViewModel` and saved instance state.

In short, dealing with UI state loss by blocking configuration changes is bad form. We are only mentioning it so that you will recognize it as such if you see it out in the wild.

# 5

# Debugging Android Apps

In this chapter, you will find out what to do when apps get buggy. You will learn how to use Logcat, Android Lint, and the debugger that comes with Android Studio.

To practice debugging, the first step is to break something. In `MainActivity.kt`, comment out the code in **onCreate(Bundle?)** where you find questionTextView by its ID.

## Listing 5.1 Commenting out a crucial line (MainActivity.kt)

```
override fun onCreate(savedInstanceState: Bundle?) {
    ...
    trueButton = findViewById(R.id.true_button)
    falseButton = findViewById(R.id.false_button)
    nextButton = findViewById(R.id.next_button)
    // questionTextView = findViewById(R.id.question_text_view)
    ...
}
```

Run GeoQuiz and see what happens. The app will crash and burn almost immediately.

On versions before Android Pie (API 28), an error message appears telling you that the app crashed. On a device running Android Pie, if you watch the screen, you may see the app appear for a brief moment before vanishing without a word. In this case, launch the app again by pressing the GeoQuiz icon on the launcher screen. This time, when the app crashes you will see a message like the one shown in Figure 5.1.

Figure 5.1  GeoQuiz is about to E.X.P.L.O.D.E.

Of course, you know exactly what is wrong with your app. But if you did not, it might help to look at your app from a new perspective.

# Exceptions and Stack Traces

Expand the Logcat tool window so that you can see what has happened. If you scroll up and down in Logcat, you should eventually find an expanse of red, as shown in Figure 5.2. This is a standard AndroidRuntime exception report.

If you do not see much in Logcat and cannot find the exception, you may need to select the No Filters option in the filter dropdown. On the other hand, if you see too much in Logcat, you can adjust the Log Level to Error, which will show only the most severe log messages. You can also search for the text fatal exception, which will bring you straight to the exception that caused the app to crash.

## Figure 5.2 Exception and stack trace in Logcat

The report tells you the top-level exception and its stack trace, then the exception that caused that exception and *its* stack trace, and so on until it finds an exception with no cause.

It may seem strange to see a java.lang exception in the stack trace, since you are writing Kotlin code. When building for Android, Kotlin code is compiled to the same kind of low-level bytecode to which Java code is compiled. During that process, many Kotlin exceptions are mapped to java.lang exception classes under the hood through type-aliasing. **kotlin.RuntimeException** is the superclass of **kotlin.UninitializedPropertyAccessException**, and it is aliased to **java.lang.RuntimeException** when running on Android.

In most of the code you will write, that last exception with no cause is the interesting one. Here, the exception without a cause is a **kotlin.UninitializedPropertyAccessException**. The line just below this exception is the first line in its stack trace. This line tells you the class and function where the exception occurred as well as what file and line number the exception occurred on. Click the blue link, and Android Studio will take you to that line in your source code.

The line to which you are taken is the first use of the questionTextView variable, inside **updateQuestion()**. The name **UninitializedPropertyAccessException** gives you a hint to the problem: This variable was not initialized.

Uncomment the line initializing `questionTextView` to fix the bug.

## Listing 5.2  Uncommenting a crucial line (`MainActivity.kt`)

```
override fun onCreate(savedInstanceState: Bundle?) {
    ...
    trueButton = findViewById(R.id.true_button)
    falseButton = findViewById(R.id.false_button)
    nextButton = findViewById(R.id.next_button)
    // questionTextView = findViewById(R.id.question_text_view)
    ...
}
```

When you encounter runtime exceptions, remember to look for the last exception in Logcat and the first line in its stack trace that refers to code that you have written. That is where the problem occurred, and it is the best place to start looking for answers.

If a crash occurs while a device is not plugged in, all is not lost. The device will store the latest lines written to the log. The length and expiration of the stored log depends on the device, but you can usually count on retrieving log results within 10 minutes. Just plug in the device and select it in the Devices view. Logcat will fill itself with the stored log.

# Diagnosing misbehaviors

Problems with your apps will not always be crashes. In some cases, they will be misbehaviors. For example, suppose that every time you pressed the NEXT button, nothing happened. That would be a noncrashing, misbehaving bug.

In `MainActivity.kt`, make a change to the `nextButton` listener to comment out the code that increments the question index.

## Listing 5.3  Forgetting a critical line of code (`MainActivity.kt`)

```
override fun onCreate(savedInstanceState: Bundle?) {
    ...
    nextButton.setOnClickListener {
        // quizViewModel.moveToNext()
        updateQuestion()
    }
    ...
}
```

Run GeoQuiz and press the NEXT button. You should see no effect.

This bug is trickier than the last bug. It is not throwing an exception, so fixing the bug is not a simple matter of making the exception go away. On top of that, this misbehavior could be caused in two different ways: The index might not be changed, or **updateQuestion()** might not be called.

You know what caused this bug, because you just introduced it intentionally. But if this type of bug popped up on its own and you had no idea what was causing the problem, you would need to track down the culprit. In the next few sections, you will see two ways to do this: diagnostic logging of a stack trace and using the debugger to set a breakpoint.

# Logging stack traces

In **MainActivity**, add a log statement to **updateQuestion()**.

## Listing 5.4 **Exception** for fun and profit (MainActivity.kt)

```
private fun updateQuestion() {
    Log.d(TAG, "Updating question text", Exception())
    val questionTextResId = quizViewModel.currentQuestionText
    questionTextView.setText(questionTextResId)
}
```

The **Log.d(String, String, Throwable)** version of **Log.d** logs the entire stack trace, like the **UninitializedPropertyAccessException** you saw earlier. The stack trace will tell you where the call to **updateQuestion()** was made.

The exception that you pass to **Log.d(String, String, Throwable)** does not have to be a thrown exception that you caught. You can create a brand new **Exception** and pass it to the function without ever throwing it, and you will get a report of where the exception was created.

Run GeoQuiz, press the NEXT button, and then check the output in Logcat (Figure 5.3).

## Figure 5.3 The results

The top line in the stack trace is the line where you logged out the **Exception**. A few lines after that you can see where **updateQuestion()** was called from within your **onClick(View)** implementation. Click the link on this line, and you will be taken to where you commented out the line to increment your question index. But do not get rid of the bug; you are going to use the debugger to find it again in a moment.

Logging out stack traces is a powerful tool, but it is also a verbose one. Leave a bunch of these hanging around, and soon Logcat will be an unmanageable mess. Also, a competitor might steal your ideas by reading your stack traces to understand what your code is doing.

On the other hand, sometimes a stack trace showing what your code does is exactly what you need. If you are seeking help with a problem at stackoverflow.com or forums.bignerdranch.com, it often helps to include a stack trace. You can copy and paste lines directly from Logcat.

Before continuing, delete the log statement in MainActivity.kt.

## Listing 5.5  Farewell, old friend (MainActivity.kt)

```
private fun updateQuestion() {
    Log.d(TAG, "Updating question text", Exception())
    val questionTextResId = quizViewModel.currentQuestionText
    questionTextView.setText(questionTextResId)
}
```

# Setting breakpoints

Now you will use the debugger that comes with Android Studio to track down the same bug. You will set a *breakpoint* on **updateQuestion()** to see whether it was called. A breakpoint pauses execution before the line executes and allows you to examine line by line what happens next.

In MainActivity.kt, return to the **updateQuestion()** function. Next to the first line of this function, click the gray gutter area in the lefthand margin. You should now see a red circle in the left gutter like the one shown in Figure 5.4. This is a breakpoint. You can also toggle a breakpoint on and off by placing the cursor on the desired line and pressing Command-F8 (Ctrl-F8).

## Figure 5.4  A breakpoint

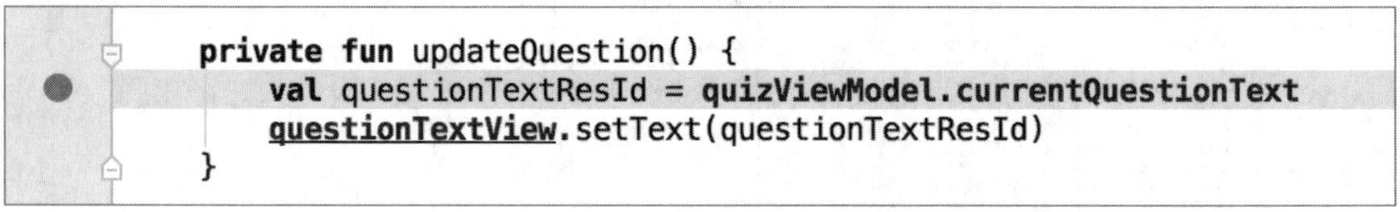

```
private fun updateQuestion() {
    val questionTextResId = quizViewModel.currentQuestionText
    questionTextView.setText(questionTextResId)
}
```

To engage the debugger and trigger your breakpoint, you need to debug your app instead of running it. To debug your app, click the Debug 'app' button (Figure 5.5). You can also navigate to Run → Debug 'app' in the menu bar. Your device will report that it is waiting for the debugger to attach, and then it will proceed normally.

## Figure 5.5  Debug app buttons

In some circumstances, you may want to debug a running app without relaunching it. You can attach the debugger to a running application by clicking the Attach Debugger to Android Process button shown in Figure 5.5 or by navigating to Run → Attach to process.... Choose your app's process on the dialog that appears and click OK, and the debugger will attach. Note that breakpoints are only active when the debugger is attached, so any breakpoints that are hit before you attach the debugger will be ignored.

You want to debug GeoQuiz from the start of your code, which is why you used the Debug 'app' option. Shortly after your app is up and running with the debugger attached, it will pause. Firing up GeoQuiz called `MainActivity.onCreate(Bundle?)`, which called `updateQuestion()`, which hit your breakpoint. (If you had attached the debugger to the process after it had started, then the app likely would not pause, because `MainActivity.onCreate(Bundle?)` would have executed before you could attach the debugger.)

In Figure 5.6, you can see that `MainActivity.kt` is now open in the editor tool window and that the line with the breakpoint where execution has paused is highlighted. The debug tool window at the bottom of the screen is now visible. It contains the Frames and Variables views. (If the debug tool window did not open automatically, you can open it by clicking Debug at the bottom of the Android Studio window.)

### Figure 5.6  Stop right there!

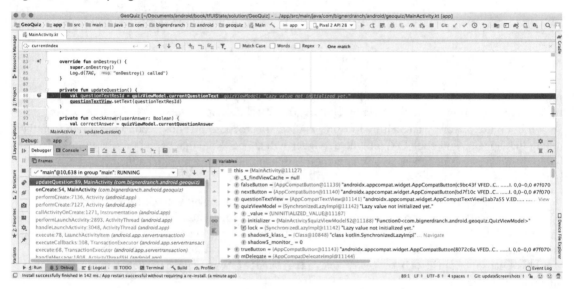

You can use the arrow buttons at the top of the debug tool window (Figure 5.7) to step through your program. You can use the Evaluate Expression button to execute simple Kotlin statements on demand during debugging, which is a powerful tool.

### Figure 5.7  Debug tool window controls

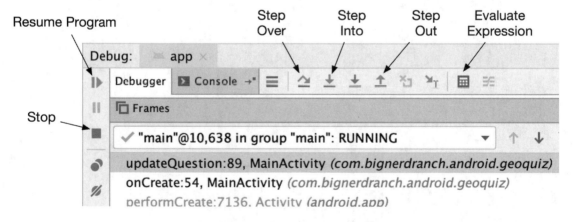

You can see from the stack trace on the left that **updateQuestion()** has been called from inside **onCreate(Bundle?)**. But you are interested in investigating the NEXT button's behavior, so click the Resume Program button to continue execution. Then press the NEXT button in GeoQuiz to see if your breakpoint is hit and execution is stopped. (It should be.)

Now that you are stopped at an interesting point of execution, you can take a look around. The Variables view allows you to examine the values of the objects in your program. At the top, you should see the value this (the **MainActivity** instance itself).

Expand the this variable to see all the variables declared in **MainActivity**, in **MainActivity**'s superclass (**Activity**), in **Activity**'s superclass, in its super-superclass, and so on. For now, focus on the variables that you created.

You are only interested in one value: quizViewModel.currentIndex. Scroll down in the variables view until you see quizViewModel. Expand quizViewModel and look for currentIndex (Figure 5.8).

## Figure 5.8  Inspecting variable values at runtime

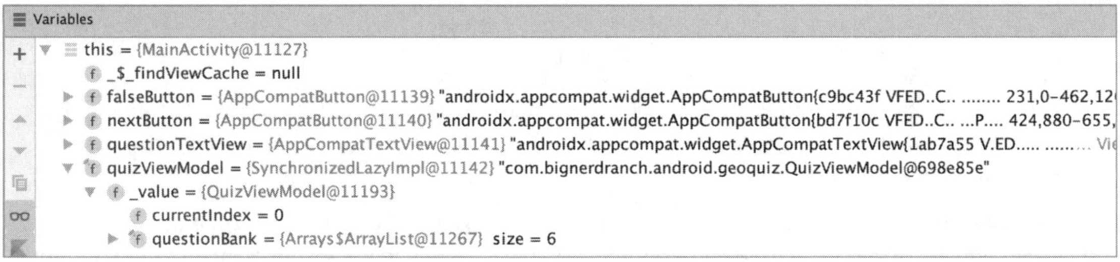

```
≡ Variables
+  ▼  ≡ this = {MainActivity@11127}
        (f) _$_findViewCache = null
   ▶  (f) falseButton = {AppCompatButton@11139} "androidx.appcompat.widget.AppCompatButton{c9bc43f VFED..C.. ......... 231,0–462,12
   ▶  (f) nextButton = {AppCompatButton@11140} "androidx.appcompat.widget.AppCompatButton{bd7f10c VFED..C.. ...P.... 424,880–655,
   ▶  (f) questionTextView = {AppCompatTextView@11141} "androidx.appcompat.widget.AppCompatTextView{1ab7a55 V.ED..... ......... Vi∈
   ▼  (f) quizViewModel = {SynchronizedLazyImpl@11142} "com.bignerdranch.android.geoquiz.QuizViewModel@698e85e"
      ▼  (f) _value = {QuizViewModel@11193}
            (f) currentIndex = 0
         ▶  (f) questionBank = {Arrays$ArrayList@11267}  size = 6
```

You would expect currentIndex to have a value of 1. You pressed the NEXT button, which should have resulted in currentIndex being incremented from 0 to 1. However, as shown in Figure 5.8, currentIndex still has a value of 0.

Check the code in the editor tool window. The code in **MainActivity.updateQuestion()** simply updates the question text based the contents of **QuizViewModel**. There is no problem there. So where does the bug originate?

To continue your investigation, you need to step out of this function to determine what code was executed just before **MainActivity.updateQuestion()**. To do this, click the Step Out button.

Check the editor tool window. It has now jumped you over to your nextButton's **OnClickListener**, right after **updateQuestion()** was called. Pretty nifty.

As you already knew, the problematic behavior is a result of `quizViewModel.moveToNext()` never being called (because you commented it out). You will want to fix this implementation – but before you make any changes to code, you should stop debugging your app. If you edit your code while debugging, the code running with the debugger attached will be out of date compared to what is in the editor tool window, so the debugger can show misleading information compared to the updated code.

You can stop debugging in two ways: You can stop the program, or you can simply disconnect the debugger. To stop the program, click the Stop button shown in Figure 5.7.

Now return your `OnClickListener` to its former glory.

## Listing 5.6  Returning to normalcy (`MainActivity.kt`)

```kotlin
override fun onCreate(savedInstanceState: Bundle?) {
    ...
    nextButton.setOnClickListener {
        // quizViewModel.moveToNext()
        updateQuestion()
    }
    ...
}
```

You have tried out two ways of tracking down a misbehaving line of code: stack trace logging and setting a breakpoint in the debugger. Which is better? Each has its uses, and one or the other will probably end up being your favorite.

Logging out stack traces has the advantage that you can see stack traces from multiple places in one log. The downside is that to learn something new you have to add new log statements, rebuild, deploy, and navigate through your app to see what happened.

The debugger is more convenient. If you run your app with the debugger attached (or attach the debugger to the application's process after it has started), then you can set a breakpoint while the application is running and poke around to get information about multiple issues.

# Android-Specific Debugging

Most Android debugging is just like Kotlin debugging. However, you will sometimes run into issues with Android-specific parts, such as resources, that the Kotlin compiler knows nothing about. In this section, you will learn about two kinds of Android-specific issues: Android Lint issues and issues with the R class.

## Using Android Lint

Android Lint (or just "Lint") is a *static analyzer* for Android code. A static analyzer is a program that examines your code to find defects without running it. Lint uses its knowledge of the Android frameworks to look deeper into your code and find problems that the compiler cannot. In many cases, Lint's advice is worth taking.

In Chapter 7, you will see Lint warn you about compatibility problems. Lint can also perform type-checking for objects that are defined in XML.

You can manually run Lint to see all of the potential issues in your project, including those that are less serious. Select Analyze → Inspect Code... from the menu bar. You will be asked which parts of your project you would like to inspect. Choose Whole project and click OK. Android Studio will run Android Lint as well as a few other static analyzers on your code, such as spelling and Kotlin checks.

Once the scan is complete, you will see categories of potential issues in the inspection tool window. Expand the Android and Lint categories to see Lint's information about your project (Figure 5.9).

Figure 5.9  Lint warnings

(Do not be concerned if you see a different number of Lint warnings. The Android toolchain is constantly evolving, and new checks may have been added to Lint, new restrictions may have been added to the Android framework, and newer versions of tools and dependencies may have become available.)

Expand Internationalization and then, under it, expand Bidirectional Text to see more detailed information on this issue in your project. Click on Using left/right instead of start/end attributes to learn about this particular warning (Figure 5.10).

## Figure 5.10  Lint warning description

Lint is warning you that using `right` and `left` values for layout attributes could be problematic if your app is used on a device set to a language that reads from right to left instead of left to right. (You will learn about making your app ready for international use in Chapter 17.)

Dig further to see which file and line or lines of code caused the warning. Expand Using left/right instead of start/end attributes. Click on the offending file, `activity_main.xml`, to see the snippet of code with the problem (Figure 5.11).

## Figure 5.11 Viewing the code that caused the warning

Double-click on the warning description that appears under the filename. This will open `res/layout/land/activity_main.xml` in the editor tool window and place the cursor on the line causing the warning:

```
<Button
        android:id="@+id/next_button"
        android:layout_width="wrap_content"
        android:layout_height="wrap_content"
        android:layout_gravity="bottom|right"
        android:text="@string/next_button"
        android:drawableEnd="@drawable/arrow_right"
        android:drawablePadding="4dp"/>
```

The line Lint is concerned about sets the gravity of the NEXT button so that it appears in the bottom-right corner of the landscape layout. To fix the warning, change the value `bottom|right` to `bottom|end`. This way, the button will be positioned on the bottom left on a device set to a language that reads right to left instead of left to right.

## Listing 5.7 Addressing bidirectional text warning (res/layout/land/activity_main.xml)

```
...
<Button
        android:id="@+id/next_button"
        android:layout_width="wrap_content"
        android:layout_height="wrap_content"
        android:layout_gravity="bottom|right"
        android:layout_gravity="bottom|end"
        android:text="@string/next_button"
        android:drawableEnd="@drawable/arrow_right"
        android:drawablePadding="4dp"/>
...
```

Rerun Lint to confirm that the bidirectional text issue you just fixed is no longer listed in the Lint results. To preview how the layout will look on devices with right to left locales, open the Design tab in the editor tool window. Change the selection in the Locale for Preview dropdown from Default (en-us) to Preview Right to Left (Figure 5.12). If you do not see the Locale for Preview dropdown, click >> at the top of the preview pane to expand preview options.

Figure 5.12  Previewing left to right and right to left

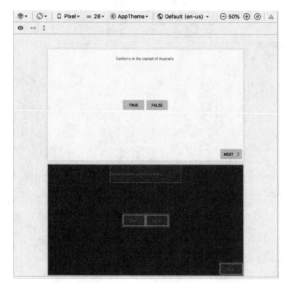
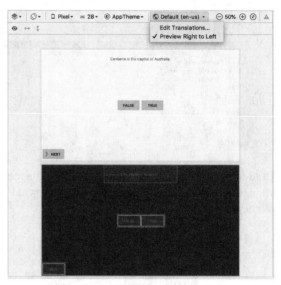

For the most part, your app will execute just fine even if you do not address the things Lint warns you about. Often, though, addressing Lint warnings can help prevent problems in the future or make your users' experience better. We recommend you take all Lint warnings seriously, even if you ultimately decide not to address them (as in this case). Otherwise you could get used to ignoring Lint and miss a serious problem.

The Lint tool provides detailed information about each issue it finds and provides suggestions for how to address it. We leave it to you as an exercise to review the issues Lint found in GeoQuiz. You can ignore the issues, fix them as Lint recommends, or use the Suppress button in the problem description pane to suppress the warnings in the future. For the remainder of the GeoQuiz chapters, we will assume you left the remaining Lint issues unaddressed.

# Issues with the R class

You are familiar with build errors that occur when you reference resources before adding them or delete resources that other files refer to. Usually, resaving the files once the resource is added or the references are removed will cause Android Studio to rebuild without any fuss.

Sometimes, however, these build errors will persist or appear seemingly out of nowhere. If this happens to you, here are some things you can try:

*Recheck the validity of the XML in your resource files*

> If your R.java file was not generated for the last build, you will see errors in your project wherever you reference a resource. Often, this is caused by a typo in one of your XML files. Layout XML is not always validated, so typos in these files may not be pointedly brought to your attention. Finding the typo and resaving the file should cause R.java to regenerate.

*Clean your project*

> Select Build → Clean Project. Android Studio will rebuild the project from scratch, which often results in an error-free build. We can all use a deep clean every now and then.

*Sync your project with Gradle*

> If you make changes to your build.gradle file, you will need to sync those changes to update your project's build settings. Select File → Sync Project with Gradle Files. Android Studio will rebuild the project from scratch with the correct project settings, which can help to resolve issues after changing your Gradle configuration.

*Run Android Lint*

> Pay close attention to the warnings from Lint. With this tool, you will often discover unexpected issues.

If you are still having problems with resources (or having different problems), give the error messages and your layout files a fresh look. It is easy to overlook mistakes in the heat of the moment. Check out any Lint errors and warnings as well. A cool-headed reconsideration of the error messages may turn up a bug or typo.

Finally, if you are stuck or having other issues with Android Studio, check the archives at stackoverflow.com or visit the forum for this book at forums.bignerdranch.com.

# Challenge: Exploring the Layout Inspector

For support debugging layout file issues, the layout inspector can be used to interactively inspect how a layout file is rendered to the screen. To use the layout inspector, make sure GeoQuiz is running in the emulator and select Tools → Layout Inspector from the menu bar. Once the inspector is activated, you can explore the properties of your layout by clicking the elements within the layout inspector view.

# Challenge: Exploring the Profiler

The profiler tool window creates detailed reports for how your application is using an Android device's resources, such as CPU and memory. It is useful when assessing and tuning the performance of your app.

To view the profiler tool window, run your app on a connected Android device or emulator and select View → Tool Windows → Profiler from the menu bar. Once the profiler is open, you can see a timeline with sections for CPU, memory, network, and energy.

Click into a section to see more details about your app's usage of that resource. On the CPU view, make sure to hit the Record button to capture more information about CPU usage. Once you have performed any interactions with your app that you would like to record, hit the Stop button to stop the recording.

# 6

# Your Second Activity

In this chapter, you will add a second activity to GeoQuiz. An activity controls a screen of information, and this activity will add a second screen that offers users a chance to cheat on the current question by showing the answer. Figure 6.1 shows the new activity.

Figure 6.1 **CheatActivity** offers the chance to peek at the answer

If users choose to view the answer and then return to the **MainActivity** and answer the question, they will get a new message, shown in Figure 6.2.

## Figure 6.2 **MainActivity** knows if you've been cheating

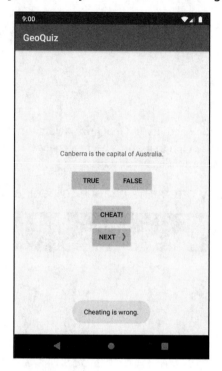

Why is this a good Android programming exercise? Because you will learn how to:

- Create a new activity and a new layout for it.

- Start an activity from another activity. *Starting* an activity means asking the OS to create an activity instance and call its **onCreate(Bundle?)** function.

- Pass data between the parent (starting) activity and the child (started) activity.

# Setting Up a Second Activity

There is a lot to do in this chapter. Fortunately, some of the grunt work can be done for you by Android Studio's New Activity wizard.

Before you invoke the magic, open `res/values/strings.xml` and add all the strings you will need for this chapter.

Listing 6.1  Adding strings (`res/values/strings.xml`)

```
<resources>
    ...
    <string name="incorrect_toast">Incorrect!</string>
    <string name="warning_text">Are you sure you want to do this?</string>
    <string name="show_answer_button">Show Answer</string>
    <string name="cheat_button">Cheat!</string>
    <string name="judgment_toast">Cheating is wrong.</string>

</resources>
```

## Creating a new activity

Creating an activity typically involves touching at least three files: the Kotlin class file, an XML layout file, and the application manifest. If you touch those files in the wrong ways, Android can get mad. To ensure that you do it right, you can use Android Studio's New Activity wizard.

Launch the New Activity wizard by right-clicking on the `app/java` folder in the project tool window. Choose New → Activity → Empty Activity, as shown in Figure 6.3.

Figure 6.3  The New Activity menu

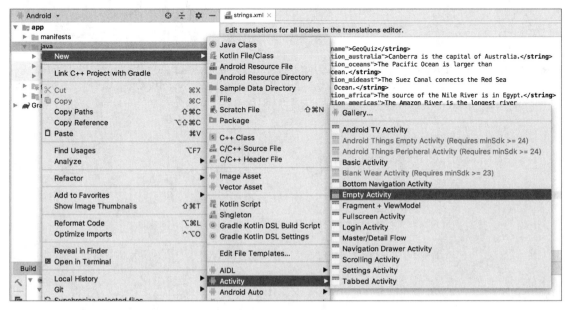

You should then see a dialog like Figure 6.4. Set Activity Name to CheatActivity. This is the name of your `Activity` subclass. Layout Name will be automatically set to activity_cheat. This will be the base name of the layout file the wizard creates.

Figure 6.4  The New Empty Activity wizard

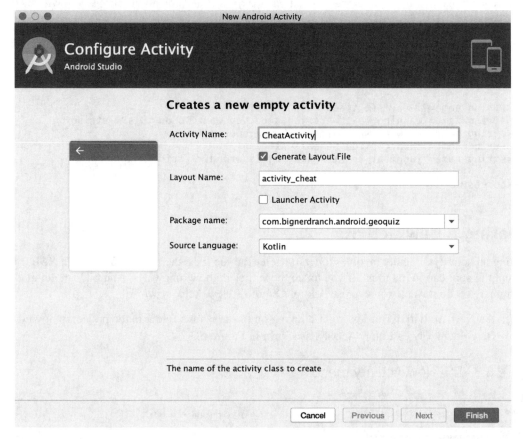

The defaults for the remaining fields are fine, but take care to ensure that the package name is what you expect. This determines where `CheatActivity.kt` will live on the filesystem. Click the Finish button to make the magic happen.

Now it is time to make the UI look good. The screenshot at the beginning of the chapter shows you what **CheatActivity**'s view should look like. Figure 6.5 shows the widget definitions.

## Figure 6.5  Diagram of layout for **CheatActivity**

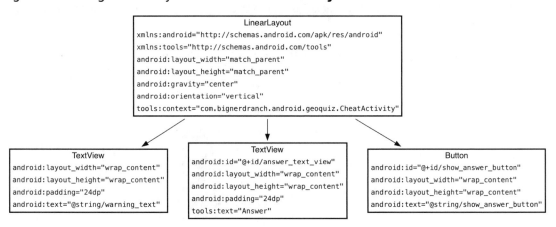

Open res/layout/activity_cheat.xml and switch to the Text view.

Try creating the XML for the layout using Figure 6.5 as a guide. Replace the sample layout with a new **LinearLayout** and so on down the tree. You can check your work against Listing 6.2.

## Listing 6.2  Filling out the second activity's layout (res/layout/activity_cheat.xml)

```
<LinearLayout xmlns:android="http://schemas.android.com/apk/res/android"
    xmlns:tools="http://schemas.android.com/tools"
    android:layout_width="match_parent"
    android:layout_height="match_parent"
    android:gravity="center"
    android:orientation="vertical"
    tools:context="com.bignerdranch.android.geoquiz.CheatActivity">

    <TextView
        android:layout_width="wrap_content"
        android:layout_height="wrap_content"
        android:padding="24dp"
        android:text="@string/warning_text"/>

    <TextView
        android:id="@+id/answer_text_view"
        android:layout_width="wrap_content"
        android:layout_height="wrap_content"
        android:padding="24dp"
        tools:text="Answer"/>

    <Button
        android:id="@+id/show_answer_button"
        android:layout_width="wrap_content"
        android:layout_height="wrap_content"
        android:text="@string/show_answer_button"/>

</LinearLayout>
```

You will not be creating a landscape alternative for `activity_cheat.xml`, but there is a way to preview how the default layout will appear in landscape.

In the Design tab of the editor tool window, find the button in the toolbar above the preview pane that looks like a device with curved arrows. Click this button to change the orientation of the preview to landscape (Figure 6.6).

## Figure 6.6  Previewing `activity_cheat.xml` in landscape

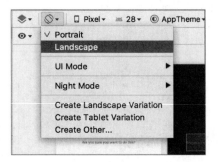

The default layout works well enough in both orientations, so let's move on to fleshing out the activity subclass.

# A new activity subclass

`CheatActivity.kt` may have opened automatically in the editor tool window. If it did not, open it from the project tool window.

The **CheatActivity** class already includes a basic implementation of **onCreate(Bundle?)** that passes the resource ID of the layout defined in `activity_cheat.xml` to **setContentView(…)**.

**CheatActivity** will eventually do more in its **onCreate(Bundle?)** function. For now, let's take a look at another thing the New Activity wizard did for you: declaring **CheatActivity** in the application's manifest.

# Declaring activities in the manifest

The *manifest* is an XML file containing metadata that describes your application to the Android OS. The file is always named `AndroidManifest.xml`, and it lives in the `app/manifests` directory of your project.

In the project tool window, find and open `manifests/AndroidManifest.xml`. You can also use Android Studio's Find File dialog by pressing Command-Shift-O (Ctrl-Shift-N) and starting to type the filename. Once it has guessed the right file, press Return to open it.

Every activity in an application must be declared in the manifest so that the OS can access it.

When you used the New Project wizard to create **MainActivity**, the wizard declared the activity for you. Likewise, the New Activity wizard declared **CheatActivity** by adding the XML highlighted in Listing 6.3.

## Listing 6.3 Declaring **CheatActivity** in the manifest (manifests/AndroidManifest.xml)

```
<manifest xmlns:android="http://schemas.android.com/apk/res/android"
    package="com.bignerdranch.android.geoquiz">

    <application
        android:allowBackup="true"
        android:icon="@mipmap/ic_launcher"
        android:label="@string/app_name"
        android:roundIcon="@mipmap/ic_launcher_round"
        android:supportsRtl="true"
        android:theme="@style/AppTheme">
        <activity android:name=".CheatActivity">
        </activity>
        <activity android:name=".MainActivity">
            <intent-filter>
                <action android:name="android.intent.action.MAIN" />

                <category android:name="android.intent.category.LAUNCHER" />
            </intent-filter>
        </activity>
    </application>

</manifest>
```

The `android:name` attribute is required, and the dot at the start of this attribute's value tells the OS that this activity's class is in the package specified in the `package` attribute in the `manifest` element at the top of the file.

You will sometimes see a fully qualified `android:name` attribute, like `android:name="com.bignerdranch.android.geoquiz.CheatActivity"`. The long-form notation is identical to the version in Listing 6.3.

There are many interesting things in the manifest, but for now, let's stay focused on getting **CheatActivity** up and running. You will learn about the different parts of the manifest in later chapters.

# Adding a cheat button to MainActivity

The plan is for the user to press a button in **MainActivity** to get an instance of **CheatActivity** onscreen. So you need new buttons in res/layout/activity_main.xml and res/layout-land/activity_main.xml.

You can see in Figure 6.2 that the new CHEAT! button is positioned above the NEXT button. In the default layout, define the new button as a direct child of the root **LinearLayout**, right before the definition of the NEXT button.

**Listing 6.4  Adding a cheat button to the default layout (res/layout/activity_main.xml)**

```
    ...
</LinearLayout>

<Button
    android:id="@+id/cheat_button"
    android:layout_width="wrap_content"
    android:layout_height="wrap_content"
    android:layout_marginTop="24dp"
    android:text="@string/cheat_button" />

<Button
    android:id="@+id/next_button"
    .../>

</LinearLayout>
```

In the landscape layout, have the new button appear at the bottom and center of the root **FrameLayout**.

**Listing 6.5  Adding a cheat button to the landscape layout (res/layout-land/activity_main.xml)**

```
    ...
</LinearLayout>

<Button
    android:id="@+id/cheat_button"
    android:layout_width="wrap_content"
    android:layout_height="wrap_content"
    android:layout_gravity="bottom|center_horizontal"
    android:text="@string/cheat_button" />

<Button
    android:id="@+id/next_button"
    .../>

</FrameLayout>
```

Now, in `MainActivity.kt`, add a variable, get a reference, and set a **View.OnClickListener** stub for the CHEAT! button.

## Listing 6.6  Wiring up the cheat button (MainActivity.kt)

```kotlin
class MainActivity : AppCompatActivity() {

    private lateinit var trueButton: Button
    private lateinit var falseButton: Button
    private lateinit var nextButton: Button
    private lateinit var cheatButton: Button
    private lateinit var questionTextView: TextView
    ...
    override fun onCreate(savedInstanceState: Bundle?) {
        ...
        nextButton = findViewById(R.id.next_button)
        cheatButton = findViewById(R.id.cheat_button)
        questionTextView = findViewById(R.id.question_text_view)
        ...
        nextButton.setOnClickListener {
            quizViewModel.moveToNext()
            updateQuestion()
        }

        cheatButton.setOnClickListener {
            // Start CheatActivity
        }

        updateQuestion()
    }
    ...
}
```

Now you can get to the business of starting **CheatActivity**.

# Starting an Activity

The simplest way one activity can start another is with the **startActivity(Intent)** function.

You might guess that **startActivity(Intent)** is a static function that you call on the **Activity** subclass that you want to start. But it is not. When an activity calls **startActivity(Intent)**, this call is sent to the OS.

In particular, it is sent to a part of the OS called the **ActivityManager**. The **ActivityManager** then creates the **Activity** instance and calls its **onCreate(Bundle?)** function, as shown in Figure 6.7.

Figure 6.7  Starting an activity

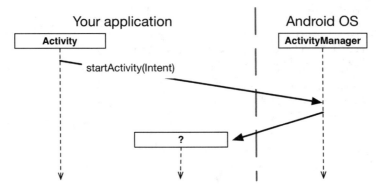

How does the **ActivityManager** know which **Activity** to start? That information is in the **Intent** parameter.

# Communicating with intents

An *intent* is an object that a *component* can use to communicate with the OS. The only components you have seen so far are activities, but there are also services, broadcast receivers, and content providers.

Intents are multipurpose communication tools, and the **Intent** class provides different constructors depending on what you are using the intent to do.

In this case, you are using an intent to tell the **ActivityManager** which activity to start, so you will use this constructor: Intent(packageContext: Context, class: Class<?>).

Within cheatButton's listener, create an **Intent** that includes the **CheatActivity** class. Then pass the intent into **startActivity(Intent)**.

Listing 6.7  Starting **CheatActivity** (MainActivity.kt)

```
cheatButton.setOnClickListener {
    // Start CheatActivity
    val intent = Intent(this, CheatActivity::class.java)
    startActivity(intent)
}
```

The **Class** argument you pass to the **Intent** constructor specifies the activity class that the **ActivityManager** should start. The **Context** argument tells the **ActivityManager** which application package the activity class can be found in.

Before starting the activity, the **ActivityManager** checks the package's manifest for a declaration with the same name as the specified **Class**. If it finds a declaration, it starts the activity, and all is well. If it does not, you get a nasty **ActivityNotFoundException**, which will crash your app. This is why all of your activities must be declared in the manifest.

Run GeoQuiz. Press the CHEAT! button, and an instance of your new activity will appear onscreen. Now press the Back button. This will destroy the **CheatActivity** and return you to the **MainActivity**.

## Explicit and implicit intents

When you create an **Intent** with a **Context** and a **Class** object, you are creating an *explicit intent*. You use explicit intents to start activities within your application.

It may seem strange that two activities within your application must communicate via the **ActivityManager**, which is outside of your application. However, this pattern makes it easy for an activity in one application to work with an activity in another application.

When an activity in your application wants to start an activity in another application, you create an *implicit intent*. You will use implicit intents in Chapter 15.

# Passing Data Between Activities

Now that you have a **MainActivity** and a **CheatActivity**, you can think about passing data between them. Figure 6.8 shows what data you will pass between the two activities.

Figure 6.8  The conversation between **MainActivity** and **CheatActivity**

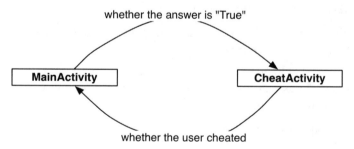

The **MainActivity** will inform the **CheatActivity** of the answer to the current question when the **CheatActivity** is started.

When the user presses the Back button to return to the **MainActivity**, the **CheatActivity** will be destroyed. In its last gasp, it will send data to the **MainActivity** about whether the user cheated.

You will start with passing data from **MainActivity** to **CheatActivity**.

# Using intent extras

To inform the **CheatActivity** of the answer to the current question, you will pass it the value of:

```
questionBank[currentIndex].answer
```

You will send this value as an *extra* on the **Intent** that is passed into **startActivity(Intent)**.

Extras are arbitrary data that the calling activity can include with an intent. You can think of them like constructor arguments, even though you cannot use a custom constructor with an activity subclass. (Android creates activity instances and is responsible for their lifecycle.) The OS forwards the intent to the recipient activity, which can then access the extras and retrieve the data, as shown in Figure 6.9.

## Figure 6.9  Intent extras: communicating with other activities

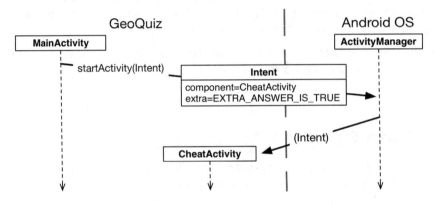

An extra is structured as a key-value pair, like the one you used to save out the value of currentIndex in **MainActivity.onSaveInstanceState(Bundle)**.

To add an extra to an intent, you use **Intent.putExtra(…)**. In particular, you will be calling **putExtra(name: String, value: Boolean)**.

**Intent.putExtra(…)** comes in many flavors, but it always has two arguments. The first argument is always a String key, and the second argument is the value, whose type will vary. It returns the **Intent** itself, so you can chain multiple calls if you need to.

In CheatActivity.kt, add a key for the extra.

## Listing 6.8  Adding an extra constant (CheatActivity.kt)

```
private const val EXTRA_ANSWER_IS_TRUE =
        "com.bignerdranch.android.geoquiz.answer_is_true"

class CheatActivity : AppCompatActivity() {
    ...
}
```

An activity may be started from several different places, so you should define keys for extras on the activities that retrieve and use them. Using your package name as a qualifier for your extra, as shown in Listing 6.8, prevents name collisions with extras from other apps.

Now you could return to **MainActivity** and put the extra on the intent, but there is a better approach. There is no reason for **MainActivity**, or any other code in your app, to know the implementation details of what **CheatActivity** expects as extras on its **Intent**. Instead, you can encapsulate that work into a **newIntent(…)** function.

Create this function in **CheatActivity** now. Place the function inside a companion object.

## Listing 6.9 A **newIntent(…)** function for **CheatActivity** (CheatActivity.kt)

```
class CheatActivity : AppCompatActivity() {

    override fun onCreate(savedInstanceState: Bundle?) {
        ...
    }

    companion object {
        fun newIntent(packageContext: Context, answerIsTrue: Boolean): Intent {
            return Intent(packageContext, CheatActivity::class.java).apply {
                putExtra(EXTRA_ANSWER_IS_TRUE, answerIsTrue)
            }
        }
    }
}
```

This function allows you to create an **Intent** properly configured with the extras **CheatActivity** will need. The answerIsTrue argument, a Boolean, is put into the intent with a private name using the EXTRA_ANSWER_IS_TRUE constant. You will extract this value momentarily.

A companion object allows you to access functions without having an instance of a class, similar to static functions in Java. Using a **newIntent(…)** function inside a companion object like this for your activity subclasses will make it easy for other code to properly configure their launching intents.

Speaking of other code, use this new function in **MainActivity**'s cheat button listener now.

## Listing 6.10 Launching **CheatActivity** with an extra (MainActivity.kt)

```
cheatButton.setOnClickListener {
    // Start CheatActivity
    val intent = Intent(this, CheatActivity::class.java)
    val answerIsTrue = quizViewModel.currentQuestionAnswer
    val intent = CheatActivity.newIntent(this@MainActivity, answerIsTrue)
    startActivity(intent)
}
```

You only need one extra, but you can put multiple extras on an **Intent** if you need to. If you do, add more arguments to your **newIntent(…)** function to stay consistent with the pattern.

To retrieve the value from the extra, you will use **Intent.getBooleanExtra(String, Boolean)**.

The first argument is the name of the extra. The second argument of **getBooleanExtra(…)** is a default answer if the key is not found.

In **CheatActivity**, retrieve the value from the extra in **onCreate(Bundle?)** and store it in a member variable.

## Listing 6.11  Using an extra (CheatActivity.kt)

```kotlin
class CheatActivity : AppCompatActivity() {

    private var answerIsTrue = false

    override fun onCreate(savedInstanceState: Bundle?) {
        super.onCreate(savedInstanceState)
        setContentView(R.layout.activity_cheat)

        answerIsTrue = intent.getBooleanExtra(EXTRA_ANSWER_IS_TRUE, false)
    }
    ...
}
```

Note that **Activity.getIntent()** always returns the **Intent** that started the activity. This is what you sent when calling **startActivity(Intent)**.

Finally, wire up the answer **TextView** and the SHOW ANSWER button to use the retrieved value.

## Listing 6.12  Enabling cheating (CheatActivity.kt)

```kotlin
class CheatActivity : AppCompatActivity() {

    private lateinit var answerTextView: TextView
    private lateinit var showAnswerButton: Button

    private var answerIsTrue = false

    override fun onCreate(savedInstanceState: Bundle?) {
        ...

        answerIsTrue = intent.getBooleanExtra(EXTRA_ANSWER_IS_TRUE, false)
        answerTextView = findViewById(R.id.answer_text_view)
        showAnswerButton = findViewById(R.id.show_answer_button)
        showAnswerButton.setOnClickListener {
            val answerText = when {
                answerIsTrue -> R.string.true_button
                else -> R.string.false_button
            }
            answerTextView.setText(answerText)
        }
    }
    ...
}
```

This code is pretty straightforward. You set the **TextView**'s text using **TextView.setText(Int)**. **TextView.setText(…)** has many variations, and here you use the one that accepts the resource ID of a string resource.

Run GeoQuiz. Press CHEAT! to get to **CheatActivity**. Then press SHOW ANSWER to reveal the answer to the current question.

# Getting a result back from a child activity

At this point, the user can cheat with impunity. Let's fix that by having the **CheatActivity** tell the **MainActivity** whether the user chose to view the answer.

When you want to hear back from the child activity, you call the **Activity.startActivityForResult(Intent, Int)** function.

The first parameter is the same intent as before. The second parameter is the *request code*. The request code is a user-defined integer that is sent to the child activity and then received back by the parent. It is used when an activity starts more than one type of child activity and needs to know who is reporting back. **MainActivity** will only ever start one type of child activity, but using a constant for the request code is a best practice that will set you up well for future changes.

In **MainActivity**, modify cheatButton's listener to call **startActivityForResult(Intent, int)**.

## Listing 6.13  Calling **startActivityForResult(…)** (MainActivity.kt)

```
private const val TAG = "MainActivity"
private const val KEY_INDEX = "index"
private const val REQUEST_CODE_CHEAT = 0

class MainActivity : AppCompatActivity() {
    ...
    override fun onCreate(savedInstanceState: Bundle?) {
        ...
        cheatButton.setOnClickListener {
            ...
            startActivity(intent)
            startActivityForResult(intent, REQUEST_CODE_CHEAT)
        }

        updateQuestion()
    }
    ...
}
```

## Setting a result

There are two functions you can call in the child activity to send data back to the parent:

```
setResult(resultCode: Int)
setResult(resultCode: Int, data: Intent)
```

Typically, the *result code* is one of two predefined constants: `Activity.RESULT_OK` or `Activity.RESULT_CANCELED`. (You can use another constant, `RESULT_FIRST_USER`, as an offset when defining your own result codes.)

Setting result codes is useful when the parent needs to take different action depending on how the child activity finished.

For example, if a child activity had an OK button and a Cancel button, the child activity would set a different result code depending on which button was pressed. Then the parent activity would take a different action depending on the result code.

Calling **setResult(…)** is not required of the child activity. If you do not need to distinguish between results or receive arbitrary data on an intent, then you can let the OS send a default result code. A result code is always returned to the parent if the child activity was started with **startActivityForResult(…)**. If **setResult(…)** is not called, then when the user presses the Back button, the parent will receive `Activity.RESULT_CANCELED`.

## Sending back an intent

In this implementation, you are interested in passing some specific data back to **MainActivity**. So you are going to create an **Intent**, put an extra on it, and then call **Activity.setResult(Int, Intent)** to get that data into **MainActivity**'s hands.

In **CheatActivity**, add a constant for the extra's key and a private function that does this work. Then call this function in the SHOW ANSWER button's listener.

### Listing 6.14  Setting a result (CheatActivity.kt)

```kotlin
const val EXTRA_ANSWER_SHOWN = "com.bignerdranch.android.geoquiz.answer_shown"
private const val EXTRA_ANSWER_IS_TRUE =
        "com.bignerdranch.android.geoquiz.answer_is_true"

class CheatActivity : AppCompatActivity() {
    ...
    override fun onCreate(savedInstanceState: Bundle?) {
        ...
        showAnswerButton.setOnClickListener {
            ...
            answerTextView.setText(answerText)
            setAnswerShownResult(true)
        }
    }

    private fun setAnswerShownResult(isAnswerShown: Boolean) {
        val data = Intent().apply {
            putExtra(EXTRA_ANSWER_SHOWN, isAnswerShown)
        }
        setResult(Activity.RESULT_OK, data)
    }
    ...
}
```

When the user presses the SHOW ANSWER button, the **CheatActivity** packages up the result code and the intent in the call to **setResult(Int, Intent)**.

Then, when the user presses the Back button to return to the **MainActivity**, the **ActivityManager** calls the following function on the parent activity:

```
onActivityResult(requestCode: Int, resultCode: Int, data: Intent)
```

The parameters are the original request code from **MainActivity** and the result code and intent passed into **setResult(Int, Intent)**.

Figure 6.10 shows this sequence of interactions.

## Figure 6.10  Sequence diagram for GeoQuiz

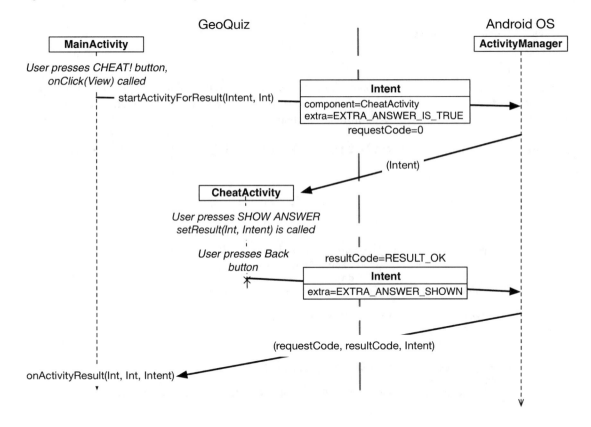

The final step is to override **onActivityResult(Int, Int, Intent)** in **MainActivity** to handle the result.

## Handling a result

In QuizViewModel.kt, add a new property to hold the value that **CheatActivity** is passing back. The user's cheat status is part of the UI state. Stashing the value in **QuizViewModel** instead of **MainActivity** means the value will persist across a configuration change rather than being destroyed with the activity, as discussed in Chapter 4.

Listing 6.15  Tracking cheating in **QuizViewModel** (QuizViewModel.kt)

```kotlin
class QuizViewModel : ViewModel() {

    var currentIndex = 0
    var isCheater = false
    ...
}
```

Next, in MainActivity.kt, override **onActivityResult(…)** to pull the value out of the result sent back from **CheatActivity**. Check the request code and result code to be sure they are what you expect. This, again, is a best practice to make future maintenance easier.

Listing 6.16  Implementing **onActivityResult(…)** (MainActivity.kt)

```kotlin
class MainActivity : AppCompatActivity() {
    ...
    override fun onCreate(savedInstanceState: Bundle?) {
        ...
    }

    override fun onActivityResult(requestCode: Int,
                                  resultCode: Int,
                                  data: Intent?) {
        super.onActivityResult(requestCode, resultCode, data)

        if (resultCode != Activity.RESULT_OK) {
            return
        }

        if (requestCode == REQUEST_CODE_CHEAT) {
            quizViewModel.isCheater =
                data?.getBooleanExtra(EXTRA_ANSWER_SHOWN, false) ?: false
        }
    }
    ...
}
```

Finally, modify the **checkAnswer(Boolean)** function in **MainActivity** to check whether the user cheated and to respond appropriately.

## Listing 6.17  Changing toast message based on value of isCheater (MainActivity.kt)

```
class MainActivity : AppCompatActivity() {
    ...
    private fun checkAnswer(userAnswer: Boolean) {
        val correctAnswer: Boolean = quizViewModel.currentQuestionAnswer

        val messageResId = if (userAnswer == correctAnswer) {
            R.string.correct_toast
        } else {
            R.string.incorrect_toast
        }
        val messageResId = when {
            quizViewModel.isCheater -> R.string.judgment_toast
            userAnswer == correctAnswer -> R.string.correct_toast
            else -> R.string.incorrect_toast
        }
        Toast.makeText(this, messageResId, Toast.LENGTH_SHORT)
                .show()
    }
}
```

Run GeoQuiz. Press CHEAT!, then press SHOW ANSWER on the cheat screen. Once you cheat, press the Back button. Try answering the current question. You should see the judgment toast appear.

What happens if you go to the next question? Still a cheater. If you wish to relax your rules around cheating, try your hand at the challenge outlined in the section called Challenge: Tracking Cheat Status by Question.

At this point GeoQuiz is feature complete. In the next chapter, Chapter 7, you will add some flair to GeoQuiz by including an activity transition animation when displaying **CheatActivity**. In doing so you will learn how to include the newest Android features available while still supporting older versions of Android in the same application.

# How Android Sees Your Activities

Let's look at what is going on OS-wise as you move between activities. First, when you click on the GeoQuiz app in the launcher, the OS does not start the application; it starts an activity in the application. More specifically, it starts the application's *launcher activity*. For GeoQuiz, **MainActivity** is the launcher activity.

When the New Project wizard created the GeoQuiz application and **MainActivity**, it made **MainActivity** the launcher activity by default. Launcher activity status is specified in the manifest by the intent-filter element in **MainActivity**'s declaration (Listing 6.18).

## Listing 6.18 **MainActivity** declared as launcher activity (manifests/AndroidManifest.xml)

```
<manifest xmlns:android="http://schemas.android.com/apk/res/android"
    ... >

    <application
        ... >
        <activity android:name=".CheatActivity">
        </activity>
        <activity android:name=".MainActivity">
            <intent-filter>
                <action android:name="android.intent.action.MAIN"/>

                <category android:name="android.intent.category.LAUNCHER"/>
            </intent-filter>
        </activity>
    </application>

</manifest>
```

After the instance of **MainActivity** is onscreen, the user can press the CHEAT! button. When this happens, an instance of **CheatActivity** is started – on top of the **MainActivity**. These activities exist in a stack (Figure 6.11).

Pressing the Back button in **CheatActivity** pops this instance off the stack, and the **MainActivity** resumes its position at the top, as shown in Figure 6.11.

## Figure 6.11  GeoQuiz's back stack

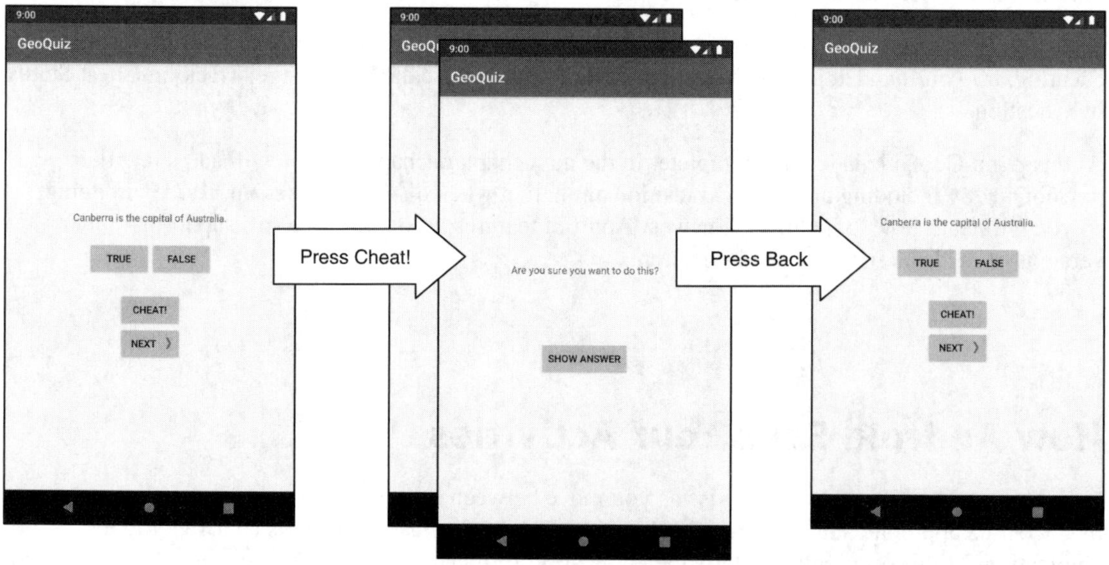

A call to **Activity.finish()** in **CheatActivity** would also pop the **CheatActivity** off the stack.

If you run GeoQuiz and press the Back button from the **MainActivity**, the **MainActivity** will be popped off the stack and you will return to the last screen you were viewing before running GeoQuiz (Figure 6.12).

## Figure 6.12  Looking at the Home screen

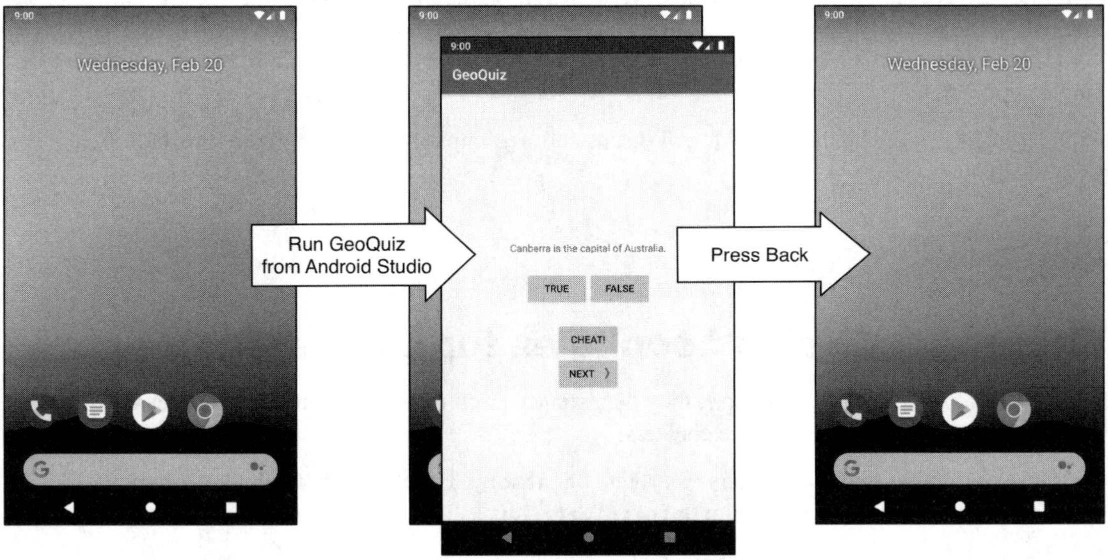

If you started GeoQuiz from the launcher application, pressing the Back button from **MainActivity** will return you to the launcher (Figure 6.13).

## Figure 6.13  Running GeoQuiz from the launcher

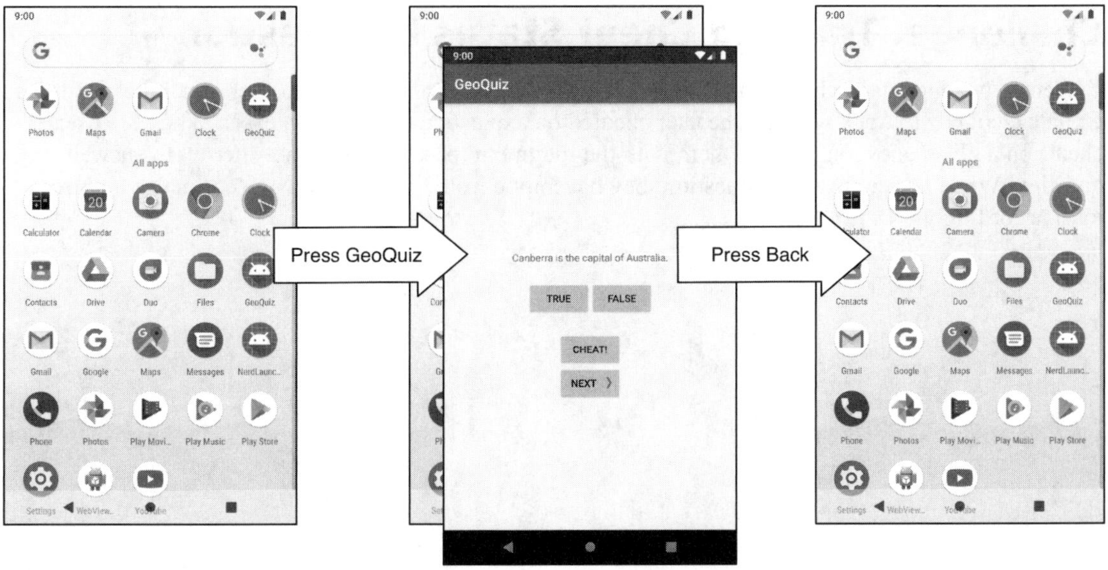

Pressing the Back button from the launcher will return you to the screen you were looking at before you opened the launcher.

What you are seeing here is that the **ActivityManager** maintains a *back stack* and that this back stack is not just for your application's activities. Activities for all applications share the back stack, which is one reason the **ActivityManager** is involved in starting your activities and lives with the OS and not your application. The stack represents the use of the OS and device as a whole rather than the use of a single application.

(Wondering about the Up button? We will discuss how to implement and configure this button in Chapter 14.)

# Challenge: Closing Loopholes for Cheaters

Cheaters never win. Unless, of course, they persistently circumvent your anticheating measures. Which they probably will. Because they are cheaters.

GeoQuiz has a major loophole. Users can rotate **CheatActivity** after they cheat to clear out the cheating result. When they go back to **MainActivity**, it is as if they never cheated at all.

Fix this bug by persisting **CheatActivity**'s UI state across rotation and process death using the techniques you learned in Chapter 4.

# Challenge: Tracking Cheat Status by Question

Currently, when the user cheats on a single question, they are considered a cheater on all the questions. Update GeoQuiz to track whether the user cheated on a question-by-question basis. When the user cheats on a given question, present them with the judgment toast any time they attempt to answer that question. When a user answers a question they have not cheated on yet, show the correct or incorrect toast accordingly.

# 7
# Android SDK Versions and Compatibility

Now that you have gotten your feet wet with GeoQuiz, let's review some background information about the different versions of Android. The information in this chapter is important to have under your belt as you continue with the book and develop more complex and realistic apps.

## Android SDK Versions

Table 7.1 shows the SDK versions, the associated versions of the Android firmware, and the percentage of devices running them as of May 2019.

Table 7.1  Android API levels, firmware versions, and percent of devices in use

| API level | Codename | Device firmware version | % of devices in use |
|-----------|----------|-------------------------|---------------------|
| 28 | Pie | 9.0 | 10.4 |
| 27 | Oreo | 8.1 | 15.4 |
| 26 | | 8.0 | 12.9 |
| 25 | Nougat | 7.1 | 7.8 |
| 24 | | 7.0 | 11.4 |
| 23 | Marshmallow | 6.0 | 16.9 |
| 22 | Lollipop | 5.1 | 11.5 |
| 21 | | 5.0 | 3.0 |
| 19 | KitKat | 4.4 | 6.9 |
| 18 | Jelly Bean | 4.3 | 0.5 |
| 17 | | 4.2 | 1.5 |
| 16 | | 4.1 | 1.2 |
| 15 | Ice Cream Sandwich | 4.0.3, 4.0.4 | 0.3 |
| 10 | Gingerbread | 2.3.3 - 2.3.7 | 0.3 |

(Note that versions of Android with less than 0.1 percent distribution are omitted from this table.)

Most "codenamed" releases are followed by incremental releases. For instance, Ice Cream Sandwich was initially released as Android 4.0 (API level 14). It was almost immediately replaced with incremental releases culminating in Android 4.0.3 and 4.0.4 (API level 15).

The percentage of devices using each version changes constantly, of course, but the figures do reveal an important trend: Android devices running older versions are not immediately upgraded or replaced when a newer version is available. As of May 2019, almost 11 percent of devices are still running KitKat or an earlier version. KitKat (Android 4.4) was released in October 2013.

(If you are curious, the data in Table 7.1 is available at `developer.android.com/about/dashboards/index.html`, where it is periodically updated.)

Why do so many devices still run older versions of Android? Most of it has to do with heavy competition among Android device manufacturers and US carriers. Carriers want features and phones that no other network has. Device manufacturers feel this pressure, too – all of their phones are based on the same OS, but they want to stand out from the competition. The combination of pressures from the market and the carriers means that there is a bewildering array of devices with proprietary, one-off modifications of Android.

A device with a proprietary version of Android is not able to run a new version of Android released by Google. Instead, it must wait for a compatible proprietary upgrade. That upgrade might not be available until months after Google releases its version, if it is ever available. Manufacturers often choose to spend resources on newer devices rather than keeping older ones up to date.

# Compatibility and Android Programming

The delay in upgrades combined with regular new releases makes compatibility an important issue in Android programming. To reach a broad market, Android developers must create apps that perform well on devices running the most current version of Android plus the three to four previous versions of Android – as well as on different device form factors.

Targeting different sizes of devices is easier than you might think. Phone screens are a variety of sizes, but the Android layout system does a good job at adapting. If you need to provide custom resources or layouts based on screen size, you can use configuration qualifiers to do the job (as you will see in Chapter 17). However, for Android TV and Wear OS by Google devices (both of which also run Android), the differences in UI are large enough that you need to rethink the user interaction patterns and design of your app.

## A sane minimum

The oldest version of Android that the exercises in this book support is API level 21 (Lollipop). There are references to legacy versions of Android, but the focus is on what we consider to be modern versions (API level 21+). With the distribution of Gingerbread, Ice Cream Sandwich, Jelly Bean, and KitKat dropping month by month, the amount of work required to support those older versions eclipses the value they can provide.

Incremental releases cause little problem with backward compatibility. Major versions can be a different story. The work required to support 5.x devices is not terribly significant. If you also need to support 4.x devices, you will have to spend time working through the differences in those versions. Luckily, Google has provided libraries to ease the pain. You will learn about these libraries in later chapters.

When you created the GeoQuiz project, you set a minimum SDK version within the New Project wizard, as shown in Figure 7.1. (Note that Android uses the terms "SDK version" and "API level" interchangeably.)

## Figure 7.1  Remember me?

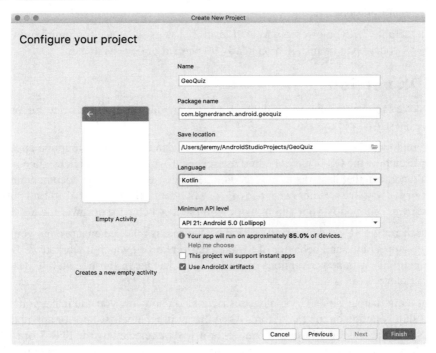

In addition to the minimum supported version, you can also set the *target* version and the *compile* version. Let's explain the default choices and see how to change them.

All these properties are set in the build.gradle file in your app module. The compile version lives exclusively in this file. The minimum SDK version and target SDK version are set in the build.gradle file, but they are used to overwrite or set values in your AndroidManifest.xml file.

Open the build.gradle file in your app module. Notice the values for compileSdkVersion, minSdkVersion, and targetSdkVersion:

```
compileSdkVersion 28
defaultConfig {
    applicationId "com.bignerdranch.android.geoquiz"
    minSdkVersion 21
    targetSdkVersion 28
```

# Minimum SDK version

The `minSdkVersion` value is a hard floor below which the OS should refuse to install the app.

By setting this version to API level 21 (Lollipop), you give Android permission to install GeoQuiz on devices running Lollipop or higher. Android will refuse to install GeoQuiz on a device running anything lower than Lollipop.

Looking again at Table 7.1, you can see why API level 21 is a good choice for a minimum SDK version: It allows your app to be installed on nearly 90 percent of devices in use.

# Target SDK version

The `targetSdkVersion` value tells Android which API level your app is *designed* to run on. Most often this will be the latest Android release.

When would you lower the target SDK? New SDK releases can change how your app appears on a device or even how the OS behaves behind the scenes. If you have already designed an app, you should confirm that it works as expected on new releases. Check the documentation at `developer.android.com/reference/android/os/Build.VERSION_CODES.html` to find potential problems. Then you can modify your app to work with the new behavior or lower the target SDK.

Not increasing the target SDK when a new version of Android is released ensures that your app will still run with the appearance and behavior of the targeted version on which it worked well. This option exists for compatibility with newer versions of Android, as changes in subsequent releases are ignored until the `targetSdkVersion` is increased.

One important thing to note is that Google has restrictions on how low you can make your target SDK if you want to ship your app on the Play Store. As of this writing, any new apps or app updates must have a target SDK of at least API level 26 (Oreo) – or it will be rejected by the Play Store. This ensures that users can benefit from the performance and security improvements in recent versions of Android. These version requirements will increase over time, as new versions of Android are released, so make sure you keep an eye on the documentation to know when you need to update your target version.

# Compile SDK version

The last SDK setting is the `compileSdkVersion`. This setting is not used to update the `AndroidManifest.xml` file. Whereas the minimum and target SDK versions are placed in the manifest when you build your app to advertise those values to the OS, the compile SDK version is private information between you and the compiler.

Android's features are exposed through the classes and functions in the SDK. The compile SDK version specifies which version to use when building your code. When Android Studio is looking to find the classes and functions you refer to in your imports, the compile SDK version determines which SDK version it checks against.

The best choice for a compile SDK version is the latest API level available. However, you can change the compile SDK version of an existing application if you need to. For instance, you might want to update the compile SDK version when a new version of Android is released so that you can use the new functions and classes it introduces.

You can modify the minimum SDK version, target SDK version, and compile SDK version in your `build.gradle` file. Remember that you must sync your project with the Gradle changes before they will be reflected.

# Adding code from later APIs safely

The difference between GeoQuiz's minimum SDK version and compile SDK version leaves you with a compatibility gap to manage. For example, what happens if you call code from an SDK version that is later than the minimum SDK of Lollipop (API level 21)? When your app is installed and run on a Lollipop device, it will crash.

This used to be a testing nightmare. However, thanks to improvements in Android Lint, potential problems caused by calling newer code on older devices can be caught at compile time. If you use code from a higher version than your minimum SDK, Android Lint will report build errors.

Right now, all of GeoQuiz's simple code was introduced in API level 21 or earlier. Let's add some code from after API level 21 (Lollipop) and see what happens.

Open `MainActivity.kt`. In the **OnClickListener** for the CHEAT! button, add the following code to use a fancy reveal animation when **CheatActivity** comes on to the screen.

### Listing 7.1  Adding activity animation code (`MainActivity.kt`)

```
class MainActivity : AppCompatActivity() {
    ...
    override fun onCreate(savedInstanceState: Bundle?) {
        ...
        cheatButton.setOnClickListener { view ->
            // Start CheatActivity
            val answerIsTrue = quizViewModel.currentQuestionAnswer
            val intent = CheatActivity.newIntent(this@MainActivity, answerIsTrue)
            val options = ActivityOptions
                    .makeClipRevealAnimation(view, 0, 0, view.width, view.height)

            startActivityForResult(intent, REQUEST_CODE_CHEAT, options.toBundle())
        }

        updateQuestion()
    }
    ...
}
```

You use the **ActivityOptions** class to customize how you want your activity to be started. In the code above, you call **makeClipRevealAnimation(…)** to specify that the **CheatActivity** should use a reveal animation. The values you pass into **makeClipRevealAnimation(…)** specify the view object to use as the source of the animation (the CHEAT! button, in this case), the x and y position (relative to the source view) to start displaying the new activity, and the initial width and height of the new activity.

Note that you named the lambda argument `view`, rather than using the default name `it`. In the context of setting a click listener, the argument to the lambda represents the view that was clicked. Naming the argument is not required, but it can help improve the readability of your code. We recommend you name the lambda argument when the body of the lambda uses the argument and it is not immediately clear to a new reader of the code what the argument represents.

Finally, you called **options.toBundle()** to package the **ActivityOptions** up into a **Bundle** object and then passed them to **startActivityForResult(…)**. The **ActivityManager** uses the options bundle to determine how to bring your activity into view.

Notice that a Lint error appears on the line where you call
**ActivityOptions.makeClipRevealAnimation(…)**, in the form of a red squiggly under the function name and, when you click on the function, a red lightbulb icon. The **makeClipRevealAnimation(…)** function was added to the Android SDK in API level 23, so this code would crash on a device running API 22 or lower.

Because your compile SDK version is API level 28, the compiler itself has no problem with this code. Android Lint, on the other hand, knows about your minimum SDK version, and so it complains.

The error message reads something like Call requires API level 23 (Current min is 21). You can still run the code with this warning (try it and see), but Lint knows it is not safe.

How do you get rid of this error? One option is to raise the minimum SDK version to 23. However, raising the minimum SDK version is not really dealing with this compatibility problem as much as ducking it. If your app cannot be installed on API level 23 and older devices, then you no longer have a compatibility problem – but you also no longer have those users.

A better option is to wrap the higher API code in a conditional statement that checks the device's version of Android.

### Listing 7.2  Checking the device's Android version first (`MainActivity.kt`)

```kotlin
class MainActivity : AppCompatActivity() {
    ...
    @SuppressLint("RestrictedApi")
    override fun onCreate(savedInstanceState: Bundle?) {
        ...
        cheatButton.setOnClickListener { view ->
            ...
            if (Build.VERSION.SDK_INT >= Build.VERSION_CODES.M) {
                val options = ActivityOptions
                        .makeClipRevealAnimation(view, 0, 0, view.width, view.height)

                startActivityForResult(intent, REQUEST_CODE_CHEAT, options.toBundle())
            } else {
                startActivityForResult(intent, REQUEST_CODE_CHEAT)
            }
        }

        updateQuestion()
    }
}
```

The `Build.VERSION.SDK_INT` constant is the device's version of Android. You compare that version with the constant that stands for the M (Marshmallow) release. (Version codes are listed at `developer.android.com/reference/android/os/Build.VERSION_CODES.html`.)

Now your reveal code will only be called when the app is running on a device with API level 23 or higher. You have made your code safe for API level 21, and Android Lint should now be content.

Run GeoQuiz on a Marshmallow or higher device, cheat on a question, and check out your new animation.

The transition animations are pretty quick, and you may not be able to tell the difference between your new one and the original. To make seeing the difference easier, you can tweak your device to slow down the transitions. Open the Settings app and dive into the developer options (System → Advanced → Developer options). Find Transition animation scale (under Drawing), select it, and set the value to Animation Scale 10x (Figure 7.2).

Figure 7.2  Slowing down transitions

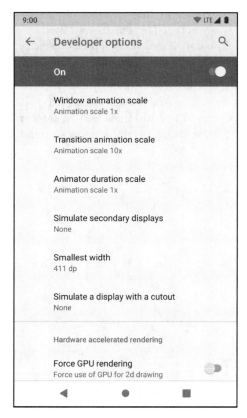

This will slow down your transitions by a factor of 10, which should make it apparent how different the new transition is. Return to GeoQuiz and rerun the app to see your new transition in slow mo. Undo your changes to **MainActivity** if you want to see what the original transition looks like as well. Before moving on, return to the developer options and return the transition animation scale back to 1x.

You can also run GeoQuiz on a Lollipop device (virtual or otherwise). It will not have the same reveal animation, but you can confirm that the app still runs safely.

You will see another example of guarding newer APIs in Chapter 27.

# Jetpack libraries

While guarding API levels works, it is not optimal for a couple reasons. First, it is more work for you as a developer to support different paths in your app for different versions. Second, it means that users of your app will have a different experience based on the version their device is running.

In Chapter 4, you learned about the Jetpack libraries and AndroidX. In addition to offering new features (like `ViewModel`), the Jetpack libraries offer backward compatibility for new features on older devices and provide (or attempt to provide) consistent behavior when possible across Android versions. At the very least, using the libraries allows you to write as few conditional API checks as possible.

Many of the AndroidX libraries in Jetpack are modifications of previous support libraries. You should strive to use these libraries any time you can. This makes your life as a developer easier, because you no longer have to guard against different API versions and handle each case separately. Your users also benefit, because they will have the same experience no matter what version their device is running.

Unfortunately, the Jetpack libraries are not a compatibility cure-all, because not all the features you will want to use are available in them. The Android team does a good job of adding new APIs to the Jetpack libraries as time goes on, but you will still find cases where a certain API is unavailable. In this case, you will need to use explicit version checks until a Jetpack version of the feature is added.

# Using the Android Developer Documentation

Android Lint errors will tell you what API level your incompatible code is from. But you can also find out which API level particular classes and functions belong to in Android's developer documentation.

It is a good idea to get comfortable using the developer documentation right away. There is far too much in the Android SDKs to keep in your head. And, with new versions appearing regularly, you will need to learn what is new and how to use it.

The Android developer documentation is an excellent and voluminous source of information. The main page of the documentation is developer.android.com. It is split into six parts: Platform, Android Studio, Google Play, Android Jetpack, Docs, and News. It is all worth perusing when you get a chance. Each section outlines different aspects of Android development, from just getting started to deploying your app to the Play Store.

| Platform | Information on the basic platform, focusing on the supported form factors and the different Android versions. |
| --- | --- |
| Android Studio | Articles on the IDE to help learn the different tools and workflows to make your life easier. |
| Google Play | Tips and tricks for deploying your apps as well as making your apps more successful with users. |
| Android Jetpack | Information about the Jetpack libraries and how the Android team is striving to improve the app development experience. Some of the Jetpack libraries are used in this book, but you should explore this section for the full list. |
| Docs | The main page for the developer documentation. Here you will find information on the individual classes in the framework as well as a trove of tutorials and codelabs that you can work through to improve and hone your skills. |
| News | Articles and posts to keep you up to date on the latest happenings in Android. |

You can also download the documentation to access it offline. In Android Studio's SDK Manager (Tools → SDK Manager), select the SDK Tools tab. Check Documentation for Android SDK and click Apply. You will be informed of the size of the download and asked to confirm. Once the download has finished, you can access the documentation on your filesystem. The directory where you downloaded the SDKs (which you can check in the SDK Manager, if you do not know it) will have a new docs directory that contains the complete documentation.

On the documentation website, determine what API level makeClipRevealAnimation(…) belongs to by searching for its name using the search bar at the top right. Select the ActivityOptions result (which is likely the first search result), and you will be taken to the class reference page shown in Figure 7.3. On the right side of this page are links to its different sections.

Figure 7.3 **ActivityOptions** reference page

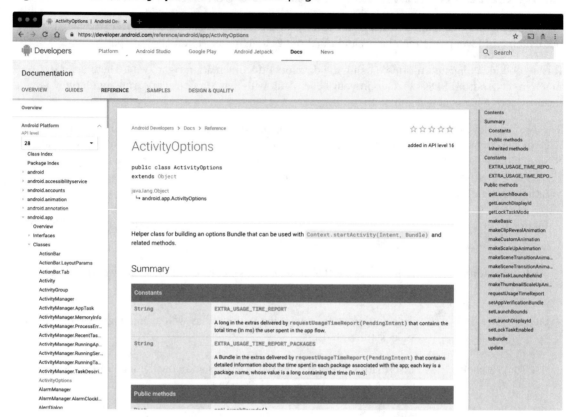

Scroll down, find the **makeClipRevealAnimation(…)** function, and click on the function name to see a description. To the right of the function signature, you can see that **makeClipRevealAnimation(…)** was introduced in API level 23.

If you want to see which **ActivityOptions** methods are available in, say, API level 21, you can filter the reference by API level. On the lefthand side of the page, where the classes are indexed by package, find where it says API level: 28. Click the adjacent control and select 21 from the list. Everything that Android has introduced after API level 21 will be grayed out.

The API level filter is much more useful for a class that is available at the API level that you are using. Search for the reference page on the **Activity** class in the documentation. Change the API level filter back down to API level 21 and notice that many methods are available at that level – though some have been added since that API, such as **onMultiWindowModeChanged(…)**, which is an addition to the SDK in Nougat that allows you to be notified when the activity changes from full-screen mode to multi-window mode and vice versa.

As you continue through this book, visit the developer documentation often. You will certainly need the documentation to tackle the challenge exercises, but you should also explore it whenever you get curious about particular classes, functions, or other topics. Android is constantly updating and improving the documentation, so there is always something new to learn.

# Challenge: Reporting the Device's Android Version

Add a **TextView** widget to the GeoQuiz layout that reports to the user what API level the device is running. Figure 7.4 shows what the final result should look like.

Figure 7.4  Finished challenge

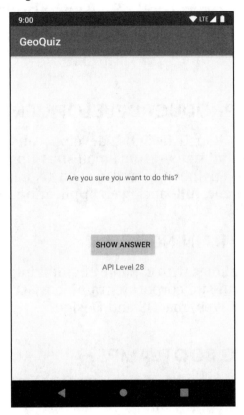

You cannot set this **TextView**'s text in the layout, because you will not know the device's Android version until runtime. Find the **TextView** function for setting text in the **TextView** reference page in Android's documentation. You are looking for a function that accepts a single argument – a string (or a CharSequence).

Use other XML attributes listed in the **TextView** reference to adjust the size or typeface of the text.

# Challenge: Limited Cheats

Allow the user to cheat a maximum of three times. Keep track of the user's cheat occurrences and display the number of remaining cheat tokens below the cheat button. If no tokens remain, disable the cheat button.

Of the top 25 apps in the U.S., 19 are built by companies that brought in Big Nerd Ranch to train their developers.

### APP & PRODUCT DEVELOPMENT

Big Nerd Ranch designs, develops and deploys applications for clients of all sizes—from small start-ups to large corporations. Our in-house engineering and design teams possess expertise in iOS, Android and full-stack web application development.

### TEAM TRAINING

For companies with capable engineering teams, Big Nerd Ranch can provide on-site corporate training in iOS, Android, Front-End Web, Back-End Web, macOS and Design.

### CODING BOOTCAMPS

Our all-inclusive, immersive bootcamps are like none other. As soon as you arrive, we take care of everything, from the airport shuttle to hotels to meals. Our Georgia and California retreats are perfect for intermediate to advanced developers who can't spend months away from home.

### FRONTIER SCREENCASTS

Take advantage of bite-sized tutorials on a variety of topics, including Converting Your Java Project to Kotlin. Our authors and developers have prepared a variety of topics to keep you leveled up. New screencasts released weekly. Ask about our free trial.

**www.bignerdranch.com**

# 8

# UI Fragments and the Fragment Manager

In this chapter, you will start building an application named CriminalIntent. CriminalIntent records the details of "office crimes" – things like leaving dirty dishes in the break room sink or walking away from an empty shared printer after documents have printed.

With CriminalIntent, you can make a record of a crime including a title, a date, and a photo. You can also identify a suspect from your contacts and lodge a complaint via email, Twitter, Facebook, or another app. After documenting and reporting a crime, you can proceed with your work free of resentment and ready to focus on the business at hand.

CriminalIntent is a complex app that will take 11 chapters to complete. It will have a *list-detail interface*: The main screen will display a list of recorded crimes, and users will be able to add new crimes or select an existing crime to view and edit its details (Figure 8.1).

Figure 8.1  CriminalIntent, a list-detail app

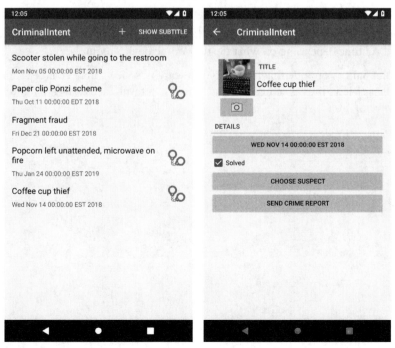

# The Need for UI Flexibility

You might imagine that a list-detail application consists of two activities: one managing the list and the other managing the detail view. Pressing on a crime in the list would start an instance of the detail activity. Pressing the Back button would destroy the detail activity and return you to the list, where you could select another crime.

That would work, but what if you wanted more sophisticated presentation and navigation between screens?

Consider the possibility of CriminalIntent running on a large device. Some devices have screens large enough to show the list and detail at the same time – at least in landscape orientation (Figure 8.2).

Figure 8.2  Ideal list-detail interface for varying screen widths

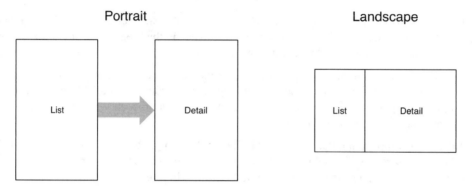

Or imagine a user is viewing a crime and wants to see the next crime in the list. It would be better if they could select a different crime from the list without navigating back to the previous screen first.

What these scenarios have in common is UI flexibility: the ability to compose and recompose an activity's view at runtime depending on what the user or the device requires.

Activities were not built to provide this flexibility. An activity's views may change at runtime, but the code to control those views must live inside the activity. As a result, activities are tightly coupled to the particular screen being used.

# Introducing Fragments

You can ensure that your app is flexible by moving the app's UI management from the activity to one or more *fragments*.

A fragment is a controller object that an activity can deputize to perform tasks. Most commonly, the task is managing a UI. The UI can be an entire screen or just one part of the screen.

A fragment managing a UI is known as a *UI fragment*. A UI fragment has a view of its own that is inflated from a layout file. The fragment's view contains the interesting UI elements that the user wants to see and interact with.

Instead of containing the UI, the activity's view can hold a container for the fragment. The fragment's view is inserted into the container once it is inflated. In this chapter, the activity will host a single fragment, but an activity can have multiple containers in its view for different fragments.

You can use the fragment (or fragments) associated with the activity to compose and recompose the screen as your app and users require. The activity's view technically stays the same throughout its lifetime, and no laws of Android are violated.

Let's see how this would work in a list-detail application to display the list and detail together. You would compose the activity's view from a list fragment and a detail fragment. The detail view would show the details of the selected list item.

Selecting another item should display a new detail view. This is easy with fragments; the activity will replace the detail fragment with another detail fragment (Figure 8.3). No activities need to die for this major view change to happen.

## Figure 8.3  Swapping out a detail fragment

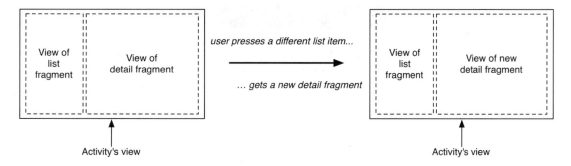

Using UI fragments separates the UI of your app into building blocks, which is useful for more than just list-detail applications. Working with individual blocks, it is easy to build tab interfaces, tack on animated sidebars, and more. Additionally, some of the new Android Jetpack APIs, such as the navigation controller, work best with fragments. So using fragments sets you up to integrate nicely with Jetpack APIs.

# Starting CriminalIntent

In this chapter, you are going to start on the detail part of CriminalIntent. Figure 8.4 shows you what CriminalIntent will look like at the end of this chapter.

Figure 8.4  CriminalIntent at the end of this chapter

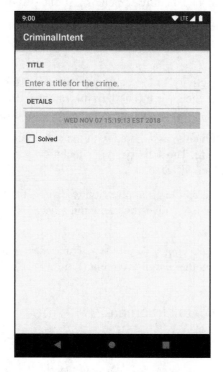

The screen shown in Figure 8.4 will be managed by a UI fragment named **CrimeFragment**. An instance of **CrimeFragment** will be *hosted* by an activity named **MainActivity**.

For now, think of hosting as the activity providing a spot in its view hierarchy to contain the fragment and its view (Figure 8.5). A fragment is incapable of getting a view onscreen itself. Only when it is inserted in an activity's hierarchy will its view appear.

Figure 8.5 **MainActivity** hosting a **CrimeFragment**

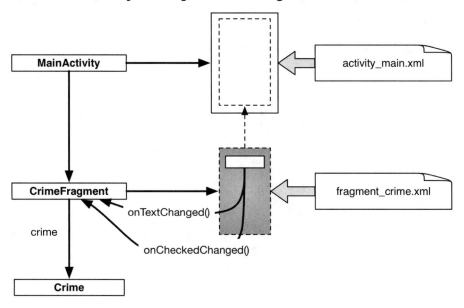

CriminalIntent will be a large project, and one way to keep your head wrapped around a project is with an object diagram. Figure 8.6 gives you the big picture of CriminalIntent. You do not have to memorize these objects and their relationships, but it is good to have an idea of where you are heading before you start.

You can see that **CrimeFragment** will do the sort of work that your activities did in GeoQuiz: create and manage the UI and interact with the model objects.

## Figure 8.6  Object diagram for CriminalIntent (for this chapter)

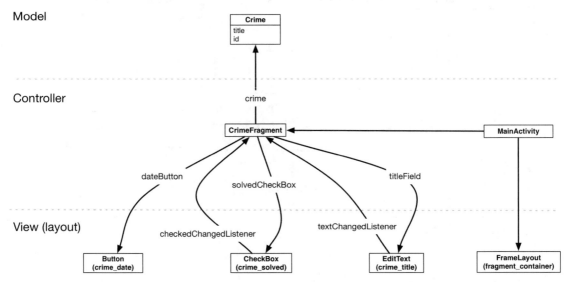

Three of the classes shown in Figure 8.6 are classes that you will write: **Crime**, **CrimeFragment**, and **MainActivity**.

An instance of **Crime** will represent a single office crime. In this chapter, a crime will have a title, an ID, a date, and a Boolean that indicates whether the crime has been solved. The title is a descriptive name, like "Toxic sink dump" or "Someone stole my yogurt!" The ID will uniquely identify an instance of **Crime**.

For this chapter, you will keep things very simple and use a single instance of **Crime**. **CrimeFragment** will have a property (crime) to hold this isolated incident.

**MainActivity**'s view will consist of a **FrameLayout** that defines the spot where the **CrimeFragment**'s view will appear.

**CrimeFragment**'s view will consist of a **LinearLayout** with a few child views inside of it, including an **EditText**, a **Button**, and a **CheckBox**. **CrimeFragment** will have a property for each of these views and will set listeners on them to update the model layer when there are changes.

# Creating a new project

Enough talk; time to build a new app. Create a new Android application (File → New → New Project...). Select the Empty Activity template (Figure 8.7). Click Next.

Figure 8.7  Creating the CriminalIntent application

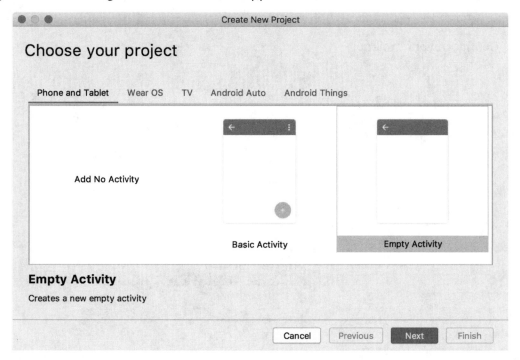

Configure your project as shown in Figure 8.8. Name the application CriminalIntent. Make sure the Package name is com.bignerdranch.android.criminalintent and the Language is Kotlin. Select API 21: Android 5.0 (Lollipop) from the Minimum API level dropdown. Finally, check the box to Use AndroidX artifacts.

## Figure 8.8  Configuring the CriminalIntent project

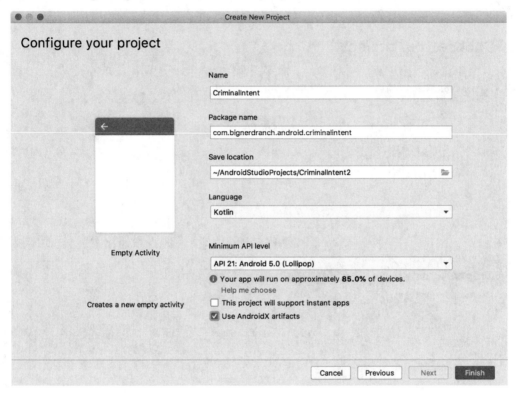

Click Finish to generate the project.

Before proceeding with **MainActivity**, create the model layer for CriminalIntent by writing the **Crime** class.

# Creating a Data Class

In the project tool window, right-click the com.bignerdranch.android.criminalintent package and select New → Kotlin File/Class to create a file named Crime.kt.

In Crime.kt, add fields to represent the crime's ID, title, date, and status and a constructor that initializes the ID and date fields. In addition to the fields, add the data keyword to the class definition to make **Crime** a data class.

Listing 8.1  Adding the **Crime** data class (Crime.kt)

```
data class Crime(val id: UUID = UUID.randomUUID(),
                 var title: String = "",
                 var date: Date = Date(),
                 var isSolved: Boolean = false)
```

When importing **Date**, you will be presented with multiple options. Make sure to import **java.util.Date**.

**UUID** is a utility class included in the Android framework. It provides an easy way to generate universally unique ID values. In the constructor, you generate a random unique ID by calling **UUID.randomUUID()**.

Initializing the **Date** variable using the default **Date** constructor sets date to the current date. This will be the default date for a crime.

That is all you need for the **Crime** class and for CriminalIntent's model layer in this chapter.

At this point, you have created the model layer and an activity that is capable of hosting a support fragment. Now you will get into the details of how the activity performs its duties as host.

# Creating a UI Fragment

The steps to create a UI fragment are the same as those you followed to create an activity:

- compose a UI by defining widgets in a layout file

- create the class and set its view to be the layout that you defined

- wire up the widgets inflated from the layout in code

## Defining CrimeFragment's layout

`CrimeFragment`'s view will display the information contained within an instance of `Crime`.

First, define the strings that the user will see in res/values/strings.xml.

### Listing 8.2  Adding strings (res/values/strings.xml)

```
<resources>
    <string name="app_name">CriminalIntent</string>
    <string name="crime_title_hint">Enter a title for the crime.</string>
    <string name="crime_title_label">Title</string>
    <string name="crime_details_label">Details</string>
    <string name="crime_solved_label">Solved</string>
</resources>
```

Next, you will define the UI. The layout for **CrimeFragment** will consist of a vertical **LinearLayout** that contains two **TextView**s, an **EditText**, a **Button**, and a **CheckBox**.

To create a layout file, right-click the res/layout folder in the project tool window and select New → Layout resource file. Name this file fragment_crime.xml and enter LinearLayout as the root element.

Android Studio creates the file and adds the **LinearLayout** for you. Add the widgets that make up the fragment's layout to res/layout/fragment_crime.xml.

## Listing 8.3 Layout file for fragment's view (res/layout/fragment_crime.xml)

```
<LinearLayout xmlns:android="http://schemas.android.com/apk/res/android"
    xmlns:tools="http://schemas.android.com/tools"
    android:orientation="vertical"
    android:layout_width="match_parent"
    android:layout_height="match_parent"
    android:layout_margin="16dp">

    <TextView
            style="?android:listSeparatorTextViewStyle"
            android:layout_width="match_parent"
            android:layout_height="wrap_content"
            android:text="@string/crime_title_label"/>

    <EditText
            android:id="@+id/crime_title"
            android:layout_width="match_parent"
            android:layout_height="wrap_content"
            android:hint="@string/crime_title_hint"/>

    <TextView
            style="?android:listSeparatorTextViewStyle"
            android:layout_width="match_parent"
            android:layout_height="wrap_content"
            android:text="@string/crime_details_label"/>

    <Button
            android:id="@+id/crime_date"
            android:layout_width="match_parent"
            android:layout_height="wrap_content"
            tools:text="Wed Nov 14 11:56 EST 2018"/>

    <CheckBox
            android:id="@+id/crime_solved"
            android:layout_width="match_parent"
            android:layout_height="wrap_content"
            android:text="@string/crime_solved_label"/>

</LinearLayout>
```

(The first **TextView**'s definition includes some new syntax related to view style: style="?
android:listSeparatorTextViewStyle". Fear not. You will learn the meaning behind this syntax in the section called Styles, themes, and theme attributes in Chapter 10.)

Recall that the `tools` namespace allows you to provide information that the preview is able to display. In this case, you are adding text to the date button so that it will not be empty in the preview. Check the Design tab to see a preview of your fragment's view (Figure 8.9).

Figure 8.9  Previewing updated crime fragment layout

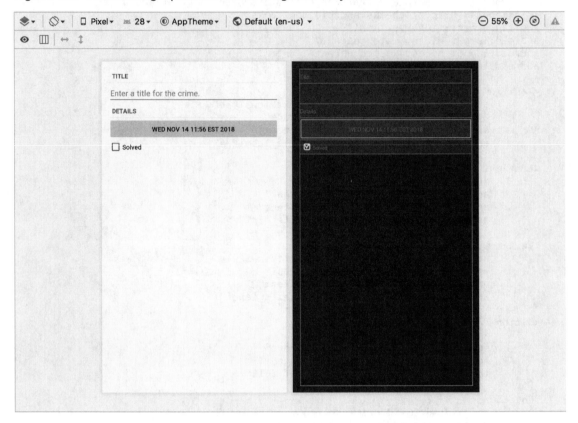

# Creating the CrimeFragment class

Create another Kotlin file for the **CrimeFragment** class. This time, select Class as the kind, and Android Studio will stub out the class definition for you. Turn the class into a fragment by subclassing the **Fragment** class.

## Listing 8.4  Subclassing the **Fragment** class (CrimeFragment.kt)

```
class CrimeFragment : Fragment() {
}
```

As you subclass the **Fragment** class, you will notice that Android Studio finds two classes with the **Fragment** name. You will see **android.app.Fragment** and **androidx.fragment.app.Fragment**. The **android.app.Fragment** is the version of fragments built into the Android OS. You will use the Jetpack version, so be sure to select **androidx.fragment.app.Fragment**, as shown in Figure 8.10. (Recall that the Jetpack libraries are in packages that begin with androidx.)

## Figure 8.10  Choosing the Jetpack **Fragment** class

If you do not see this dialog, try clicking into the **Fragment** class name. If the dialog still does not appear, you can manually import the correct class: Add the line import androidx.fragment.app.Fragment at the top of the file.

If, on the other hand, you have an import for **android.app.Fragment**, remove that line of code. Then import the correct **Fragment** class with Option-Return (Alt-Enter).

## Different types of fragments

New Android apps should always be built using the Jetpack (androidx) version of fragments. If you maintain older apps, you may see two other versions of fragments being used: the framework version and the v4 support library version. These are legacy versions of the **Fragment** class, and you should consider migrating apps that use them to the current Jetpack version.

Fragments were introduced in API level 11, along with the first Android tablets and the sudden need for UI flexibility. The framework implementation of fragments was built into devices running API level 11 or higher. Shortly afterward, a **Fragment** implementation was added to the v4 support library to enable fragment support on older devices. With each new version of Android, both of these fragment versions were updated with new features and security patches.

But as of Android 9.0 (API 28), the framework version of fragments is deprecated. No further updates will be made to this version, so you should not use it for new projects. Also, the earlier support library fragments have been moved to the Jetpack libraries. No further updates will be made to the support libraries after version 28. All future updates will apply to the Jetpack version, instead of the framework or v4 support fragments.

So: Always use the Jetpack fragments in your new projects, and migrate existing projects to ensure they stay current with new features and bug fixes.

## Implementing fragment lifecycle functions

**CrimeFragment** is a controller that interacts with model and view objects. Its job is to present the details of a specific crime and update those details as the user changes them.

In GeoQuiz, your activities did most of their controller work in activity lifecycle functions. In CriminalIntent, this work will be done by fragments in fragment lifecycle functions. Many of these functions correspond to the **Activity** functions you already know, such as **onCreate(Bundle?)**. (You will learn more about the fragment lifecycle in the section called The FragmentManager and the fragment lifecycle later in this chapter.)

In CrimeFragment.kt, add a property for the **Crime** instance and an implementation of **Fragment.onCreate(Bundle?)**.

Android Studio can provide some assistance when overriding functions. Begin typing the name of the **onCreate(Bundle?)** function. Android Studio will provide a list of suggestions, as shown in Figure 8.11.

### Figure 8.11  Overriding the **onCreate(Bundle?)** function

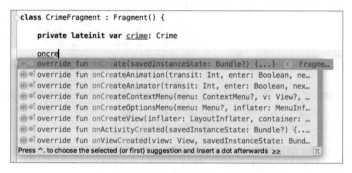

Press Return to select the option to override the **onCreate(Bundle?)** function, and Android Studio will create the declaration for you, including the call to the superclass implementation. Update your code to create a new **Crime**, matching Listing 8.5.

### Listing 8.5  Overriding **Fragment.onCreate(Bundle?)** (CrimeFragment.kt)

```
class CrimeFragment : Fragment() {

    private lateinit var crime: Crime

    override fun onCreate(savedInstanceState: Bundle?) {
        super.onCreate(savedInstanceState)
        crime = Crime()
    }
}
```

There are a couple of things to notice in this implementation. First, **Fragment.onCreate(Bundle?)** is public; Kotlin functions default to public when no visibility modifier is included in the definition. This differs from the **Activity.onCreate(Bundle?)** function, which is protected. **Fragment.onCreate(Bundle?)** and other **Fragment** lifecycle functions must be public, because they will be called by whatever activity is hosting the fragment.

Second, similar to an activity, a fragment has a bundle to which it saves and retrieves its state. You can override **Fragment.onSaveInstanceState(Bundle)** for your own purposes, just as you can override **Activity.onSaveInstanceState(Bundle)**.

Also, note what does *not* happen in **Fragment.onCreate(Bundle?)**: You do not inflate the fragment's view. You configure the fragment instance in **Fragment.onCreate(Bundle?)**, but you create and configure the fragment's view in another fragment lifecycle function: **onCreateView(LayoutInflater, ViewGroup?, Bundle?)**.

This function is where you inflate the layout for the fragment's view and return the inflated **View** to the hosting activity. The **LayoutInflater** and **ViewGroup** parameters are necessary to inflate the layout. The **Bundle** will contain data that this function can use to re-create the view from a saved state.

In CrimeFragment.kt, add an implementation of **onCreateView(…)** that inflates fragment_crime.xml. You can use the same trick from Figure 8.11 to fill out the function declaration.

## Listing 8.6 Overriding **onCreateView(…)** (CrimeFragment.kt)

```kotlin
class CrimeFragment : Fragment() {

    private lateinit var crime: Crime

    override fun onCreate(savedInstanceState: Bundle?) {
        super.onCreate(savedInstanceState)
        crime = Crime()
    }

    override fun onCreateView(
        inflater: LayoutInflater,
        container: ViewGroup?,
        savedInstanceState: Bundle?
    ): View? {
        val view = inflater.inflate(R.layout.fragment_crime, container, false)
        return view
    }
}
```

Within **onCreateView(…)**, you explicitly inflate the fragment's view by calling **LayoutInflater.inflate(…)** and passing in the layout resource ID. The second parameter is your view's parent, which is usually needed to configure the widgets properly. The third parameter tells the layout inflater whether to immediately add the inflated view to the view's parent. You pass in false because the fragment's view will be hosted in the activity's container view. The fragment's view does not need to be added to the parent view immediately – the activity will handle adding the view later.

## Wiring up widgets in a fragment

You are now going to hook up the **EditText**, **CheckBox**, and **Button** in your fragment. The **onCreateView(…)** function is the place to wire up these widgets.

Start with the **EditText**. After the view is inflated, get a reference to the **EditText** using **findViewById**.

## Listing 8.7  Wiring up the **EditText** widget (CrimeFragment.kt)

```kotlin
class CrimeFragment : Fragment() {

    private lateinit var crime: Crime
    private lateinit var titleField: EditText
    ...
    override fun onCreateView(
        inflater: LayoutInflater,
        container: ViewGroup?,
        savedInstanceState: Bundle?
    ): View? {
        val view = inflater.inflate(R.layout.fragment_crime, container, false)

        titleField = view.findViewById(R.id.crime_title) as EditText

        return view
    }
}
```

Getting references in **Fragment.onCreateView(…)** works nearly the same as in **Activity.onCreate(Bundle?)**. The only difference is that you call **View.findViewById(Int)** on the fragment's view. The **Activity.findViewById(Int)** function that you used before is a convenience function that calls **View.findViewById(Int)** behind the scenes. The **Fragment** class does not have a corresponding convenience function, so you have to call the real thing.

Once the reference is set, add a listener in the **onStart()** lifecycle callback.

## Listing 8.8  Adding a listener to the **EditText** widget (CrimeFragment.kt)

```kotlin
class CrimeFragment : Fragment() {
    ...
    override fun onCreateView(
        inflater: LayoutInflater,
        container: ViewGroup?,
        savedInstanceState: Bundle?
    ): View? {
        ...
    }

    override fun onStart() {
        super.onStart()

        val titleWatcher = object : TextWatcher {

            override fun beforeTextChanged(
                sequence: CharSequence?,
                start: Int,
                count: Int,
                after: Int
            ) {
                // This space intentionally left blank
            }

            override fun onTextChanged(
                sequence: CharSequence?,
                start: Int,
                before: Int,
                count: Int
            ) {
                crime.title = sequence.toString()
            }

            override fun afterTextChanged(sequence: Editable?) {
                // This one too
            }
        }

        titleField.addTextChangedListener(titleWatcher)
    }
}
```

Setting listeners in a fragment works exactly the same as in an activity. Here, you create an anonymous class that implements the verbose **TextWatcher** interface. **TextWatcher** has three functions, but you only care about one: **onTextChanged(…)**.

In **onTextChanged(…)**, you call **toString()** on the CharSequence that is the user's input. This function returns a string, which you then use to set the **Crime**'s title.

Notice that the **TextWatcher** listener is set up in **onStart()**. Some listeners are triggered not only when the user interacts with them but also when data is set on them when the view state is restored, such as on rotation. Listeners that react to data input, such as the **TextWatcher** for an **EditText** or an **OnCheckChangedListener** for a **CheckBox**, are susceptible to this behavior.

Listeners that only react to user interaction, such as an **OnClickListener**, are not susceptible to this, because they are not impacted by setting data on a view. This is the reason you did not encounter this in GeoQuiz. That app only used click listeners, which are not triggered on rotation, so you could set everything up in **onCreate(…)** – before any state restoration.

View state is restored after **onCreateView(…)** and before **onStart()**. When the state is restored, the contents of the **EditText** will get set to whatever value is currently in `crime.title`. At this point, if you have already set a listener on the **EditText** (such as in **onCreate(…)** or **onCreateView(…)**), **TextWatcher**'s **beforeTextChanged(…)**, **onTextChanged(…)**, and **afterTextChanged(…)** functions will execute. Setting the listener in **onStart()** avoids this behavior since the listener is hooked up after the view state is restored.

Next, connect the **Button** to display the date of the crime.

## Listing 8.9  Setting **Button** text (CrimeFragment.kt)

```kotlin
class CrimeFragment : Fragment() {

    private lateinit var crime: Crime
    private lateinit var titleField: EditText
    private lateinit var dateButton: Button
    ...
    override fun onCreateView(
        inflater: LayoutInflater,
        container: ViewGroup?,
        savedInstanceState: Bundle?
    ): View? {
        val view = inflater.inflate(R.layout.fragment_crime, container, false)

        titleField = view.findViewById(R.id.crime_title) as EditText
        dateButton = view.findViewById(R.id.crime_date) as Button

        dateButton.apply {
            text = crime.date.toString()
            isEnabled = false
        }

        return view
    }
}
```

Disabling the button ensures that it will not respond in any way to the user pressing it. It also changes its appearance to advertise its disabled state. In Chapter 13, you will enable the button and allow the user to choose the date of the crime.

Moving on to the **CheckBox**, get a reference to it in **onCreateView(…)**. Then, set a listener in **onStart()** that will update the solvedCheckBox field of the **Crime**, as shown in Listing 8.10. Even though the **OnClickListener** is not triggered by the state restoration of the fragment, putting it in **onStart** helps keep all of your listeners in one place and easy to find.

## Listing 8.10 Listening for **CheckBox** changes (CrimeFragment.kt)

```
class CrimeFragment : Fragment() {

    private lateinit var crime: Crime
    private lateinit var titleField: EditText
    private lateinit var dateButton: Button
    private lateinit var solvedCheckBox: CheckBox
    ...
    override fun onCreateView(
        inflater: LayoutInflater,
        container: ViewGroup?,
        savedInstanceState: Bundle?
    ): View? {
        val view = inflater.inflate(R.layout.fragment_crime, container, false)

        titleField = view.findViewById(R.id.crime_title) as EditText
        dateButton = view.findViewById(R.id.crime_date) as Button
        solvedCheckBox = view.findViewById(R.id.crime_solved) as CheckBox
        ...
    }

    override fun onStart() {
        ...
        titleField.addTextChangedListener(titleWatcher)

        solvedCheckBox.apply {
            setOnCheckedChangeListener { _, isChecked ->
                crime.isSolved = isChecked
            }
        }
    }
}
```

Your code for **CrimeFragment** is now complete. It would be great if you could run CriminalIntent and play with the code you have written. But you cannot. Fragments cannot put their views onscreen on their own. To realize your efforts, you first have to add a **CrimeFragment** to **MainActivity**.

# Hosting a UI Fragment

To host a UI fragment, an activity must:

- define a spot in its layout for the fragment's view

- manage the lifecycle of the fragment instance

You can attach fragments to your activities in code. You determine when the fragment is added to the activity and what happens to it after that. You can remove the fragment, replace it with another, and then add the first fragment back again.

The code details will come later in the chapter. First, you are going to define **MainActivity**'s layout.

## Defining a container view

You will be adding a UI fragment in the hosting activity's code, but you still need to make a spot for the fragment's view in the activity's view hierarchy. Locate **MainActivity**'s layout at res/layout/ activity_main.xml. Open this file and replace the default layout with a **FrameLayout**. Your XML should match Listing 8.11.

Listing 8.11  Creating the fragment container layout
(res/layout/activity_main.xml)

```
<androidx.constraintlayout.widget.ConstraintLayout
        xmlns:android="http://schemas.android.com/apk/res/android"
        xmlns:tools="http://schemas.android.com/tools"
        xmlns:app="http://schemas.android.com/apk/res-auto"
        android:layout_width="match_parent"
        android:layout_height="match_parent"
        tools:context=".MainActivity">

    <TextView
            android:layout_width="wrap_content"
            android:layout_height="wrap_content"
            android:text="Hello World!"
            app:layout_constraintBottom_toBottomOf="parent"
            app:layout_constraintLeft_toLeftOf="parent"
            app:layout_constraintRight_toRightOf="parent"
            app:layout_constraintTop_toTopOf="parent"/>

</androidx.constraintlayout.widget.ConstraintLayout>
<FrameLayout
        xmlns:android="http://schemas.android.com/apk/res/android"
        android:id="@+id/fragment_container"
        android:layout_width="match_parent"
        android:layout_height="match_parent"/>
```

This **FrameLayout** will be the *container view* for a **CrimeFragment**. Notice that the container view is completely generic; it does not name the **CrimeFragment** class. You can and will use this same layout to host other fragments.

Note that while activity_main.xml consists solely of a container view for a single fragment, an activity's layout can be more complex and define multiple container views as well as widgets of its own.

Run CriminalIntent to check your code. You will see an empty **FrameLayout** below a toolbar containing the app name (Figure 8.12).

Figure 8.12 An empty **FrameLayout**

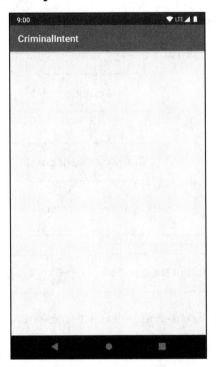

The **FrameLayout** is empty because the **MainActivity** is not yet hosting a fragment. Later, you will write code that puts a fragment's view inside this **FrameLayout**. But first, you need to create a fragment.

(The toolbar at the top of your app is included automatically because of the way you configured your activity. You will learn more about the toolbar in Chapter 14.)

# Adding a UI fragment to the FragmentManager

When the **Fragment** class was introduced in Honeycomb, the **Activity** class was changed to include a piece called the **FragmentManager**. The **FragmentManager** handles two things: a list of fragments and a back stack of fragment transactions (which you will learn about shortly) (Figure 8.13). It is responsible for adding the fragments' views to the activity's view hierarchy and driving the fragments' lifecycles.

Figure 8.13  The **FragmentManager**

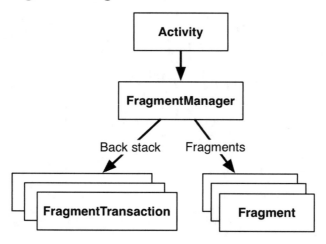

For CriminalIntent, you will only be concerned with the **FragmentManager**'s list of fragments.

## Fragment transactions

Now that you have the **FragmentManager**, add the following code to give it a fragment to manage. (We will step through this code afterward. Just get it in for now.)

Listing 8.12  Adding a **CrimeFragment** (MainActivity.kt)

```kotlin
class MainActivity : AppCompatActivity() {

    override fun onCreate(savedInstanceState: Bundle?) {
        super.onCreate(savedInstanceState)
        setContentView(R.layout.activity_main)

        val currentFragment =
            supportFragmentManager.findFragmentById(R.id.fragment_container)

        if (currentFragment == null) {
            val fragment = CrimeFragment()
            supportFragmentManager
                .beginTransaction()
                .add(R.id.fragment_container, fragment)
                .commit()
        }
    }
}
```

To add a fragment to an activity in code, you make explicit calls to the activity's **FragmentManager**. You can access the activity's fragment manager using the supportFragmentManager property. You use supportFragmentManager because you are using the Jetpack library and the **AppCompatActivity** class. The name is prefixed with "support" because the property originated in the v4 support library, but the support library has since been repackaged as an androidx library within Jetpack.

The best place to start understanding the rest of the code you just added is not at the beginning. Instead, find the **add(…)** operation and the code around it. This code creates and commits a *fragment transaction*.

```
if (currentFragment == null) {
    val fragment = CrimeFragment()
    supportFragmentManager
        .beginTransaction()
        .add(R.id.fragment_container, fragment)
        .commit()
}
```

Fragment transactions are used to add, remove, attach, detach, or replace fragments in the fragment list. They allow you to group multiple operations together, such as adding multiple fragments to different containers at the same time. They are the heart of how you use fragments to compose and recompose screens at runtime.

The **FragmentManager** maintains a back stack of fragment transactions that you can navigate. If your fragment transaction includes multiple operations, they are reversed when the transaction is removed from the back stack. This provides more control over your UI state when you group your fragment operations into a single transaction.

The **FragmentManager.beginTransaction()** function creates and returns an instance of **FragmentTransaction**. The **FragmentTransaction** class uses a *fluent interface* – functions that configure **FragmentTransaction** return a **FragmentTransaction** instead of Unit, which allows you to chain them together. So the code highlighted above says, "Create a new fragment transaction, include one add operation in it, and then commit it."

The **add(…)** function is the meat of the transaction. It has two parameters: a container view ID and the newly created **CrimeFragment**. The container view ID should look familiar. It is the resource ID of the **FrameLayout** that you defined in activity_main.xml.

A container view ID serves two purposes:

- It tells the **FragmentManager** where in the activity's view the fragment's view should appear.

- It is used as a unique identifier for a fragment in the **FragmentManager**'s list.

When you need to retrieve the **CrimeFragment** from the **FragmentManager**, you ask for it by container view ID:

```
val currentFragment =
    supportFragmentManager.findFragmentById(R.id.fragment_container)

if (currentFragment == null) {
    val fragment = CrimeFragment()
    supportFragmentManager
        .beginTransaction()
        .add(R.id.fragment_container, fragment)
        .commit()
}
```

It may seem odd that the **FragmentManager** identifies the **CrimeFragment** using the resource ID of a **FrameLayout**. But identifying a UI fragment by the resource ID of its container view is built into how the **FragmentManager** operates. If you are adding multiple fragments to an activity, you would typically create separate containers with separate IDs for each of those fragments.

Now we can summarize the code you added in Listing 8.12 from start to finish:

First, you ask the **FragmentManager** for the fragment with a container view ID of R.id.fragment_container. If this fragment is already in the list, the **FragmentManager** will return it.

Why would a fragment already be in the list? The call to **MainActivity.onCreate(Bundle?)** could be in response to **MainActivity** being *re-created* after being destroyed on rotation or to reclaim memory. When an activity is destroyed, its **FragmentManager** saves out its list of fragments. When the activity is re-created, the new **FragmentManager** retrieves the list and re-creates the listed fragments to make everything as it was before.

On the other hand, if there is no fragment with the given container view ID, then fragment will be null. In this case, you create a new **CrimeFragment** and a new fragment transaction that adds the fragment to the list.

**MainActivity** is now hosting a **CrimeFragment**. Run CriminalIntent to prove it. You should see the view defined in `fragment_crime.xml`, as shown in Figure 8.14.

Figure 8.14  **CrimeFragment**'s view hosted by **MainActivity**

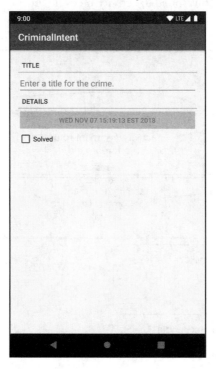

## The FragmentManager and the fragment lifecycle

Figure 8.15 shows the fragment lifecycle. The fragment lifecycle is similar to the activity lifecycle: It has stopped, paused, and resumed states, and it has functions you can override to get things done at critical points – many of which correspond to activity lifecycle functions.

### Figure 8.15  Fragment lifecycle diagram

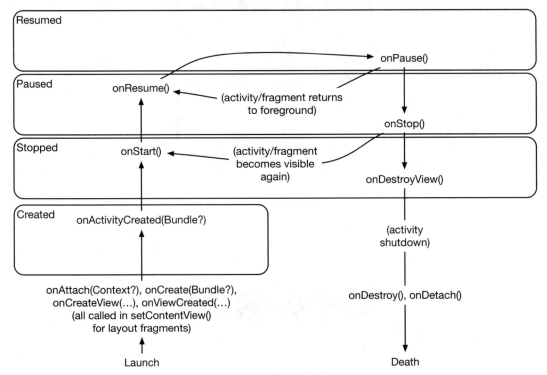

The correspondence is important. Because a fragment works on behalf of an activity, its state should reflect the activity's state. Thus, it needs corresponding lifecycle functions to handle the activity's work.

One critical difference between the fragment lifecycle and the activity lifecycle is that fragment lifecycle functions are called by the **FragmentManager** of the hosting activity, not the OS. The OS knows nothing about the fragments that an activity is using to manage things. Fragments are the activity's internal business. The **onAttach(Context?)**, **onCreate(Bundle?)**, **onCreateView(…)**, and **onViewCreated(…)** functions are called when you add the fragment to the **FragmentManager**.

The **onActivityCreated(Bundle?)** function is called after the hosting activity's **onCreate(Bundle?)** function has executed. You are adding the **CrimeFragment** in **MainActivity.onCreate(Bundle?)**, so this function will be called after the fragment has been added.

What happens if you add a fragment while the activity is already resumed? In that case, the **FragmentManager** immediately walks the fragment through whatever steps are necessary to get it caught up to the activity's state. For example, as a fragment is added to an activity that is already resumed, that fragment gets calls to **onAttach(Context?)**, **onCreate(Bundle?)**, **onCreateView(…)**, **onViewCreated(…)**, **onActivityCreated(Bundle?)**, **onStart()**, and then **onResume()**.

Once the fragment's state is caught up to the activity's state, the hosting activity's `FragmentManager` will call further lifecycle functions around the same time it receives the corresponding calls from the OS to keep the fragment's state aligned with that of the activity.

# Application Architecture with Fragments

Designing your app with fragments the right way is supremely important. Many developers, after first learning about fragments, try to use them for each and every component in their application. This is the wrong way to use fragments.

Fragments are intended to encapsulate major components in a reusable way. A major component in this case would be on the level of an entire screen of your application. If you have a significant number of fragments onscreen at once, your code will be littered with fragment transactions and unclear responsibility. A better architectural solution for reuse with smaller components is to extract them into a custom view (a class that subclasses `View` or one of its subclasses).

Use fragments responsibly. A good rule of thumb is to have no more than two or three fragments on the screen at a time (Figure 8.16).

Figure 8.16  Less is more

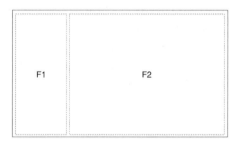
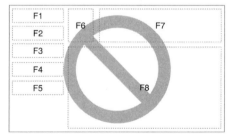

## Deciding whether to use fragments

Fragments are the topic of a lot of discussion in the Android community. Some people are very opposed to the additional complexity involved with fragments and their lifecycles, so they never use them in their projects. An issue with this approach is that there are several APIs in Android that rely on fragments, such as **ViewPager** and the Jetpack Navigation library. If you need to use these options in your app, then you must use fragments to get their benefits.

If you do not need fragment-dependent APIs, fragments are more useful in larger applications that have more requirements. For simple, single-screen applications, the complexity introduced by fragments and their lifecycle is often unnecessary.

One thing to consider when starting a new app is that adding fragments later can be a minefield. Changing an activity to an activity hosting a UI fragment is not difficult, but there are swarms of annoying gotchas. Keeping some interfaces managed by activities and having others managed by fragments only makes things worse, because you have to keep track of this meaningless distinction. It is far easier to write your code using fragments from the beginning and not worry about the pain and annoyance of reworking it later, or having to remember which style of controller you are using in each part of your application.

Therefore, when it comes to fragments, we have a different principle: Almost always use fragments. If you know that the app you are building will remain very small, the extra effort of using fragments may not be worth it, so they can be left out. For larger apps, the complexity introduced is offset by the flexibility fragments provide, making it easier to justify having them in the project.

From here on, some of the apps in this book will use fragments and others will not. You will build some small applications during a single chapter, and you will make building these apps easier by *not* using fragments. However, the larger apps in this book do use fragments to give you extra experience using them and to make the apps easier to extend in the future.

# 9

# Displaying Lists with RecyclerView

CriminalIntent's model layer currently consists of a single instance of **Crime**. In this chapter, you will update CriminalIntent to work with a list of crimes. The list will display each **Crime**'s title and date, as shown in Figure 9.1.

Figure 9.1  A list of crimes

Figure 9.2 shows the overall plan for CriminalIntent in this chapter.

## Figure 9.2  CriminalIntent with a list of crimes

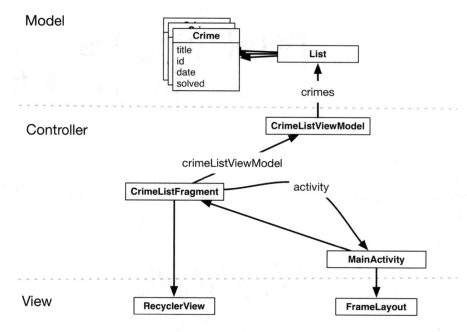

In the controller layer, you have a new **ViewModel** that will encapsulate the data for the new screen. **CrimeListViewModel** will store a list of **Crime** objects.

Displaying a list of crimes requires a new fragment in CriminalIntent's controller layer: **CrimeListFragment**. **MainActivity** will host an instance of **CrimeListFragment**, which will in turn display the list of crimes on the screen.

(Where is **CrimeFragment** in Figure 9.2? It is part of the detail view, so we are not showing it here. In Chapter 12, you will connect the list and detail parts of CriminalIntent.)

In Figure 9.2, you can also see the view objects associated with **MainActivity** and **CrimeListFragment**. The activity's view will consist of the same single fragment-containing **FrameLayout**. The fragment's view will consist of a **RecyclerView**. You will learn more about the **RecyclerView** class later in the chapter.

# Adding a New Fragment and ViewModel

The first step is to add a new **ViewModel** to store the **List** of **Crime** objects you will eventually display on the screen. As you learned in Chapter 4, the **ViewModel** class is part of the lifecycle-extensions library. So begin by adding the lifecycle-extensions dependency to your app/build.gradle file.

## Listing 9.1 Adding lifecycle-extensions dependency (app/build.gradle)

```
dependencies {
    ...
    implementation 'androidx.appcompat:appcompat:1.1.0-alpha02'
    implementation 'androidx.core:core-ktx:1.1.0-alpha04'
    implementation 'androidx.lifecycle:lifecycle-extensions:2.0.0'
    ...
}
```

Do not forget to sync your Gradle files after making this change.

Next, create a new Kotlin class called **CrimeListViewModel**. Update the new **CrimeListViewModel** class to extend from **ViewModel**. Add a property to store a list of **Crime**s. In the init block, populate the list with dummy data.

## Listing 9.2 Generating crimes (CrimeListViewModel.kt)

```
class CrimeListViewModel : ViewModel() {

    val crimes = mutableListOf<Crime>()

    init {
        for (i in 0 until 100) {
            val crime = Crime()
            crime.title = "Crime #$i"
            crime.isSolved = i % 2 == 0
            crimes += crime
        }
    }
}
```

Eventually, the **List** will contain user-created **Crime**s that can be saved and reloaded. For now, you populate the **List** with 100 boring **Crime** objects.

The **CrimeListViewModel** is not a solution for long-term storage of data, but it does encapsulate all the data necessary to populate **CrimeListFragment**'s view. In Chapter 11, you will learn more about long-term data storage when you update CriminalIntent to store the crime list in a database.

The next step is to add a new **CrimeListFragment** class and associate it with **CrimeListViewModel**. Create the **CrimeListFragment** class and make it a subclass of **androidx.fragment.app.Fragment**.

### Listing 9.3  Implementing **CrimeListFragment** (CrimeListFragment.kt)

```
private const val TAG = "CrimeListFragment"

class CrimeListFragment : Fragment() {

    private val crimeListViewModel: CrimeListViewModel by lazy {
        ViewModelProviders.of(this).get(CrimeListViewModel::class.java)
    }

    override fun onCreate(savedInstanceState: Bundle?) {
        super.onCreate(savedInstanceState)
        Log.d(TAG, "Total crimes: ${crimeListViewModel.crimes.size}")
    }

    companion object {
        fun newInstance(): CrimeListFragment {
            return CrimeListFragment()
        }
    }
}
```

For now, **CrimeListFragment** is an empty shell of a fragment. It logs the number of crimes found in **CrimeListViewModel**. You will flesh this fragment out later in the chapter.

One good practice to follow is to provide a **newInstance(…)** function that your activities can call to get an instance of your fragment. This is similar to the **newIntent()** function you used in GeoQuiz. You will see how to pass data to your fragments in Chapter 12.

## ViewModel lifecycle with fragments

In Chapter 4 you learned about the **ViewModel** lifecycle when used with an activity. This lifecycle is slightly different when the **ViewModel** is used with a fragment. It still only has two states, created or destroyed/nonexistent, but it is now tied to the lifecycle of the fragment instead of the activity.

The **ViewModel** will remain active as long as the fragment's view is onscreen. The **ViewModel** will persist across rotation (even though the fragment instance will not) and be accessible to the new fragment instance.

The **ViewModel** will be destroyed when the fragment is destroyed. This can happen when the user presses the Back button to dismiss the screen. It can also happen if the hosting activity replaces the fragment with a different one. Even though the same activity is on the screen, both the fragment and its associated **ViewModel** will be destroyed, since they are no longer needed.

One special case is when you add the fragment transaction to the back stack. When the activity replaces the current fragment with a different one, if the transaction is added to the back stack, the fragment instance and its **ViewModel** will not be destroyed. This maintains your state: If the user presses the Back button, the fragment transaction is reversed. The original fragment instance is put back on the screen, and all the data in the **ViewModel** is preserved.

Next, update **MainActivity** to host an instance of **CrimeListFragment** instead of **CrimeFragment**.

## Listing 9.4  Adding **CrimeListFragment** with a fragment transaction (MainActivity.kt)

```
class MainActivity : AppCompatActivity() {

    override fun onCreate(savedInstanceState: Bundle?) {
        ...
        if (currentFragment == null) {
            val fragment = CrimeFragment() CrimeListFragment.newInstance()
            supportFragmentManager
                .beginTransaction()
                .add(R.id.fragment_container, fragment)
                .commit()
        }
    }
}
```

For now, you have hardcoded **MainActivity** to always display a **CrimeListFragment**. In Chapter 12 you will update **MainActivity** to swap out **CrimeListFragment** and **CrimeFragment** on demand as the user navigates through the app.

Run CriminalIntent, and you will see **MainActivity**'s **FrameLayout** hosting an empty **CrimeListFragment**, as shown in Figure 9.3.

## Figure 9.3  Blank **MainActivity** screen

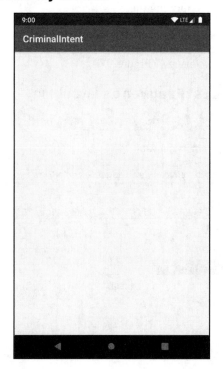

Search the Logcat output for **CrimeListFragment**. You will see a log statement showing the total number of crimes available:

```
2019-02-25 15:19:39.950 26140-26140/com.bignerdranch.android.criminalintent
    D/CrimeListFragment: Total crimes: 100
```

# Adding a RecyclerView

You want **CrimeListFragment** to display a list of crimes to the user. To do this you will use a **RecyclerView**.

The **RecyclerView** class lives in another Jetpack library. The first step to using a **RecyclerView** is to add the RecyclerView library as a dependency.

Listing 9.5  Adding RecyclerView dependency (`app/build.gradle`)

```
dependencies {
    ...
    implementation 'androidx.lifecycle:lifecycle-extensions:2.0.0'
    implementation 'androidx.recyclerview:recyclerview:1.0.0'
    ...
}
```

Again, sync your Gradle files before moving on.

Your **RecyclerView** will live in **CrimeListFragment**'s layout file. First, you must create the layout file. Create a new layout resource file named fragment_crime_list. For the Root element, specify androidx.recyclerview.widget.RecyclerView (Figure 9.4).

Figure 9.4  Adding **CrimeListFragment**'s layout file

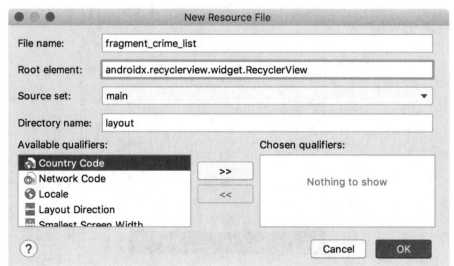

In the new `layout/fragment_crime_list.xml` file, add an ID attribute to the **RecyclerView**. Collapse the close tag into the opening tag, since you will not add any children to the **RecyclerView**.

## Listing 9.6  Adding **RecyclerView** to a layout file (`layout/fragment_crime_list.xml`)

```
<androidx.recyclerview.widget.RecyclerView
        xmlns:android="http://schemas.android.com/apk/res/android"
        android:id="@+id/crime_recycler_view"
        android:layout_width="match_parent"
        android:layout_height="match_parent">
        android:layout_height="match_parent"/>

</androidx.recyclerview.widget.RecyclerView>
```

Now that **CrimeListFragment**'s view is set up, hook up the view to the fragment. Modify **CrimeListFragment** to use this layout file and to find the **RecyclerView** in the layout file, as shown in Listing 9.7.

## Listing 9.7  Setting up the view for **CrimeListFragment** (`CrimeListFragment.kt`)

```
class CrimeListFragment : Fragment() {

    private lateinit var crimeRecyclerView: RecyclerView

    private val crimeListViewModel: CrimeListViewModel by lazy {
        ViewModelProviders.of(this).get(CrimeListViewModel::class.java)
    }

    override fun onCreate(savedInstanceState: Bundle?) {
        super.onCreate(savedInstanceState)
        Log.d(TAG, "Total crimes: ${crimeListViewModel.crimes.size}")
    }

    override fun onCreateView(
        inflater: LayoutInflater,
        container: ViewGroup?,
        savedInstanceState: Bundle?
    ): View? {
        val view = inflater.inflate(R.layout.fragment_crime_list, container, false)

        crimeRecyclerView =
            view.findViewById(R.id.crime_recycler_view) as RecyclerView
        crimeRecyclerView.layoutManager = LinearLayoutManager(context)

        return view
    }
}
```

Note that as soon as you create your **RecyclerView**, you give it another object called a **LayoutManager**. **RecyclerView** requires a **LayoutManager** to work. If you forget to give it one, it will crash.

**RecyclerView** does not position items on the screen itself. It delegates that job to the **LayoutManager**. The **LayoutManager** positions every item and also defines how scrolling works. So if **RecyclerView** tries to do those things when the **LayoutManager** is not there, the **RecyclerView** will immediately fall over and die.

There are a few built-in **LayoutManager**s to choose from, and you can find more as third-party libraries. You are using the **LinearLayoutManager**, which will position the items in the list vertically. Later on in this book, you will use **GridLayoutManager** to arrange items in a grid instead.

Run the app. You should again see a blank screen, but now you are looking at an empty **RecyclerView**.

## Creating an Item View Layout

**RecyclerView** is a subclass of **ViewGroup**. It displays a list of child **View** objects, called *item views*. Each item view represents a single object from the list of data backing the recycler view (in your case, a single crime from the crime list). Depending on the complexity of what you need to display, these child **View**s can be complex or very simple.

For your first implementation, each item in the list will display the title and date of a **Crime**, as shown in Figure 9.5.

Figure 9.5  A **RecyclerView** with child **View**s

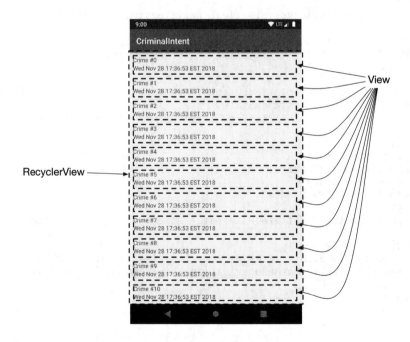

Each item displayed on the **RecyclerView** will have its own view hierarchy, exactly the way **CrimeFragment** has a view hierarchy for the entire screen. Specifically, the **View** object on each row will be a **LinearLayout** containing two **TextView**s.

You create a new layout for a list item view the same way you do for the view of an activity or a fragment. In the project tool window, right-click the res/layout directory and choose New → Layout resource file. Name the file list_item_crime, set the root element to LinearLayout, and click OK.

Update your layout file to add padding to the **LinearLayout** and to add the two **TextView**s, as shown in Listing 9.8.

### Listing 9.8  Updating the list item layout file (layout/`list_item_crime.xml`)

```
<LinearLayout xmlns:android="http://schemas.android.com/apk/res/android"
              android:orientation="vertical"
              android:layout_width="match_parent"
              android:layout_height="match_parent">
              android:layout_height="wrap_content"
              android:padding="8dp">

    <TextView
            android:id="@+id/crime_title"
            android:layout_width="match_parent"
            android:layout_height="wrap_content"
            android:text="Crime Title"/>

    <TextView
            android:id="@+id/crime_date"
            android:layout_width="match_parent"
            android:layout_height="wrap_content"
            android:text="Crime Date"/>

</LinearLayout>
```

Take a look at the design preview, and you will see that you have created exactly one row of the completed product. In a moment, you will see how **RecyclerView** will create those rows for you.

# Implementing a ViewHolder

The **RecyclerView** expects an item view to be wrapped in an instance of **ViewHolder**. A **ViewHolder** stores a reference to an item's view (and sometimes references to specific widgets within that view).

Define a view holder by adding an inner class in **CrimeListFragment** that extends from **RecyclerView.ViewHolder**.

### Listing 9.9  The beginnings of a **ViewHolder** (CrimeListFragment.kt)

```
class CrimeListFragment : Fragment() {
    ...
    override fun onCreateView(
        inflater: LayoutInflater,
        container: ViewGroup?,
        savedInstanceState: Bundle?
    ): View? {
        ...
    }

    private inner class CrimeHolder(view: View)
        : RecyclerView.ViewHolder(view) {

    }
}
```

In **CrimeHolder**'s constructor, you take in the view to hold on to. Immediately, you pass it as the argument to the **RecyclerView.ViewHolder** constructor. The base **ViewHolder** class will then hold on to the view in a property named itemView (Figure 9.6).

Figure 9.6  The **ViewHolder** and its itemView

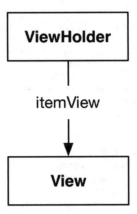

A **RecyclerView** never creates **View**s by themselves. It always creates **ViewHolder**s, which bring their itemViews along for the ride (Figure 9.7).

Figure 9.7  The **ViewHolder** visualized

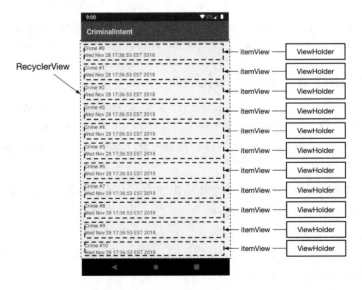

When the **View** for each item is simple, **ViewHolder** has few responsibilities. For more complicated **View**s, the **ViewHolder** makes wiring up the different parts of itemView to a **Crime** simpler and more efficient. (For example, you do not need to search through the item view hierarchy to get a handle to the title text view every time you need to set the title.)

Update **CrimeHolder** to find the title and date text views in itemView's hierarchy when an instance is first created. Store references to the text views in properties.

Listing 9.10  Pulling out views in the constructor (`CrimeListFragment.kt`)

```kotlin
private inner class CrimeHolder(view: View)
    : RecyclerView.ViewHolder(view) {

    val titleTextView: TextView = itemView.findViewById(R.id.crime_title)
    val dateTextView: TextView = itemView.findViewById(R.id.crime_date)
}
```

The updated view holder now stashes references to the title and date text views so you can easily change the value displayed later without having to go back through the item's view hierarchy (Figure 9.8).

Figure 9.8  The **ViewHolder** re-visualized

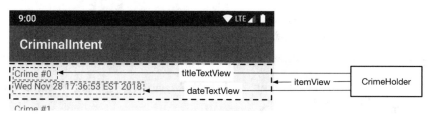

Note that the **CrimeHolder** assumes that the view passed to its constructor has child text views with the IDs `R.id.crime_title` and `R.id.crime_date`. You may be wondering, "Who (or what) creates crime holder instances, and can I safely assume the view hierarchy passed to the constructor contains the child widgets I expect?" You will learn the answer to these questions in just a moment.

# Implementing an Adapter to Populate the RecyclerView

Figure 9.7 is somewhat simplified. **RecyclerView** does not create **ViewHolder**s itself. Instead, it asks an *adapter*. An adapter is a controller object that sits between the **RecyclerView** and the data set that the **RecyclerView** should display.

The adapter is responsible for:

- creating the necessary **ViewHolder**s when asked

- binding **ViewHolder**s to data from the model layer when asked

The recycler view is responsible for:

- asking the adapter to create a new **ViewHolder**

- asking the adapter to bind a **ViewHolder** to the item from the backing data at a given position

Time to create your adapter. Add a new inner class named **CrimeAdapter** to **CrimeListFragment**. Add a primary constructor that expects a list of crimes as input and stores the crime list passed in a property, as shown in Listing 9.11.

In your new **CrimeAdapter**, you are also going to override three functions: **onCreateViewHolder(…)**, **onBindViewHolder(…)**, and **getItemCount()**. To save you typing (and typos), Android Studio can generate these overrides for you. Once you have typed the initial line of the new code, put your cursor on **CrimeAdapter** and press Option-Return (Alt-Enter). Select Implement members from the pop-up. In the Implement members dialog, select all three function names and click OK. Then you only need to fill in the bodies as shown.

### Listing 9.11  Creating **CrimeAdapter** (CrimeListFragment.kt)

```kotlin
class CrimeListFragment : Fragment() {
    ...
    private inner class CrimeHolder(view: View)
        : RecyclerView.ViewHolder(view) {
        ...
    }

    private inner class CrimeAdapter(var crimes: List<Crime>)
        : RecyclerView.Adapter<CrimeHolder>() {

        override fun onCreateViewHolder(parent: ViewGroup, viewType: Int)
                : CrimeHolder {
            val view = layoutInflater.inflate(R.layout.list_item_crime, parent, false)
            return CrimeHolder(view)
        }

        override fun getItemCount() = crimes.size

        override fun onBindViewHolder(holder: CrimeHolder, position: Int) {
            val crime = crimes[position]
            holder.apply {
                titleTextView.text = crime.title
                dateTextView.text = crime.date.toString()
            }
        }
    }
}
```

**Adapter.onCreateViewHolder(…)** is responsible for creating a view to display, wrapping the view in a view holder, and returning the result. In this case, you inflate list_item_view.xml and pass the resulting view to a new instance of **CrimeHolder**. (For now, you can ignore **onCreateViewHolder(…)**'s parameters. You only need these values if you are doing something fancy, like displaying different types of views within the same recycler view. See the section called Challenge: RecyclerView ViewTypes at the end of this chapter for more information.)

**Adapter.onBindViewHolder(holder: CrimeHolder, position: Int)** is responsible for populating a given holder with the crime from a given position. In this case, you get the crime from the crime list at the requested position. You then use the title and data from that crime to set the text in the corresponding text views.

When the recycler view needs to know how many items are in the data set backing it (such as when the recycler view first spins up), it will ask its adapter by calling **Adapter.getItemCount()**. Here, **getItemCount()** returns the number of items in the list of crimes to answer the recycler view's request.

The **RecyclerView** itself does not know anything about the **Crime** object or the list of **Crime** objects to be displayed. Instead, the **CrimeAdapter** knows all of a **Crime**'s intimate and personal details. The adapter also knows about the list of crimes that backs the recycler view (Figure 9.9).

Figure 9.9 **Adapter** sits between recycler view and data set

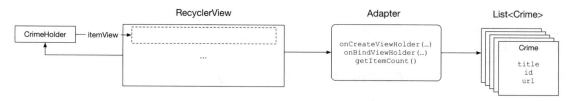

When the **RecyclerView** needs a view object to display, it will have a conversation with its adapter. Figure 9.10 shows an example of a conversation that a **RecyclerView** might initiate.

Figure 9.10 A scintillating **RecyclerView**-**Adapter** conversation

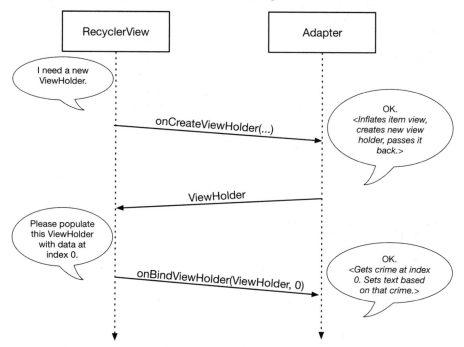

The **RecyclerView** calls the adapter's **onCreateViewHolder(ViewGroup, Int)** function to create a new **ViewHolder**, along with its juicy payload: a **View** to display. The **ViewHolder** (and its itemView) that the adapter creates and hands back to the **RecyclerView** has not yet been populated with data from a specific item in the data set.

Next, the **RecyclerView** calls **onBindViewHolder(ViewHolder, Int)**, passing a **ViewHolder** into this function along with the position. The adapter will look up the model data for that position and *bind* it to the **ViewHolder**'s **View**. To bind it, the adapter fills in the **View** to reflect the data in the model object.

After this process is complete, **RecyclerView** will place a list item on the screen.

# Setting the RecyclerView's adapter

Now that you have an **Adapter**, connect it to your **RecyclerView**. Implement a function called **updateUI** that sets up **CrimeListFragment**'s UI. For now, it will create a **CrimeAdapter** and set it on the **RecyclerView**.

Listing 9.12  Setting an **Adapter** (CrimeListFragment.kt)

```kotlin
class CrimeListFragment : Fragment() {

    private lateinit var crimeRecyclerView: RecyclerView
    private var adapter: CrimeAdapter? = null
    ...
    override fun onCreateView(
        inflater: LayoutInflater,
        container: ViewGroup?,
        savedInstanceState: Bundle?
    ): View? {
        val view = inflater.inflate(R.layout.fragment_crime_list, container, false)

        crimeRecyclerView =
                view.findViewById(R.id.crime_recycler_view) as RecyclerView
        crimeRecyclerView.layoutManager = LinearLayoutManager(context)

        updateUI()

        return view
    }

    private fun updateUI() {
        val crimes = crimeListViewModel.crimes
        adapter = CrimeAdapter(crimes)
        crimeRecyclerView.adapter = adapter
    }
    ...
}
```

In later chapters, you will add more to **updateUI()** as configuring your UI gets more involved.

Run CriminalIntent and scroll through your new **RecyclerView**, which should look like Figure 9.11.

Figure 9.11 **RecyclerView** populated with **Crime**s

Swipe or drag down and you will see even more views scroll across your screen. Every visible **CrimeHolder** should display a distinct **Crime**. (If your rows are much taller than these, or if you only see one row on the screen, then double-check that the layout_height on your row's **LinearLayout** is set to wrap_content.)

When you fling the view up, the scrolling animation should feel as smooth as warm butter. This effect is a direct result of keeping **onBindViewHolder(…)** small and efficient, doing only the minimum amount of work necessary. Take heed: Always be efficient in your **onBindViewHolder(…)**. Otherwise, your scroll animation could feel as chunky as cold Parmesan cheese.

# Recycling Views

Figure 9.11 shows 11 rows of **View**s. You can swipe to scroll through 100 **View**s to see all of your **Crime**s. Does that mean that you have 100 **View** objects in memory? Thanks to your **RecyclerView**, no.

Creating a **View** for every item in the list all at once could easily become unworkable. As you can imagine, a list can have far more than 100 items, and your list items can be much more involved than your simple implementation here. Also, a **Crime** only needs a **View** when it is onscreen, so there is no need to have 100 **View**s ready and waiting. It would make far more sense to create view objects only as you need them.

**RecyclerView** does just that. Instead of creating 100 **View**s, it creates just enough to fill the screen. When a view is scrolled off the screen, **RecyclerView** reuses it rather than throwing it away. In short, it lives up to its name: It recycles views over and over.

Because of this, **onCreateViewHolder(ViewGroup, Int)** will happen a lot less often than **onBindViewHolder(ViewHolder, Int)**. Once enough **ViewHolder**s have been created, **RecyclerView** stops calling **onCreateViewHolder(…)**. Instead, it saves time and memory by recycling old **ViewHolder**s and passing those into **onBindViewHolder(ViewHolder, Int)**.

# Cleaning Up Binding List Items

Right now, the **Adapter** binds crime data directly to a crime holder's text views in
**Adapter.onBindViewHolder(…)**. This works fine, but it is better to more cleanly separate concerns
between the view holder and the adapter. The adapter should know as little as possible about the inner
workings and details of the view holder.

We recommend you place all the code that will do the real work of binding inside your **CrimeHolder**.
First, add a property to stash the **Crime** being bound. While you are at it, make the existing text view
properties private. Add a **bind(Crime)** function to **CrimeHolder**. In this new function, cache the crime
being bound into a property and set the text values on titleTextView and dateTextView.

Listing 9.13 Writing a **bind(Crime)** function (CrimeListFragment.kt)

```kotlin
private inner class CrimeHolder(view: View)
    : RecyclerView.ViewHolder(view) {

    private lateinit var crime: Crime

    private val titleTextView: TextView = itemView.findViewById(R.id.crime_title)
    private val dateTextView: TextView = itemView.findViewById(R.id.crime_date)

    fun bind(crime: Crime) {
        this.crime = crime
        titleTextView.text = this.crime.title
        dateTextView.text = this.crime.date.toString()
    }
}
```

When given a **Crime** to bind, **CrimeHolder** will now update the title **TextView** and date **TextView** to
reflect the state of the **Crime**.

Next, call your newly minted **bind(Crime)** function each time the **RecyclerView** requests that a given
**CrimeHolder** be bound to a particular crime.

Listing 9.14 Calling the **bind(Crime)** function (CrimeListFragment.kt)

```kotlin
private inner class CrimeAdapter(var crimes: List<Crime>)
    : RecyclerView.Adapter<CrimeHolder>() {

    override fun onCreateViewHolder(parent: ViewGroup, viewType: Int): CrimeHolder {
        ...
    }

    override fun onBindViewHolder(holder: CrimeHolder, position: Int) {
        val crime = crimes[position]
        holder.apply {
            titleTextView.text = crime.title
            dateTextView.text = crime.date.toString()
        }
        holder.bind(crime)
    }

    override fun getItemCount() = crimes.size
}
```

Run CriminalIntent one more time. The result should look the same as it did in Figure 9.11.

# Responding to Presses

As icing on the **RecyclerView** cake, CriminalIntent should also respond to a press on these list items. In Chapter 12, you will launch the detail view for a **Crime** when the user presses on that **Crime** in the list. For now, show a **Toast** when the user takes action on a **Crime**.

As you may have noticed, **RecyclerView**, while powerful and capable, has precious few real responsibilities. (May it be an example to us all.) The same goes here: Handling touch events is mostly up to you. If you need them, **RecyclerView** can forward along raw touch events. But most of the time this is not necessary.

Instead, you can handle them like you normally do: by setting an **OnClickListener**. Since each **View** has an associated **ViewHolder**, you can make your **ViewHolder** the **OnClickListener** for its **View**.

Modify the **CrimeHolder** to handle presses for the entire row.

Listing 9.15  Detecting presses in **CrimeHolder** (CrimeListFragment.kt)

```kotlin
private inner class CrimeHolder(view: View)
    : RecyclerView.ViewHolder(view), View.OnClickListener {

    private lateinit var crime: Crime

    private val titleTextView: TextView = itemView.findViewById(R.id.crime_title)
    private val dateTextView: TextView = itemView.findViewById(R.id.crime_date)

    init {
        itemView.setOnClickListener(this)
    }

    fun bind(crime: Crime) {
        this.crime = crime
        titleTextView.text = this.crime.title
        dateTextView.text = this.crime.date.toString()
    }

    override fun onClick(v: View) {
        Toast.makeText(context, "${crime.title} pressed!", Toast.LENGTH_SHORT)
                .show()
    }
}
```

In Listing 9.15, the **CrimeHolder** itself is implementing the **OnClickListener** interface. On the itemView, which is the **View** for the entire row, the **CrimeHolder** is set as the receiver of click events.

Run CriminalIntent and press on an item in the list. You should see a **Toast** indicating that the item was pressed.

# For the More Curious: ListView and GridView

The core Android OS includes **ListView**, **GridView**, and **Adapter** classes. Until the release of Android 5.0, these were the preferred ways to create lists or grids of items.

The API for these components is very similar to that of a **RecyclerView**. The **ListView** or **GridView** class is responsible for scrolling a collection of items, but it does not know much about each of those items. The **Adapter** is responsible for creating each of the **View**s in the list. However, **ListView** and **GridView** do not enforce that you use the **ViewHolder** pattern (though you can – and should – use it).

These old implementations are replaced by the **RecyclerView** implementation because of the complexity required to alter the behavior of a **ListView** or **GridView**.

Creating a horizontally scrolling **ListView**, for example, is not included in the **ListView** API and requires a lot of work. Creating custom layout and scrolling behavior with a **RecyclerView** is still a lot of work, but **RecyclerView** was built to be extended, so it is not quite so bad.

Another key feature of **RecyclerView** is the animation of items in the list. Animating the addition or removal of items in a **ListView** or **GridView** is a complex and error-prone task. **RecyclerView** makes this much easier, includes a few built-in animations, and allows for easy customization of these animations.

For example, if you found out that the crime at position 0 moved to position 5, you could animate that change like so:

```
recyclerView.adapter.notifyItemMoved(0, 5)
```

# Challenge: RecyclerView ViewTypes

For this advanced challenge, you will create two types of rows in your **RecyclerView**: a normal row and a row for more serious crimes. To implement this, you will work with the *view type* feature available in **RecyclerView.Adapter**. Add a new property, requiresPolice, to the **Crime** object and use it to determine which view to load on the **CrimeAdapter** by implementing the **getItemViewType(Int)** function (developer.android.com/reference/android/support/v7/ widget/RecyclerView.Adapter.html#getItemViewType).

In the **onCreateViewHolder(ViewGroup, Int)** function, you will also need to add logic that returns a different **ViewHolder** based on the new viewType value returned by **getItemViewType(Int)**. Use the original layout for crimes that do not require police intervention and a new layout with a streamlined interface containing a button that says "contact police" for crimes that do.

193

# 10

# Creating User Interfaces with Layouts and Widgets

In this chapter, you will learn more about layouts and widgets while adding some style to your list items in the **RecyclerView**. You will also learn how to use the graphical layout editor to arrange widgets within a **ConstraintLayout**. Figure 10.1 shows what **CrimeListFragment**'s view will look like once you chisel down your existing app to build up your masterpiece.

Figure 10.1  CriminalIntent, now with beautiful pictures

In previous chapters you used nested layout hierarchies to arrange your widgets. For example, the layout/activity_main.xml file you created for GeoQuiz in Chapter 1 nested a **LinearLayout** within another **LinearLayout**. This nesting is hard for you as a developer to read and edit. Worse, nesting can degrade your app's performance. Nested layouts can take a long time for the Android OS to measure and lay out, meaning your users might experience a delay before they see your views onscreen.

Flat, or non-nested, layouts are quicker for the OS to measure and lay out. And this is one of the areas where **ConstraintLayout** really shines. You can create beautifully intricate layouts without using nesting.

Before you dive in to **ConstraintLayout**, you must do a little legwork and learn a little background. You will need a copy of that fancy handcuff image from Figure 10.1 in your project. Open the solutions file (www.bignerdranch.com/solutions/AndroidProgramming4e.zip) and the 10_LayoutsAndWidgets/CriminalIntent/app/src/main/res directory. Copy each density version of ic_solved.png into the appropriate drawable folder in your project.

# Introducing ConstraintLayout

With **ConstraintLayout**, instead of using nested layouts you add a series of *constraints* to your layout. A constraint is like a rubber band: It pulls two things toward each other. So, for example, if you have an **ImageView**, you can attach a constraint from its right edge to the right edge of its parent (the **ConstraintLayout** itself), as shown in Figure 10.2. The constraint will hold the **ImageView** to the right.

Figure 10.2 **ImageView** with a constraint on the right edge

You can create a constraint from all four edges of your **ImageView** (left, top, right, and bottom). If you have opposing constraints, they will equal out, and your **ImageView** will be right in the center of the two constraints (Figure 10.3).

Figure 10.3 **ImageView** with opposing constraints

So that is the big picture: To place views where you want them to go in a **ConstraintLayout**, you give them constraints.

What about sizing widgets? For that, you have three options: Let the widget decide (your old friend `wrap_content`), decide for yourself, or let your widget expand to fit your constraints.

With those tools, you can achieve a great many layouts with a single **ConstraintLayout**, no nesting required. As you go through this chapter, you will see how to use constraints with your `list_item_crime.xml` layout file.

# Introducing the Graphical Layout Editor

So far, you have created layouts by typing XML. In this section, you will use Android Studio's graphical layout tool.

Open `layout/list_item_crime.xml` and select the Design tab at the bottom of the file (Figure 10.4).

## Figure 10.4  Views in the graphical layout tool

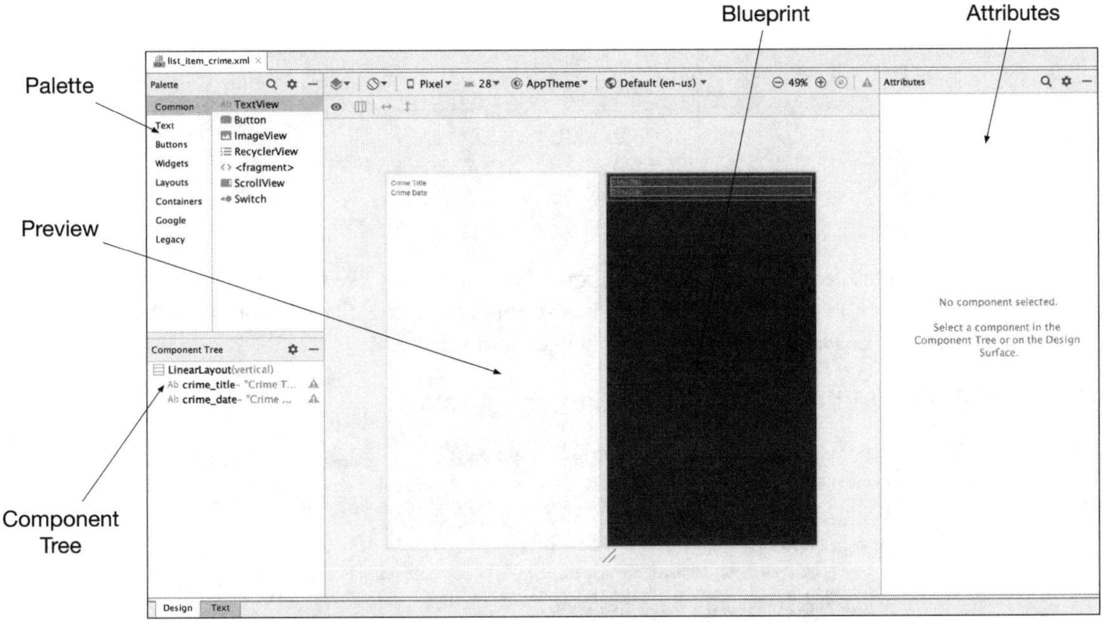

In the middle of the graphical layout editor is the preview you have seen before. To the right of the preview is the Blueprint, which, as you saw in Chapter 1, is like the preview but shows an outline of each of your views. This can be useful when you need to see how big each view is, not just what it is displaying.

On the lefthand side of the screen is the palette, which contains all the widgets you could wish for, organized by category. The component tree is in the bottom left. The tree shows how the widgets are organized in the layout. If you do not see the palette or component tree, click on the tabs on the left side of the preview to open the windows.

On the right side of the screen is the *attributes view*. Here, you can view and edit the attributes of the widget selected in the component tree.

The first thing you need to do is convert list_item_crime.xml to use a **ConstraintLayout**. Right-click on your root **LinearLayout** in the component tree and select Convert LinearLayout to ConstraintLayout (Figure 10.5).

Figure 10.5  Converting the root view to a **ConstraintLayout**

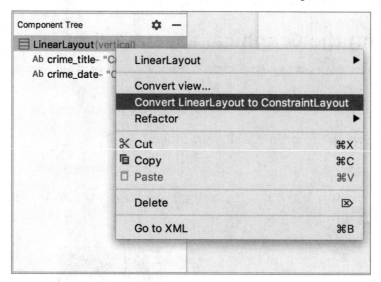

Android Studio will ask you in a pop-up how aggressive you would like this conversion process to be (Figure 10.6). Since list_item_crime.xml is a simple layout file, there is not much that Android Studio can optimize. Leave the default values checked and select OK.

Figure 10.6  Converting with the default configuration

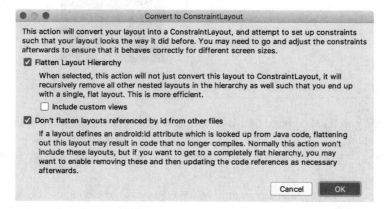

Be patient. The conversion process might take a little while. But when it is complete, you will have a fine, new **ConstraintLayout** to work with (Figure 10.7).

## Figure 10.7  Life as a **ConstraintLayout**

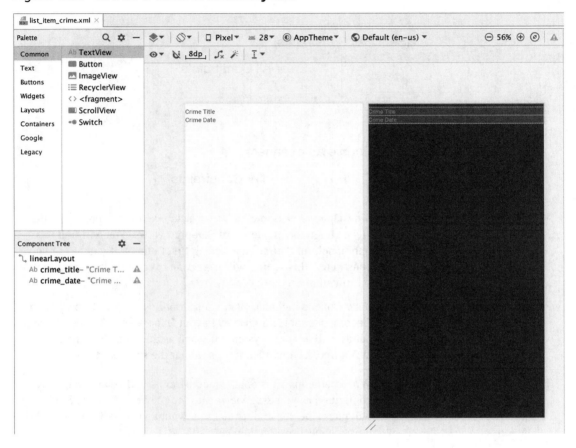

(Wondering why the component tree says you have a linearLayout? We will get to that in a moment.)

The toolbar above the preview has a few editing controls (Figure 10.8). You may need to click into the preview to see all the controls.

## Figure 10.8  Constraint controls

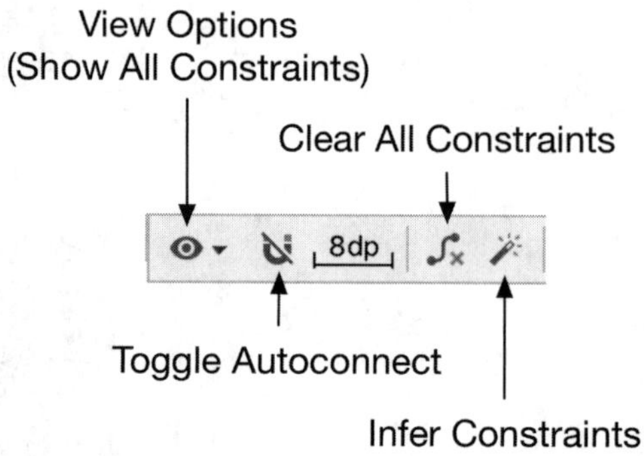

View Options
(Show All Constraints)

Clear All Constraints

Toggle Autoconnect

Infer Constraints

| View Options | View Options → Show All Constraints reveals the constraints that are set up in the preview and Blueprint views. You will find this option helpful at times and unhelpful at others. If you have many constraints, this setting will trigger an overwhelming amount of information. |
|---|---|
| | View Options includes other useful options, such as Show Layout Decorations. Selecting Show Layout Decorations displays the app bar as well as some system UI (such as the status bar) the user sees at runtime. You will learn more about the app bar in Chapter 14. |
| Toggle Autoconnect | When autoconnect is enabled, constraints will be automatically configured as you drag views into the preview. Android Studio will guess the constraints that you want a view to have and make those connections on demand. |
| Clear All Constraints | This button removes all existing constraints in the layout file. You will use this shortly. |
| Infer Constraints | This option is similar to autoconnect in that Android Studio will automatically create constraints for you, but it is only triggered when you select this button. Autoconnect is active any time you add a view to your layout file. |

# Using ConstraintLayout

When you converted `list_item_crime.xml` to use **ConstraintLayout**, Android Studio automatically added the constraints it thinks will replicate the behavior of your old layout. However, to learn how constraints work you are going to start from scratch.

Select the top-level view in the component tree, labeled linearLayout. Why does it say linearLayout, when you converted it to a **ConstraintLayout**? That is the ID the **ConstraintLayout** converter supplied. linearLayout is, in fact, your **ConstraintLayout**. You can check the XML version of your layout if you want to confirm this.

With linearLayout selected in the component tree, click the Clear All Constraints button (shown in Figure 10.8). You will immediately see red warning flags, including one at the top right of the screen. Click on it to see what that is all about (Figure 10.9).

Figure 10.9 **ConstraintLayout** warnings

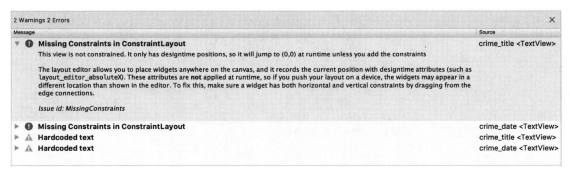

When views do not have enough constraints, **ConstraintLayout** cannot know exactly where to put them. Your **TextView**s have no constraints at all, so they each have a warning that says they will not appear in the right place at runtime.

As you go through the chapter, you will add those constraints back to fix those warnings. In your own work, keep an eye on that warning indicator to avoid unexpected behavior at runtime.

## Making room

You need to make some room to work in the graphical layout editor. Your two **TextView**s are taking up the entire area, which will make it hard to wire up anything else. Time to shrink those two widgets.

Select crime_title in the component tree and look at the attributes view on the right (Figure 10.10). If this pane is not open for you, click the Attributes tab on the right to open it.

Figure 10.10  Title **TextView**'s attributes

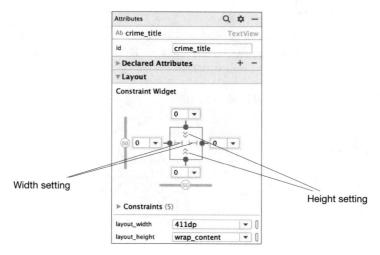

The vertical and horizontal sizes of your **TextView** are governed by the height setting and width setting, respectively. These can be set to one of three view size settings (Figure 10.11), each of which corresponds to a value for layout_width or layout_height.

Figure 10.11  Three view size settings

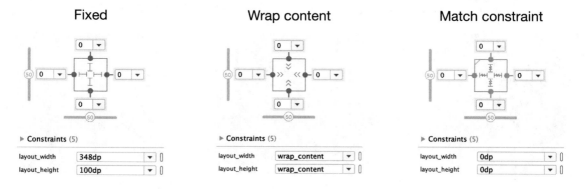

## Table 10.1 View size setting types

| Setting type | Setting value | Usage |
|---|---|---|
| fixed | Xdp | Specifies an explicit size (that will not change) for the view. The size is specified in dp units. (If you need a refresher on dp units, see the section called Screen Pixel Densities in Chapter 2.) |
| wrap content | wrap_content | Assigns the view its "desired" size. For a **TextView**, this means that the size will be just big enough to show its contents. |
| match constraint | match_constraint | Allows the view to stretch to meet the specified constraints. |

Both the title and date **TextView**s are set to a large fixed width, which is why they are taking up the whole screen. Adjust the width and height of both of these widgets. With crime_title still selected in the component tree, click the width setting until it cycles around to the wrap content setting. If necessary, adjust the height setting until the height is also set to wrap content (Figure 10.12).

## Figure 10.12 Adjusting the title width and height

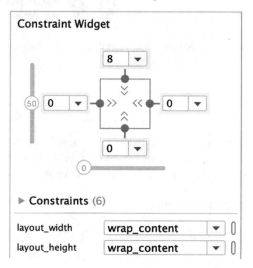

203

Repeat the process with the crime_date widget to set its width and height.

Now the two widgets are the correct size (Figure 10.13), but they will still overlap when the app runs because they have no constraints. Note that the positioning you see in the preview differs from what you see when you run the app. The preview allows you to position the views to make it easier to add your constraints, but these positions are only valid in the preview, not at runtime.

Figure 10.13  Correctly sized **TextView**s

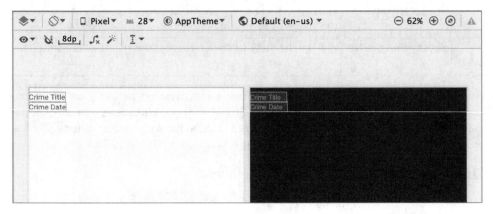

You will add constraints to correctly position your **TextView**s later. First, you will add the third view you need in your layout.

## Adding widgets

With your other widgets out of the way, you can add the handcuffs image to your layout. Add an **ImageView** to your layout file. In the palette, find ImageView in the Common category (Figure 10.14). Drag it into your component tree as a child of the ConstraintLayout, just underneath crime_date.

Figure 10.14  Finding the **ImageView**

In the pop-up, expand the Project section and choose ic_solved as the resource for the **ImageView** (Figure 10.15). This image will be used to indicate which crimes have been solved. Click OK.

Figure 10.15  Choosing the **ImageView**'s resource

The **ImageView** is now a part of your layout, but it has no constraints. So while the graphical layout editor gives it a position, that position does not really mean anything.

Time to add some constraints. Click on your **ImageView** in the preview pane. (You may want to zoom the preview in to get a better look. The zoom controls are in the toolbar above the constraint tools.) You will see dots on each side of the **ImageView** (Figure 10.16). Each of these dots represents a *constraint handle*.

Figure 10.16  **ImageView**'s constraint handles

You want the **ImageView** to be anchored in the right side of the view. To accomplish this, you need to create constraints from the top, right, and bottom edges of the **ImageView**.

Before adding constraints, drag the **ImageView** to the right and down to move it away from the **TextView**s (Figure 10.17). Do not worry about where you place the **ImageView**. This placement will be ignored once you get your constraints in place.

Figure 10.17  Moving a widget temporarily

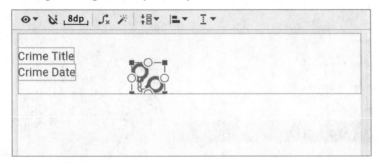

First, you are going to set a constraint between the top of the **ImageView** and the top of the **ConstraintLayout**. In the preview, drag the top constraint handle from the **ImageView** to the top of the **ConstraintLayout**. The handle will display an arrow and turn green (Figure 10.18).

Figure 10.18  Part of the way through creating a top constraint

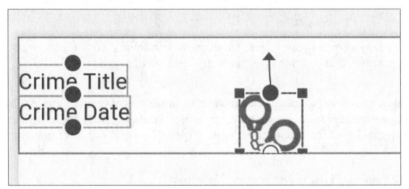

Keep dragging. Watch for the constraint handle to turn blue, then release the mouse to create the constraint (Figure 10.19).

Figure 10.19  Creating a top constraint

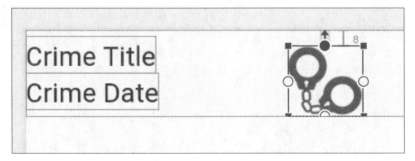

Be careful to avoid clicking when the mouse cursor is a corner shape – this will resize your **ImageView** instead. Also, make sure you do not inadvertently attach the constraint to one of your **TextView**s. If you do, click on the constraint handle to delete the bad constraint, then try again.

When you let go and set the constraint, the view will snap into position to account for the presence of the new constraint. This is how you move views around in a **ConstraintLayout** – by setting and removing constraints.

Verify that your **ImageView** has a top constraint connected to the top of the **ConstraintLayout** by hovering over the **ImageView** with your mouse. It should look like Figure 10.20.

Figure 10.20 **ImageView** with a top constraint

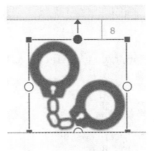

Do the same for the bottom constraint handle, dragging it from the **ImageView** to the bottom of the root view (Figure 10.21), again taking care to avoid attaching it to the **TextView**s.

Figure 10.21 **ImageView** with top and bottom constraints

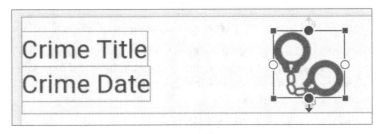

Finally, drag the right constraint handle from the **ImageView** to the right side of the root view. That should set all of your constraints. Your constraints should look like Figure 10.22.

Figure 10.22 **ImageView**'s three constraints

## ConstraintLayout's inner workings

Any edits that you make with the graphical layout editor are reflected in the XML behind the scenes. You can still edit the raw **ConstraintLayout** XML, but the graphical layout editor will often be easier for adding the initial constraints. **ConstraintLayout** is much more verbose than other **ViewGroup**s, so adding the initial constraints manually can be a lot of work. Working directly with the XML can be more useful when you need to make smaller changes to the layout.

(The graphical layout tools are useful, especially with **ConstraintLayout**. Not everyone is a fan, though. You do not have to choose sides – you can switch between the graphical layout editor and directly editing XML at any time. Use whichever tool you prefer to create the layouts in this book. You can decide for yourself how to create it – XML, graphical layout editor, or some of each.)

Switch to the text view to see what happened to the XML when you created the three constraints on your **ImageView**:

```
<androidx.constraintlayout.widget.ConstraintLayout
        ... >
    ...
    <ImageView
        android:id="@+id/imageView"
        android:layout_width="wrap_content"
        android:layout_height="wrap_content"
        android:layout_marginTop="8dp"
        android:layout_marginEnd="8dp"
        android:layout_marginBottom="8dp"
        app:layout_constraintBottom_toBottomOf="parent"
        app:layout_constraintEnd_toEndOf="parent"
        app:layout_constraintTop_toTopOf="parent"
        app:srcCompat="@drawable/ic_solved" />

</android.support.constraint.ConstraintLayout>
```

(You will still see errors related to the two **TextView**s. Leave them as is – you will fix them later.)

All of the widgets are direct children of the single **ConstraintLayout** – there are no nested layouts. If you had created the same layout using **LinearLayout**, you would have had to nest one inside another. As we said earlier, reducing nesting also reduces the time needed to render the layout, and that results in a quicker, more seamless user experience.

Take a closer look at the top constraint on the **ImageView**:

```
app:layout_constraintTop_toTopOf="parent"
```

This attribute begins with layout_. All attributes that begin with layout_ are known as *layout parameters*. Unlike other attributes, layout parameters are directions to that widget's *parent*, not the widget itself. They tell the parent layout how to arrange the child element within itself. You have seen a few layout parameters so far, like layout_width and layout_height.

The name of the constraint is constraintTop. This means that this is the top constraint on your **ImageView**.

Finally, the attribute ends with toTopOf="parent". This means that this constraint is connected to the top edge of the parent. The parent here is the **ConstraintLayout**.

Whew, what a mouthful. Time to leave the raw XML behind and return to the graphical layout editor.

# Editing properties

Your **ImageView** is now positioned correctly. Next up: Position and size the title **TextView**.

First, select Crime Date in the preview and drag it out of the way (Figure 10.23). Remember that any changes you make to the position in the preview will not be represented when the app is running. At runtime, only constraints remain.

## Figure 10.23 Get out of here, date

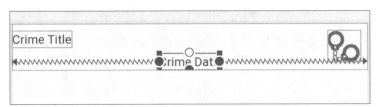

Now, select crime_title in the component tree. This will also highlight Crime Title in the preview.

You want Crime Title to be at the top left of your layout, positioned to the left of your new **ImageView**. That requires three constraints:

- from the left side of your view to the left side of the parent

- from the top of your view to the top of the parent

- from the right of your view to the left side of the new **ImageView**

Modify your layout so that all of these constraints are in place (Figure 10.24). If a constraint does not work as you expected, key Command-Z (Ctrl-Z) to undo and try again.

## Figure 10.24 **TextView** constraints

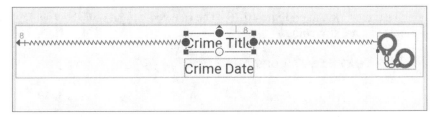

Now you are going to add margins to the constraints on your **TextView**. With Crime Title selected in the preview pane, check out the attributes pane to the right. Since you added constraints to the top, left, and right of the **TextView**, dropdown menus appear to allow you to select the margin for each constraint (Figure 10.25). Select 16dp for the left and top margins, and select 8dp for the right margin.

Figure 10.25  Adding margins to **TextView**

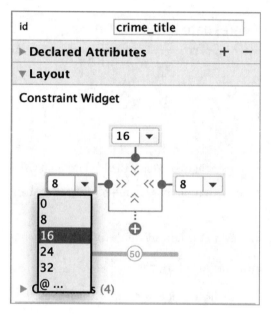

Notice that Android Studio defaulted to either a 16dp or a 8dp value for the margins. These values follow Android's material design guidelines. You can find all of the Android design guidelines at developer.android.com/design/index.html. Your Android apps should follow these guidelines as closely as possible.

Verify that your constraints look like Figure 10.26. (The selected widget will show squiggly lines for any of its constraints that are stretching.)

Figure 10.26  Title **TextView**'s constraints

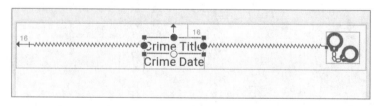

Now that the constraints are set up, you can restore the title **TextView** to its full glory. Adjust its horizontal view setting to `match_constraint` to allow the title **TextView** to fill all of the space available within its constraints. Adjust the vertical view setting to `wrap_content`, if it is not already, so that the **TextView** will be just tall enough to show the title of the crime. Verify that your settings match those shown in Figure 10.27.

Figure 10.27 `crime_title` view settings

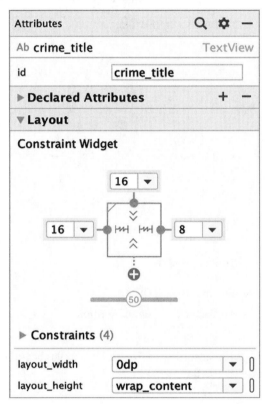

Now, add constraints to the date **TextView**. Select crime_date in the component tree. Repeat the steps from the title **TextView** to add three constraints:

- from the left side of your view to the left side of the parent, with a 16dp margin

- from the top of your view to the bottom of the crime title, with an 8dp margin

- from the right of your view to the left side of the **ImageView**, with an 8dp margin

After adding the constraints, adjust the properties of the **TextView**. You want the width of your date **TextView** to be match_constraint and the height to be wrap_content, just like the title **TextView**. Verify that your settings match those shown in Figure 10.28.

Figure 10.28  `crime_date` view settings

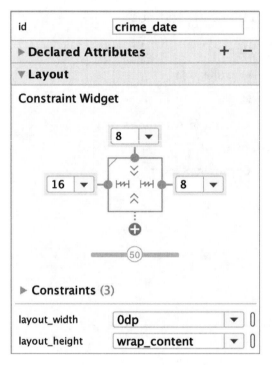

Your layout in the preview should look similar to Figure 10.1, at the beginning of the chapter. Up close, your preview should match Figure 10.29.

Figure 10.29  Final constraints up close

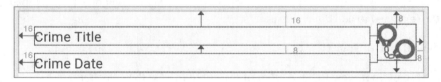

Switch to the text view in the editor tool window to review the XML resulting from the changes you made in the graphical layout editor. Red underlines no longer appear under each of the **TextView** tags. This is because the **TextView** widgets are now adequately constrained, so the **ConstraintLayout** that contains them can figure out where to properly position the widgets at runtime.

Two yellow warning indicators remain related to the **TextView**s, and if you explore them you will see that the warnings have to do with their hardcoded strings. These warnings would be important for a production application, but for CriminalIntent you can disregard them. (If you prefer, feel free to follow the advice to extract the hardcoded text into string resources. This will resolve the warnings.)

Additionally, one warning remains on the **ImageView**, indicating that you failed to set a content description. For now, you can disregard this warning as well. You will address this issue when you learn about content descriptions in Chapter 18. In the meantime, your app will function fine, although the image will not be accessible to users utilizing a screen reader.

Run CriminalIntent and verify that you see all three components lined up nicely in each row of your **RecyclerView** (Figure 10.30).

Figure 10.30  Now with three views per row

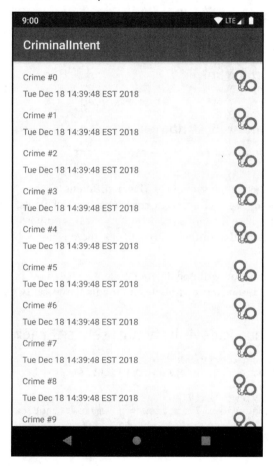

# Making list items dynamic

Now that the layout includes the right constraints, update the **ImageView** so that the handcuffs are only shown on crimes that have been solved.

First, update the ID of your **ImageView**. When you added the **ImageView** to your **ConstraintLayout**, it was given a default name. That name is not very descriptive. Select your **ImageView** and, in the attributes pane, update the ID attribute to crime_solved (Figure 10.31). You will be asked whether Android Studio should update all usages of the ID; select **Yes**.

### Figure 10.31  Updating the image ID

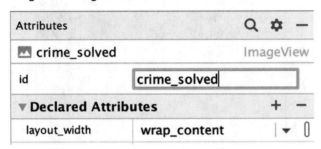

You may notice that you are using the same view IDs in different layouts. The crime_solved ID is used in both the list_item_crime.xml and fragment_crime.xml layouts. You may think reusing IDs would be an issue, but in this case it is not a problem. Layout IDs only need to be unique in the same layout. Since your IDs are defined in different layout files, there is no problem using the same ID in both.

With a proper ID in place, now you will update your code. Open CrimeListFragment.kt. In **CrimeHolder**, add an **ImageView** instance variable and toggle its visibility based on the solved status of the crime.

### Listing 10.1  Updating handcuff visibility (CrimeListFragment.kt)

```
private inner class CrimeHolder(view: View)
    : RecyclerView.ViewHolder(view), View.OnClickListener {
    ...
    private val dateTextView: TextView
    private val solvedImageView: ImageView = itemView.findViewById(R.id.crime_solved)

    init {
        ...
    }

    fun bind(crime: Crime) {
        this.crime = crime
        titleTextView.text = this.crime.title
        dateTextView.text = this.crime.date.toString()
        solvedImageView.visibility = if (crime.isSolved) {
            View.VISIBLE
        } else {
            View.GONE
        }
    }
    ...
}
```

Run CriminalIntent and verify that the handcuffs now appear on every other row. (Check **CrimeListViewModel** if you do not recall why this would be the case.)

# More on Layout Attributes

Now you are going to add a few more tweaks to the design of list_item_crime.xml and, in the process, answer some lingering questions you might have about widgets and attributes.

Navigate back to the design view of list_item_crime.xml. Select crime_title and adjust some of its attributes: Expand the textAppearance section and set the textSize attribute to 18sp. Set the textColor attribute to @android:color/black (Figure 10.32).

Figure 10.32  Updating the title color and size

You can type these values directly into the fields in the attributes pane, choose from the dropdown (in the case of textSize), or click the ... button next to the field to pick a dimension resource.

Run CriminalIntent and be amazed at how much better everything looks with a fresh coat of paint (Figure 10.33).

Figure 10.33  Fresh paint

# Styles, themes, and theme attributes

A *style* is an XML resource that contains attributes that describe how a widget should look and behave. For example, the following is a style resource that configures a widget with a larger-than-normal text size:

```
<style name="BigTextStyle">
  <item name="android:textSize">20sp</item>
  <item name="android:padding">3dp</item>
</style>
```

You can create your own styles (and you will in Chapter 21). You add them to a styles file in `res/values/` and refer to them in layouts like this: `@style/my_own_style`.

Take another look at the **TextView** widgets in `layout/fragment_crime.xml` (not the `list_item_crime.xml` file you have been working in for this chapter). Each has a `style` attribute that refers to a style created by Android. This particular style makes the **TextView**s look like list separators and comes from the app's *theme*. A theme is a collection of styles. Structurally, a theme is itself a style resource whose attributes point to other style resources.

Android provides platform themes that your apps can use. When you created CriminalIntent, the wizard set up a theme for the app that is referenced on the `application` tag in the manifest.

You can apply a style from the app's theme to a widget using a *theme attribute reference*. This is what you are doing in `fragment_crime.xml` when you use the value `?android:listSeparatorTextViewStyle`.

In a theme attribute reference, you tell Android's runtime resource manager, "Go to the app's theme and find the attribute named `listSeparatorTextViewStyle`. This attribute points to another style resource. Put the value of that resource here."

Every Android theme will include an attribute named `listSeparatorTextViewStyle`, but its definition will be different depending on the overall look and feel of the particular theme. Using a theme attribute reference ensures that the **TextView**s will have the correct look and feel for your app.

You will learn more about how styles and themes work in Chapter 21.

# For the More Curious: Margins vs Padding

In both GeoQuiz and CriminalIntent, you have given widgets margin and padding attributes. Beginning developers sometimes get confused about these two. Now that you understand what a layout parameter is, the difference is easier to explain.

Margin attributes are layout parameters. They determine the distance between widgets. Given that a widget can only know about itself, margins must be the responsibility of the widget's parent.

Padding, on the other hand, is not a layout parameter. The android:padding attribute tells the widget how much bigger than its contents it should draw itself. For example, say you wanted the date button to be spectacularly large without changing its text size (Figure 10.34).

Figure 10.34  I like big buttons and I cannot lie...

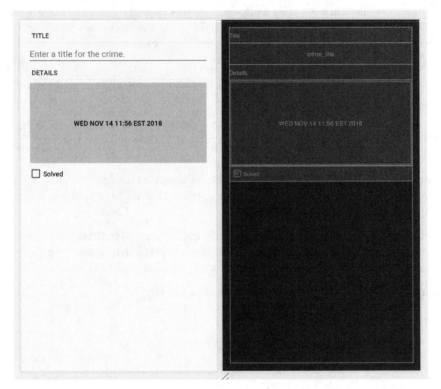

You could add the following attribute to the **Button**:

```
<Button
    android:id="@+id/crime_date"
    android:layout_width="match_parent"
    android:layout_height="wrap_content"
    android:padding="80dp"
    tools:text="Wed Nov 14 11:56 EST 2018"/>
```

Alas, you should probably remove this attribute before continuing.

# For the More Curious: New Developments in ConstraintLayout

`ConstraintLayout` has additional capabilities to help arrange its child views. In this chapter you positioned views by constraining them to the parent as well as to other, sibling views. `ConstraintLayout` also includes helper views, such as **Guideline**s, that simplify arranging views on the screen.

Guidelines do not display on the app screen; they are just a tool to help you position views the way you need. There are both horizontal and vertical guidelines, and they can be placed at a specific location on the screen using dp values or by setting them to be a percentage of the screen. Other views can be constrained to the guideline to ensure that they appear at the same location, even if the screen size is different.

Figure 10.35 shows an example of using a vertical **Guideline**. It is positioned at 20 percent of the width of the parent. Both the crime title and date have a left constraint to the **Guideline** instead of to the parent.

Figure 10.35  Using a **Guideline**

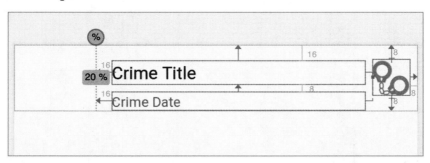

**MotionLayout** is an extension of **ConstraintLayout** that simplifies adding animations to your views. To use **MotionLayout**, you create a MotionScene file that describes how the animations should be performed and which views map to each other in the starting and ending layouts. You can also set **Keyframe**s that provide intermediary views in the animation. **MotionLayout** can animate from the starting view through the various keyframes you provide, then ensure that the view animates to the ending layout appropriately.

# Challenge: Formatting the Date

The **Date** object is more of a timestamp than a conventional date. A timestamp is what you see when you call **toString()** on a **Date**, so that is what you have in each of your **RecyclerView** rows. While timestamps make for good documentation, it might be nicer if the rows just displayed the date as humans think of it – like "Jul 22, 2019." You can do this with an instance of the **android.text.format.DateFormat** class. The place to start is the reference page for this class in the Android documentation.

You can use functions in the **DateFormat** class to get a common format. Or you can prepare your own format string. For a more advanced challenge, create a format string that will display the day of the week as well – for example, "Monday, Jul 22, 2019."

# 11

# Databases and the Room Library

Almost every application needs a place to save data for the long term. In this chapter you will implement a database for CriminalIntent and seed it with dummy data. Then you will update the app to pull crime data from the database and display it in the crime list (Figure 11.1).

## Figure 11.1  Displaying crimes from the database

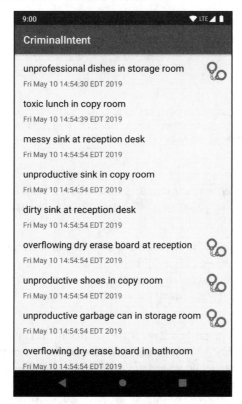

In Chapter 4 you learned how to persist transient UI state data across rotation and process death using **ViewModel** and saved instance state. These two approaches are great for small amounts of data tied to the UI. However, these approaches should not be used for storing non-UI data or data that is not tied to an activity or fragment instance and needs to persist regardless of UI state.

Instead, store your non-UI app data either locally (on the filesystem or in a database, as you will do for CriminalIntent) or on a web server.

# Room Architecture Component Library

Room is a Jetpack architecture component library that simplifies database setup and access. It allows you to define your database structure and queries using annotated Kotlin classes.

Room is composed of an API, annotations, and a compiler. The API contains classes you extend to define your database and build an instance of it. You use the annotations to indicate things like which classes need to be stored in the database, which class represents your database, and which class specifies the accessor functions to your database tables. The compiler processes the annotated classes and generates the implementation of your database.

To use Room, you first need to add the dependencies it requires. Add the `room-runtime` and `room-compiler` dependencies to your `app/build.gradle` file.

## Listing 11.1  Adding dependencies (`app/build.gradle`)

```
apply plugin: 'kotlin-android-extensions'

apply plugin: 'kotlin-kapt'

android {
    ...
}
...
dependencies {
    ...
    implementation 'androidx.core:core-ktx:1.1.0-alpha04'
    implementation 'androidx.room:room-runtime:2.1.0-alpha04'
    kapt 'androidx.room:room-compiler:2.1.0-alpha04'
    ...
}
```

Near the top of the file, you added a new Android Studio *plug-in*. Plug-ins are a way to add functionality to the IDE. Check out `plugins.jetbrains.com/androidstudio` for more plug-ins you can add.

`kotlin-kapt` stands for "Kotlin annotation processor tool." When libraries generate code for you, you will often want to use those generated classes directly in your code. But by default, those generated classes are not visible to Android Studio, so you will see an error if you try to import them. Adding the `kotlin-kapt` plug-in makes library-generated files visible to Android Studio so that you can import them in your own classes.

The first dependency you added, `room-runtime`, is for the Room API containing all the classes and annotations you will need to define your database. The second dependency, `room-compiler`, is for the Room compiler, which will generate your database implementation based on the annotations you specify. The compiler uses the `kapt` keyword, instead of `implementation`, so that the generated classes from the compiler are visible to Android Studio, thanks to the `kotlin-kapt` plug-in.

Do not forget to sync your Gradle files. With your dependencies in place, you can move on to preparing your model layer for storage in the database.

# Creating a Database

There are three steps to creating a database with Room:

- annotating your model class to make it a database entity

- creating the class that will represent the database itself

- creating a type converter so that your database can handle your model data

Room makes each of these steps straightforward, as you are about to see.

## Defining entities

Room structures the database tables for your application based on the *entities* you define. Entities are model classes you create, annotated with the @Entity annotation. Room will create a database table for any class with that annotation.

Since you want to store crime objects in your database, update **Crime** to be a Room entity. Open Crime.kt and add two annotations:

Listing 11.2  Making **Crime** an entity (Crime.kt)

```
@Entity
data class Crime(@PrimaryKey val id: UUID = UUID.randomUUID(),
                var title: String = "",
                var date: Date = Date(),
                var isSolved: Boolean = false)
```

The first annotation, @Entity, is applied at the class level. This entity annotation indicates that the class defines the structure of a table, or set of tables, in the database. In this case, each row in the table will represent an individual **Crime**. Each property defined on the class will be a column in the table, with the name of the property as the name of the column. The table that stores your crimes will have four columns: id, title, date, and isSolved.

The other annotation you added is @PrimaryKey, which you added to the id property. This annotation specifies which column in your database is the *primary key*. The primary key in a database is a column that holds data that is unique for each entry, or row, so that it can be used to look up individual entries. The id property is unique for every **Crime**, so by adding @PrimaryKey to this property you will be able to query a single crime from the database using its id.

Now that your **Crime** class is annotated, you can move on to creating your database class.

# Creating a database class

Entity classes define the structure of database tables. A single entity class could be used across multiple databases, should your app have more than one database. That case is not common, but it is possible. For this reason, an entity class is not used by Room to create a table unless you explicitly associate it with a database, which you will do shortly.

First, create a new package called database for your database-specific code. In the project tool window, right-click the com.bignerdranch.android.criminalintent folder and choose New → Package. Name your new package database.

Now, create a new class called **CrimeDatabase** in the database package and define the class as shown below.

## Listing 11.3  Initial **CrimeDatabase** class (database/CrimeDatabase.kt)

```
@Database(entities = [ Crime::class ], version=1)
abstract class CrimeDatabase : RoomDatabase() {
}
```

The @Database annotation tells Room that this class represents a database in your app. The annotation itself requires two parameters. The first parameter is a list of entity classes, which tells Room which entity classes to use when creating and managing tables for this database. In this case, you only pass the **Crime** class, since it is the only entity in the app.

The second parameter is the version of the database. When you first create a database, the version should be 1. As you develop your app in the future, you may add new entities and new properties to existing entities. When this happens, you will need to modify your entities list and increment your database version to tell Room something has changed. (You will do this in Chapter 15.)

The database class itself is empty at this point. **CrimeDatabase** extends from **RoomDatabase** and is marked as abstract, so you cannot make an instance of it directly. You will learn how to use Room to get a database instance you can use later in this chapter.

## Creating a type converter

Room uses SQLite under the hood. SQLite is an open source relational database, like MySQL or PostgreSQL. (SQL, short for Structured Query Language, is a standard language used for interacting with databases. People pronounce "SQL" as either "sequel" or as an initialism, "S-Q-L.") Unlike other databases, SQLite stores its data in simple files you can read and write using the SQLite library. Android includes this SQLite library in its standard library, along with some additional helper classes.

Room makes using SQLite even easier and cleaner, serving as an object-relational mapping (or ORM) layer between your Kotlin objects and database implementation. For the most part, you do not need to know or care about SQLite when using Room, but if you want to learn more you can visit www.sqlite.org, which has complete SQLite documentation.

Room is able to store primitive types with ease in the underlying SQLite database tables, but other types will cause issues. Your **Crime** class relies on the **Date** and **UUID** objects, which Room does not know how to store by default. You need to give the database a hand so it knows how to store these types and how to pull them out of the database table correctly.

To tell Room how to convert your data types, you specify a *type converter*. A type converter tells Room how to convert a specific type to the format it needs to store in the database. You will need two functions, which you will annotate with @TypeConverter, for each type: One tells Room how to convert the type to store it in the database, and the other tells Room how to convert from the database representation back to the original type.

Create a class called **CrimeTypeConverters** in the database package and add two functions each for the **Date** and **UUID** types.

## Listing 11.4 Adding **TypeConverter** functions (database/CrimeTypeConverters.kt)

```kotlin
class CrimeTypeConverters {

    @TypeConverter
    fun fromDate(date: Date?): Long? {
        return date?.time
    }

    @TypeConverter
    fun toDate(millisSinceEpoch: Long?): Date? {
        return millisSinceEpoch?.let {
            Date(it)
        }
    }

    @TypeConverter
    fun toUUID(uuid: String?): UUID? {
        return UUID.fromString(uuid)
    }

    @TypeConverter
    fun fromUUID(uuid: UUID?): String? {
        return uuid?.toString()
    }
}
```

The first two functions handle the **Date** object, and the second two handle the **UUID**s. Make sure you import the java.util.Date version of the **Date** class.

Declaring the converter functions does not enable your database to use them. You must explicitly add the converters to your database class.

## Listing 11.5 Enabling **TypeConverter**s (database/CrimeDatabase.kt)

```kotlin
@Database(entities = [ Crime::class ], version=1)
@TypeConverters(CrimeTypeConverters::class)
abstract class CrimeDatabase : RoomDatabase() {
}
```

By adding the @TypeConverters annotation and passing in your **CrimeTypeConverters** class, you tell your database to use the functions in that class when converting your types.

With that, your database and table definitions are complete.

# Defining a Data Access Object

A database table does not do much good if you cannot edit or access its contents. The first step to interacting with your database tables is to create a *data access object*, or DAO. A DAO is an interface that contains functions for each database operation you want to perform. In this chapter, CriminalIntent's DAO needs two query functions: one to return a list of all crimes in the database and another to return a single crime matching a given **UUID**.

Add a file named `CrimeDao.kt` to the `database` package. In it, define an empty interface named **CrimeDao** annotated with Room's @Dao annotation.

## Listing 11.6  Creating an empty DAO (`database/CrimeDao.kt`)

```
@Dao
interface CrimeDao {
}
```

The @Dao annotation lets Room know that **CrimeDao** is one of your data access objects. When you hook **CrimeDao** up to your database class, Room will generate implementations of the functions you add to this interface.

Speaking of adding functions, now is the time. Add two query functions to **CrimeDao**.

## Listing 11.7  Adding database query functions (`database/CrimeDao.kt`)

```
@Dao
interface CrimeDao {

    @Query("SELECT * FROM crime")
    fun getCrimes(): List<Crime>

    @Query("SELECT * FROM crime WHERE id=(:id)")
    fun getCrime(id: UUID): Crime?
}
```

The @Query annotation indicates that **getCrimes()** and **getCrime(UUID)** are meant to pull information out of the database, rather than inserting, updating, or deleting items from the database. The return type of each query function in the DAO interface reflects the type of result the query will return.

The @Query annotation expects a string containing a SQL command as input. In most cases you only need to know minimal SQL to use Room, but if you are interested in learning more check out the SQL Syntax section at www.sqlite.org.

SELECT * FROM crime asks Room to pull all columns for all rows in the crime database table. SELECT * FROM crime WHERE id=(:id) asks Room to pull all columns from only the row whose id matches the ID value provided.

With that, the **CrimeDao** is complete, at least for now. In Chapter 12 you will add a function to update an existing crime. In Chapter 14 you will add a function to insert a new crime.

Next, you need to register your DAO class with your database class. Since the **CrimeDao** is an interface, Room will handle generating the concrete version of the class for you. But for that to work, you need to tell your database class to generate an instance of the DAO.

To hook up your DAO, open `CrimeDatabase.kt` and add an abstract function that has **CrimeDao** as the return type.

### Listing 11.8  Registering the DAO in the database (database/CrimeDatabase.kt)

```
@Database(entities = [ Crime::class ], version=1)
@TypeConverters(CrimeTypeConverters::class)
abstract class CrimeDatabase : RoomDatabase() {

    abstract fun crimeDao(): CrimeDao
}
```

Now, when the database is created, Room will generate a concrete implementation of the DAO that you can access. Once you have a reference to the DAO, you can call any of the functions defined on it to interact with your database.

# Accessing the Database Using the Repository Pattern

To access your database, you will use the *repository pattern* recommended by Google in its Guide to App Architecture (`developer.android.com/jetpack/docs/guide`).

A *repository* class encapsulates the logic for accessing data from a single source or a set of sources. It determines how to fetch and store a particular set of data, whether locally in a database or from a remote server. Your UI code will request all the data from the repository, because the UI does not care how the data is actually stored or fetched. Those are implementation details of the repository itself.

Since CriminalIntent is a simpler app, the repository will only handle fetching data from the database.

Create a class called **CrimeRepository** in the `com.bignerdranch.android.criminalintent` package and define a companion object in the class.

### Listing 11.9  Implementing a repository (CrimeRepository.kt)

```
class CrimeRepository private constructor(context: Context) {

    companion object {
        private var INSTANCE: CrimeRepository? = null

        fun initialize(context: Context) {
            if (INSTANCE == null) {
                INSTANCE = CrimeRepository(context)
            }
        }

        fun get(): CrimeRepository {
            return INSTANCE ?:
            throw IllegalStateException("CrimeRepository must be initialized")
        }
    }
}
```

**CrimeRepository** is a *singleton*. This means there will only ever be one instance of it in your app process.

A singleton exists as long as the application stays in memory, so storing any properties on the singleton will keep them available throughout any lifecycle changes in your activities and fragments. Be careful with singleton classes, as they are destroyed when Android removes your application from memory. The **CrimeRepository** singleton is not a solution for long-term storage of data. Instead, it gives the app an owner for the crime data and provides a way to easily pass that data between controller classes.

To make **CrimeRepository** a singleton, you add two functions to its companion object. One initializes a new instance of the repository, and the other accesses the repository. You also mark the constructor as private to ensure no components can go rogue and create their own instance.

The getter function is not very nice if you have not called **initialize()** before it. It will throw an **IllegalStateException**, so you need to make sure that you initialize your repository when your application is starting.

To do work as soon as your application is ready, you can create an **Application** subclass. This allows you to access lifecycle information about the application itself. Create a class called **CriminalIntentApplication** that extends **Application** and override **Application.onCreate()** to set up the repository initialization.

## Listing 11.10  Creating an application subclass (CriminalIntentApplication.kt)

```kotlin
class CriminalIntentApplication : Application() {

    override fun onCreate() {
        super.onCreate()
        CrimeRepository.initialize(this)
    }
}
```

Similar to **Activity.onCreate(…)**, **Application.onCreate()** is called by the system when your application is first loaded in to memory. That makes it a good place to do any kind of one-time initialization operations.

The application instance does not get constantly destroyed and re-created, like your activity or fragment classes. It is created when the app launches and destroyed when your app process is destroyed. The only lifecycle function you will override in CriminalIntent is **onCreate()**.

In a moment, you are going to pass the application instance to your repository as a **Context** object. This object is valid as long as your application process is in memory, so it is safe to hold a reference to it in the repository class.

But in order for your application class to be used by the system, you need to register it in your manifest. Open `AndroidManifest.xml` and specify the `android:name` property to set up your application.

## Listing 11.11 Hooking up the application subclass (manifests/AndroidManifest.xml)

```
<manifest xmlns:android="http://schemas.android.com/apk/res/android"
        package="com.bignerdranch.android.criminalintent">

    <application
            android:name=".CriminalIntentApplication"
            android:allowBackup="true"
            ... >
    ...
    </application>

</manifest>
```

With the application class registered in the manifest, the OS will create an instance of **CriminalIntentApplication** when launching your app. The OS will then call **onCreate()** on the **CriminalIntentApplication** instance. Your **CrimeRepository** will be initialized, and you can access it from your other components.

Next, add two properties on your **CrimeRepository** to store references to your database and DAO objects.

## Listing 11.12 Setting up repository properties (CrimeRepository.kt)

```
private const val DATABASE_NAME = "crime-database"

class CrimeRepository private constructor(context: Context) {

    private val database : CrimeDatabase = Room.databaseBuilder(
        context.applicationContext,
        CrimeDatabase::class.java,
        DATABASE_NAME
    ).build()

    private val crimeDao = database.crimeDao()

    companion object {
        ...
    }
}
```

**Room.databaseBuilder()** creates a concrete implementation of your abstract **CrimeDatabase** using three parameters. It first needs a **Context** object, since the database is accessing the filesystem. You pass in the application context because, as discussed above, the singleton will most likely live longer than any of your activity classes.

The second parameter is the database class that you want Room to create. The third is the name of the database file you want Room to create for you. You are using a private string constant defined in the same file, since no other components need to access it.

Next, fill out your **CrimeRepository** so your other components can perform any operations they need to on your database. Add a function to your repository for each function in your DAO.

## Listing 11.13  Adding repository functions (`CrimeRepository.kt`)

```
class CrimeRepository private constructor(context: Context) {

    ...
    private val crimeDao = database.crimeDao()

    fun getCrimes(): List<Crime> = crimeDao.getCrimes()

    fun getCrime(id: UUID): Crime? = crimeDao.getCrime(id)

    companion object {
        ...
    }
}
```

Since Room provides the query implementations in the DAO, you call through to those implementations from your repository. This helps keep your repository code short and easy to understand.

This may seem like a lot of work for little gain, since the repository is just calling through to functions on your **CrimeDao**. But fear not; you will be adding functionality soon to encapsulate additional work the repository needs to handle.

# Testing Queries

With your repository in place, there is one last step before you can test your query functions. Currently, your database is empty, because you have not added any crimes to it. To speed things up, you will upload existing database files to your emulator to populate your database. The database files have been provided for you in the solutions file for this chapter (`www.bignerdranch.com/solutions/ AndroidProgramming4e.zip`).

You could programmatically generate and insert dummy data into the database, like the 100 dummy crimes you have been using. However, you have not yet implemented a DAO function to insert new database entries (you will do so in Chapter 14). Uploading a preexisting database file allows you to easily seed the database without altering your app's code unnecessarily. Plus, it gives you practice using the Device File Explorer to view the contents of your emulator's local storage system.

Having said that, there is one drawback to this method of testing. You can only access your app's private files (where the database files are located) when you are on an emulator (or a "rooted" device). You cannot upload the database files to a typical physical device.

# Uploading test data

Each application on an Android device has a directory in the device's *sandbox*. Keeping files in the sandbox protects them from being accessed by other applications or even the prying eyes of users (unless the device has been rooted, in which case the user can get to whatever they like).

An application's sandbox directory is a child of the device's data/data directory named after the application package. For CriminalIntent, the full path to the sandbox directory is data/data/com.bignerdranch.android.criminalintent.

To upload the files, make sure the emulator is running and open the Device File Explorer toolbar window in Android Studio by clicking its tab in the bottom right of the window. The file explorer pane will show all of the files currently on the emulator (Figure 11.2).

Figure 11.2  Device File Explorer window

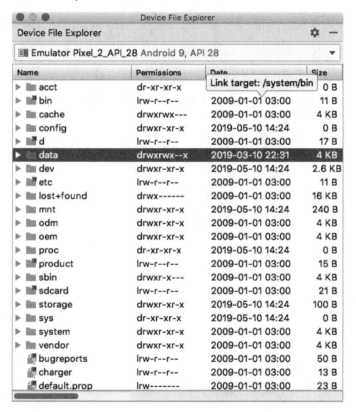

To find the folder for CriminalIntent, open the data/data/ folder and find the subfolder with the name matching the package ID of the project (Figure 11.3). Files in this folder are private to your app by default, so no other apps can read them. This is where you will upload the database files.

## Figure 11.3  App sandbox folder

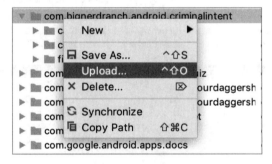

To upload the databases folder, right-click on the package-name folder and select Upload... (Figure 11.4).

## Figure 11.4  Uploading database files

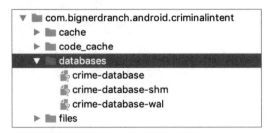

This will show you a file navigator where you can select the files to upload. Navigate to the solutions folder for this chapter. Make sure you upload the entire databases folder. Room needs the files to be in a folder called databases, or it will not work. When you finish the upload, your app sandbox folder should look like Figure 11.5.

## Figure 11.5  Uploaded database files

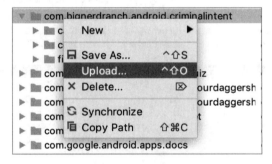

With your database files uploaded, you now have data you can query using your repository. Currently, your `CrimeListViewModel` creates 100 fake crimes to display in the list. Remove the code that generates the fake crimes and replace it with a call to the `getCrimes()` function on your `CrimeRepository`.

## Listing 11.14 Accessing the repository in **ViewModel** (CrimeListViewModel.kt)

```
class CrimeListViewModel : ViewModel() {

    val crimes = mutableListOf<Crime>()

    init {
        for (i in 0 until 100) {
            val crime = Crime()
            crime.title = "Crime #$i"
            crime.isSolved = i % 2 == 0
            crimes += crime
        }
    }

    private val crimeRepository = CrimeRepository.get()
    val crimes = crimeRepository.getCrimes()
}
```

Now, run your app to see the outcome. You may be surprised to find … your app crashes.

Do not worry, this is the expected behavior. (At least, it is what *we* expected. Sorry.) Take a look at the exception in Logcat to see what happened.

```
java.lang.IllegalStateException: Cannot access database on the main thread since
it may potentially lock the UI for a long period of time.
```

This error originates from the Room library. Room is unhappy with your attempt to access the database on the main thread. Throughout the remainder of this chapter, you will learn about the threading model Android uses, as well as the purpose of the main thread and considerations for the type of work you run on the main thread. Additionally, you will move your database interactions to a background thread. That will make Room happy and get rid of the exception, which will in turn fix the crash.

# Application Threads

Reading from the database does not happen immediately. Because access can take so long, Room disallows all database operations on the main thread. If you try to violate this rule, Room will throw the **IllegalStateException** you have just seen.

Why? To understand that, you need to understand what a thread is, what the main thread is, and what the main thread does.

A thread is a single sequence of execution. Code running within a single thread will execute one step after another. Every Android app starts life with a *main thread*. The main thread, however, is not a preordained list of steps. Instead, it sits in an infinite loop and waits for events initiated by the user or the system. Then it executes code in response to those events as they occur (Figure 11.6).

## Figure 11.6  Regular threads vs the main thread

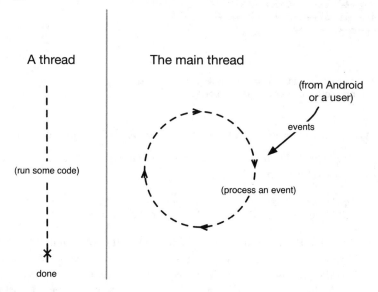

Imagine that your app is an enormous shoe store and that you only have one employee – The Flash. (Who hasn't dreamed of that?) There are a lot of things to do in a store to keep the customers happy: arranging the merchandise, fetching shoes for customers, wielding the Brannock device. The Flash is so fast that everyone is taken care of in a timely fashion, even though there is only one guy doing all the work.

For this situation to work, The Flash cannot spend too much time doing any one thing. What if a shipment of shoes goes missing? Someone will have to spend a lot of time on the phone straightening it out. Your customers will get mighty impatient waiting for shoes while The Flash is on hold.

The Flash is like the main thread in your application. It runs all the code that updates the UI. This includes the code executed in response to different UI-related events – activity startup, button presses, and so on. (Because the events are all related to the UI in some way, the main thread is sometimes called the *UI thread*.)

The event loop keeps the UI code in sequence. It makes sure that none of these operations step on each other, while still ensuring that the code is executed in a timely fashion. So far, all of the code you have written has been executed on the main thread.

# Background threads

Database access is a lot like a phone call to your shoe distributor: It takes a long time compared to other tasks. During that time, the UI will be completely unresponsive, which might result in an *application not responding*, or ANR.

An ANR occurs when Android's watchdog determines that the main thread has failed to respond to an important event, like pressing the Back button. To the user, it looks like Figure 11.7.

## Figure 11.7 Application not responding

In your store, you would solve the problem by (naturally) hiring a second Flash to call the shoe distributor. In Android, you do something similar – you create a *background thread* and access the database from there.

There are two important rules to consider when you start adding background threads to your apps:

- *All long-running tasks should be done on a background thread.* This ensures that your main thread is free to handle UI-related tasks to keep the UI responsive for your users.

- *The UI can only be updated from the main thread.* You will get an error if you try to modify the UI from a background thread, so you need to make sure any data generated from a background thread is sent to the main thread to update the UI.

There are many ways to execute work on a background thread on Android. You will learn how to make asynchronous network requests in Chapter 24, use **Handler**s to perform many small background operations in Chapter 25, and perform periodic background work with WorkManager in Chapter 27.

For CriminalIntent, you will use two options to execute your database calls in the background. In this chapter you will use **LiveData** to wrap your query data. In Chapter 12 and Chapter 14 you will use **Executor** to insert and update data.

# Using LiveData

**LiveData** is a data holder class found in the Jetpack `lifecycle-extensions` library. Room is built to work with **LiveData**. Since you already included the `lifecycle-extensions` library in your `app/build.gradle` file in Chapter 4, you have access to the **LiveData** class in your project.

**LiveData**'s goal is to simplify passing data between different parts of your application, such as from your **CrimeRepository** to the fragment that needs to display the crime data. **LiveData** also enables passing data between threads. This makes it a perfect fit for respecting the threading rules we laid out above.

When you configure queries in your Room DAO to return **LiveData**, Room will automatically execute those query operations on a background thread and then publish the results to the **LiveData** object when the query is done. You can set your activity or fragment up to observe the **LiveData** object, in which case your activity or fragment will be notified on the main thread of results when they are ready.

In this chapter, you will focus on using the cross-thread communication functionality of **LiveData** to perform your database queries. To begin, open `CrimeDao.kt` and update the return type of your query functions to return a **LiveData** object that wraps the original return type.

### Listing 11.15  Returning **LiveData** in the DAO (database/CrimeDao.kt)

```kotlin
@Dao
interface CrimeDao {

    @Query("SELECT * FROM crime")
    fun getCrimes(): List<Crime>
    fun getCrimes(): LiveData<List<Crime>>

    @Query("SELECT * FROM crime WHERE id=(:id)")
    fun getCrime(id: UUID): Crime?
    fun getCrime(id: UUID): LiveData<Crime?>
}
```

By returning an instance of **LiveData** from your DAO class, you signal Room to run your query on a background thread. When the query completes, the **LiveData** object will handle sending the crime data over to the main thread and notify any observers.

Next, update **CrimeRepository** to return **LiveData** from its query functions.

### Listing 11.16  Returning **LiveData** from the repository (CrimeRepository.kt)

```kotlin
class CrimeRepository private constructor(context: Context) {
    ...
    private val crimeDao = database.crimeDao()

    fun getCrimes(): List<Crime> = crimeDao.getCrimes()
    fun getCrimes(): LiveData<List<Crime>> = crimeDao.getCrimes()

    fun getCrime(id: UUID): Crime? = crimeDao.getCrime(id)
    fun getCrime(id: UUID): LiveData<Crime?> = crimeDao.getCrime(id)
    ...
}
```

# Observing LiveData

To display the crimes from the database in the crime list screen, update **CrimeListFragment** to observe the **LiveData** returned from **CrimeRepository.getCrimes()**.

First, open CrimeListViewModel.kt and rename the crimes property so it is more clear what data the property holds.

## Listing 11.17  Accessing the repository in the **ViewModel** (CrimeListViewModel.kt)

```
class CrimeListViewModel : ViewModel() {

    private val crimeRepository = CrimeRepository.get()
    val crimes crimeListLiveData = crimeRepository.getCrimes()
}
```

Next, clean up **CrimeListFragment** to reflect the fact that **CrimeListViewModel** now exposes the **LiveData** returned from your repository (Listing 11.18). Remove the **onCreate(…)** implementation, since it references crimeListViewModel.crimes, which no longer exists (and since you no longer need the logging you put in place there). In **updateUI()**, remove the reference to crimeListViewModel.crimes and add a parameter to accept a list of crimes as input.

Finally, remove the call to **updateUI()** from **onCreateView(…)**. You will implement a call to **updateUI()** from another place shortly.

## Listing 11.18  Removing references to the old version of **ViewModel** (CrimeListFragment.kt)

```
private const val TAG = "CrimeListFragment"

class CrimeListFragment : Fragment() {
    ...
    override fun onCreate(savedInstanceState: Bundle?) {
        super.onCreate(savedInstanceState)
        Log.d(TAG, "Total crimes: ${crimeListViewModel.crimes.size}")
    }
    ...
    override fun onCreateView(
        ...
    ): View? {
        ...
        crimeRecyclerView.layoutManager = LinearLayoutManager(context)

        updateUI()

        return view
    }

    private fun updateUI() {
    private fun updateUI(crimes: List<Crime>) {
        val crimes = crimeListViewModel.crimes
        adapter = CrimeAdapter(crimes)
        crimeRecyclerView.adapter = adapter
    }
    ...
}
```

Now, update **CrimeListFragment** to observe the **LiveData** that wraps the list of crimes returned from the database. Since the fragment will have to wait for results from the database before it can populate the recycler view with crimes, initialize the recycler view adapter with an empty crime list to start. Then set up the recycler view adapter with the new list of crimes when new data is published to the **LiveData**.

## Listing 11.19 Hooking up the **RecyclerView** (CrimeListFragment.kt)

```kotlin
private const val TAG = "CrimeListFragment"

class CrimeListFragment : Fragment() {

    private lateinit var crimeRecyclerView: RecyclerView
    private var adapter: CrimeAdapter? = null
    private var adapter: CrimeAdapter? = CrimeAdapter(emptyList())
    ...
    override fun onCreateView(
        ...
    ): View? {
        ...
        crimeRecyclerView.layoutManager = LinearLayoutManager(context)
        crimeRecyclerView.adapter = adapter
        return view
    }

    override fun onViewCreated(view: View, savedInstanceState: Bundle?) {
        super.onViewCreated(view, savedInstanceState)
        crimeListViewModel.crimeListLiveData.observe(
            viewLifecycleOwner,
            Observer { crimes ->
                crimes?.let {
                    Log.i(TAG, "Got crimes ${crimes.size}")
                    updateUI(crimes)
                }
            })
    }
    ...
}
```

The **LiveData.observe(LifecycleOwner, Observer)** function is used to register an observer on the **LiveData** instance and tie the life of the observation to the life of another component, such as an activity or fragment.

The second parameter to the **observe(…)** function is an **Observer** implementation. This object is responsible for reacting to new data from the **LiveData**. In this case, the observer's code block is executed whenever the **LiveData**'s list of crimes gets updated. The observer receives a list of crimes from the **LiveData** and prints a log statement if the property is not null.

If you never unsubscribe or cancel your **Observer** from listening to the **LiveData**'s changes, your **Observer** implementation might try to update your fragment's view when the view is in an invalid state (such as when the view is being torn down). And if you attempt to update an invalid view, your app can crash.

This is where the **LifecycleOwner** parameter to **LiveData.observe(…)** comes in. The lifetime of the **Observer** you provide is scoped to the lifetime of the Android component represented by the **LifecycleOwner** you provide. In the code above, you scope the observer to the life of the fragment's view.

As long as the *lifecycle owner* you scope your observer to is in a valid lifecycle state, the **LiveData** object will notify the observer of any new data coming in. The **LiveData** object will automatically unregister the **Observer** when the associated lifecycle is no longer in a valid state. Because **LiveData** reacts to changes in a lifecycle, it is called a *lifecycle-aware component*. You will learn more about lifecycle-aware components in Chapter 25.

A lifecycle owner is a component that implements the **LifecycleOwner** interface and contains a **Lifecycle** object. A **Lifecycle** is an object that keeps track of an Android lifecycle's current state. (Recall that activities, fragments, views, and even the application process itself all have their own lifecycle.) The lifecycle states, such as created and resumed, are enumerated in **Lifecycle.State**. You can query a **Lifecycle**'s state using **Lifecycle.getCurrentState()** or register to be notified of changes in state.

The AndroidX **Fragment** is a lifecycle owner directly – **Fragment** implements **LifecycleOwner** and has a **Lifecycle** object representing the state of the fragment instance's lifecycle.

A fragment's view lifecycle is owned and tracked separately by **FragmentViewLifecycleOwner**. Each **Fragment** has an instance of **FragmentViewLifecycleOwner** that keeps track of the lifecycle of that fragment's view.

In the code above, you scope the observation to the fragment's view lifecycle, rather than the lifecycle of the fragment itself, by passing the viewLifecycleOwner to the observe(…) function. The fragment's view lifecycle, though separate from the lifecycle of the **Fragment** instance itself, mirrors the lifecycle of the fragment. It is possible to change this default behavior by *retaining* the fragment (which you will not do in CriminalIntent). You will learn more about the view lifecycle and retaining fragments in Chapter 25.

**Fragment.onViewCreated(…)** is called after **Fragment.onCreateView(…)** returns, signaling that the fragment's view hierarchy is in place. You observe the **LiveData** from **onViewCreated(…)** to ensure that your view is ready to display the crime data. This is also the reason you pass the viewLifecycleOwner to the **observe()** function, rather than the fragment itself. You only want to receive the list of crimes while your view is in a good state, so using the view's lifecycle owner ensures that you will not receive updates when your view is not on the screen.

When the list of crimes is ready, the observer you defined prints a log message and sends the list to the **updateUI()** function to prepare the adapter.

With everything in place, run CriminalIntent. You should no longer see the crash you saw earlier. Instead, you should see the fake crimes from the database file you uploaded to your emulator (Figure 11.8).

## Figure 11.8 Database crimes

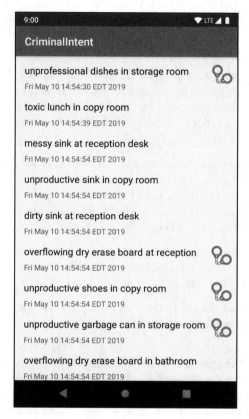

In the next chapter you will connect the crime list and crime detail screens and populate the crime detail screen with data for the crime you clicked on from the database.

# Challenge: Addressing the Schema Warning

If you look through your build logs, you will find a warning about your app not providing a schema export directory:

```
warning: Schema export directory is not provided to the annotation processor
so we cannot export the schema. You can either provide `room.schemaLocation`
annotation processor argument OR set exportSchema to false.
```

A database *schema* represents the structure of the database, including what tables are in the database, what columns are in those tables, and any constraints on and relationships between those tables. Room supports exporting your database schema into a file so you can store it in a source control. Exporting your schema is often useful so that you have a versioned history of your database.

The warning you see means that you are not providing a file location where Room can save your database schema. You can either provide a schema location to the @Database annotation, or you can disable the export to remove the warning. For this challenge, resolve the schema warning by choosing one of these options.

To provide a location for the export, you provide a path for the annotation processor's room.schemaLocation property. To do this, add the following kapt{} block to your app/build.gradle file:

```
...
android {
    ...
    buildTypes {
        ...
    }
    kapt {
        arguments {
            arg("room.schemaLocation", "some/path/goes/here/")
        }
    }
}
...
```

To disable the export, set exportSchema to false:

```
@Database(entities = [ Crime::class ], version=1, exportSchema = false)
@TypeConverters(CrimeTypeConverters::class)
abstract class CrimeDatabase : RoomDatabase() {

    abstract fun crimeDao(): CrimeDao
}
```

# For the More Curious: Singletons

The singleton pattern, as used in the **CrimeRepository**, is very common in Android. Singletons get a bad rap because they can be misused in a way that makes an app hard to maintain.

Singletons are often used in Android because they outlive a single fragment or activity. A singleton will still exist across rotation and will exist as you move between activities and fragments in your application.

Singletons also make a convenient owner of your model objects. Imagine a more complex CriminalIntent application with many activities and fragments modifying crimes. When one controller modifies a crime, how would you make sure that updated crime was sent over to the other controllers?

If the **CrimeRepository** is the owner of crimes and all modifications to crimes pass through it, propagating changes is much easier. As you transition between controllers, you can pass the crime ID as an identifier for a particular crime and have each controller pull the full crime object from the **CrimeRepository** using that ID.

However, singletons do have a few downsides. For example, while they allow for an easy place to stash data with a longer lifetime than a controller, singletons do have a lifetime. Singletons will be destroyed, along with all of their instance variables, as Android reclaims memory at some point after you switch out of an application. Singletons are not a long-term storage solution. (Writing the files to disk or sending them to a web server is.)

Singletons can also make your code hard to unit test (you will learn more about unit testing in Chapter 20). There is not a great way to replace the **CrimeRepository** instance in this chapter with a mock version of itself. In practice, Android developers usually solve this problem using a tool called a *dependency injector*. This tool allows for objects to be shared as singletons, while still making it possible to replace them when needed. To learn more about dependency injection, read the section called For the More Curious: Managing Dependencies in Chapter 24.

And, as we said, singletons have the potential to be misused. It can be tempting to use singletons for everything, because they are convenient – you can get to them wherever you are, and you can store in them whatever information you need to get at later. But when you do that, you are avoiding answering important questions: Where is this data used? Where is this function important?

A singleton does not answer those questions. So whoever comes after you will open up your singleton and find something that looks like somebody's disorganized junk drawer. Batteries, zip ties, old photographs? What is all this here for? Make sure that anything in your singleton is truly global and has a strong reason for being there.

On balance, singletons are a key component of a well-architected Android app – when used correctly.

# 12

# Fragment Navigation

In this chapter, you will get the list and the detail parts of CriminalIntent working together. When a user presses an item in the list of crimes, **MainActivity** will swap out **CrimeListFragment** with a new instance of **CrimeFragment**. **CrimeFragment** will display the details for the crime that was pressed (Figure 12.1).

Figure 12.1  Swapping **CrimeListFragment** for **CrimeFragment**

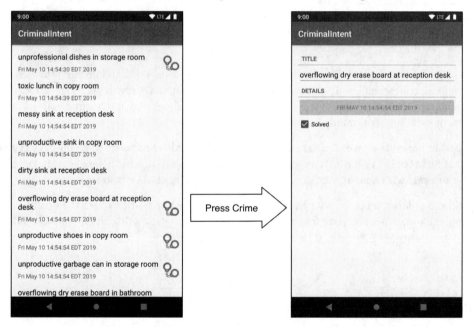

To get this working you will learn how to implement navigation by having the hosting activity change out fragments in response to user actions. You will also learn how to pass data to a fragment instance using *fragment arguments*. Finally, you will learn how to use **LiveData** *transformations* to load immutable data in response to UI changes.

# Single Activity: Fragment Boss

In GeoQuiz, you had one activity (**MainActivity**) start another activity (**CheatActivity**). In CriminalIntent, you are instead going to use a *single activity architecture*. An app that uses single activity architecture has one activity and multiple fragments. The activity's job is to swap fragments in and out in response to user events.

To implement the navigation from **CrimeListFragment** to **CrimeFragment** in response to the user pressing on a crime in the list, you might think to initiate a fragment transaction on the hosting activity's fragment manager in **CrimeListFragment**'s **CrimeHolder.onClick(View)**. This **onClick(View)** would get **MainActivity**'s **FragmentManager** and commit a fragment transaction that replaces **CrimeListFragment** with **CrimeFragment**.

The code in your **CrimeListFragment.CrimeHolder** would look like this:

```
fun onClick(view: View) {
    val fragment = CrimeFragment.newInstance(crime.id)
    val fm = activity.supportFragmentManager
    fm.beginTransaction()
        .replace(R.id.fragment_container, fragment)
        .commit()
}
```

This works, but it is not how stylish Android programmers do things. Fragments are intended to be standalone, composable units. If you write a fragment that adds fragments to the activity's **FragmentManager**, then that fragment is making assumptions about how the hosting activity works, and your fragment is no longer a standalone, composable unit.

For example, in the code above, **CrimeListFragment** adds a **CrimeFragment** to **MainActivity** and assumes that **MainActivity** has a fragment_container in its layout. This is business that should be handled by **CrimeListFragment**'s hosting activity instead of **CrimeListFragment**.

To maintain the independence of your fragments, you will delegate work back to the hosting activity by defining callback interfaces in your fragments. The hosting activities will implement these interfaces to perform fragment-bossing duties and layout-dependent behavior.

## Fragment callback interfaces

To delegate functionality back to the hosting activity, a fragment typically defines a custom callback interface named **Callbacks**. This interface defines work that the fragment needs done by its boss, the hosting activity. Any activity that will host the fragment must implement this interface.

With a callback interface, a fragment is able to call functions on its hosting activity without having to know anything about which activity is hosting it.

Use a callback interface to delegate on-click events from **CrimeListFragment** back to its hosting activity. First, open **CrimeListFragment** and define a **Callbacks** interface with a single callback function. Add a callbacks property to hold an object that implements **Callbacks**. Override **onAttach(Context)** and **onDetach()** to set and unset the callbacks property.

## Listing 12.1 Adding a callback interface (CrimeListFragment.kt)

```kotlin
class CrimeListFragment : Fragment() {

    /**
     * Required interface for hosting activities
     */
    interface Callbacks {
        fun onCrimeSelected(crimeId: UUID)
    }

    private var callbacks: Callbacks? = null

    private lateinit var crimeRecyclerView: RecyclerView
    private var adapter: CrimeAdapter = CrimeAdapter(emptyList())
    private val crimeListViewModel: CrimeListViewModel by lazy {
        ViewModelProviders.of(this).get(CrimeListViewModel::class.java)
    }

    override fun onAttach(context: Context) {
        super.onAttach(context)
        callbacks = context as Callbacks?
    }

    override fun onCreateView(
        ...
    ): View? {
        ...
    }

    override fun onViewCreated(view: View, savedInstanceState: Bundle?) {
        ...
    }

    override fun onDetach() {
        super.onDetach()
        callbacks = null
    }
    ...
}
```

The **Fragment.onAttach(Context)** lifecycle function is called when a fragment is attached to an activity. Here you stash the **Context** argument passed to **onAttach(…)** in your callbacks property. Since **CrimeListFragment** is hosted in an activity, the **Context** object passed to **onAttach(…)** is the activity instance hosting the fragment.

Remember, **Activity** is a subclass of **Context**, so **onAttach(…)** passes a **Context** as a parameter, which is more flexible. Ensure that you use the **onAttach(Context)** signature for **onAttach(…)** and not the deprecated **onAttach(Activity)** function, which may be removed in future versions of the API.

Similarly, you set the variable to null in the corresponding waning lifecycle function, **Fragment.onDetach()**. You set the variable to null here because afterward you cannot access the activity or count on the activity continuing to exist.

Note that **CrimeListFragment** performs an unchecked cast of its activity to **CrimeListFragment.Callbacks**. This means that the hosting activity *must* implement **CrimeListFragment.Callbacks**. That is not a bad dependency to have, but it is important to document it.

Now **CrimeListFragment** has a way to call functions on its hosting activity. It does not matter which activity is doing the hosting. As long as the activity implements **CrimeListFragment.Callbacks**, everything in **CrimeListFragment** can work the same.

Next, update the click listener for individual items in the crime list so that pressing a crime notifies the hosting activity via the **Callbacks** interface. Call **onCrimeSelected(Crime)** in **CrimeHolder.onClick(View)**.

## Listing 12.2  Calling all callbacks! (CrimeListFragment.kt)

```
class CrimeListFragment : Fragment() {
    ...
    private inner class CrimeHolder(view: View)
        : RecyclerView.ViewHolder(view), View.OnClickListener {
        ...
        fun bind(crime: Crime) {
            ...
        }

        override fun onClick(v: View?) {
            Toast.makeText(context, "${crime.title} clicked!", Toast.LENGTH_SHORT)
                .show()
            callbacks?.onCrimeSelected(crime.id)
        }
    }
    ...
}
```

Finally, update **MainActivity** to implement **CrimeListFragment.Callbacks**. Log a debug statement in **onCrimeSelected(UUID)** for now.

## Listing 12.3  Implementing callbacks (MainActivity.kt)

```
private const val TAG = "MainActivity"
class MainActivity : AppCompatActivity(),
    CrimeListFragment.Callbacks {

    override fun onCreate(savedInstanceState: Bundle?) {
        ...
    }

    override fun onCrimeSelected(crimeId: UUID) {
        Log.d(TAG, "MainActivity.onCrimeSelected: $crimeId")
    }
}
```

Run CriminalIntent. Search or filter Logcat to view **MainActivity**'s log statements. Each time you press a crime in the list you should see a log statement indicating the click event was propagated from **CrimeListFragment** to **MainActivity** through **Callbacks.onCrimeSelected(UUID)**.

# Replacing a fragment

Now that your callback interface is wired up correctly, update **MainActivity**'s
**onCrimeSelected(UUID)** to swap out the **CrimeListFragment** with an instance of **CrimeFragment**
when the user presses a crime in **CrimeListFragment**'s list. For now, ignore the crime ID passed to the
callback.

## Listing 12.4  Replacing **CrimeListFragment** with **CrimeFragment** (MainActivity.kt)

```kotlin
class MainActivity : AppCompatActivity(),
    CrimeListFragment.Callbacks {

    override fun onCreate(savedInstanceState: Bundle?) {
        ...
    }

    override fun onCrimeSelected(crimeId: UUID) {
        Log.d(TAG, "MainActivity.onCrimeSelected: $crimeId")
        val fragment = CrimeFragment()
        supportFragmentManager
            .beginTransaction()
            .replace(R.id.fragment_container, fragment)
            .commit()
    }
}
```

**FragmentTransaction.replace(Int, Fragment)** replaces the fragment hosted in the activity (in
the container with the integer resource ID specified) with the new fragment provided. If a fragment
is not already hosted in the container specified, the new fragment is added, just as if you had called
**FragmentTransaction.add(Int, fragment)**.

Run CriminalIntent. Press a crime in the list. You should see the crime detail screen appear (Figure 12.2).

## Figure 12.2  A blank **CrimeFragment**

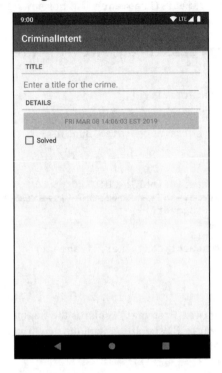

For now, the crime detail screen is empty, because you have not told **CrimeFragment** which **Crime** to display. You will populate the detail screen shortly. But first, you need to file down a remaining sharp edge in your navigation implementation.

Press the Back button. This dismisses **MainActivity**. This is because the only item in your app's back stack is the **MainActivity** instance that was launched when you launched the app.

Users will expect that pressing the Back button from the crime detail screen will bring them back to the crime list. To implement this behavior, add the replace transaction to the back stack.

## Listing 12.5  Adding fragment transaction to the back stack (**MainActivity.kt**)

```
class MainActivity : AppCompatActivity(),
    CrimeListFragment.Callbacks {
    ...
    override fun onCrimeSelected(crimeId: UUID) {
        val fragment = CrimeFragment()
        supportFragmentManager
            .beginTransaction()
            .replace(R.id.fragment_container, fragment)
            .addToBackStack(null)
            .commit()
    }
}
```

When you add a transaction to the back stack, this means that when the user presses the Back button the transaction will be reversed. So, in this case, **CrimeFragment** will be replaced with **CrimeListFragment**.

You can name the back stack state you are adding by passing a String to **FragmentTransaction.addToBackStack(String)**. Doing so is optional and, since you do not care about the name in this implementation, you pass null.

Run your app. Select a crime from the list to launch **CrimeFragment**. Press the Back button to go back to **CrimeListFragment**. Enjoy the simple pleasure of your app's navigation matching what users will expect.

# Fragment Arguments

**CrimeListFragment** now notifies its hosting activity (**MainActivity**) when a crime is selected and passes along the ID of the selected crime.

That is all fine and dandy. But what you really need is a way to pass the selected crime ID from **MainActivity** to **CrimeFragment**. This way, **CrimeFragment** can pull data for that crime from the database and populate the UI with that data.

Fragment arguments offer a solution to this problem – they allow you to stash pieces of data someplace that belongs to the fragment. The "someplace" that belongs to a fragment is known as its *arguments bundle*. The fragment can retrieve data from the arguments bundle without relying on its parent activity or some other outside source.

Fragment arguments help you keep your fragment encapsulated. A well-encapsulated fragment is a reusable building block that can easily be hosted in any activity.

To create fragment arguments, you first create a **Bundle** object. This bundle contains key-value pairs that work just like the intent extras of an **Activity**. Each pair is known as an argument. Next, you use type-specific "put" functions of **Bundle** (similar to those of **Intent**) to add arguments to the bundle:

```
val args = Bundle().apply {
  putSerializable(ARG_MY_OBJECT, myObject)
  putInt(ARG_MY_INT, myInt)
  putCharSequence(ARG_MY_STRING, myString)
}
```

Every fragment instance can have a fragment arguments **Bundle** object attached to it.

# Attaching arguments to a fragment

To attach the arguments bundle to a fragment, you call **Fragment.setArguments(Bundle)**. Attaching arguments to a fragment must be done after the fragment is created but before it is added to an activity.

To accomplish this, Android programmers follow a convention of adding a companion object that contains the **newInstance(…)** function to the **Fragment** class. This function creates the fragment instance and bundles up and sets its arguments.

When the hosting activity needs an instance of that fragment, you have it call the **newInstance(…)** function rather than calling the constructor directly. The activity can pass in any required parameters to **newInstance(…)** that the fragment needs to create its arguments.

In **CrimeFragment**, write a **newInstance(UUID)** function that accepts a **UUID**, creates an arguments bundle, creates a fragment instance, and then attaches the arguments to the fragment.

### Listing 12.6 Writing a **newInstance(UUID)** function (CrimeFragment.kt)

```
private const val ARG_CRIME_ID = "crime_id"

class CrimeFragment : Fragment() {
    ...
    override fun onStart() {
        ...
    }

    companion object {

        fun newInstance(crimeId: UUID): CrimeFragment {
            val args = Bundle().apply {
                putSerializable(ARG_CRIME_ID, crimeId)
            }
            return CrimeFragment().apply {
                arguments = args
            }
        }
    }
}
```

Update **MainActivity** to call **CrimeFragment.newInstance(UUID)** when it needs to create a **CrimeFragment**. Pass along the **UUID** that was received in **MainActivity.onCrimeSelected(UUID)**.

### Listing 12.7 Using **CrimeFragment.newInstance(UUID)** (MainActivity.kt)

```
class MainActivity : AppCompatActivity(),
    CrimeListFragment.Callbacks {
    ...
    override fun onCrimeSelected(crimeId: UUID) {
        val fragment = CrimeFragment()
        val fragment = CrimeFragment.newInstance(crimeId)
        supportFragmentManager
            .beginTransaction()
            .replace(R.id.fragment_container, fragment)
            .addToBackStack(null)
            .commit()
    }
}
```

Notice that the need for independence does not go both ways. **MainActivity** has to know plenty about **CrimeFragment**, including that it has a **newInstance(UUID)** function. This is fine. Hosting activities should know the specifics of how to host their fragments, but fragments should not have to know specifics about their activities. At least, not if you want to maintain the flexibility of independent fragments.

# Retrieving arguments

To access a fragment's arguments, reference the **Fragment** property named `arguments`. Then use one of the type-specific "get" functions of **Bundle** to pull individual values out of the arguments bundle.

Back in **CrimeFragment.onCreate(…)**, retrieve the **UUID** from the fragment arguments. For now, log the ID so you can verify that the argument was attached as expected.

## Listing 12.8  Getting crime ID from the arguments (`CrimeFragment.kt`)

```kotlin
private const val TAG = "CrimeFragment"
private const val ARG_CRIME_ID = "crime_id"

class CrimeFragment : Fragment() {
    ...
    override fun onCreate(savedInstanceState: Bundle?) {
        super.onCreate(savedInstanceState)
        crime = Crime()
        val crimeId: UUID = arguments?.getSerializable(ARG_CRIME_ID) as UUID
        Log.d(TAG, "args bundle crime ID: $crimeId")
        // Eventually, load crime from database
    }
    ...
}
```

Run CriminalIntent. The app will behave the same, but you should feel all warm and fuzzy inside for passing the crime ID along to **CrimeFragment** while still maintaining **CrimeFragment**'s independence.

# Using LiveData Transformations

Now that **CrimeFragment** has the crime ID, it needs to pull the crime object from the database so it can display the crime's data. Since this requires a database lookup that you do not want to repeat unnecessarily on rotation, add a **CrimeDetailViewModel** to manage the database query.

When **CrimeFragment** requests to load a crime with a given ID, its **CrimeDetailViewModel** should kick off a **getCrime(UUID)** database request. When the request completes, **CrimeDetailViewModel** should notify **CrimeFragment** and pass along the crime object that resulted from the query.

Create a new class named **CrimeDetailViewModel** and expose a **LiveData** property to store and publish the **Crime** pulled from the database. Use **LiveData** to implement a relationship where changing the crime ID triggers a new database query.

Listing 12.9  Adding **ViewModel** for **CrimeFragment**
(CrimeDetailViewModel.kt)

```
class CrimeDetailViewModel() : ViewModel() {

    private val crimeRepository = CrimeRepository.get()
    private val crimeIdLiveData = MutableLiveData<UUID>()

    var crimeLiveData: LiveData<Crime?> =
        Transformations.switchMap(crimeIdLiveData) { crimeId ->
            crimeRepository.getCrime(crimeId)
        }

    fun loadCrime(crimeId: UUID) {
        crimeIdLiveData.value = crimeId
    }
}
```

The crimeRepository property stores a handle to the **CrimeRepository**. This is not necessary, but later on **CrimeDetailViewModel** will communicate with the repository in more than one place, so the property will prove useful at that point.

crimeIdLiveData stores the ID of the crime currently displayed (or about to be displayed) by **CrimeFragment**. When **CrimeDetailViewModel** is first created, the crime ID is not set. Eventually, **CrimeFragment** will call **CrimeDetailViewModel.loadCrime(UUID)** to let the **ViewModel** know which crime it needs to load.

Note that you explicitly defined crimeLiveData's type as **LiveData<Crime?>**. Since crimeLiveData is publicly exposed, you should ensure it is not exposed as a **MutableLiveData**. In general, **ViewModel**s should never expose **MutableLiveData**.

It may seem strange to wrap the crime ID in **LiveData**, since it is private to **CrimeDetailViewModel**. What within this **CrimeDetailViewModel**, you may wonder, needs to listen for changes to the private ID value?

The answer lies in the live data **Transformation** statement. A *live data transformation* is a way to set up a trigger-response relationship between two **LiveData** objects. A transformation function takes two inputs: a **LiveData** object used as a *trigger* and a *mapping function* that must return a **LiveData** object. The transformation function returns a new **LiveData** object, which we call the *transformation result*, whose value gets updated every time a new value gets set on the trigger **LiveData** instance.

The transformation result's value is calculated by executing the mapping function. The value property on the **LiveData** returned from the mapping function is used to set the value property on the live data transformation result.

Using a transformation this way means the **CrimeFragment** only has to observe the exposed CrimeDetailViewModel.crimeLiveData one time. When the fragment changes the ID it wants to display, the **ViewModel** just publishes the new crime data to the existing live data stream.

Open CrimeFragment.kt. Associate **CrimeFragment** with **CrimeDetailViewModel**. Request that the **ViewModel** load the **Crime** in **onCreate(…)**.

## Listing 12.10 Hooking **CrimeFragment** up to **CrimeDetailViewModel** (CrimeFragment.kt)

```
class CrimeFragment : Fragment() {

    private lateinit var crime: Crime
    ...
    private lateinit var solvedCheckBox: CheckBox
    private val crimeDetailViewModel: CrimeDetailViewModel by lazy {
        ViewModelProviders.of(this).get(CrimeDetailViewModel::class.java)
    }

    override fun onCreate(savedInstanceState: Bundle?) {
        super.onCreate(savedInstanceState)
        crime = Crime()
        val crimeId: UUID = arguments?.getSerializable(ARG_CRIME_ID) as UUID
        Log.d(TAG, "args bundle crime ID: $crimeId")
        // Eventually, load crime from database
        crimeDetailViewModel.loadCrime(crimeId)
    }
    ...
}
```

Next, observe **CrimeDetailViewModel**'s crimeLiveData and update the UI any time new data is published.

## Listing 12.11  Observing changes (CrimeFragment.kt)

```
class CrimeFragment : Fragment() {

    private lateinit var crime: Crime
    ...

    override fun onCreateView(
        ...
    ): View? {
        ...
    }

    override fun onViewCreated(view: View, savedInstanceState: Bundle?) {
        super.onViewCreated(view, savedInstanceState)
        crimeDetailViewModel.crimeLiveData.observe(
            viewLifecycleOwner,
            Observer { crime ->
                crime?.let {
                    this.crime = crime
                    updateUI()
                }
            })
    }

    override fun onStart() {
        ...
    }

    private fun updateUI() {
        titleField.setText(crime.title)
        dateButton.text = crime.date.toString()
        solvedCheckBox.isChecked = crime.isSolved
    }
    ...
}
```

(Be sure to import **androidx.lifecycle.Observer**.)

You may have noticed that **CrimeFragment** has its own **Crime** state stored in its crime property. The values in this crime property represent the edits the user is currently making. The crime in CrimeDetailViewModel.crimeLiveData represents the data as it is currently saved in the database. **CrimeFragment** "publishes" the user's edits when the fragment moves to the stopped state by writing the updated data to the database.

Run your app. Press a crime in the list. If all goes as planned, you should see the crime detail screen appear, populated with data from the crime you pressed in the list (Figure 12.3).

## Figure 12.3  CriminalIntent's back stack

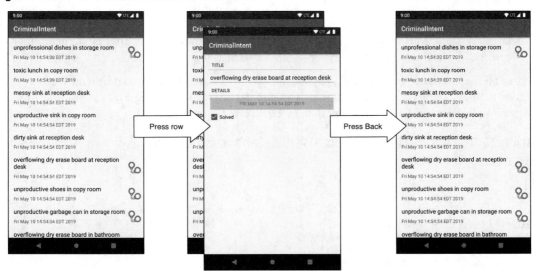

When **CrimeFragment** displays, you may see the checkbox animating to the checked state if you are viewing a crime marked as solved. This is expected, since the checkbox state gets set as the result of an asynchronous operation. The database query for the crime kicks off when the user first launches **CrimeFragment**. When the database query completes, the fragment's crimeDetailViewModel.crimeLiveData observer is notified and in turn updates the data displayed in the widgets.

Clean this up by skipping over the animation when you programmatically set the checkbox checked state. You do this by calling **View.jumpDrawablesToCurrentState()**. Note that if the lag as the crime detail screen loads is unacceptable based on your app's requirements, you could pre-load the crime data into memory ahead of time (as the app launches, for example) and stash it in a shared place. For CriminalIntent, the lag is very slight, so the simple solution of skipping the animation is enough.

## Listing 12.12  Skipping checkbox animation (CrimeFragment.kt)

```
class CrimeFragment : Fragment() {
    ...
    private fun updateUI() {
        titleField.setText(crime.title)
        dateButton.text = crime.date.toString()
        solvedCheckBox.isChecked = crime.isSolved
        solvedCheckBox.apply {
            isChecked = crime.isSolved
            jumpDrawablesToCurrentState()
        }
    }
    ...
}
```

Run your app again. Press a solved crime in the list. Notice the checkbox no longer animates as the screen spins up. If you press the checkbox, the animation does happen, as desired.

Now, edit the crime's title. Press the Back button to go back to the crime list screen. Sadly, the changes you made were not saved. Luckily, this is easy to fix.

# Updating the Database

The database serves as the single source of truth for crime data. In CriminalIntent, when the user leaves the detail screen, any edits they made should be saved to the database. (Other apps might have other requirements, like having a "save" button or saving updates as the user types.)

First, add a function to your **CrimeDao** to update an existing crime. While you are at it, also add a function to insert a new crime. You will mostly ignore the insert function for now, but you will use it in Chapter 14 when you add a menu option to the UI to create new crimes.

## Listing 12.13  Adding update and insert database functions (database/CrimeDao.kt)

```
@Dao
interface CrimeDao {

    @Query("SELECT * FROM crime")
    fun getCrimes(): LiveData<List<Crime>>

    @Query("SELECT * FROM crime WHERE id=(:id)")
    fun getCrime(id: UUID): LiveData<Crime?>

    @Update
    fun updateCrime(crime: Crime)

    @Insert
    fun addCrime(crime: Crime)
}
```

The annotations for these functions do not require any parameters. Room can generate the appropriate SQL command for these operations.

The **updateCrime()** function uses the @Update annotation. This function takes in a crime object, uses the ID stored in that crime to find the associated row, and then updates the data in that row based on the new data in the crime object.

The **addCrime()** function uses the @Insert annotation. The parameter is the crime you want to add to the database table.

Next, update the repository to call through to the new insert and update DAO functions. Recall that Room automatically executes the database queries for **CrimeDao.getCrimes()** and **CrimeDao.getCrime(UUID)** on a background thread because those DAO functions return **LiveData**. In those cases, **LiveData** handles ferrying the data over to your main thread so you can update your UI.

You cannot, however, rely on Room to automatically run your insert and update database interactions on a background thread for you. Instead, you must execute those DAO calls on a background thread explicitly. A common way to do this is to use an *executor*.

# Using an executor

An **Executor** is an object that references a thread. An executor instance has a function called **execute** that accepts a block of code to run. The code you provide in the block will run on whatever thread the executor points to.

You are going to create an executor that uses a new thread (which will always be a background thread). Any code in the block will run on that thread, so you can perform your database operations there safely.

You cannot implement an executor in the **CrimeDao** directly, because Room generates the function implementations for you based on the interface you define. Instead, implement the executor in **CrimeRepository**. Add a property to the executor to hold a reference, then execute your insert and update functions using the executor.

Listing 12.14 Inserting and updating with an executor (`CrimeRepository.kt`)

```
class CrimeRepository private constructor(context: Context) {
    ...
    private val crimeDao = database.crimeDao()
    private val executor = Executors.newSingleThreadExecutor()

    fun getCrimes(): LiveData<List<Crime>> = crimeDao.getCrimes()

    fun getCrime(id: UUID): LiveData<Crime?> = crimeDao.getCrime(id)

    fun updateCrime(crime: Crime) {
        executor.execute {
            crimeDao.updateCrime(crime)
        }
    }

    fun addCrime(crime: Crime) {
        executor.execute {
            crimeDao.addCrime(crime)
        }
    }
    ...
}
```

The **newSingleThreadExecutor()** function returns an executor instance that points to a new thread. Any work you execute with the executor will therefore happen off the main thread.

Both **updateCrime()** and **addCrime()** wrap their calls to the DAO inside the **execute {}** block. This pushes these operations off the main thread so you do not block your UI.

# Tying database writes to the fragment lifecycle

Last but not least, update your app to write the values the user enters in the crime detail screen to the database when the user navigates away from the screen.

Open `CrimeDetailViewModel.kt` and add a function to save a crime object to the database.

Listing 12.15  Adding save capability (`CrimeDetailViewModel.kt`)

```
class CrimeDetailViewModel() : ViewModel() {
    ...
    fun loadCrime(crimeId: UUID) {
        crimeIdLiveData.value = crimeId
    }

    fun saveCrime(crime: Crime) {
        crimeRepository.updateCrime(crime)
    }
}
```

`saveCrime(Crime)` accepts a **Crime** and writes it to the database. Since **CrimeRepository** handles running the update request on a background thread, the database integration here is very simple.

Now, update **CrimeFragment** to save the user's edited crime data to the database.

Listing 12.16  Saving in **onStop()** (`CrimeFragment.kt`)

```
class CrimeFragment : Fragment() {
    ...
    override fun onStart() {
        ...
    }

    override fun onStop() {
        super.onStop()
        crimeDetailViewModel.saveCrime(crime)
    }

    private fun updateUI() {
        ...
    }
    ...
}
```

`Fragment.onStop()` is called any time your fragment moves to the stopped state (that is, any time the fragment moves entirely out of view). This means the data will get saved when the user finishes the detail screen (such as by pressing the Back button). The data will also be saved when the user switches tasks (such as by pressing the Home button or using the overview screen). Thus, saving in `onStop()` meets the requirement of saving the data whenever the user leaves the detail screen and also ensures that, if the process is killed due to memory pressure, the edited data is not lost.

Run CriminalIntent and select a crime from the list. Change data in that crime. Press the Back button and pat yourself on the back for your most recent success: The changes you made on the detail screen are now reflected in the list screen. In the next chapter, you will hook up the date button on the detail screen to allow the user to select the date when the crime occurred.

# For the More Curious: Why Use Fragment Arguments?

In this chapter you added a **newInstance(…)** function to your fragment to pass along arguments when creating a new instance of fragment. While this pattern is helpful from a code organization standpoint, it is also necessary in the case of fragment arguments. You cannot use a constructor to pass arguments to a fragment instance.

For instance, you might consider adding a one-argument constructor to **CrimeFragment** that expects a **UUID** crime ID as input, rather than adding a **newInstance(UUID)** function. However, this approach is flawed. When a configuration change occurs, the current activity's fragment manager automatically re-creates the fragment that was hosted before the configuration change occurred. The fragment manager then adds that new fragment instance to the new activity.

When the fragment manager re-creates the fragment after a configuration change, it calls the fragment's default, parameterless constructor. This means that after rotation, the new fragment instance would not receive the crime ID data.

So how are fragment arguments any different? Fragment arguments are stored across fragment death. The fragment manager reattaches the arguments to the new fragment it re-creates after rotation. That new fragment can then use the arguments bundle to re-create its state.

This all seems so complicated. Why not just set an instance variable on the **CrimeFragment** when it is created?

Because it would not always work. When the OS re-creates your fragment – either across a configuration change or when the user has switched out of your app and the OS reclaims memory – all of your instance variables will be lost. Also, remember that there is no way to cheat low-memory death, no matter how hard you try.

If you want something that works in all cases, you have to persist your arguments.

One option is to use the saved instance state mechanism. You can store the crime ID as a normal instance variable, save the crime ID in **onSaveInstanceState(Bundle)**, and snag it from the **Bundle** in **onCreate(Bundle?)**. This will work in all situations.

However, that solution is hard to maintain. If you revisit this fragment in a few years and add another argument, you may not remember to save the argument in **onSaveInstanceState(Bundle)**. Going this route is less explicit.

Android developers prefer the fragment arguments solution because it is very explicit and clear in its intentions. In a few years, you will come back and know that the crime ID is an argument and is safely shuttled along to new instances of this fragment. If you add another argument, you will know to stash it in the arguments bundle.

# For the More Curious: Navigation Architecture Component Library

As you have seen, there are several ways of navigating users through your app. You can have multiple activities, one for each screen, and start them as the user interacts with your UI. You can also go with a single activity that hosts several fragments that make up your UI instead.

In an effort to simplify app navigation, the Android team introduced the Navigation architecture component library as part of Jetpack. This library simplifies the implementation of your navigation by providing a GUI-based editor where you can configure your navigation flow (Figure 12.4).

## Figure 12.4  Navigation editor

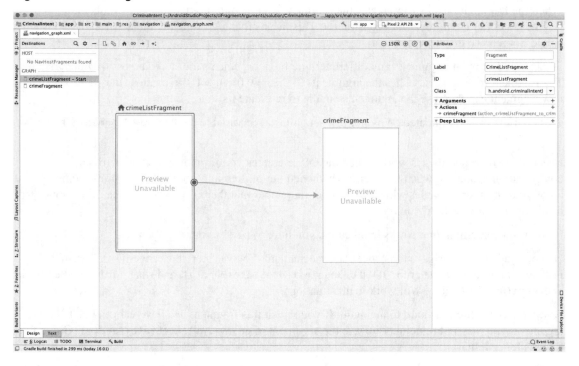

The Navigation library is opinionated about how you should implement navigation in your project. It prefers navigation using fragments with a single activity over using an activity for each screen. You can provide the arguments your fragments need directly in the navigation editor tool.

For a big challenge, create a copy of CriminalIntent and implement the app's navigation using the Navigation architecture component (developer.android.com/topic/libraries/architecture/navigation). The documentation will be very useful on your journey. There are many parts involved, but once your setup is complete it is simple to add new screens to your app and hook up the actions between them.

As of this writing, the stable version of the Navigation architecture component was just officially released. The timing did not allow us to incorporate it into this edition, but this tool has major promise, and we believe it will be the way of the future for many Android developers. We recommend you try it out and see what you think. We are in the process of doing that as well.

# Challenge: Efficient RecyclerView Reloading

Right now, when the user returns to the list screen after editing a single crime, **CrimeListFragment** redraws all of the visible crimes in the recycler view. This is wildly inefficient, because at most one **Crime** will have changed.

Update **CrimeListFragment**'s **RecyclerView** implementation to redraw only the row associated with the changed crime. To do this, update **CrimeAdapter** to extend from **androidx.recyclerview.widget.ListAdapter<Crime, CrimeHolder>** instead of **RecyclerView.Adapter<CrimeHolder>**.

**ListAdapter** is a **RecyclerView.Adapter** that figures out the difference between the current data set backing the recycler view and a new data set you apply to back the recycler view. The comparison happens on a background thread, so it does not slow down the UI. **ListAdapter** in turn tells the recycler view to only redraw rows for data that has changed.

**ListAdapter** uses **androidx.recyclerview.widget.DiffUtil** to determine which parts of the data set have changed. To finish this challenge, you will need to provide a **DiffUtil.ItemCallback<Crime>** implementation to your **ListAdapter**.

You will also need to update **CrimeListFragment** to submit an updated crime list to the recycler view's adapter, rather than reassigning the recycler view's adapter to a new adapter object every time you want to update the UI. You can submit a new list by calling **ListAdapter.submitList(MutableList<T>?)**. Or you can set up **LiveData** and observe the changes.

See the API reference pages for **androidx.recyclerview.widget.DiffUtil** and **androidx.recyclerview.widget.ListAdapter** on developer.android.com/reference/kotlin for more details on how to use these tools.

# 13
# Dialogs

Dialogs demand attention and input from the user. They are useful for presenting a choice or important information. In this chapter, you will add a dialog in which users can change the date of a crime. Pressing the date button in **CrimeFragment** will present this dialog (Figure 13.1).

## Figure 13.1 A dialog for picking the date of a crime

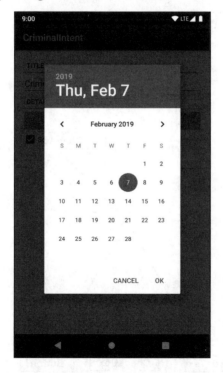

The dialog in Figure 13.1 is an instance of **DatePickerDialog**, a subclass of **AlertDialog**. **DatePickerDialog** displays a date selection prompt to the user and provides a listener interface you can implement to capture the selection. For creating more custom dialogs, **AlertDialog** is the all-purpose **Dialog** subclass that you will use most often.

# Creating a DialogFragment

When displaying a **DatePickerDialog**, it is a good idea to wrap it in an instance of **DialogFragment**, a subclass of **Fragment**. It is possible to display a **DatePickerDialog** without a **DialogFragment**, but it is not recommended. Having the **DatePickerDialog** managed by the **FragmentManager** gives you more options for presenting the dialog.

In addition, a bare **DatePickerDialog** will vanish if the device is rotated. If the **DatePickerDialog** is wrapped in a fragment, then the dialog will be re-created and put back onscreen after rotation.

For CriminalIntent, you are going to create a **DialogFragment** subclass named **DatePickerFragment**. Within **DatePickerFragment**, you will create and configure an instance of **DatePickerDialog**. **DatePickerFragment** will be hosted by **MainActivity**.

Figure 13.2 shows you an overview of these relationships.

Figure 13.2  Object diagram for two fragments hosted by **MainActivity**

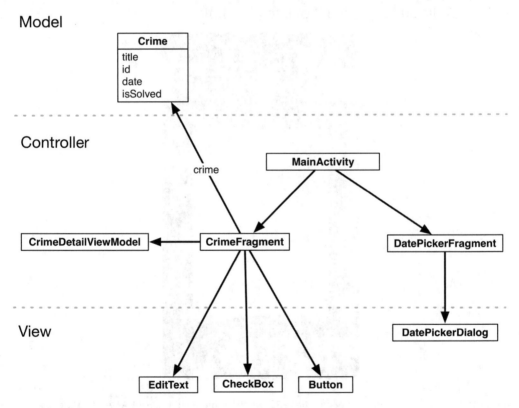

Your first tasks are:

- creating the **DatePickerFragment** class
- building a **DatePickerFragment**
- getting the dialog onscreen via the **FragmentManager**

Later in this chapter, you will pass the necessary data between **CrimeFragment** and **DatePickerFragment**.

Create a new class named **DatePickerFragment** and make its superclass **DialogFragment**. Be sure to choose the Jetpack version of **DialogFragment**: `androidx.fragment.app.DialogFragment`.

**DialogFragment** includes the following function:

```
onCreateDialog(savedInstanceState: Bundle?): Dialog
```

The **FragmentManager** of the hosting activity calls this function as part of putting the **DialogFragment** onscreen.

In `DatePickerFragment.kt`, add an implementation of **onCreateDialog(Bundle?)** that builds a **DatePickerDialog** initialized with the current date (Listing 13.1).

## Listing 13.1  Creating a **DialogFragment** (DatePickerFragment.kt)

```kotlin
class DatePickerFragment : DialogFragment() {

    override fun onCreateDialog(savedInstanceState: Bundle?): Dialog {
        val calendar = Calendar.getInstance()
        val initialYear = calendar.get(Calendar.YEAR)
        val initialMonth = calendar.get(Calendar.MONTH)
        val initialDay = calendar.get(Calendar.DAY_OF_MONTH)

        return DatePickerDialog(
            requireContext(),
            null,
            initialYear,
            initialMonth,
            initialDay
        )
    }
}
```

The **DatePickerDialog** constructor takes in several parameters. The first is a context object, which is required to access the necessary resources for the view. The second parameter is for the date listener, which you will add later in this chapter. The last three parameters are the year, month, and day that the date picker should be initialized to. Until you know the date of the crime, you can just initialize it to the current date.

# Showing a DialogFragment

Like all fragments, instances of **DialogFragment** are managed by the **FragmentManager** of the hosting activity.

To get a **DialogFragment** added to the **FragmentManager** and put onscreen, you can call either of the following functions on the fragment instance:

```
show(manager: FragmentManager, tag: String)
show(transaction: FragmentTransaction, tag: String)
```

The string parameter uniquely identifies the **DialogFragment** in the **FragmentManager**'s list. Whether you use the **FragmentManager** or **FragmentTransaction** version is up to you. If you pass in a **FragmentTransaction**, you are responsible for creating and committing that transaction. If you pass in a **FragmentManager**, a transaction will automatically be created and committed for you.

Here, you will pass in a **FragmentManager**.

In **CrimeFragment**, add a constant for the **DatePickerFragment**'s tag.

Then, in **onCreateView(…)**, remove the code that disables the date button. Set a **View.OnClickListener** that shows a **DatePickerFragment** when the date button is pressed in **onStart()**.

Listing 13.2  Showing your **DialogFragment** (CrimeFragment.kt)

```
private const val TAG = "CrimeFragment"
private const val ARG_CRIME_ID = "crime_id"
private const val DIALOG_DATE = "DialogDate"

class CrimeFragment : Fragment() {
    ...
    override fun onCreateView(inflater: LayoutInflater,
                             container: ViewGroup?,
                             savedInstanceState: Bundle?): View? {
        ...
        solvedCheckBox = view.findViewById(R.id.crime_solved) as CheckBox

        dateButton.apply {
            text = crime.date.toString()
            isEnabled = false
        }

        return view
    }
    ...
    override fun onStart() {
        ...
        solvedCheckBox.apply {
            ...
        }

        dateButton.setOnClickListener {
            DatePickerFragment().apply {
                show(this@CrimeFragment.requireFragmentManager(), DIALOG_DATE)
            }
        }
    }
    ...
}
```

this@CrimeFragment is needed to call **requireFragmentManager()** from the **CrimeFragment** instead of the **DatePickerFragment**. this references the **DatePickerFragment** inside the apply block, so you need to specify the this from the outer scope.

**DialogFragment**'s **show(FragmentManager, String)** requires a non-null value for the fragment manager argument. The Fragment.fragmentManager property is nullable, so you cannot pass it directly to **show(…)**. Instead, you use **Fragment**'s **requireFragmentManager()** function, whose return type is a non-null **FragmentManager**. If the fragment's fragmentManager property is null when **Fragment.requireFragmentManager()** is called, the function will throw an **IllegalStateException** stating that the fragment is not currently associated with a fragment manager.

Run CriminalIntent and press the date button to see the dialog (Figure 13.3).

## Figure 13.3  A configured dialog

Your dialog is onscreen and looks good. In the next section, you will wire it up to present the **Crime**'s date and allow the user to change it.

# Passing Data Between Two Fragments

You have passed data between two activities using intent extras, passed data between a fragment and an activity using a callbacks interface, and passed data from an activity to a fragment using fragment arguments. Now you need to pass data between two fragments that are hosted by the same activity – **CrimeFragment** and **DatePickerFragment** (Figure 13.4).

Figure 13.4  Conversation between **CrimeFragment** and **DatePickerFragment**

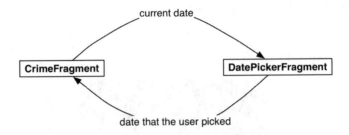

To get the **Crime**'s date to **DatePickerFragment**, you are going to write a **newInstance(Date)** function and make the **Date** an argument on the fragment.

To get the new date back to the **CrimeFragment** so that it can update the model layer and its own view, you will declare a callbacks interface function in **DatePickerFragment** that accepts the new date parameter, as shown in Figure 13.5.

Figure 13.5  Sequence of events between **CrimeFragment** and **DatePickerFragment**

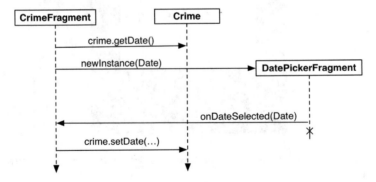

# Passing data to DatePickerFragment

To get data into your **DatePickerFragment**, you are going to stash the date in **DatePickerFragment**'s arguments bundle, where the **DatePickerFragment** can access it.

Creating and setting fragment arguments is typically done in a **newInstance(…)** function, as you saw in Chapter 12. In DatePickerFragment.kt, add a **newInstance(Date)** function in a companion object.

Listing 13.3  Adding a **newInstance(Date)** function (DatePickerFragment.kt)

```
private const val ARG_DATE = "date"

class DatePickerFragment : DialogFragment() {

    override fun onCreateDialog(savedInstanceState: Bundle?): Dialog {
        ...
    }

    companion object {
        fun newInstance(date: Date): DatePickerFragment {
            val args = Bundle().apply {
                putSerializable(ARG_DATE, date)
            }

            return DatePickerFragment().apply {
                arguments = args
            }
        }
    }
}
```

In **CrimeFragment**, remove the call to the **DatePickerFragment** constructor and replace it with a call to **DatePickerFragment.newInstance(Date)**.

Listing 13.4  Adding a call to **newInstance(…)** (CrimeFragment.kt)

```
override fun onStart() {
    ...
    dateButton.setOnClickListener {
        DatePickerFragment().apply {
        DatePickerFragment.newInstance(crime.date).apply {
            show(this@CrimeFragment.requireFragmentManager(), DIALOG_DATE)
        }
    }
}
```

**DatePickerFragment** needs to initialize the **DatePickerDialog** using the information held in the **Date**. However, initializing the **DatePickerDialog** requires Ints for the month, day, and year. **Date** is more of a timestamp and cannot provide Ints like this directly.

To get the Ints you need, you provide the **Date** to the **Calendar** object. Then you can retrieve the required information from the **Calendar**.

In **onCreateDialog(Bundle?)**, get the **Date** from the arguments and use it and the **Calendar** to initialize the **DatePickerDialog**.

## Listing 13.5  Extracting the date and initializing **DatePickerDialog** (DatePickerFragment.kt)

```
class DatePickerFragment : DialogFragment() {

    override fun onCreateDialog(savedInstanceState: Bundle?): Dialog {
        val date = arguments?.getSerializable(ARG_DATE) as Date
        val calendar = Calendar.getInstance()
        calendar.time = date
        val initialYear = calendar.get(Calendar.YEAR)
        val initialMonth = calendar.get(Calendar.MONTH)
        val initialDate = calendar.get(Calendar.DAY_OF_MONTH)

        return DatePickerDialog(
            requireContext(),
            null,
            initialYear,
            initialMonth,
            initialDate
        )
    }
    ...
}
```

Now **CrimeFragment** is successfully telling **DatePickerFragment** what date to show. You can run CriminalIntent and make sure that everything works as before.

# Returning data to CrimeFragment

To have **CrimeFragment** receive the date back from **DatePickerFragment**, you need a way to keep track of the relationship between the two fragments.

With activities, you call **startActivityForResult(…)**, and the **ActivityManager** keeps track of the parent-child activity relationship. When the child activity dies, the **ActivityManager** knows which activity should receive the result.

## Setting a target fragment

You can create a similar connection by making **CrimeFragment** the *target fragment* of **DatePickerFragment**. This connection is automatically re-established after both **CrimeFragment** and **DatePickerFragment** are destroyed and re-created by the OS. To create this relationship, you call the following **Fragment** function:

```
setTargetFragment(fragment: Fragment, requestCode: Int)
```

This function accepts the fragment that will be the target and a request code just like the one you send in **startActivityForResult(…)**.

The **FragmentManager** keeps track of the target fragment and request code. You can retrieve them by accessing the targetFragment and targetRequestCode properties on the fragment that has set the target.

In CrimeFragment.kt, create a constant for the request code and then make **CrimeFragment** the target fragment of the **DatePickerFragment** instance.

## Listing 13.6 Setting a target fragment (CrimeFragment.kt)

```
private const val DIALOG_DATE = "DialogDate"
private const val REQUEST_DATE = 0

class CrimeFragment : Fragment() {
    ...
    override fun onStart() {
        ...
        dateButton.setOnClickListener {
            DatePickerFragment.newInstance(crime.date).apply {
                setTargetFragment(this@CrimeFragment, REQUEST_DATE)
                show(this@CrimeFragment.requireFragmentManager(), DIALOG_DATE)
            }
        }
    }
    ...
}
```

## Sending data to the target fragment

Now that you have a connection between **CrimeFragment** and **DatePickerFragment**, you need to send the date back to **CrimeFragment**. You are going to create a callbacks interface in **DatePickerFragment** that **CrimeFragment** will implement.

In **DatePickerFragment**, create a callbacks interface with a single function called **onDateSelected()**.

## Listing 13.7  Creating a callbacks interface (DatePickerFragment.kt)

```kotlin
class DatePickerFragment : DialogFragment() {

    interface Callbacks {
        fun onDateSelected(date: Date)
    }

    override fun onCreateDialog(savedInstanceState: Bundle?): Dialog {
        ...
    }
    ...
}
```

Next, implement the **Callbacks** interface in **CrimeFragment**. In **onDateSelected()**, set the date on the crime property and update the UI.

## Listing 13.8  Implementing the callbacks interface (CrimeFragment.kt)

```kotlin
class CrimeFragment : Fragment(), DatePickerFragment.Callbacks {
    ...
    override fun onStop() {
        ...
    }

    override fun onDateSelected(date: Date) {
        crime.date = date
        updateUI()
    }
    ...
}
```

Now that **CrimeFragment** can respond to new dates, **DatePickerFragment** needs to send the new date when the user selects one. In **DatePickerFragment**, add a listener to the **DatePickerDialog** that sends the date back to **CrimeFragment** (Listing 13.9).

## Listing 13.9  Sending back the date (DatePickerFragment.kt)

```kotlin
class DatePickerFragment : DialogFragment() {
    ...
    override fun onCreateDialog(savedInstanceState: Bundle?): Dialog {
        val dateListener = DatePickerDialog.OnDateSetListener {
                _: DatePicker, year: Int, month: Int, day: Int ->

            val resultDate : Date = GregorianCalendar(year, month, day).time

            targetFragment?.let { fragment ->
                (fragment as Callbacks).onDateSelected(resultDate)
            }
        }

        val date = arguments?.getSerializable(ARG_DATE) as Date
        ...
        return DatePickerDialog(
            requireContext(),
            null,
            dateListener,
            initialYear,
            initialMonth,
            initialDate
        )
    }
    ...
}
```

The **OnDateSetListener** is used to receive the date the user selects. The first parameter is for the **DatePicker** the result is coming from. Since you are not using that parameter in this case, you name it _. This is a Kotlin convention to denote parameters that are unused.

The selected date is provided in year, month, and day format, but you need a **Date** to send back to **CrimeFragment**. You pass these values to the **GregorianCalendar** and access the time property to get a **Date** object.

Once you have the date, it needs to be sent back to **CrimeFragment**. The targetFragment property stores the fragment instance that started your **DatePickerFragment**. Since it is nullable, you wrap it in a safe-call let block. You then cast the fragment instance to your **Callbacks** interface and call the **onDateSelected()** function, passing in your new date.

Now the circle is complete. The dates must flow. He who controls the dates controls time itself. Run CriminalIntent to ensure that you can, in fact, control the dates. Change the date of a **Crime** and confirm that the new date appears in **CrimeFragment**'s view. Then return to the list of crimes and check the **Crime**'s date to ensure that the model layer was updated.

# Challenge: More Dialogs

Write another dialog fragment named **TimePickerFragment** that allows the user to select what time of day the crime occurred using a **TimePicker** widget. Add another button to **CrimeFragment** to display a **TimePickerFragment**.

# 14

# The App Bar

A key component of any well-designed Android app is the *app bar*. The app bar includes actions that the user can take, provides an additional mechanism for navigation, and also provides design consistency and branding.

In this chapter, you will add a menu option to the app bar that lets users add a new crime (Figure 14.1).

Figure 14.1 CriminalIntent's app bar

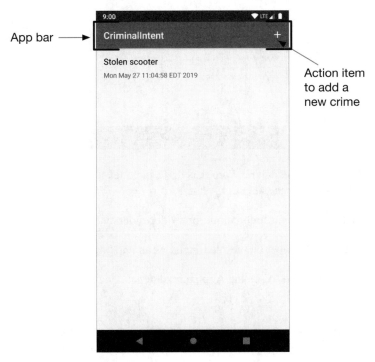

The app bar is often referred to as either the *action bar* or *toolbar*, depending on who you ask. You will learn more about these overlapping terms in the section called For the More Curious: App Bar vs Action Bar vs Toolbar near the end of this chapter.

# AppCompat Default App Bar

CriminalIntent already has a simple app bar in place (Figure 14.2).

Figure 14.2  The app bar

This is because Android Studio sets all new projects up to include an app bar by default for all activities that extend from **AppCompatActivity**. It does this by:

- adding the Jetpack AppCompat foundation library dependency

- applying one of the AppCompat themes that includes an app bar

Open your app/build.gradle file to see the AppCompat dependency:

```
dependencies {
    ...
    implementation 'androidx.appcompat:appcompat:1.0.0-beta01'
    ...
```

"AppCompat" is short for "application compatibility." The Jetpack AppCompat foundation library contains classes and resources that are core to providing a consistent-looking UI across different versions of Android. You can explore what is contained in each of the AppCompat subpackages on the official API listings at developer.android.com/reference/kotlin/androidx/packages.

Android Studio automatically sets your app's *theme* to `Theme.AppCompat.Light.DarkActionBar` when it creates your project. The theme, which specifies default styling for your entire app, is set in `res/values/styles.xml`:

```
<resources>

    <!-- Base application theme. -->
    <style name="AppTheme" parent="Theme.AppCompat.Light.DarkActionBar">
      <!-- Customize your theme here. -->
      <item name="colorPrimary">@color/colorPrimary</item>
      <item name="colorPrimaryDark">@color/colorPrimaryDark</item>
      <item name="colorAccent">@color/colorAccent</item>
    </style>

</resources>
```

The theme for your application is specified at the application level and optionally per activity in your manifest. Open `manifests/AndroidManifest.xml` and look at the `<application>` tag. Notice the `android:theme` attribute. You should see something similar to this:

```
<manifest ... >
    <application
        ...
        android:theme="@style/AppTheme" >
        ...
    </application>
</manifest>
```

You will learn much more about styles and themes in Chapter 21. Now it is time to add actions to the app bar.

# Menus

The top-right area of the app bar is reserved for the app bar's menu. The menu consists of *action items* (sometimes also referred to as *menu items*), which can perform an action on the current screen or on the app as a whole. You will add an action item to allow the user to create a new crime.

Your new action item will require a string resource for its label. Open `res/values/strings.xml` and add a string label describing your new action.

Listing 14.1  Adding a string for menu (`res/values/strings.xml`)

```
<resources>
    ...
    <string name="crime_solved_label">Solved</string>
    <string name="new_crime">New Crime</string>

</resources>
```

# Defining a menu in XML

Menus are a type of resource, similar to layouts. You create an XML description of a menu and place the file in the res/menu directory of your project. Android generates a resource ID for the menu file that you then use to inflate the menu in code.

In the project tool window, right-click the res directory and select New → Android resource file. Name the menu resource fragment_crime_list, change the Resource type to Menu, and click OK (Figure 14.3).

## Figure 14.3  Creating a menu file

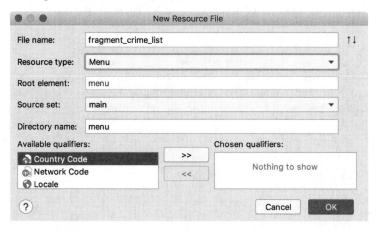

Here, you use the same naming convention for menu files as you do for layout files. Android Studio will generate res/menu/fragment_crime_list.xml, which has the same name as your **CrimeListFragment**'s layout file but lives in the menu folder. In the new file, switch to the text view and add an item element, as shown in Listing 14.2.

## Listing 14.2  Creating a menu resource for **CrimeListFragment** (res/menu/fragment_crime_list.xml)

```
<menu xmlns:android="http://schemas.android.com/apk/res/android"
    xmlns:app="http://schemas.android.com/apk/res-auto">
    <item
        android:id="@+id/new_crime"
        android:icon="@android:drawable/ic_menu_add"
        android:title="@string/new_crime"
        app:showAsAction="ifRoom|withText"/>
</menu>
```

The showAsAction attribute refers to whether the item will appear in the app bar itself or in the *overflow menu*. You have piped together two values, ifRoom and withText, so the item's icon and text will appear in the app bar if there is room. If there is room for the icon but not the text, then only the icon will be visible. If there is no room for either, then the item will be relegated to the overflow menu.

If you have items in the overflow menu, those items will be represented by the three dots on the far-right side of the app bar, as shown in Figure 14.4.

## Figure 14.4 Overflow menu in the app bar

Other options for showAsAction include always and never. Using always is not recommended; it is better to use ifRoom and let the OS decide. Using never is a good choice for less-common actions. In general, you should only put action items that users will access frequently in the app bar to avoid cluttering the screen.

## The app namespace

Notice that fragment_crime_list.xml uses the xmlns tag to define a new namespace, app, which is separate from the usual android namespace declaration. This app namespace is then used to specify the showAsAction attribute.

This unusual namespace declaration exists for legacy reasons with the AppCompat library. The app bar APIs (called "action bar" at the time) were first added in Android 3.0. Originally, the AppCompat library was created to bundle a compatibility version of the action bar into apps supporting earlier versions of Android, so that the action bar would exist on any device, even those that did not support the native action bar. On devices running Android 2.3 or older, menus and their corresponding XML did exist, but the android:showAsAction attribute was only added with the release of the action bar.

The AppCompat library defines its own custom showAsAction attribute and does not look for the native showAsAction attribute.

# Creating the menu

In code, menus are managed by callbacks from the **Activity** class. When the menu is needed, Android calls the **Activity** function **onCreateOptionsMenu(Menu)**.

However, your design calls for code to be implemented in a fragment, not an activity. **Fragment** comes with its own set of menu callbacks, which you will implement in **CrimeListFragment**. The functions for creating the menu and responding to the selection of an action item are:

```
onCreateOptionsMenu(menu: Menu, inflater: MenuInflater)
onOptionsItemSelected(item: MenuItem): Boolean
```

In CrimeListFragment.kt, override **onCreateOptionsMenu(Menu, MenuInflater)** to inflate the menu defined in fragment_crime_list.xml.

## Listing 14.3  Inflating a menu resource (CrimeListFragment.kt)

```
class CrimeListFragment : Fragment() {
    ...
    override fun onDetach() {
        super.onDetach()
        callbacks = null
    }

    override fun onCreateOptionsMenu(menu: Menu, inflater: MenuInflater) {
        super.onCreateOptionsMenu(menu, inflater)
        inflater.inflate(R.menu.fragment_crime_list, menu)
    }
    ...
}
```

Within this function, you call **MenuInflater.inflate(Int, Menu)** and pass in the resource ID of your menu file. This populates the **Menu** instance with the items defined in your file.

Notice that you call through to the superclass implementation of **onCreateOptionsMenu(…)**. This is not required, but we recommend calling through as a matter of convention. That way, any menu functionality defined by the superclass will still work. However, it is only a convention – the base **Fragment** implementation of this function does nothing.

The **FragmentManager** is responsible for calling **Fragment.onCreateOptionsMenu(Menu, MenuInflater)** when the activity receives its **onCreateOptionsMenu(…)** callback from the OS. You must explicitly tell the **FragmentManager** that your fragment should receive a call to **onCreateOptionsMenu(…)**. You do this by calling the following **Fragment** function:

```
setHasOptionsMenu(hasMenu: Boolean)
```

Define **CrimeListFragment.onCreate(Bundle?)** and let the **FragmentManager** know that **CrimeListFragment** needs to receive menu callbacks.

## Listing 14.4  Receiving menu callbacks (CrimeListFragment.kt)

```
class CrimeListFragment : Fragment() {
    ...
    override fun onAttach(context: Context) {
        ...
    }

    override fun onCreate(savedInstanceState: Bundle?) {
        super.onCreate(savedInstanceState)
        setHasOptionsMenu(true)
    }
    ...
}
```

You can run CriminalIntent now to see your menu (Figure 14.5).

## Figure 14.5  Icon for the New Crime action item in the app bar

Where is the action item's text? Most phones only have enough room for the icon in portrait orientation. You can long-press an icon in the app bar to reveal its title (Figure 14.6).

Figure 14.6  Long-pressing an icon in the app bar shows the title

In landscape orientation, there is room in the app bar for the icon and the text (Figure 14.7).

Figure 14.7  Icon and text in the landscape app bar

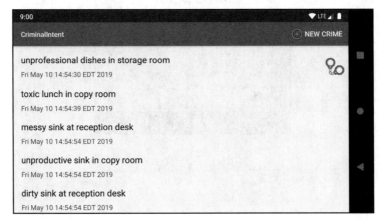

# Responding to menu selections

To respond to the user pressing the New Crime action item, you need a way for **CrimeListFragment** to add a new crime to the database. Add a function to **CrimeListViewModel** to wrap a call to the repository's **addCrime(Crime)** function.

Listing 14.5  Adding a new crime (CrimeListViewModel.kt)

```
class CrimeListViewModel : ViewModel() {

    private val crimeRepository = CrimeRepository.get()
    val crimeListLiveData = crimeRepository.getCrimes()

    fun addCrime(crime: Crime) {
        crimeRepository.addCrime(crime)
    }
}
```

When the user presses an action item, your fragment receives a callback to the function **onOptionsItemSelected(MenuItem)**. This function receives an instance of **MenuItem** that describes the user's selection.

Although your menu only contains one action item, menus often have more than one. You can determine which action item has been selected by checking the ID of the **MenuItem** and then respond appropriately. This ID corresponds to the ID you assigned to the **MenuItem** in your menu file.

In CrimeListFragment.kt, implement **onOptionsItemSelected(MenuItem)** to respond to **MenuItem** selection by creating a new **Crime**, saving it to the database, and then notifying the parent activity that the new crime has been selected.

Listing 14.6  Responding to menu selection (CrimeListFragment.kt)

```
class CrimeListFragment : Fragment() {
    ...
    override fun onCreateOptionsMenu(menu: Menu, inflater: MenuInflater) {
        super.onCreateOptionsMenu(menu, inflater)
        inflater.inflate(R.menu.fragment_crime_list, menu)
    }

    override fun onOptionsItemSelected(item: MenuItem): Boolean {
        return when (item.itemId) {
            R.id.new_crime -> {
                val crime = Crime()
                crimeListViewModel.addCrime(crime)
                callbacks?.onCrimeSelected(crime.id)
                true
            }
            else -> return super.onOptionsItemSelected(item)
        }
    }
    ...
}
```

Notice that this function returns a Boolean value. Once you have handled the **MenuItem**, you should return true to indicate that no further processing is necessary. If you return false, menu processing will continue by calling the hosting activity's **onOptionsItemSelected(MenuItem)** function (or, if the activity hosts other fragments, the **onOptionsItemSelected** function will get called on those fragments). The default case calls the superclass implementation if the item ID is not in your implementation.

In this brave new world where you can add crimes yourself, the seed database data you uploaded is no longer necessary. Remove the database files to start fresh with an empty list of crimes: Open the Device File Explorer tool window. Expand the data/data folder. Locate and expand the folder with your package name. Right-click the databases folder and choose Delete from the menu that appears. When you are done, the database folder will be gone (Figure 14.8).

## Figure 14.8  No more database files

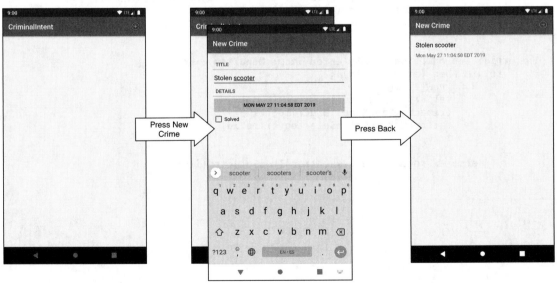

Note that the folders remaining in the data/data/*your.package.name* folder may look slightly different from the ones in Figure 14.8. That is OK, so long as the databases folder is gone.

Run CriminalIntent. You should see an empty list to start with. Try out your new menu item to add a new crime. You should see the new crime appear in the crime list (Figure 14.9).

## Figure 14.9  New crime flow

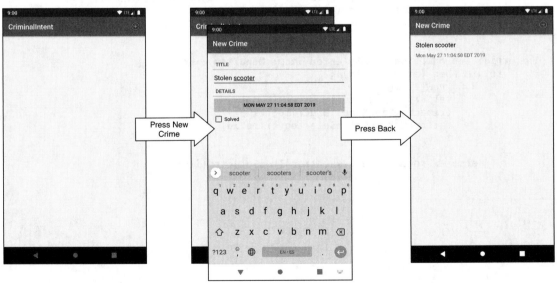

The empty list that you see before you add any crimes can be disconcerting. If you tackle the challenge in the section called Challenge: An Empty View for the RecyclerView at the end of this chapter, you will present a helpful clue when the list is empty.

# Using the Android Asset Studio

In the `android:icon` attribute, the value `@android:drawable/ic_menu_add` references a *system icon*. A system icon is one that is found on the device rather than in your project's resources.

In a prototype, referencing a system icon works fine. However, in an app that will be released, it is better to be sure of what your user will see instead of leaving it up to each device. System icons can change drastically across devices and OS versions, and some devices might have system icons that do not fit with the rest of your app's design.

One alternative is to create your own icons from scratch. You will need to prepare versions for each screen density and possibly for other device configurations. For more information, visit Android's Icon Design Guidelines at `developer.android.com/design/style/iconography.html`.

A second alternative is to find system icons that meet your app's needs and copy them directly into your project's drawable resources.

System icons can be found in your Android SDK directory. On a Mac, this is typically `/Users/`*user*`/Library/Android/sdk`. On Windows, the default location is `\Users\`*user*`\sdk`. You can also verify your SDK location by opening the project structure window (File → Project Structure) and checking the Android SDK location shown.

In your SDK directory, you will find Android's resources, including `ic_menu_add`. These resources are found in `/platforms/android-XX/data/res`, where XX represents the API level of the Android version. For example, for API level 28, Android's resources are found in `platforms/android-28/data/res`.

The third and easiest alternative is to use the Android Asset Studio, which is included in Android Studio. The Asset Studio allows you to create and customize an image to use in the app bar.

Right-click on your drawable directory in the project tool window and select New → Image Asset to bring up the Asset Studio (Figure 14.10).

Here, you can generate a few types of icons. Try it out by making a new icon for the New Crime action item. In the Icon Type field, choose Action Bar and Tab Icons. Next, name your asset ic_menu_add and set the Asset Type option to Clip Art.

Update the Theme to use HOLO_DARK. Since your app bar uses a dark theme, your image should appear as a light color. These changes are shown in Figure 14.10; note that while we are also showing the clip art you are about to select, your screen will feature the adorable Android logo.

## Figure 14.10  The Asset Studio

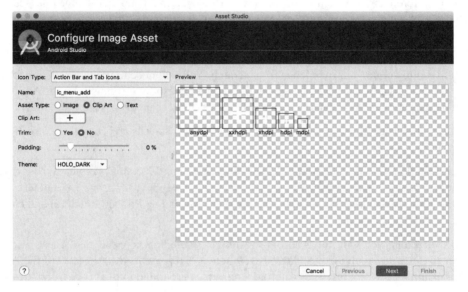

Select the Clip Art button to pick your clip art. In the clip art window, choose the image that looks like a plus sign (Figure 14.11). (You can enter "add" in the search box at the top left to save yourself some hunting.)

## Figure 14.11  Clip art options – where is that plus sign?

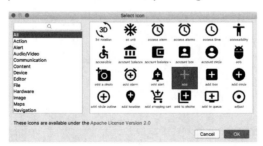

Back on the main screen, click Next to move to the last step of the wizard. The Asset Studio will show you a preview of the work that it will do (Figure 14.12). Notice that an hdpi, mdpi, xhdpi, xxhdpi, and anydpi icon will be created for you. Jim-dandy.

Figure 14.12 The Asset Studio's generated files

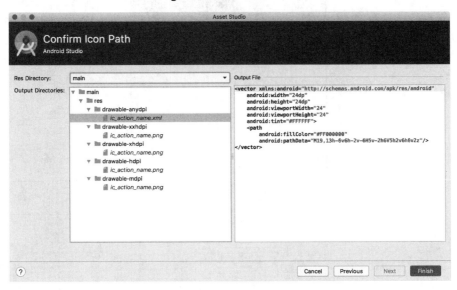

Select Finish to generate the images. Then, in your layout file, modify your icon attribute to reference the new resource in your project.

Listing 14.7 Referencing a local resource
(res/menu/fragment_crime_list.xml)

```
<item
    android:id="@+id/new_crime"
    android:icon="@android:drawable/ic_menu_add"
    android:icon="@drawable/ic_menu_add"
    android:title="@string/new_crime"
    app:showAsAction="ifRoom|withText"/>
```

Run your app and relish your newly updated icon, which will now look the same no matter which version of Android your user has installed (Figure 14.13).

Figure 14.13  Updated icon in place

# For the More Curious: App Bar vs Action Bar vs Toolbar

You will often hear people refer to the app bar as the "toolbar" or the "action bar." And the official Android documentation uses these terms interchangeably. But are the app bar, action bar, and toolbar really the same thing? In short, no. The terms are related, but they are not exactly equivalent.

The UI design element itself is called an app bar. Prior to Android 5.0 (Lollipop, API level 21), the app bar was implemented using the **ActionBar** class. The terms action bar and app bar came to be treated as one and the same. Starting with Android 5.0 (Lollipop, API level 21), the **Toolbar** class was introduced as the preferred method for implementing the app bar.

As of this writing, AppCompat uses the Jetpack **Toolbar** widget to implement the app bar (Figure 14.14).

## Figure 14.14 Layout inspector view of app bar

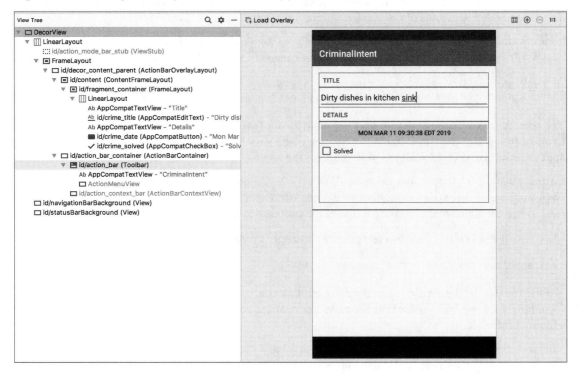

The **ActionBar** and **Toolbar** are very similar components. The toolbar builds on top of the action bar. It has a tweaked UI and is more flexible in the ways that you can use it.

The action bar has many constraints. It will always appear at the top of the screen. There can only be one action bar. The size of the action bar is fixed and should not be changed. The toolbar does not have these constraints.

In this chapter, you used a toolbar that was provided by one of the AppCompat themes. Alternatively, you can manually include a toolbar as a normal view in your activity or fragment's layout file. You can place this toolbar anywhere you like, and you can even include multiple toolbars on the screen at the same time. This flexibility allows for interesting designs; for example, imagine if each fragment that you use maintained its own toolbar. When you host multiple fragments on the screen at the same time, each of them could bring along its own toolbar instead of sharing a single toolbar at the top of the screen.

Another interesting addition with the toolbar is the ability to place **View**s inside the toolbar and also to adjust the height of the toolbar. This allows for much more flexibility in the way that your app works.

Equipped with this bit of history about the app bar-related APIs, you are now armed to more easily navigate the official developer documentation about this topic. And perhaps you can even spread the love and help clarify the overlap in these terms to future Android developers, since it is very confusing without the historical perspective.

# For the More Curious: Accessing the AppCompat App Bar

As you saw in this chapter, you can change the contents of the app bar by adding menu items. You can also change other attributes of the app bar at runtime, such as the title it displays.

To access the AppCompat app bar, you reference your **AppCompatActivity**'s supportFragmentManager property. From **CrimeFragment**, it would look something like this:

```
val appCompatActivity = activity as AppCompatActivity
val appBar = appCompatActivity.supportActionBar as Toolbar
```

The activity that is hosting the fragment is cast to an **AppCompatActivity**. Recall that because CriminalIntent uses the AppCompat library, you made your **MainActivity** a subclass of **AppCompatActivity**, which allows you to access the app bar.

Casting supportActionBar to a **Toolbar** allows you to call any **Toolbar** functions. (Remember, AppCompat uses a **Toolbar** to implement the app bar. But it used to use an **ActionBar**, as you just read, hence the somewhat-confusing name of the property to access the app bar).

Once you have a reference to the app bar, you can apply changes like so:

```
appBar.setTitle(R.string.some_cool_title)
```

See the **Toolbar** API reference page for a list of other functions you can apply to alter the app bar (assuming your app bar is a **Toolbar**) at developer.android.com/reference/androidx/appcompat/widget/Toolbar.

Note that if you need to alter the contents of the app bar's menu while the activity is still displayed, you can trigger the **onCreateOptionsMenu(Menu, MenuInflater)** callback by calling the **invalidateOptionsMenu()** function. You can change the contents of the menu programmatically in the **onCreateOptionsMenu** callback, and those changes will appear once the callback is complete.

# Challenge: An Empty View for the RecyclerView

Currently, when CriminalIntent launches it displays an empty **RecyclerView** – a big white void. You should give users something to interact with when there are no items in the list.

For this challenge, display a message like There are no crimes and add a button to the view that will trigger the creation of a new crime.

Use the visibility property that exists on any **View** class to show and hide this new placeholder view when appropriate.

# 15

# Implicit Intents

In Android, you can start an activity in another application on the device using an *intent*. In an *explicit intent*, you specify the class of the activity to start, and the OS will start it. In an *implicit intent*, you describe the job that you need done, and the OS will start an activity in an appropriate application for you.

In CriminalIntent, you will use implicit intents to enable picking a suspect for a `Crime` from the user's list of contacts and sending a text-based report of a crime. The user will choose a suspect from whatever contacts app is installed on the device and will be offered a choice of apps to send the crime report (Figure 15.1).

## Figure 15.1  Opening contacts and text-sending apps

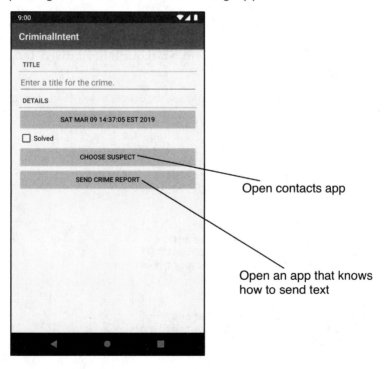

Using implicit intents to harness other applications is far easier than writing your own implementations for common tasks. Users also appreciate being able to use apps they already know and like in conjunction with your app.

Before you can create these implicit intents, there is some setup to do in CriminalIntent:

- add CHOOSE SUSPECT and SEND CRIME REPORT buttons to **CrimeFragment**'s layouts

- add a suspect property to the **Crime** class that will hold the name of a suspect

- create a crime report using a set of *format resource strings*

# Adding Buttons

Update **CrimeFragment**'s layout to include new buttons for accusation and tattling: namely, a suspect button and a report button. First, add the strings that these buttons will display.

### Listing 15.1  Adding button strings (`res/values/strings.xml`)

```
<resources>
    ...
    <string name="new_crime">New Crime</string>
    <string name="crime_suspect_text">Choose Suspect</string>
    <string name="crime_report_text">Send Crime Report</string>
</resources>
```

In `res/layout/fragment_crime.xml`, add two button widgets, as shown in Listing 15.2.

### Listing 15.2  Adding CHOOSE SUSPECT and SEND CRIME REPORT buttons (`res/layout/fragment_crime.xml`)

```
<LinearLayout xmlns:android="http://schemas.android.com/apk/res/android"
          ... >
    ...
    <CheckBox
            android:id="@+id/crime_solved"
            android:layout_width="match_parent"
            android:layout_height="wrap_content"
            android:text="@string/crime_solved_label"/>

    <Button
            android:id="@+id/crime_suspect"
            android:layout_width="match_parent"
            android:layout_height="wrap_content"
            android:text="@string/crime_suspect_text"/>

    <Button
            android:id="@+id/crime_report"
            android:layout_width="match_parent"
            android:layout_height="wrap_content"
            android:text="@string/crime_report_text"/>
</LinearLayout>
```

Preview the updated layout or run CriminalIntent to confirm that your new buttons are in place.

# Adding a Suspect to the Model Layer

Next, open Crime.kt and give **Crime** a property that will hold the name of a suspect.

## Listing 15.3 Adding a suspect property (Crime.kt)

```
@Entity
data class Crime(@PrimaryKey val id: UUID = UUID.randomUUID(),
                 var title: String = "",
                 var date: Date = Date(),
                 var isSolved: Boolean = false,
                 var suspect: String = "")
```

Now you need to add an additional property to your crime database. This requires incrementing the version of your **CrimeDatabase** class, as well as telling Room how to migrate your database between the versions.

To tell Room how to change your database from one version to another, you provide a **Migration**. Open CrimeDatabase.kt, add a migration, and increment the version.

## Listing 15.4 Adding database migration (database/CrimeDatabase.kt)

```
@Database(entities = [ Crime::class ], version=1 version=2)
@TypeConverters(CrimeTypeConverters::class)
abstract class CrimeDatabase : RoomDatabase() {

    abstract fun crimeDao(): CrimeDao
}

val migration_1_2 = object : Migration(1, 2) {
    override fun migrate(database: SupportSQLiteDatabase) {
        database.execSQL(
            "ALTER TABLE Crime ADD COLUMN suspect TEXT NOT NULL DEFAULT ''"
        )
    }
}
```

Since your initial database version is set to 1, you bump it up to 2. You then create a **Migration** object that contains instructions for updating your database.

The **Migration** class constructor takes in two parameters. The first is the database version you are migrating from, and the second is the version you are migrating to. In this case, you provide the version numbers 1 and 2.

The only function you need to implement in your **Migration** object is
**migrate(SupportSQLiteDatabase)**. You use the database parameter to execute any SQL commands necessary to upgrade your tables. (Room uses SQLite under the hood, as you read in Chapter 11.) The ALTER TABLE command you wrote adds the new suspect column to the crime table.

After you create your **Migration**, you need to provide it to your database when it is created. Open CrimeRepository.kt and provide the migration to Room when creating your **CrimeDatabase** instance.

### Listing 15.5  Providing migration to Room (CrimeRepository.kt)

```
class CrimeRepository private constructor(context: Context) {

    private val database : CrimeDatabase = Room.databaseBuilder(
        context.applicationContext,
        CrimeDatabase::class.java,
        DATABASE_NAME
    ).build()
    ).addMigrations(migration_1_2)
        .build()
    private val crimeDao = database.crimeDao()
    ...
}
```

To set up the migration, you call **addMigrations(…)** before calling the **build()** function. **addMigrations()** takes in a variable number of **Migration** objects, so you can pass all of your migrations in when you declare them.

When your app launches and Room builds the database, it will first check the version of the existing database on the device. If this version does not match the one you define in the @Database annotation, Room will search for the appropriate migrations to update the database to the latest version.

It is important to provide migrations for converting your database. If you do not provide migrations, Room will delete the old version of the database and re-create a new version. This means that all the data will be lost, leading to very unhappy users.

Once your migration is in place, run CriminalIntent to make sure everything builds correctly. The app behavior should be the same as before you applied the migration, and you should see the crime you added in Chapter 14. You will make use of the newly added column shortly.

# Using a Format String

The last preliminary step is to create a template crime report that can be configured with the specific crime's details. Because you will not know a crime's details until runtime, you must use a format string with placeholders that can be replaced at runtime. Here is the format string you will use:

```
%1$s! The crime was discovered on %2$s. %3$s, and %4$s
```

%1$s, %2$s, etc. are placeholders that expect string arguments. In code, you will call **getString(…)** and pass in the format string and four other strings in the order in which they should replace the placeholders.

First, in strings.xml, add the strings shown in Listing 15.6.

## Listing 15.6 Adding string resources (`res/values/strings.xml`)

```xml
<resources>
    ...
    <string name="crime_suspect_text">Choose Suspect</string>
    <string name="crime_report_text">Send Crime Report</string>
    <string name="crime_report">%1$s!
      The crime was discovered on %2$s. %3$s, and %4$s
    </string>
    <string name="crime_report_solved">The case is solved</string>
    <string name="crime_report_unsolved">The case is not solved</string>
    <string name="crime_report_no_suspect">there is no suspect.</string>
    <string name="crime_report_suspect">the suspect is %s.</string>
    <string name="crime_report_subject">CriminalIntent Crime Report</string>
    <string name="send_report">Send crime report via</string>
</resources>
```

In `CrimeFragment.kt`, add a function that creates four strings and then pieces them together and returns a complete report.

## Listing 15.7 Adding a **getCrimeReport()** function (`CrimeFragment.kt`)

```kotlin
private const val REQUEST_DATE = 0
private const val DATE_FORMAT = "EEE, MMM, dd"

class CrimeFragment : Fragment(), DatePickerFragment.Callbacks {
    ...
    private fun updateUI() {
        ...
    }

    private fun getCrimeReport(): String {
        val solvedString = if (crime.isSolved) {
            getString(R.string.crime_report_solved)
        } else {
            getString(R.string.crime_report_unsolved)
        }

        val dateString = DateFormat.format(DATE_FORMAT, crime.date).toString()
        var suspect = if (crime.suspect.isBlank()) {
            getString(R.string.crime_report_no_suspect)
        } else {
            getString(R.string.crime_report_suspect, crime.suspect)
        }

        return getString(R.string.crime_report,
                crime.title, dateString, solvedString, suspect)
    }

    companion object {
        ...
    }
}
```

(Note that there are multiple **DateFormat** classes. Make sure you import **android.text.format.DateFormat**.)

Now the preliminaries are complete, and you can turn to implicit intents.

# Using Implicit Intents

An **Intent** is an object that describes to the OS something that you want it to do. With the *explicit* intents that you have created thus far, you explicitly name the activity that you want the OS to start, like:

```
val intent = Intent(this, CheatActivity::class.java)
startActivity(intent)
```

With an *implicit* intent, you describe to the OS the job that you want done. The OS then starts the activity that has advertised itself as capable of doing that job. If the OS finds more than one capable activity, then the user is offered a choice.

## Parts of an implicit intent

Here are the critical parts of an intent that you can use to define the job you want done:

the *action* that you are trying to perform

> These are typically constants from the **Intent** class. For example, if you want to view a URL, you can use Intent.ACTION_VIEW for your action. To send something, you use Intent.ACTION_SEND.

the location of any *data*

> This can be something outside the device, like the URL of a web page, but it can also be a URI to a file or a *content URI* pointing to a record in a **ContentProvider**.

the *type* of data that the action is for

> This is a MIME type, like text/html or audio/mpeg3. If an intent includes a location for data, then the type can usually be inferred from that data.

optional *categories*

> If the action is used to describe *what* to do, the category usually describes *where*, *when*, or *how* you are trying to use an activity. Android uses the category android.intent.category.LAUNCHER to indicate that an activity should be displayed in the top-level app launcher. The android.intent.category.INFO category, on the other hand, indicates an activity that shows information about a package to the user but should not show up in the launcher.

So, for example, a simple implicit intent for viewing a website would include an action of Intent.ACTION_VIEW and a data **Uri** that is the URL of a website.

Based on this information, the OS will launch the appropriate activity of an appropriate application. (If it finds more than one candidate, the user gets a choice.)

An activity would advertise itself as an appropriate activity for ACTION_VIEW via an intent filter in the manifest. If you wanted to write a browser app, for instance, you would include the following intent filter in the declaration of the activity that should respond to ACTION_VIEW:

```
<activity
    android:name=".BrowserActivity"
    android:label="@string/app_name" >
    <intent-filter>
        <action android:name="android.intent.action.VIEW" />
        <category android:name="android.intent.category.DEFAULT" />
        <data android:scheme="http" android:host="www.bignerdranch.com" />
    </intent-filter>
</activity>
```

To respond to implicit intents, an activity must have the DEFAULT category explicitly set in an intent filter. The action element in the intent filter tells the OS that the activity is capable of performing the job, and the DEFAULT category tells the OS that this activity should be considered for the job when the OS is asking for volunteers. This DEFAULT category is implicitly added to every implicit intent. (In Chapter 23, you will see that this is not the case when Android is not asking for a volunteer.)

Implicit intents can also include extras, just like explicit intents. But any extras on an implicit intent are not used by the OS to find an appropriate activity.

Note that the action and data parts of an intent can also be used in conjunction with an explicit intent. That would be the equivalent of telling a particular activity to do something specific.

# Sending a crime report

Let's see how this works by creating an implicit intent to send a crime report in CriminalIntent. The job you want done is sending plain text; the crime report is a string. So the implicit intent's action will be ACTION_SEND. It will not point to any data or have any categories, but it will specify a type of text/plain.

In **CrimeFragment**'s **onCreateView(…)**, get a reference to the SEND CRIME REPORT button, then set a listener on it in **CrimeFragment**'s **onStart()**. Within the listener's implementation, create an implicit intent and pass it into **startActivity(Intent)**.

## Listing 15.8  Sending a crime report (CrimeFragment.kt)

```
class CrimeFragment : Fragment(), DatePickerFragment.Callbacks {
    ...
    private lateinit var solvedCheckBox: CheckBox
    private lateinit var reportButton: Button
    ...
    override fun onCreateView(
        ...
    ): View? {
        ...
        dateButton = view.findViewById(R.id.crime_date) as Button
        solvedCheckBox = view.findViewById(R.id.crime_solved) as CheckBox
        reportButton = view.findViewById(R.id.crime_report) as Button

        return view
    }
    ...
    override fun onStart() {
        ...
        dateButton.setOnClickListener {
            ...
        }

        reportButton.setOnClickListener {
            Intent(Intent.ACTION_SEND).apply {
                type = "text/plain"
                putExtra(Intent.EXTRA_TEXT, getCrimeReport())
                putExtra(
                    Intent.EXTRA_SUBJECT,
                    getString(R.string.crime_report_subject))
            }.also { intent ->
                startActivity(intent)
            }
        }
    }
    ...
}
```

Here you use the **Intent** constructor that accepts a string that is a constant defining the action. There are other constructors that you can use depending on what kind of implicit intent you need to create. You can find them all on the **Intent** reference page in the documentation. There is no constructor that accepts a type, so you set it explicitly.

You include the text of the report and the string for the subject of the report as extras. Note that these extras use constants defined in the **Intent** class. Any activity responding to this intent will know these constants and what to do with the associated values.

Starting an activity from a fragment works nearly the same as starting an activity from another activity. You call **Fragment**'s **startActivity(Intent)** function, which calls the corresponding **Activity** function behind the scenes.

Run CriminalIntent and press the SEND CRIME REPORT button. Because this intent will likely match many activities on the device, you will probably see a list of activities presented in a chooser (Figure 15.2). You may need to scroll down in the list to see all of the activities.

Figure 15.2  Activities volunteering to send your crime report

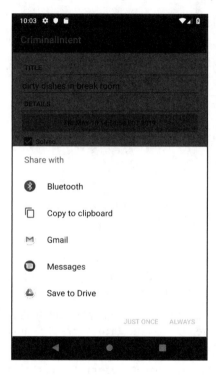

If you are offered a choice, make a selection. You will see your crime report loaded into the app that you chose. All you have to do is address and send it.

Note that apps like Gmail and Google Drive require you to log in with a Google account. It is simpler to choose the Messages app, which does not require you to log in. Press New message in the Select conversation dialog window, type any phone number in the To field, and press the Send to *phone number* label that appears (Figure 15.3). You will see the crime report in the body of the message.

## Figure 15.3  Sending a crime report with the Messages app

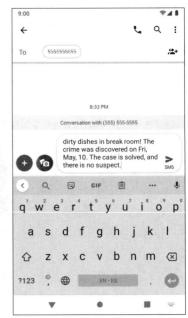

If, on the other hand, you do not see a chooser, that means one of two things. Either you have already set a default app for an identical implicit intent, or your device has only a single activity that can respond to this intent.

Often, it is best to go with the user's default app for an action. In CriminalIntent, however, you always want the user to have a choice for ACTION_SEND. Today a user might want to be discreet and email the crime report, but tomorrow they may prefer public shaming via Twitter.

You can create a chooser to be shown every time an implicit intent is used to start an activity. After you create your implicit intent as before, you call the **Intent.createChooser(Intent, String)** function and pass in the implicit intent and a string for the chooser's title.

Then you pass the intent returned from **createChooser(…)** into **startActivity(…)**.

In CrimeFragment.kt, create a chooser to display the activities that respond to your implicit intent.

## Listing 15.9  Using a chooser (CrimeFragment.kt)

```kotlin
reportButton.setOnClickListener {
    Intent(Intent.ACTION_SEND).apply {
        type = "text/plain"
        putExtra(Intent.EXTRA_TEXT, getCrimeReport())
        putExtra(
            Intent.EXTRA_SUBJECT,
            getString(R.string.crime_report_subject))
    }.also { intent ->
        startActivity(intent)
        val chooserIntent =
                Intent.createChooser(intent, getString(R.string.send_report))
        startActivity(chooserIntent)
    }
}
```

Run CriminalIntent again and press the SEND CRIME REPORT button. As long as you have more than one activity that can handle your intent, you will be offered a list to choose from (Figure 15.4).

Figure 15.4  Sending text with a chooser

## Asking Android for a contact

Now you are going to create another implicit intent that enables users to choose a suspect from their contacts. This implicit intent will have an action and a location where the relevant data can be found. The action will be Intent.ACTION_PICK. The data for contacts is at ContactsContract.Contacts.CONTENT_URI. In short, you are asking Android to help pick an item in the contacts database.

You expect a result back from the started activity, so you will pass the intent via **startActivityForResult(…)** along with a request code. In CrimeFragment.kt, add a constant for the request code and a member variable for the CHOOSE SUSPECT button.

### Listing 15.10  Adding a field for the CHOOSE SUSPECT button (CrimeFragment.kt)

```
private const val REQUEST_DATE = 0
private const val REQUEST_CONTACT = 1
private const val DATE_FORMAT = "EEE, MMM, dd"

class CrimeFragment : Fragment(), DatePickerFragment.Callbacks {
    ...
    private lateinit var reportButton: Button
    private lateinit var suspectButton: Button
    ...
}
```

At the end of **onCreateView(…)**, get a reference to the button. Then, in **onStart()**, set a click listener on the button. Pass the implicit intent into **startActivityForResult(…)** in the click listener implementation. Create an implicit intent for requesting a contact. Also, if a suspect is assigned, show the name on the CHOOSE SUSPECT button.

## Listing 15.11 Sending an implicit intent (`CrimeFragment.kt`)

```
class CrimeFragment : Fragment(), DatePickerFragment.Callbacks {
    ...
    override fun onCreateView(
        ...
    ): View? {
        ...
        reportButton = view.findViewById(R.id.crime_report) as Button
        suspectButton = view.findViewById(R.id.crime_suspect) as Button

        return view
    }
    ...
    override fun onStart() {
        ...
        reportButton.setOnClickListener {
            ...
        }

        suspectButton.apply {
            val pickContactIntent =
                    Intent(Intent.ACTION_PICK, ContactsContract.Contacts.CONTENT_URI)

            setOnClickListener {
                startActivityForResult(pickContactIntent, REQUEST_CONTACT)
            }
        }
    }
    ...
}
```

You will be using `pickContactIntent` one more time in a bit, which is why you declared it outside the **OnClickListener**.

Next, modify **updateUI()** to set the text on the CHOOSE SUSPECT button if the crime has a suspect.

## Listing 15.12 Setting CHOOSE SUSPECT button text (`CrimeFragment.kt`)

```
private fun updateUI() {
    titleField.setText(crime.title)
    dateButton.text = crime.date.toString()
    solvedCheckBox.apply {
        isChecked = crime.isSolved
        jumpDrawablesToCurrentState()
    }
    if (crime.suspect.isNotEmpty()) {
        suspectButton.text = crime.suspect
    }
}
```

Run CriminalIntent and press the CHOOSE SUSPECT button. You should see a list of contacts (Figure 15.5).

## Figure 15.5  A list of possible suspects

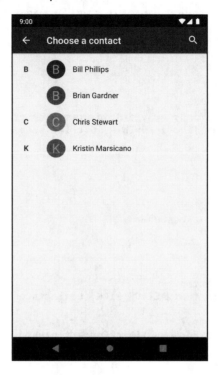

If you have a different contacts app installed, your screen will look different. Again, this is one of the benefits of implicit intents. You do not have to know the name of the contacts application to use it from your app. Users can install whatever app they like best, and the OS will find and launch it.

## Getting data from the contacts list

Now you need to get a result back from the contacts application. Contacts information is shared by many applications, so Android provides an in-depth API for working with contacts information through a **ContentProvider**. Instances of this class wrap databases and make the data available to other applications. You can access a **ContentProvider** through a **ContentResolver**. (The contacts database is a large topic in itself. We will not cover it here. If you would like to know more, read the Content Provider API guide at developer.android.com/guide/topics/providers/content-provider-basics.)

Because you started the activity for a result with ACTION_PICK, you will receive an intent via **onActivityResult(…)**. This intent includes a data URI. The URI is a locator that points at the single contact the user picked.

In CrimeFragment.kt, implement **onActivityResult(…)** to retrieve the contact's name from the contacts application. This is a large block of new code; we will explain it step by step after you enter it.

## Listing 15.13 Pulling the contact's name out (`CrimeFragment.kt`)

```kotlin
class CrimeFragment : Fragment(), DatePickerFragment.Callbacks {
    ...
    private fun updateUI() {
        ...
    }

    override fun onActivityResult(requestCode: Int, resultCode: Int, data: Intent?) {
        when {
            resultCode != Activity.RESULT_OK -> return

            requestCode == REQUEST_CONTACT && data != null -> {
                val contactUri: Uri? = data.data
                // Specify which fields you want your query to return values for
                val queryFields = arrayOf(ContactsContract.Contacts.DISPLAY_NAME)
                // Perform your query - the contactUri is like a "where" clause here
                val cursor = requireActivity().contentResolver
                    .query(contactUri, queryFields, null, null, null)
                cursor?.use {
                    // Verify cursor contains at least one result
                    if (it.count == 0) {
                        return
                    }

                    // Pull out the first column of the first row of data -
                    // that is your suspect's name
                    it.moveToFirst()
                    val suspect = it.getString(0)
                    crime.suspect = suspect
                    crimeDetailViewModel.saveCrime(crime)
                    suspectButton.text = suspect
                }
            }
        }
    }
    ...
}
```

In Listing 15.13, you create a query that asks for all the display names of the contacts in the returned data. Then you query the contacts database and get a **Cursor** object to work with. Once you verify that the cursor returned contains at least one row, you call **Cursor.moveToFirst()** to move the cursor to the first row. Finally, you call **Cursor.getString(Int)** to pull the contents of the first column in that first row as a string. This string will be the name of the suspect, and you use it to set the **Crime**'s suspect and the text of the CHOOSE SUSPECT button.

You also save the crime to the database as soon as you receive the suspect data. The reason you need to do this is subtle. When **CrimeFragment** is resumed, your **onViewCreated(…)** function will be called, and you will query the crime from the database. But **onActivityResult(…)** is called before **onViewCreated(…)**, so when the database crime is received it will overwrite the crime with the suspect information. To avoid losing the suspect data, you write the crime with the suspect as soon as it is ready.

Now the information will be persisted in the database. **CrimeFragment** will still receive the old database crime first, but the **LiveData** will quickly be notified of the new crime information once the update completes.

In a moment, you are going to run your app. Be sure to run it on a device that has a contacts app – use the emulator if your Android device does not have one. If you are using the emulator, add a few contacts using its Contacts app before you run CriminalIntent. Then run your app.

Pick a suspect. The name of the suspect you chose should appear on the CHOOSE SUSPECT button. Then send a crime report. The suspect's name should appear in the crime report (Figure 15.6).

## Figure 15.6  Suspect name on button and in crime report

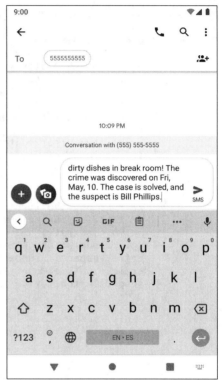

## Contacts permissions

How are you getting permission to read from the contacts database? The contacts app is extending its permissions to you. The contacts app has full permissions to the contacts database. When the contacts app returns a data URI in an **Intent** to the parent activity, it also adds the flag Intent.FLAG_GRANT_READ_URI_PERMISSION. This flag signals to Android that the parent activity in CriminalIntent should be allowed to use this data one time. This works well because you do not really need access to the entire contacts database. You only need access to one contact inside that database.

# Checking for responding activities

The first implicit intent you created in this chapter will always be responded to in some way – there may be no way to send a report, but the chooser will still display properly. However, that is not the case for the second example: Some devices or users may not have a contacts app. This is a problem, because if the OS cannot find a matching activity, then the app will crash.

The fix is to check with part of the OS called the **PackageManager** first. Do this in **onStart()**.

Listing 15.14  Guarding against no contacts app (`CrimeFragment.kt`)

```
override fun onStart() {
    ...
    suspectButton.apply {
        val pickContactIntent =
            Intent(Intent.ACTION_PICK, ContactsContract.Contacts.CONTENT_URI)

        setOnClickListener {
            startActivityForResult(pickContactIntent, REQUEST_CONTACT)
        }

        val packageManager: PackageManager = requireActivity().packageManager
        val resolvedActivity: ResolveInfo? =
            packageManager.resolveActivity(pickContactIntent,
                PackageManager.MATCH_DEFAULT_ONLY)
        if (resolvedActivity == null) {
            isEnabled = false
        }
    }
}
```

**PackageManager** knows about all the components installed on your Android device, including all of its activities. (You will run into the other components later on in this book.) By calling **resolveActivity(Intent, Int)**, you ask it to find an activity that matches the **Intent** you gave it. The MATCH_DEFAULT_ONLY flag restricts this search to activities with the CATEGORY_DEFAULT flag, just like **startActivity(Intent)** does.

If this search is successful, it will return an instance of **ResolveInfo** telling you all about which activity it found. On the other hand, if the search returns null, the game is up – no contacts app. So you disable the useless CHOOSE SUSPECT button.

If you would like to verify that your filter works but you do not have a device without a contacts application, temporarily add an additional category to your intent. This category does nothing, but it will prevent any contacts applications from matching your intent.

Listing 15.15  Adding dummy code to verify filter (`CrimeFragment.kt`)

```
override fun onStart() {
    ...
    suspectButton.apply {
        ...
        pickContactIntent.addCategory(Intent.CATEGORY_HOME)
        val packageManager: PackageManager = requireActivity().packageManager
        ...
    }
}
```

Run CriminalIntent again, and you should see the CHOOSE SUSPECT button disabled (Figure 15.7).

Figure 15.7  Disabled CHOOSE SUSPECT button

Delete the dummy code once you are done verifying this behavior.

Listing 15.16  Deleting dummy code (`CrimeFragment.kt`)

```
override fun onStart() {
    ...
    suspectButton.apply {
        ...
        pickContactIntent.addCategory(Intent.CATEGORY_HOME)
        val packageManager: PackageManager = requireActivity().packageManager
        ...
    }
}
```

# Challenge: Another Implicit Intent

Instead of sending a crime report, an angry user may prefer a phone confrontation with the suspect. Add a new button that calls the named suspect.

You will need the phone number out of the contacts database. This will require you to query another table in the **ContactsContract** database called **CommonDataKinds.Phone**. Check out the documentation for **ContactsContract** and **ContactsContract.CommonDataKinds.Phone** for more information on how to query for this information.

A couple of tips: To query for additional data, you can use the android.permission.READ_CONTACTS permission. This is a *runtime permission*, so you need to explicitly ask the user's permission to access their contacts. If you would like to know more, read the Request App Permissions guide at developer.android.com/training/permissions/requesting.

With that permission in hand, you can read the ContactsContract.Contacts._ID to get a contact ID on your original query. You can then use that ID to query the **CommonDataKinds.Phone** table.

Once you have the phone number, you can create an implicit intent with a telephone URI:

```
Uri number = Uri.parse("tel:5551234");
```

The action can be Intent.ACTION_DIAL or Intent.ACTION_CALL. What is the difference? ACTION_CALL pulls up the phone app and immediately calls the number sent in the intent; ACTION_DIAL just enters the number and waits for the user to initiate the call.

We recommend using ACTION_DIAL. It is the kinder, gentler option. ACTION_CALL may be restricted and will definitely require a permission. Your user may also appreciate the chance to cool down before starting the call.

# 16

# Taking Pictures with Intents

Now that you know how to work with implicit intents, you can document crimes in even more detail. With a picture of the crime, you can share the gory details with everyone. Taking a picture will involve a couple of new tools, used in combination with a tool you recently got to know: the implicit intent.

An implicit intent can be used to start up the user's favorite camera application and receive a new picture from it. But where do you put the picture the camera takes? And once the picture comes in, how do you display it? In this chapter, you will answer both of those questions.

## A Place for Your Photo

The first step is to build out a place for your photo to live on the crime detail screen. You will need two new **View** objects: an **ImageView** to display the photo and a **Button** to press to take a new photo (Figure 16.1).

Figure 16.1  New UI

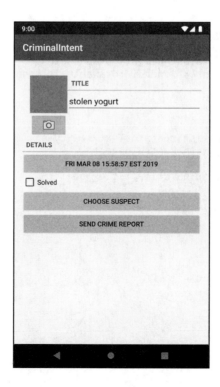

Dedicating an entire row to a thumbnail and a button would make your app look clunky and unprofessional. You do not want that, so you will arrange things nicely.

Add new views to res/layout/fragment_crime.xml to build out this new area. Start with the lefthand side, adding an **ImageView** for the picture and an **ImageButton** to take a picture.

## Listing 16.1  Adding an image and camera button to the layout (res/layout/fragment_crime.xml)

```
<LinearLayout xmlns:android="http://schemas.android.com/apk/res/android"
              ... >
    <LinearLayout
            android:layout_width="match_parent"
            android:layout_height="wrap_content"
            android:orientation="horizontal"
            android:layout_marginStart="16dp"
            android:layout_marginTop="16dp">

        <LinearLayout
                android:layout_width="wrap_content"
                android:layout_height="wrap_content"
                android:orientation="vertical">

            <ImageView
                    android:id="@+id/crime_photo"
                    android:layout_width="80dp"
                    android:layout_height="80dp"
                    android:scaleType="centerInside"
                    android:cropToPadding="true"
                    android:background="@android:color/darker_gray"/>

            <ImageButton
                    android:id="@+id/crime_camera"
                    android:layout_width="match_parent"
                    android:layout_height="wrap_content"
                    android:src="@android:drawable/ic_menu_camera"/>
        </LinearLayout>
    </LinearLayout>

    <TextView
            style="?android:listSeparatorTextViewStyle"
            android:layout_width="match_parent"
            android:layout_height="wrap_content"
            android:text="@string/crime_title_label"/>
    ...
</LinearLayout>
```

Now set up the righthand side, moving your title **TextView** and **EditText** into a new **LinearLayout** child to the **LinearLayout** you just built.

## Listing 16.2  Updating the title layout (res/layout/fragment_crime.xml)

```xml
<LinearLayout xmlns:android="http://schemas.android.com/apk/res/android"
              ... >
    <LinearLayout
            android:layout_width="match_parent"
            android:layout_height="wrap_content"
            android:orientation="horizontal"
            android:layout_marginStart="16dp"
            android:layout_marginTop="16dp">

        <LinearLayout
                android:layout_width="wrap_content"
                android:layout_height="wrap_content"
                android:orientation="vertical">
            ...
        </LinearLayout>
    </LinearLayout>

        <LinearLayout
                android:orientation="vertical"
                android:layout_width="0dp"
                android:layout_height="wrap_content"
                android:layout_weight="1">

            <TextView
                    style="?android:listSeparatorTextViewStyle"
                    android:layout_width="match_parent"
                    android:layout_height="wrap_content"
                    android:text="@string/crime_title_label"/>

            <EditText
                    android:id="@+id/crime_title"
                    android:layout_width="match_parent"
                    android:layout_height="wrap_content"
                    android:hint="@string/crime_title_hint"/>
        </LinearLayout>
    </LinearLayout>
    ...
</LinearLayout>
```

Run CriminalIntent and press on a crime to see its details. You should see your new UI looking just like Figure 16.1.

Looks great. Now, to respond to presses on your **ImageButton** and to control the content of your **ImageView**, you need properties referring to each of them. In **CrimeFragment**, call **findViewById(Int)** as usual on your inflated fragment_crime.xml to find your new views and wire them up.

## Listing 16.3  Adding properties (CrimeFragment.kt)

```kotlin
class CrimeFragment : Fragment() {
    ...
    private lateinit var suspectButton: Button
    private lateinit var photoButton: ImageButton
    private lateinit var photoView: ImageView
    private val crimeDetailViewModel: CrimeDetailViewModel by lazy {
        ViewModelProviders.of(this).get(CrimeDetailViewModel::class.java)
    }
    ...
    override fun onCreateView(
        inflater: LayoutInflater,
        container: ViewGroup?,
        savedInstanceState: Bundle?
    ): View? {
        ...
        suspectButton = view.findViewById(R.id.crime_suspect) as Button
        photoButton = view.findViewById(R.id.crime_camera) as ImageButton
        photoView = view.findViewById(R.id.crime_photo) as ImageView

        return view

    }
    ...
}
```

And with that, you are done with the UI for the time being. (You will wire those buttons up in a minute or two.)

# File Storage

Your photo needs more than a place on the screen. Full-size pictures are too large to stick inside a SQLite database, much less an **Intent**. They will need a place to live on your device's filesystem.

Luckily, you have a place to stash these files: your private storage. Recall that your database is saved to your app's private storage. With functions like **Context.getFileStreamPath(String)** and **Context.getFilesDir()**, you can do the same thing with regular files, too (which will live in a subfolder adjacent to the databases subfolder your database lives in).

These are the basic file and directory functions in the **Context** class:

**getFilesDir(): File**

> returns a handle to the directory for private application files

**openFileInput(name: String): FileInputStream**

> opens an existing file in the files directory for input

**openFileOutput(name: String, mode: Int): FileOutputStream**

> opens a file in the files directory for output, possibly creating it

**getDir(name: String, mode: Int): File**

> gets (and possibly creates) a subdirectory within the files directory

**fileList(…): Array<String>**

> gets a list of filenames in the main files directory, such as for use with **openFileInput(String)**

**getCacheDir(): File**

> returns a handle to a directory you can use specifically for storing cache files; you should take care to keep this directory tidy and use as little space as possible

There is a catch. Because these files are private, *only your own application* can read or write to them. As long as no other app needs to access those files, these functions are sufficient.

However, they are not sufficient if another application needs to write to your files. This is the case for CriminalIntent, because the external camera app will need to save the picture it takes as a file in your app.

In those cases, the functions above do not go far enough: While there is a Context.MODE_WORLD_READABLE flag you can pass into **openFileOutput(String, Int)**, it is deprecated and not completely reliable in its effects on newer devices. Once upon a time you could also transfer files using publicly accessible external storage, but this has been locked down in recent versions of Android for security reasons.

If you need to share files with or receive files from other apps, you need to expose those files through a **ContentProvider**. A **ContentProvider** allows you to expose content URIs to other apps. They can then download from or write to those content URIs. Either way, you are in control and always have the option to deny those reads or writes if you so choose.

# Using FileProvider

When all you need to do is receive a file from another application, implementing an entire **ContentProvider** is overkill. Fortunately, Google has provided a convenience class called **FileProvider** that takes care of everything except the configuration work.

The first step is to declare **FileProvider** as a **ContentProvider** hooked up to a specific *authority*. Do this by adding a content provider declaration to your Android manifest.

## Listing 16.4  Adding a **FileProvider** declaration (manifests/AndroidManifest.xml)

```
<activity android:name=".MainActivity">
    ...
</activity>
<provider
        android:name="androidx.core.content.FileProvider"
        android:authorities="com.bignerdranch.android.criminalintent.fileprovider"
        android:exported="false"
        android:grantUriPermissions="true">
</provider>
```

The authority is a location – a place that files will be saved to. The string you choose for android:authorities must be unique across the entire system. To help ensure this, the convention is to prepend the authority string with your package name. (We show the package name com.bignerdranch.android.criminalintent above. If your app's package name is different, use your package name instead.)

By hooking up **FileProvider** to your authority, you give other apps a target for their requests. By adding the exported="false" attribute, you keep anyone from using your provider except you or anyone you grant permission to. And by adding the grantUriPermissions attribute, you add the ability to grant other apps permission to write to URIs on this authority when you send them out in an intent. (Keep an eye out for this later.)

Now that you have told Android where your **FileProvider** is, you also need to tell your **FileProvider** which files it is exposing. This bit of configuration is done with an extra XML resource file. Right-click your app/res folder in the project tool window and select New → Android resource file. Enter files for the name, and for Resource type select XML. Click OK and Android Studio will add and open the new resource file.

In the text view of your new res/xml/files.xml, add details about the file path (Listing 16.5).

## Listing 16.5  Filling out the paths description (res/xml/files.xml)

```
<PreferenceScreen xmlns:android="http://schemas.android.com/apk/res/android">

</PreferenceScreen>
<paths>
    <files-path name="crime_photos" path="."/>
</paths>
```

This XML file says, "Map the root path of my private storage as crime_photos." You will not use the crime_photos name – **FileProvider** uses that internally.

Now, hook up `files.xml` to your **FileProvider** by adding a meta-data tag in your AndroidManifest.xml.

### Listing 16.6  Hooking up the paths description (manifests/AndroidManifest.xml)

```
<provider
        android:name="androidx.core.content.FileProvider"
        android:authorities="com.bignerdranch.android.criminalintent.fileprovider"
        android:exported="false"
        android:grantUriPermissions="true">
    <meta-data
            android:name="android.support.FILE_PROVIDER_PATHS"
            android:resource="@xml/files"/>
</provider>
```

# Designating a picture location

Time to give your pictures a place to live on disk locally. First, add a computed property to **Crime** to get a well-known filename.

### Listing 16.7  Adding the filename property (Crime.kt)

```
@Entity
data class Crime(@PrimaryKey val id: UUID = UUID.randomUUID(),
                 var title: String = "",
                 var date: Date = Date(),
                 var isSolved: Boolean = false,
                 var suspect: String = "") {

    val photoFileName
        get() = "IMG_$id.jpg"
}
```

**photoFileName** does not include the path to the folder the photo will be stored in. However, the filename will be unique, since it is based on the **Crime**'s ID.

Next, find where the photos should live. **CrimeRepository** is responsible for everything related to persisting data in CriminalIntent, so it is a natural owner for this idea. Add a **getPhotoFile(Crime)** function to **CrimeRepository** that provides a complete local file path for **Crime**'s image.

### Listing 16.8  Finding the photo file location (CrimeRepository.kt)

```
class CrimeRepository private constructor(context: Context) {
    ...
    private val executor = Executors.newSingleThreadExecutor()
    private val filesDir = context.applicationContext.filesDir

    fun addCrime(crime: Crime) {
        ...
    }

    fun getPhotoFile(crime: Crime): File = File(filesDir, crime.photoFileName)
    ...
}
```

This code does not create any files on the filesystem. It only returns **File** objects that point to the right locations. Later on, you will use **FileProvider** to expose these paths as URIs.

Finally, add a function to **CrimeDetailViewModel** to expose the file information to **CrimeFragment**.

## Listing 16.9  Exposing a file through **CrimeDetailViewModel** (CrimeDetailViewModel.kt)

```
class CrimeDetailViewModel : ViewModel() {
    ...
    fun saveCrime(crime: Crime) {
        crimeRepository.updateCrime(crime)
    }

    fun getPhotoFile(crime: Crime): File {
        return crimeRepository.getPhotoFile(crime)
    }
}
```

# Using a Camera Intent

The next step is to actually take the picture. This is the easy part: You get to use an implicit intent again.

Start by stashing the location of the photo file. You will use it a few more times, so this will save a bit of work.

## Listing 16.10  Grabbing the photo file location (CrimeFragment.kt)

```
class CrimeFragment : Fragment(), DatePickerFragment.Callbacks {

    private lateinit var crime: Crime
    private lateinit var photoFile: File
    ...
    override fun onViewCreated(view: View, savedInstanceState: Bundle?) {
        ...
        crimeDetailViewModel.crimeLiveData.observe(
            viewLifecycleOwner,
            Observer { crime ->
                crime?.let {
                    this.crime = crime
                    photoFile = crimeDetailViewModel.getPhotoFile(crime)
                    updateUI()
                }
            })
    }
    ...
}
```

Next you will hook up the camera button to actually take the picture. The camera intent is defined in **MediaStore**, Android's lord and master of all things media related. You will send an intent with an action of MediaStore.ACTION_IMAGE_CAPTURE, and Android will fire up a camera activity and take a picture for you.

But hold that thought for one minute.

# Firing the intent

Now you are ready to fire the camera intent. The action you want is called `ACTION_IMAGE_CAPTURE`, and it is defined in the **MediaStore** class. **MediaStore** defines the public interfaces used in Android for interacting with common media – images, videos, and music. This includes the image capture intent, which fires up the camera.

By default, `ACTION_IMAGE_CAPTURE` will dutifully fire up the camera application and take a picture, but it will not be a full-resolution picture. Instead, it will take a small-resolution thumbnail picture and stick it inside the **Intent** object returned in **onActivityResult(…)**.

For a full-resolution output, you need to tell it where to save the image on the filesystem. This can be done by passing a **Uri** pointing to where you want to save the file in `MediaStore.EXTRA_OUTPUT`. This **Uri** will point to a location serviced by **FileProvider**.

First, create a new property for the photo URI and initialize it after you have a reference to the `photoFile`.

### Listing 16.11 Adding a photo URI property (`CrimeFragment.kt`)

```kotlin
class CrimeFragment : Fragment(), DatePickerFragment.Callbacks {

    private lateinit var crime: Crime
    private lateinit var photoFile: File
    private lateinit var photoUri: Uri
    ...
    override fun onViewCreated(view: View, savedInstanceState: Bundle?) {
        ...
        crimeDetailViewModel.crimeLiveData.observe(
            viewLifecycleOwner,
            Observer { crime ->
                crime?.let {
                    this.crime = crime
                    photoFile = crimeDetailViewModel.getPhotoFile(crime)
                    photoUri = FileProvider.getUriForFile(requireActivity(),
                        "com.bignerdranch.android.criminalintent.fileprovider",
                        photoFile)
                    updateUI()
                }
            })
    }
    ...
}
```

Calling **FileProvider.getUriForFile(…)** translates your local file path into a **Uri** the camera app can see. The function takes in your activity, provider authority, and photo file to create the URI that points to the file. The authority string you pass to **FileProvider.getUriForFile(…)** must match the authority string you defined in the manifest (Listing 16.4).

Next, write an implicit intent to ask for a new picture to be taken into the location saved in photoUri (Listing 16.12). Add code to ensure that the button is disabled if there is no camera app or if there is no location to save the photo to. (To determine whether there is a camera app available, you will query **PackageManager** for activities that respond to your camera implicit intent, as discussed in the section called Checking for responding activities in Chapter 15.)

## Listing 16.12  Firing a camera intent (CrimeFragment.kt)

```kotlin
private const val REQUEST_CONTACT = 1
private const val REQUEST_PHOTO = 2
private const val DATE_FORMAT = "EEE, MMM, dd"

class CrimeFragment : Fragment(), DatePickerFragment.Callbacks {
    ...
    override fun onStart() {
        ...
        suspectButton.apply {
            ...
        }

        photoButton.apply {
            val packageManager: PackageManager = requireActivity().packageManager

            val captureImage = Intent(MediaStore.ACTION_IMAGE_CAPTURE)
            val resolvedActivity: ResolveInfo? =
                packageManager.resolveActivity(captureImage,
                        PackageManager.MATCH_DEFAULT_ONLY)
            if (resolvedActivity == null) {
                isEnabled = false
            }

            setOnClickListener {
                captureImage.putExtra(MediaStore.EXTRA_OUTPUT, photoUri)

                val cameraActivities: List<ResolveInfo> =
                    packageManager.queryIntentActivities(captureImage,
                            PackageManager.MATCH_DEFAULT_ONLY)

                for (cameraActivity in cameraActivities) {
                    requireActivity().grantUriPermission(
                        cameraActivity.activityInfo.packageName,
                        photoUri,
                        Intent.FLAG_GRANT_WRITE_URI_PERMISSION)
                }

                startActivityForResult(captureImage, REQUEST_PHOTO)
            }
        }

        return view
    }
    ...
}
```

To actually write to photoUri, you need to grant the camera app permission. To do this, you grant the Intent.FLAG_GRANT_WRITE_URI_PERMISSION flag to every activity your cameraImage intent can resolve to. That grants them all a write permission specifically for this one **Uri**. Adding the android:grantUriPermissions attribute in your provider declaration was necessary to open this bit of functionality. Later, you will revoke this permission to close up that gap in your armor again.

Run CriminalIntent and press the camera button to run your camera app (Figure 16.2).

Figure 16.2 [Insert your camera app here]

# Scaling and Displaying Bitmaps

With that, you are successfully taking pictures. Your image will be saved to a file on the filesystem for you to use.

Your next step is to take this file, load it up, and show it to the user. To do this, you need to load it into a reasonably sized **Bitmap** object. To get a **Bitmap** from a file, all you need to do is use the **BitmapFactory** class:

```
val bitmap = BitmapFactory.decodeFile(photoFile.getPath())
```

There has to be a catch, right? Otherwise we would have put that in bold, you would have typed it in, and you would be done.

Here is the catch: When we say "reasonably sized," we mean it. A **Bitmap** is a simple object that stores literal pixel data. That means that even if the original file were compressed, there would be no compression in the **Bitmap** itself. So a 16-megapixel, 24-bit camera image – which might only be a 5 MB JPG – would blow up to 48 MB loaded into a **Bitmap** object (!).

You can get around this, but it does mean that you will need to scale the bitmap down by hand. You will first scan the file to see how big it is, next figure out how much you need to scale it by to fit it in a given area, and finally reread the file to create a scaled-down **Bitmap** object.

Create a new file called PictureUtils.kt and add a file-level function to it called getScaledBitmap(String, Int, Int) (Listing 16.13).

## Listing 16.13  Creating **getScaledBitmap(…)** (PictureUtils.kt)

```kotlin
fun getScaledBitmap(path: String, destWidth: Int, destHeight: Int): Bitmap {
    // Read in the dimensions of the image on disk
    var options = BitmapFactory.Options()
    options.inJustDecodeBounds = true
    BitmapFactory.decodeFile(path, options)

    val srcWidth = options.outWidth.toFloat()
    val srcHeight = options.outHeight.toFloat()

    // Figure out how much to scale down by
    var inSampleSize = 1
    if (srcHeight > destHeight || srcWidth > destWidth) {
        val heightScale = srcHeight / destHeight
        val widthScale = srcWidth / destWidth

        val sampleScale = if (heightScale > widthScale) {
            heightScale
        } else {
            widthScale
        }
        inSampleSize = Math.round(sampleScale)
    }

    options = BitmapFactory.Options()
    options.inSampleSize = inSampleSize

    // Read in and create final bitmap
    return BitmapFactory.decodeFile(path, options)
}
```

The key parameter above is `inSampleSize`. This determines how big each "sample" should be for each pixel – a sample size of 1 has one final horizontal pixel for each horizontal pixel in the original file, and a sample size of 2 has one horizontal pixel for every two horizontal pixels in the original file. So when `inSampleSize` is 2, the pixel count in the image is one-quarter of the pixel count in the original.

One more bit of bad news: When your fragment initially starts up, you will not know how big **PhotoView** is. Until a layout pass happens, views do not have dimensions onscreen. The first layout pass happens after **onCreate(…)**, **onStart()**, and **onResume()** initially run, which is why **PhotoView** does not know how big it is.

There are two solutions to this problem: Either you wait until a layout pass happens, or you use a conservative estimate. The conservative estimate approach is less efficient but more straightforward. Write another file-level function called **getScaledBitmap(String, Activity)** to scale a **Bitmap** for a particular **Activity**'s size.

## Listing 16.14  Writing a conservative scale function (PictureUtils.kt)

```kotlin
fun getScaledBitmap(path: String, activity: Activity): Bitmap {
    val size = Point()
    activity.windowManager.defaultDisplay.getSize(size)

    return getScaledBitmap(path, size.x, size.y)
}

fun getScaledBitmap(path: String, destWidth: Int, destHeight: Int): Bitmap {
    ...
}
```

This function checks to see how big the screen is and then scales the image down to that size. The **ImageView** you load into will always be smaller than this size, so this is a very conservative estimate.

Next, to load this **Bitmap** into your **ImageView**, add a function to **CrimeFragment** to update photoView.

## Listing 16.15  Updating photoView (CrimeFragment.kt)

```
class CrimeFragment : Fragment(), DatePickerFragment.Callbacks {
    ...
    private fun updateUI() {
        ...
    }

    private fun updatePhotoView() {
        if (photoFile.exists()) {
            val bitmap = getScaledBitmap(photoFile.path, requireActivity())
            photoView.setImageBitmap(bitmap)
        } else {
            photoView.setImageDrawable(null)
        }
    }

    override fun onActivityResult(requestCode: Int, resultCode: Int, data: Intent?) {
        ...
    }
    ...
}
```

Then call that function from inside **updateUI()** and **onActivityResult(…)**.

## Listing 16.16  Calling **updatePhotoView()** (CrimeFragment.kt)

```
class CrimeFragment : Fragment(), DatePickerFragment.Callbacks {
    ...
    private fun updateUI() {
        ...
        if (crime.suspect.isNotEmpty()) {
            suspectButton.text = crime.suspect
        }
        updatePhotoView()
    }
    ...
    override fun onActivityResult(requestCode: Int, resultCode: Int, data: Intent?) {
        when {
            resultCode != Activity.RESULT_OK -> return

            requestCode == REQUEST_CONTACT && data != null -> {
                ...
            }

            requestCode == REQUEST_PHOTO -> {
                updatePhotoView()
            }
        }
    }
    ...
}
```

Now that the camera is done writing to your file, you can revoke the permission, closing off access to your file again. Do this from **onActivityResult(…)** to revoke it when a valid result is received and also from **onDetach()** to cover the possibility of an invalid response.

## Listing 16.17  Revoking URI permissions (CrimeFragment.kt)

```kotlin
class CrimeFragment : Fragment(), DatePickerFragment.Callbacks {
    ...
    override fun onStop() {
        ...
    }

    override fun onDetach() {
        super.onDetach()
        requireActivity().revokeUriPermission(photoUri,
            Intent.FLAG_GRANT_WRITE_URI_PERMISSION)
    }

    override fun onActivityResult(requestCode: Int, resultCode: Int, data: Intent?) {
        when {
            ...

            requestCode == REQUEST_PHOTO -> {
                requireActivity().revokeUriPermission(photoUri,
                    Intent.FLAG_GRANT_WRITE_URI_PERMISSION)
                updatePhotoView()
            }
        }
    }
    ...
}
```

Run CriminalIntent again. Open a crime's detail screen and use the camera button to take a photo. You should see your image displayed in the thumbnail view (Figure 16.3).

Figure 16.3  Thumbnail proudly appearing on the crime detail screen

# Declaring Features

Your camera implementation works great now. One more task remains: Tell potential users about it. When your app uses a feature like the camera – or near-field communication, or any other feature that may vary from device to device – it is strongly recommended that you tell Android about it. This allows other apps (like the Play Store) to refuse to install your app if it uses a feature the device does not support.

To declare that you use the camera, add a `<uses-feature>` tag to your `AndroidManifest.xml` (Listing 16.18).

### Listing 16.18 Adding a `<uses-feature>` tag (manifests/AndroidManifest.xml)

```
<manifest xmlns:android="http://schemas.android.com/apk/res/android"
    package="com.bignerdranch.android.criminalintent" >

    <uses-feature android:name="android.hardware.camera"
                  android:required="false"/>
    ...
</manifest>
```

You include the optional attribute `android:required` here. Why? By default, declaring that you use a feature means that your app will not work correctly without that feature. This is not the case for CriminalIntent. You call **resolveActivity(…)** to check for a working camera app, then gracefully disable the camera button if you do not find one.

Passing in `android:required="false"` handles this situation correctly. You tell Android that your app can work fine without the camera, but that some parts will be disabled as a result.

# Challenge: Detail Display

While you can certainly see the image you display here, you cannot see it very well. For this first challenge, create a new **DialogFragment** that displays a zoomed-in version of your crime scene photo. When you press on the thumbnail, it should pull up the zoomed-in **DialogFragment**.

# Challenge: Efficient Thumbnail Load

In this chapter, you had to use a crude estimate of the size you should scale down to. This is not ideal, but it works and is quick to implement.

With the out-of-the-box APIs, you can use a tool called **ViewTreeObserver**, an object that you can get from any view in your **Activity**'s hierarchy:

```
val observer = imageView.viewTreeObserver
```

You can register a variety of listeners on a **ViewTreeObserver**, including **OnGlobalLayoutListener**. This listener fires an event whenever a layout pass happens.

For this challenge, adjust your code so that it uses the dimensions of photoView when they are valid and waits until a layout pass before initially calling **updatePhotoView()**.

# 17
# Localization

Knowing CriminalIntent is going to be a wildly popular app, you have decided to make it accessible to a larger audience. Your first step is to *localize* all of the user-facing text so your app can be read in Spanish or English.

Localization is the process of providing the appropriate resources for your app based on the user's language setting. In this chapter you will provide a Spanish version of res/values/strings.xml. When a device's language is set to Spanish, Android will automatically find and use the Spanish strings at runtime (Figure 17.1).

## Figure 17.1 IntentoCriminal

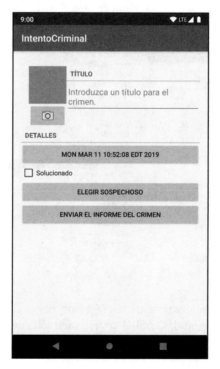

# Localizing Resources

Language settings are part of the device's configuration. (See the section called Device Configuration Changes and the Activity Lifecycle in Chapter 3 for an overview of device configuration.) Android provides qualifiers for different languages, just as it does for screen orientation, screen size, and other configuration factors. This makes localization straightforward: You create resource subdirectories with the desired language configuration qualifier and put the alternative resources in them. The Android resource system does the rest.

In your CriminalIntent project, create a new values resource file: In the project tool window, right-click res/values/ and select New → Values resource file. Enter strings for the File name. Leave the Source set option set to main and make sure Directory name is set to values.

Select Locale in the Available qualifiers list and click the >> button to move Locale to the Chosen qualifiers section. Select es: Spanish in the Language list. Any Region will be automatically selected in the Specific Region Only list – which is just what you want, so leave that selection be.

The resulting New Resource File window should look similar to Figure 17.2.

Figure 17.2  Adding a qualified strings resource file

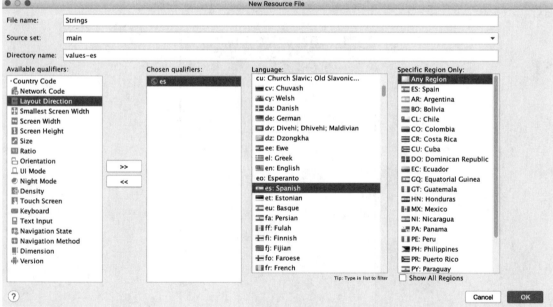

Note that Android Studio automatically changes the Directory name field to values-es. The language configuration qualifiers are taken from ISO 639-1 codes, and each consists of two characters. For Spanish, the qualifier is –es.

Click OK. The new `strings.xml` file will be listed under `res/values`, with `(es)` after its name. The strings files are grouped together in the project tool window's **Android** view (Figure 17.3).

## Figure 17.3 Viewing new `strings.xml` in Android view

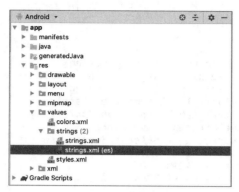

However, if you explore the directory structure, you will see that your project now contains an additional values directory: `res/values-es`. The newly generated `strings.xml` is located inside of this new directory (Figure 17.4).

## Figure 17.4 Viewing new `strings.xml` in Project view

Now it is time to make the magic happen. Add Spanish versions of all your strings to res/values-es/ strings.xml. (If you do not wish to type these strings in, copy the contents from the solutions file at www.bignerdranch.com/solutions/AndroidProgramming4e.zip.)

## Listing 17.1  Adding Spanish alternatives for string resources (res/values-es/strings.xml)

```
<resources>
    <string name="app_name">IntentoCriminal</string>
    <string name="crime_title_hint">Introduzca un título para el crimen.</string>
    <string name="crime_title_label">Título</string>
    <string name="crime_details_label">Detalles</string>
    <string name="crime_solved_label">Solucionado</string>
    <string name="new_crime">Crimen Nuevo</string>
    <string name="crime_suspect_text">Elegir Sospechoso</string>
    <string name="crime_report_text">Enviar el Informe del Crimen</string>
    <string name="crime_report">%1$s!
        El crimen fue descubierto el %2$s. %3$s, y %4$s
    </string>
    <string name="crime_report_solved">El caso está resuelto</string>
    <string name="crime_report_unsolved">El caso no está resuelto</string>
    <string name="crime_report_no_suspect">no hay sospechoso.</string>
    <string name="crime_report_suspect">el/la sospechoso/a es %s.</string>
    <string name="crime_report_subject">IntentoCriminal Informe del Crimen</string>
    <string name="send_report">Enviar el informe del crimen a través de</string>
</resources>
```

That is all you have to do to provide localized string resources for your app. To confirm, change your device's settings to Spanish by opening Settings and finding the language settings. Depending on your version of Android, these settings will be labeled Language and input, Language and Keyboard, or something similar.

When you get to a list of language options, choose a setting for Español. The region (España or Estados Unidos) will not matter, because the qualification -es matches both. (Note that on newer versions of Android, users can select multiple languages and assign a priority order. If you are on a newer device, make sure Español appears first in your language settings list.)

Now run CriminalIntent and bask in the glory of your newly localized app. When you are done basking, return your device's language setting to English. Look for Ajustes or Configuración (Settings) in the launcher and find the setting that includes Idioma (Language).

# Default resources

The configuration qualifier for English is -en. In a fit of localization, you might think to rename your existing values directory to values-en. This is not a good idea, but pretend for a moment you did just that: Your hypothetical update means your app now has an English strings.xml in values-en and a Spanish strings.xml in values-es.

Your newly updated app will build just fine. It will also run just fine on devices with the language set to Spanish or English. But what happens if the user's device language is set to Italian? Bad things. Very bad things. If the app is allowed to run, Android will not find string resources that match the current configuration. This will cause your app to crash with a **Resources.NotFoundException**.

Android Studio takes steps to save you from this fate. The Android Asset Packaging Tool (AAPT) does many checks while packaging up your resources. If AAPT finds that you are using resources that are not included in the default resource files, it will throw an error at compile time:

```
Android resource linking failed

warn: removing resource
com.bignerdranch.android.criminalintent:string/crime_title_label
without required default value.

AAPT: error: resource string/crime_title_label
(aka com.bignerdranch.android.criminalintent:string/crime_title_label)
not found.

error: failed linking file resources.
```

The moral of the story is this: Provide a *default resource* for each of your resources. Resources in unqualified resource directories are your default resources. Default resources will be used if no match for the current device configuration is found. Your app will misbehave if Android looks for a resource and cannot find either one that matches the device configuration or a default.

## Screen density works differently

The exception to providing default resources is for screen density. A project's drawable directories are typically qualified for screen density with -mdpi, -xxhdpi, etc., as you have seen. However, Android's decision about which drawable resource to use is not a simple matter of matching the device's screen density or defaulting to an unqualified directory if there is no match.

The choice is based on a combination of screen size and density, and Android may choose a drawable from a directory that is qualified with a lower or higher density than the device and then scale the drawable. There are more details in the docs at developer.android.com/guide/practices/screens_support.html, but the important point is that putting default drawable resources in res/drawable/ is not necessary.

# Checking string coverage using the Translations Editor

As the number of languages you support grows, making sure you provide a version of each string for each language becomes more difficult. Luckily, Android Studio provides a handy Translations Editor to see all of your translations in one place. Before starting, open your default strings.xml and comment out crime_title_label and crime_details_label (Listing 17.2).

## Listing 17.2 Commenting out strings (res/values/strings.xml)

```
<resources>
    <string name="app_name">CriminalIntent</string>
    <string name="crime_title_hint">Enter a title for the crime.</string>
    <!--<string name="crime_title_label">Title</string>-->
    <!--<string name="crime_details_label">Details</string>-->
    <string name="crime_solved_label">Solved</string>
    ...
</resources>
```

To launch the Translations Editor, right-click one of the strings.xml files in the project tool window and select **Open Translations Editor**. The Translations Editor displays all of the app's strings and the translation status for each of the languages your app currently provides any qualified string values for. Since crime_title_label and crime_details_label are commented out, you will see those field names in red (Figure 17.5).

## Figure 17.5 Using the Translations Editor to check your string coverage

| Key | Resource Folder | Untranslatable | Default Value | Spanish (es) |
|---|---|---|---|---|
| crime_title_hint | app/src/main/res | ☐ | Enter a title for the crime. | Introduzca un título para el crimen. |
| app_name | app/src/main/res | ☐ | CriminalIntent | IntentoCriminal |
| crime_title_label | app/src/main/res | ☐ | | Título |
| crime_details_label | app/src/main/res | ☐ | | Detalles |
| crime_solved_label | app/src/main/res | ☐ | Solved | Solucionado |
| new_crime | app/src/main/res | ☐ | New Crime | Crimen Nuevo |
| crime_suspect_text | app/src/main/res | ☐ | Choose Suspect | Elegir Sospechoso |
| crime_report_text | app/src/main/res | ☐ | Send Crime Report | Enviar el Informe del Crimen |
| crime_report | app/src/main/res | ☐ | %1$s![...] | %1$s![...] |
| crime_report_solved | app/src/main/res | ☐ | The case is solved | El caso está resuelto |
| crime_report_unsolved | app/src/main/res | ☐ | The case is not solved | El caso no está resuelto |
| crime_report_no_suspect | app/src/main/res | ☐ | there is no suspect. | no hay sospechoso. |
| crime_report_suspect | app/src/main/res | ☐ | the suspect is %s. | el/la sospechoso/a es %s. |
| crime_report_subject | app/src/main/res | ☐ | CriminalIntent Crime Report | IntentoCriminal Informe del Crimen |
| send_report | app/src/main/res | ☐ | Send crime report via | Enviar el informe del crimen a través de |

This provides an easy list of resources to add to your project. Find missing resources in any locale configuration and add them to the related strings file.

Although you can add strings right in the Translations Editor, in your case you only need to uncomment crime_title_label and crime_details_label. Do that before moving on.

# Targeting a region

You can qualify a resource directory with a language-plus-region qualifier that targets resources even more specifically. For instance, the qualifier for Spanish spoken in Spain is -es-rES, where the r denotes a region qualifier and ES is the ISO 3166-1-alpha-2 code for Spain. Configuration qualifiers are not case sensitive, but it is good to follow Android's convention here: Use a lowercase language code and an uppercase region code prefixed with a lowercase r.

Note that a language-region qualifier, such as -es-rES, may look like two distinct configuration qualifiers that have been combined, but it is just one. The region is not a valid qualifier on its own.

A resource qualified with both a locale and region has two opportunities for matching a user's locale. An exact match occurs when both the language and region qualifiers match the user's locale. If no exact match is found, the system will strip off the region qualifier and look for an exact match for the language only.

The selection of resources when there is not an exact match can vary depending on the device's Android version. Figure 17.6 shows the locale resource resolution strategy before and after Android Nougat.

## Figure 17.6 Locale resolution (pre- and post-Nougat)

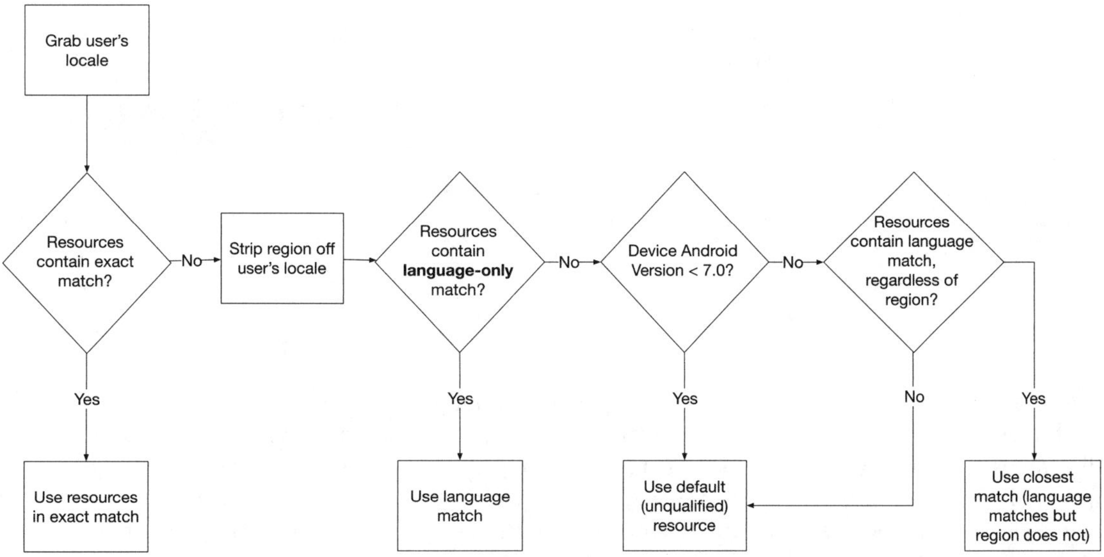

On devices running pre-Nougat versions of Android, if no language match is found, the default (unqualified resource) is used – period.

Nougat and later versions have enhanced locale support, with more locales and the ability to select more than one locale in the device's settings. The system also uses a more intelligent resource resolution strategy for locale with the aim of showing the correct language as often as possible, even if the app does not provide an exact region match or a nonqualified language match. If no exact match is found on a device running Nougat, and no language-only match is found, the system will look for a resource qualified with the same language but a different region and will use the best match of resources that meet those criteria.

Consider an example. Suppose you set the language on your device to Spanish and your region to Chile (Figure 17.7). An app on your device contains Spanish `strings.xml` files tailored for Spain and Mexico (in `values-es-rES` and `values-es-rMX`). The default `values` directory contains an English `strings.xml`.

If your device is running pre-Nougat Android, you will see the English contents of the default `values` directory. But if your device is running Nougat or later, you will have a better experience: You will see the contents of `values-es-rMX/strings.xml` – which means you will see Spanish, though not tailored to Chile.

## Figure 17.7  Locale resolution example (pre- and post-Nougat)

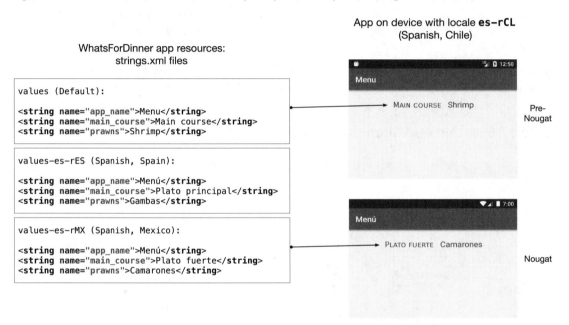

This example is a bit contrived. But it brings up an important point: Provide strings in as general a context as possible, using language-only qualified directories as much as possible and region-qualified directories only when necessary. Rather than maintaining all Spanish user-facing strings in region-qualified directories, this example app would be better off storing most of the Spanish strings in a language-only qualified `values-es` directory and providing region-qualified strings only for words and phrases that are different in the different regional dialects.

This not only makes maintaining the strings files easier for the programmer but also helps the system resolve the resources on both pre-Nougat devices and Nougat or later devices (by providing a language-only match). Note that this advice goes for all types of alternative resources in the `values` directories: Provide shared resources in more general directories and include only the resources that need to be tailored in more specifically qualified directories.

# Configuration Qualifiers

You have now seen and used several configuration qualifiers for providing alternative resources: language (such as `values-es`), screen orientation (`layout-land`), and screen density (`drawable-mdpi`).

The device configurations that Android provides configuration qualifiers to target resources for are:

1. mobile country code (MCC), optionally followed by mobile network code (MNC)
2. language code, optionally followed by region code
3. layout direction
4. smallest width
5. available width
6. available height
7. screen size
8. screen aspect
9. round screen (API level 23 and above)
10. wide color gamut
11. high dynamic range
12. screen orientation
13. UI mode
14. night mode
15. screen density (dpi)
16. touchscreen type
17. keyboard availability
18. primary text input method
19. navigation key availability
20. primary non-touch navigation method
21. API level

You can find descriptions of these characteristics and examples of specific configuration qualifiers at `developer.android.com/guide/topics/resources/providing-resources.html#AlternativeResources`.

Not all qualifiers are supported by earlier versions of Android. Luckily the system implicitly adds a platform version qualifier to qualifiers that were introduced after Android 1.0. So if, for example, you use the `round` qualifier, Android will automatically include the `v23` qualifier, because round screen qualifiers were added in API level 23. This means you do not have to worry about problems on older devices when you introduce resources qualified for newer devices.

## Prioritizing alternative resources

Given the many types of configuration qualifiers for targeting resources, there may be times when the device configuration will match more than one alternative resource. When this happens, qualifiers are given precedence in the order shown in the list above.

To see this prioritizing in action, add another alternative resource to CriminalIntent – a longer English version of the crime_title_hint string resource – to be displayed when the current configuration's width is at least 600dp. The crime_title_hint resource is displayed in the crime title text box before the user enters any text. When CriminalIntent is running on a screen that is at least 600dp (such as on a tablet, or perhaps in landscape mode on a smaller device), this change will display a more descriptive, engaging hint for the title field.

Create a new values resource file called strings. Follow the steps from the section called Localizing Resources earlier in this chapter to create the resource file, but select Screen Width in the Available qualifiers list and click the >> button to move Screen Width to the Chosen qualifiers section. In the Screen width box that appears, enter 600. The directory name will automatically be set to values-w600dp; -w600dp will match any device where the current available screen width is 600dp or more, meaning a device may match when in landscape mode but not in portrait mode. (To learn more about screen size qualifiers, read the section called For the More Curious: More on Determining Device Size near the end of this chapter.) Your dialog should look like Figure 17.8.

### Figure 17.8  Adding strings for a wider screen

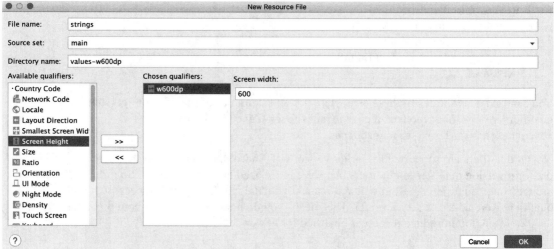

Now, add a longer value for `crime_title_hint` to `res/values-w600dp/strings.xml`.

## Listing 17.3 Creating an alternative string resource for a wider screen (`res/values-w600dp/strings.xml`)

```
<resources>
    <string name="crime_title_hint">
        Enter a meaningful, memorable title for the crime.
    </string>
</resources>
```

The only string resource you want to be different on wider screens is `crime_title_hint`. That is why `crime_title_hint` is the only string you specified in `values-w600dp`. As we said earlier, you should provide alternatives for only those string resources (and other `values` resources) that will be different based on some configuration qualification. You do not need to duplicate strings when they are the same. More than that, you *should* not: Those duplicated strings would only end up being a maintenance hassle down the road.

Now you have three versions of `crime_title_hint`: a default version in `res/values/strings.xml`, a Spanish alternative in `res/values-es/strings.xml`, and a wide-screen alternative in `res/values-w600dp/strings.xml`.

With your device's language set to Spanish, run CriminalIntent and rotate to landscape (Figure 17.9). The Spanish language alternative has precedence, so you see the string from `res/values-es/strings.xml` instead of `res/values-w600dp/strings.xml`.

## Figure 17.9 Android prioritizes language over available screen width

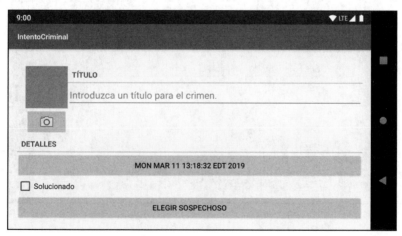

If you like, change your settings back to English and check the app again to confirm that the alternative wide-screen string appears as expected.

## Multiple qualifiers

You may have noticed that the New Resource File dialog has many available qualifiers. You can put more than one qualifier on a resource directory. When using multiple qualifiers on directories, you must put them in the order of their precedence. Thus, values-es-w600dp is a valid directory name, but values-w600dp-es is not. (When you use the New Resource File dialog, it correctly configures the directory name for you.)

Create a directory for a wide-screen Spanish string. It should be named values-es-w600dp and have a file named strings.xml. Add a string resource for crime_title_hint to values-es-w600dp/strings.xml (Listing 17.4).

### Listing 17.4  Creating a wide-screen Spanish string resource (res/values-es-w600dp/strings.xml)

```
<resources>
    <string name="crime_title_hint">
        Introduzca un título significativo y memorable para el crimen.
    </string>
</resources>
```

Now, with your language set to Spanish, run CriminalIntent to confirm that your new alternative resource appears on cue (Figure 17.10).

### Figure 17.10  Spanish wide-screen string resource

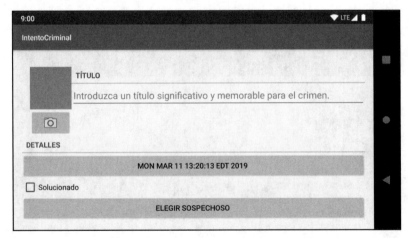

# Finding the best-matching resources

Let's walk through how Android determined which version of `crime_title_hint` to display in this run. First, consider the four alternatives for the string resource named `crime_title_hint` and an example landscape device configuration for a Pixel 2 set to Spanish language and with an available screen width greater than 600dp:

**Device configuration**

- Language: es (Spanish)
- Available height: 411dp
- Available width: 731dp
- (etc.)

**App values for `crime_title_hint`**

- `values`
- `values-es`
- `values-es-w600dp`
- `values-w600dp`

## Ruling out incompatible directories

The first step that Android takes to find the best resource is to rule out any resource directory that is incompatible with the current configuration.

None of the four choices is incompatible with the current configuration. (If you rotated the device to portrait, the available width would become 411dp, and the resource directories `values-w600dp/` and `values-es-w600dp/` would be incompatible and thus ruled out.)

## Stepping through the precedence table

After the incompatible resource directories have been ruled out, Android starts working through the precedence table shown in the section called Configuration Qualifiers earlier in this chapter, starting with the highest priority qualifier: MCC. If there is a resource directory with an MCC qualifier, then all resource directories that *do not* have an MCC qualifier are ruled out. If there is still more than one matching directory, then Android considers the next-highest precedence qualifier and continues until only one directory remains.

In our example, no directories contain an MCC qualifier, so no directories are ruled out, and Android moves down the list to the language qualifier. Two directories (`values-es` and `values-es-w600dp`) contain the matching language qualifier -es. The `values` and `values-w600dp` directories do not contain a language qualifier and thus are ruled out.

(However, as you read earlier in this chapter, the unqualified `values` directory serves as the default resource, or fallback. So while it is ruled out for now due to lack of a language qualifier, `values` could still end up being the best match if the other values directories have a mismatch in one or more of the lower-order qualifiers.)

**Device configuration**

- Language: es (Spanish)
- Available height: 411dp
- Available width: 731dp
- (etc.)

**App values for `crime_title_hint`**

- ~~values~~ (not language specific)
- `values-es`
- `values-es-w600dp`
- ~~values-w600dp~~ (not language specific)

Because there are multiple values still in the running, Android keeps stepping down the qualifier list. When it reaches available width, it finds one directory with an available width qualifier and one without. It rules out values-es, leaving only values-es-w600dp:

**Device configuration**

- Language: es (Spanish)
- Available height: 411dp
- Available width: 731dp
- (etc.)

**App values for `crime_title_hint`**

- ~~values~~ (not language or width specific)
- ~~values-es~~ (not width specific)
- **values-es-w600dp** (best match)
- ~~values-w600dp~~ (not language specific)

Thus, Android uses the resource in values-es-w600dp.

# Testing Alternative Resources

It is important to test your app on different device configurations to see how your layouts and other resources look on those configurations. You can test on both real and virtual devices. You can also use the graphical layout tool.

The graphical layout tool has many options for previewing how a layout will appear in different configurations. You can preview the layout on different screen sizes, device types, API levels, languages, and more.

To see these options, open res/layout/fragment_crime.xml in the graphical layout tool. Then try some of the settings in the toolbar shown in Figure 17.11.

**Figure 17.11  Using the graphical layout tool to preview various device configurations**

You can see all of your default resources in action by setting a device or emulator to a language that you have not localized any resources for. Run your app and put it through its paces. Visit all of the views and rotate them.

Before continuing to the next chapter, you may want to change your device's language back to English.

Congratulations! Now your CriminalIntent app can be enjoyed fully in both Spanish and English. Crimes will be logged. Cases will be solved. And all in the comfort of your user's native language (so long as that is either Spanish or English). And adding support for more languages is simply a matter of including additional qualified strings files.

# For the More Curious: More on Determining Device Size

Android provides three qualifiers that allow you to test for the dimensions of the device. Table 17.1 shows these new qualifiers.

Table 17.1  Discrete screen dimension qualifiers

| Qualifier format | Description |
|---|---|
| wXXXdp | available width: width greater than or equal to XXX dp |
| hXXXdp | available height: height greater than or equal to XXX dp |
| swXXXdp | smallest width: width or height (whichever is smaller) greater than or equal to XXX dp |

Let's say that you wanted to specify a layout that would only be used if the display were at least 300dp wide. In that case, you could use an available width qualifier and put your layout file in res/layout-w300dp (the "w" is for "width"). You can do the same thing for height by using an "h" (for "height").

However, the height and width may swap depending on the orientation of the device. To detect a particular size of screen, you can use sw, which stands for *smallest width*. This specifies the smallest dimension of your screen. Depending on the device's orientation, this can be either width or height. If the screen is 1024x800, then sw is 800. If the screen is 800x1024, sw is still 800.

# Challenge: Localizing Dates

You may have noticed that, regardless of the device's locale, the dates displayed in CriminalIntent are always formatted in the default US style, with the month before the day. Take your localization a step further by formatting the dates according to the locale configuration. It is easier than you might think.

Check out the developer documentation on the **DateFormat** class, which is provided as part of the Android framework. **DateFormat** provides a date-time formatter that will take into consideration the current locale. You can control the output further by using configuration constants built into **DateFormat**.

# 18

# Accessibility

In this chapter you will make CriminalIntent more *accessible*. An accessible app is usable by anyone, regardless of any impairments in vision, mobility, or hearing. These impairments may be permanent, but they could also be temporary or situational: Dilated eyes after an eye exam can make focusing difficult. Greasy hands while cooking may mean you do not want to touch the screen. And if you are at a loud concert, the music drowns out any sounds made by your device. The more accessible an app is, the more pleasant it is to use for everyone.

Making an app fully accessible is a tall order. But that is no excuse not to try. In this chapter you will take some steps to make CriminalIntent more usable for people with a visual impairment. This is a good place to begin learning about accessibility issues and accessible app design.

The changes you make in this chapter will not alter the appearance of the app. Instead, the changes will make your app easier to explore with *TalkBack*.

# TalkBack

TalkBack is an Android screen reader made by Google. It speaks out the contents of a screen based on what the user is doing.

TalkBack works because it is an *accessibility service*, which is a special component that can read information from the screen (no matter which app you are using). Anyone can write their own accessibility service, but TalkBack is the most popular.

To use TalkBack, install the Android Accessibility Suite through the Play Store app on your emulator or device (Figure 18.1). If you choose to use an emulator, you must use an emulator image that has the Play Store installed.

Figure 18.1  Android Accessibility Suite

Next, make sure the device's sound output is not muted – but you may want to grab headphones, because once TalkBack is enabled the device will do a lot of "talking."

To enable TalkBack, launch Settings and press Accessibility. Press on TalkBack under the Screen readers heading. Then press the Use service switch near the top right of the screen to turn TalkBack on (Figure 18.2).

## Figure 18.2  TalkBack settings screen

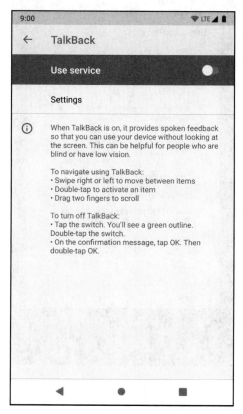

Android presents a dialog asking for permission to access certain information, such as observing the user's actions, and to alter certain settings, such as turning on Explore by Touch (Figure 18.3). Press OK.

Figure 18.3  Giving TalkBack permission

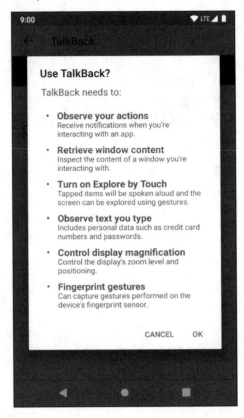

If this is your first time using TalkBack on the device, you will be brought through a tutorial. When you return to the TalkBack settings menu, exit it by pressing the Up button in the toolbar (the left-pointing arrow).

You will notice something different right away. A green outline appears around the Up button (Figure 18.4) and the device speaks: "Navigate Up button. Double-tap to activate."

## Figure 18.4  TalkBack enabled

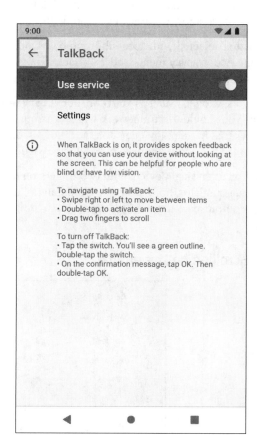

(Although "press" is the usual terminology for Android devices, TalkBack uses "tap." Also, TalkBack uses double-taps, which are not commonly used in Android.)

The green outline indicates which UI element has *accessibility focus*. Only one UI element can have accessibility focus at a time. When a UI element receives focus, TalkBack will provide information about that element.

When TalkBack is enabled, a single press (or "tap") gives an element accessibility focus. Double-tapping anywhere on the screen activates the element that has focus. So double-tapping anywhere when the Up button has focus navigates up, double-tapping when a checkbox has focus toggles its check state, and so on. (Also, if your device locks, you can unlock it by pressing the lock icon and then double-tapping anywhere on the screen.)

## Explore by Touch

By turning TalkBack on, you have also enabled TalkBack's Explore by Touch mode. This means the device will speak information about an item immediately after it is pressed. (This assumes that the item pressed specifies information TalkBack can read, which you will learn more about shortly.)

Leave the Up button selected with accessibility focus. Double-tap anywhere on the screen. The device returns you to the Accessibility menu, and TalkBack announces information about what is showing and what has accessibility focus: "Accessibility. Navigate Up button. Double-tap to activate."

Android framework widgets, such as `Toolbar`, `RecyclerView`, and `Button`, have basic TalkBack support built in. You should use framework widgets as much as possible so you can leverage the accessibility work that has already been done for those widgets. It is possible to properly respond to accessibility events for custom widgets, but that is beyond the scope of this book.

To scroll the list on a physical device, hold two fingers on the screen and drag them up or down. To scroll the list on an emulator, hold down the Command (Ctrl) button on the keyboard, click on one of the two larger, semitransparent circles that appear, and drag up or down with your mouse or trackpad (Figure 18.5).

### Figure 18.5  Scrolling on the emulator

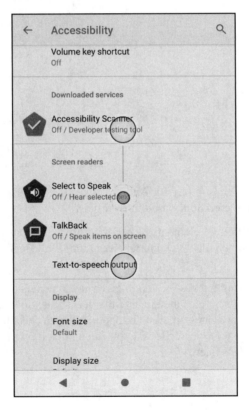

Depending on the length of the list, you will hear tones that change as you scroll. These tones are *earcons*, sounds used to give meta information about the interaction.

# Linear navigation by swiping

Imagine what it must be like to explore an app by touch for the first time. You would not know where things are located. What if the only way to learn what was on the screen was to press all around until you landed on an element that TalkBack could read? You might end up pressing on the same thing multiple times – worse, you might miss elements altogether.

Luckily, there is a way to explore the UI linearly, and in fact this is the more common way to use TalkBack: Swiping right moves accessibility focus to the next item on the screen. Swiping left moves accessibility focus to the previous item on the screen. This allows the user to walk through each item on the screen in a linear fashion, rather than trial-and-error poking around in hopes of landing on something meaningful.

Try it out for yourself. Launch CriminalIntent and go to the crime list screen. By default, accessibility focus will be given to the + action item in the app bar. (If not, press on the + to give it accessibility focus.) The device reads out, "CriminalIntent. New Crime. Double-tap to activate." (Figure 18.6).

Figure 18.6  New Crime action item selected

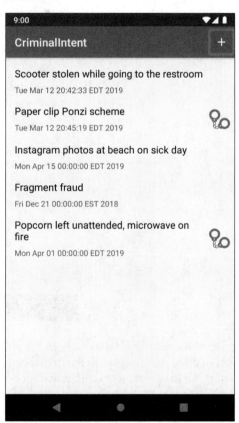

For framework widgets, such as menu items and buttons, TalkBack will read the visible text content displayed on the widget by default. But the New Crime menu item is just an icon and does not have any visible text. In this case, TalkBack looks for other information in the widget. You specified a `title` in your menu XML, and that is what TalkBack reads to the user. TalkBack will also provide details about actions the user can take on the widget and sometimes information about what kind of widget it is.

Now swipe left. Accessibility focus moves to the CriminalIntent title in the app bar. TalkBack announces, "CriminalIntent" (Figure 18.7).

## Figure 18.7  App bar title selected

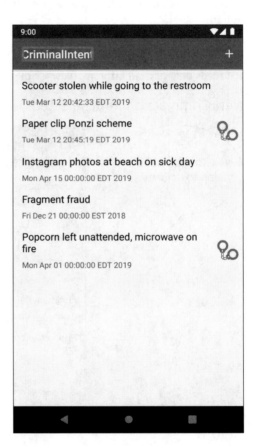

Swipe right, and TalkBack reads information about the + (New Crime) menu button again. Swipe right a second time; accessibility focus moves to the first crime in the list. Swipe left, and focus moves back to the + menu button. Android does its best to move accessibility focus in an order that makes sense.

# Making Non-Text Elements Readable by TalkBack

With the New Crime button selected, double-tap anywhere on the screen to launch the crime details screen.

## Adding content descriptions

On the crime details screen, press the image capture button to give it accessibility focus (Figure 18.8). TalkBack announces, "Unlabeled button. Double-tap to activate." (You may get slightly different results depending on the version of Android you are using.)

Figure 18.8  Image capture button selected

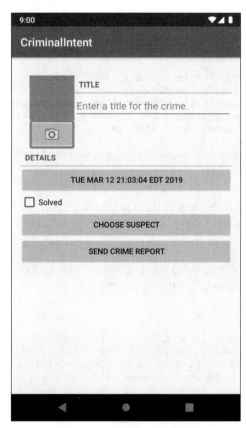

The camera button does not display any text, so TalkBack describes the button as well as it can. While this is TalkBack's best effort, the information is not very helpful to a user with a vision impairment.

Luckily, this problem is very easy to fix. You are going to specify details for TalkBack to read by adding a *content description* to the **ImageButton**. A content description is a piece of text that describes the widget and is read by TalkBack. (While you are at it, you are going to add a content description for the **ImageView** that displays the selected picture, too.)

You can set a widget's content description in the XML layout file by setting a value for the attribute android:contentDescription. That is what you are going to do next. You can also set it in your UI setup code, using *someView*.setContentDescription(*someString*), which you will do later in this chapter.

The text you set should be meaningful without being overly wordy. Remember, TalkBack users will be listening to the audio, which is linear. They can speed up the pace of TalkBack's speech output, but even so you want to avoid adding extraneous information and wasting users' time. For example, if you are setting the description for a framework widget, avoid including information about what kind of widget it is (like "a button"), because TalkBack already knows and includes that information.

First, some housekeeping. Add the content description strings to the unqualified res/values/strings.xml.

### Listing 18.1  Adding content description strings (res/values/strings.xml)

```
<resources>
    ...
    <string name="crime_details_label">Details</string>
    <string name="crime_solved_label">Solved</string>
    <string name="crime_photo_button_description">Take photo of crime scene</string>
    <string name="crime_photo_no_image_description">
        Crime scene photo (not set)
    </string>
    <string name="crime_photo_image_description">Crime scene photo (set)</string>
    ...
</resources>
```

Android Studio will underline the newly added strings in red, warning you that you have not defined the Spanish version of these new strings. To fix this, add the content description strings to res/values-es/strings.xml.

### Listing 18.2  Adding Spanish content description strings (res/values-es/strings.xml)

```
<resources>
    ...
    <string name="crime_details_label">Detalles</string>
    <string name="crime_solved_label">Solucionado</string>
    <string name="crime_photo_button_description">
        Tomar foto de la escena del crimen
    </string>
    <string name="crime_photo_no_image_description">
        Foto de la escena del crimen (no establecida)
    </string>
    <string name="crime_photo_image_description">
        Foto de la escena del crimen (establecida)
    </string>
    ...
</resources>
```

Next, open res/layout/fragment_crime.xml and set the content description for the **ImageButton**.

## Listing 18.3 Setting the content description for **ImageButton** (res/layout/fragment_crime.xml)

```
<ImageButton
    android:id="@+id/crime_camera"
    android:layout_width="match_parent"
    android:layout_height="wrap_content"
    android:src="@android:drawable/ic_menu_camera"
    android:contentDescription="@string/crime_photo_button_description"/>
```

Run CriminalIntent and press the camera button. TalkBack helpfully announces, "Take photo of crime scene button. Double-tap to activate." This spoken information is much more helpful than "unlabeled button."

Next, press the crime scene image (which at the moment is just the gray placeholder). You might expect the accessibility focus to move to the **ImageView**, but the green border does not appear. TalkBack remains silent rather than announcing information about the **ImageView**. What gives?

## Making a widget focusable

The problem is that the **ImageView** is not registered to receive focus. Some widgets, such as **Button**s, are focusable by default. Other widgets, such **ImageView**s, are not. You can make a view focusable by setting its android:focusable attribute to true or by adding a click listener. You can also make a view focusable by adding an android:contentDescription.

Make the crime photo's **ImageView** focusable by giving it a content description.

### Listing 18.4  Making the photo **ImageView** focusable with a content description (res/layout/fragment_crime.xml)

```
<ImageView
  android:id="@+id/crime_photo"
  ...
  android:background="@android:color/darker_gray"
  android:contentDescription="@string/crime_photo_no_image_description" />
```

Run CriminalIntent again and press on the crime photo. The **ImageView** now accepts focus, and TalkBack announces, "Crime scene photo (not set)" (Figure 18.9).

### Figure 18.9  Focusable **ImageView**

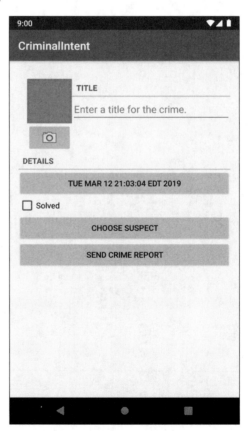

Crime scene photo (not set).

# Creating a Comparable Experience

You should specify a content description for any UI widget that provides information to the user but does not use text to do it (such as an image). If there is a widget that does not provide any value other than decoration, you should explicitly tell TalkBack to ignore it by setting its content description to null.

You might think, "If a user cannot see, why do they need to know whether there is an image?" But you should not make assumptions about your users. More importantly, you should make sure a user with a visual impairment gets the same amount of information and functionality as a user without one. The overall experience and flow may be different, but all users should be able to get the same functionality from the app.

Good accessibility design is not about reading out every single thing on the screen. Instead, it focuses on comparable experiences. Which pieces of information and context are important?

Right now, the user experience related to the crime photo is limited. TalkBack will always announce that the image is not set, even if an image is indeed set. To see this for yourself, press the camera button and then double-tap anywhere on the screen to activate it. The camera app launches, and TalkBack announces, "Camera." Capture a photo by pressing on the shutter button and then double-tapping anywhere on the screen.

Accept the photo. (The steps will be different depending on which camera app you are using, but remember that you will need to press to select a button and then double-tap anywhere to activate it.) The crime details screen will appear with the updated photo. Press the photo to give it accessibility focus. TalkBack announces, "Crime scene photo (not set)."

To provide more relevant information to TalkBack users, dynamically set the content description of the **ImageView** in **updatePhotoView()**.

## Listing 18.5  Dynamically setting the content description (`CrimeFragment.kt`)

```kotlin
class CrimeFragment : Fragment() {
    ...
    private fun updatePhotoView() {
        if (photoFile.exists()) {
            val bitmap = getScaledBitmap(photoFile.path, requireActivity())
            photoView.setImageBitmap(bitmap)
            photoView.contentDescription =
                getString(R.string.crime_photo_image_description)
        } else {
            photoView.setImageDrawable(null)
            photoView.contentDescription =
                getString(R.string.crime_photo_no_image_description)
        }
    }
    ...
}
```

Now, whenever the photo view is updated, **updatePhotoView()** will update the content description. If photoFile is empty, it will set the content description to indicate that there is no photo. Otherwise, it will set the content description to indicate that a photo is present.

Run CriminalIntent. View the crime detail screen for the crime you just added a photo to. Press on the photo of the crime scene (Figure 18.10). TalkBack proudly announces, "Crime scene photo (set)."

Figure 18.10  Focusable **ImageView** with a dynamic description

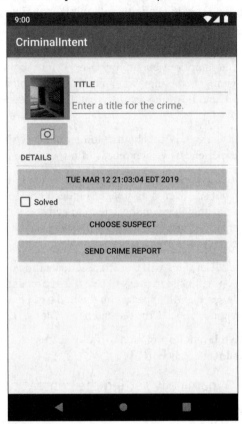

Congratulations on making your app more accessible. One of the most common reasons developers cite for not making their apps more accessible is lack of awareness about the topic. You are now aware and can see how easy it is to make your apps more usable to TalkBack users. And, as a bonus, improving your app's TalkBack support means it will also be more likely to support other accessibility services, such as BrailleBack.

Designing and implementing an accessible app may seem overwhelming. People make entire careers out of being accessibility engineers. But rather than forgoing accessibility altogether because you fear you will not do it right, start with the basics: Make sure every meaningful piece of content is reachable and readable by TalkBack. Make sure TalkBack users get enough context to understand what is going on in your app – without having to listen to extraneous information that wastes their time. And, most importantly, listen to your users and learn from them.

With that, you have reached the end of your time with CriminalIntent. In 11 chapters, you have created a complex application that uses fragments, talks to other apps, takes pictures, stores data, and even speaks Spanish. Why not celebrate with a piece of cake?

Just be sure to clean up after yourself. You never know who might be watching.

# For the More Curious: Using Accessibility Scanner

In this chapter you focused on making your app more accessible using TalkBack. But this is not the whole story. Accommodating people with visual impairments is just one subset of accessibility.

Testing your application for accessibility should really involve user tests by people who actually use accessibility services on a regular basis. But even if this is not possible, you should still do your best to make your app accessible.

Google's Accessibility Scanner analyzes apps and evaluates how accessible they are. It provides suggestions based on its findings. Try it out on CriminalIntent.

Begin by installing the Accessibility Scanner app on your device (Figure 18.11).

Figure 18.11  Installing Accessibility Scanner

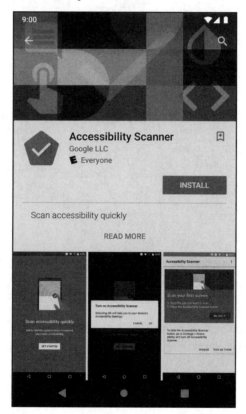

Once you have Accessibility Scanner installed and running and you see the blue check mark icon hovering over your screen, the real fun can begin. Launch CriminalIntent from the app launcher or overview screen, leaving the check mark alone. Once CriminalIntent appears, make sure it is displaying a crime details screen (Figure 18.12).

## Figure 18.12  Launching CriminalIntent for analysis

Press the check mark, and Accessibility Scanner will go to work. (You may need to give it certain permissions first; accept any permissions that are requested.) You will see a progress spinner while the analysis happens. Once the analysis is complete, a window showing suggestions will appear (Figure 18.13).

Figure 18.13  Accessibility Scanner results summary

The **EditText** and **CheckBox** have outlines around them. This indicates that the scanner found potential accessibility problems with those widgets. Press on the **CheckBox** to view accessibility suggestions for that widget. Press the down arrow to drill into the details (Figure 18.14).

Figure 18.14  Accessibility Scanner **CheckBox** recommendations

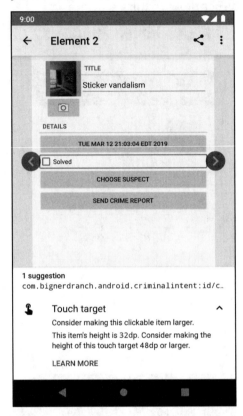

Accessibility Scanner suggests you increase the size of the **CheckBox**. The recommended minimum size for all touch targets is 48dp. The **CheckBox**'s height is smaller, which you can easily fix by specifying an android:minHeight attribute for the widget.

You can learn more about Accessibility Scanner's recommendation by pressing LEARN MORE.

To turn Accessibility Scanner off, go to Settings. Press Accessibility, then press Accessibility Scanner. Press the toggle to turn the scanner off (Figure 18.15).

Figure 18.15  Turning Accessibility Scanner off

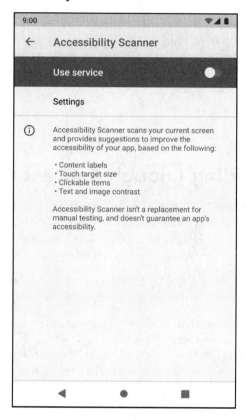

# Challenge: Improving the List

On the crime list screen, TalkBack reads the title and date of each item. However, it does not indicate whether the crime is solved. Fix this problem by giving the handcuff icon a content description.

Note that the readout is a bit lengthy, given the date format, and that the solved status is read at the very end – or not at all, if the crime is not solved. To take this challenge one step further, instead of having TalkBack read off the contents of the two **TextView**s and the content description of the icon (if the icon is present), add a dynamic content description to each row in the recycler view. In the description, summarize the data the user sees in the row.

# Challenge: Providing Enough Context for Data Entry

The date button and CHOOSE SUSPECT button both suffer from a similar problem. Users, whether using TalkBack or not, are not explicitly told what the button with the date on it is for. Similarly, once users select a contact as the suspect, they are no longer told or shown what the button represents. Users can probably infer the meaning of the buttons and the text on those buttons, but should they have to?

This is one of the nuances of UI design. It is up to you (or your design team) to figure out what makes the most sense for your application – to balance simplicity of the UI with ease of use.

For this challenge, update the implementation of the details screen so that users do not lose context about what the data they have chosen means. This could be as simple as adding labels for each field. To do this, you could add a **TextView** label for each button. Then you would tell TalkBack that the **TextView** is a label for the **Button** using the android:labelFor attribute.

```
<TextView
    android:id="@+id/crime_date_label"
    android:layout_width="match_parent"
    android:layout_height="wrap_content"
    android:text="Date"
    android:labelFor="@+id/crime_date"/>
<Button
    android:id="@+id/crime_date"
    android:layout_width="match_parent"
    android:layout_height="wrap_content"
    tools:text="Wed Nov 14 11:56 EST 2018"/>
```

The android:labelFor attribute tells TalkBack that the **TextView** serves as a label to the view specified by the ID value. labelFor is defined on the **View** class, so you can associate any view as the label for any other view. Note that you must use the @+id syntax here because you are referring to an ID that has not been defined at that point in the file. You could now remove the + from the android:id="@+id/crime_title" line in the **EditText**'s definition, but it is not necessary to do so.

# Challenge: Announcing Events

By adding dynamic content descriptions to the crime scene photo **ImageView**, you improved the crime scene photo experience. But the onus is on the TalkBack user to press on the **ImageView** to check its status. A sighted user has the benefit of seeing the image change (or not) when returning from the camera app.

You can provide a similar experience via TalkBack by announcing what happened as a result of the camera app closing. Read up on the **View.announceForAccessibility(…)** function in the documentation and use it in CriminalIntent at the appropriate time.

You might consider making the announcement in **onActivityResult(…)**. If you do, there will be some timing issues related to the activity lifecycle. You can get around these by delaying the announcement for a small amount of time by posting a **Runnable** (which you will learn more about in Chapter 25). It might look something like this:

```
someView.postDelayed(Runnable {
    // code for making announcements here
}, SOME_DURATION_IN_MILLIS)
```

You could avoid using a **Runnable** by instead using some other mechanism for knowing when to announce the change. For example, you might consider making the announcement in **onResume()** instead – though you would then need to keep track of whether the user has just returned from the camera app.

# 19

# Data Binding and MVVM

This chapter starts a new project called BeatBox (Figure 19.1). BeatBox is not a box for musical beats. It helps you beat your opponents in the sport of boxing. It does not help with the easy part, though: the part where you train to be faster and stronger than your foe. It helps with the hard part: yelling in a manner calculated to frighten your opponent into submission.

Figure 19.1  BeatBox at the end of this chapter

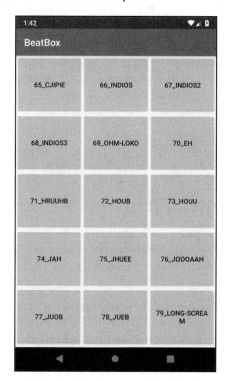

In this project, you will learn how to use a Jetpack architecture component library called *data binding*. You will use data binding to implement an architecture called *Model-View-View Model*, or MVVM. In addition, you will see how to use the assets system to store a sound file.

# Different Architectures: Why Bother?

Every app you have written so far has used a simple version of MVC. And, so far – if we have done our job well – every app has made sense to you. So why change? What is the problem?

The MVC architecture we have shown you works just fine for small, simple apps. It makes it easy to add new features and easy to think about the moving pieces of the app. It creates a solid foundation for development, gets your app up and running quickly, and works well in the early phases of a project.

The problem arises when your project grows larger than what we show in this book – as real-world projects do. Large fragments and activities are difficult to build on top of and difficult to understand. New features and bug fixes take longer. At some point, those controllers must be broken down into smaller pieces.

How do you do that? You figure out the different jobs your big controller classes are doing, and you give each job its own class. Instead of one big class, you have instances of a few classes doing the work as a team.

How do you determine what those different jobs are, then? The answer to that question is the definition of your architecture. People use descriptions like "Model-View-Controller" and "Model-View-View Model" to describe at a high level the ways they answer this question. But answering this question is always your responsibility, so your architecture is always uniquely yours.

BeatBox, as we said, is designed with an MVVM architecture. We are fans of MVVM because it does a great job of lifting a lot of boring controller code out into the layout file, where you can easily see which parts of your interface are dynamic. At the same time, it pulls the non-boring dynamic controller code into a *view model class*, where it can be more easily tested and verified.

How large each view model should be is always a judgment call. If your view model grows too large, you can break it down further. Your architecture is yours, not ours.

# MVVM View Models vs Jetpack ViewModels

Before you get started on your new project, a note about terminology: The view model that is a part of MVVM is not the same as the Jetpack **ViewModel** class that you learned about in Chapter 4 and Chapter 9. To avoid confusion, we will always format the name of the Jetpack class as "**ViewModel**" and the MVVM concept as "view model."

Recall that the Jetpack **ViewModel** is a specific class for maintaining data in fragments and activities, even across their volatile lifecycles. The view model in MVVM is a more conceptual part of the architecture. View models may be implemented using Jetpack **ViewModel**s, but – as you will see through most of this chapter – they can also be implemented without using the **ViewModel** class.

# Creating BeatBox

Time to get started. The first step is to create your BeatBox app.

In Android Studio, select File → New → New Project... to create a new project. Start with the Empty Activity option for Phone and Tablet. Call this app BeatBox and give it a package name of com.bignerdranch.android.beatbox. Select the option to Use AndroidX artifacts and leave the rest of the defaults as they are.

The activity will display a grid of buttons in a **RecyclerView**. Add the androidx.recyclerview:recyclerview:1.0.0 dependency to your app/build.gradle file (do not forget to sync the file). Replace the autogenerated contents of res/layout/activity_main.xml with a single **RecyclerView**.

## Listing 19.1  Updating the layout file for **MainActivity** (res/layout/activity_main.xml)

```
<androidx.constraintlayout.widget.ConstraintLayout
    ...
    tools:context=".MainActivity">
    ...
</androidx.constraintlayout.widget.ConstraintLayout>
<androidx.recyclerview.widget.RecyclerView
        xmlns:android="http://schemas.android.com/apk/res/android"
        android:id="@+id/recycler_view"
        android:layout_width="match_parent"
        android:layout_height="match_parent" />
```

Run your app. You should see a blank screen, reassuring you that you plugged everything together correctly to this point. Pat yourself on the back before you dive into the new territory of data binding.

# Implementing Simple Data Binding

The next job is to hook up your **RecyclerView**. This is a job that you have done before. But this time, you will use data binding to speed up your work.

Data binding provides several benefits that make life easier when working with layouts. In simple cases, like the one you will see in this section, it allows you to access views without needing to call **findViewById(…)**. Later, you will see more advanced uses of data binding, including how it helps you implement MVVM.

Start by enabling data binding and applying the kotlin-kapt plug-in in your app's build.gradle file.

## Listing 19.2  Enabling data binding (app/build.gradle)

```
apply plugin: 'kotlin-kapt'

android {
    ...
    buildTypes {
        ...
    }
    dataBinding {
        enabled = true
    }
}
```

Note that applying the kotlin-kapt plug-in allows data binding to perform annotation processing on Kotlin. You will see why that is important later in this chapter.

To use data binding in a layout file, you have to make the file a data binding layout file. You do that by wrapping the entire XML file in a <layout> tag. Make that change to activity_main.xml, as shown in Listing 19.3.

## Listing 19.3  Wrapping it up (res/layout/activity_main.xml)

```
<layout xmlns:android="http://schemas.android.com/apk/res/android">
    <androidx.recyclerview.widget.RecyclerView
        xmlns:android="http://schemas.android.com/apk/res/android"
        android:id="@+id/recycler_view"
        android:layout_width="match_parent"
        android:layout_height="match_parent"/>
</layout>
```

The <layout> tag is your signal to the data binding library that it should work on your layout file. For layouts with this tag, the library will generate a *binding class* for you. By default, this class is named after your layout file, but instead of using snake_case, it is switched to the CamelCase class naming style and suffixed with Binding.

So the data binding library should have already generated a binding class for your activity_main.xml file called **ActivityMainBinding**. This class is what you will use for data binding: Instead of inflating a view hierarchy with **setContentView(Int)**, you will inflate an instance of **ActivityMainBinding**. **ActivityMainBinding** will hold on to the view hierarchy for you in a property called root. In addition to that, the binding holds on to named references for each view you tagged with an android:id in your layout file.

So your **ActivityMainBinding** class has two references: root, which refers to the entire layout, and recyclerView, which refers to just your **RecyclerView** (Figure 19.2).

## Figure 19.2  Your binding class

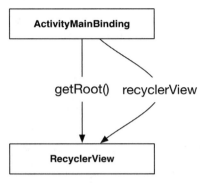

Your layout only has one view, of course, so both references point at the same view: your **RecyclerView**.

Now to use your binding class. Update **onCreate(Bundle?)** in **MainActivity** and use **DataBindingUtil** to inflate an instance of **ActivityMainBinding** (Listing 19.4).

You will need to import **ActivityMainBinding** like any other class. If Android Studio cannot find **ActivityMainBinding**, this means it was not autogenerated for some reason. Force Android Studio to generate the class by selecting Build → Rebuild Project. If the class is not generated after forcing the project to rebuild, restart Android Studio.

## Listing 19.4  Inflating a binding class (MainActivity.kt)

```
class MainActivity : AppCompatActivity() {

    override fun onCreate(savedInstanceState: Bundle?) {
        super.onCreate(savedInstanceState)
        setContentView(R.layout.activity_main)

        val binding: ActivityMainBinding =
            DataBindingUtil.setContentView(this, R.layout.activity_main)
    }
}
```

With your binding class created, you can now access your **RecyclerView** and configure it.

## Listing 19.5  Configuring **RecyclerView** (MainActivity.kt)

```
class MainActivity : AppCompatActivity() {

    override fun onCreate(savedInstanceState: Bundle?) {
        super.onCreate(savedInstanceState)

        val binding: ActivityMainBinding =
            DataBindingUtil.setContentView(this, R.layout.activity_main)

        binding.recyclerView.apply {
            layoutManager = GridLayoutManager(context, 3)
        }
    }
}
```

Next, create the layout file for the buttons, res/layout/list_item_sound.xml. You will be using data binding here as well, so surround your layout with a <layout> tag.

Listing 19.6  Creating the sound layout (res/layout/list_item_sound.xml)

```xml
<layout xmlns:android="http://schemas.android.com/apk/res/android"
        xmlns:tools="http://schemas.android.com/tools">
    <Button
        android:layout_width="match_parent"
        android:layout_height="120dp"
        tools:text="Sound name"/>
</layout>
```

Next, create a **SoundHolder** wired up to list_item_sound.xml.

Listing 19.7  Creating **SoundHolder** (MainActivity.kt)

```kotlin
class MainActivity : AppCompatActivity() {

    override fun onCreate(savedInstanceState: Bundle?) {
        ...
    }

    private inner class SoundHolder(private val binding: ListItemSoundBinding) :
            RecyclerView.ViewHolder(binding.root) {
    }
}
```

Your **SoundHolder** expects the binding class you just implicitly created: **ListItemSoundBinding**.

And now create an **Adapter** hooked up to **SoundHolder**.

Listing 19.8  Creating **SoundAdapter** (MainActivity.kt)

```kotlin
class MainActivity : AppCompatActivity() {
    ...
    private inner class SoundHolder(private val binding: ListItemSoundBinding) :
            RecyclerView.ViewHolder(binding.root) {
    }

    private inner class SoundAdapter() :
        RecyclerView.Adapter<SoundHolder>() {

        override fun onCreateViewHolder(parent: ViewGroup, viewType: Int):
                SoundHolder {
            val binding = DataBindingUtil.inflate<ListItemSoundBinding>(
                layoutInflater,
                R.layout.list_item_sound,
                parent,
                false
            )
            return SoundHolder(binding)
        }

        override fun onBindViewHolder(holder: SoundHolder, position: Int) {
        }

        override fun getItemCount() = 0
    }
}
```

Finally, wire up **SoundAdapter** in **onCreate(Bundle?)**.

### Listing 19.9  Wiring up **SoundAdapter** (MainActivity.kt)

```
override fun onCreate(savedInstanceState: Bundle?) {
    super.onCreate(savedInstanceState)

    val binding: ActivityMainBinding =
        DataBindingUtil.setContentView(this, R.layout.activity_main)

    binding.recyclerView.apply {
        layoutManager = GridLayoutManager(context, 3)
        adapter = SoundAdapter()
    }
}
```

You have now used data binding to set up the recycler view. Unfortunately, it does not have anything to show yet. It is time to fix that by giving it some sound files to display.

# Importing Assets

First, you need to add the sound files to your project so your code can use them at runtime. Rather than use the resources system for this job, you will use raw *assets*. You can think of assets as stripped-down resources: They are packaged into your APK like resources, but without any of the configuration system tooling that goes on top of resources.

In some ways, that is good. Because there is no configuration system, you can name assets whatever you want and organize them with your own folder structure. In other ways, though, it is bad. Without a configuration system, you cannot automatically respond to changes in pixel density, language, or orientation, nor can you automatically use the assets in layout files or other resources.

Usually resources are the better deal. However, in cases where you only access files programmatically, assets can come out ahead. Most games use assets for graphics and sound, for example – and so will BeatBox.

Your first step will be to import your assets. Create an assets folder inside your project by right-clicking on your app module and selecting New → Folder → Assets Folder. In the dialog that pops up, leave the Change Folder Location checkbox unchecked and leave the Target Source Set set to main (Figure 19.3).

## Figure 19.3  Creating the assets folder

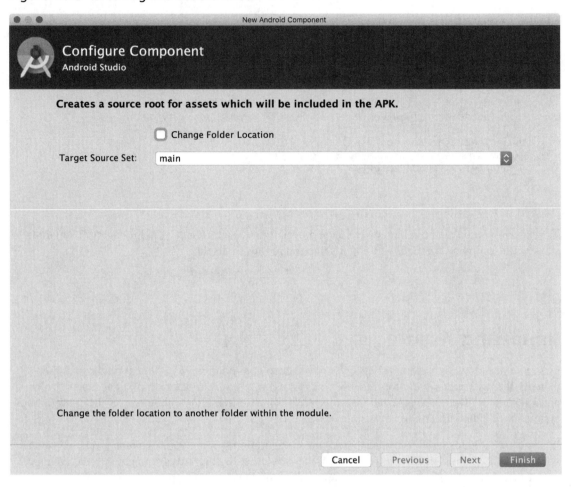

Click Finish to create your assets folder.

Next, right-click on assets to create a subfolder for your sounds by selecting New → Directory. Enter sample_sounds for the directory name (Figure 19.4).

## Figure 19.4  Creating the sample_sounds folder

Everything inside the assets folder will be deployed with your app. For the sake of convenience and organization, you created a subfolder called sample_sounds. Unlike with resources, a subfolder is not required for assets. You include it to organize your sounds.

So where can you find the sounds? You will be using a Creative Commons-licensed sound set we initially found provided by the user plagasul at freesound.org/people/plagasul/packs/3/. We have put them in a zip file for you at bignerdranch.com/solutions/sample_sounds.zip.

Download the zip file and unzip its contents. Copy or move the unzipped sound files into assets/sample_sounds (Figure 19.5).

## Figure 19.5  Imported assets

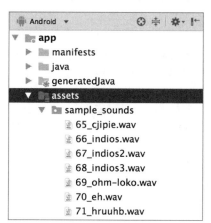

(Make sure only .wav files are in there, by the way – not the .zip file you got them from.)

Build your app to make sure everything is hunky-dory. The next step will be to list those assets and show them to the user.

# Accessing Assets

BeatBox will end up doing a lot of work related to asset management: finding assets, keeping track of them, and eventually playing them as sounds. To manage all this, create a new class called **BeatBox** in com.bignerdranch.android.beatbox. Go ahead and add a couple of constants: one for logging and one to remember which folder you saved your boxing grunts in.

### Listing 19.10  New **BeatBox** class (BeatBox.kt)

```
private const val TAG = "BeatBox"
private const val SOUNDS_FOLDER = "sample_sounds"

class BeatBox {

}
```

Assets are accessed using the **AssetManager** class. You can get an **AssetManager** from any **Context**. Since **BeatBox** will need one, give it a constructor that takes in an **AssetManager** and stashes it for later.

### Listing 19.11  Stashing an **AssetManager** for safekeeping (BeatBox.kt)

```
private const val TAG = "BeatBox"
private const val SOUNDS_FOLDER = "sample_sounds"

class BeatBox(private val assets: AssetManager) {

}
```

When accessing assets, in general you do not need to worry about which **Context** you are using. In every situation you are likely to encounter in practice, every **Context**'s **AssetManager** will be wired up to the same set of assets.

To get a listing of what you have in your assets, you can use the **list(String)** function. Write a function called **loadSounds()** that looks in your assets with **list(String)**.

### Listing 19.12  Looking at assets (BeatBox.kt)

```
class BeatBox(private val assets: AssetManager) {

    fun loadSounds(): List<String> {
        try {
            val soundNames = assets.list(SOUNDS_FOLDER)!!
            Log.d(TAG, "Found ${soundNames.size} sounds")
            return soundNames.asList()
        } catch (e: Exception) {
            Log.e(TAG, "Could not list assets", e)
            return emptyList()
        }
    }
}
```

**AssetManager.list(String)** lists filenames contained in the folder path you pass in. By passing in your sounds folder, you should see every .wav file you put in there.

To verify that this is working correctly, create an instance of **BeatBox** in **MainActivity** and invoke the **loadSounds()** function.

### Listing 19.13  Creating a **BeatBox** instance (MainActivity.kt)

```kotlin
class MainActivity : AppCompatActivity() {

    private lateinit var beatBox: BeatBox

    override fun onCreate(savedInstanceState: Bundle?) {
        super.onCreate(savedInstanceState)

        beatBox = BeatBox(assets)
        beatBox.loadSounds()

        val binding: ActivityMainBinding =
            DataBindingUtil.setContentView(this, R.layout.activity_main)

        binding.recyclerView.apply {
            layoutManager = GridLayoutManager(context, 3)
            adapter = SoundAdapter()
        }
    }
    ...
}
```

Run your app, and you should see some log output telling you how many sound files were found. We provided 22 .wav files, so you should see:

```
...1823–1823/com.bignerdranch.android.beatbox D/BeatBox: Found 22 sounds
```

# Wiring Up Assets for Use

Now that you have your asset filenames, you should present them to the user. Eventually, you will want the files to be played, so it makes sense to have an object responsible for keeping track of the filename, the name the user should see, and any other information related to that sound.

Create a **Sound** class to hold all of this.

### Listing 19.14  Creating **Sound** object (Sound.kt)

```kotlin
private const val WAV = ".wav"

class Sound(val assetPath: String) {

    val name = assetPath.split("/").last().removeSuffix(WAV)
}
```

In the constructor, you do a little work to make a presentable name for your sound. First, you split off the filename using **String.split(String).last()**. Once you have done that, you use **String.removeSuffix(String)** to strip off the file extension, too.

Next, build up a list of **Sound**s in **BeatBox.loadSounds()**.

## Listing 19.15  Creating **Sound**s (BeatBox.kt)

```kotlin
class BeatBox(private val assets: AssetManager) {

    val sounds: List<Sound>

    init {
      sounds = loadSounds()
    }

    fun loadSounds(): List<String>List<Sound> {

        val soundNames: Array<String>

        try {
            val soundNames = assets.list(SOUNDS_FOLDER)!!
            Log.d(TAG, "Found ${soundNames.size} sounds")
            return soundNames.asList()
        } catch (e: Exception) {
            Log.e(TAG, "Could not list assets", e)
            return emptyList()
        }
        val sounds = mutableListOf<Sound>()
        soundNames.forEach { filename ->
            val assetPath = "$SOUNDS_FOLDER/$filename"
            val sound = Sound(assetPath)
            sounds.add(sound)
        }
        return sounds
    }
}
```

Now, wire up **SoundAdapter** to the **List** of **Sound**s.

## Listing 19.16  Hooking up to the **Sound** list (MainActivity.kt)

```kotlin
private inner class SoundAdapter(private val sounds: List<Sound>) :
        RecyclerView.Adapter<SoundHolder>() {

    ...

    override fun onBindViewHolder(holder: SoundHolder, position: Int) {
    }

    override fun getItemCount() = 0sounds.size
}
```

And now pass in **BeatBox**'s sounds in **onCreate(Bundle?)**.

## Listing 19.17  Passing in **Sound**s to the adapter (MainActivity.kt)

```
override fun onCreate(savedInstanceState: Bundle?) {
    ...

    binding.recyclerView.apply {
        layoutManager = GridLayoutManager(context, 3)
        adapter = SoundAdapter(beatBox.sounds)
    }
}
```

Finally, remove the **BeatBox.loadSounds()** function call in **onCreate**.

## Listing 19.18  Removing **BeatBox.loadSounds()** from **onCreate(…)** (MainActivity.kt)

```
override fun onCreate(savedInstanceState: Bundle?) {
    ...
    beatBox = BeatBox(assets)
    beatBox.loadSounds()
    ...
}
```

Since **BeatBox.loadSounds()** is no longer being called from outside of **BeatBox**'s initializer block, there is no need to keep this function public. To be a good citizen and avoid inadvertently calling **loadSounds()** from other parts of the code, update its visibility modifier to private.

## Listing 19.19  Updating **BeatBox.loadSounds()**'s visibility modifier to private (BeatBox.kt)

```
class BeatBox(private val assets: AssetManager) {
    ...
    private fun loadSounds(): List<Sound> {
        ...
    }
}
```

With that, you should see a grid of buttons when you run BeatBox (Figure 19.6).

Figure 19.6  Empty buttons

To populate the buttons with titles, you will use some additional tools from your new data binding utility belt.

# Binding to Data

With data binding, you can declare data objects within your layout file:

```
<layout xmlns:android="http://schemas.android.com/apk/res/android"
        xmlns:tools="http://schemas.android.com/tools">
    <data>
        <variable
            name="crime"
            type="com.bignerdranch.android.criminalintent.Crime"/>
    </data>
    ...
</layout>
```

And then use values from those objects directly in your layout file by using the *binding mustache* operator, @{}:

```
<CheckBox
    android:id="@+id/list_item_crime_solved_check_box"
    android:layout_width="wrap_content"
    android:layout_height="wrap_content"
    android:layout_alignParentRight="true"
    android:checked="@{crime.isSolved()}"
    android:padding="4dp"/>
```

In an object diagram, that would look like Figure 19.7:

Figure 19.7  The ties that bind

Your goal right now is to put the sound names on their buttons. The most direct way to do that using data binding is to bind directly to a **Sound** object in list_item_sound.xml (Figure 19.8):

Figure 19.8  Direct hookup

However, this causes some architectural issues. To see why, look at it from an MVC perspective (Figure 19.9).

## Figure 19.9  Broken MVC

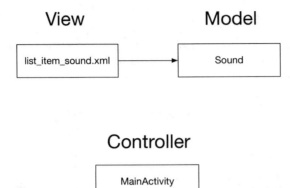

The guiding principle behind any architecture is the *Single Responsibility Principle*. It says that each class you make should have exactly one responsibility. MVC gave you an idea of what those responsibilities should be: The model represents how your app works, the controller decides how to display your app, and the view displays it on the screen the way you want it to look.

Using data binding as shown in Figure 19.8 would break this division of responsibilities, because the **Sound** model object would likely end up with code that prepares the data for the view to display. This would quickly make your app a mess, as Sound.kt would become littered with two kinds of code: code that represents how your app works and code that prepares data for the view to display.

Instead of muddying up the responsibility of **Sound**, you will introduce a new object called a view model to use with data binding. This view model will take on the responsibility of preparing the data for the view to display (Figure 19.10).

## Figure 19.10  Model-View-View Model

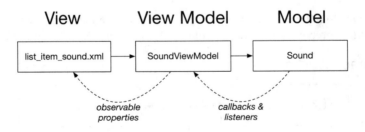

This architecture, as we have said, is called MVVM, short for Model-View-View Model. Most of the work your controller classes once did at runtime to format data for display will go in the view model. Wiring widgets up with that data will be handled directly in the layout file using data binding to that view model. Your activity or fragment will be in charge of things like initializing the binding and the view model and creating the link between the two.

There is no controller with MVVM; rather, activities and fragments are considered part of the view.

# Creating a view model

Let's create your view model. Create a new class called **SoundViewModel** and give it two properties: a **Sound** for it to use and a **BeatBox** to (eventually) play that sound with.

Listing 19.20  Creating **SoundViewModel** (SoundViewModel.kt)

```kotlin
class SoundViewModel {

    var sound: Sound? = null
        set(sound) {
            field = sound
        }
}
```

These properties are the interface your adapter will use. For the layout file, you will want an additional function to get the title that the button should display. Add it now to **SoundViewModel**.

Listing 19.21  Adding binding functions (SoundViewModel.kt)

```kotlin
class SoundViewModel {

    var sound: Sound? = null
        set(sound) {
            field = sound
        }

    val title: String?
        get() = sound?.name
}
```

## Binding to a view model

Now to integrate the view model into your layout file. The first step is to declare a property on your layout file, like so:

### Listing 19.22  Declaring the view model property (res/layout/list_item_sound.xml)

```
<layout xmlns:android="http://schemas.android.com/apk/res/android"
        xmlns:tools="http://schemas.android.com/tools">
    <data>
        <variable
            name="viewModel"
            type="com.bignerdranch.android.beatbox.SoundViewModel"/>
    </data>
    ...
</layout>
```

This defines a property named viewModel on your binding class, including a getter and setter. Within your binding class, you can use viewModel in binding expressions.

### Listing 19.23  Binding your button title (res/layout/list_item_sound.xml)

```
<layout xmlns:android="http://schemas.android.com/apk/res/android"
        xmlns:tools="http://schemas.android.com/tools">
    <data>
        <variable
            name="viewModel"
            type="com.bignerdranch.android.beatbox.SoundViewModel"/>
    </data>
    <Button
        android:layout_width="match_parent"
        android:layout_height="120dp"
        android:text="@{viewModel.title}"
        tools:text="Sound name"/>
</layout>
```

Within the binding mustache, you can write simple Java expressions, including chained function calls, math, and most anything else you want to include.

The last step is to hook up your view model. Create a **SoundViewModel** and attach it to your binding class. Then add a binding function to your **SoundHolder**.

### Listing 19.24  Hooking up the view model (MainActivity.kt)

```
private inner class SoundHolder(private val binding: ListItemSoundBinding) :
        RecyclerView.ViewHolder(binding.root) {

    init {
        binding.viewModel = SoundViewModel()
    }

    fun bind(sound: Sound) {
        binding.apply {
            viewModel?.sound = sound
            executePendingBindings()
        }
    }
}
```

Inside your constructor, you construct and attach your view model. Then, in your **bind** function, you update the data that view model is working with.

Calling **executePendingBindings()** is not normally necessary. Here, though, you are updating binding data inside a **RecyclerView**, which updates views at a very high speed. By calling this function, you force the layout to immediately update itself, rather than waiting a millisecond or two. This keeps your **RecyclerView** in sync with its **RecyclerView.Adapter**.

Finally, finish hooking up your view model by implementing **onBindViewHolder(…)**.

## Listing 19.25  Calling **bind(Sound)** (MainActivity.kt)

```
private inner class SoundAdapter(private val sounds: List<Sound>) :
        RecyclerView.Adapter<SoundHolder>() {
    ...
    override fun onBindViewHolder(holder: SoundHolder, position: Int) {
        val sound = sounds[position]
        holder.bind(sound)
    }

    override fun getItemCount() = sounds.size
}
```

Run your app, and you will see titles on all the buttons on your screen (Figure 19.11).

## Figure 19.11  Button titles filled in

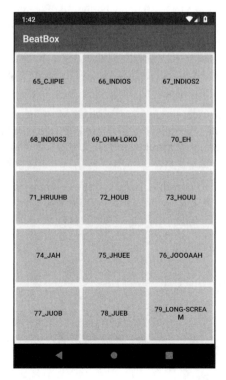

# Observable data

All may appear to be well, but darkness lies hidden in your code. You can see it if you scroll down (Figure 19.12).

## Figure 19.12  Déjà vu

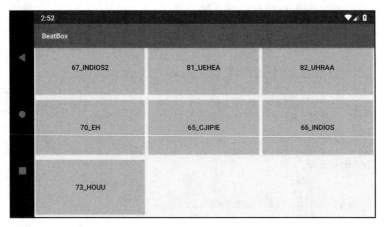

Did you see an item 67_INDIOS2 at the top, and then one that looks just like it at the bottom? Scroll up and down repeatedly, and you will see other file titles repeatedly appearing in unexpected, seemingly random places. If you do not see this, rotate the device into landscape mode and try again to see how deep the rabbit hole goes. Remember: We only offered you the truth – nothing more…

Worry not! This is not a glitch in the Matrix. This is happening because your layout has no way of knowing that you updated **SoundViewModel**'s **Sound** inside **SoundHolder.bind(Sound)**. In other words, the view model is not properly pushing data to your layout file as shown in Figure 19.10. In addition to having a clear division of responsibilities, this step is the secret sauce that separates MVVM from other architectures like MVC, as discussed in the section called Different Architectures: Why Bother? earlier in this chapter.

Your next job will be to make the view model communicate with the layout file when a change occurs. To do this, your view model needs to implement data binding's **Observable** interface. This interface lets your binding class set listeners on your view model so that it can automatically receive callbacks when its fields are modified.

Implementing the whole interface is possible, but it requires extra work. We do not shy away from extra work here at Big Nerd Ranch, but we prefer to avoid it when we can. So we will instead show you how to do it the easy way, with data binding's **BaseObservable** class.

Three steps are required:

1. Subclass **BaseObservable** in your view model.

2. Annotate your view model's bindable properties with @Bindable.

3. Call **notifyChange()** or **notifyPropertyChanged(Int)** each time a bindable property's value changes.

In **SoundViewModel**, this is only a few lines of code. Update **SoundViewModel** to be observable.

## Listing 19.26 Making view model observable (SoundViewModel.kt)

```kotlin
class SoundViewModel : BaseObservable() {

    var sound: Sound? = null
        set(sound) {
            field = sound
            notifyChange()
        }

    @get:Bindable
    val title: String?
        get() = sound?.name
}
```

When you call **notifyChange()** here, it notifies your binding class that all of the **Bindable** properties on your objects have been updated. The binding class then runs the code inside the binding mustaches again to repopulate the view. So now, when the value of sound is set, **ListItemSoundBinding** will be notified and call **Button.setText(String)** as you specified in list_item_sound.xml.

Above, we mentioned another function: **notifyPropertyChanged(Int)**. The **notifyPropertyChanged(Int)** function does the same thing as **notifyChange()**, except it is more particular. By writing **notifyChange()**, you say, "All of my bindable properties have changed; please update everything." By writing **notifyPropertyChanged(BR.title)**, you can instead say, "Only title's value has changed."

**BR.title** is a constant that is generated by the data binding library. The **BR** class name is short for "binding resource." Each property you annotate with **@Bindable** results in a generated BR constant with the same name.

Here are a few other examples:

```kotlin
@get:Bindable val title: String // yields BR.title
@get:Bindable val volume: Int // yields BR.volume
@get:Bindable val etcetera: String // yields BR.etcetera
```

You may be thinking that using **Observable** seems similar to using **LiveData**, as you learned about in Chapter 11 – and you would be right. In fact, you can use **LiveData** with data binding instead of the **Observable** interface. You will find out more about this in the section called For the More Curious: LiveData and Data Binding at the end of this chapter.

Run BeatBox one more time. This time, you should see the right thing when you scroll around (Figure 19.13).

Figure 19.13  All done

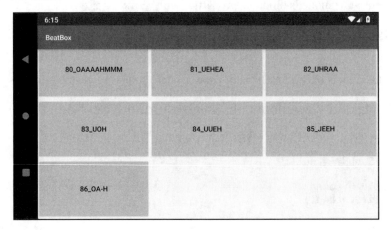

# For the More Curious: More About Data Binding

Complete coverage of data binding is outside the scope of this book. And yet, reader, we must nevertheless try.

## Lambda expressions

You can write short callbacks directly in your layout file by using *lambda expressions*. These are simplified versions of Java's lambda expressions:

```
<Button
    android:layout_width="match_parent"
    android:layout_height="120dp"
    android:text="@{viewModel.title}"
    android:onClick="@{(view) -> viewModel.onButtonClick()}"
    tools:text="Sound name"/>
```

Like Java 8 lambda expressions, these are turned into implementations for the interface you use them for. (In this case, **View.OnClickListener**.) Unlike Java 8 lambda expressions, these expressions must use this exact syntax: The parameter must be in parentheses, and you must have exactly one expression on the right-hand side.

Also, unlike in Java lambdas, you can omit the lambda parameters if you are not using them. So this works fine, too:

```
android:onClick="@{() -> viewModel.onButtonClick()}"
```

## Syntactic sugar

You also get a few additional bits of handy syntax for data binding. Particularly handy is the ability to use backticks for double quotes:

```
android:text="@{`File name: ` + viewModel.title}"
```

Here, `File name` means the same thing as "File name".

Binding expressions also have a null coalescing operator:

```
android:text="@{`File name: ` + viewModel.title ?? `No file`}"
```

In the event that title is null, the ?? operator will yield the value "No file" instead.

In addition, automatic null handling is provided for you in data binding expressions. Even if viewModel is null in the code above, data binding will provide appropriate null checks so that it does not crash the app. Instead of crashing, the subexpression viewModel.title will yield "null".

# BindingAdapters

By default, data binding interprets a binding expression as a property invocation. So this:

```
android:text="@{`File name: ` + viewModel.title ?? `No file`}"
```

Is translated into an invocation of the **setText(String)** function.

Sometimes that is not enough, and you want some custom behavior to be applied for a particular attribute. In those cases, you can write a **BindingAdapter**:

```
@BindingAdapter("app:soundName")
fun bindAssetSound(button: Button, assetFileName: String ) {
    ...
}
```

Simply create a file-level function anywhere in your project and annotate it with @BindingAdapter, passing in the name of the attribute you want to bind as a parameter to the annotation and the **View** to which the annotation applies as the first parameter to the function. (Yes, this really works.)

In the example above, whenever data binding encounters a **Button** with an app:soundName attribute containing a *binding expression*, it will call your function, passing the **Button** and the result of the binding expression.

You can even create **BindingAdapter**s for more generalized views, such as **View** or **ViewGroup**. In this case the **BindingAdapter** will apply to that **View** and all of its subclasses.

For example, if you wanted to define an attribute app:isGone that would set the visibility of any **View** based on a Boolean value, you could do that like so:

```
@BindingAdapter("app:isGone")
fun bindIsGone(view: View, isGone: Boolean ) {
    view.visibility = if (isGone) View.GONE else View.VISIBLE
}
```

Because **View** is the first argument to **bindIsGone**, this attribute is available to **View** and all subclasses of **View** in your app module. This means you can use it with **Button**s, **TextView**s, **LinearLayout**s, and so on.

You will probably think of one or two operations you would like to use data binding with on the standard library widgets. Many common operations already have binding adapters defined – for example, **TextViewBindingAdapter** provides additional attributes for **TextView**. You can read these binding adapters yourself by viewing the source in Android Studio. So, before you write your own solution, type Command-Shift-O (Ctrl-Shift-O) to search for a class, open up the associated binding adapters file, and check to see whether it already exists.

# For the More Curious: LiveData and Data Binding

**LiveData** and data binding are similar in that they both provide a way to observe data and react when that data changes. In fact, it is possible to work with both **LiveData** and data binding together, in tandem. The example below shows the changes that you would make to **SoundViewModel** to bind the title property as **LiveData** instead of an **Observable** property.

```
class SoundViewModel : BaseObservable() {

    val title: MutableLiveData<String?> = MutableLiveData()

    var sound: Sound? = null
        set(sound) {
            field = sound
            notifyChange()
            title.postValue(sound?.name)
        }

    @get:Bindable
    val title: String?
        get() = sound?.name
}
```

In this example, it is no longer necessary to subclass **BaseObservable** or provide @Bindable annotations, because **LiveData** has its own mechanisms for notifying observers. However, as you learned in Chapter 11, **LiveData** does require a **LifecycleOwner**. To tell the data binding framework which lifecycle owner to use when observing the title property, you would update **SoundAdapter**, setting the lifecycleOwner property after creating the binding:

```
private inner class SoundAdapter(private val sounds: List<Sound>) :
        RecyclerView.Adapter<SoundHolder>() {
    ...
    override fun onCreateViewHolder(parent: ViewGroup, viewType: Int):
            SoundHolder {
        val binding = DataBindingUtil.inflate<ListItemSoundBinding>(
            layoutInflater,
            R.layout.list_item_sound,
            parent,
            false
        )

        binding.lifecycleOwner = this@MainActivity

        return SoundHolder(binding)
    }
}
```

This would set **MainActivity** as the lifecycle owner. No changes to the view would be required as long as the property name, title, remained the same.

# 20

# Unit Testing and Audio Playback

One reason MVVM architecture is so appealing is that it makes a critical programming practice easier: *unit testing*. Unit testing is the practice of writing small programs that verify the standalone behavior of each unit of your main app. Because BeatBox's units are each classes, classes are what your unit tests will test.

In this chapter, you will finally play all of the .wav files you loaded in the previous chapter. As you build and integrate sound playback, you will write unit tests for your **SoundViewModel**'s integration with **BeatBox**.

Android's audio APIs are low level, for the most part, but there is a tool practically tailor-made for the app you are writing: **SoundPool**. **SoundPool** can load a large set of sounds into memory and control the maximum number of sounds that are playing back at any one time. So, if your app's user gets a bit too excited and mashes all the buttons at the same time, it will not break your app or overtax the user's phone.

Ready? Time to get started.

## Creating a SoundPool

Your first job is to build out sound playback inside **BeatBox**. To do that, first create a **SoundPool** object (Listing 20.1).

Listing 20.1 Creating a **SoundPool** (BeatBox.kt)

```
private const val TAG = "BeatBox"
private const val SOUNDS_FOLDER = "sample_sounds"
private const val MAX_SOUNDS = 5

class BeatBox(private val assets: AssetManager) {

    val sounds: List<Sound>
    private val soundPool = SoundPool.Builder()
        .setMaxStreams(MAX_SOUNDS)
        .build()

    init {
        sounds = loadSounds()
    }
    ...
}
```

A **Builder** is used to create a **SoundPool** instance. The **setMaxStreams(Int)** option on the builder specifies how many sounds can play at any given time. Here, you pass in 5. If five sounds are playing and you try to play a sixth one, the **SoundPool** will stop playing the oldest one.

In addition to the max streams option, the **SoundPool** builder allows you to specify different attributes of the audio stream with the **setAudioAttributes(AudioAttributes)** option. Check the documentation for more information on what this does. The default audio attributes work well enough in this example, so you can leave this option out for now.

# Accessing Assets

Recall that your sound files are stored in your app's assets. Before you access those files to play the audio, let's discuss a bit more about how assets work.

Your **Sound** object has an asset file path defined on it. Asset file paths will not work if you try to open them with a **File**; you must use them with an **AssetManager**:

```
val assetPath = sound.assetPath

val assetManager = context.assets

val soundData = assetManager.open(assetPath)
```

This gives you a standard **InputStream** for the data, which you can use like any other **InputStream** in Kotlin.

Some APIs require **FileDescriptor**s instead. This is what you will use with **SoundPool**. If you need that, you can call **AssetManager.openFd(String)** instead:

```
val assetPath = sound.assetPath

val assetManager = context.assets

// AssetFileDescriptors are different from FileDescriptors...
val assetFileDescriptor = assetManager.openFd(assetPath)

// ... but you can get a regular FileDescriptor easily if you need to
val fileDescriptor = assetFileDescriptor.fileDescriptor
```

# Loading Sounds

The next thing to do with your **SoundPool** is to load it up with sounds. The main benefit of using a **SoundPool** over some other methods of playing audio is that **SoundPool** responds quickly: When you tell it to play a sound, it will play the sound immediately, with no lag.

The trade-off for that is that you must load sounds into your **SoundPool** before you play them. Each sound you load will get its own integer ID. To track this ID, add a soundId property to **Sound**.

### Listing 20.2  Adding a sound ID property (Sound.kt)

```
class Sound(val assetPath: String, var soundId: Int? = null) {
    val name = assetPath.split("/").last().removeSuffix(WAV)
}
```

By making soundId a nullable type (Int?), you make it possible to say that a **Sound** has no value set for soundId by assigning it a null value.

Now to load your sounds. Add a **load(Sound)** function to **BeatBox** to load a **Sound** into your **SoundPool**.

### Listing 20.3  Loading sounds into **SoundPool** (BeatBox.kt)

```
class BeatBox(private val assets: AssetManager) {
    ...
    private fun loadSounds(): List<Sound> {
        ...
    }

    private fun load(sound: Sound) {
        val afd: AssetFileDescriptor = assets.openFd(sound.assetPath)
        val soundId = soundPool.load(afd, 1)
        sound.soundId = soundId
    }
}
```

Calling **soundPool.load(AssetFileDescriptor, Int)** loads a file into your **SoundPool** for later playback. To keep track of the sound and play it back again (or unload it), **soundPool.load(…)** returns an Int ID, which you stash in the soundId field you just defined.

Be aware that since calling **openFd(String)** can throw **IOException**, **load(Sound)** can throw **IOException**, too. This means you will need to handle that exception any time **load(Sound)** is called.

Now load up all your sounds by calling **load(Sound)** inside **BeatBox.loadSounds()**.

### Listing 20.4  Loading up all your sounds (BeatBox.kt)

```
private fun loadSounds(): List<Sound> {
    ...
    val sounds = mutableListOf<Sound>()
    soundNames.forEach { filename ->
        val assetPath = "$SOUNDS_FOLDER/$filename"
        val sound = Sound(assetPath)
        sounds.add(sound)
        try {
            load(sound)
            sounds.add(sound)
        } catch (ioe: IOException) {
            Log.e(TAG, "Cound not load sound $filename", ioe)
        }
    }
    return sounds
}
```

Run BeatBox to make sure that all the sounds loaded correctly. If they did not, you will see red exception logs in Logcat.

# Playing Sounds

**BeatBox** also needs to be able to play sounds. Add the **play(Sound)** function to **BeatBox**.

## Listing 20.5  Playing sounds back (BeatBox.kt)

```
class BeatBox(private val assets: AssetManager) {
    ...
    init {
        sounds = loadSounds()
    }

    fun play(sound: Sound) {
        sound.soundId?.let {
            soundPool.play(it, 1.0f, 1.0f, 1, 0, 1.0f)
        }
    }
    ...
}
```

Before playing your soundId, you check to make sure it is not null. This might happen if the **Sound** failed to load.

Once you are sure you have a non-null value, you play the sound by calling **SoundPool.play(Int, Float, Float, Int, Int, Float)**. Those parameters are, respectively: the sound ID, volume on the left, volume on the right, priority, whether the audio should loop, and playback rate. For full volume and normal playback rate, you pass in **1.0**. Passing in **0** for the looping value says "do not loop." (You can pass in −1 if you want it to loop forever. We speculate that this would be incredibly annoying.)

With that function written, you are now ready to integrate sound playback into **SoundViewModel**. You will perform this integration in a test-first manner – that is, you will first write a failing unit test and then implement the integration to make the test pass.

# Test Dependencies

Before you write your test, you will need to add a couple of tools to your testing environment: Mockito and Hamcrest. Mockito is a Java framework that makes it easy to create simple *mock objects*. These mock objects will help you isolate your tests of **SoundViewModel** so that you do not accidentally test other objects at the same time.

Hamcrest is a library of *matchers*. Matchers are tools that make it easy to "match" conditions in your code and fail if your code does not match what you expect. You will use them to verify that your code works as you expect it to.

A version of Hamcrest is automatically included with the JUnit library, and JUnit is automatically included as a dependency when you create a new Android Studio project. This means that you only need to add the dependencies for Mockito to your test build. Open your app module's `build.gradle` file and add the Mockito dependencies (Listing 20.6). Sync your files when you are done.

## Listing 20.6 Adding Mockito dependencies (`app/build.gradle`)

```
dependencies {
    ...
    implementation 'androidx.recyclerview:recyclerview:1.0.0'
    testImplementation 'org.mockito:mockito-core:2.25.0'
    testImplementation 'org.mockito:mockito-inline:2.25.0'
}
```

The `testImplementation` scope means that this dependency will only be included in test builds of your app. That way, you do not bloat your APK with additional unused code.

`mockito-core` includes all of the functions you will use to create and configure your mock objects. `mockito-inline` is a special dependency that will make Mockito easier to use with Kotlin.

By default, all Kotlin classes are final. This means that you cannot inherit from these classes unless you explicitly mark them as open. Unfortunately, Mockito makes heavy use of inheritance when mocking classes. This means that Mockito cannot mock your Kotlin classes out of the box. The `mockito-inline` dependency includes functionality that allows Mockito to mock final classes and functions, working around this inheritance problem. This allows you to mock your Kotlin classes without needing to change your source files.

# Creating a Test Class

The most convenient way to write unit tests is within a *testing framework*. The framework makes it easier to write and run a suite of tests together and see their output in Android Studio.

JUnit is almost universally used as a testing framework on Android and has convenient integrations into Android Studio. Your first job is to create a class for your JUnit tests to live in. To do this, open up SoundViewModel.kt and key in Command-Shift-T (Ctrl-Shift-T). Android Studio attempts to navigate to a test class associated with the class you are looking at. If there is no test class (as is the case here), you are given the option to create a new test class (Figure 20.1).

Figure 20.1  Trying to open a test class

```
class SoundViewModel : BaseObservable() {
                        Choose Test for SoundViewModel (0 found)   📌
    var sound: Sound
        set(sound) {    Create New Test...
            field = sound
            notifyChange()
        }

    @get:Bindable
    val title: String?
        get() = sound?.name
}
```

Choose Create New Test... to create the new test class. Select JUnit4 for your testing library and check the box marked setUp/@Before. Leave all the other fields as they are (Figure 20.2).

Figure 20.2  Creating a new test class

Click OK to continue to the next dialog.

The last step is to choose what kind of test class you will create. Tests in the androidTest folder are called *instrumentation tests*. Instrumentation tests run on an Android device or emulator. The advantage of this is that you can test your app against the same system frameworks and APIs that your APK will be running against once the app is released. The downside is that instrumentation tests take longer to set up and run, because they are running against a full version of the Android OS.

Tests in the test folder are often referred to as unit tests. These tests run on a Java Virtual Machine, or JVM, without any of the Android runtime. Leaving out that baggage makes them quick.

The term "unit test" on Android is overloaded. It is sometimes used to describe a type of test that verifies a single class or unit of functionality in isolation. At other times, it is used to describe any test residing in the test directory. Unfortunately, a test in that directory might verify a single class or unit – but it might be an *integration test*, which tests a section of an app with many pieces working together. You will learn more about integration tests in the section called For the More Curious: Integration Testing near the end of this chapter.

For the remainder of this chapter, we will use the term *JVM test* for a test of either type that lives in the test folder and runs on the JVM. We will reserve *unit test* for only those tests that verify a single class or unit.

Unit tests are the smallest kind of test you can write: a test of one component by itself. They should not need your entire app or a device to run, and they should run quickly enough for you to run them repeatedly as you work. Because of this, they are rarely run as instrumentation tests. With this in mind, choose the test folder for your test class (Figure 20.3) and click OK.

## Figure 20.3 Selecting a destination directory

# Setting Up Your Test

Now to build out your **SoundViewModel** test. Android Studio has created a class file for you, called SoundViewModelTest.kt. (You can find this class under the source set labeled test inside your app module.) The template starts out with a single function called **setUp()**:

```
class SoundViewModelTest {

    @Before
    fun setUp() {
    }
}
```

A test needs to do the same work for most objects: build an instance of the object to test and create any other objects that object depends on. Instead of writing this same code for every test, JUnit provides an annotation called @Before. Code written inside a function marked @Before will be run once before each test executes. By convention, most JUnit test classes have one function marked @Before named **setUp()**.

## Setting up the test subject

Inside your **setUp()** function, you will construct an instance of **SoundViewModel** to test. To do that, you need an instance of **Sound**, because **SoundViewModel** needs a sound object to know how to display a title.

Create your **SoundViewModel** and a **Sound** for it to use (Listing 20.7). Since **Sound** is a simple data object with no behavior to break, it is safe not to mock it.

Listing 20.7  Creating a **SoundViewModel** test subject
(SoundViewModelTest.java)

```
class SoundViewModelTest {

    private lateinit var sound: Sound
    private lateinit var subject: SoundViewModel

    @Before
    fun setUp() {
        sound = Sound("assetPath")
        subject = SoundViewModel()
        subject.sound = sound
    }
}
```

Anywhere else in this book, you would have named your **SoundViewModel** soundViewModel. Here, though, you have named it subject. This is a convention we like to use in our tests at Big Nerd Ranch, for two reasons:

- It makes it clear that subject is the object under test (and the other objects are not).

- If any functions on **SoundViewModel** are ever moved to a different class (say, **BeatBoxSoundViewModel**), the test functions can be cut and pasted over without renaming soundViewModel to beatBoxSoundViewModel.

# Writing Tests

Now that your initial **setUp()** function is written, you are ready to write your tests. A test is a function in your test class annotated with @Test.

Start by writing a test that asserts existing behavior in **SoundViewModel**: The title property is connected to the **Sound**'s name property. Write a function that tests this (Listing 20.8).

## Listing 20.8  Testing the title property (SoundViewModelTest.kt)

```kotlin
class SoundViewModelTest {
    ...
    @Before
    fun setUp() {
        ...
    }

    @Test
    fun exposesSoundNameAsTitle() {
        assertThat(subject.title, `is`(sound.name))
    }
}
```

Two functions will show up red: the **assertThat(…)** function and the **is(…)** function. Key in Option-Return (Alt-Enter) on **assertThat(…)** and select **Assert.assertThat(…)** from org.junit. Do the same for the **is(…)** function, selecting **Is.is** from org.hamcrest.

This test uses the **is(…)** Hamcrest matcher with JUnit's **assertThat(…)** function. The code reads almost like a sentence: "Assert that subject's title property is the same value as sound's name property." If those two functions return different values, the test fails.

To run your unit tests, right-click on the **SoundViewModelTest** class name and select Run 'SoundViewModelTest'. Android Studio's bottom pane shows the results (Figure 20.4).

## Figure 20.4  Passing tests

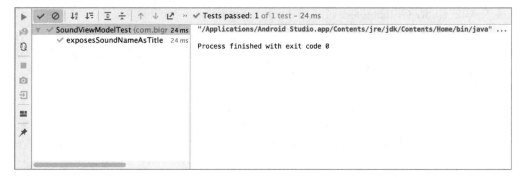

By default, the test display only shows details for failing tests, since those are the only tests that are interesting. So this output means that everything is A-OK – your tests ran, and they passed.

# Testing object interactions

Now for the real work: building out the interactions between **SoundViewModel** and your new
**BeatBox.play(Sound)** function. A common way to go about this is to write a test that shows what you
expect a new function to do *before* you have written the function. You are going to write a new function
on **SoundViewModel** called **onButtonClicked()** that calls **BeatBox.play(Sound)**. Write a test function
that calls **onButtonClicked()** (Listing 20.9).

### Listing 20.9  Writing a test for **onButtonClicked()** (SoundViewModelTest.kt)

```
class SoundViewModelTest {
    ...
    @Test
    fun exposesSoundNameAsTitle() {
        assertThat(subject.title, `is`(sound.name))
    }

    @Test
    fun callsBeatBoxPlayOnButtonClicked() {
        subject.onButtonClicked()
    }
}
```

That function does not exist yet, so it shows up in red. Put your cursor over it and key in Option-Return
(Alt-Enter). Then select Create member function 'SoundViewModel.onButtonClicked', and the function
will be created for you.

### Listing 20.10  Creating **onButtonClicked()** (SoundViewModel.kt)

```
class SoundViewModel : BaseObservable() {
    fun onButtonClicked() {
        TODO("not implemented") //To change ...
    }
    ...
}
```

For now, leave it empty (or delete the TODO, if Android Studio adds one) and key in Command-Shift-T
(Ctrl-Shift-T) to return to **SoundViewModelTest**.

Your test calls the function, but it should also verify that the function does what you say it does: calls
**BeatBox.play(Sound)**. The first step to implementing this is to provide **SoundViewModel** with a
**BeatBox** object.

You could create an instance of **BeatBox** in your test and pass it to the view model constructor.
But if you do that in a unit test, you create a problem: If **BeatBox** is broken, then tests you write in
**SoundViewModel** that use **BeatBox** might break, too. That is not what you want. **SoundViewModel**'s unit
tests should only fail when **SoundViewModel** is broken.

In other words, you want to test the behavior of **SoundViewModel** and its interactions with other classes
in isolation. This is a key tenet of unit testing.

The solution is to use a *mocked* **BeatBox**. This mock object will be a subclass of **BeatBox** that has all the same functions as **BeatBox** – but none of those functions will do anything. That way, your test of **SoundViewModel** can verify that **SoundViewModel** itself is using **BeatBox** correctly, without depending at all on how **BeatBox** works.

To create a mock object with Mockito, you call the **mock(Class)** static function, passing in the class you want to mock. Create a mock of **BeatBox** and a field to store it in **SoundViewModelTest** (Listing 20.11).

### Listing 20.11  Creating a mock **BeatBox** (SoundViewModelTest.kt)

```
class SoundViewModelTest {

    private lateinit var beatBox: BeatBox
    private lateinit var sound: Sound
    private lateinit var subject: SoundViewModel

    @Before
    fun setUp() {
        beatBox = mock(BeatBox::class.java)
        sound = Sound("assetPath")
        subject = SoundViewModel()
        subject.sound = sound
    }
    ...
}
```

The **mock(Class)** function will need to be imported, just like a class reference. This function will automatically create a mocked-out version of **BeatBox** for you. Pretty slick.

With the mock **BeatBox** ready, you can finish writing your test to verify that the play function is called. Mockito can help you do this odd-sounding job. All Mockito mock objects keep track of which of their functions have been called, as well as what parameters were passed in for each call. Mockito's **verify(Object)** function can then check to see whether those functions were called the way you expected them to be called.

Call **verify(Object)** to ensure that **onButtonClicked()** calls **BeatBox.play(Sound)** with the **Sound** object you hooked up to your **SoundViewModel** (Listing 20.12).

### Listing 20.12  Verifying that **BeatBox.play(Sound)** is called (SoundViewModelTest.kt)

```
class SoundViewModelTest {
    ...
    @Test
    fun callsBeatBoxPlayOnButtonClicked() {
        subject.onButtonClicked()

        verify(beatBox).play(sound)
    }
}
```

**verify(Object)** uses a fluent interface. It is an abbreviation for the following code:

```
verify(beatBox)
beatBox.play(sound)
```

Calling **verify(beatBox)** says, "I am about to verify that a function was called on beatBox." The next function call is then interpreted as, "Verify that this function was called like this." So your call to **verify(…)** here means, "Verify that the **play(…)** function was called on beatBox with this specific sound as a parameter."

No such thing has happened, of course. **SoundViewModel.onButtonClicked()** is empty, so **beatBox.play(Sound)** has not been called. Also, **SoundViewModel** does not even hold a reference to beatBox, so it cannot call any functions on it. This means that your test *should* fail. Because you are writing the test first, that is a good thing – if your test does not fail at first, it must not be testing anything.

Run your test to see it fail. You can follow the same steps from earlier, or key in Control-R (Shift-F10) to repeat the last run command you performed. The result is shown in Figure 20.5.

## Figure 20.5  Failing test output

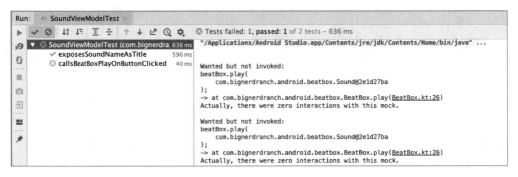

The output says that your test expected a call to **beatBox.play(Sound)** but did not receive it:

```
Wanted but not invoked:
beatBox.play(
    com.bignerdranch.android.beatbox.Sound@3571b748
);
-> at ….callsBeatBoxPlayOnButtonClicked(SoundViewModelTest.java:28)
Actually, there were zero interactions with this mock.
```

Under the hood, **verify(Object)** made an assertion, just like **assertThat(…)** did. When that assertion failed, it caused the test to fail and logged this output describing what went wrong.

Now to fix your test. First, create a constructor property for **SoundViewModel** that accepts a **BeatBox** instance.

## Listing 20.13  Providing a **BeatBox** to **SoundViewModel** (SoundViewModel.kt)

```kotlin
class SoundViewModel(private val beatBox: BeatBox) : BaseObservable() {
    ...
}
```

This change will cause two errors in your code: one in your tests and one in your production code. Fix the production error first. Open MainActivity.kt and provide the beatBox object to your view models when they are created in **SoundHolder** (Listing 20.14).

### Listing 20.14  Fixing the error in **SoundHolder** (MainActivity.kt)

```
private inner class SoundHolder(private val binding: ListItemSoundBinding) :
    RecyclerView.ViewHolder(binding.root) {

    init {
        binding.viewModel = SoundViewModel(beatBox)
    }

    fun bind(sound: Sound) {
        ...
    }
}
```

Next, provide the mock version of **BeatBox** to your view model in your test class (Listing 20.15).

### Listing 20.15  Providing the mock **BeatBox** in test (SoundViewModelTest.kt)

```
class SoundViewModelTest {
    ...
    @Before
    fun setUp() {
        beatBox = mock(BeatBox::class.java)
        sound = Sound("assetPath")
        subject = SoundViewModel(beatBox)
        subject.sound = sound
    }
    ...
}
```

This gets you halfway to a passing test. Next, implement **onButtonClicked()** to do what the test expects (Listing 20.16).

### Listing 20.16  Implementing **onButtonClicked()** (SoundViewModel.kt)

```
class SoundViewModel(private val beatBox: BeatBox) : BaseObservable() {
    ...
    fun onButtonClicked() {
        sound?.let {
            beatBox.play(it)
        }
    }
}
```

Rerun your test. This time you should see green, indicating that all your tests passed (Figure 20.6).

### Figure 20.6  All green, all good

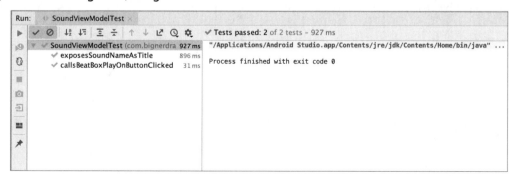

# Data Binding Callbacks

One last step remains to get your buttons working: You need to hook **onButtonClicked()** up to your buttons.

Remember how you used data binding to put data into your UI? You can also use it to hook up click listeners and the like by using lambda expressions. (To refresh your memory on lambda expressions, see the section called Lambda expressions in Chapter 19.)

Add a data binding callback expression to hook your buttons up to **SoundViewModel.onButtonClicked()**.

### Listing 20.17  Hooking up your buttons (list_item_sound.xml)

```
<Button
    android:layout_width="match_parent"
    android:layout_height="120dp"
    android:onClick="@{() -> viewModel.onButtonClicked()}"
    android:text="@{viewModel.title}"
    tools:text="Sound name"/>
```

The next time you run BeatBox, your buttons should play sounds for you. However, if you try to run BeatBox with the green run button now, your tests will run again. This is because running the tests changed your *run configuration* – the setting that determines what Android Studio will do when you click the run button.

To run your BeatBox app, click the run configuration selector next to the run button and switch back over to the app run configuration (Figure 20.7).

### Figure 20.7  Changing your run configuration

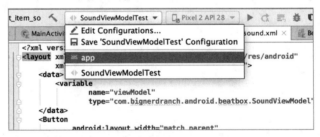

Now run BeatBox and click on your buttons. You should hear your app make aggressive yelling sounds. Do not be afraid – this is what BeatBox was meant to do.

# Unloading Sounds

The app works, but to be a good citizen you should clean up your **SoundPool** by calling
**SoundPool.release()** when you are done with it (Listing 20.18).

Listing 20.18  Releasing your **SoundPool** (BeatBox.kt)

```kotlin
class BeatBox(private val assets: AssetManager) {
    ...
    fun play(sound: Sound) {
        ...
    }

    fun release() {
        soundPool.release()
    }

    private fun loadSounds(): List<Sound> {
        ...
    }
    ...
}
```

Then, add a matching **BeatBox.release()** function in **MainActivity** (Listing 20.19).

Listing 20.19  Releasing your **BeatBox** (MainActivity.kt)

```kotlin
class MainActivity : AppCompatActivity() {

    private lateinit var beatBox: BeatBox

    override fun onCreate(savedInstanceState: Bundle?) {
        ...
    }

    override fun onDestroy() {
        super.onDestroy()
        beatBox.release()
    }
    ...
}
```

Run your app again to make sure it works correctly with your new **release()** function. If you play a
long sound and rotate the screen or hit the Back button, you should now hear the sound stop.

# For the More Curious: Integration Testing

We said earlier that **SoundViewModelTest** is a unit test and that your other option was to create an integration test. So: What is an integration test?

In a unit test, the item under test is an individual class. In an integration test, the item under test is a section of your app, with many pieces working together. Both of these tests are important and serve different purposes. Unit tests ensure correct behavior of each class unit and your expectations of how these units will interact with each other. Integration tests verify that the individually tested pieces actually do integrate together properly and function as expected.

Integration tests can be written for non-UI parts of your app, such as database interactions, but on Android they are most commonly written to test the app at the UI level by interacting with its UI and verifying expectations. They are usually written screen by screen. For example, you might test that when the **MainActivity** screen is fired up, the first button displays the name of the first file from sample_sounds: 65_cjipie.

Integration testing against the UI requires framework classes such as activities and fragments. It may also require system services, file systems, and other pieces not available to a JVM test. For this reason, integration tests are most often implemented as instrumentation tests on Android.

Integration tests should pass when the app *does* what you expect, not when the app is *implemented* how you expect. Changing the name of a button ID does not affect what the application does, but if you write an integration test that says, "Call **findViewById(R.id.button)** and make sure the button it finds is displaying the right text," that test will break. So instead of using standard Android framework tools like **findViewById(Int)**, UI integration tests are most often written with a UI testing framework that makes it easier to say things like, "Make sure there is a button with the text I expect on the screen somewhere."

Espresso is a UI testing framework from Google for testing Android apps. You can include it by adding com.android.support.test.espresso:espresso-core as an androidTestImplementation artifact in your app/build.gradle file. Android Studio includes this dependency by default on new projects.

Once you have Espresso included as a dependency, you can use it to make assertions about an activity you have fired up to test. Here is an example test showing how to assert that a view exists on the screen, using the first sample_sounds test filename:

```
@RunWith(AndroidJUnit4::class)
class MainActivityTest {

    @get:Rule
    val activityRule = ActivityTestRule(MainActivity::class.java)

    @Test
    fun showsFirstFileName() {
        onView(withText("65_cjipie"))
                .check(matches(isDisplayed()))
    }
}
```

A couple of annotations get this code up and running. The `@RunWith(AndroidJUnit4.class)` annotation up top specifies that this is an Android instrumentation test that might want to work with activities and other Android runtime toys. After that, the `@get:Rule` annotation on `activityRule` signals to JUnit that it should fire up an instance of **MainActivity** before running each test.

With that setup done, you can make assertions about **MainActivity** in your test. In **showsFirstFileName()**, the line `onView(withText("65_cjipie"))` finds a view with the text `65_cjipie` on it to perform a test operation on. The call to `check(matches(isDisplayed()))` after that asserts that the view is visible on the screen – if there is no view with that text, the check will fail. The `check(…)` function is Espresso's way to make **assertThat(…)**-type assertions about views.

Often you will want to click on a view, then make an assertion to verify the result of your click. You can also use Espresso to click on views or otherwise interact with them:

```
onView(withText("65_cjipie"))
        .perform(click())
```

When you interact with a view, Espresso will wait until your application is *idle* before continuing your test. Espresso has built-in ways of detecting when your UI is done updating, but if you need Espresso to wait longer, you can use a subclass of **IdlingResource** to signal to Espresso that your app has not settled down quite yet.

For more information about how to use Espresso to manipulate and test the UI, see the Espresso documentation at `developer.android.com/training/testing/espresso`.

Remember, integration tests and unit tests each serve different purposes. Most people prefer to start with unit tests because they help you define and verify the behavior of the individual parts of your app. Integration tests depend on those individually tested parts and verify that the parts work well together as a whole. Each gives you a distinct, important view of the health of your app, so the best shops do both kinds of testing.

# For the More Curious: Mocks and Testing

Mocking has a much different role in integration testing than it does in unit testing. Mock objects exist to isolate the component under test by pretending to be other, unrelated components. Unit testing tests an individual class; each class will have its own distinct dependencies, so each test class has a different set of mock objects. Since the mock objects are different in each test class, and the behavior rarely matters, mock frameworks that make it easy to create simple mock objects (like Mockito) are a great fit for unit tests.

Integration tests, on the other hand, are meant to test a larger piece of the app as a whole. Instead of isolating pieces of the app from each other, you use mocks to isolate the app from anything external it might interact with – for example, by providing a web service with fake data and responses. In BeatBox, you would provide a fake **SoundPool** that could tell you when a particular sound file was played. Because the mocks are larger and shared among many tests, and because it is more common to implement mock behavior, it is better to avoid automatic mocking frameworks for integration tests and instead manually write mock objects.

In either case, the same rule applies: Mock out the entities at the boundary of the component under test. This focuses the scope of your test and keeps it from breaking except when the component itself is broken.

# Challenge: Playback Speed Control

In this challenge, you will add playback speed control to BeatBox to greatly expand the user's repertoire of possible sounds (Figure 20.8). Within **MainActivity**, wire up a **SeekBar** to control the rate value **SoundPool**'s **play(Int, Float, Float, Int, Int, Float)** function accepts.

Figure 20.8  BeatBox with playback speed control

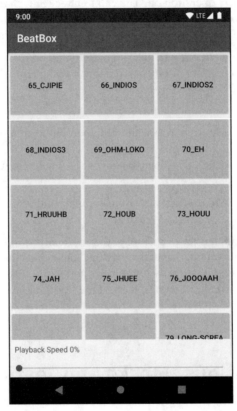

To make this happen, check out the docs at developer.android.com/reference/android/widget/SeekBar.html.

# Challenge: Play Sound Across Rotation

Currently, BeatBox will stop playing the sound if you rotate the device. This challenge will fix that.

The main issue in the current app is where you save your **BeatBox** object. Your **MainActivity** holds a reference to your **BeatBox**, but it is destroyed and re-created across rotation. This means that your initial **BeatBox** releases the **SoundPool** and re-creates it every time you rotate.

You have already seen how to persist information across rotation in GeoQuiz and CriminalIntent. Add a Jetpack **ViewModel** to BeatBox to keep your **BeatBox** object alive across rotation.

You can expose the **BeatBox** object as a public property from your **ViewModel**. This way, **MainActivity** can access the **BeatBox** instance from the Jetpack **ViewModel** to hand it to the data binding view model.

# 21

# Styles and Themes

Now that BeatBox sounds intimidating, it is time to make it look intimidating, too.

So far, BeatBox sticks with the default UI styles. The buttons are stock. The colors are stock. The app does not stand out. It does not have its own brand.

We can restyle it. We have the technology.

Figure 21.1 shows the better, stronger, faster – or at least more stylish – BeatBox.

Figure 21.1  A themed BeatBox

# Color Resources

Begin by defining a few colors that you will use throughout this chapter. Edit your res/values/
colors.xml file to match Listing 21.1.

## Listing 21.1  Defining a few colors (res/values/colors.xml)

```
<resources>
    <color name="colorPrimary">#008577</color>
    <color name="colorPrimaryDark">#00574B</color>
    <color name="colorAccent">#D81B60</color>

    <color name="red">#F44336</color>
    <color name="dark_red">#C3352B</color>
    <color name="gray">#607D8B</color>
    <color name="soothing_blue">#0083BF</color>
    <color name="dark_blue">#005A8A</color>
</resources>
```

Color resources are a convenient way to specify color values in one place that you reference throughout
your application.

# Styles

Now, update the buttons in BeatBox with a *style*. A style is a set of attributes that you can apply to a
widget.

Navigate to res/values/styles.xml and add a style named **BeatBoxButton** (Listing 21.2). (When you
created BeatBox, your new project should have come with a built-in styles.xml file. If your project
did not, create the file.)

## Listing 21.2  Adding a style (res/values/styles.xml)

```
<resources>

    <style name="AppTheme" parent="Theme.AppCompat.Light.DarkActionBar">
        <!-- Customize your theme here. -->
        <item name="colorPrimary">@color/colorPrimary</item>
        <item name="colorPrimaryDark">@color/colorPrimaryDark</item>
        <item name="colorAccent">@color/colorAccent</item>
    </style>

    <style name="BeatBoxButton">
        <item name="android:background">@color/dark_blue</item>
    </style>

</resources>
```

Here, you create a style called **BeatBoxButton**. This style defines a single attribute,
android:background, and sets it to a dark blue color. You can apply this style to as many widgets as
you like and then update the attributes of all of those widgets in this one place.

Now that the style is defined, apply **BeatBoxButton** to your buttons.

### Listing 21.3 Using a style (res/layout/list_item_sound.xml)

```
<Button
    style="@style/BeatBoxButton"
    android:layout_width="match_parent"
    android:layout_height="120dp"
    android:onClick="@{() -> viewModel.onButtonClicked()}"
    android:text="@{viewModel.title}"
    tools:text="Sound name"/>
```

Run BeatBox, and you will see that all of your buttons now have a dark blue background color (Figure 21.2).

### Figure 21.2 BeatBox with button styles

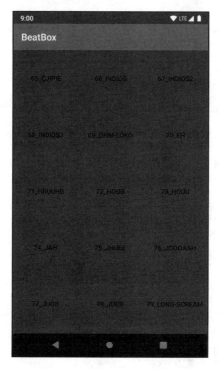

You can create a style for any set of attributes that you want to reuse in your application. Pretty handy.

# Style inheritance

Styles also support inheritance: A style can inherit and override attributes from another style.

Create a new style called **BeatBoxButton.Strong** that inherits from **BeatBoxButton** and also bolds the text.

## Listing 21.4  Inheriting from **BeatBoxButton** (res/values/styles.xml)

```
<style name="BeatBoxButton">
    <item name="android:background">@color/dark_blue</item>
</style>

<style name="BeatBoxButton.Strong">
    <item name="android:textStyle">bold</item>
</style>
```

(While you could have added the android:textStyle attribute to the **BeatBoxButton** style directly, you created **BeatBoxButton.Strong** to demonstrate style inheritance.)

The naming convention here is a little strange. When you name your style **BeatBoxButton.Strong**, you are saying that your theme inherits attributes from **BeatBoxButton**.

There is also an alternative inheritance naming style. You can specify a parent when declaring the style:

```
<style name="BeatBoxButton">
    <item name="android:background">@color/dark_blue</item>
</style>

<style name="StrongBeatBoxButton" parent="@style/BeatBoxButton">
    <item name="android:textStyle">bold</item>
</style>
```

Stick with the **BeatBoxButton.Strong** style in BeatBox.

Update res/layout/list_item_sound.xml to use your newer, stronger style.

## Listing 21.5  Using a bolder style (res/layout/list_item_sound.xml)

```
<Button
    style="@style/BeatBoxButton.Strong"
    android:layout_width="match_parent"
    android:layout_height="120dp"
    android:onClick="@{() -> viewModel.onButtonClicked()}"
    android:text="@{viewModel.title}"
    tools:text="Sound name"/>
```

Run BeatBox and verify that your button text is indeed bold, as in Figure 21.3.

## Figure 21.3  A bolder BeatBox

# Themes

Styles are cool. They allow you to define a set of attributes in one place and then apply them to as many widgets as you want. The downside of styles is that you have to apply them to each and every widget, one at a time. What if you had a more complex app with lots of buttons in lots of layouts? Adding your **BeatBoxButton** style to them all could be a huge task.

That is where themes come in. Themes take styles a step further: They allow you to define a set of attributes in one place, like a style – but then those attributes are automatically applied throughout your app. Theme attributes can store a reference to concrete resources, such as colors, and they can also store a reference to styles. In a theme, you can say, for example, "I want all buttons to use this style." And then you do not need to find every button widget and tell it to use the theme.

## Modifying the theme

When you created BeatBox, it was given a default theme. Navigate to `manifests/AndroidManifest.xml` and look at the `theme` attribute on the `application` tag:

```
<manifest xmlns:android="http://schemas.android.com/apk/res/android"
    package="com.bignerdranch.android.beatbox" >

    <application
        android:allowBackup="true"
        android:icon="@mipmap/ic_launcher"
        android:label="@string/app_name"
        android:roundIcon="@mipmap/ic_launcher_round"
        android:supportsRtl="true"
        android:theme="@style/AppTheme">
        ...
    </application>

</manifest>
```

The `theme` attribute is pointing to a theme called **AppTheme**. **AppTheme** was declared in the `styles.xml` file that you modified earlier.

As you can see, a theme is also a style. But themes specify different attributes than a style does (as you will see in a moment). Themes are also given superpowers by being declared in the manifest. This is what causes the theme to be applied across the entire app automatically.

Navigate to the definition of the **AppTheme** theme by Command-clicking (Ctrl-clicking) on `@style/AppTheme`. Android Studio will take you to `res/values/styles.xml`:

```
<resources>

    <style name="AppTheme" parent="Theme.AppCompat.Light.DarkActionBar">
        ...
    </style>

    <style name="BeatBoxButton">
        <item name="android:background">@color/dark_blue</item>
    </style>
    ...
</resources>
```

When you choose Use AndroidX artifacts in new projects created in Android Studio, they are given an **AppCompat** theme. **AppTheme** is inheriting attributes from **Theme.AppCompat.Light.DarkActionBar**. Within **AppTheme**, you can add or override additional values from the parent theme.

The AppCompat library comes with three main themes:

- **Theme.AppCompat** – a dark theme

- **Theme.AppCompat.Light** – a light theme

- **Theme.AppCompat.Light.DarkActionBar** – a light theme with a dark app bar

Change the parent theme to **Theme.AppCompat** to give BeatBox a dark theme as its base.

### Listing 21.6  Changing to a dark theme (res/values/styles.xml)

```
<resources>

    <style name="AppTheme" parent="Theme.AppCompat.Light.DarkActionBar">
        ...
    </style>
    ...
</resources>
```

Run BeatBox to see your new dark theme (Figure 21.4).

### Figure 21.4  A dark BeatBox

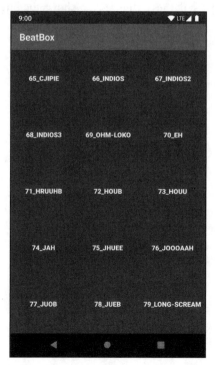

# Adding Theme Colors

With the base theme squared away, it is time to customize the attributes of BeatBox's **AppTheme**.

In the styles.xml file, you will see three attributes. Update them to match Listing 21.7.

### Listing 21.7  Setting theme attributes (res/values/styles.xml)

```
<style name="AppTheme" parent="Theme.AppCompat">
    <!-- Customize your theme here. -->
    <item name="colorPrimary">@color/colorPrimaryred</item>
    <item name="colorPrimaryDark">@color/colorPrimaryDarkdark_red</item>
    <item name="colorAccent">@color/colorAccentgray</item>
</style>
```

These theme attributes look similar to the style attributes that you set up earlier, but they specify different properties. Style attributes specify properties for an individual widget, such as the textStyle that you used to bold the button text. Theme attributes have a larger scope: They are properties that are set on the theme that any widget can access. For example, the app bar will look at the colorPrimary attribute on the theme to set its background color.

These three attributes have a large impact. The colorPrimary attribute is the primary color for your app's brand. This color will be used as the app bar's background and in a few other places.

colorPrimaryDark is used to color the status bar, which shows up at the top of the screen. Typically colorPrimaryDark will be a slightly darker version of your colorPrimary color. Status bar theming is a feature that was added to Android in Lollipop. Keep in mind that the status bar will be black on older devices (no matter what the theme specifies). Figure 21.5 shows the effect of these two theme attributes on BeatBox.

### Figure 21.5  BeatBox with custom AppCompat color attributes

Finally, you set `colorAccent` to a gray color. `colorAccent` should contrast with your `colorPrimary` attribute; it is used to tint some widgets, such as an **EditText**.

You will not see the `colorAccent` attribute affect BeatBox, because **Button**s do not support tinting. But you still specify `colorAccent`, because it is a good idea to think about these three color attributes together. These colors should mesh, and the default `colorAccent` attribute from your parent theme may clash with the other colors that you specified. This sets you up well for any future additions.

Run BeatBox to see the new colors. Your app should look like Figure 21.5.

# Overriding Theme Attributes

Now that the colors are worked out, it is time to dive in and see what theme attributes exist that you can override. Be warned, theme spelunking is tough. There is little to no documentation about which attributes exist, which ones you can override yourself, and even what the attributes do. You are going off the map here. It is a good thing you have this book to be your guide.

Your first goal is to change the background color of BeatBox by altering the theme. While you could navigate to `res/layout/fragment_beat_box.xml` and manually set the `android:background` attribute on your **RecyclerView** – and then repeat the process in every other fragment and activity layout file that might exist – this would be wasteful. Wasteful of your time, obviously, but also wasteful of app effort.

The theme is always setting a background color. By setting another color on top of that, you are doing extra work. You are also writing code that is hard to maintain by duplicating the background attribute throughout the app.

## Theme spelunking

Instead, you want to override the background color attribute on your theme. To discover the name of this attribute, take a look at how this attribute is set by your parent theme: **Theme.AppCompat**.

You might be thinking, "How will I know which attribute to override if I don't know its name?" You will not. You will read the names of the attributes until one makes you think, "That one sounds right." Then you will override that attribute, run the app, and hope that you chose wisely.

What you want to do is search through the ancestors of your theme. To do this, you will keep on navigating up to one parent after another until you find a suitable attribute.

Open your `styles.xml` file and Command-click (Ctrl-click) on **Theme.AppCompat**. Let's see how deep the rabbit hole goes.

(If you are unable to navigate through your theme attributes directly in Android Studio, or you want to do this outside of Android Studio, you can find Android's theme sources in the directory *your-SDK-directory*/platforms/android-28/data/res/values directory.)

At the time of this writing, you are brought to a very large file with a focus on this line:

```
<style name="Theme.AppCompat" parent="Base.Theme.AppCompat" />
```

**Theme.AppCompat** inherits attributes from **Base.Theme.AppCompat**. Interestingly, **Theme.AppCompat** does not override any attributes itself. It just points to its parent.

Command-click (Ctrl-click) on **Base.Theme.AppCompat**. Android Studio will tell you that this theme is resource qualified. There are a few different versions of this theme depending on the version of Android that you are on.

Choose the values/values.xml version (Figure 21.6), and you will be brought to **Base.Theme.AppCompat**'s definition.

## Figure 21.6  Choosing the parent

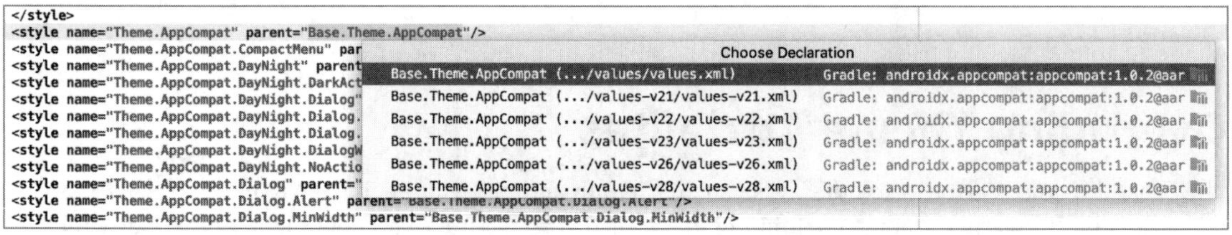

```
</style>
<style name="Theme.AppCompat" parent="Base.Theme.AppCompat"/>
<style name="Theme.AppCompat.CompactMenu" par
<style name="Theme.AppCompat.DayNight" parent                        Choose Declaration
<style name="Theme.AppCompat.DayNight.DarkAct
<style name="Theme.AppCompat.DayNight.Dialog     Base.Theme.AppCompat (.../values/values.xml)      Gradle: androidx.appcompat:appcompat:1.0.2@aar
<style name="Theme.AppCompat.DayNight.Dialog.    Base.Theme.AppCompat (.../values-v21/values-v21.xml)   Gradle: androidx.appcompat:appcompat:1.0.2@aar
<style name="Theme.AppCompat.DayNight.Dialog.    Base.Theme.AppCompat (.../values-v22/values-v22.xml)   Gradle: androidx.appcompat:appcompat:1.0.2@aar
<style name="Theme.AppCompat.DayNight.DialogW    Base.Theme.AppCompat (.../values-v23/values-v23.xml)   Gradle: androidx.appcompat:appcompat:1.0.2@aar
<style name="Theme.AppCompat.DayNight.NoActio    Base.Theme.AppCompat (.../values-v26/values-v26.xml)   Gradle: androidx.appcompat:appcompat:1.0.2@aar
<style name="Theme.AppCompat.Dialog" parent="   Base.Theme.AppCompat (.../values-v28/values-v28.xml)   Gradle: androidx.appcompat:appcompat:1.0.2@aar
<style name="Theme.AppCompat.Dialog.Alert" parent="Base.Theme.AppCompat.Dialog.Alert"/>
<style name="Theme.AppCompat.Dialog.MinWidth" parent="Base.Theme.AppCompat.Dialog.MinWidth"/>
```

Choosing the unqualified version may seem strange here since your app's minimum supported API version is 21. You chose the unqualified version because the background theme attribute has been around much longer than API 21, meaning it must exist in the original **Base.Theme.AppCompat** version.

```
<style name="Base.Theme.AppCompat" parent="Base.V7.Theme.AppCompat">
</style>
```

**Base.Theme.AppCompat** is another theme that exists only for its name and does not override any attributes. Continue along to its parent theme: **Base.V7.Theme.AppCompat**.

```
<style name="Base.V7.Theme.AppCompat" parent="Platform.AppCompat">
    <item name="viewInflaterClass">
            androidx.appcompat.app.AppCompatViewInflater</item>
    <item name="windowNoTitle">false</item>
    <item name="windowActionBar">true</item>
    <item name="windowActionBarOverlay">false</item>
    ...
</style>
```

You are getting closer. Scan through the list of attributes in **Base.V7.Theme.AppCompat**.

You will not see an attribute that seems to change the background color. Navigate to **Platform.AppCompat**. You will see that this is resource qualified. Again, choose the values/values.xml version.

```
<style name="Platform.AppCompat" parent="android:Theme.Holo">
    <item name="android:windowNoTitle">true</item>
    <item name="android:windowActionBar">false</item>

    <item name="android:buttonBarStyle">?attr/buttonBarStyle</item>
    <item name="android:buttonBarButtonStyle">?attr/buttonBarButtonStyle</item>
    <item name="android:borderlessButtonStyle">?attr/borderlessButtonStyle</item>
    ...
</style>
```

Here you see that the parent of the **Platform.AppCompat** theme is **android:Theme.Holo**. Notice that the parent theme is not referenced just as **Theme**. Instead it has the android namespace in front of it.

You can think of the AppCompat library as something that lives within your own app. When you build your project, you include the AppCompat library, and it brings along a bunch of XML and Kotlin (and Java) files. Those files are just like the files that you wrote yourself. If you want to refer to something in the AppCompat library, you do it directly. You would just write **Theme.AppCompat**, because those files exist in your app.

Themes that exist in the Android OS, like **Theme**, have to be declared with the namespace that points to their location. The AppCompat library uses **android:Theme** because the theme exists in the Android OS.

You have finally arrived. Here you see many attributes that you can override in your theme. You can of course navigate to **Platform.AppCompat**'s parent, **Theme.Holo**, but this is not necessary. You will find the attribute you need in this theme.

Just above the text color attributes, windowBackground is declared. It seems likely that this attribute is the background for the theme.

```
<style name="Platform.AppCompat" parent="android:Theme.Holo">
    ...

    <!-- Window colors -->
    ...
    <item name="android:windowBackground">@color/background_material_dark</item>
```

This is the attribute that you want to override in BeatBox. Navigate back to your styles.xml file and override the windowBackground attribute.

## Listing 21.8  Setting the window background (res/values/styles.xml)

```
<style name="AppTheme" parent="Theme.AppCompat">
    <!-- Customize your theme here. -->
    <item name="colorPrimary">@color/red</item>
    <item name="colorPrimaryDark">@color/dark_red</item>
    <item name="colorAccent">@color/gray</item>

    <item name="android:windowBackground">@color/soothing_blue</item>
</style>
```

Notice that you must use the android namespace when overriding this attribute, because windowBackground is declared in the Android OS.

Run BeatBox, scroll down to the bottom of your recycler view, and verify that the background (where it is not covered with a button) is a soothing blue, as in Figure 21.7.

## Figure 21.7  BeatBox with a themed background

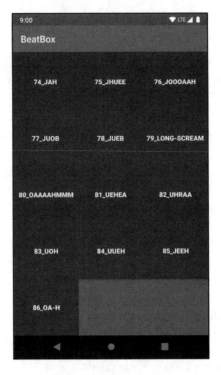

The steps that you just went through to find the windowBackground attribute are the same steps that every Android developer takes when modifying an app's theme. You will not find much documentation on these attributes. Most people go straight to the source to see what is available.

To recap, you navigated through the following themes:

- Theme.AppCompat

- Base.Theme.AppCompat

- Base.V7.Theme.AppCompat

- Platform.AppCompat

You navigated through the theme hierarchy until you arrived at AppCompat's root theme. As you become more familiar with your theme options, you may opt to skip ahead to the appropriate theme in the future. But it is nice to follow the hierarchy so you can see your theme's roots.

Be aware that this theme hierarchy may change over time. But the task of walking the hierarchy will not. You follow your theme hierarchy until you find the attribute that you want to override.

# Modifying Button Attributes

Earlier you customized the buttons in BeatBox by manually setting a `style` attribute in the `res/layout/list_item_sound.xml` file. If you have a more complex app, with buttons throughout many activities or fragments, setting a `style` attribute on each and every button does not scale well. You can take your theme a step further by defining a style in your theme for every button in your app.

Before adding a button style to your theme, remove the `style` attribute from `list_item_sound.xml`.

### Listing 21.9  Be gone! We have a better way (res/layout/list_item_sound.xml)

```
<Button
    style="@style/BeatBoxButton.Strong"
    android:layout_width="match_parent"
    android:layout_height="120dp"
    android:onClick="@{() -> viewModel.onButtonClicked()}"
    android:text="@{viewModel.title}"
    tools:text="Sound name"/>
```

Run BeatBox again and verify that your buttons are back to the old, bland look (Figure 21.8).

### Figure 21.8  BeatBox with old, bland buttons

Go theme spelunking again. This time, you are looking for buttonStyle. You will find it in
**Base.V7.Theme.AppCompat**.

```
<style name="Base.V7.Theme.AppCompat" parent="Platform.AppCompat">
    ...
    <!-- Button styles -->
    <item name="buttonStyle">@style/Widget.AppCompat.Button</item>
    <item name="buttonStyleSmall">@style/Widget.AppCompat.Button.Small</item>
    ...
</style>
```

buttonStyle specifies the style of any normal button within your app.

The buttonStyle attribute points to a style resource rather than a value. When you updated the
windowBackground attribute, you passed in a value: the color. In this case, buttonStyle should point
to a style. Navigate to **Widget.AppCompat.Button** to see the button style. (If you cannot Command-
click [Ctrl-click] on the style, just search for it in the same values.xml file and you will find its style
declaration.)

```
<style name="Widget.AppCompat.Button" parent="Base.Widget.AppCompat.Button"/>
```

**Widget.AppCompat.Button** does not define any attributes itself. Navigate to its parent to see the goods.
You will find that there are two versions of the base style. Choose the values/values.xml version.

```
<style name="Base.Widget.AppCompat.Button" parent="android:Widget">
    <item name="android:background">@drawable/abc_btn_default_mtrl_shape</item>
    <item name="android:textAppearance">?android:attr/textAppearanceButton</item>
    <item name="android:minHeight">48dip</item>
    <item name="android:minWidth">88dip</item>
    <item name="android:focusable">true</item>
    <item name="android:clickable">true</item>
    <item name="android:gravity">center_vertical|center_horizontal</item>
</style>
```

Every **Button** that you use in BeatBox is given these attributes.

Duplicate what happens in Android's own theme in BeatBox. Change the parent of **BeatBoxButton** to
inherit from the existing button style (Listing 21.10). Also, remove your **BeatBoxButton.Strong** style
from earlier.

## Listing 21.10  Creating a button style (res/values/styles.xml)

```
<resources>

    <style name="AppTheme" parent="Theme.AppCompat">
        <item name="colorPrimary">@color/red</item>
        <item name="colorPrimaryDark">@color/dark_red</item>
        <item name="colorAccent">@color/gray</item>

        <item name="android:windowBackground">@color/soothing_blue</item>
    </style>

    <style name="BeatBoxButton" parent="Widget.AppCompat.Button">
        <item name="android:background">@color/dark_blue</item>
    </style>

    <style name="BeatBoxButton.Strong">
        <item name="android:textStyle">bold</item>
    </style>

</resources>
```

You specified a parent of **Widget.AppCompat.Button**. You want your button to inherit all of the properties that a normal button would receive and then selectively modify attributes.

If you do not specify a parent theme for **BeatBoxButton**, you will notice that your buttons devolve into something that does not look like a button at all. Properties you expect to see, such as the text centered in the button, will be lost.

Now that you have fully defined **BeatBoxButton**, it is time to use it. Look back at the buttonStyle attribute that you found earlier when digging through Android's themes. Duplicate this attribute in your own theme.

## Listing 21.11  Using the **BeatBoxButton** style (res/values/styles.xml)

```
<resources>

    <style name="AppTheme" parent="Theme.AppCompat">
        <!-- Customize your theme here. -->
        <item name="colorPrimary">@color/red</item>
        <item name="colorPrimaryDark">@color/dark_red</item>
        <item name="colorAccent">@color/gray</item>

        <item name="android:windowBackground">@color/soothing_blue</item>
        <item name="buttonStyle">@style/BeatBoxButton</item>
    </style>

    <style name="BeatBoxButton" parent="Widget.AppCompat.Button">
        <item name="android:background">@color/dark_blue</item>
    </style>

</resources>
```

Notice that you do not use the android: prefix when defining buttonStyle. This is because the buttonStyle attribute that you are overriding is implemented in the AppCompat library.

You are now overriding the buttonStyle attribute and substituting your own style: **BeatBoxButton**.

Run BeatBox and notice that all of your buttons are dark blue (Figure 21.9). You changed the look of every normal button in BeatBox without modifying any layout files directly. Behold the power of theme attributes in Android!

Figure 21.9  The completely themed BeatBox

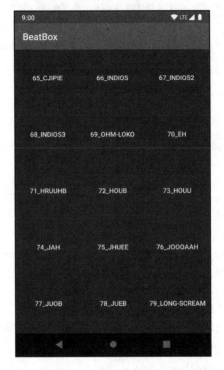

It sure would be nice if the buttons were more clearly buttons. In the next chapter, you will fix this issue and make those buttons really shine.

# For the More Curious: More on Style Inheritance

The description of style inheritance earlier in this chapter does not explain the full story. You may have noticed a switch in inheritance style as you were exploring the theme hierarchy. The AppCompat themes used the name of the theme to indicate inheritance until you arrive at the **Platform.AppCompat** theme.

```
<style name="Platform.AppCompat" parent="android:Theme.Holo">
    ...
</style>
```

Here, the inheritance naming style changes to the more explicit parent attribute style. Why?

Specifying the parent theme in the theme name only works for themes that exist in the same package. So you will see the Android OS themes use the theme-name inheritance style most of the time, and you will see the AppCompat library do the same. But once the AppCompat library crosses over to a parent outside of itself, the explicit parent attribute is used.

In your own applications, it is a good idea to follow the same convention. Specify your theme parent in the name of your theme if you are inheriting from one of your own themes. If you inherit from a style or theme in the Android OS, explicitly specify the parent attribute.

# For the More Curious: Accessing Theme Attributes

Once attributes are declared in your theme, you can access them in XML or in code.

To access a theme attribute in XML, you use the notation that you saw on the listSeparatorTextViewStyle attribute in Chapter 8. When referencing a concrete value in XML, such as a color, you use the @ notation. @color/gray points to a specific resource.

When referencing a resource in the theme, you use the ? notation:

```
<Button xmlns:android="http://schemas.android.com/apk/res/android"
    xmlns:tools="http://schemas.android.com/tools"
    android:id="@+id/list_item_sound_button"
    android:layout_width="match_parent"
    android:layout_height="120dp"
    android:background="?attr/colorAccent"
    tools:text="Sound name"/>
```

The ? notation says to use the resource that the colorAccent attribute on your theme points to. In your case, this would be the gray color that you defined in your colors.xml file.

You can also use theme attributes in code, although it is much more verbose.

```
val theme: Resources.Theme = activity.theme
val attrsToFetch = intArrayOf(R.attr.colorAccent)
val a: TypedArray = theme.obtainStyledAttributes(R.style.AppTheme, attrsToFetch)
val accentColor = a.getInt(0, 0)
a.recycle()
```

On the **Theme** object, you ask to resolve the attribute R.attr.colorAccent that is defined in your **AppTheme**, which is **R.style.AppTheme**. This call returns a **TypedArray**, which holds your data. On the **TypedArray**, you ask for an Int value to pull out the accent color. From here, you can use that color to change the background of a button, for example.

The app bar and buttons in BeatBox are doing exactly this to style themselves based on your theme attributes.

# 22

# XML Drawables

Now that BeatBox has been themed, it is time to do something about those buttons.

Currently, the buttons do not show any kind of response when you press on them, and they are just blue boxes. In this chapter, you will use *XML drawables* to take BeatBox to the next level (Figure 22.1).

## Figure 22.1 BeatBox makeover

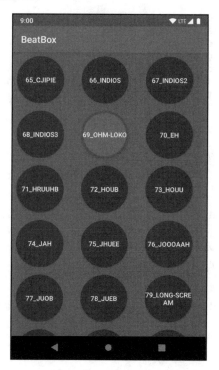

Android calls anything that is intended to be drawn to the screen a "drawable," whether it is an abstract shape, a clever bit of code that subclasses the **Drawable** class, or a bitmap image. In this chapter, you will see shape drawables, state list drawables, and layer list drawables. All three are defined in XML files, so we group them in the category of XML drawables.

# Making Uniform Buttons

Before creating any XML drawables, modify `res/layout/list_item_sound.xml` to prep your buttons for the changes to come.

## Listing 22.1  Spacing the buttons out (`res/layout/list_item_sound.xml`)

```
<layout xmlns:android="http://schemas.android.com/apk/res/android"
        xmlns:tools="http://schemas.android.com/tools">
    <data>
        <variable
                name="viewModel"
                type="com.bignerdranch.android.beatbox.SoundViewModel"/>
    </data>
    <FrameLayout
            android:layout_width="match_parent"
            android:layout_height="wrap_content"
            android:layout_margin="8dp">
        <Button
                android:layout_width="match_parent"
                android:layout_height="120dp"
                android:layout_width="100dp"
                android:layout_height="100dp"
                android:layout_gravity="center"
                android:onClick="@{() -> viewModel.onButtonClicked()}"
                android:text="@{viewModel.title}"
                tools:text="Sound name"/>
    </FrameLayout>
</layout>
```

You gave each button a width and height of 100dp so that when the buttons are circles later on they will not be skewed.

Your recycler view will always show three columns, no matter what the screen size is. If there is extra room, the recycler view will stretch those columns to fit the device. You do not want the recycler view to stretch your buttons, so you wrapped your buttons in a frame layout. The frame layout will be stretched and the buttons will not.

Run BeatBox, and you will see that your buttons are all the same size and have some space between them (Figure 22.2).

Figure 22.2  Spaced-out buttons

# Shape Drawables

Now, make your buttons round with a *shape drawable*.

Since XML drawables are not density specific, they are placed in the default drawable folder instead of a density-specific one. In the project tool window, create a new file in res/drawable called button_beat_box_normal.xml (Listing 22.2). (Why is this one "normal"? Because soon it will have a not-so-normal friend.)

Listing 22.2  Making a round shape drawable
(res/drawable/button_beat_box_normal.xml)

```
<shape xmlns:android="http://schemas.android.com/apk/res/android"
        android:shape="oval">

    <solid android:color="@color/dark_blue"/>

</shape>
```

This file creates an oval shape drawable that is filled in with a dark blue color. There are additional customization options with shape drawables, including rectangles, lines, and gradients. Check out the documentation at developer.android.com/guide/topics/resources/drawable-resource.html for details.

Apply `button_beat_box_normal` as the background for your buttons.

## Listing 22.3  Modifying the background drawable (`res/values/styles.xml`)

```
<resources>

    <style name="AppTheme" parent="Theme.AppCompat">
        ...
    </style>

    <style name="BeatBoxButton" parent="Widget.AppCompat.Button">
        <item name="android:background">@color/dark_blue</item>
        <item name="android:background">@drawable/button_beat_box_normal</item>
    </style>

</resources>
```

Run BeatBox. Your buttons are now nice circles (Figure 22.3).

## Figure 22.3  Circular buttons

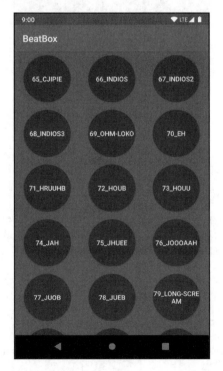

Press a button. You will hear the sound, but the button will not change its appearance. It would be better if the button looked different once it was pressed.

# State List Drawables

To fix this, define a new shape drawable that will be used for the pressed state of the button.

Create `button_beat_box_pressed.xml` in `res/drawable`. Make this pressed drawable the same as the normal version but with a red background color.

### Listing 22.4 Defining a pressed shape drawable (res/drawable/button_beat_box_pressed.xml)

```
<shape xmlns:android="http://schemas.android.com/apk/res/android"
       android:shape="oval">

    <solid android:color="@color/red"/>

</shape>
```

Next, you are going to use this pressed version when the user presses the button. To do this, you will use a *state list drawable*.

A state list drawable is a drawable that points to other drawables based on the state of something. A button has a pressed and an unpressed state. You will use a state list drawable to specify one drawable as the background when pressed and a different drawable when not pressed.

Define a state list drawable in a new file in your `res/drawable` folder.

### Listing 22.5 Creating a state list drawable (res/drawable/button_beat_box.xml)

```
<selector xmlns:android="http://schemas.android.com/apk/res/android">
    <item android:drawable="@drawable/button_beat_box_pressed"
          android:state_pressed="true"/>
    <item android:drawable="@drawable/button_beat_box_normal" />
</selector>
```

Now, modify your button style to use this new state list drawable as the button background.

### Listing 22.6 Applying a state list drawable (res/values/styles.xml)

```
<resources>

    <style name="AppTheme" parent="Theme.AppCompat">
        ...
    </style>

    <style name="BeatBoxButton" parent="Widget.AppCompat.Button">
        <item name="android:background">@drawable/button_beat_box_normal</item>
        <item name="android:background">@drawable/button_beat_box</item>
    </style>

</resources>
```

When the button is in the pressed state, `button_beat_box_pressed` will be used as the background. Otherwise, `button_beat_box_normal` will be the background of the button.

Run BeatBox and press a button. The button's background changes (Figure 22.4). Pretty slick, right?

## Figure 22.4  BeatBox, now with a pressed button state

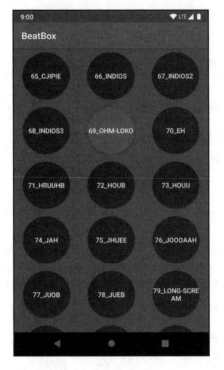

State list drawables are a handy customization tool. Many other states are also supported, including disabled, focused, and activated. Check out the documentation at developer.android.com/reference/android/graphics/drawable/StateListDrawable for details.

# Layer List Drawables

BeatBox is looking good. You now have round buttons, and they visually respond to presses. Time for something a little more advanced.

*Layer list drawables* allow you to combine two XML drawables into one. Armed with this tool, add a dark ring around your button when it is in the pressed state.

### Listing 22.7  Using a layer list drawable (res/drawable/button_beat_box_pressed.xml)

```
<layer-list xmlns:android="http://schemas.android.com/apk/res/android">
    <item>
        <shape xmlns:android="http://schemas.android.com/apk/res/android"
            android:shape="oval">

          <solid android:color="@color/red"/>
        </shape>
    </item>
    <item>
        <shape android:shape="oval">

            <stroke android:width="4dp"
                    android:color="@color/dark_red"/>
        </shape>
    </item>
</layer-list>
```

You specified two drawables in this layer list drawable. The first drawable is a red circle, as it was before this change. The second drawable will be drawn on top of the first. In the second drawable, you specified another oval with a stroke width of 4dp. This will create a ring of dark red.

These two drawables combine to form the layer list drawable. You can combine more than two drawables in a layer list to make something even more complex.

Run BeatBox and press on a button or two. You will see a nice ring around the pressed interface (Figure 22.5). Even slicker.

Figure 22.5  BeatBox complete

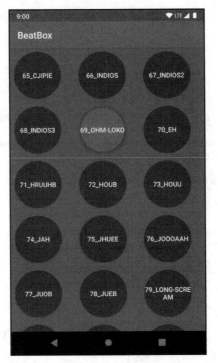

With the layer list drawable addition, BeatBox is now complete. Remember how plain BeatBox used to look? You now have something special and uniquely identifiable. Making your app a pleasure to look at makes it fun to use, and that will pay off in popularity.

# For the More Curious: Why Bother with XML Drawables?

You will always want a pressed state for your buttons, so state list drawables are a critical component of any Android app. But what about shape drawables and layer list drawables? Should you use them?

XML drawables are flexible. You can use them for many purposes, and you can easily update them in the future. With a combination of layer list drawables and shape drawables, you can create complex backgrounds without using an image editor. If you decide to change the color scheme in BeatBox, updating the colors in an XML drawable is easy.

In this chapter, you defined your XML drawables in the `drawable` directory with no resource qualifiers for the screen density. This is because XML drawables are density independent. With a standard background that is an image, you will typically create multiple versions of that same image in different densities so that the image will look crisp on most devices. XML drawables only need to be defined once and will look crisp at any screen density.

# For the More Curious: Mipmap Images

Resource qualifiers and drawables are handy. When you need an image in your app, you generate the image in a few different sizes and add the versions to your resource-qualified folders: drawable-mdpi, drawable-hdpi, etc. Then you reference the image by name, and Android figures out which density to use based on the current device.

However, there is a downside to this system. The APK file that you release to the Play Store will contain all of the images in your drawable directories at each density that you added to your project – even though many of them will not be used. That is a lot of bloat.

To reduce this bloat, you can generate separate APKs for each screen density. You would have an mdpi APK of your app, an hdpi APK, and so on. (For more information on APK splitting, see the tools documentation at developer.android.com/studio/build/configure-apk-splits.html.)

But there is one exception. You want to maintain every density of your launcher icon.

A launcher on Android is a Home screen application. (You will learn much more about launchers in Chapter 23.) When you press the Home button on your device, you are taken to the launcher.

Some newer launchers display app icons at a larger size than launchers have traditionally displayed them. To make the larger icons look nice, these launchers will take an icon from the next density bucket up. For example, if your device is an hdpi device, the launcher will use the xhdpi icon to represent your app. But if the xhdpi version has been stripped from your APK, the launcher will have to fall back to the lower-resolution version.

Scaled-up low-res icons look fuzzy. You want your icon to look crisp.

The *mipmap* directory is Android's solution to this problem. When APK splitting is enabled, mipmaps are not pruned from the APKs. Otherwise, mipmaps are identical to drawables.

New projects in Android Studio are automatically set up to use a mipmap resource for their launcher icon (Figure 22.6).

## Figure 22.6  Mipmap icons

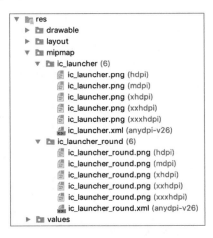

We recommend putting just your launcher icon in the various mipmap directories. All other images belong in the drawable directories.

# For the More Curious: 9-Patch Images

Sometimes (or maybe often), you will fall back to regular old image files for your button backgrounds. But what happens to those image files when your button can be displayed at many different sizes? If the width of the button is greater than the width of its background image, the image just stretches, right? Is that always going to look good?

Uniformly stretching your background image will not always look right. Sometimes you need more control over how the image will stretch.

In this section, you will convert BeatBox to use a *9-patch* image as the background for the buttons (more on what that means in just a moment). This is not because it is necessarily a better solution for BeatBox – it is a way for you to see how a 9-patch works for those times when you want to use an image file. Make a copy of the project to work in, if you like.

First, modify `list_item_sound.xml` to allow the button size to change based on the available space (Listing 22.8).

## Listing 22.8 Letting those buttons stretch (res/layout/list_item_sound.xml)

```
<layout xmlns:android="http://schemas.android.com/apk/res/android"
        xmlns:tools="http://schemas.android.com/tools">
    <data>
        <variable
                name="viewModel"
                type="com.bignerdranch.android.beatbox.SoundViewModel"/>
    </data>
    <FrameLayout
            android:layout_width="match_parent"
            android:layout_height="wrap_content"
            android:layout_margin="8dp">
        <Button
                android:layout_width="100dp"
                android:layout_height="100dp"
                android:layout_width="match_parent"
                android:layout_height="match_parent"
                android:layout_gravity="center"
                android:onClick="@{() -> viewModel.onButtonClicked()}"
                android:text="@{viewModel.title}"
                tools:text="Sound name"/>
    </FrameLayout>
</layout>
```

Now the buttons will take up the available space, leaving an 8dp margin. The image in Figure 22.7, with a snazzy folded corner and shadow, will be your new button background.

### Figure 22.7  New button background image (res/drawable-xxhdpi/ic_button_beat_box_default.png)

In the solutions file for this chapter (www.bignerdranch.com/solutions/ AndroidProgramming4e.zip), you can find this image along with a pressed version in the drawable-xxhdpi folder. Copy these two images into your project's drawable-xxhdpi folder and apply them as your button background by modifying button_beat_box.xml (Listing 22.9).

### Listing 22.9  Applying the new button background images (res/drawable/button_beat_box.xml)

```
<selector xmlns:android="http://schemas.android.com/apk/res/android">
    <item android:drawable="@drawable/button_beat_box_pressed"
    <item android:drawable="@drawable/ic_button_beat_box_pressed"
        android:state_pressed="true"/>
    <item android:drawable="@drawable/button_beat_box_normal"
    <item android:drawable="@drawable/ic_button_beat_box_default"
</selector>
```

Run BeatBox, and you will see the new button background (Figure 22.8).

## Figure 22.8  BeastBox

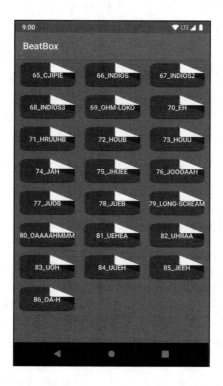

Whoa. That looks … bad.

Why does it look like that? Android is uniformly stretching ic_button_beat_box_default.png, including the dog-eared edge and the rounded corners. It would look better if you could specify which parts of the image to stretch and which parts not to stretch. This is where 9-patch images come in.

A 9-patch image file is specially formatted so that Android knows which portions can and cannot be scaled. Done properly, this ensures that the edges and corners of your background remain consistent with the image as it was created.

Why are they called 9-patches? A 9-patch breaks your image into a three-by-three grid – a grid with nine sections, or patches. The corners of the grid remain unscaled, the sides are only scaled in one dimension, and the center is scaled in both dimensions, as shown in Figure 22.9.

## Figure 22.9  How a 9-patch scales

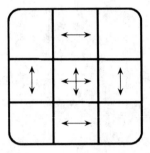

A 9-patch image is like a regular PNG image in everything except two aspects: Its filename ends with .9.png, and it has an additional one-pixel border around the edge. This border is used to specify the location of the center square of the 9-patch. Border pixels are drawn black to indicate the center and transparent to indicate the edges.

You can create a 9-patch using any image editor, with the draw9patch tool provided as part of the Android SDK, or using Android Studio.

First, convert your two new background images to 9-patch images by right-clicking on ic_button_beat_box_default.png in the project tool window and selecting Refactor → Rename... to rename the file to ic_button_beat_box_default.9.png. (If Android Studio warns you that a resource with the same name already exists, click Continue.) Then, repeat the process to rename the pressed version to ic_button_beat_box_pressed.9.png.

Next, double-click on the default image in the project tool window to open it in Android Studio's built-in 9-patch editor, as shown in Figure 22.10. (If Android Studio does not open the editor, try closing the file and collapsing your drawable folder in the project tool window. Then re-open the default image.)

In the 9-patch editor, first check the Show patches option to make your patches more visible. Now, fill in black pixels on the top and left borders to mark the stretchable regions of the image (Figure 22.10). You can also drag the edges of the colored overlay to match the figure.

Figure 22.10  Creating a 9-patch image

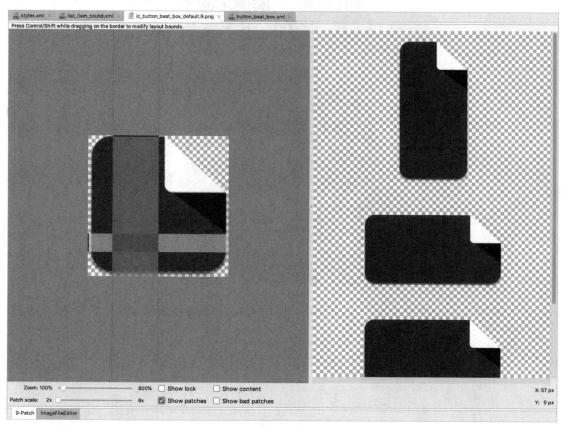

The black line at the top of the image specifies a region to stretch if this image is stretched horizontally. The line on the left indicates which pixels to stretch if the image is stretched vertically. The previews to the right show what your image will look like when stretched in various ways.

Repeat the process with the pressed version. Run BeatBox to see your new 9-patch image in action (Figure 22.11).

## Figure 22.11  New and improved

So the top and left borders of your 9-patch image indicate the areas of the image to stretch. What about the bottom and right borders? You can use them to define an optional content region for the 9-patch image. The content region is the area where content (usually text) should be rendered. If you do not include a content region, it defaults to be the same as your stretchable region.

Use the content area to center the text within the buttons below the folded corner, not just the stretchable region. Go back to ic_button_beat_box_default.9.png and add the right and bottom lines as shown in Figure 22.12. Enable the Show content setting in the 9-patch editor. This setting updates the preview to highlight the areas of the image that will hold your text.

## Figure 22.12  Defining the content area

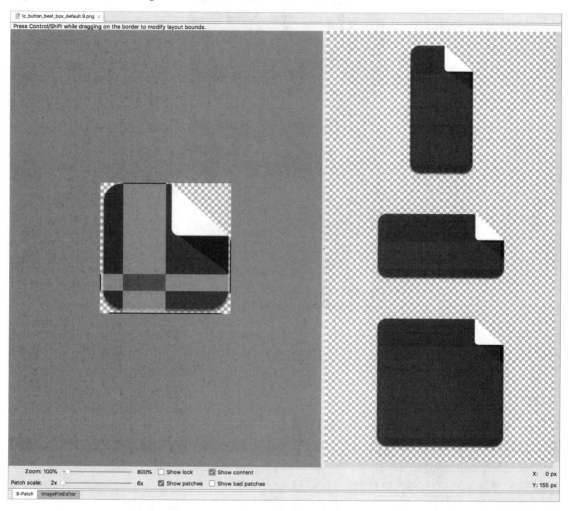

Repeat the process for the pressed version of the image. Be extra sure that both your images are updated with the correct content area lines. When 9-patch images are specified through state list drawables (as they are in BeatBox), the content area does not behave as you might expect. Android will set the content area when the background is initialized and will not change the content area while you press on the button. That means that the content area from one of your two images is ignored! The image that Android will take the content area from is not defined, so it is best to make sure that all of your 9-patch images in a state list drawable have the same content area.

Run BeatBox to see your nicely centered text (Figure 22.13).

Figure 22.13  Newer and more improved

Try rotating to landscape. The images are even more stretched, but your button backgrounds still look good and your text is still centered.

# Challenge: Button Themes

After completing the 9-patch image update, you may notice that something is not quite right with the background of your buttons. Behind the dog ear, you can see something that looks like a shadow. As you press the button, it appears to come closer to your finger.

Your challenge is to remove that shadow. Use your new theme spelunking skills to determine how the shadow is applied. Is there some other type of button style that you can use as your parent for the `BeatBoxButton` style?

# 23

# More About Intents and Tasks

In this chapter, you will use implicit intents to create a launcher app to replace Android's default launcher app. Figure 23.1 shows what this app, NerdLauncher, will look like.

Figure 23.1  NerdLauncher final product

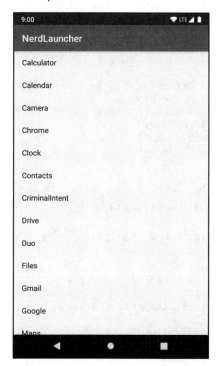

NerdLauncher will display a list of apps on the device. The user will press a list item to launch the app.

To get it working correctly, you will deepen your understanding of intents, intent filters, and the interaction of applications in the Android environment.

# Setting Up NerdLauncher

In Android Studio, select File → New Project... to create a new project. Start with the Add No Activity option for Phone and Tablet. Name the app NerdLauncher and give it a package name of com.bignerdranch.android.nerdlauncher. Select the option to Use AndroidX artifacts and leave the rest of the defaults as they are.

Once Android Studio has initialized the project, create a new empty activity using File → New → Activity → Empty Activity. Name the activity NerdLauncherActivity and check the Launcher Activity box.

**NerdLauncherActivity** will display a list of application names in a **RecyclerView**. Add the androidx.recyclerview:recyclerview:1.0.0 dependency to app/build.gradle, as you did in Chapter 9. If you would like to use newer versions of RecyclerView, you can find the latest release versions at developer.android.com/jetpack/androidx/releases/recyclerview.

Replace the contents of layout/activity_nerd_launcher.xml with the **RecyclerView** shown in Listing 23.1.

## Listing 23.1  Updating the **NerdLauncherActivity** layout (layout/activity_nerd_launcher.xml)

```xml
<?xml version="1.0" encoding="utf-8"?>
<androidx.recyclerview.widget.RecyclerView
    xmlns:android="http://schemas.android.com/apk/res/android"
    android:id="@+id/app_recycler_view"
    android:layout_width="match_parent"
    android:layout_height="match_parent"/>
```

Open NerdLauncherActivity.kt and stash a reference to the **RecyclerView** object in a property. (You will hook data up to the **RecyclerView** in just a bit.)

## Listing 23.2  Basic **NerdLauncherActivity** implementation (NerdLauncherActivity.kt)

```kotlin
class NerdLauncherActivity : AppCompatActivity() {

    private lateinit var recyclerView: RecyclerView

    override fun onCreate(savedInstanceState: Bundle?) {
        super.onCreate(savedInstanceState)
        setContentView(R.layout.activity_nerd_launcher)

        recyclerView = findViewById(R.id.app_recycler_view)
        recyclerView.layoutManager = LinearLayoutManager(this)
    }
}
```

Run your app to make sure everything is hooked up correctly to this point. If so, you will be the proud owner of an app titled NerdLauncher, displaying an empty **RecyclerView** (Figure 23.2).

Figure 23.2  NerdLauncher beginnings

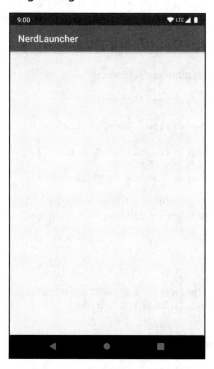

# Resolving an Implicit Intent

NerdLauncher will show the user a list of launchable apps on the device. (A launchable app is an app the user can open by clicking an icon on the Home screen or launcher screen.) To do so, it will query the system for launchable main activities.

The **PackageManager**, which you learned about in Chapter 15, is used to resolve the activities. Launchable main activities are simply activities with intent filters that include a MAIN action and a LAUNCHER category. You have seen this intent filter in the manifests/AndroidManifest.xml file in your previous projects:

```
<intent-filter>
    <action android:name="android.intent.action.MAIN" />
    <category android:name="android.intent.category.LAUNCHER" />
</intent-filter>
```

When you made **NerdLauncherActivity** a launcher activity, these intent filters were added for you automatically. (Check the manifest, if you like.)

In `NerdLauncherActivity.kt`, add a function named **setupAdapter()** and call that function from **onCreate(…)**. (Ultimately this function will create a **RecyclerView.Adapter** instance and set it on your **RecyclerView** object. For now, it will just generate a list of application data.)

Also, create an implicit intent and get a list of activities that match the intent from the **PackageManager**. Log the number of activities that the **PackageManager** returns.

## Listing 23.3  Querying the **PackageManager** (NerdLauncherActivity.kt)

```kotlin
private const val TAG = "NerdLauncherActivity"

class NerdLauncherActivity : AppCompatActivity() {

    private lateinit var recyclerView: RecyclerView

    override fun onCreate(savedInstanceState: Bundle?) {
        super.onCreate(savedInstanceState)
        setContentView(R.layout.activity_nerd_launcher)

        recyclerView = findViewById(R.id.app_recycler_view)
        recyclerView.layoutManager = LinearLayoutManager(this)

        setupAdapter()
    }

    private fun setupAdapter() {
        val startupIntent = Intent(Intent.ACTION_MAIN).apply {
            addCategory(Intent.CATEGORY_LAUNCHER)
        }

        val activities = packageManager.queryIntentActivities(startupIntent, 0)

        Log.i(TAG, "Found ${activities.size} activities")
    }
}
```

Here you create an implicit intent with the action set to `ACTION_MAIN`. You add `CATEGORY_LAUNCHER` to the intent's categories.

Calling **PackageManager.queryIntentActivities(Intent, Int)** returns a list containing the **ResolveInfo** for all the activities that have a filter matching the given intent. You can specify flags to modify the results. For example, the `PackageManager.GET_SHARED_LIBRARY_FILES` flag causes the query to include extra data (paths to libraries that are associated with each matching application) in the results. Here you pass `0`, indicating you do not want to modify the results.

Run NerdLauncher and check Logcat to see how many apps the **PackageManager** returned. (We got 30 the first time we tried it.)

In CriminalIntent, you used an implicit intent to send a crime report. You presented an activity chooser by creating an implicit intent, wrapping it in a chooser intent, and sending it to the OS with **startActivity(Intent)**:

```
val intent = Intent(Intent.ACTION_SEND)
... // Create and put intent extras
chooserIntent = Intent.createChooser(intent, getString(R.string.send_report)
startActivity(chooserIntent)
```

You may be wondering why you are not using that approach here. The short explanation is that the MAIN/LAUNCHER intent filter may or may not match a MAIN/LAUNCHER implicit intent that is sent via **startActivity(Intent)**.

**startActivity(Intent)** does not mean, "Start an activity matching this implicit intent." It means, "Start the *default* activity matching this implicit intent." When you send an implicit intent via **startActivity(Intent)** (or **startActivityForResult(…)**), the OS secretly adds the Intent.CATEGORY_DEFAULT category to the intent.

Thus, if you want an intent filter to match implicit intents sent via **startActivity(Intent)**, you must include the DEFAULT category in that intent filter.

An activity that has the MAIN/LAUNCHER intent filter is the main entry point for the app that it belongs to. It only wants the job of main entry point for that application. It typically does not care about being the "default" main entry point, so it does not have to include the CATEGORY_DEFAULT category.

Because MAIN/LAUNCHER intent filters may not include CATEGORY_DEFAULT, you cannot reliably match them to an implicit intent sent via **startActivity(Intent)**. Instead, you use the intent to query the **PackageManager** directly for activities with the MAIN/LAUNCHER intent filter.

The next step is to display the labels of these activities in **NerdLauncherFragment**'s **RecyclerView**. An activity's *label* is its display name – something the user should recognize. Given that these activities are launcher activities, the label is most likely the application name.

You can find the labels for the activities, along with other metadata, in the **ResolveInfo** objects that the **PackageManager** returned.

First, sort the **ResolveInfo** objects returned from the **PackageManager** alphabetically by label using the **ResolveInfo.loadLabel(PackageManager)** function.

## Listing 23.4 Sorting alphabetically (NerdLauncherActivity.kt)

```
class NerdLauncherActivity : AppCompatActivity() {
    ...
    private fun setupAdapter() {
        val startupIntent = Intent(Intent.ACTION_MAIN).apply {
            addCategory(Intent.CATEGORY_LAUNCHER)
        }

        val activities = packageManager.queryIntentActivities(startupIntent, 0)
        activities.sortWith(Comparator { a, b ->
            String.CASE_INSENSITIVE_ORDER.compare(
                a.loadLabel(packageManager).toString(),
                b.loadLabel(packageManager).toString()
            )
        })

        Log.i(TAG, "Found ${activities.size} activities")
    }
}
```

Now define a **ViewHolder** that displays an activity's label. Store the activity's **ResolveInfo** in a property (you will use it more than once later on).

## Listing 23.5  Implementing **ViewHolder** (NerdLauncherActivity.kt)

```
class NerdLauncherActivity : AppCompatActivity() {
    ...
    private fun setupAdapter() {
        ...
    }

    private class ActivityHolder(itemView: View) :
            RecyclerView.ViewHolder(itemView) {

        private val nameTextView = itemView as TextView
        private lateinit var resolveInfo: ResolveInfo

        fun bindActivity(resolveInfo: ResolveInfo) {
            this.resolveInfo = resolveInfo
            val packageManager = itemView.context.packageManager
            val appName = resolveInfo.loadLabel(packageManager).toString()
            nameTextView.text = appName
        }
    }
}
```

Next add a **RecyclerView.Adapter** implementation.

## Listing 23.6  Implementing **RecyclerView.Adapter** (NerdLauncherActivity.kt)

```kotlin
class NerdLauncherActivity : AppCompatActivity() {
    ...
    private class ActivityHolder(itemView: View) :
            RecyclerView.ViewHolder(itemView) {
        ...
    }

    private class ActivityAdapter(val activities: List<ResolveInfo>) :
            RecyclerView.Adapter<ActivityHolder>() {

        override fun onCreateViewHolder(container: ViewGroup, viewType: Int):
                ActivityHolder {
            val layoutInflater = LayoutInflater.from(container.context)
            val view = layoutInflater
                .inflate(android.R.layout.simple_list_item_1, container, false)
            return ActivityHolder(view)
        }

        override fun onBindViewHolder(holder: ActivityHolder, position: Int) {
            val resolveInfo = activities[position]
            holder.bindActivity(resolveInfo)
        }

        override fun getItemCount(): Int {
            return activities.size
        }
    }
}
```

Here you inflate android.R.layout.simple_list_item_1 in **onCreateViewHolder(…)**. The simple_list_item_1 layout file is part of the Android framework, which is why you reference it as android.R.layout instead of R.layout. This file contains a single **TextView**.

Last, but not least, update **setupAdapter()** to create an instance of **ActivityAdapter** and set it as the **RecyclerView**'s adapter.

## Listing 23.7  Setting **RecyclerView**'s adapter (NerdLauncherActivity.kt)

```kotlin
class NerdLauncherActivity : AppCompatActivity() {
    ...
    private fun setupAdapter() {
        ...
        Log.i(TAG, "Found ${activities.size} activities")
        recyclerView.adapter = ActivityAdapter(activities)
    }
    ...
}
```

Run NerdLauncher, and you will see a **RecyclerView** populated with activity labels (Figure 23.3).

Figure 23.3  All your activities are belong to us

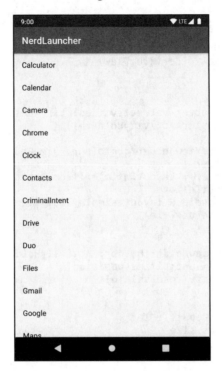

# Creating Explicit Intents at Runtime

You used an implicit intent to gather the desired activities and present them in a list. The next step is to start the selected activity when the user presses its list item. You will start the activity using an explicit intent.

To create the explicit intent, you need to get the activity's package name and class name from the **ResolveInfo**. You can get this data from a part of the **ResolveInfo** called **ActivityInfo**. (You can learn what data is available in different parts of **ResolveInfo** from its reference page: developer.android.com/reference/kotlin/android/content/pm/ResolveInfo.html)

Update **ActivityHolder** to implement a click listener. When an activity in the list is pressed, use the **ActivityInfo** for that activity to create an explicit intent. Then use that explicit intent to launch the selected activity.

## Listing 23.8 Launching a pressed activity (NerdLauncherActivity.kt)

```kotlin
class NerdLauncherActivity : AppCompatActivity() {
    ...
    private class ActivityHolder(itemView: View) :
            RecyclerView.ViewHolder(itemView),
            View.OnClickListener {

        private val nameTextView = itemView as TextView
        private lateinit var resolveInfo: ResolveInfo

        init {
            nameTextView.setOnClickListener(this)
        }

        fun bindActivity(resolveInfo: ResolveInfo) {
            ...
        }

        override fun onClick(view: View) {
            val activityInfo = resolveInfo.activityInfo

            val intent = Intent(Intent.ACTION_MAIN).apply {
                setClassName(activityInfo.applicationInfo.packageName,
                    activityInfo.name)
            }

            val context = view.context
            context.startActivity(intent)
        }
    }
    ...
}
```

Notice that in this intent you are sending an action as part of an explicit intent. Most apps will behave the same whether you include the action or not. However, some may change their behavior. The same activity can display different interfaces depending on how it is started. As a programmer, it is best to declare your intentions clearly and let the activities you start do what they will.

In Listing 23.8, you get the package name and class name from the metadata and use them to create an explicit intent using the **Intent** function:

```kotlin
fun setClassName(packageName: String, className: String): Intent
```

This is different from how you have created explicit intents in the past. Before, you used an **Intent** constructor that accepts a **Context** and a **Class** object:

```kotlin
Intent(packageContext: Context, cls: Class<?>)
```

This constructor uses its parameters to get what the **Intent** really needs – a **ComponentName**. A **ComponentName** is a package name and a class name stuck together. When you pass in an **Activity** and a **Class** to create an **Intent**, the constructor determines the fully qualified package name from the **Activity**.

```kotlin
fun setComponent(component: ComponentName): Intent
```

However, it is less code to use **setClassName(…)**, which creates the component name behind the scenes.

Run NerdLauncher and launch some apps.

# Tasks and the Back Stack

Android uses tasks to keep track of the state within each running application. Each application opened from Android's default launcher app gets its own task. This is the desired behavior – but, unfortunately for your NerdLauncher, it is not the default behavior. Before you foray into forcing applications to launch into their own tasks, let's discuss what tasks are and how they work.

A *task* is a stack of activities that the user is concerned with. The activity at the bottom of the stack is called the *base activity*, and whatever activity is on top is the activity that the user sees. When you press the Back button, you are popping the top activity off the stack. If you are looking at the base activity and press the Back button, it will send you to the Home screen.

By default, new activities are started in the current task. In CriminalIntent, whenever you started a new activity, that activity was added to the current task (as shown in Figure 23.4). This was true even if the activity was not part of the CriminalIntent application, like when you started an activity to select a crime suspect.

Figure 23.4  CriminalIntent task

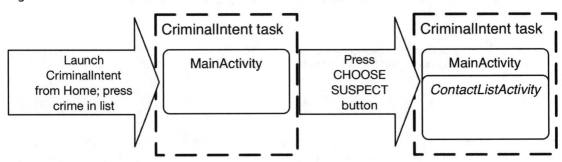

The benefit of adding an activity to the current task is that the user can navigate back through the task instead of the application hierarchy (as shown in Figure 23.5).

Figure 23.5  Pressing the Back button in CriminalIntent

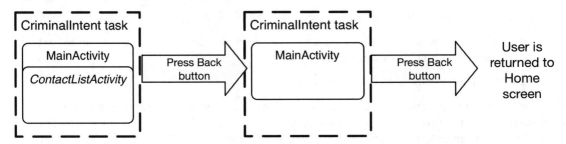

# Switching between tasks

Using the overview screen, you can switch between tasks without affecting each task's state. For instance, if you start entering a new contact and switch to checking your Twitter feed, you will have two tasks started. If you switch back to editing contacts, your place in both tasks will be saved.

Try switching tasks using the overview screen on your device or emulator. First, launch CriminalIntent from the Home screen or from your app launcher. (If your device or emulator no longer has CriminalIntent installed, open your CriminalIntent project in Android Studio and run it from there. If you skipped over the CriminalIntent chapters and did not build the app, you can access the code in the solutions file at www.bignerdranch.com/solutions/AndroidProgramming4e.zip.)

Select a crime from the crime list. Then push the Home button to return to the Home screen. Next, launch BeatBox from the Home screen or from your app launcher (or, if necessary, from Android Studio). Finally, open the overview screen using the Recents button (next to the Home button) (Figure 23.6).

Figure 23.6  Overview screen on Nougat (left) and Pie (right)

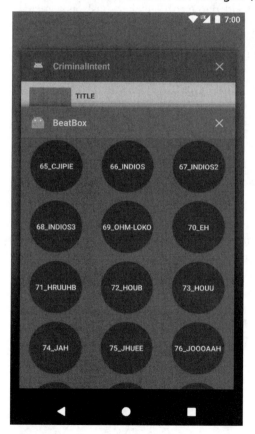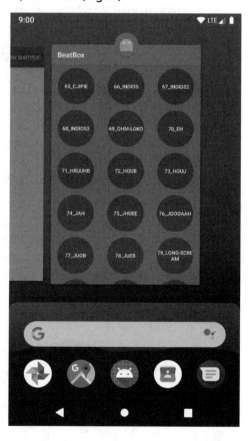

The overview screen on the left in Figure 23.6 is what users will see if they are running Android Nougat (API level 24). The overview screen on the right is what users running Android Pie (API level 28) will see (so long as they do not have the Swipe up on Home option enabled, as discussed in Chapter 3).

In both cases, the entry displayed for each app (known as a *card*) represents the app's task. A screenshot of the activity at the top of each task's back stack is displayed. You can press on the BeatBox or CriminalIntent card to return to the app (and to whatever activity you were interacting with in that app).

You can clear an app's task by swiping on the card entry to remove the card from the task list. Clearing the task removes all activities from the application's back stack.

Try clearing CriminalIntent's task, then relaunching the app. You will see the list of crimes instead of the crime you were editing before you cleared the task.

## Starting a new task

When you start an activity, sometimes you want the activity added to the current task. Other times, you want it started in a new task that is independent of the activity that started it.

Right now, any activity started from NerdLauncher is added to NerdLauncher's task, as depicted in Figure 23.7.

Figure 23.7  NerdLauncher's task contains CriminalIntent

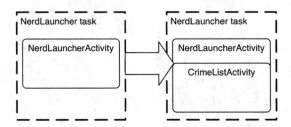

You can confirm this by clearing all the tasks displayed in the overview screen. Then start NerdLauncher and click on the CriminalIntent entry to launch the CriminalIntent app. Open the overview screen again. You will only see one task in the overview screen even though you started a different app.

When CriminalIntent's **MainActivity** was started, it was added to NerdLauncher's task (Figure 23.8). If you press the NerdLauncher task, you will be returned to whatever CriminalIntent screen you were looking at before starting the overview screen.

Figure 23.8  CriminalIntent not in its own task

This will not do. Instead, you want NerdLauncher to start activities in new tasks (Figure 23.9). That way, each application opened by pressing an item in the NerdLauncher list gets its own task, and users can switch between running applications via the overview screen, NerdLauncher, or the Home screen, as they prefer.

Figure 23.9  Launching CriminalIntent into its own task

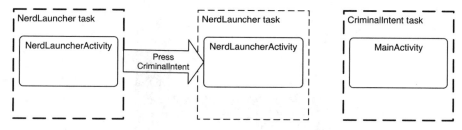

To start a new task when you start a new activity, add a flag to the intent in `NerdLauncherActivity.kt`.

## Listing 23.9  Adding a new task flag to the intent (`NerdLauncherActivity.kt`)

```
class NerdLauncherActivity : AppCompatActivity() {
    ...
    private class ActivityHolder(itemView: View) :
            RecyclerView.ViewHolder(itemView),
            View.OnClickListener {
        ...
        override fun onClick(view: View) {
            val activityInfo = resolveInfo.activityInfo

            val intent = Intent(Intent.ACTION_MAIN).apply {
                setClassName(activityInfo.applicationInfo.packageName,
                    activityInfo.name)
                addFlags(Intent.FLAG_ACTIVITY_NEW_TASK)
            }

            val context = view.context
            context.startActivity(intent)
        }
    }
    ...
}
```

Clear the tasks listed in your overview screen. Run NerdLauncher and start CriminalIntent. This time, when you pull up the overview screen, you will see a separate task for CriminalIntent (Figure 23.10).

## Figure 23.10  CriminalIntent now in its own task

If you start CriminalIntent from NerdLauncher again, you will not create a second CriminalIntent task. The FLAG_ACTIVITY_NEW_TASK flag by itself creates one task per activity. **MainActivity** already has a task running, so Android will switch to that task instead of starting a new one.

Try this out. Open the detail screen for one of the crimes in CriminalIntent. Use the overview screen to switch to NerdLauncher. Press on CriminalIntent in the list. You will be right back where you were in the CriminalIntent app, viewing the details for a single crime.

# Using NerdLauncher as a Home Screen

Who wants to start an app to start other apps? It would make more sense to offer NerdLauncher as a replacement for the device's Home screen. Open NerdLauncher's `AndroidManifest.xml` file and add to its main intent filter.

Listing 23.10  Changing **NerdLauncherActivity**'s categories
(manifests/AndroidManifest.xml)

```xml
<intent-filter>
    <action android:name="android.intent.action.MAIN" />
    <category android:name="android.intent.category.LAUNCHER" />
    <category android:name="android.intent.category.HOME" />
    <category android:name="android.intent.category.DEFAULT" />
</intent-filter>
```

By adding the HOME and DEFAULT categories, **NerdLauncherActivity** is asking to be offered as an option for the Home screen. Press the Home button, and NerdLauncher will be offered as an option (Figure 23.11).

Figure 23.11  Selecting a Home app

If you make NerdLauncher the Home screen, you can easily change it back later. Launch the Settings app from NerdLauncher. Go to Settings → Apps & Notification. Select NerdLauncher from the app list. (If you do not see NerdLauncher listed, select See all apps to expand the list and scroll until you find NerdLauncher.)

Once you have selected NerdLauncher, you should be on the App Info screen. Expand the Advanced settings list and select Open by default. Press the CLEAR DEFAULTS button. The next time you press the Home button, you will be able to select another default.

# For the More Curious: Processes vs Tasks

All objects need memory and a virtual machine to live in. A *process* is a place created by the OS for your application's objects to live in and for your application to run.

Processes may own resources managed by the OS, like memory, network sockets, and open files. Processes also have at least one, possibly many, threads of execution. And, on Android, your process will always have exactly one virtual machine running.

Before Android 4.4 (KitKat), Dalvik was the process virtual machine used by the Android OS. Whenever a process started, a new instance of a Dalvik virtual machine would spawn to house that process. Android Runtime (ART) has since replaced Dalvik, becoming the accepted process virtual machine from Android 5.0 (Lollipop) on.

While there are some obscure exceptions, in general every application component in Android is associated with exactly one process. Your application is created with its own process, and this is the default process for all components in your application.

(You can assign individual components to different processes, but we recommend sticking to the default process. If you think you need something running in a different process, you can usually achieve the same ends with multi-threading, which is more straightforward to program in Android than using multiple processes.)

Every activity instance lives in exactly one process and is referenced by exactly one task. But that is where the similarities between processes and tasks end. Tasks contain only activities and often consist of activities living in different application processes. Processes, on the other hand, contain all running code and objects for a single application.

It can be easy to confuse processes and tasks because there is some overlap between the two ideas and both are often referred to by an application name. For instance, when you launched CriminalIntent from NerdLauncher, the OS created a CriminalIntent process and a new task for which `MainActivity` was the base activity. In the overview screen, this task was labeled CriminalIntent.

The task that an activity is referenced by can be different from the process it lives in. For example, consider the CriminalIntent and Contacts applications and walk through the following scenario.

Open CriminalIntent, select a crime from the list (or add a new crime), and then press CHOOSE SUSPECT. This launches the Contacts application to choose a contact. The contact list activity is added to the CriminalIntent task. This means that when your user presses the Back button to navigate between different activities, they may be unknowingly switching between processes, which is nifty.

However, the contact list activity instance is actually created in the memory space of the Contacts app's process, and it runs on the virtual machine living in the Contacts application's process. (The states of the activity instances and task references of this scenario are depicted in Figure 23.12.)

Figure 23.12 Task referencing multiple processes

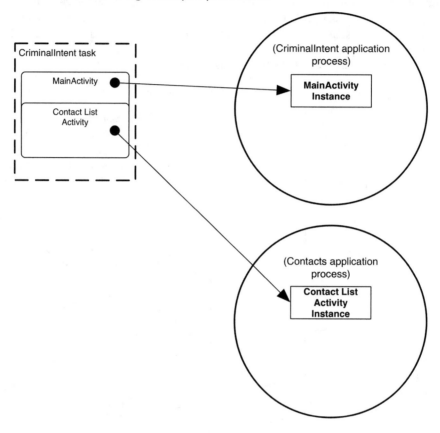

To explore the idea of processes versus tasks further, leave CriminalIntent up and running on the contact list screen. (Make sure the Contacts app itself is not listed on the overview screen. If so, clear the Contacts app task.) Press the Home button. Launch the Contacts app from the Home screen. Select a contact from the list of contacts (or select to add a new contact).

When you do this, new contact list activity and contact details instances will be created in the Contacts application's process. A new task will be created for the Contacts application, and that task will reference the new contact list and contact details activity instances (as shown in Figure 23.13).

## Figure 23.13  Process referenced by multiple tasks

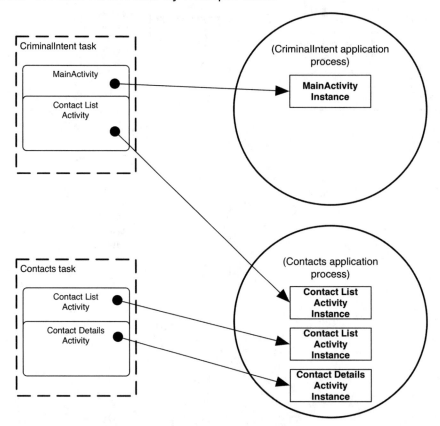

In this chapter, you created tasks and switched between them. What about replacing Android's default overview screen, as you are able to do with the Home screen? Unfortunately, Android does not provide a way to do this. Also, you should know that apps advertised on the Play Store as "task killers" are, in fact, process killers. Such apps kill a particular process, which means they may be killing activities referenced by other applications' tasks.

# For the More Curious: Concurrent Documents

If you tried testing the overview screen with CriminalIntent and sharing crime data with other apps, you may have noticed some interesting behavior. When you opt to send a crime report from CriminalIntent, the activity for the app you select from the chooser is added to its own task rather than to CriminalIntent's task (Figure 23.14).

Figure 23.14  Gmail launched into a separate task

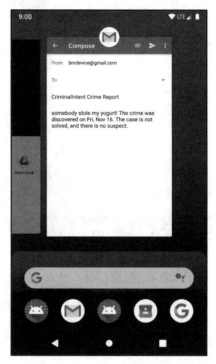

The implicit intent chooser creates a new, separate task for activities launched with the `android.intent.action.SEND` or `android.intent.action.SEND_MULTIPLE` actions.

This behavior uses a notion called *concurrent documents*. Concurrent documents allow any number of tasks to be dynamically created for an app at runtime. Note that this behavior was introduced on Android Lollipop (API level 21), so if you test it on an older device you will not see the concurrent documents in the overview screen. Prior to Lollipop, apps could only have a predefined set of tasks, each of which had to be named in the manifest.

A prime example of concurrent documents in practice is the Google Drive app. You can open and edit multiple documents, each of which gets its own task in the overview screen (Figure 23.15).

Figure 23.15  Multiple Google Drive tasks

You can start multiple "documents" (tasks) from your own app by either adding the Intent.FLAG_ACTIVITY_NEW_DOCUMENT flag to an intent before calling **startActivity(…)** or by setting the documentLaunchMode on the activity in the manifest, like so:

```
<activity
    android:name=".CrimePagerActivity"
    android:label="@string/app_name"
    android:parentActivityName=".MainActivity"
    android:documentLaunchMode="intoExisting" />
```

Using this approach, only one task per document will be created (so if you issue an intent with the same data as an already existing task, no new task will be created). You can force a new task to always be created, even if one already exists for a given document, by either adding the Intent.FLAG_ACTIVITY_MULTIPLE_TASK flag along with the Intent.FLAG_ACTIVITY_NEW_DOCUMENT flag before issuing the intent or by using always as the value for documentLaunchMode in your manifest.

# Challenge: Icons

You used **ResolveInfo.loadLabel(PackageManager)** in this chapter to present useful names in your launcher. **ResolveInfo** provides a similar function called **loadIcon()** that retrieves an icon to display for each application. For a small challenge, add an icon for each application to NerdLauncher.

# 24

# HTTP and Background Tasks

The apps that dominate the brains of users are networked apps. Those people fiddling with their phones instead of talking to each other at dinner? They are maniacally checking their newsfeeds, responding to text messages, or playing networked games.

To get started with networking in Android, you are going to create a new app called PhotoGallery. PhotoGallery is a client for the photo-sharing site Flickr. It will fetch and display the most interesting public photos of the day according to Flickr. Figure 24.1 gives you an idea of what the app will look like.

Figure 24.1  Complete PhotoGallery

(We have added a filter to our PhotoGallery implementation to show only photos listed on Flickr as having no known copyright restrictions. Visit flickr.com/commons/usage/ to learn more about unrestricted images. All other photos on Flickr are the property of the person who posted them and are subject to usage restrictions depending on the license specified by the owner. To read more about permissions for using images that you retrieve from Flickr, visit flickr.com/creativecommons/.)

You will spend several chapters with PhotoGallery. In this chapter, you will learn how to use the Retrofit library to make web requests to REST APIs and the Gson library to deserialize the response to these requests from JSON into Kotlin objects. Almost all day-to-day programming of web services these days is based on the HTTP networking protocol. Retrofit provides a type-safe way to access HTTP and HTTP/2 web services easily from Android apps.

By the end of the chapter, you will be fetching, parsing, and displaying photo titles from Flickr (Figure 24.2). Retrieving and displaying photos will happen in Chapter 25.

## Figure 24.2  PhotoGallery at the end of the chapter

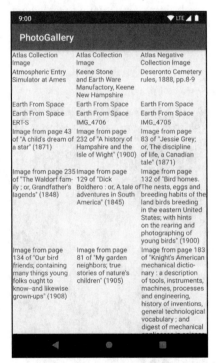

# Creating PhotoGallery

Create a new Android application project. As you have done before, choose Phone and Tablet as the target form factor and select the option to add no activity. Name the project PhotoGallery. Make sure the Package name is com.bignerdranch.android.photogallery, the Language is Kotlin, and the Minimum API level is API 21: Android 5.0 (Lollipop). Check the box to Use AndroidX artifacts.

Once the project has initialized, click on app in the project tool window and add an empty activity (File → New → Activity → Empty Activity) named PhotoGalleryActivity. Check the box to make **PhotoGalleryActivity** a Launcher Activity.

**PhotoGalleryActivity** will host a **PhotoGalleryFragment**, which you will create shortly. First, open res/layout/activity_photo_gallery.xml and replace the auto-generated contents with a single **FrameLayout**. This frame layout will serve as the container for the hosted fragment. Give the frame layout an ID of fragmentContainer. When you are done, the contents of activity_photo_gallery.xml should match Listing 24.1.

## Listing 24.1 Adding a fragment container (res/layout/activity_photo_gallery.xml)

```xml
<?xml version="1.0" encoding="utf-8"?>
<FrameLayout
        xmlns:android="http://schemas.android.com/apk/res/android"
        xmlns:tools="http://schemas.android.com/tools"
        android:id="@+id/fragmentContainer"
        android:layout_width="match_parent"
        android:layout_height="match_parent"
        tools:context=".PhotoGalleryActivity"/>
```

In PhotoGalleryActivity.kt, update **onCreate(…)** to check whether a fragment is already hosted in the fragment container. If not, create an instance of **PhotoGalleryFragment** and add it to the container. (Bear with the error that this code will cause for the moment. It will go away after you create the **PhotoGalleryFragment** class.)

## Listing 24.2 Setting up the activity (PhotoGalleryActivity.kt)

```kotlin
class PhotoGalleryActivity : AppCompatActivity() {

    override fun onCreate(savedInstanceState: Bundle?) {
        super.onCreate(savedInstanceState)
        setContentView(R.layout.activity_photo_gallery)

        val isFragmentContainerEmpty = savedInstanceState == null
        if (isFragmentContainerEmpty) {
            supportFragmentManager
                .beginTransaction()
                .add(R.id.fragmentContainer, PhotoGalleryFragment.newInstance())
                .commit()
        }
    }
}
```

In CriminalIntent, you checked whether a fragment was already hosted in the container by calling **findFragmentById(…)** on the fragment container ID. This check was necessary because the fragment manager automatically creates and adds hosted fragments back to the activity after a configuration change or after a system-initiated process death. You only want to add the fragment to the container if there is not already a fragment there.

**PhotoGalleryActivity** takes a different approach to determining whether a fragment is already hosted: It checks to see whether the savedInstanceState bundle passed to **onCreate(…)** is null. Recall that, if the bundle is null, this is a fresh launch of the activity and you can safely assume no fragments were automatically restored and rehosted. If the bundle is not null, it means the activity is being reconstructed after a system-initiated destruction (such as rotation or process death) and any fragments that were hosted before the destruction were re-created and added back to their respective containers.

Either approach works to find out whether a fragment is already hosted in the activity's single container, and you will likely see the check done both ways out in the wild. Which to use is mostly a matter of style preference.

Checking savedInstanceState allows you to use information you already have to determine whether a fragment is hosted. However, it assumes the reader of your code understands how savedInstanceState and fragment restoration across configuration changes works.

Checking for the fragment's existence using **supportFragmentManager.findFragmentById(R.id.fragment_container)** is more explicit and easier to parse for people new to Android. However, it involves unnecessarily interacting with the fragment manager in the scenario where a fragment already exists in the container.

Now set up the fragment's view. PhotoGallery will display its results in a **RecyclerView**, using the built-in **GridLayoutManager** to arrange the items in a grid. First, add the RecyclerView library as a dependency, as you did in Chapter 9. Open the app module's build.gradle file and add the recycler view Gradle dependency (Listing 24.3). After you make these changes, sync the Gradle file using Android Studio's prompt.

## Listing 24.3  Adding a RecyclerView dependency (app/build.gradle)

```
dependencies {
    ...
    implementation 'androidx.constraintlayout:constraintlayout:2.0.0-alpha2'
    implementation 'androidx.recyclerview:recyclerview:1.0.0'
    ...
}
```

Next, right-click the res/layout folder in the project tool window and select New → Layout resource file. Name this file fragment_photo_gallery.xml and enter androidx.recyclerview.widget.RecyclerView as the root element. When the file is created, set the recycler view's android:id to @ +id/photo_recycler_view. Fold the closing tag into the opening tag, since you will not be placing anything between them. When you are done, the contents of res/layout/ fragment_photo_gallery.xml should match Listing 24.4.

## Listing 24.4  Adding a recycler view to the fragment layout (res/layout/fragment_photo_gallery.xml)

```
<?xml version="1.0" encoding="utf-8"?>
<androidx.recyclerview.widget.RecyclerView
        xmlns:android="http://schemas.android.com/apk/res/android"
        android:id="@+id/photo_recycler_view"
        android:layout_width="match_parent"
        android:layout_height="match_parent"/>
```

Finally, create the **PhotoGalleryFragment** class. Inflate the layout you just created and initialize a member variable referencing the **RecyclerView**. Set the recycler view's layoutManager to a new instance of **GridLayoutManager**. For now, hardcode the number of columns to 3. (In the section called Challenge: Dynamically Adjusting the Number of Columns at the end of this chapter, you will be tasked with adapting the number of columns to suit the screen width.) When you are done, your fragment code should match Listing 24.5.

## Listing 24.5  Setting up the fragment (PhotoGalleryFragment.kt)

```
class PhotoGalleryFragment : Fragment() {

    private lateinit var photoRecyclerView: RecyclerView

    override fun onCreateView(
        inflater: LayoutInflater,
        container: ViewGroup?,
        savedInstanceState: Bundle?
    ): View {
        val view = inflater.inflate(R.layout.fragment_photo_gallery, container, false)

        photoRecyclerView = view.findViewById(R.id.photo_recycler_view)
        photoRecyclerView.layoutManager = GridLayoutManager(context, 3)

        return view
    }

    companion object {
        fun newInstance() = PhotoGalleryFragment()
    }
}
```

Run PhotoGallery to make sure everything is wired up correctly before moving on. If all is well, you will have a very nice blank screen.

# Networking Basics with Retrofit

Retrofit is an open-source library created and maintained by Square (`square.github.io/retrofit`). Under the hood, it uses the OkHttp library as its HTTP client (`square.github.io/okhttp`).

Retrofit helps you build an HTTP gateway class. You write an interface with annotated instance methods, and Retrofit creates the implementation. Retrofit's implementation handles making an HTTP request and parsing the HTTP response into an **OkHttp.ResponseBody**. But this is limiting: It would be better if you could work with your app's data types. To support this, Retrofit lets you register a response converter, which Retrofit then uses to marshal your data types into the request and un-marshal your data types from the response.

Add the Retrofit dependency to your app module's `build.gradle` file. Sync your Gradle file once you make the change.

### Listing 24.6  Adding the Retrofit dependency (`app/build.gradle`)

```
dependencies {
    implementation fileTree(dir: 'libs', include: ['*.jar'])
    implementation"org.jetbrains.kotlin:kotlin-stdlib-jdk7:$kotlin_version"
    ...
    implementation 'com.squareup.retrofit2:retrofit:2.5.0'
}
```

Before retrofitting (pun intended) the Flickr REST API, you will first configure Retrofit to fetch and log the contents of a web page URL – specifically, Flickr's home page. Using Retrofit involves a bunch of moving parts. Starting simple will allow you to see the foundations. Later, you will build on this basic implementation to build your Flickr requests and *deserialize* the responses – meaning convert the linear, serialized data into non-serial pieces of data. That non-serial data will be your model objects.

# Defining an API interface

It is time to define the API calls you want your app to be able to make. First, create a new package for your API-specific code. In the project tool window, right-click the com.bignerdranch.android.photogallery folder and choose New → Package. Name your new package api.

Next, add a Retrofit API interface to your new package. A Retrofit API interface is a standard Kotlin interface that uses Retrofit annotations to define API calls. Right-click the api folder in the project tool window. Choose New → Kotlin File/Class and name the file FlickrApi. Leave the Kind dropdown set to File. In the new file, define an interface named **FlickrApi** and add a single function representing a GET request.

### Listing 24.7 Adding a Retrofit API interface (api/FlickrApi.kt)

```
interface FlickrApi {

    @GET("/")
    fun fetchContents(): Call<String>
}
```

If you are given a choice when importing **Call**, select retrofit2.Call.

Each function in the interface maps to a specific HTTP request and must be annotated with an *HTTP request method annotation*. An HTTP request method annotation tells Retrofit the HTTP request type (also known as an "HTTP verb") that the function in your API interface maps to. The most common request types are @GET, @POST, @PUT, @DELETE, and @HEAD. (For an exhaustive list of available types, see the API docs at square.github.io/retrofit/2.x/retrofit).

The @GET("/") annotation in the code above configures the **Call** returned by **fetchContents()** to perform a GET request. The "/" is the *relative path* – a path string representing the relative URL from the base URL of your API endpoint. Most HTTP request method annotations include a relative path. In this case, the relative path of "/" means the request will be sent to the base URL, which you will provide shortly.

By default, all Retrofit web requests return a **retrofit2.Call** object. A **Call** object represents a single web request that you can execute. Executing a **Call** produces one corresponding web response. (You can also configure Retrofit to return RxJava **Observable**s instead, but that is outside the scope of this book.)

The type you use as **Call**'s generic type parameter specifies the data type you would like Retrofit to deserialize the HTTP response into. By default, Retrofit deserializes the response into an **OkHttp.ResponseBody**. Specifying **Call<String>** tells Retrofit that you want the response deserialized into a String object instead.

# Building the Retrofit object and creating an API instance

The Retrofit instance is responsible for implementing and creating instances of your API interface. To make web requests based on the API interface you defined, you need Retrofit to implement and instantiate your **FlickrApi** interface.

First, build and configure a Retrofit instance. Open PhotoGalleryFragment.kt. In **onCreate(…)**, build a Retrofit object and use it to create a concrete implementation of your **FlickrApi** interface.

## Listing 24.8  Using the Retrofit object to create an instance of the API (PhotoGalleryFragment.kt)

```
class PhotoGalleryFragment : Fragment() {

    private lateinit var photoRecyclerView: RecyclerView

    override fun onCreate(savedInstanceState: Bundle?) {
        super.onCreate(savedInstanceState)

        val retrofit: Retrofit = Retrofit.Builder()
            .baseUrl("https://www.flickr.com/")
            .build()

        val flickrApi: FlickrApi = retrofit.create(FlickrApi::class.java)
    }
    ...
}
```

**Retrofit.Builder()** is a fluent interface that makes it easy to configure and build your Retrofit instance. You provide a base URL for your endpoint using the **baseUrl(…)** function. Here, you provide the Flickr home page: "https://www.flickr.com/". Make sure to include the appropriate protocol with the URL (here, https://). Also, always include a trailing / to ensure Retrofit correctly appends the relative paths you provide in your API interface onto the base URL.

Calling **build()** returns a Retrofit instance, configured based on the settings you specified using the builder object. Once you have a Retrofit object, you use it to create an instance of your API interface. Note that Retrofit does not generate any code at compile time – instead, it does all the work at runtime. When you call **retrofit.create(…)**, Retrofit uses the information in the API interface you specify, along with the information you specified when building the Retrofit instance, to create and instantiate an anonymous class that implements the interface on the fly.

## Adding a String converter

By default, Retrofit deserializes web responses into **okhttp3.ResponseBody** objects. But for logging the contents of a web page, it is much easier to work with a plain ol' String. To get Retrofit to deserialize the response into strings instead, you will specify a *converter* when building your Retrofit object.

A converter knows how to decode a **ResponseBody** object into some other object type. You could create a custom converter, but you do not have to. Lucky for you, Square created an open-source converter, called the scalars converter, that can convert the response into a string. You will use it to deserialize Flickr responses into string objects.

To use the scalars converter, first add the dependency to your app module's `build.gradle` file. Do not forget to sync the file after you add the dependency.

## Listing 24.9  Adding the scalar converter dependency (app/build.gradle)

```
dependencies {
    ...
    implementation 'com.squareup.retrofit2:retrofit:2.5.0'
    implementation 'com.squareup.retrofit2:converter-scalars:2.5.0'
}
```

Now, create an instance of the scalar converter factory and add it to your Retrofit object.

## Listing 24.10  Adding the converter to the Retrofit object (PhotoGalleryFragment.kt)

```
class PhotoGalleryFragment : Fragment() {

    private lateinit var photoRecyclerView: RecyclerView

    override fun onCreate(savedInstanceState: Bundle?) {
        super.onCreate(savedInstanceState)

        val retrofit: Retrofit = Retrofit.Builder()
            .baseUrl("https://www.flickr.com/")
            .addConverterFactory(ScalarsConverterFactory.create())
            .build()

        val flickrApi: FlickrApi = retrofit.create(FlickrApi::class.java)
    }
    ...
}
```

`Retrofit.Builder`'s `addConverterFactory(…)` function expects an instance of `Converter.Factory`. A converter factory knows how to create and return instances of a particular converter. `ScalarsConverterFactory.create()` returns an instance of the scalars converter factory (`retrofit2.converter.scalars.ScalarsConverterFactory`), which in turn will provide instances of a scalar converter when Retrofit needs it.

More specifically, since you specified `Call<String>` as the return type for `FlickrApi.fetchContents()`, the scalar converter factory will provide an instance of the string converter (`retrofit2.converter.scalars.StringResponseBodyConverter`). In turn, your Retrofit object will use the string converter to convert the `ResponseBody` object into a `String` before returning the `Call` result.

Square provides other handy open-source converters for Retrofit. Later in this chapter, you will use the Gson converter. You can see the other available converters, and information on creating your own custom converter, at `square.github.io/retrofit`.

# Executing a web request

Up to this point, you have been writing code to configure your network request. Now is the moment you have been waiting for: executing a web request and logging the result. First, call **fetchContents()** to generate a **retrofit2.Call** object representing an executable web request.

## Listing 24.11  Getting a **Call** representing a request (PhotoGalleryFragment.kt)

```kotlin
class PhotoGalleryFragment : Fragment() {

    private lateinit var photoRecyclerView: RecyclerView

    override fun onCreate(savedInstanceState: Bundle?) {
        ...
        val flickrApi: FlickrApi = retrofit.create(FlickrApi::class.java)

        val flickrHomePageRequest: Call<String> = flickrApi.fetchContents()
    }
    ...
}
```

Note that calling **fetchContents()** on the **FlickrApi** instance does not cause any networking to happen. Instead, **fetchContents()** returns a **Call<String>** object representing a web request. You can execute the **Call** at any time in the future. Retrofit determines the details of the call object based on the API interface you provided (**FlickrApi**) and the Retrofit object you created.

To execute the web request represented by the **Call** object, call the **enqueue(…)** function in **onCreate(savedInstanceState: Bundle?)** and pass an instance of **retrofit2.Callback**. While you are at it, add a TAG constant.

## Listing 24.12  Executing the request asynchronously (PhotoGalleryFragment.kt)

```kotlin
private const val TAG = "PhotoGalleryFragment"

class PhotoGalleryFragment : Fragment() {

    private lateinit var photoRecyclerView: RecyclerView

    override fun onCreate(savedInstanceState: Bundle?) {
        ...
        val flickrHomePageRequest : Call<String> = bnrInterface.fetchContents()

        flickrHomePageRequest.enqueue(object : Callback<String> {
            override fun onFailure(call: Call<String>, t: Throwable) {
                Log.e(TAG, "Failed to fetch photos", t)
            }

            override fun onResponse(
                call: Call<String>,
                response: Response<String>
            ) {
                Log.d(TAG, "Response received: ${response.body()}")
            }
        })
    }
}
```

Retrofit makes it easy to respect the two most important Android threading rules:

1. Execute long-running operations on a background thread, never on the main thread.

2. Update the UI from the main thread only, never from a background thread.

`Call.enqueue(…)` executes the web request represented by the `Call` object. Most importantly, it executes the request *on a background thread*. Retrofit manages the background thread for you, so you do not have to worry about it.

The thread maintains a queue, or list, of work to do. When you call `Call.enqueue(…)`, Retrofit adds your request to its queue of work. You can enqueue multiple requests, and Retrofit will process them one by one until the queue is empty. (You will learn more about creating and managing background threads in Chapter 25.)

The `Callback` object you pass to `enqueue(…)` is where you define what you want to happen after the request completes and the response comes back. When the request running on the background thread is complete, Retrofit calls one of the callback functions you provided on the main (UI) thread: If a response is received from the server, it calls `Callback.onResponse(…)`; if not, it calls `Callback.onFailure(…)`.

The `Response` Retrofit passes to `onResponse()` contains the result contents in its body. The type of the result will match the return type you specified on the corresponding function in the API interface. In this case, `fetchContents()` returns `Call<String>`, so `response.body()` returns a `String`.

The `Call` object passed to `onResponse()` and `onFailure()` is the original call object used to initiate the request.

You can force a request to execute synchronously by calling `Call.execute()`. Just make sure the execution happens on a background thread and not on the main UI thread. As you learned in Chapter 11, Android disallows all networking on the main thread. If you try to do it, Android will throw a `NetworkOnMainThreadException`.

# Asking permission to network

One more thing is required to get networking up and running: You have to ask permission. Just as users would not want you secretly taking their pictures, they also do not want you secretly downloading ASCII pictures of farm animals.

To ask permission to network, add the following permission to your `manifests/AndroidManifest.xml` file.

## Listing 24.13  Adding networking permission to the manifest (manifests/AndroidManifest.xml)

```
<manifest xmlns:android="http://schemas.android.com/apk/res/android"
        package="com.bignerdranch.android.photogallery" >

    <uses-permission android:name="android.permission.INTERNET" />

    <application>
        ...
    </application>

</manifest>
```

Android treats the `INTERNET` permission as "normal," since so many apps require it. As a result, all you need to do to use this permission is declare it in your manifest. More dangerous permissions (like the one allowing you to know the device's location) also require a runtime request.

Run your code, and you should see the amazing Flickr home page HTML pop up in Logcat, as shown in Figure 24.3. (Finding your log statements within the Logcat window can be tricky. It helps to search for something specific. In this case, enter PhotoGalleryFragment in the Logcat search box, as shown.)

## Figure 24.3  Flickr.com HTML in Logcat

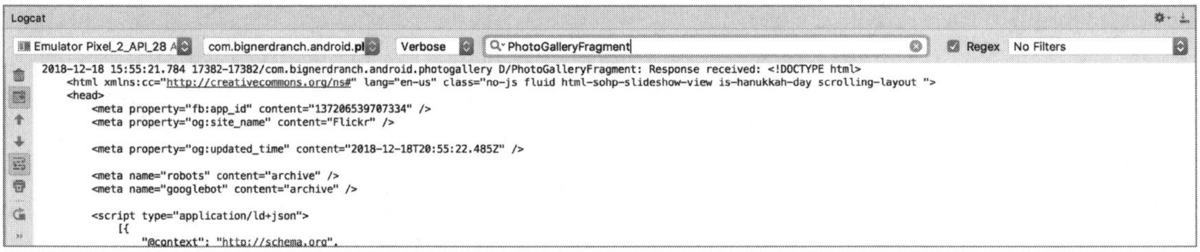

# Moving toward the repository pattern

Right now, your networking code is embedded in your fragment. Before you move on, move the Retrofit configuration code and API direct access to a new class.

Create a new Kotlin file named FlickrFetchr.kt. Add a property to stash a **FlickrApi** instance. Cut the Retrofit configuration code and API interface instantiation code from **PhotoGalleryFragment** and paste it into an init block in the new class (these are the two lines that start with val retrofit: Retrofit = ... and flickrApi = ... in Listing 24.14). Split the flickrApi declaration and assignment into two separate lines to declare flickrApi as a private property on **FlickrFetchr**. This is so that you can access it elsewhere in the class (outside of the init block) – but not outside of the class.

When you are done, **FlickrFetchr** should match Listing 24.14.

## Listing 24.14  Creating **FlickrFetchr** (FlickrFetchr.kt)

```kotlin
private const val TAG = "FlickrFetchr"

class FlickrFetchr {

    private val flickrApi: FlickrApi

    init {
        val retrofit: Retrofit = Retrofit.Builder()
            .baseUrl("https://www.flickr.com/")
            .addConverterFactory(ScalarsConverterFactory.create())
            .build()

        flickrApi = retrofit.create(FlickrApi::class.java)
    }
}
```

If you have not already, cut the redundant Retrofit configuration code from **PhotoGalleryFragment** (Listing 24.15). This will cause an error, which you will fix once you finish fleshing out **FlickrFetchr**.

### Listing 24.15 Cutting Retrofit setup from the fragment (PhotoGalleryFragment.kt)

```
class PhotoGalleryFragment : Fragment() {

    private lateinit var photoRecyclerView: RecyclerView

    override fun onCreate(savedInstanceState: Bundle?) {
        super.onCreate(savedInstanceState)

        val retrofit: Retrofit = Retrofit.Builder()
            .baseUrl("https://www.flickr.com/")
            .addConverterFactory(ScalarsConverterFactory.create())
            .build()

        val flickrApi: FlickrApi = retrofit.create(FlickrApi::class.java)

        val flickrHomePageRequest : Call<String> = flickrApi.fetchContents()

        ...
    }
    ...
}
```

Next, add a function named **fetchContents()** to **FlickrFetchr** to wrap the Retrofit API function you defined for fetching the Flickr home page. (You can copy most of the code below from **PhotoGalleryFragment**, but make sure to adjust the pasted result to match Listing 24.16.)

## Listing 24.16 Adding **fetchContents()** to **FlickrFetchr** (FlickrFetchr.kt)

```kotlin
private const val TAG = "FlickrFetchr"

class FlickrFetchr {

    private val flickrApi: FlickrApi

    init {
        ...
    }

    fun fetchContents(): LiveData<String> {
        val responseLiveData: MutableLiveData<String> = MutableLiveData()
        val flickrRequest: Call<String> = flickrApi.fetchContents()

        flickrRequest.enqueue(object : Callback<String> {

            override fun onFailure(call: Call<String>, t: Throwable) {
                Log.e(TAG, "Failed to fetch photos", t)
            }

            override fun onResponse(
                call: Call<String>,
                response: Response<String>
            ) {
                Log.d(TAG, "Response received")
                responseLiveData.value = response.body()
            }
        })

        return responseLiveData
    }
}
```

In **fetchContents()**, you instantiate responseLiveData to an empty **MutableLiveData<String>** object. You then enqueue a web request to fetch the Flickr page and return responseLiveData immediately (before the request completes). When the request successfully completes, you publish the result by setting responseLiveData.value. This way other components, such as **PhotoGalleryFragment**, can observe the **LiveData** returned from **fetchContents()** to eventually receive the web request results.

Note that the return type for **fetchContents()** is a non-mutable **LiveData<String>**. You should avoid exposing mutable live data objects when at all possible to limit other components from changing the live data's contents. The data should flow in one direction through the **LiveData**.

**FlickrFetchr** will wrap most of the networking code in PhotoGallery (right now it is small and simple, but it will grow over the next several chapters). **fetchContents()** enqueues the network request and wraps the result in **LiveData**. Now other components in your app, such as **PhotoGalleryFragment** (or some **ViewModel** or activity, etc.), can create an instance of **FlickrFetchr** and request photo data without having to know about the Retrofit or the source the data is coming from.

Update **PhotoGalleryFragment** to use **FlickrFetchr** to see this magic in action (Listing 24.17).

## Listing 24.17  Using **FlickrFetchr** in **PhotoGalleryFragment** (PhotoGalleryFragment.kt)

```
class PhotoGalleryFragment : Fragment() {

    private lateinit var photoRecyclerView: RecyclerView

    override fun onCreate(savedInstanceState: Bundle?) {
        super.onCreate(savedInstanceState)

        val flickrHomePageRequest : Call<String> = flickrApi.fetchContents()

        flickrHomePageRequest.enqueue(object : Callback<String> {
            override fun onFailure(call: Call<String>, t: Throwable) {
                Log.e(TAG, "Failed to fetch photos", t)
            }

            override fun onResponse(
                call: Call<String>,
                response: Response<String>
            ) {
                Log.d(TAG, "Response received: ${response.body()}")
            }
        })

        val flickrLiveData: LiveData<String> = FlickrFetchr().fetchContents()
        flickrLiveData.observe(
            this,
            Observer { responseString ->
                Log.d(TAG, "Response received: $responseString")
            })
    }
    ...
}
```

This refactor moves your app closer to following the repository pattern recommended by Google in its Guide to App Architecture (developer.android.com/jetpack/docs/guide). **FlickrFetchr** serves as a very basic repository. A repository class encapsulates the logic for accessing data from a single source or a set of sources. It determines how to fetch and store a particular set of data, whether locally in a database or from a remote server. Your UI code will request all of the data from the repository, because the UI does not care how the data is actually stored or fetched. Those are implementation details of the repository itself.

Right now, all of your app's data comes directly from the Flickr web server. However, in the future you might decide to cache that data in a local database. In that case, the repository would manage getting the data from the right place. Other components in your app can use the repository to get data without having to know where the data is coming from.

Take a moment to run your app and verify that it still works correctly. You should see the contents of the Flickr home page print to Logcat, as shown in Figure 24.3.

# Fetching JSON from Flickr

JSON stands for JavaScript Object Notation. It is a popular data format, particularly for web services. You can get more information about JSON as a format at json.org.

Flickr offers a fine JSON API. All the details you need are available in the documentation at flickr.com/services/api. Pull it up in your favorite web browser and find the list of **Request Formats**. You will be using the simplest – REST. The REST API endpoint is api.flickr.com/ services/rest, and you can invoke the methods Flickr provides on this endpoint.

Back on the main page of the API documentation, find the list of **API Methods**. Scroll down to the **interestingness** section and click on flickr.interestingness.getList. The documentation will report that this method "returns the list of interesting photos for the most recent day or a user-specified date." That is exactly what you want for PhotoGallery.

The only required parameter for the **getList** method is an API key. To get an API key, return to flickr.com/services/api and follow the link for **API Keys**. You will need a Yahoo ID to log in. Once you are logged in, request a new, noncommercial API key. This usually only takes a moment. Your API key will look something like 4f721bgafa75bf6d2cb9af54f937bb70. (You do not need the "Secret," which is only used when an app will access user-specific information or images.)

Once you have a key, you have all you need to make a request to the Flickr web service. Your GET request URL will look something like this:

```
https://api.flickr.com/services/rest/?method=flickr.interestingness.getList
    &api_key=yourApiKeyHere&format=json&nojsoncallback=1&extras=url_s
```

The Flickr response is in XML format by default. To get a valid JSON response, you need to specify values for both the format and nojsoncallback parameters. Setting nojsoncallback to 1 tells Flickr to exclude the enclosing method name and parentheses from the response it sends back. This lets your Kotlin code more easily parse the response.

Specifying the parameter called extras with the value url_s tells Flickr to include the URL for the small version of the picture if it is available.

Copy the example URL into your browser, replacing *yourApiKeyHere* with your actual API key. This will allow you to see an example of what the response data will look like, as shown in Figure 24.4.

## Figure 24.4  Sample JSON output

Time to update your existing networking code to request recent interesting photos data from the Flickr REST API instead of requesting the contents of Flickr's home page. First, add a function to your **FlickrApi** API interface. Again, replace *yourApiKeyHere* with your API key. For now, hardcode the URL query parameters in the relative path string. (Later, you will abstract these query parameters out and add them in programmatically.)

## Listing 24.18  Defining the "fetch recent interesting photos" request (api/FlickrApi.kt)

```
interface FlickrApi {

    @GET("/")
    fun fetchContents() : Call<String>

    @GET(
        "services/rest/?method=flickr.interestingness.getList" +
                "&api_key=yourApiKeyHere" +
                "&format=json" +
                "&nojsoncallback=1" +
                "&extras=url_s"
    )
    fun fetchPhotos(): Call<String>
}
```

Notice that you added values for the method, api_key, format, nojsoncallback, and extras parameters.

Next, update the Retrofit instance configuration code in **FlickrFetchr**. Change the base URL from Flickr's home page to the base API endpoint. Rename the **fetchContents()** function to **fetchPhotos()** and call through to the new **fetchPhotos()** function on the API interface.

## Listing 24.19  Updating the base URL (FlickrFetchr.kt)

```
class FlickrFetchr {

    private val flickrApi: FlickrApi

    init {
        val retrofit: Retrofit = Retrofit.Builder()
            .baseUrl("https://www.api.flickr.com/")
            .addConverterFactory(ScalarsConverterFactory.create())
            .build()

        flickrApi = retrofit.create(FlickrApi::class.java)
    }

    fun fetchContents()fetchPhotos(): LiveData<String> {
        val responseLiveData: MutableLiveData<String> = MutableLiveData()
        val flickrRequest: Call<String> = flickrApi.fetchContents()fetchPhotos()
        ...
    }
}
```

Note that the base URL you set is `api.flickr.com`, but the endpoints you want to hit are at `api.flickr.com/services/rest`. This is because you specified the `services` and `rest` parts of the path in your `@GET` annotation in **FlickrApi**. The path and other information you included in the `@GET` annotation will be appended onto the URL by Retrofit before it issues the web request.

Finally, update **PhotoGalleryFragment** to execute the web request so that it fetches recent interesting photos instead of the contents of Flickr's home page. Replace the **fetchContents()** call with a call to the new **fetchPhotos()** function. For now, serialize the response into a string, as you did previously.

### Listing 24.20 Executing the "fetch recent interesting photos" request (PhotoGalleryFragment.kt)

```kotlin
class PhotoGalleryFragment : Fragment() {

    private lateinit var photoRecyclerView: RecyclerView

    override fun onCreate(savedInstanceState: Bundle?) {
        super.onCreate(savedInstanceState)

        val flickrLiveData: LiveData<String> = FlickrFetchr().fetchContentsPhotos()
        ...
    }
    ...
}
```

Making these few tweaks to your existing code renders your app ready to fetch and log Flickr data. Run PhotoGallery, and you should see rich, fertile Flickr JSON in Logcat, like Figure 24.5. (It will help to search for PhotoGalleryFragment in the Logcat search box.)

### Figure 24.5 Flickr JSON in Logcat

(Logcat can be finicky. Do not panic if you do not get results like ours. Sometimes the connection to the emulator is not quite right and the log messages do not get printed out. Usually it clears up over time, but sometimes you have to rerun your application or even restart your emulator.)

As of this writing, the Android Studio Logcat window does not wrap the output automatically. Scroll to the right to see more of the extremely long JSON response string. Or wrap the Logcat contents by clicking the Use Soft Wraps button shown in Figure 24.5.

Now that you have such fine JSON data from Flickr, what should you do with it? You will do what you do with all data – put it in one or more model objects. The model class you are going to create for PhotoGallery is called **GalleryItem**. A gallery item holds meta information for a single photo, including the title, the ID, and the URL to download the image from.

Create the **GalleryItem** data class and add the following code:

## Listing 24.21 Creating a model object class (GalleryItem.kt)

```kotlin
data class GalleryItem(
    var title: String = "",
    var id: String = "",
    var url: String = ""
)
```

Now that you have defined a model object, it is time to create and populate instances of that object with data from the JSON output you got from Flickr.

## Deserializing JSON text into model objects

The JSON response displayed in your browser and Logcat window is hard to read. If you *pretty print* the response (format it with white space), it looks something like the text on the left in Figure 24.6.

## Figure 24.6 JSON text, JSON hierarchy, and corresponding model objects

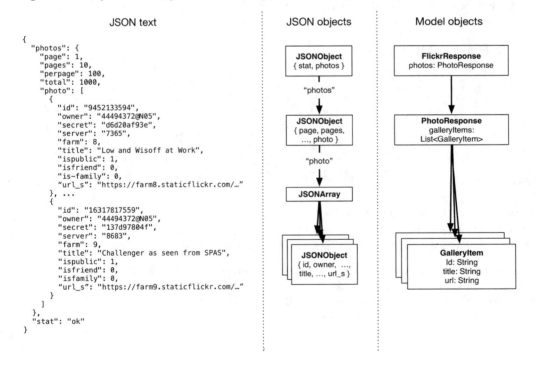

A JSON object is a set of name-value pairs enclosed between curly braces, { }. A JSON array is a comma-separated list of JSON objects enclosed in square brackets, [ ]. You can have objects nested within each other, resulting in a hierarchy.

Android includes the standard org.json package, which has classes that provide access to creating and parsing JSON text (such as **JSONObject** and **JSONArray**). However, lots of smart people have created libraries to simplify the process of converting JSON text to Java objects and back again.

One such library is Gson (github.com/google/gson). Gson maps JSON data to Kotlin objects for you automatically. This means you do not need to write any parsing code. Instead, you define Kotlin classes that map to the JSON hierarchy of objects and let Gson do the rest.

Square created a Gson converter for Retrofit that makes it easy to plug Gson into your Retrofit implementation. First, add the Gson and Retrofit Gson converter library dependencies to your app module's Gradle file. As always, be sure to sync the file when you are done.

## Listing 24.22  Adding Gson dependencies (app/build.gradle)

```
dependencies {
    ...
    implementation 'com.squareup.retrofit2:retrofit:2.5.0'
    implementation 'com.squareup.retrofit2:converter-scalars:2.5.0'
    implementation 'com.google.code.gson:gson:2.8.5'
    implementation 'com.squareup.retrofit2:converter-gson:2.4.0'
}
```

Next, create model objects that map to the JSON data in the Flickr response. You already have **GalleryItem**, which maps almost directly to an individual object in the "photo" JSON array. By default, Gson maps JSON object names to property names. If your property names match the JSON object names directly, you can leave them as is.

But your property names do not need to match the JSON object names. Take your GalleryItem.url property, versus the "url_s" field in the JSON data. GalleryItem.url is more meaningful in the context of your codebase, so it is better to keep it. In this case, you can add a @SerializedName annotation to the property to tell Gson which JSON field the property maps to.

Update **GalleryItem** now to do just that.

## Listing 24.23  Overriding default name-property mapping (GalleryItem.kt)

```
data class GalleryItem(
    var title: String = "",
    var id: String = "",
    @SerializedName("url_s") var url: String = ""
)
```

Now, create a **PhotoResponse** class to map to the "photos" object in the JSON data. Place the new class in the api package, since this class is a side effect of how you implement deserialization of the Flickr API, rather than a model object the rest of your app cares about.

Include a property called galleryItems to store a list of gallery items and annotate it with @SerializedName("photo"). Gson will automatically create a list and populate it with gallery item objects based on the JSON array named "photo". (Right now, the only data you care about in this particular object is the array of photo data in the "photo" JSON object. Later in this chapter, you will want to capture the paging data if you choose to do the challenge in the section called Challenge: Paging.)

### Listing 24.24 Adding **PhotoResponse** (PhotoResponse.kt)

```
class PhotoResponse {
    @SerializedName("photo")
    lateinit var galleryItems: List<GalleryItem>
}
```

Finally, add a class named **FlickrResponse** to the api package. This class will map to the outermost object in the JSON data (the one at the top of the JSON object hierarchy, denoted by the outermost { }). Add a property to map to the "photos" field.

### Listing 24.25 Adding **FlickrResponse** (FlickrResponse.kt)

```
class FlickrResponse {
    lateinit var photos: PhotoResponse
}
```

The diagram in Figure 24.6 shows how the objects you created map to the JSON data.

Now it is time to make the magic happen: to configure Retrofit to use Gson to deserialize your data into the model objects you just defined. First, update the return type specified in the Retrofit API interface to match the model object you defined to map to the outermost JSON object. This indicates to Gson that it should use the **FlickrResponse** to deserialize the JSON response data.

### Listing 24.26 Updating **fetchPhoto()**'s return type (FlickrApi.kt)

```
interface FlickrApi {

    @GET(...)
    fun fetchPhotos(): Call<StringFlickrResponse>
}
```

Next, update **FlickrFetchr**. Swap out the scalar converter factory for a Gson converter factory. Update **fetchPhotos()** to return **LiveData** that wraps a list of gallery items. Change the **LiveData** and **MutableLiveData** type specifiers from String to **List<GalleryItem>**. Change the **Call** and **Callback** type specifiers from String to **FlickrResponse**. Finally, update **onResponse(…)** to dig the gallery item list out of the response and update the live data object with the list.

## Listing 24.27  Updating **FlickrFetchr** for Gson (FlickrFetchr.kt)

```kotlin
class FlickrFetchr {

    private val flickrApi: FlickrApi

    init {
        val retrofit: Retrofit = Retrofit.Builder()
            .baseUrl("https://api.flickr.com/")
            .addConverterFactory(ScalarsConverterFactoryGsonConverterFactory.create())
            .build()

        flickrApi = retrofit.create(FlickrApi::class.java)
    }

    fun fetchPhotos(): LiveData<StringList<GalleryItem>> {
        val responseLiveData: MutableLiveData<String> = MutableLiveData()
        val responseLiveData: MutableLiveData<List<GalleryItem>> = MutableLiveData()
        val flickrRequest: Call<StringFlickrResponse> = flickrApi.fetchPhotos()

        flickrRequest.enqueue(object : Callback<StringFlickrResponse> {

            override fun onFailure(call: Call<StringFlickrResponse>, t: Throwable) {
                Log.e(TAG, "Failed to fetch photos", t)
            }

            override fun onResponse(
                call: Call<StringFlickrResponse>,
                response: Response<StringFlickrResponse>
            ) {
                Log.d(TAG, "Response received")
                responseLiveData.value = response.body()
                val flickrResponse: FlickrResponse? = response.body()
                val photoResponse: PhotoResponse? = flickrResponse?.photos
                var galleryItems: List<GalleryItem> = photoResponse?.galleryItems
                    ?: mutableListOf()
                galleryItems = galleryItems.filterNot {
                    it.url.isBlank()
                }
                responseLiveData.value = galleryItems
            }
        })

        return responseLiveData
    }
}
```

Note that Flickr does not always return a valid url_s value for each image. The code above filters out gallery items with blank URL values using filterNot{…}.

Last, update the **LiveData** type specifier in **PhotoGalleryFragment**.

## Listing 24.28  Updating type specifiers in **PhotoGalleryFragment** (PhotoGalleryFragment.kt)

```
class PhotoGalleryFragment : Fragment() {

    private lateinit var photoRecyclerView: RecyclerView

    override fun onCreate(savedInstanceState: Bundle?) {
        super.onCreate(savedInstanceState)

        val flickrLiveData: LiveData<String> = FlickrFetchr().fetchPhotos()
        val flickrLiveData: LiveData<List<GalleryItem>> = FlickrFetchr().fetchPhotos()
        flickrLiveData.observe(
            this,
            Observer { responseStringgalleryItems ->
                Log.d(TAG, "Response received: $responseStringgalleryItems")
            })
    }
    ...
}
```

Run PhotoGallery to test your JSON parsing code. You should see the **toString()** output of the gallery item list printed to Logcat. If you want explore the results further, set a breakpoint on the logging line in **Observer** and use the debugger to drill down through galleryItems (Figure 24.7).

## Figure 24.7  Exploring the Flickr response

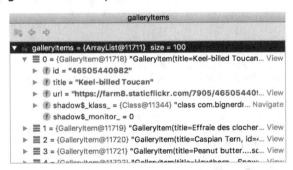

If you run into an **UninitializedPropertyAccessException**, make sure that your web request is properly formatted. In some cases (such as when the API key is invalid), the Flickr API will return a response with a good response code (200) but an empty response body, and Gson will fail to initialize your late-initialized models.

# Networking Across Configuration Changes

Now that you have your app deserializing JSON into model objects, take a closer look at how your implementation behaves when a configuration change occurs. Run your app, make sure auto-rotate is turned on for your device or emulator, and then rotate the device quickly five or so times in a row. Inspect the Logcat output, filtering by PhotoGalleryFragment and turning soft wraps off (Figure 24.8).

## Figure 24.8  Logcat output across multiple rotations

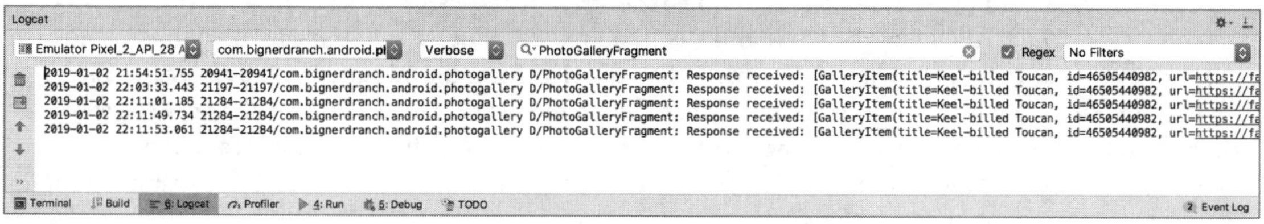

What is going on here? A new network request is made every time you rotate the device. This is because you kick off the request in **onCreate(…)**. Since the fragment is destroyed and re-created every time you rotate, a new request is issued to (unnecessarily) re-download the data. This is problematic because you are doing duplicate work – you should instead issue a download request when the fragment is first created. That same request (and the resulting data) should persist across rotation to ensure a speedy user experience (and to avoid unnecessarily using up the user's data if they are not on WiFi).

Instead of launching a new web request every time a configuration changes occurs, you need to fetch the photo data once, when the fragment is initially created and displayed onscreen. Then you can allow the web request to continue to execute when a configuration change occurs by caching the results in memory for the perceived life of the fragment, across any and all configuration changes (such as rotation). Finally, you can use these cached results when available rather than making a new request.

**ViewModel** is the right tool to help you with this job. (If you need a refresher on **ViewModel**, refer back to Chapter 4.)

First, add the lifecycle-extensions dependency to app/build.gradle.

## Listing 24.29  Adding the lifecycle-extensions dependency (app/build.gradle)

```
dependencies {
    ...
    implementation 'androidx.appcompat:appcompat:1.0.2'
    implementation 'androidx.lifecycle:lifecycle-extensions:2.0.0'
    ...
}
```

Next, create a **ViewModel** class named **PhotoGalleryViewModel**. Add a property to store a live data object holding a list of gallery items. Kick off a web request to fetch photo data when the **ViewModel** is first initialized, and stash the resulting live data in the property you created. When you are done, your code should match Listing 24.30.

493

## Listing 24.30 Shiny new **ViewModel** (PhotoGalleryViewModel.kt)

```kotlin
class PhotoGalleryViewModel : ViewModel() {

    val galleryItemLiveData: LiveData<List<GalleryItem>>

    init {
        galleryItemLiveData = FlickrFetchr().fetchPhotos()
    }
}
```

You call **FlickrFetchr().fetchPhotos()** in **PhotoGalleryViewModel**'s init{} block. This kicks off
the request for photo data when the **ViewModel** is first created. Since the **ViewModel** is only created
once in the span of lifecycle owner's lifetime (when queried from the **ViewModelProviders** class for
the first time), the request will only be made once (when the user launches **PhotoGalleryFragment**).
When the user rotates the device or some other configuration change happens, the **ViewModel** will
remain in memory, and the re-created version of the fragment will be able to access the results of the
original request through the **ViewModel**.

With this design, the **FlickrFetchr** repository will continue to execute the request even if the user
backs out of the fragment's hosting activity early. In your app, the result of the request will just be
ignored. But in a production app, you might cache the results in a database or some other local storage,
so it would make sense to let the fetch continue to completion.

If you instead wanted to stop an in-flight **FlickrFetchr** request when the user exits the fragment,
you could update **FlickrFetchr** to stash the **Call** object representing the web request and cancel the
request when the **ViewModel** is removed from memory. See the section called For the More Curious:
Canceling Requests later in this chapter for more details.

Update **PhotoGalleryFragment.onCreate(…)** to get access to the **ViewModel**. Stash a reference
to the **ViewModel** in a property. Remove the existing code that interacts with **FlickrFetchr**, since
**PhotoGalleryViewModel** handles that now.

## Listing 24.31 Getting a **ViewModel** instance from the provider (PhotoGalleryFragment.kt)

```kotlin
class PhotoGalleryFragment : Fragment() {

    private lateinit var photoGalleryViewModel: PhotoGalleryViewModel
    private lateinit var photoRecyclerView: RecyclerView

    override fun onCreate(savedInstanceState: Bundle?) {
        super.onCreate(savedInstanceState)

        val flickrLiveData: LiveData<List<GalleryItem>> = FlickrFetchr().fetchPhotos()
        flickrLiveData.observe(
            this,
            Observer { galleryItems ->
                Log.d(TAG, "Response received: $galleryItems")
            })

        photoGalleryViewModel =
                ViewModelProviders.of(this).get(PhotoGalleryViewModel::class.java)
    }

    ...
}
```

Recall that the first time a **ViewModel** is requested for a given lifecycle owner, a new instance of the **ViewModel** is created. When **PhotoGalleryFragment** is destroyed and re-created due to a configuration change like rotation, the existing **ViewModel** persists. Successive requests for the **ViewModel** return the same instance that was originally created.

Now, update **PhotoGalleryFragment** to observe **PhotoGalleryViewModel**'s live data once the fragment's view is created. For now, log a statement indicating the data was received. Eventually you will use these results to update your recycler view contents.

## Listing 24.32 Observing the **ViewModel**'s live data (PhotoGalleryFragment.kt)

```kotlin
class PhotoGalleryFragment : Fragment() {
    ...
    override fun onCreateView(
        ...
    ): View {
        ...
    }

    override fun onViewCreated(view: View, savedInstanceState: Bundle?) {
        super.onViewCreated(view, savedInstanceState)
        photoGalleryViewModel.galleryItemLiveData.observe(
            viewLifecycleOwner,
            Observer { galleryItems ->
                Log.d(TAG, "Have gallery items from ViewModel $galleryItems")
                // Eventually, update data backing the recycler view
            })
    }
    ...
}
```

Eventually you will update UI-related things (such as the recycler view adapter) in response to data changes. Starting the observation in **onViewCreated(…)** ensures that the UI widgets and other related objects will be ready. It also ensures that you properly handle the situation where the fragment becomes detached and its view gets destroyed. In this scenario, the view will be re-created when the fragment is reattached, and the live data subscription will be added to the new view once it is created.

(Out in the wild, you might also see the observation kicked off in **onCreateView(…)** or **onActivityCreated(…)**, which should work fine but is less explicit about the relationship between the live data being observed and the life of the view.)

Passing viewLifecycleOwner as the **LifecycleOwner** parameter to **LiveData.observe(LifecycleOwner, Observer)** ensures that the **LiveData** object will remove your observer when the fragment's view is destroyed.

Run your app. Filter Logcat by FlickrFetchr. Rotate the emulator multiple times. You should only see FlickrFetchr: Response received printed to the Logcat window one time, no matter how many times you rotate.

# Displaying Results in RecyclerView

For your last task in this chapter, you will switch to the view layer and get **PhotoGalleryFragment**'s **RecyclerView** to display some titles.

First, define a **ViewHolder** class within **PhotoGalleryFragment**.

## Listing 24.33  Adding a **ViewHolder** implementation (PhotoGalleryFragment.kt)

```kotlin
class PhotoGalleryFragment : Fragment() {
    ...
    override fun onViewCreated(view: View, savedInstanceState: Bundle?) {
        ...
    }

    private class PhotoHolder(itemTextView: TextView)
        : RecyclerView.ViewHolder(itemTextView) {

        val bindTitle: (CharSequence) -> Unit = itemTextView::setText
    }
    ...
}
```

Next, add a **RecyclerView.Adapter** to provide **PhotoHolder**s as needed based on a list of **GalleryItem**s.

## Listing 24.34  Adding a **RecyclerView.Adapter** implementation (PhotoGalleryFragment.kt)

```kotlin
class PhotoGalleryFragment : Fragment() {
    ...
    private class PhotoHolder(itemTextView: TextView)
        : RecyclerView.ViewHolder(itemTextView) {

        val bindTitle: (CharSequence) -> Unit = itemTextView::setText
    }

    private class PhotoAdapter(private val galleryItems: List<GalleryItem>)
        : RecyclerView.Adapter<PhotoHolder>() {

        override fun onCreateViewHolder(
                parent: ViewGroup,
                viewType: Int
        ): PhotoHolder {
            val textView = TextView(parent.context)
            return PhotoHolder(textView)
        }

        override fun getItemCount(): Int = galleryItems.size

        override fun onBindViewHolder(holder: PhotoHolder, position: Int) {
            val galleryItem = galleryItems[position]
            holder.bindTitle(galleryItem.title)
        }
    }
    ...
}
```

Now that you have the appropriate nuts and bolts in place for **RecyclerView**, add code to attach an adapter with updated gallery item data when the live data observer callback fires.

## Listing 24.35 Adding an adapter to the recycler view when data is available or changed (PhotoGalleryFragment.kt)

```kotlin
class PhotoGalleryFragment : Fragment() {
    ...
    override fun onViewCreated(view: View, savedInstanceState: Bundle?) {
        super.onViewCreated(view, savedInstanceState)
        photoGalleryViewModel.galleryItemLiveData.observe(
            this,
            Observer { galleryItems ->
                Log.d(TAG, "Have gallery items from ViewModel $galleryItems")
                // Eventually, update data backing the recycler view
                photoRecyclerView.adapter = PhotoAdapter(galleryItems)
            })

        return view
    }
    ...
}
```

With that, your work for this chapter is complete. Run PhotoGallery, and you should see text displayed for each **GalleryItem** you downloaded (similar to Figure 24.2).

# For the More Curious: Alternate Parsers and Data Formats

Gson is a popular parser for JSON, but it is not the only one you can use. Moshi (github.com/square/moshi) is another popular library from Square that also handles parsing JSON data. Moshi borrows some ideas from Gson and attempts to make them faster and more efficient. Square created a converter for Moshi so that it can work directly with Retrofit.

Retrofit does not limit you to just using JSON as your data format. You can also use XML or even Protobufs, if you want. There are many serialization libraries available for Retrofit, so you can use the one that best fits your data transfer configuration.

# For the More Curious: Canceling Requests

In your current implementation, **PhotoGalleryFragment** asks its **ViewModel**, **PhotoGalleryViewModel**, to start a web request to download photo data. If the user presses the Back button quickly enough after launching your application, it is possible that the web request will continue even after the user exits the activity. This will not cause a memory leak, because **FlickrFetchr** does not hold references to any UI-related components, nor to the **ViewModel**.

However, since you are ignoring the results, allowing the request to continue will cause some minimal wasted battery, wasted CPU cycles, and possibly some wasted paid data usage if the user is on a metered network. Granted, there is no major harm in this case, since the data size you are fetching is very small.

In most production applications, you would likely let the request continue, as you do here. But rather than ignoring the result, you would cache it somewhere locally, like in a database.

Since you are not caching the results in your current implementation, you could instead cancel an in-flight request when the **ViewModel** is destroyed. To do so, you would stash the **Call** object representing an in-flight web request. Then you would cancel the web request by calling **Call.cancel()** on the call object(s) you stashed:

```
class SomeRespositoryClass {

    private lateinit var someCall: Call<SomeResponseType>
    ...
    fun cancelRequestInFlight() {
        if (::someCall.isInitialized) {
            someCall.cancel()
        }
    }
}
```

When you cancel a **Call** object, the corresponding **Callback.onFailure(…)** method will be called. You can check the value of **Call.isCancelled** to determine whether the failure was due to a canceled request (a value of true means the request was indeed canceled).

To hook into the **ViewModel** lifecycle, and more specifically to cancel calls when a **ViewModel** is destroyed, you override **ViewModel.onCleared()**. This function is called when the **ViewModel** is about to be destroyed (such as when the user backs out of the activity using the Back button).

```
class SomeViewModel : ViewModel() {

    private val someRepository = SomeRespositoryClass()
    ...
    override fun onCleared() {
        super.onCleared()
        someRepository.cancelRequestInFlight()
    }
    ...
}
```

# For the More Curious: Managing Dependencies

**FlickrFetchr** provides a layer of abstraction over the source of Flickr photo metadata. Other components (such as **PhotoGalleryFragment**) use this abstraction to fetch Flickr data without worrying about where the data is coming from.

**FlickrFetchr** itself does not know how to download JSON data from Flickr. Instead, **FlickrFetchr** relies on **FlickrApi** to know the endpoint URL, to connect to that endpoint, and to perform the actual work of downloading the JSON data. **FlickrFetchr** is said to have a *dependency* on **FlickrApi**.

You are initializing **FlickrApi** inside the **FlickrFetchr** init block:

```
class FlickrFetchr {
    ...
    private val flickrApi: FlickrApi

    init {
        val retrofit: Retrofit = Retrofit.Builder()
                .baseUrl("https://www.flickr.com/")
                .addConverterFactory(ScalarsConverterFactory.create())
                .build()

        flickrApi = retrofit.create(FlickrApi::class.java)
    }

    fun fetchContents(): LiveData<String> {
        ...
    }
}
```

This works well for a simple application, but there are a few potential issues to consider.

First, it is difficult to unit test **FlickrFetchr**. Recall from Chapter 20 that the goal of a unit test is to verify the behavior of a class and its interactions with other classes. To properly unit test **FlickrFetchr**, you need to isolate it from the real **FlickrApi**. But this is a difficult – if not impossible – task, because **FlickrApi** is initialized inside of the **FlickrFetchr** init block.

Hence, there is no way to provide a mock instance of **FlickrApi** to **FlickrFetchr** for testing purposes. This is problematic, because any test you run against **fetchContents()** will result in a network request. The success of your tests would be dependent on network state and the availability of the Flickr back-end API at the time of running the test.

Another issue is that **FlickrApi** is tedious to instantiate. You must build and configure an instance of **Retrofit** before you can build an instance of **FlickrApi**. This implementation requires you to duplicate five lines of Retrofit configuration code anywhere you want to create a **FlickrApi** instance.

Finally, creating a new instance of **FlickrApi** everywhere you want to use it results in unnecessary object creation. Object creation is expensive relative to the scarce resources available on a mobile device. Whenever practical, you should share instances of a class across your app and avoid needless object allocation. **FlickrApi** is a perfect candidate for sharing, since there is no variable instance state.

*Dependency injection* (or DI) is a design pattern that addresses these issues by centralizing the logic for creating dependencies, such as **FlickrApi**, and supplying the dependencies to the classes that need them. By applying DI to PhotoGallery, you could easily pass an instance of **FlickrApi** into **FlickrFetchr** each time a new instance of **FlickrFetchr** was constructed. Using DI would allow you to:

- encapsulate the initialization logic of **FlickrApi** into a common place outside of **FlickrFetchr**

- use a singleton instance of **FlickrApi** throughout the app

- substitute a mock version of **FlickrApi** when unit testing

Applying the DI pattern to **FlickrFetchr** might look something like this:

```
class FlickrFetchr(flickrApi: FlickrApi) {
    fun fetchContents(): LiveData<String> {
        ...
    }
}
```

Note that DI does not enforce the singleton pattern for all dependencies. **FlickrFetchr** is passed an instance of **FlickrApi** on construction. This mechanism for constructing **FlickrFetchr** gives you the flexibility to provide a new instance or a shared instance of **FlickrApi** based on your use case.

DI is a broad topic with many facets that extend well beyond Android. This section just scratches the surface. There are entire books dedicated to the concept of DI and many libraries to make DI easier to implement. If you want to use DI in your app, you should consider using one of these libraries. It will help guide you through the process of DI and reduce the amount of code you need to write to implement the pattern.

At the time of this writing, Dagger 2 is the official Google-recommended library for implementing DI on Android. You can find detailed documentation, code samples, and tutorials about DI with Dagger 2 at google.github.io/dagger.

501

# Challenge: Adding a Custom Gson Deserializer

The JSON response from Flickr contains multiple layers of nested data (Figure 24.6). In the section called Deserializing JSON text into model objects, you created model objects to map directly to the JSON hierarchy. But what if you did not care about the data in the outer layers? Wouldn't it be nice to avoid cluttering your codebase with unnecessary model objects?

By default, Gson maps all of the JSON data directly to your model objects by matching Kotlin property names (or @SerializedName annotations) to JSON field names. You can customize this behavior by defining a custom **com.google.gson.JsonDeserializer**.

For this challenge, implement a custom deserializer to strip out the outermost layer of JSON data (the layer that maps to **FlickrResponse**). The deserializer should return a **PhotoResponse** object populated based on the JSON data. To do this, create a new class that extends from **com.google.gson.JsonDeserializer** and override the **deserialize(…)** function:

```
class PhotoDeserializer : JsonDeserializer<PhotoResponse> {

    override fun deserialize(
        json: JsonElement,
        typeOfT: Type?,
        context: JsonDeserializationContext?
    ): PhotoResponse {
        // Pull photos object out of JsonElement
        // and convert to PhotoResponse object
    }
}
```

Check out the Gson API documentation to learn how to parse through the **JsonElement** and convert it to a model object. (Hint: Look closely at the docs for **JsonElement**, **JsonObject**, and **Gson**.)

Once you create the deserializer, update the **FlickrFetchr** initialization code:

- Use **GsonBuilder** to create a **Gson** instance and register your custom deserializer as a type adapter.

- Create a **retrofit2.converter.gson.GsonConverterFactory** instance that uses the **Gson** instance as its converter.

- Update the Retrofit instance configuration to use this custom Gson converter factory instance.

Finally, remove **FlickrResponse** from your project and update any dependent code accordingly.

# Challenge: Paging

By default, getList returns one page of 100 results. There is an additional parameter you can use called page that will let you return page two, page three, and so on.

For this challenge, research the Jetpack Paging Library (developer.android.com/topic/libraries/architecture/paging) and use it to implement paging for PhotoGallery. This library provides a framework for loading your app's data when it is needed. While you could implement this functionality manually, the paging library will be less work and less prone to error.

# Challenge: Dynamically Adjusting the Number of Columns

Currently, the number of columns displayed in the grid is fixed at three. Update your code to provide a dynamic number of columns so more columns appear in landscape and on larger devices.

A simple approach could involve providing an integer resource qualified for different orientations and/or screen sizes. This is similar to the way you provided different strings for different screen sizes in Chapter 17. Integer resources should be placed in the res/values folder(s). Check out the Android developer documentation for more details.

But providing qualified resources does not offer much in the way of granularity. For a more difficult challenge (and a more flexible implementation), calculate and set the number of columns each time the fragment's view is created. Calculate the number of columns based on the current width of the RecyclerView and some predetermined constant column width.

There is only one catch: You cannot calculate the number of columns in onCreateView(…), because the RecyclerView will not be sized yet. Instead, implement a ViewTreeObserver.OnGlobalLayoutListener and put your column calculation code in onGlobalLayout(). Add the listener to your RecyclerView using addOnGlobalLayoutListener().

# 25

# Loopers, Handlers, and HandlerThread

Now that you have downloaded and parsed JSON data from Flickr, your next task is to download and display images. In this chapter, you will learn how to use **Looper**, **Handler**, and **HandlerThread** to dynamically download and display photos in PhotoGallery. Along the way you will gain a deeper understanding of your app's main thread and further explore restrictions around what work can be done on the main thread versus what work can be done on a background thread. Finally, you will learn how to communicate between the main thread and a background thread.

## Preparing RecyclerView to Display Images

The current **PhotoHolder** in **PhotoGalleryFragment** simply provides **TextView**s for the **RecyclerView**'s **GridLayoutManager** to display. Each **TextView** displays the caption of a **GalleryItem**.

To display photos, you are going to update **PhotoHolder** to provide **ImageView**s instead. Eventually, each **ImageView** will display a photo downloaded from the url of a **GalleryItem**.

Start by creating a new layout file for your gallery items called list_item_gallery.xml. This layout will consist of a single **ImageView** (Listing 25.1).

Listing 25.1 Gallery item layout (res/layout/list_item_gallery.xml)

```xml
<?xml version="1.0" encoding="utf-8"?>
<ImageView xmlns:android="http://schemas.android.com/apk/res/android"
           android:layout_width="match_parent"
           android:layout_height="120dp"
           android:layout_gravity="center"
           android:scaleType="centerCrop"/>
```

These **ImageView**s will be managed by **RecyclerView**'s **GridLayoutManager**, which means that their width will vary. Their height, on the other hand, will remain fixed. To make the most of the **ImageView**'s space, you have set its scaleType to centerCrop. This setting centers the image and then scales it up so that the smaller dimension is equal to the view and the larger one is cropped on both sides.

Next, update **PhotoHolder** to hold an **ImageView** instead of a **TextView**. Replace bindTitle with a function reference to set the **ImageView**'s **Drawable**.

### Listing 25.2  Updating **PhotoHolder** (PhotoGalleryFragment.kt)

```
class PhotoGalleryFragment : Fragment() {
    ...
    private class PhotoHolder(private val itemTextView: TextView)
        : RecyclerView.ViewHolder(itemTextView) {
    private class PhotoHolder(private val itemImageView: ImageView)
        : RecyclerView.ViewHolder(itemImageView) {

        val bindTitle: (CharSequence) -> Unit = itemTextView::setText
        val bindDrawable: (Drawable) -> Unit  = itemImageView::setImageDrawable
    }
    ...
}
```

Previously, the **PhotoHolder** constructor assumed it would be passed a **TextView**. The new version instead expects an **ImageView**.

Update **PhotoAdapter**'s **onCreateViewHolder(…)** to inflate the list_item_gallery.xml file you created and pass it to **PhotoHolder**'s constructor. Add the inner keyword so **PhotoAdapter** can access the parent activity's layoutInflater property directly. (You could get the inflater from parent.context, but you will need access to other properties and functions in the parent activity later, and using inner makes that easier.)

### Listing 25.3  Updating **PhotoAdapter**'s **onCreateViewHolder(…)** (PhotoGalleryFragment.kt)

```
class PhotoGalleryFragment : Fragment() {
    ...
    private inner class PhotoAdapter(private val galleryItems: List<GalleryItem>)
        : RecyclerView.Adapter<PhotoHolder>() {

        override fun onCreateViewHolder(
            parent: ViewGroup,
            viewType: Int
        ): PhotoHolder {
            val textView = TextView(activity)
            return PhotoHolder(textView)
            val view = layoutInflater.inflate(
                R.layout.list_item_gallery,
                parent,
                false
            ) as ImageView
            return PhotoHolder(view)
        }
        ...
    }
    ...
}
```

Next, you will need a placeholder image for each **ImageView** to display until you download an image to replace it. Find bill_up_close.png in the solutions file (www.bignerdranch.com/solutions/ AndroidProgramming4e.zip) and put it in res/drawable.

Update **PhotoAdapter**'s **onBindViewHolder(…)** to set the placeholder image as the **ImageView**'s **Drawable**.

### Listing 25.4  Binding the default image (PhotoGalleryFragment.kt)

```
class PhotoGalleryFragment : Fragment() {
    ...
    private inner class PhotoAdapter(private val galleryItems: List<GalleryItem>)
        : RecyclerView.Adapter<PhotoHolder>() {
        ...
        override fun onBindViewHolder(holder: PhotoHolder, position: Int) {
            val galleryItem = galleryItems[position]
            holder.bindTitle(galleryItem.title)
            val placeholder: Drawable = ContextCompat.getDrawable(
                requireContext(),
                R.drawable.bill_up_close
            ) ?: ColorDrawable()
            holder.bindDrawable(placeholder)
        }
    }
    ...
}
```

Notice that you are providing a blank **ColorDrawable** object if **ContextCompat.getDrawable(…)** returns null.

Run PhotoGallery, and you should see an array of close-up Bills, as in Figure 25.1.

### Figure 25.1  A Billsplosion

# Preparing to Download Bytes from a URL

Your Retrofit API interface does not support downloading an image yet. Patch that hole now. Add a new function that accepts a URL string as input and returns an executable call object (**retrofit2.Call**) whose result will be an **okhttp3.ResponseBody**.

### Listing 25.5  Updating **FlickrApi** (api/FlickrApi.kt)

```
interface FlickrApi {
    ...
    @GET
    fun fetchUrlBytes(@Url url: String): Call<ResponseBody>
}
```

This new API function looks a little different. It accepts a URL as input and uses that parameter value directly when determining where to download the data from. Using a parameterless @GET annotation combined with annotating the first parameter in **fetchUrlBytes(…)** with @Url causes Retrofit to override the base URL completely. Instead, Retrofit will use the URL passed to the **fetchUrlBytes(…)** function.

Add a function to **FlickrFetchr** to fetch the bytes from a given URL and decode them into a **Bitmap** (Listing 25.6 ).

### Listing 25.6  Adding image downloading to **FlickrFetchr** (FlickrFetchr.kt)

```
class FlickrFetchr {
    ...
    @WorkerThread
    fun fetchPhoto(url: String): Bitmap? {
        val response: Response<ResponseBody> = flickrApi.fetchUrlBytes(url).execute()
        val bitmap = response.body()?.byteStream()?.use(BitmapFactory::decodeStream)
        Log.i(TAG, "Decoded bitmap=$bitmap from Response=$response")
        return bitmap
    }
}
```

Here, you use **Call.execute()**, which executes the web request synchronously. As you have learned, networking on the main thread is not allowed. The @WorkerThread annotation indicates that this function should only be called on a background thread.

However, the annotation itself does not take care of making a thread or putting the work on a background thread. That is your job. (The @WorkerThread annotation will show a Lint error if the function you call it from is annotated with @MainThread or @UiThread. However, as of this writing, Android lifecycle functions are not annotated with @MainThread or @UiThread, even though all lifecycle functions execute on the main thread.) Eventually, you will call **fetchPhoto(String)** from a background thread you create.

You pull a **java.io.InputStream** from the response body using the **ResponseBody.byteStream()** function. Once you have the byte stream, you pass it to **BitmapFactory.decodeStream(InputStream)**, which will create a **Bitmap** from the bytes in the stream.

The response and byte stream must be closed. Since **InputStream** implements **Closeable**, the Kotlin standard library function **use(…)** will clean things up when **BitmapFactory.decodeStream(…)** returns.

Finally, you return the bitmap that **BitmapFactory** constructed. With that, your API interface and repository are ready to download images.

But there is still (a lot) more work to do.

# Downloading Lots of Small Things

Currently, PhotoGallery's networking works like this: **PhotoGalleryViewModel** calls **FlickrFetchr().fetchPhotos()** to download JSON data from Flickr. **FlickrFetchr** immediately returns an empty **LiveData<List<GalleryItem>>** object and enqueues an asynchronous Retrofit request to retrieve the data from Flickr. That network request executes on a background thread.

When the data download is complete, **FlickrFetchr** parses the JSON data into a list of **GalleryItem**s and publishes the list to the live data object it returned. Each **GalleryItem** now has a URL where a thumbnail-size photo lives.

The next step is to go and get those thumbnails. How will you go about this? **FlickrFetchr** requests only 100 URLs by default, so your **GalleryItem** list holds at most 100 URLs. So one option would be to download the images one after another until you have all 100, notify the **ViewModel**, and ultimately display the images en masse in the **RecyclerView**.

However, downloading the thumbnails all at once would cause two problems. The first is that it could take a while, and the UI would not be updated until the downloading was complete. On a slow connection, users would be staring at a wall of Bills for a long time.

The second problem is the cost of having to store the entire set of images. One hundred thumbnails will fit into memory easily. But what if it were 1,000? What if you wanted to implement infinite scrolling? Eventually, you would run out of space.

Given these problems, real-world apps often download images only when they need to be displayed onscreen. Downloading on demand puts the responsibility on the **RecyclerView** and its adapter. The adapter triggers the image downloading as part of its **onBindViewHolder(…)** implementation.

OK, so how will you go about *that*? You could enqueue a separate asynchronous Retrofit request for each image download. However, you would need to keep track of all the **Call** objects and manage their lives in relation to each view holder and to the fragment itself.

Instead you are going to create a dedicated background thread. This thread will receive and process download requests one at a time, and it will provide the resulting image for each individual request as the corresponding download completes. Since all the requests are managed by the background thread, you can easily clean up all the requests or stop the thread altogether, rather than having to manage a whole bunch of separate requests.

# Assembling a Background Thread

Create a new class called **ThumbnailDownloader** that extends **HandlerThread**. Then give it a constructor, a stub implementation of a function called **queueThumbnail()**, and an override of the **quit()** function that signals when your thread has quit. (Toward the end of the chapter, you will need this bit of information.)

Listing 25.7  Initial thread code (ThumbnailDownloader.kt)

```kotlin
private const val TAG = "ThumbnailDownloader"

class ThumbnailDownloader<in T>
    : HandlerThread(TAG) {

    private var hasQuit = false

    override fun quit(): Boolean {
        hasQuit = true
        return super.quit()
    }

    fun queueThumbnail(target: T, url: String) {
        Log.i(TAG, "Got a URL: $url")
    }
}
```

Notice that you gave the class a single generic argument, <T>. Your **ThumbnailDownloader**'s user, **PhotoGalleryFragment** in this case, will need to use some object to identify each download and to determine which UI element to update with the image once it is downloaded. Rather than locking the user into a specific type of object as the identifier, using a generic makes the implementation more flexible.

The **queueThumbnail()** function expects an object of type T to use as the identifier for the download and a String containing the URL to download. This is the function you will have **PhotoAdapter** call in its **onBindViewHolder(…)** implementation.

# Making your thread lifecycle aware

Since the sole purpose of **ThumbnailDownloader** is to download and serve images to **PhotoGalleryFragment**, tie the life of the thread to the user's *perceived lifetime* of the fragment. In other words, spin the thread up when the user first launches the screen. Spin the thread down when the user finishes with the screen (e.g., by pressing the Back button or dismissing the task). Do not destroy and then re-create the thread when the user rotates the device – retain the thread instance across configuration changes.

The life of a **ViewModel** matches the user's perceived life of the fragment. However, managing the thread in **PhotoGalleryViewModel** would make the implementation more complex than necessary and also cause some challenges with leaking views down the line. It would make more sense to push the thread management to some other component, such as the repository (**FlickrFetchr**). In a real-world app, you would likely do just that. But in this case, doing so would detract from the goal of understanding **HandlerThread**.

Instead, for the purposes of this chapter, directly tie a **ThumbnailDownloader** instance to your **PhotoGalleryFragment**. First, retain **PhotoGalleryFragment** so that the life of the fragment instance matches the user's perceived life of the fragment.

## Listing 25.8 Retaining **PhotoGalleryFragment** (PhotoGalleryFragment.kt)

```kotlin
class PhotoGalleryFragment : Fragment() {
    ...
    override fun onCreate(savedInstanceState: Bundle?) {
        super.onCreate(savedInstanceState)

        retainInstance = true
        ...
    }
    ...
}
```

(In general, you should avoid retaining fragments. You are only doing it here because retaining the fragment simplifies the implementation so you can focus on learning how **HandlerThread** works. You will learn more about the implications of retaining a fragment in the section called Retained Fragments later in this chapter.)

Now that the fragment is retained, start the thread when **PhotoGalleryFragment.onCreate(…)** is called and quit the thread when **PhotoGalleryFragment.onDestroy()** is called. You could achieve this by adding code to **PhotoGalleryFragment**'s lifecycle functions directly, but this would add unnecessary complexity to your fragment class. Instead, abstract the code into **ThumbnailDownloader** by making **ThumbnailDownloader** *lifecycle aware*.

A lifecycle-aware component, known as a *lifecycle observer*, observes the lifecycle of a *lifecycle owner*. **Activity** and **Fragment** are examples of lifecycle owners – they have a lifecycle and implement the **LifecycleOwner** interface.

Update **ThumbnailDownloader** to implement the **LifecycleObserver** interface and observe the **onCreate(…)** and **onDestroy** functions of its lifecycle owner. Have **ThumbnailDownloader** start itself when **onCreate(…)** is called and stop itself when **onDestroy()** is called.

## Listing 25.9  Making **ThumbnailDownloader** lifecycle aware (ThumbnailDownloader.kt)

```
private const val TAG = "ThumbnailDownloader"

class ThumbnailDownloader<in T>
    : HandlerThread(TAG), LifecycleObserver {

    private var hasQuit = false

    override fun quit(): Boolean {
        hasQuit = true
        return super.quit()
    }

    @OnLifecycleEvent(Lifecycle.Event.ON_CREATE)
    fun setup() {
        Log.i(TAG, "Starting background thread")
    }

    @OnLifecycleEvent(Lifecycle.Event.ON_DESTROY)
    fun tearDown() {
        Log.i(TAG, "Destroying background thread")
    }

    fun queueThumbnail(target: T, url: String) {
        Log.i(TAG, "Got a URL: $url")
    }
}
```

Implementing **LifecycleObserver** means you can register **ThumbnailDownloader** to receive lifecycle callbacks from any **LifecycleOwner**. You use the @OnLifecycleEvent(Lifecycle.Event) annotation to associate a function in your class with a lifecycle callback. Lifecycle.Event.ON_CREATE registers **ThumbnailDownloader.setup()** to be called when **LifecycleOwner.onCreate(…)** is called. Lifecycle.Event.ON_DESTROY registers **ThumbnailDownloader.tearDown()** to be called when **LifecycleOwner.onDestroy()** is called.

You can view a list of available **Lifecycle.Event** constants by visiting the API reference page (developer.android.com/reference/android/arch/lifecycle/Lifecycle.Event).

(By the way, **LifecycleObserver**, **Lifecycle.Event**, and **OnLifecycleEvent** are part of Jetpack, in the android.arch.lifecycle package. You already have access to these classes because you added the lifecycle-extensions dependency to your Gradle file in Chapter 24.)

Next, you need to create an instance of **ThumbnailDownloader** and register it to receive lifecycle callbacks from **PhotoGalleryFragment**. Do that in PhotoGalleryFragment.kt.

## Listing 25.10  Creating a **ThumbnailDownloader** (PhotoGalleryFragment.kt)

```
class PhotoGalleryFragment : Fragment() {

    private lateinit var photoGalleryViewModel: PhotoGalleryViewModel
    private lateinit var photoRecyclerView: RecyclerView
    private lateinit var thumbnailDownloader: ThumbnailDownloader<PhotoHolder>

    override fun onCreate(savedInstanceState: Bundle?) {
        super.onCreate(savedInstanceState)

        retainInstance = true

        photoGalleryViewModel =
                ViewModelProviders.of(this).get(PhotoGalleryViewModel::class.java)

        thumbnailDownloader = ThumbnailDownloader()
        lifecycle.addObserver(thumbnailDownloader)
    }
    ...
    override fun onViewCreated(view: View, savedInstanceState: Bundle?) {
        ...
    }

    override fun onDestroy() {
        super.onDestroy()
        lifecycle.removeObserver(
            thumbnailDownloader
        )
    }
    ...
}
```

You can specify any type for **ThumbnailDownloader**'s generic argument. However, recall that this argument specifies the type of the object that will be used as the identifier for your download. In this case, the **PhotoHolder** makes for a convenient identifier, since it is also the target where the downloaded images will eventually go.

Since **Fragment** implements **LifecycleOwner**, it has a lifecycle property.
You use this property to add an observer to the fragment's **Lifecycle**. Calling **lifecycle.addObserver(thumbnailDownloader)** registers the thumbnail downloader instance to receive the fragment's lifecycle callbacks. Now, when **PhotoGalleryFragment.onCreate(…)** is called, **ThumbnailDownloader.setup()** gets called. When **PhotoGalleryFragment.onDestroy()** is called, **ThumbnailDownloader.tearDown()** gets called.

You call **lifecycle.removeObserver(thumbnailDownloader)** in **Fragment.onDestroy()** to remove thumbnailDownloader as a lifecycle observer when the fragment instance is destroyed. You could rely on garbage collection to get rid of the fragment's lifecycle and lifecycle observers when the garbage collector frees the fragment's (and possibly activity's) object graph. However, we prefer deterministic resource deallocation over waiting for the next time scavenging happens. This helps keep bugs close to the event that triggered them.

Run your app. You should still see a wall of close-up Bills. Check your log statements for the message ThumbnailDownloader: Starting background thread to verify that **ThumbnailDownloader.setup()** got executed one time. Press the Back button to exit the application and finish (and destroy) **PhotoGalleryActivity** (and the **PhotoGalleryFragment** it hosts). Check your log statements again; the message ThumbnailDownloader: Destroying background thread verifies that **ThumbnailDownloader.tearDown()** got executed one time.

## Starting and stopping a HandlerThread

Now that **ThumbnailDownloader** is observing **PhotoGalleryFragment**'s lifecycle, update **ThumbnailDownloader** to start itself when **PhotoGalleryFragment.onCreate(…)** is called and stop itself when **PhotoGalleryFragment.onDestroy()** is called.

### Listing 25.11  Starting and stopping the **ThumbnailDownloader** thread (ThumbnailDownloader.kt)

```
class ThumbnailDownloader<in T>
    : HandlerThread(TAG), LifecycleObserver {
    ...
    @OnLifecycleEvent(Lifecycle.Event.ON_CREATE)
    fun setup() {
        Log.i(TAG, "Starting background thread")
        start()
        looper
    }

    @OnLifecycleEvent(Lifecycle.Event.ON_DESTROY)
    fun tearDown() {
        Log.i(TAG, "Destroying background thread")
        quit()
    }

    fun queueThumbnail(target: T, url: String) {
        Log.i(TAG, "Got a URL: $url")
    }
}
```

A couple of safety notes. One: Notice that you access looper after calling **start()** on your **ThumbnailDownloader** (you will learn more about the **Looper** in a moment). This is a way to ensure that the thread's guts are ready before proceeding, to obviate a potential (though rarely occurring) race condition. Until you first access looper, there is no guarantee that **onLooperPrepared()** has been called, so there is a possibility that calls to **queueThumbnail(…)** will fail due to a null **Handler**.

Safety note number two: You call **quit()** to terminate the thread. This is critical. If you do not quit your **HandlerThread**s, they will never die. Like zombies. Or rock and roll.

Finally, within **PhotoAdapter.onBindViewHolder(…)**, call the thread's **queueThumbnail()** function and pass in the target **PhotoHolder** where the image will ultimately be placed and the **GalleryItem**'s URL to download from.

### Listing 25.12 Hooking up **ThumbnailDownloader** (PhotoGalleryFragment.kt)

```
class PhotoGalleryFragment : Fragment() {
    ...
    private inner class PhotoAdapter(private val galleryItems: List<GalleryItem>)
        : RecyclerView.Adapter<PhotoHolder>() {
        ...
        override fun onBindViewHolder(holder: PhotoHolder, position: Int) {
            val galleryItem = galleryItems[position]
            ...
            thumbnailDownloader.queueThumbnail(holder, galleryItem.url)
        }
    }
}
```

Run PhotoGallery again and check out Logcat. When you scroll around the **RecyclerView**, you should see lines in Logcat signaling that **ThumbnailDownloader** is getting each one of your download requests. You will still see a wall of Bills in the app (do not fear, you will fix this soon enough).

Now that you have a **HandlerThread** up and running, the next step is to communicate between your app's main thread and your new background thread.

# Messages and Message Handlers

Your dedicated thread will download photos, but how will it work with the **RecyclerView**'s adapter to display them when it cannot directly access the main thread? (Recall that background threads are not allowed to execute code that modifies the view – only the main thread is permitted do that. The main thread cannot execute long-running tasks – only a background thread is permitted to do that.)

Think back to the shoe store with two Flashes. Background Flash has wrapped up his phone call to the distributor. He needs to tell Main Flash that the shoes are back in stock. If Main Flash is busy, Background Flash cannot do this right away. He would have to wait by the register to catch Main Flash at a spare moment. This would work, but it would not be very efficient.

The better solution is to give each Flash an inbox. Background Flash writes a message about the shoes being in stock and puts it on top of Main Flash's inbox. Main Flash does the same thing when he wants to tell Background Flash that the stock of shoes has run out.

The inbox idea turns out to be really handy. The Flash (either Flash, that is) may have something that needs to be done soon, but not right at the moment. In that case, he can put a message in his own inbox and then handle it when he has time.

In Android, the inbox that threads use is called a *message queue*. A thread that works by using a message queue is called a *message loop*; it loops again and again looking for new messages on its queue (Figure 25.2).

## Figure 25.2  Flash dance

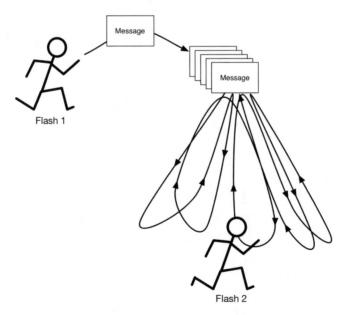

A message loop consists of a thread and a *looper*. The **Looper** is the object that manages a thread's message queue.

The main thread is a message loop and has a looper. Everything your main thread does is performed by its looper, which grabs messages off of its message queue and performs the task they specify (Figure 25.3).

### Figure 25.3  Main thread is a **HandlerThread**

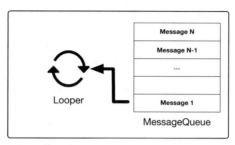

You are going to create a background thread that is also a message loop. You will use a class called **HandlerThread** that prepares a **Looper** for you.

The main thread and your background thread will communicate with each other by placing messages in each other's queue using **Handler**s (Figure 25.4).

### Figure 25.4  Communicating with **Handler**s

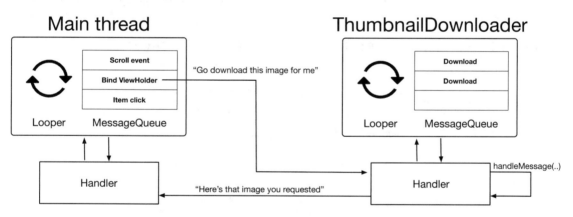

Before you create a message, you need to understand what a **Message** is and the relationship it has with its **Handler** (often called its *message handler*).

## Message anatomy

Let's start by looking closely at messages. The messages that a Flash might put in an inbox (its own inbox or that of another Flash) are not supportive notes, like, "You run very fast, Flash." They are tasks that need to be handled.

A message is an instance of **Message** and contains several fields. Three are relevant to your implementation:

what       a user-defined Int that describes the message

obj        a user-specified object to be sent with the message

target     the **Handler** that will handle the message

The target of a **Message** is an instance of **Handler**. You can think of the name **Handler** as being short for "message handler." When you create a **Message**, it will automatically be attached to a **Handler**. And when your **Message** is ready to be processed, **Handler** will be the object in charge of making it happen.

## Handler anatomy

To do any real work with messages, you first need an instance of **Handler**. A **Handler** is not just a target for processing your **Message**s. A **Handler** is your interface for creating and posting **Message**s, too. Take a look at Figure 25.5.

### Figure 25.5  **Looper**, **Handler**, **HandlerThread**, and **Message**s

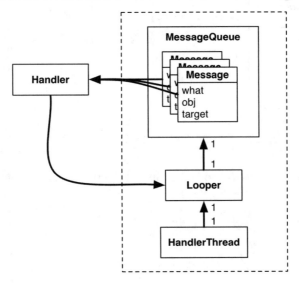

**Message**s must be posted and consumed on a **Looper**, because the **Looper** owns the inbox of **Message** objects. So the **Handler** always has a reference to its coworker, the **Looper**.

A **Handler** is attached to exactly one **Looper**, and a **Message** is attached to exactly one target **Handler**, called its *target*. A **Looper** has a whole queue of **Message**s. Multiple **Message**s can reference the same target **Handler** (Figure 25.5).

Multiple **Handler**s can be attached to one **Looper** (Figure 25.6). This means that your **Handler**'s **Message**s may be living side by side with another **Handler**'s messages.

Figure 25.6  Multiple **Handler**s, one **Looper**

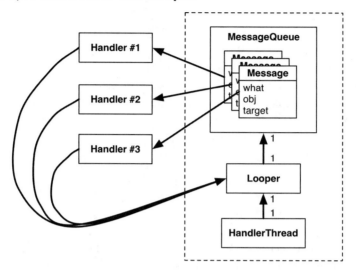

## Using handlers

Usually, you do not set a message's target **Handler** by hand. It is better to build the message by calling **Handler.obtainMessage(…)**. You pass the other message fields into this function, and it automatically sets the target to the **Handler** object the function was called on for you.

**Handler.obtainMessage(…)** pulls from a common recycling pool to avoid creating new **Message** objects, so it is also more efficient than creating new instances.

Once you have obtained a **Message**, you call **sendToTarget()** to send the **Message** to its **Handler**. The **Handler** will then put the **Message** on the end of **Looper**'s message queue.

In this case, you are going to obtain a message and send it to its target within the implementation of **queueThumbnail()**. The message's what will be a constant defined as MESSAGE_DOWNLOAD. The message's obj will be an object of type T, which will be used to identify the download. In this case, obj will be the **PhotoHolder** that the adapter passed in to **queueThumbnail()**.

When the looper pulls a **Message** from the queue, it gives the message to the message's target **Handler** to handle. Typically, the message is handled in the target's implementation of **Handler.handleMessage(…)**.

Figure 25.7 shows the object relationships involved.

## Figure 25.7 Creating a **Message** and sending it

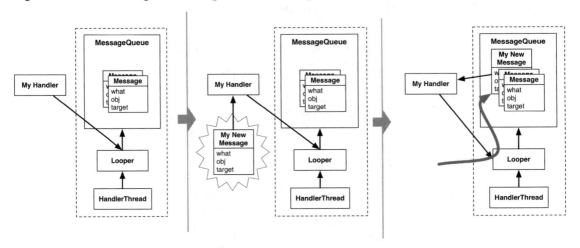

In this case, your implementation of **handleMessage(...)** will use **FlickrFetchr** to download bytes from the URL and then turn those bytes into a bitmap.

First, add the constant and properties shown in Listing 25.13.

## Listing 25.13 Adding a constant and properties (ThumbnailDownloader.kt)

```kotlin
private const val TAG = "ThumbnailDownloader"
private const val MESSAGE_DOWNLOAD = 0

class ThumbnailDownloader<in T>
    : HandlerThread(TAG), LifecycleObserver {

    private var hasQuit = false
    private lateinit var requestHandler: Handler
    private val requestMap = ConcurrentHashMap<T, String>()
    private val flickrFetchr = FlickrFetchr()
    ...
}
```

MESSAGE_DOWNLOAD will be used to identify messages as download requests. (**ThumbnailDownloader** will set this as the what on any new download messages it creates.)

The newly added requestHandler will store a reference to the **Handler** responsible for queueing download requests as messages onto the **ThumbnailDownloader** background thread. This handler will also be in charge of processing download request messages when they are pulled off the queue.

The requestMap property is a **ConcurrentHashMap**, a thread-safe version of **HashMap**. Here, using a download request's identifying object of type T as a key, you can store and retrieve the URL associated with a particular request. (In this case, the identifying object is a **PhotoHolder**, so the request response can be easily routed back to the UI element where the downloaded image should be placed.)

The `flickrFetchr` property stores a reference to a **FlickrFetchr** instance. This way all of the Retrofit setup code will only execute once during the lifetime of the thread. (Creating and configuring a new Retrofit instance every time you make a web request can slow your app down, especially if you are doing many requests in rapid succession.)

Next, add code to **queueThumbnail(…)** to update `requestMap` and to post a new message to the background thread's message queue.

## Listing 25.14  Obtaining and sending a message (ThumbnailDownloader.kt)

```kotlin
class ThumbnailDownloader<in T>
    : HandlerThread(TAG), LifecycleObserver {
    ...
    fun queueThumbnail(target: T, url: String) {
        Log.i(TAG, "Got a URL: $url")
        requestMap[target] = url
        requestHandler.obtainMessage(MESSAGE_DOWNLOAD, target)
            .sendToTarget()
    }
}
```

You obtain a message directly from `requestHandler`, which automatically sets the new **Message** object's `target` field to `requestHandler`. This means `requestHandler` will be in charge of processing the message when it is pulled off the message queue. The message's what field is set to `MESSAGE_DOWNLOAD`. Its `obj` field is set to the `T` target value (a **PhotoHolder**, in this case) that is passed to **queueThumbnail(…)**.

The new message represents a download request for the specified `T` target (a **PhotoHolder** from the **RecyclerView**). Recall that **RecyclerView**'s adapter implementation in **PhotoGalleryFragment** calls **queueThumbnail(…)** from **onBindViewHolder(…)**, passing along the **PhotoHolder** the image is being downloaded for and the URL location of the image to download.

Notice that the message itself does not include the URL. Instead, you update `requestMap` with a mapping between the request identifier (**PhotoHolder**) and the URL for the request. Later you will pull the URL from `requestMap` to ensure that you are always downloading the most recently requested URL for a given **PhotoHolder** instance. (This is important because **ViewHolder** objects in **RecyclerView**s are recycled and reused.)

Finally, initialize requestHandler and define what that **Handler** will do when downloaded messages are pulled off the queue and passed to it.

## Listing 25.15  Handling a message (ThumbnailDownloader.kt)

```kotlin
class ThumbnailDownloader<in T>
    : HandlerThread(TAG), LifecycleObserver {
    ...
    private val requestMap = ConcurrentHashMap<T, String>()
    private val flickrFetchr = FlickrFetchr()

    @Suppress("UNCHECKED_CAST")
    @SuppressLint("HandlerLeak")
    override fun onLooperPrepared() {
        requestHandler = object : Handler() {
            override fun handleMessage(msg: Message) {
                if (msg.what == MESSAGE_DOWNLOAD) {
                    val target = msg.obj as T
                    Log.i(TAG, "Got a request for URL: ${requestMap[target]}")
                    handleRequest(target)
                }
            }
        }
    }
    ...
    fun queueThumbnail(target: T, url: String) {
        ...
    }

    private fun handleRequest(target: T) {
        val url = requestMap[target] ?: return
        val bitmap = flickrFetchr.fetchPhoto(url) ?: return
    }
}
```

When importing **Message**, make sure to select android.os.Message from the options presented.

You implemented **Handler.handleMessage(…)** in your **Handler** subclass within **onLooperPrepared()**. **HandlerThread.onLooperPrepared()** is called before the **Looper** checks the queue for the first time. This makes it a good place to create your **Handler** implementation.

Within **Handler.handleMessage(…)**, you check the message type, retrieve the obj value (which will be of type T and serves as the identifier for the request), and then pass it to **handleRequest(…)**. (Recall that **Handler.handleMessage(…)** will get called when a download message is pulled off the queue and ready to be processed.)

The **handleRequest()** function is a helper function where the downloading happens. Here you check for the existence of a URL. Then you pass the URL to the **FlickrFetchr.fetchPhoto(…)** function that you created with such foresight at the beginning of this chapter.

The @Suppress("UNCHECKED_CAST") annotation tells the Lint checker that you are well aware that you are casting msg.obj to type T without first checking whether msg.obj is indeed of type T. This is OK for now because you are the only developer dealing with your PhotoGallery code. You control messages added to the queue, and you know that at this point all the messages you queue have their obj field set to a **PhotoHolder** instance (which matches the T specified on **ThumbnailDownloader**).

The way you create the **Handler** implementation above technically creates an inner class. Inner classes hold a reference to their outer class (**ThumbnailDownloader** in this case), which can in turn cause the outer class to leak if the lifetime of the inner class is longer than the intended lifetime of the outer class.

This is only problematic if your handler is attached to the main thread's looper. You suppress a **HandlerLeak** warning using @SuppressLint("HandlerLeak"), since the handler you create is attached to the looper of a background thread. If the handler were instead attached to the main thread's looper, it might not be garbage-collected. If it were to leak, since it also holds a reference to the **ThumbnailDownloader**, your app would leak the **ThumbnailDownloader** instance as well.

In general, you should only suppress Lint warnings if you truly understand the warning and why suppressing it in the given scenario is safe.

Run PhotoGallery and check Logcat for your confirming log statements.

Of course, the request will not be completely handled until you set the bitmap on the **PhotoHolder** that originally came from **PhotoAdapter**. However, that is UI work, so it must be done on the main thread.

Everything you have seen so far uses handlers and messages on a single thread – **ThumbnailDownloader** putting messages in **ThumbnailDownloader**'s own inbox. In the next section, you will see how **ThumbnailDownloader** can use a **Handler** to post requests to a separate thread (namely, the main thread).

## Passing handlers

So far you are able to schedule work on the background thread from the main thread using **ThumbnailDownloader**'s requestHandler. This flow is shown in Figure 25.8.

Figure 25.8 Scheduling work on **ThumbnailDownloader** from the main thread

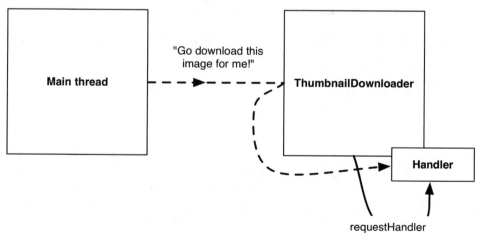

You can also schedule work on the main thread from the background thread using a **Handler** attached to the main thread. This flow looks like Figure 25.9.

## Figure 25.9  Scheduling work on the main thread from **ThumbnailDownloader**'s thread

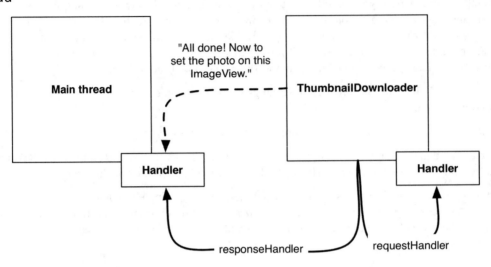

The main thread is a message loop with handlers and a **Looper**. When you create a **Handler** in the main thread, it will be associated with the main thread's **Looper**. You can then pass that **Handler** to another thread. The passed **Handler** maintains its loyalty to the **Looper** of the thread that created it. Any messages the **Handler** is responsible for will be handled on the main thread's queue.

In ThumbnailDownloader.kt, add the responseHandler property seen above to hold a **Handler** passed from the main thread. Then replace the constructor with one that accepts a **Handler** (which will be stored in responseHandler) and a function type that will be used as a callback to communicate the responses (downloaded images) with the requester (the main thread).

## Listing 25.16  Adding the responseHandler (ThumbnailDownloader.kt)

```
class ThumbnailDownloader<in T>(
    private val responseHandler: Handler,
    private val onThumbnailDownloaded: (T, Bitmap) -> Unit
) : HandlerThread(TAG), LifecycleObserver {
    ...
}
```

The function type property defined in your new constructor will eventually be called when an image has been fully downloaded and is ready to be added to the UI. Using this listener delegates the responsibility of what to do with the downloaded image to a class other than **ThumbnailDownloader** (in this case, to **PhotoGalleryFragment**). Doing so separates the downloading task from the UI updating task (putting the images into **ImageView**s), so that **ThumbnailDownloader** could be used for downloading into other kinds of **View** objects as needed.

Next, modify **PhotoGalleryFragment** to pass a **Handler** attached to the main thread to **ThumbnailDownloader**. Also, pass an anonymous function to handle the downloaded image once it is complete.

## Listing 25.17 Hooking up to response **Handler** (PhotoGalleryFragment.kt)

```
class PhotoGalleryFragment : Fragment() {
    ...
    override fun onCreate(savedInstanceState: Bundle?) {
        ...
        thumbnailDownloader = ThumbnailDownloader()
        val responseHandler = Handler()
        thumbnailDownloader =
                ThumbnailDownloader(responseHandler) { photoHolder, bitmap ->
                    val drawable = BitmapDrawable(resources, bitmap)
                    photoHolder.bindDrawable(drawable)
                }
        lifecycle.addObserver(thumbnailDownloader)
    }
    ...
}
```

Remember that by default, the **Handler** will attach itself to the **Looper** for the current thread. Because this **Handler** is created in **onCreate(…)**, it will be attached to the main thread's **Looper**.

Now **ThumbnailDownloader** has access via responseHandler to a **Handler** that is tied to the main thread's **Looper**. It also has your function type implementation to do the UI work with the returning **Bitmap**s. Specifically, the function passed to the **onThumbnailDownloaded** higher-order function sets the **Drawable** of the originally requested **PhotoHolder** to the newly downloaded **Bitmap**.

You could send a custom **Message** back to the main thread requesting to add the image to the UI, similar to how you queued a request on the background thread to download the image. However, this would require another subclass of **Handler**, with an override of **handleMessage(…)**.

Instead, use another handy **Handler** function – **post(Runnable)**.

**Handler.post(Runnable)** is a convenience function for posting **Message**s that look like this:

```
var myRunnable: Runnable = object : Runnable {
    override fun run() {
        // Your code here
    }
}
var msg: Message = Message.obtain(someHandler, myRunnable)
// Sets msg.callback to myRunnable
```

When a **Message** has its callback field set, it is not routed to its target **Handler** when pulled off the message queue. Instead, the **run()** function of the **Runnable** stored in callback is executed directly.

In **ThumbnailDownloader.handleRequest()**, post a **Runnable** to the main thread's queue through responseHandler (Listing 25.18).

## Listing 25.18  Downloading and displaying images (ThumbnailDownloader.kt)

```kotlin
class ThumbnailDownloader<in T>(
    private val responseHandler: Handler,
    private val onThumbnailDownloaded: (T, Bitmap) -> Unit
) : HandlerThread(TAG), LifecycleObserver {
    ...
    private fun handleRequest(target: T) {
        val url = requestMap[target] ?: return
        val bitmap = flickrFetchr.fetchPhoto(url) ?: return

        responseHandler.post(Runnable {
            if (requestMap[target] != url || hasQuit) {
                return@Runnable
            }

            requestMap.remove(target)
            onThumbnailDownloaded(target, bitmap)
        })
    }
}
```

Because responseHandler is associated with the main thread's **Looper**, all of the code inside of **Runnable**'s **run()** will be executed on the main thread.

So what does this code do? First, you double-check the requestMap. This is necessary because the **RecyclerView** recycles its views. By the time **ThumbnailDownloader** finishes downloading the **Bitmap**, **RecyclerView** may have recycled the **PhotoHolder** and requested a different URL for it. This check ensures that each **PhotoHolder** gets the correct image, even if another request has been made in the meantime.

Next, you check hasQuit. If **ThumbnailDownloader** has already quit, it may be unsafe to run any callbacks.

Finally, you remove the **PhotoHolder**-URL mapping from the requestMap and set the bitmap on the target **PhotoHolder**.

# Listening to the View Lifecycle

Before running PhotoGallery and seeing your hard-won images, there is one last danger you need to account for. If the user rotates the screen, **ThumbnailDownloader** may be hanging on to invalid **PhotoHolder**s. Your app could crash if **ThumbnailDownloader** tries to send a bitmap to a **PhotoHolder** that was part of a view that was destroyed across rotation.

Fix this leak by clearing all the requests out of your queue when the fragment's view is destroyed. To do this, **ThumbnailDownloader** needs to know about the fragment's view lifecycle. (Recall that the lifecycles for the fragment and its view diverge, since you are retaining the fragment: The view will be destroyed across rotation, but the fragment instance itself will not.)

First, refactor your existing fragment lifecycle observer code to make room for a second lifecycle observer implementation.

### Listing 25.19  Refactoring your fragment lifecycle observer (ThumbnailDownloader.kt)

```
class ThumbnailDownloader<in T>(
    private val responseHandler: Handler,
    private val onThumbnailDownloaded: (T, Bitmap) -> Unit
) : HandlerThread(TAG), LifecycleObserver {

    val fragmentLifecycleObserver: LifecycleObserver =
        object : LifecycleObserver {

            @OnLifecycleEvent(Lifecycle.Event.ON_CREATE)
            fun setup() {
                Log.i(TAG, "Starting background thread")
                start()
                looper
            }

            @OnLifecycleEvent(Lifecycle.Event.ON_DESTROY)
            fun tearDown() {
                Log.i(TAG, "Destroying background thread")
                quit()
            }
        }

    private var hasQuit = false
    ...
    @OnLifecycleEvent(Lifecycle.Event.ON_CREATE)
    fun setup() {
        start()
        looper
    }

    @OnLifecycleEvent(Lifecycle.Event.ON_DESTROY)
    fun tearDown() {
        Log.i(TAG, "Background thread destroyed")
        quit()
    }
    ...
}
```

Next, define a new observer that will eventually listen to lifecycle callbacks from the fragment's view.

## Listing 25.20  Adding a view lifecycle observer (ThumbnailDownloader.kt)

```kotlin
class ThumbnailDownloader<in T>(
    private val responseHandler: Handler,
    private val onThumbnailDownloaded: (T, Bitmap) -> Unit
) : HandlerThread(TAG) {

    val fragmentLifecycleObserver: LifecycleObserver =
        object : LifecycleObserver {
            ...
        }

    val viewLifecycleObserver: LifecycleObserver =
        object : LifecycleObserver {

            @OnLifecycleEvent(Lifecycle.Event.ON_DESTROY)
            fun clearQueue() {
                Log.i(TAG, "Clearing all requests from queue")
                requestHandler.removeMessages(MESSAGE_DOWNLOAD)
                requestMap.clear()
            }
        }
    ...
}
```

When observing a fragment's view lifecycle, Lifecycle.Event.ON_DESTROY maps to
**Fragment.onDestroyView()**. (To learn how the other **Lifecycle.Event** constants map
to the fragment's lifecycle callbacks when you observe the fragment's view lifecycle, see
**getViewLifecycleOwner** in the API reference for **Fragment** at developer.android.com/reference/
kotlin/androidx/fragment/app/Fragment.)

Now update **PhotoGalleryFragment** to register the refactored fragment observer. Also, register the newly added lifecycle observer to listen for the fragment's view lifecycle.

## Listing 25.21  Registering the view lifecycle observer (PhotoGalleryFragment.kt)

```kotlin
class PhotoGalleryFragment : Fragment() {
    ...
    override fun onCreate(savedInstanceState: Bundle?) {
        ...
        thumbnailDownloader =
            ThumbnailDownloader(responseHandler) {
            ...
        }
        lifecycle.addObserver(thumbnailDownloader.fragmentLifecycleObserver)
    }

    override fun onCreateView(
            inflater: LayoutInflater,
            container: ViewGroup?,
            savedInstanceState: Bundle?
    ): View {
        viewLifecycleOwner.lifecycle.addObserver(
            thumbnailDownloader.viewLifecycleObserver
        )
        ...
    }
    ...
}
```

You can safely observe the view lifecycle in **Fragment.onCreateView(…)** so long as you return a non-null view at the end of the **onCreateView(…)** function. See the section called Challenge: Observing View LifecycleOwner LiveData near the end of this chapter to learn more about observing viewLifecycleOwner, which offers more flexibility in configuring the view lifecycle observation.

Finally, unregister `thumbnailDownloader` as a fragment view lifecycle observer in
**Fragment.onDestroyView()**. Update the existing code that unregisters `thumbnailDownloader` as a
fragment lifecycle observer to reflect your recent refactor.

## Listing 25.22  Unregistering the view lifecycle observer (PhotoGalleryFragment.kt)

```kotlin
class PhotoGalleryFragment : Fragment() {
    ...
    override fun onDestroyView() {
        super.onDestroyView()
        viewLifecycleOwner.lifecycle.removeObserver(
            thumbnailDownloader.viewLifecycleObserver
        )
    }

    override fun onDestroy() {
        super.onDestroy()
        lifecycle.removeObserver(
            thumbnailDownloader.fragmentLifecycleObserver
        )
    }
    ...
}
```

As with the fragment `lifecycle` observers, you do not have to explicitly unregister fragment
`viewLifecycleOwner.lifecycle` observers. The fragment's view lifecycle registry, which keeps track
of all of the view lifecycle observers, gets nulled out when the fragment's view is destroyed. However,
just as before, we prefer to explicitly unregister observers rather than rely on garbage collection.

With that, your work for this chapter is complete. Run PhotoGallery. Scroll around to see images
dynamically loading (Figure 25.10).

Figure 25.10 Images on display

PhotoGallery has achieved its basic goal of displaying images from Flickr. In the next few chapters, you will add more functionality, like searching for photos and opening each photo's Flickr page in a web view.

# Retained Fragments

By default, the retainInstance property of a fragment is false. This means it is not retained but is destroyed and re-created on rotation along with the activity that hosts it. Calling **setRetainInstance(true)** retains the fragment. When a fragment is retained, the fragment is not destroyed with the activity. Instead, it is preserved and passed along intact to the new activity.

When you retain a fragment, you can count on all of its instance variables to keep the same values. When you reach for them, they are simply there.

## Rotation and retained fragments

Let's take a closer look at how retained fragments work. Retained fragments take advantage of the fact that a fragment's view can be destroyed and re-created without having to destroy the fragment itself.

During a configuration change, the **FragmentManager** first destroys the views of the fragments in its list. Fragment views always get destroyed and re-created on a configuration change for the same reasons that activity views are destroyed and re-created: If you have a new configuration, then you might need new resources. Just in case better matching resources are now available, you rebuild the view from scratch.

Next, the **FragmentManager** checks the retainInstance property of each fragment. If it is false, which it is by default, then the **FragmentManager** destroys the fragment instance. The fragment and its view will be re-created by the new **FragmentManager** of the new activity "on the other side" (Figure 25.11).

## Figure 25.11  Default rotation with a UI fragment

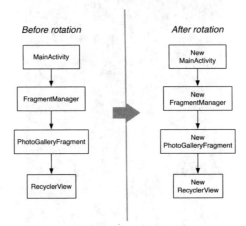

On the other hand, if retainInstance is true, then the fragment's view is destroyed, but the fragment itself is not. When the new activity is created, the new **FragmentManager** finds the retained fragment and re-creates its view (Figure 25.12).

## Figure 25.12  Rotation with a retained UI fragment

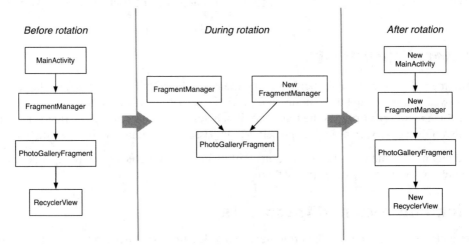

A retained fragment is not destroyed, but it is *detached* from the dying activity. This puts the fragment in a retained state. The fragment still exists, but it is not hosted by any activity (Figure 25.13).

## Figure 25.13 Fragment lifecycle

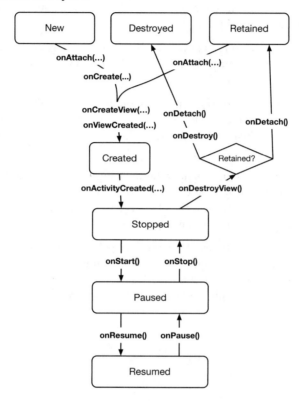

The retained state is entered when two conditions are met:

- **setRetainInstance(true)** has been called on the fragment

- the hosting activity is being destroyed for a configuration change (typically rotation)

A fragment is only in the retained state for an extremely brief interval – the time between being detached from the old activity and being reattached to the new activity that is immediately created.

## Whether to retain

Retained fragments: pretty nifty, right? Yes! They are indeed nifty. They appear to solve all the problems that pop up from activities and fragments being destroyed on rotation. When the device configuration changes, you get the most appropriate resources by creating a brand-new view, and you have an easy way to retain data and objects.

You may wonder why you would not retain every fragment or why fragments are not retained by default. In general, we do not recommend using this mechanism unless you absolutely need to, for a few reasons.

The first reason is simply that retained fragments are more complicated than unretained fragments. When something goes wrong with them, it takes longer to get to the bottom of what went wrong. Programs are always more complicated than you want them to be, so if you can get by without this complication, you are better off.

The second reason is that fragments that handle rotation using saved instance state handle all lifecycle situations, but retained fragments only handle the case when an activity is destroyed for a configuration change. If your activity is destroyed because the OS needs to reclaim memory, then all your retained fragments are destroyed, too, which may mean that you lose some data.

The third reason is that the **ViewModel** class replaces the need for retained fragments in most cases. Use a **ViewModel** instead of a retained fragment to persist UI-related state across a configuration change. **ViewModel** gives the same benefit of retained state across a configuration change without the drawbacks of introducing a more complicated lifecycle for your fragment.

# For the More Curious: Solving the Image Downloading Problem

This book is here to teach you mostly about the tools in the standard Android library. If you are open to using more third-party libraries (in addition to Retrofit and the others we have introduced), there are a few libraries that can save you a whole lot of time in various scenarios, including the image downloading work you implemented in PhotoGallery.

Admittedly, the solution you implemented in this chapter is far from perfect. And when you start to need caching, transformations, and better performance, it is natural to ask whether someone else has solved this problem before you. The answer is yes: Someone has. There are several libraries available that solve the image-loading problem. We currently use Picasso (`square.github.io/picasso`) for image loading in our production applications.

Picasso lets you do everything from this chapter with just a few function calls:

```
private class PhotoHolder(private val itemImageView: ImageView)
    : RecyclerView.ViewHolder(itemView) {
        ...
        fun bindGalleryItem(galleryItem: GalleryItem) {
            Picasso.get()
                    .load(galleryItem.url)
                    .placeholder(R.drawable.bill_up_close)
                    .into(itemImageView)
        }
        ...
    }
```

The fluent interface requires you get an instance of Picasso using **get()**. You can specify the URL of the image to download using **load(String)** and the **ImageView** object to load the result into using **into(ImageView)**. There are many other configurable options, such as specifying an image to display until the requested image is fully downloaded (using **placeholder(Int)** or **placeholder(drawable)**).

In **PhotoAdapter.onBindViewHolder(…)**, you would replace the existing code with a call through to the new **bindGalleryItem(…)** function.

Picasso does all of the work of **ThumbnailDownloader** (along with the **ThumbnailDownloader.ThumbnailDownloadListener<T>** callback) and the image-related work of **FlickrFetchr**. This means you could remove **ThumbnailDownloader** if you used Picasso (you would still need **FlickrFetchr** for downloading the JSON data). In addition to simplifying your code, Picasso supports more advanced features such as image transformations and disk caching with minimal effort on your part.

You can add Picasso to your project as a library dependency, just as you have done for other dependencies (like RecyclerView).

A downside of Picasso is that it is intentionally limited so that it can remain small. As a result, it cannot download and display animated images. If you have that need, then check out Google's Glide library or Facebook's Fresco library. Between the two, Glide has the smaller footprint, but Fresco has the edge on performance.

# For the More Curious: StrictMode

There are some things you simply should not do in your Android app – mistakes that lead directly to crashes and security holes. For example, executing a network request on the main thread would probably result in an ANR error in poor network conditions.

Instead of Android happily allowing you to invoke a network request on the application's main thread, you get a `NetworkOnMainThread` exception and log message instead. This is because of `StrictMode`, which noticed your mistake and helpfully let you know about it. `StrictMode` was introduced to help you detect this and many other programming mistakes and security problems in your code.

Without any configuration, networking on the main thread is guarded against. `StrictMode` can also help you detect other mistakes that could drag down your application's performance. To enable all of `StrictMode`'s recommended policies, call `StrictMode.enableDefaults()` (developer.android.com/reference/android/os/StrictMode.html#enableDefaults()).

Once `StrictMode.enableDefaults()` has been called, you will hear about the following violations in Logcat:

- networking on the main thread
- disk reads and writes on the main thread
- activities kept alive beyond their natural lifecycle (also known as an "activity leak")
- unclosed SQLite database cursors
- cleartext network traffic not wrapped in SSL/TLS

For custom control over what happens when policy violations occur, you can configure the `ThreadPolicy.Builder` and `VmPolicy.Builder` classes. You can specify whether you want an exception to occur, a dialog to be shown, or a statement to be logged to alert you to the violation.

# Challenge: Observing View LifecycleOwner LiveData

`PhotoGalleryFragment` calls `viewLifecycleOwner.lifecycle.observe(…)` in `Fragment.onCreateView(…)`. This is simple and works fine so long as the view you return from `onCreateView(…)` is not null.

You cannot directly observe the view's lifecycle in `Fragment.onCreate(…)`, because the view lifecycle is only valid from when `Fragment.onCreateView(…)` is called until `Fragment.onDestroyView(…)` is called. However, you can observe the lifecycle of a fragment's view by calling `Fragment.getViewLifecycleOwnerLiveData()`, which returns a `LiveData<LifecycleOwner>`. The fragment's `viewLifecycleOwner` is published to the live data once a non-null view is returned from `Fragment.onCreateView(…)` and is set to null after `Fragment.onDestroyView(…)` is called.

For this challenge, refactor your code to observe the fragment's `viewLifecycleOwner` through the `LiveData<LifecycleOwner>` returned from `Fragment.getViewLifecycleOwnerLiveData()`. The newly added observer relationship should be tied to the life of the fragment instance. When a non-null value is published, observe the fragment's view lifecycle, accessible through `viewLifecycleOwner.lifecycle`.

# Challenge: Improving ThumbnailDownloader's Lifecycle Awareness

**LiveData** is a lifecycle-aware component that removes itself as an observer automatically based on events from its lifecycle owner. Update **ThumbnailDownloader** so that it will remove itself as an observer automatically when the lifecycle it observes emits an ON_DESTROY event. To do this, **ThumbnailDownloader** will need a reference to each of the lifecycles it observes.

The fact that **ThumbnailDownloader** observes both the fragment lifecycle and the fragment view lifecycle tightly couples **ThumbnailDownloader** to **Fragment**. There are many different ways to clean this up, but here we ask you to take one small step: Refactor **ThumbnailDownloader** so that it only observes the fragment lifecycle. Then have the fragment clear the queue when **Fragment.onDestroyView()** is called. This way, your downloader could more easily be used with an activity, too.

# Challenge: Preloading and Caching

Users accept that not everything can be instantaneous. (Well, most users.) Even so, programmers strive for perfection.

To approach instantaneity, most real-world apps augment the code you have here in two ways: adding a caching layer and preloading images.

A cache is a place to stash a certain number of **Bitmap** objects so that they stick around even when you are done using them. A cache can only hold so many items, so you need a strategy to decide what to keep when your cache runs out of room. Many caches use a strategy called LRU, or "least recently used." When you are out of room, the cache gets rid of the least recently used item.

The Android support library has a class called **LruCache** that implements an LRU strategy. For the first challenge, use **LruCache** to add a simple cache to **ThumbnailDownloader**. Whenever you download the **Bitmap** for a URL, stick it in the cache. Then, when you are about to download a new image, check the cache first to see whether you already have it around.

Once you have built a cache, you can preload things into it before you actually need them. That way, there is no delay for **Bitmap**s to download before displaying them.

Preloading is tricky to implement well, but it makes a huge difference for the user. For a second, more difficult challenge, for every **GalleryItem** you display, preload **Bitmap**s for the previous 10 and the next 10 **GalleryItem**s.

# 26

# SearchView and SharedPreferences

Your next task with PhotoGallery is to search photos on Flickr. You will learn how to integrate search into your app using **SearchView**. **SearchView** is an *action view* class – a view that can be embedded right in your **Toolbar**. You will also learn how to easily store data to the device's filesystem using **SharedPreferences**.

By the end of this chapter, the user will be able to press on the **SearchView**, type in a query, and submit it. Submitting the query will send the query string to Flickr's search API and populate the **RecyclerView** with the search results (Figure 26.1). The query string itself will be persisted to the filesystem. This means the user's last query will be accessible across restarts of the app and even the device.

Figure 26.1  App preview

# Searching Flickr

Let's begin with the Flickr side of things. To search Flickr, you call the **flickr.photos.search** method. Here is what a GET request to search for the text "cat" looks like:

```
https://api.flickr.com/services/rest/?method=flickr.photos.search
&api_key=xxx&format=json&nojsoncallback=1&extras=url_s&safe_search=1&text=cat
```

The method is set to **flickr.photos.search**. The text parameter is set to whatever string you are searching for ("cat," in this case). Setting safesearch to 1 filters potentially offensive results from the search data sent back.

Some of the parameter-value pairs, such as format=json, are constant across both the **flickr.photos.search** and **flickr.interestingness.getList** request URLs. You are going to abstract these shared parameter-value pairs out into an *interceptor*. An interceptor does what you might expect – it intercepts a request or response and allows you to manipulate the contents or take some action before the request or response completes.

Create a new **Interceptor** class named **PhotoInterceptor** in your api folder. Override **intercept(chain)** to access a request, add the shared parameter-value pairs to it, and overwrite the original URL with the newly built URL. (Do not neglect to include your API key, which you created in Chapter 24, in place of *yourApiKeyHere*. You can copy it from api/FlickrApi.kt.)

## Listing 26.1  Adding an interceptor to insert URL constants (api/PhotoInterceptor.kt)

```kotlin
private const val API_KEY = "yourApiKeyHere"

class PhotoInterceptor : Interceptor {

    override fun intercept(chain: Interceptor.Chain): Response {
        val originalRequest: Request = chain.request()

        val newUrl: HttpUrl = originalRequest.url().newBuilder()
                .addQueryParameter("api_key", API_KEY)
                .addQueryParameter("format", "json")
                .addQueryParameter("nojsoncallback", "1")
                .addQueryParameter("extras", "url_s")
                .addQueryParameter("safesearch", "1")
                .build()

        val newRequest: Request = originalRequest.newBuilder()
                .url(newUrl)
                .build()

        return chain.proceed(newRequest)
    }
}
```

Android Studio presents you with multiple options when importing **Request** and **Response**. Select the okhttp3 options in both cases.

Here, you call **chain.request()** to access the original request. **originalRequest.url()** pulls the original URL from the request, and you use **HttpUrl.Builder** to add the query parameters to it.

**HttpUrl.Builder** creates a new **Request** based on the original request and overwrites the original URL with the new one. Finally, you call **chain.proceed(newRequest)** to produce a **Response**. If you did not call **chain.proceed(…)**, the network request would not happen.

Now open FlickrFetchr.kt and add the interceptor to your **Retrofit** configuration.

## Listing 26.2 Adding an interceptor to your Retrofit configuration (FlickrFetchr.kt)

```kotlin
class FlickrFetchr {

    private val flickrApi: FlickrApi

    init {
        val client = OkHttpClient.Builder()
            .addInterceptor(PhotoInterceptor())
            .build()

        val retrofit: Retrofit = Retrofit.Builder()
            .baseUrl("https://api.flickr.com/")
            .addConverterFactory(GsonConverterFactory.create())
            .client(client)
            .build()

        flickrApi = retrofit.create(FlickrApi::class.java)
    }
    ...
}
```

You create an **OkHttpClient** instance and add **PhotoInterceptor** as an interceptor. Then you set the newly configured client on your **Retrofit** instance, which replaces the default client that was already in place. Now Retrofit will use the client you provided and, in turn, apply **PhotoInterceptor.intercept(…)** to any requests that are made.

You no longer need the **flickr.interestingness.getList** URL specified in **FlickrApi**. Clean that up and, instead, add a **searchPhotos()** function to define a search request to your Retrofit API configuration.

## Listing 26.3 Adding a search function to **FlickrApi** (api/FlickrApi.kt)

```kotlin
interface FlickrApi {

    @GET("services/rest/?method=flickr.interestingness.getList" +
        "&api_key=yourApiKeyHere" +
        "&format=json" +
        "&nojsoncallback=1" +
        "&extras=url_s")
    @GET("services/rest?method=flickr.interestingness.getList")
    fun fetchPhotos(): Call<FlickrResponse>

    @GET
    fun fetchUrlBytes(@Url url: String): Call<ResponseBody>

    @GET("services/rest?method=flickr.photos.search")
    fun searchPhotos(@Query("text") query: String): Call<FlickrResponse>
}
```

The @Query annotation allows you to dynamically append a query parameter appended to the URL. Here you append a query parameter named text. The value assigned to text depends on the argument passed into **searchPhotos(String)**. For example, calling **searchPhotos("robot")** would add text=robot to the URL.

Add a search function to **FlickrFetchr** to wrap the newly added **FlickrApi.searchPhotos(String)** function. Pull the code that executes a **Call** object asynchronously and wraps the result in **LiveData** into a helper function.

## Listing 26.4  Adding a search function to **FlickrFetchr** (FlickrFetchr.kt)

```kotlin
class FlickrFetchr {

    private val flickrApi: FlickrApi

    init {
        ...
    }

    fun fetchPhotos(): LiveData<List<GalleryItem>> {
        return fetchPhotoMetadata(flickrApi.fetchPhotos())
    }

    fun searchPhotos(query: String): LiveData<List<GalleryItem>> {
        return fetchPhotoMetadata(flickrApi.searchPhotos(query))
    }

    fun fetchPhotos(): LiveData<List<GalleryItem>> {
    private fun fetchPhotoMetadata(flickrRequest: Call<FlickrResponse>)
            : LiveData<List<GalleryItem>> {
        val responseLiveData: MutableLiveData<List<GalleryItem>> = MutableLiveData()
        val flickrRequest: Call<FlickrResponse> = flickrApi.fetchPhotos()

        flickrRequest.enqueue(object : Callback<FlickrResponse> {
            ...
        })

        return responseLiveData
    }
    ...
}
```

Finally, update **PhotoGalleryViewModel** to kick off a Flickr search. For now, hardcode the search term to be "planets." Hardcoding the query allows you to test out your new search code even though you have not yet provided a way to enter a query through the UI.

## Listing 26.5 Kicking off a search request (PhotoGalleryViewModel.kt)

```kotlin
class PhotoGalleryViewModel : ViewModel() {

    val galleryItemLiveData: LiveData<List<GalleryItem>>

    init {
        galleryItemLiveData = FlickrFetchr().fetchPhotos()searchPhotos("planets")
    }
}
```

While the search request URL differs from the one you used to request interesting photos, the format of the JSON data returned remains the same. This is good news, because it means you can use the same Gson configuration and model mapping code you already wrote.

Run PhotoGallery to ensure your search query works correctly. Hopefully, you will see a cool photo or two of Earth. (If you do not get results obviously related to planets, it does not mean your query is not working. Try a different search term – such as "bicycle" or "llama" – and run your app again to confirm that you are indeed seeing search results.)

# Using SearchView

Now that **FlickrFetchr** supports searching, it is time to add a way for the user to enter a query and initiate a search. Do this by adding a **SearchView**.

As we said at the beginning of the chapter, **SearchView** is an action view, meaning your entire search interface can live in your application's app bar.

Create a new menu XML file for **PhotoGalleryFragment** called res/menu/ fragment_photo_gallery.xml. This file will specify the items that should appear in the toolbar. (See Chapter 14 for detailed steps on adding the menu XML file, if you need a reminder.)

## Listing 26.6  Adding a menu XML file (res/menu/fragment_photo_gallery.xml)

```xml
<menu xmlns:android="http://schemas.android.com/apk/res/android"
    xmlns:app="http://schemas.android.com/apk/res-auto">

    <item android:id="@+id/menu_item_search"
        android:title="@string/search"
        app:actionViewClass="androidx.appcompat.widget.SearchView"
        app:showAsAction="ifRoom" />

    <item android:id="@+id/menu_item_clear"
        android:title="@string/clear_search"
        app:showAsAction="never" />
</menu>
```

You will see a couple of errors in the new XML complaining that you have not yet defined the strings you are referencing for the android:title attributes. Ignore those for now. You will fix them in a bit.

The first item entry in Listing 26.6 tells the toolbar to display a **SearchView** by specifying the value androidx.appcompat.widget.SearchView for the app:actionViewClass attribute. (Notice the usage of the app namespace for the showAsAction and actionViewClass attributes. Refer back to Chapter 14 if you are unsure of why this is used.)

The second item in Listing 26.6 will add a "Clear Search" option. This option will always display in the overflow menu because you set app:showAsAction to never. Later, you will configure this item so that, when pressed, the user's stored query will be erased from the disk. For now, you can ignore this item.

Now it is time to address the errors in your menu XML. Open res/values/strings.xml and add the missing strings.

## Listing 26.7  Adding search strings (res/values/strings.xml)

```xml
<resources>
    ...
    <string name="search">Search</string>
    <string name="clear_search">Clear Search</string>

</resources>
```

Finally, open PhotoGalleryFragment.kt. Add a call to **setHasOptionsMenu(true)** in **onCreate(…)** to register the fragment to receive menu callbacks. Override **onCreateOptionsMenu(…)** and inflate the menu XML file you created. This will add the items listed in your menu XML to the toolbar.

## Listing 26.8 Overriding **onCreateOptionsMenu(…)** (PhotoGalleryFragment.kt)

```kotlin
class PhotoGalleryFragment : Fragment() {
    ...
    override fun onCreate(savedInstanceState: Bundle?) {
        super.onCreate(savedInstanceState)

        retainInstance = true
        setHasOptionsMenu(true)
        ...
    }
    ...
    override fun onDestroy() {
        ...
    }

    override fun onCreateOptionsMenu(menu: Menu, inflater: MenuInflater) {
        super.onCreateOptionsMenu(menu, inflater)
        inflater.inflate(R.menu.fragment_photo_gallery, menu)
    }
    ...
}
```

Fire up PhotoGallery and see what the **SearchView** looks like. Pressing the search icon expands the view to display a text box where you can enter a query (Figure 26.2).

## Figure 26.2 **SearchView** collapsed and expanded

When the **SearchView** is expanded, an x icon appears on the right. Pressing the x one time clears out what you typed. Pressing the x again collapses the **SearchView** back to a single search icon.

If you try submitting a query, it will not do anything yet. Not to worry. You will make your **SearchView** more useful in just a moment.

## Responding to SearchView user interactions

When the user submits a query, your app should execute a search against the Flickr web service and refresh the images the user sees with the search results. First, update **PhotoGalleryViewModel** to keep track of the user's latest search term and update the search results when the query changes.

### Listing 26.9  Storing the most recent query in **PhotoGalleryViewModel** (PhotoGalleryViewModel.kt)

```
class PhotoGalleryViewModel : ViewModel() {

    val galleryItemLiveData: LiveData<List<GalleryItem>>

    private val flickrFetchr = FlickrFetchr()
    private val mutableSearchTerm = MutableLiveData<String>()

    init {
        mutableSearchTerm.value = "planets"

        galleryItemLiveData = FlickrFetchr().searchPhotos("planets")
                Transformations.switchMap(mutableSearchTerm) { searchTerm ->
                    flickrFetchr.searchPhotos(searchTerm)
                }
    }

    fun fetchPhotos(query: String = "") {
        mutableSearchTerm.value = query
    }
}
```

Every time the search value changes, the gallery item list should change to reflect the new results. Since both the search term and gallery item lists are wrapped in **LiveData**, you use **Transformations.switchMap(trigger: LiveData<X>, transformFunction: Function<X, LiveData<Y>>)** to implement this relationship. (If you need to brush up on **LiveData** transformations, see Chapter 12.)

You also stash an instance of **FlickrFetchr** in a property. This way, you only create an instance of **FlickrFetchr** once in the lifetime of the **ViewModel** instance. Reusing the same **FlickrFetchr** instance avoids the unnecessary overhead of re-creating a **Retrofit** and **FlickrApi** instance every time the app performs a search. This means a speedier app for your user.

Next, update **PhotoGalleryFragment** to change **PhotoGalleryViewModel**'s search term value whenever the user submits a new query through the **SearchView**. Fortunately, the **SearchView.OnQueryTextListener** interface provides a way to receive a callback when a query is submitted.

Update **onCreateOptionsMenu(…)** to add a **SearchView.OnQueryTextListener** to your **SearchView**.

## Listing 26.10 Logging **SearchView.OnQueryTextListener** events (PhotoGalleryFragment.kt)

```kotlin
class PhotoGalleryFragment : Fragment() {
    ...
    override fun onCreateOptionsMenu(menu: Menu, inflater: MenuInflater) {
        super.onCreateOptionsMenu(menu, inflater)
        inflater.inflate(R.menu.fragment_photo_gallery, menu)

        val searchItem: MenuItem = menu.findItem(R.id.menu_item_search)
        val searchView = searchItem.actionView as SearchView

        searchView.apply {

            setOnQueryTextListener(object : SearchView.OnQueryTextListener {
                override fun onQueryTextSubmit(queryText: String): Boolean {
                    Log.d(TAG, "QueryTextSubmit: $queryText")
                    photoGalleryViewModel.fetchPhotos(queryText)
                    return true
                }

                override fun onQueryTextChange(queryText: String): Boolean {
                    Log.d(TAG, "QueryTextChange: $queryText")
                    return false
                }
            })
        }
    }
    ...
}
```

When importing **SearchView**, select the androidx.appcompat.widget.SearchView option from the choices presented.

In **onCreateOptionsMenu(…)**, you pull the **MenuItem** representing the search box from the menu and store it in searchItem. Then you pull the **SearchView** object from searchItem using **getActionView()**.

Once you have a reference to the **SearchView**, you are able to set a **SearchView.OnQueryTextListener** using **setOnQueryTextListener(…)**. You must override two functions in the **SearchView.OnQueryTextListener** implementation: **onQueryTextSubmit(String)** and **onQueryTextChange(String)**.

The **onQueryTextChange(String)** callback is executed any time text in the **SearchView** text box changes. This means that it is called every time a single character changes. You will not do anything inside this callback for this app except log the input string and return false. Returning false indicates to the system that your callback override did not handle the text change. This cues the system to perform **SearchView**'s default action (which is to show relevant suggestions, if available).

The **onQueryTextSubmit(String)** callback is executed when the user submits a query. The query the user submitted is passed as input. Returning true signifies to the system that the search request has been handled. This callback is where you call into **PhotoGalleryViewModel** to trigger the photo download for your search query.

Run your app and submit a query. You should see log statements reflecting the execution of your **SearchView.OnQueryTextListener** callback functions. You should also see the images displayed change based on the search term you enter (Figure 26.3).

Figure 26.3  Working **SearchView**

Note that if you use the hardware keyboard to submit your search query on an emulator (versus the emulator's onscreen keyboard), you may see the search executed two times, one after the other. This is because there is a small bug in **SearchView**. You can ignore this behavior because it is a side effect of using the emulator and will not affect your app when it runs on a real Android device.

# Simple Persistence with SharedPreferences

In your app, there will only be one active query at a time. **PhotoGalleryViewModel** persists the query for the user's perceived life of the fragment. But the query should also be persisted between restarts of the app (even if the user turns off the device).

You will achieve this using *shared preferences*. Any time the user submits a query, you will write the search term to shared preferences, overwriting whatever query was there before. When the application first launches, you will pull the stored query from shared preferences and use it to execute a Flickr search.

Shared preferences are files on the filesystem that you read and edit using the **SharedPreferences** class. An instance of **SharedPreferences** acts like a key-value store, much like **Bundle**, except that it is backed by persistent storage. The keys are strings, and the values are atomic data types. If you look at them, you will see that the files are simple XML, but **SharedPreferences** makes it easy to ignore that implementation detail.

By the way, shared preferences files are stored in your application's sandbox, so you should not store sensitive information (like passwords) there.

Add a new file named QueryPreferences.kt to serve as a convenient interface for reading and writing the query in the shared preferences.

## Listing 26.11 Adding an object to manage a stored query (QueryPreferences.kt)

```kotlin
private const val PREF_SEARCH_QUERY = "searchQuery"

object QueryPreferences {

    fun getStoredQuery(context: Context): String {
        val prefs = PreferenceManager.getDefaultSharedPreferences(context)
        return prefs.getString(PREF_SEARCH_QUERY, "")!!
    }

    fun setStoredQuery(context: Context, query: String) {
        PreferenceManager.getDefaultSharedPreferences(context)
                .edit()
                .putString(PREF_SEARCH_QUERY, query)
                .apply()
    }
}
```

Your app only ever needs one instance of **QueryPreferences**, which can be shared across all other components. Because of this, you use the `object` keyword (instead of `class`) to specify that **QueryPreferences** is a singleton. This enforces your intention that only one instance will be created in your app. It also allows you to access the functions in the object using `ClassName.functionName(…)` syntax (as you will see shortly).

PREF_SEARCH_QUERY is used as the key for the query preference. You will use this key any time you read or write the query value.

**PreferenceManager.getDefaultSharedPreferences(Context)** returns an instance with a default name and private permissions (so that the preferences are only available from within your application). To get a specific instance of **SharedPreferences**, you can use the

`Context.getSharedPreferences(String, Int)` function. However, in practice, you will often not care too much about the specific instance, just that it is shared across the entire app.

The `getStoredQuery(Context)` function returns the query value stored in shared preferences. It does so by first acquiring the default **SharedPreferences** for the given context. (Because **QueryPreferences** does not have a **Context** of its own, the calling component will have to pass its context as input.)

Getting a value you previously stored is as simple as calling **SharedPreferences.getString(…)**, **SharedPreferences.getInt(…)**, or whichever function is appropriate for your data type. The second input to **SharedPreferences.getString(String, String)** specifies the default return value that should be used if there is no entry for the PREF_SEARCH_QUERY key.

The return type for **SharedPreferences.getString(…)** is defined as a nullable String because the compiler cannot guarantee that the value associated with PREF_SEARCH_QUERY exists and that it is not null. But you know that you never store a null value for PREF_SEARCH_QUERY – and you supply an empty String as the default value in cases where **setStoredQuery(context: Context, query: String)** has not yet been called. So it is safe to use the non-null assertion operator (!!) here without a try/catch block around it.

The **setStoredQuery(Context)** function writes the input query to the default shared preferences for the given context. In **QueryPreferences**, you call **SharedPreferences.edit()** to get an instance of **SharedPreferences.Editor**. This is the class you use to stash values in your **SharedPreferences**. It allows you to group sets of changes together in transactions, much like you do with **FragmentTransaction**. If you have a lot of changes, this will allow you to group them together into a single storage write operation.

Once you are done making all of your changes, you call **apply()** on your editor to make them visible to other users of the **SharedPreferences** file. The **apply()** function makes the change in memory immediately and then does the actual file writing on a background thread.

**QueryPreferences** is your entire persistence engine for PhotoGallery.

Now that you have a way to easily store and access the user's most recent query, update **PhotoGalleryViewModel** to read and write the query from shared preferences as necessary. Read the query when the **ViewModel** is first created and use the value to initialize mutableSearchTerm. Write the query whenever mutableSearchTerm is changed.

## Listing 26.12  Persisting query in shared preferences (PhotoGalleryViewModel.kt)

```
class PhotoGalleryViewModel : ViewModel() {
class PhotoGalleryViewModel(private val app: Application) : AndroidViewModel(app) {
    ...
    init {
        mutableSearchTerm.value = "planets"QueryPreferences.getStoredQuery(app)
        ...
    }

    fun fetchPhotos(query: String = "") {
        QueryPreferences.setStoredQuery(app, query)
        mutableSearchTerm.value = query
    }
}
```

Your **ViewModel** needs a context to use the **QueryPreferences** functions. Changing the parent class of **PhotoGalleryViewModel** from **ViewModel** to **AndroidViewModel** grants **PhotoGalleryViewModel** access to the application context. It is safe for **PhotoGalleryViewModel** to have a reference to the application context, because the app context outlives the **PhotoGalleryViewModel**.

Next, clear the stored query (set it to "") when the user selects the Clear Search item from the overflow menu.

## Listing 26.13 Clearing a stored query (PhotoGalleryFragment.kt)

```
class PhotoGalleryFragment : Fragment() {
    ...
    override fun onCreateOptionsMenu(menu: Menu, inflater: MenuInflater) {
        ...
    }

    override fun onOptionsItemSelected(item: MenuItem): Boolean {
        return when (item.itemId) {
            R.id.menu_item_clear -> {
                photoGalleryViewModel.fetchPhotos("")
                true
            }
            else -> super.onOptionsItemSelected(item)
        }
    }
    ...
}
```

Last, but not least, update **PhotoGalleryViewModel** to fetch interesting photos when the query is cleared, rather than searching based on an empty search term.

## Listing 26.14 Fetching interesting photos when the query is blank (PhotoGalleryViewModel.kt)

```
class PhotoGalleryViewModel(private val app: Application) : AndroidViewModel(app) {
    ...
    init {

        mutableSearchTerm.value = QueryPreferences.getStoredQuery(app)

        galleryItemLiveData =
                Transformations.switchMap(mutableSearchTerm) { searchTerm ->
                    if (searchTerm.isBlank()) {
                        flickrFetchr.fetchPhotos()
                    } else {
                        flickrFetchr.searchPhotos(searchTerm)
                    }
                }
    }
    ...
}
```

Search should now work like a charm. Run PhotoGallery and try searching for something fun like "unicycle." See what results you get. Then fully exit out of the app using the Back button. Heck, even reboot your phone. When you relaunch your app, you should see the results for the same search term.

# Polishing Your App

For a little bit of polish, pre-populate the search text box with the saved query when the user presses the search icon to expand the search view.

First, add a computed property to **PhotoGalleryViewModel** to expose the search term the UI is currently displaying results for.

### Listing 26.15  Exposing the search term from **PhotoGalleryViewModel** (PhotoGalleryViewModel.java)

```
class PhotoGalleryViewModel(private val app: Application) : AndroidViewModel(app) {
    ...
    private val mutableSearchTerm = MutableLiveData<String>()

    val searchTerm: String
        get() = mutableSearchTerm.value ?: ""

    init {
        ...
    }
    ...
}
```

**SearchView**'s **View.OnClickListener.onClick()** function is called when the user presses the search icon. Hook into this callback and set the **SearchView**'s query text when the view is expanded.

### Listing 26.16  Pre-populating **SearchView** (PhotoGalleryFragment.java)

```
class PhotoGalleryFragment : Fragment() {
    ...
    override fun onCreateOptionsMenu(menu: Menu, inflater: MenuInflater) {
        ...
        searchView.apply {

            setOnQueryTextListener(object : SearchView.OnQueryTextListener {
                ...
            })

            setOnSearchClickListener {
                searchView.setQuery(photoGalleryViewModel.searchTerm, false)
            }
        }
    }
    ...
}
```

Run your app and play around with submitting a few searches. Revel at the polish your last bit of code added. Of course, there is always more polish you could add...

# Editing SharedPreferences with Android KTX

Jetpack includes the Android KTX foundation library. Android KTX is a set of Kotlin extensions that allows you to leverage Kotlin language features when writing code that relies on Android APIs written in Java. Using Android KTX does not change the functionality of the existing Java APIs. But it does help you keep your Kotlin code idiomatic.

As of this writing, Android KTX only includes extensions for a subset of Android Java APIs. See the Android KTX documentation (developer.android.com/kotlin/ktx) for a list of available extension modules. However, the core Android KTX module does include an extension for editing shared preferences.

Update **QueryPreferences** to use Android KTX. First, add the core Android KTX dependency to your app module's build.gradle file.

### Listing 26.17  Adding core-ktx dependency (app/build.gradle)

```
dependencies {
    implementation fileTree(dir: 'libs', include: ['*.jar'])
    implementation"org.jetbrains.kotlin:kotlin-stdlib-jdk7:$kotlin_version"
    implementation 'androidx.core:core-ktx:1.0.0'
    ...
}
```

Next, update **QueryPreferences.setStoredQuery(…)** to use Android KTX.

### Listing 26.18  Using Android KTX (QueryPreferences.kt)

```
object QueryPreferences {
    ...
    fun setStoredQuery(context: Context, query: String) {
        PreferenceManager.getDefaultSharedPreferences(context)
            .edit() {
            .putString(PREF_SEARCH_QUERY, query)
            .apply()
            }
    }
}
```

**SharedPreferences.edit(commit: Boolean = false, action: Editor.() -> Unit)** is an extension function in core-ktx. If your code has an error, check to make sure you added an import statement for androidx.core.content.edit.

You specify the edits you want to make in the lambda argument you pass to **SharedPreferences.Editor**. Here, you write a single string using **android.content.SharedPreferences.Editor.putString(…)**.

You remove the explicit call to **SharedPreferences.Editor.apply()** because the **edit** extension function calls **apply()** for you by default. You can override this default behavior by passing true as an argument to the **edit** extension function. Doing so causes **edit** to call **SharedPreferences.Editor.commit()** instead of **SharedPreferences.Editor.apply()**.

Run your app and ensure that the functionality of PhotoGallery was not affected. Your app should behave as it did before you made the Android KTX edits. But now your shared preferences code is a shade more idiomatic. Kotlin lovers, rejoice.

# Challenge: Polishing Your App Some More

You may notice that when you submit a query there is a bit of a lag before the `RecyclerView` starts to refresh. For this challenge, make the response to the user's query submission feel more immediate. As soon as a query is submitted, hide the soft keyboard and collapse the `SearchView`.

As an extra challenge, clear the contents of the `RecyclerView` and display a loading indicator (indeterminate progress bar) as soon as a query is submitted. Get rid of the loading indicator once the JSON data has been fully downloaded. In other words, the loading indicator should not show once your code moves on to downloading individual images.

# 27

# WorkManager

PhotoGallery can now download interesting images from Flickr, find images based on a user's search query, and remember the query when the user leaves the app. In this chapter, you will add functionality to poll Flickr and determine whether there are new photos the user has not seen yet.

This work will happen in the background, meaning it will execute even if the user is not actively using your app. If there are new photos, the app will display a notification prompting the user to return to the app and see the new content.

Tools from the Jetpack WorkManager architecture component library will handle the periodic work of checking Flickr for new photos. You will create a **Worker** class to perform the actual work, then schedule it to execute on an interval. When new photos are found, you will post a **Notification** to the user with the **NotificationManager**.

## Creating a Worker

The **Worker** class is where you will put the logic you want to perform in the background. Once your worker is in place, you will create a **WorkRequest** that tells the system when you would like your work to execute.

Before you can add your worker, you first need to add the appropriate dependency in your app/ build.gradle file.

### Listing 27.1 Adding the WorkManager dependency (app/build.gradle)

```
dependencies {
    ...
    implementation 'androidx.recyclerview:recyclerview:1.0.0'
    implementation "android.arch.work:work-runtime:1.0.1"
    ...
}
```

Sync the project to download the dependency.

With your new library in place, move on to creating your **Worker**. Create a new class called **PollWorker** that extends the **Worker** base class. Your **PollWorker** will need two parameters, a **Context** and a **WorkerParameters** object. Both of these will be passed to the superclass constructor. For now, override the **doWork()** function and log a message to the console.

## Listing 27.2  Creating the worker (PollWorker.kt)

```kotlin
private const val TAG = "PollWorker"

class PollWorker(val context: Context, workerParams: WorkerParameters)
    : Worker(context, workerParams) {

    override fun doWork(): Result {
        Log.i(TAG, "Work request triggered")
        return Result.success()
    }
}
```

The **doWork()** function is called from a background thread, so you can do any long-running tasks you need to there. The return values for the function indicate the status of your operation. In this case, you return success, since the function just prints a log to the console.

**doWork()** can return a failure result if the work cannot be completed. In that case, the work request would not run again. It can also return a retry result if a temporary error was encountered and you want the work to run again in the future.

The **PollWorker** only knows how to *execute* the background work. You need another component to schedule the work.

# Scheduling Work

To schedule a **Worker** to execute, you need a **WorkRequest**. The **WorkRequest** class itself is abstract, so you need to use one of its subclasses depending on the type of work you need to execute. If you have something that only needs to execute once, use a **OneTimeWorkRequest**. If your work is something that must execute periodically, use a **PeriodicWorkRequest**.

For now, you are going to use the **OneTimeWorkRequest**. This will let you verify that your **PollWorker** is functioning correctly and learn more about creating and controlling the requests. Later you will update your app to use a **PeriodicWorkRequest**.

Open PhotoGalleryFragment.kt, create a work request, and schedule it for execution.

### Listing 27.3 Scheduling a **WorkRequest** (PhotoGalleryFragment.kt)

```
class PhotoGalleryFragment : Fragment() {
    ...
    override fun onCreate(savedInstanceState: Bundle?) {
        ...
        lifecycle.addObserver(thumbnailDownloader.fragmentLifecycleObserver)

        val workRequest = OneTimeWorkRequest
            .Builder(PollWorker::class.java)
            .build()
        WorkManager.getInstance()
            .enqueue(workRequest)
    }
    ...
}
```

The **OneTimeWorkRequest** uses a builder to construct an instance. You provide the **Worker** class to the builder that the work request will fire. Once your work request is ready, you need to schedule it with the **WorkManager** class. You call the **getInstance()** function to access the **WorkManager**, then call **enqueue(…)** with the work request as a parameter. This will schedule your work request to execute based on the request type and any constraints you add to the request.

Run your app and search for PollWorker in Logcat. You should see your log statement soon after your app starts up (Figure 27.1).

### Figure 27.1 Work log

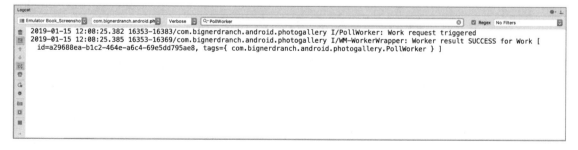

In many cases, the work you want to execute in the background is tied to the network. Maybe you are polling for new information the user has not seen yet, or you are pushing updates from the local database to save them on a remote server. While this work is important, you should make sure you are not needlessly using costly data. The best time for these requests is when the device is connected to an unmetered network.

You can use the **Constraints** class to add this information to your work requests. With this class, you can require certain conditions be met before your work can execute. Requiring a certain network type is one case. You can also require things like a sufficiently charged battery or that the device be charging.

Edit your **OneTimeWorkRequest** in **PhotoGalleryFragment** to add constraints to the request.

## Listing 27.4  Adding work constraints (PhotoGalleryFragment.kt)

```
class PhotoGalleryFragment : Fragment() {
    ...
    override fun onCreate(savedInstanceState: Bundle?) {
        ...
        lifecycle.addObserver(thumbnailDownloader.fragmentLifecycleObserver)

        val constraints = Constraints.Builder()
            .setRequiredNetworkType(NetworkType.UNMETERED)
            .build()
        val workRequest = OneTimeWorkRequest
            .Builder(PollWorker::class.java)
            .setConstraints(constraints)
            .build()
        WorkManager.getInstance()
            .enqueue(workRequest)
    }
    ...
}
```

Similar to the work request, the **Constraints** object uses a builder to configure a new instance. In this case, you specify that the device must be on an unmetered network for the work request to execute.

To test this functionality, you will need to simulate different network types on your emulator. By default, an emulator connects to a simulated WiFi network. Since WiFi is an unmetered network, if you run your app now, with the constraints in place, you should see the log message from your **PollWorker**.

To verify that the work request does not execute when the device is on a metered network, you will need to modify the network settings for your emulator. Quit PhotoGallery and pull down on the notification shade to expose the device's Quick Settings. Swiping down a second time once the notification shade is open exposes a larger, more descriptive version of the Quick Settings (Figure 27.2). It usually does not matter which version you use, but some older versions of Android require a double swipe to access network settings.

Figure 27.2 Accessing Quick Settings

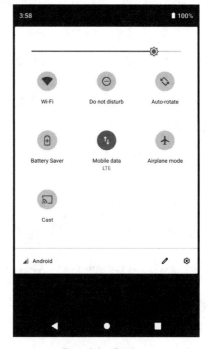

**Single Swipe**                          **Double Swipe**

Press the WiFi icon in the Quick Settings to disable the WiFi network and force the emulator to use its (simulated) cellular network, which is metered.

With the WiFi disabled, run PhotoGallery and verify that the log from `PollWorker` does not appear. Before moving on, return to the Quick Settings and re-enable the WiFi network.

# Checking for New Photos

Now that your worker is executing, you can add the logic to check for new photos. There are a couple pieces needed for this functionality. You will first need a way to save the ID of the most recent photo the user has seen, then you will need to update your worker class to pull the new photos and compare the stored ID with the newest one from the server. Your worker will also handle picking the request type if there is an existing search query.

The first change you will make is to update **QueryPreferences** to store and retrieve the latest photo ID from shared preferences.

## Listing 27.5  Saving the latest photo ID (QueryPreference.kt)

```
private const val PREF_SEARCH_QUERY = "searchQuery"
private const val PREF_LAST_RESULT_ID = "lastResultId"

object QueryPreferences {
    ...
    fun setStoredQuery(context: Context, query: String) {
        ...
    }

    fun getLastResultId(context: Context): String {
        return PreferenceManager.getDefaultSharedPreferences(context)
            .getString(PREF_LAST_RESULT_ID, "")!!
    }

    fun setLastResultId(context: Context, lastResultId: String) {
        PreferenceManager.getDefaultSharedPreferences(context).edit {
            putString(PREF_LAST_RESULT_ID, lastResultId)
        }
    }
}
```

As you did in Chapter 26, you use the non-null assertion operator (!!) when retrieving the last result ID from the default **SharedPreferences** instance in **getLastResultId(…)** because the String returned from **getString(PREF_LAST_RESULT_ID, "")** should never be null.

With the ability to store photo IDs in place, you can move on to polling for new photos. You will need to update **FlickrFetchr** to allow your **PollWorker** to perform synchronous web requests. Both the **fetchPhotos()** and **searchPhotos()** functions perform the requests asynchronously and deliver the results using **LiveData**. Since your **PollWorker** executes on a background thread, you do not need **FlickrFetchr** to do the request for you. Update **FlickrFetchr** to expose the Retrofit **Call** objects for your worker to use.

## Listing 27.6 Exposing **Call** objects (FlickrFetchr.kt)

```
class FlickrFetchr {
    ...
    fun fetchPhotosRequest(): Call<FlickrResponse> {
        return flickrApi.fetchPhotos()
    }

    fun fetchPhotos(): LiveData<List<GalleryItem>> {
        return fetchPhotoMetadata(flickrApi.fetchPhotos())
        return fetchPhotoMetadata(fetchPhotosRequest())
    }

    fun searchPhotosRequest(query: String): Call<FlickrResponse> {
        return flickrApi.searchPhotos(query)
    }

    fun searchPhotos(query: String): LiveData<List<GalleryItem>> {
        return fetchPhotoMetadata(flickrApi.searchPhotos(query))
        return fetchPhotoMetadata(searchPhotosRequest(query))
    }
    ...
}
```

With the **Call** objects exposed in **FlickrFetchr**, you can add the queries to **PollWorker**. You will need to determine which request **PollWorker** should make based on whether there is a saved search query. Once you fetch the most up-to-date photos, you will check whether the most recent photo ID matches the one you have saved. If they do not match, then you will show the user a notification.

Start by pulling out the current search query and latest photo ID from **QueryPreferences**. If there is no search query, fetch the regular photos. If there is a search query, perform the search request. For safety, use an empty list if either request fails to return any photos. Delete the log statement while you are at it, since it is no longer needed.

## Listing 27.7 Fetching recent photos (PollWorker.kt)

```
class PollWorker(val context: Context, workerParameters: WorkerParameters)
    : Worker(context, workerParameters) {

    override fun doWork(): Result {
        Log.i(TAG, "Work request triggered")
        val query = QueryPreferences.getStoredQuery(context)
        val lastResultId = QueryPreferences.getLastResultId(context)
        val items: List<GalleryItem> = if (query.isEmpty()) {
            FlickrFetchr().fetchPhotosRequest()
                .execute()
                .body()
                ?.photos
                ?.galleryItems
        } else {
            FlickrFetchr().searchPhotosRequest(query)
                .execute()
                .body()
                ?.photos
                ?.galleryItems
        } ?: emptyList()
        return Result.success()
    }
}
```

Next, return from the **doWork()** function if the items list is empty. Otherwise, check to see whether there are new photos by comparing the ID of the first item in the list with the lastResultId property. Add log statements so you can see the output of your worker. Also, update the last result ID in **QueryPreferences** if you found a new result.

## Listing 27.8  Checking for new photos (PollWorker.kt)

```kotlin
class PollWorker(val context: Context, workerParameters: WorkerParameters)
    : Worker(context, workerParameters) {

    override fun doWork(): Result {
        val query = QueryPreferences.getStoredQuery(context)
        val lastResultId = QueryPreferences.getLastResultId(context)
        val items: List<GalleryItem> = if (query.isEmpty()) {
            ...
        } else {
            ...
        }

        if (items.isEmpty()) {
            return Result.success()
        }

        val resultId = items.first().id
        if (resultId == lastResultId) {
            Log.i(TAG, "Got an old result: $resultId")
        } else {
            Log.i(TAG, "Got a new result: $resultId")
            QueryPreferences.setLastResultId(context, resultId)
        }

        return Result.success()
    }
}
```

Run your app on a device or emulator. The first time you run it, there will not be a last result ID saved in **QueryPreferences**, so you should see the log statement indicating **PollWorker** found a new result. If you quickly run the app again, you should see that your worker finds the same ID (Figure 27.3). (Make sure your Logcat is set to No Filters, as shown, and not Show only selected application.)

## Figure 27.3  Finding new and old results

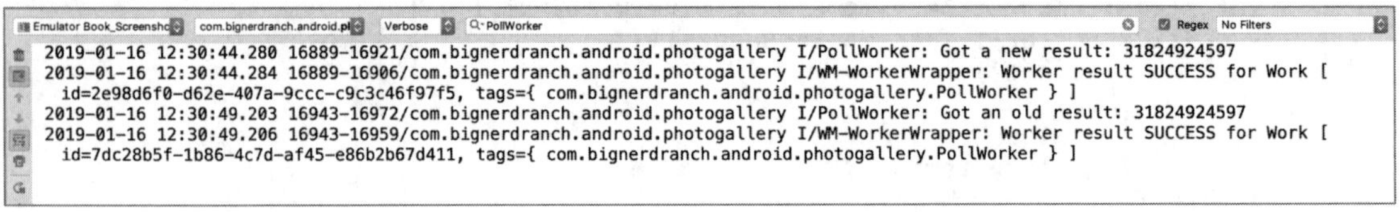

```
📱 Emulator Book_Screensho 🔻  com.bignerdranch.android.p 🔻  Verbose 🔻  Q· PollWorker                                              ☺  ☑ Regex  No Filters                    🔻
2019-01-16 12:30:44.280 16889-16921/com.bignerdranch.android.photogallery I/PollWorker: Got a new result: 31824924597
2019-01-16 12:30:44.284 16889-16906/com.bignerdranch.android.photogallery I/WM-WorkerWrapper: Worker result SUCCESS for Work [
   id=2e98d6f0-d62e-407a-9ccc-c9c3c46f97f5, tags={ com.bignerdranch.android.photogallery.PollWorker } ]
2019-01-16 12:30:49.203 16943-16972/com.bignerdranch.android.photogallery I/PollWorker: Got an old result: 31824924597
2019-01-16 12:30:49.206 16943-16959/com.bignerdranch.android.photogallery I/WM-WorkerWrapper: Worker result SUCCESS for Work [
   id=7dc28b5f-1b86-4c7d-af45-e86b2b67d411, tags={ com.bignerdranch.android.photogallery.PollWorker } ]
```

# Notifying the User

Your worker is now running and checking for new photos in the background, but the user does not know anything about it. When PhotoGallery finds new photos the user has not seen yet, it should prompt the user to open the app and see the new content.

When your app needs to communicate something to the user, the proper tool is almost always a *notification*. Notifications are items that appear in the notifications drawer, which the user can access by dragging down from the top of the screen.

Before you can create notifications on Android devices running Android Oreo (API level 26) and higher, you must create a `Channel`. A `Channel` categorizes notifications and gives the user fine-grained control over notification preferences. Rather than only having the option to turn off notifications for your entire app, the user can choose to turn off certain categories of notifications within your app. The user can also customize muting, vibration, and other notification settings channel by channel.

For example, suppose you wanted PhotoGallery to send three categories of notifications when new cute animal pictures were fetched: New Kitten Pics, New Puppy Pics, and Totes Adorbs! (for all adorable animal pictures, regardless of species). You would create three channels, one for each of the notification categories, and the user could configure them independently (Figure 27.4).

Figure 27.4  Fine-grained notification configuration for channels

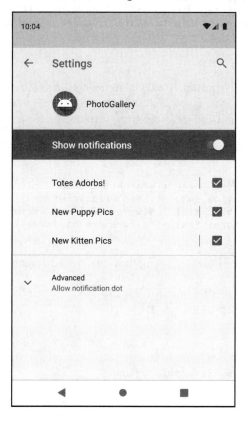

Your application must create at least one channel to support Android Oreo and higher. There is no documented upper limit on the number of channels an app can create. But be reasonable – keep the number small and meaningful for the user. Remember that the goal is to allow the user to configure notifications in your app. Adding too many channels can ultimately confuse the user and make for a poor user experience.

Add a new class named **PhotoGalleryApplication**. Extend **Application** and override **Application.onCreate()** to create and add a channel if the device is running Android Oreo or higher.

## Listing 27.9  Creating a notification channel (PhotoGalleryApplication.kt)

```kotlin
const val NOTIFICATION_CHANNEL_ID = "flickr_poll"

class PhotoGalleryApplication : Application() {

    override fun onCreate() {
        super.onCreate()
        if (Build.VERSION.SDK_INT >= Build.VERSION_CODES.O) {
            val name = getString(R.string.notification_channel_name)
            val importance = NotificationManager.IMPORTANCE_DEFAULT
            val channel =
                    NotificationChannel(NOTIFICATION_CHANNEL_ID, name, importance)
            val notificationManager: NotificationManager =
                    getSystemService(NotificationManager::class.java)
            notificationManager.createNotificationChannel(channel)
        }
    }
}
```

The channel name is a user-facing string, displayed in the notification settings screen for your app (shown in Figure 27.4). Add a string resource to res/values/strings.xml to store the channel name. While you are there, go ahead and add the other strings needed for your notification.

## Listing 27.10  Adding strings (res/values/strings.xml)

```xml
<resources>
    <string name="clear_search">Clear Search</string>
    <string name="notification_channel_name">FlickrFetchr</string>
    <string name="new_pictures_title">New PhotoGallery Pictures</string>
    <string name="new_pictures_text">You have new pictures in PhotoGallery.</string>
</resources>
```

Next, update the manifest to point to the new application class you created.

## Listing 27.11  Updating the application tag in the manifest (manifests/AndroidManifest.xml)

```xml
<manifest ... >
...
  <application
      android:name=".PhotoGalleryApplication"
      android:allowBackup="true"
      ... >

  </application>
</manifest>
```

To post a notification, you need to create a **Notification** object. **Notification**s are created by using a builder object, much like the **AlertDialog** that you used in Chapter 13. At a minimum, your **Notification** should have:

- an *icon* to show in the status bar

- a *view* to show in the notification drawer to represent the notification itself

- a *PendingIntent* to fire when the user presses the notification in the drawer

- a *NotificationChannel* to apply styling and provide user control over the notification

You will also add ticker text to the notification. This text does not display when the notification shows, but it is sent to the accessibility services so things like screen readers can notify users with visual impairments.

Once you have created a **Notification** object, you can post it by calling **notify(Int, Notification)** on the **NotificationManager** system service. The Int is the ID of the notification from your app.

First you need to add some plumbing code, shown in Listing 27.12. Open PhotoGalleryActivity.kt and add a **newIntent(Context)** function. This function will return an **Intent** instance that can be used to start **PhotoGalleryActivity**. (Eventually, **PollWorker** will call **PhotoGalleryActivity.newIntent(…)**, wrap the resulting intent in a **PendingIntent**, and set that **PendingIntent** on a notification.)

## Listing 27.12 Adding **newIntent(…)** to **PhotoGalleryActivity** (PhotoGalleryActivity.kt)

```kotlin
class PhotoGalleryActivity : AppCompatActivity() {

    override fun onCreate(savedInstanceState: Bundle?) {
        ...
    }

    companion object {
        fun newIntent(context: Context): Intent {
            return Intent(context, PhotoGalleryActivity::class.java)
        }
    }
}
```

Now make **PollWorker** notify the user that a new result is ready by creating a **Notification** and calling **NotificationManager.notify(Int, Notification)**.

## Listing 27.13  Adding a notification (PollWorker.kt)

```
class PollWorker(val context: Context, workerParameters: WorkerParameters)
    : Worker(context, workerParameters) {

    override fun doWork(): Result {
        ...
        val resultId = items.first().id
        if (resultId == lastResultId) {
            Log.i(TAG, "Got an old result: $resultId")
        } else {
            Log.i(TAG, "Got a new result: $resultId")
            QueryPreferences.setLastResultId(context, resultId)

            val intent = PhotoGalleryActivity.newIntent(context)
            val pendingIntent = PendingIntent.getActivity(context, 0, intent, 0)

            val resources = context.resources
            val notification = NotificationCompat
                .Builder(context, NOTIFICATION_CHANNEL_ID)
                .setTicker(resources.getString(R.string.new_pictures_title))
                .setSmallIcon(android.R.drawable.ic_menu_report_image)
                .setContentTitle(resources.getString(R.string.new_pictures_title))
                .setContentText(resources.getString(R.string.new_pictures_text))
                .setContentIntent(pendingIntent)
                .setAutoCancel(true)
                .build()

            val notificationManager = NotificationManagerCompat.from(context)
            notificationManager.notify(0, notification)
        }

        return Result.success()
    }
}
```

Let's go over this from top to bottom.

You use the **NotificationCompat** class to easily support notifications on both pre-Oreo and Oreo-and-above devices. **NotificationCompat.Builder** accepts a channel ID and uses the ID to set the notification's channel if the user is running Oreo or above. If the user is running a pre-Oreo version of Android, **NotificationCompat.Builder** ignores the channel. (Note that the channel ID you pass here comes from the NOTIFICATION_CHANNEL_ID constant you added to **PhotoGalleryApplication**.)

In Listing 27.9, you checked the build version SDK before you created the channel, because there is no AppCompat API for creating a channel. You do not need to do that here, because AppCompat's **NotificationCompat** does the grunt work of checking the build version for you, keeping your code clean and spiffy. This is one reason you should use an AppCompat version of the Android APIs whenever available.

You configure the ticker text and small icon by calling **setTicker(CharSequence)** and **setSmallIcon(Int)**. (The icon resource you are using is provided as part of the Android framework, denoted by the package name qualifier android in android.R.drawable.ic_menu_report_image, so you do not have to pull the icon image into your resource folder.)

After that, you configure the appearance of your **Notification** in the drawer itself. It is possible to create a completely custom look and feel, but it is easier to use the standard look for a notification, which features an icon, a title, and a text area. It will use the value from **setSmallIcon(Int)** for the icon. To set the title and text, you call **setContentTitle(CharSequence)** and **setContentText(CharSequence)**, respectively.

Next, you specify what happens when the user presses your **Notification**. This is done using a **PendingIntent** object. The **PendingIntent** you pass into **setContentIntent(PendingIntent)** will be fired when the user presses your **Notification** in the drawer. Calling **setAutoCancel(true)** tweaks that behavior a little bit: The notification will also be deleted from the notification drawer when the user presses it.

Finally, you get an instance of **NotificationManager** from the current context (NotificationManagerCompat.from) and call **NotificationManager.notify(…)** to post your notification.

The integer parameter you pass to **notify(…)** is an identifier for your notification. It should be unique across your application, but it is reusable. A notification will replace another notification with the same ID that is still in the notification drawer. If there is no existing notification with the ID, the system will show a new notification. This is how you would implement a progress bar or other dynamic visuals.

And that is it. Run your app, and you should eventually see a notification icon appear in the status bar (Figure 27.5). (You will want to clear any search terms to speed things along.)

## Figure 27.5 New photos notification

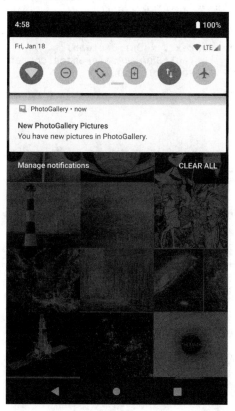

# Providing User Control over Polling

Some users may not want your app to run in the background. An important control to provide users is the ability to enable and disable background polling.

For PhotoGallery, you will add a menu item to the toolbar that will toggle your worker when selected. You will also update your work request to run your worker periodically instead of just once.

To toggle your worker, you first need to determine whether the worker is currently running. To do this, supplement your **QueryPreferences** to store a flag indicating if the worker is enabled.

### Listing 27.14  Saving **Worker** state (QueryPreferences.kt)

```
private const val PREF_SEARCH_QUERY = "searchQuery"
private const val PREF_LAST_RESULT_ID = "lastResultId"
private const val PREF_IS_POLLING = "isPolling"

object QueryPreferences {
    ...
    fun setLastResultId(context: Context, lastResultId: String) {
        ...
    }

    fun isPolling(context: Context): Boolean {
        return PreferenceManager.getDefaultSharedPreferences(context)
            .getBoolean(PREF_IS_POLLING, false)
    }

    fun setPolling(context: Context, isOn: Boolean) {
        PreferenceManager.getDefaultSharedPreferences(context).edit {
            putBoolean(PREF_IS_POLLING, isOn)
        }
    }
}
```

Next, add the string resources your options menu item needs. You will need two strings, one to prompt the user to enable polling and one to prompt them to disable it.

### Listing 27.15  Adding poll-toggling resources (res/values/strings.xml)

```
<resources>
    ...
    <string name="new_pictures_text">You have new pictures in PhotoGallery.</string>
    <string name="start_polling">Start polling</string>
    <string name="stop_polling">Stop polling</string>
</resources>
```

With your strings in place, open up your res/menu/fragment_photo_gallery.xml menu file and add a new item for your polling toggle.

## Listing 27.16 Adding a poll-toggling item (res/menu/fragment_photo_gallery.xml)

```xml
<?xml version="1.0" encoding="utf-8"?>
<menu xmlns:android="http://schemas.android.com/apk/res/android"
    xmlns:app="http://schemas.android.com/apk/res-auto">
    ...
    <item android:id="@+id/menu_item_clear"
        android:title="@string/clear_search"
        app:showAsAction="never" />

    <item android:id="@+id/menu_item_toggle_polling"
        android:title="@string/start_polling"
        app:showAsAction="ifRoom|withText"/>
</menu>
```

The default text for this item is the start_polling string. You will need to update this text if the worker is already running. Open PhotoGalleryFragment.kt and update onCreateOptionsMenu(…) to check whether the worker is already running and, if so, to set the correct title text. Also, delete the OneTimeWorkRequest logic from the onCreate(…) function, since it is no longer needed.

## Listing 27.17 Setting correct menu item text (PhotoGalleryFragment.kt)

```kotlin
class PhotoGalleryFragment : Fragment() {
    ...
    override fun onCreate(savedInstanceState: Bundle?) {
        ...
        lifecycle.addObserver(thumbnailDownloader)

        val constraints = Constraints.Builder()
            .setRequiredNetworkType(NetworkType.UNMETERED)
            .build()
        val workRequest = OneTimeWorkRequest
            .Builder(PollWorker::class.java)
            .setConstraints(constraints)
            .build()
        WorkManager.getInstance()
            .enqueue(workRequest)
    }
    ...
    override fun onCreateOptionsMenu(menu: Menu, inflater: MenuInflater) {
        ...
        searchView.apply {
            ...
        }

        val toggleItem = menu.findItem(R.id.menu_item_toggle_polling)
        val isPolling = QueryPreferences.isPolling(requireContext())
        val toggleItemTitle = if (isPolling) {
            R.string.stop_polling
        } else {
            R.string.start_polling
        }
        toggleItem.setTitle(toggleItemTitle)
    }
    ...
}
```

Finally, update **onOptionsItemSelected(…)** to respond to the poll-toggling item clicks. If the worker is not running, create a new **PeriodicWorkRequest** and schedule it with the **WorkManager**. If the worker is running, stop it.

## Listing 27.18 Handling poll-toggling item clicks (PhotoGalleryFragment.kt)

```kotlin
private const val TAG = "PhotoGalleryFragment"
private const val POLL_WORK = "POLL_WORK"

class PhotoGalleryFragment : Fragment() {
    ...
    override fun onOptionsItemSelected(item: MenuItem): Boolean {
        return when (item.itemId) {
            R.id.menu_item_clear -> {
                photoGalleryViewModel.fetchPhotos("")
                true
            }
            R.id.menu_item_toggle_polling -> {
                val isPolling = QueryPreferences.isPolling(requireContext())
                if (isPolling) {
                    WorkManager.getInstance().cancelUniqueWork(POLL_WORK)
                    QueryPreferences.setPolling(requireContext(), false)
                } else {
                    val constraints = Constraints.Builder()
                        .setRequiredNetworkType(NetworkType.UNMETERED)
                        .build()
                    val periodicRequest = PeriodicWorkRequest
                        .Builder(PollWorker::class.java, 15, TimeUnit.MINUTES)
                        .setConstraints(constraints)
                        .build()
                    WorkManager.getInstance().enqueueUniquePeriodicWork(POLL_WORK,
                        ExistingPeriodicWorkPolicy.KEEP,
                        periodicRequest)
                    QueryPreferences.setPolling(requireContext(), true)
                }
                activity?.invalidateOptionsMenu()
                return true
            }
            else -> super.onOptionsItemSelected(item)
        }
    }
    ...
}
```

If you are given a choice when importing **TimeUnit**, select java.util.concurrent.TimeUnit.

Focus first on the else block you added here. If the worker is currently *not* running, then you schedule a new work request with the **WorkManager**. In this case, you are using the **PeriodicWorkRequest** class to make your worker reschedule itself on an interval. The work request uses a builder, like the **OneTimeWorkRequest** you used previously. The builder needs the worker class to run, as well as the interval it should use to execute.

If you are thinking that 15 minutes is a long time for an interval, you are right. However, if you tried to enter a smaller interval value, you would find that your worker still executes on a 15-minute interval. This is the minimum interval allowed for a **PeriodicWorkRequest** so that the system is not tied up running the same work request all the time. This saves system resources – and the user's battery life.

The **PeriodicWorkRequest** builder accepts constraints, just like the one-time request, so you can add the unmetered network requirement. When you want to schedule the work request, you use the **WorkManager** class, but this time you use the **enqueueUniquePeriodicWork(…)** function. This function takes in a String name, a policy, and your work request. The name allows you to uniquely identify the request, which is useful when you want to cancel it.

The existing work policy tells the work manager what to do if you have already scheduled a work request with a particular name. In this case you use the KEEP option, which discards your new request in favor of the one that already exists. The other option is REPLACE, which, as the name implies, will replace the existing work request with the new one.

If the worker is already running, then you need to tell the **WorkManager** to cancel the work request. In this case, you call the **cancelUniqueWork(…)** function with the "POLL_WORK" name to remove the periodic work request.

Run the application. You should see your new menu item to toggle polling. If you do not want to wait for the 15-minute interval, you can disable the polling, wait a few seconds, then enable polling to rerun the work request.

PhotoGallery can now keep the user up to date with the latest images automatically, even when the app is not running. But there is one problem: The user will get notifications any time new images arrive – even when the app is already running. This is not desirable, because it takes the user's attention away from your app. Plus, if the user presses the notification, a new instance of **PhotoGalleryActivity** will be launched and added to your app's back stack.

You will fix this in the next chapter by preventing notifications from appearing while PhotoGallery is running. In making these updates, you will learn how to listen for broadcast intents and how to handle such intents using a broadcast receiver.

# 28

# Broadcast Intents

It is annoying and redundant to both get a notification and see the results update in the screen when you are actively viewing an app. In this chapter, you will polish PhotoGallery's polling behavior by preventing notifications about new photos from appearing while the app is running.

In making these updates, you will learn how to listen for *broadcast intents* and how to handle such intents using a *broadcast receiver*. You will also dynamically send and receive broadcast intents within your app at runtime. Finally, you will use ordered broadcasts to determine whether your application is currently running in the foreground.

## Regular Intents vs Broadcast Intents

Things are happening all the time on an Android device. WiFi is going in and out of range, packages are getting installed, and phone calls and text messages are coming and going.

There may be many components on the system that need to be aware of these kinds of events so that they can react accordingly. To notify these components, Android uses a broadcast intent to tell everyone about it.

These kinds of broadcasts, which are sent from the system, are referred to as *system broadcasts*, but you can also send and receive your own *custom broadcasts*. The mechanism for receiving both system and custom broadcasts is identical, but you will only be working with custom broadcasts in this chapter.

Broadcast intents work similarly to the intents you already know and love, except that they can be received by multiple components, called broadcast receivers, at the same time (Figure 28.1).

## Figure 28.1  Regular intents vs broadcast intents

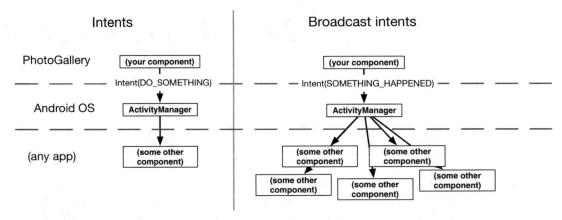

Activities and services should respond to implicit intents whenever they are used as part of a public API. When they are not part of a public API, explicit intents are almost always sufficient. Broadcast intents, on the other hand, only exist to send information to more than one listener. So while broadcast receivers *can* respond to explicit intents, they are rarely, if ever, used this way, because explicit intents can only have one receiver.

# Filtering Foreground Notifications

Your notifications work great, but they are sent even when the user already has the application open. You can use broadcast intents to change the behavior of **PollWorker** based on whether your app is in the foreground.

First, you will send a broadcast intent from your **PollWorker** whenever new photos are fetched. Next, you will register two broadcast receivers. The first receiver will be registered in your Android manifest. Whenever it receives a broadcast from **PollWorker**, it will post the notification to the user as you had done before. The second receiver will be registered dynamically so that it is only active when your application is visible to the user. Its job will be to intercept broadcasts from being delivered to the broadcast receiver in your manifest, which will prevent it from posting a notification.

It may sound unusual to use two broadcast receivers to accomplish this, but Android does not provide a mechanism to determine which activities or fragments are currently running. Since **PollWorker** cannot directly tell whether your UI is visible, you would not be able skip posting the notification using a simple if statement in **PollWorker**. Likewise, you cannot choose to conditionally send the broadcast based on whether PhotoGallery is visible, since there is not a way to determine which state your application is in. You can, however, use two receivers and set them up so that only one will react to the broadcast. That is what you will be doing.

# Sending broadcast intents

The first step is straightforward: You need to send your own broadcast intent notifying interested components that a new search results notification is ready to post. To send a broadcast intent, create an intent and pass it into **sendBroadcast(Intent)**. In this case, you will want it to broadcast an action you define, so define an action constant as well.

Update `PollWorker.kt` as shown.

## Listing 28.1 Sending a broadcast intent (`PollWorker.kt`)

```
class PollWorker(val context: Context, workerParams: WorkerParameters) :
    Worker(context, workerParams) {

    override fun doWork(): Result {
        ...
        val resultId = first().id
        if (resultId == lastResultId) {
            Log.i(TAG, "Got an old result: $resultId")
        } else {
            ...
            val notificationManager = NotificationManagerCompat.from(context)
            notificationManager.notify(0, notification)

            context.sendBroadcast(Intent(ACTION_SHOW_NOTIFICATION))
        }

        return Result.success()
    }

    companion object {
        const val ACTION_SHOW_NOTIFICATION =
            "com.bignerdranch.android.photogallery.SHOW_NOTIFICATION"
    }
}
```

# Creating and registering a standalone receiver

Although your broadcast is being sent, nobody is listening for it yet. To react to broadcasts, you will implement a **BroadcastReceiver**. There are two kinds of broadcast receivers; here you will be using a *standalone* broadcast receiver.

A standalone broadcast receiver is a receiver that is declared in the manifest. Such a receiver can be activated even if your app process is dead. Later you will learn about *dynamic* broadcast receivers, which can instead be tied to the lifecycle of a visible app component, like a fragment or activity.

Just like services and activities, broadcast receivers must be registered with the system to do anything useful. If the receiver is not registered with the system, the system will never call its **onReceive(…)** function.

Before you can register your broadcast receiver, you have to write it. Create a new Kotlin class called **NotificationReceiver** that is a subclass of **android.content.BroadcastReceiver**.

## Listing 28.2  Your first broadcast receiver (NotificationReceiver.kt)

```kotlin
private const val TAG = "NotificationReceiver"

class NotificationReceiver : BroadcastReceiver() {

    override fun onReceive(context: Context, intent: Intent) {
        Log.i(TAG, "received broadcast: ${intent.action}")
    }
}
```

A broadcast receiver is a component that receives intents, just like a service or an activity. When an intent is issued to **NotificationReceiver**, its **onReceive(…)** function will be called.

Next, open manifests/AndroidManifest.xml and hook up **NotificationReceiver** as a standalone receiver.

## Listing 28.3  Adding your receiver to the manifest (manifests/AndroidManifest.xml)

```xml
<application ... >
    <activity android:name=".PhotoGalleryActivity">
        ...
    </activity>
    <receiver android:name=".NotificationReceiver">
    </receiver>
</application>
```

To receive the broadcasts that your receiver is interested in, your receiver should also have an intent filter. This filter will behave exactly like the ones you used with implicit intents except that it will filter broadcast intents instead of regular intents. Add an intent filter to your broadcast receiver to accept intents with the SHOW_NOTIFICATION action.

## Listing 28.4  Adding an intent filter to your receiver (manifests/AndroidManifest.xml)

```xml
<receiver android:name=".NotificationReceiver">
  <intent-filter>
    <action
        android:name="com.bignerdranch.android.photogallery.SHOW_NOTIFICATION" />
  </intent-filter>
</receiver>
```

If you run PhotoGallery on a device running Android Oreo or higher after making these changes, you will not see your log. In fact, your receiver's **onReceive(…)** function will not be called at all. But on older versions of Android, your log will appear as you would expect. This is because of restrictions that newer versions of Android place on broadcasts. But have no fear – your work thus far is not in vain.

You can get around these restrictions by sending your broadcast with a permission.

# Limiting broadcasts to your app using private permissions

One issue with a broadcast like this is that anyone on the system can listen to it or trigger your receivers. You are usually not going to want either of those things to happen. Conveniently, specifying a permission on your broadcast will also make your new broadcast receiver work on newer versions of Android, so you can fix two bugs for the price of one.

You can preclude these unauthorized intrusions into your personal business by applying a custom permission to the receiver and setting the receiver's `android:exported` attribute to `"false"`. This prevents the receiver from being visible to other applications on the system. Applying a permission means only components that have requested (and been granted) permission can deliver a broadcast to the receiver.

First, declare and acquire your own permission in `AndroidManifest.xml`.

### Listing 28.5  Adding a private permission (`manifests/AndroidManifest.xml`)

```
<manifest ... >

    <permission android:name="com.bignerdranch.android.photogallery.PRIVATE"
            android:protectionLevel="signature" />

    <uses-permission android:name="android.permission.INTERNET"/>
    <uses-permission android:name="com.bignerdranch.android.photogallery.PRIVATE" />
    ...
</manifest>
```

Notice that you define a custom permission with a *protection level* of `signature`. You will learn more about protection levels in just a moment. The permission itself is a simple string, just like the intent actions, categories, and system permissions you have used. You must always acquire a permission to use it, even when you defined it yourself. Them's the rules.

Take note of the shaded constant value above, by the way. This string is the unique identifier for the custom permission, which you will use to refer to the permission elsewhere in your manifest and also from your Kotlin code when you issue a broadcast intent to the receiver. The identifier must be identical in each place. You would be wise to copy and paste it rather than typing it out by hand.

Next, apply the permission to the receiver tag and set the `exported` attribute to `"false"`.

### Listing 28.6  Applying permission and setting `exported` to `"false"` (`manifests/AndroidManifest.xml`)

```
<manifest ... >
    ...
    <application ... >
        ...
        <receiver android:name=".NotificationReceiver"
                android:permission="com.bignerdranch.android.photogallery.PRIVATE"
                android:exported="false">
                ...
        </receiver>
    </application>
</manifest>
```

Now, use your permission by defining a corresponding constant in code and then passing it into your **sendBroadcast(…)** call.

## Listing 28.7  Sending with a permission (PollWorker.kt)

```kotlin
class PollWorker(val context: Context, workerParams: WorkerParameters) :
    Worker(context, workerParams) {

    override fun doWork(): Result {
        ...
        val resultId = first().id
        if (resultId == lastResultId) {
            Log.i(TAG, "Got an old result: $resultId")
        } else {
            ...
            val notificationManager = NotificationManagerCompat.from(context)
            notificationManager.notify(0, notification)

            context.sendBroadcast(Intent(ACTION_SHOW_NOTIFICATION), PERM_PRIVATE)
        }

        return Result.success()
    }

    companion object {
        const val ACTION_SHOW_NOTIFICATION =
            "com.bignerdranch.android.photogallery.SHOW_NOTIFICATION"
        const val PERM_PRIVATE = "com.bignerdranch.android.photogallery.PRIVATE"
    }
}
```

Now, your app is the only app that can trigger that receiver. Run PhotoGallery again. You should see your log from **NotificationReceiver** appear in Logcat (though your notifications do not yet know the proper etiquette and will continue to display while the app is in the foreground – just as they did before this chapter).

## More about protection levels

Every custom permission has to specify a value for `android:protectionLevel`. Your permission's `protectionLevel` tells Android how it should be used. In your case, you used a `protectionLevel` of `signature`.

The `signature` protection level means that if another application wants to use your permission, it has to be signed with the same key as your application. This is usually the right choice for permissions you use internally in your application. Because other developers do not have your key, they cannot get access to anything this permission protects. Plus, because you *do* have your own key, you can use this permission in any other app you decide to write later.

The four available protection levels are summarized in Table 28.1:

Table 28.1 Values for `protectionLevel`

| Value | Description |
|---|---|
| normal | This is for protecting app functionality that will not do anything dangerous, like accessing secure personal data or finding out where you are on a map. The user can see the permission before choosing to install the app but is never explicitly asked to grant it. `android.permission.INTERNET` uses this permission level, and so does the permission that lets your app vibrate the user's device. |
| dangerous | This is for most of the things you would not use `normal` for – accessing personal data, accessing hardware that might be used to spy on the user, or anything else that could cause real problems. The camera permission, locations permission, and contacts permission all fall under this category. Starting in Marshmallow, `dangerous` permissions require that you call **requestPermission(…)** at runtime to ask the user to explicitly grant your app permission. |
| signature | The system grants this permission if the app is signed with the same certificate as the declaring application and denies it otherwise. If the permission is granted, the user is not notified. This is for functionality that is internal to an app – as the developer, because you have the certificate and only apps signed with the same certificate can use the permission, you have control over who uses the permission. You used it here to prevent anyone else from seeing your broadcasts. If you wanted, you could write another app that listens to them, too. |
| signatureOrSystem | This is like `signature`, but it also grants permission to all packages in the Android system image. This is for communicating with apps built into the system image. If the permission is granted, the user is not notified. Most developers will not need to use this permission level, because it is intended to be used by hardware vendors. |

# Creating and registering a dynamic receiver

Next, you need a receiver for your ACTION_SHOW_NOTIFICATION broadcast intent. The job of this receiver will be to prevent posting a notification while the user is using your app.

This receiver is only going to be registered while your activity is in the foreground. If this receiver were declared with a longer lifespan (such as the lifetime of your app's process), then you would need some other way of knowing that **PhotoGalleryFragment** is running (which would defeat the purpose of having this dynamic receiver in the first place).

The solution is to use a dynamic broadcast receiver. You register the receiver by calling `Context.registerReceiver(BroadcastReceiver, IntentFilter)` and unregister it by calling `Context.unregisterReceiver(BroadcastReceiver)`. The receiver itself is typically defined as an inner class or a lambda, like a button-click listener. However, since you need the same instance in `registerReceiver(…)` and `unregisterReceiver(…)`, you will need to assign the receiver to an instance variable.

Create a new abstract class called **VisibleFragment** with **Fragment** as its superclass. This class will be a generic fragment that hides foreground notifications. (You will write another fragment like this in Chapter 29.)

### Listing 28.8  A receiver of **VisibleFragment**'s own (VisibleFragment.kt)

```kotlin
abstract class VisibleFragment : Fragment() {

    private val onShowNotification = object : BroadcastReceiver() {
        override fun onReceive(context: Context, intent: Intent) {
            Toast.makeText(requireContext(),
                    "Got a broadcast: ${intent.action}",
                    Toast.LENGTH_LONG)
                    .show()
        }
    }

    override fun onStart() {
        super.onStart()
        val filter = IntentFilter(PollWorker.ACTION_SHOW_NOTIFICATION)
        requireActivity().registerReceiver(
            onShowNotification,
            filter,
            PollWorker.PERM_PRIVATE,
            null
        )
    }

    override fun onStop() {
        super.onStop()
        requireActivity().unregisterReceiver(onShowNotification)
    }
}
```

Note that to pass in an **IntentFilter**, you have to create one in code. Your **filter** here is identical to the filter specified by the following XML:

```xml
<intent-filter>
    <action android:name=
            "com.bignerdranch.android.photogallery.SHOW_NOTIFICATION" />
</intent-filter>
```

Any **IntentFilter** you can express in XML can also be expressed in code this way. Just call **addCategory(String)**, **addAction(String)**, **addDataPath(String)**, and so on to configure your filter.

When you use dynamically registered broadcast receivers, you must also take care to clean them up. Typically, if you register a receiver in a startup lifecycle function, you call **Context.unregisterReceiver(BroadcastReceiver)** in the corresponding shutdown function. Here, you register inside **onStart()** and unregister inside **onStop()**. If instead you registered inside **onCreate(…)**, you would unregister inside **onDestroy()**.

(Be careful with **onCreate(…)** and **onDestroy()** in retained fragments, by the way. **getActivity()** will return different values in **onCreate(…)** and **onDestroy()** if the screen has rotated. If you want to register and unregister in **Fragment.onCreate(…)** and **Fragment.onDestroy()**, use **requireActivity().getApplicationContext()** instead.)

Next, modify **PhotoGalleryFragment** to be a subclass of your new **VisibleFragment**.

## Listing 28.9  Making your fragment visible (PhotoGalleryFragment.kt)

```
class PhotoGalleryFragment : Fragment() VisibleFragment() {
    ...
}
```

Run PhotoGallery and toggle background polling a couple of times. You will see a nice toast pop up (Figure 28.2).

## Figure 28.2  Proof that your broadcast receiver exists

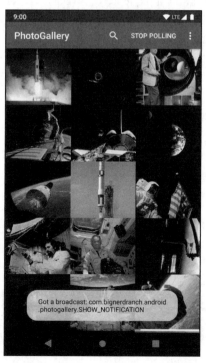

## Passing and receiving data with ordered broadcasts

Time to finally bring this baby home. The last piece is to ensure that your dynamically registered receiver always receives the PollWorker.ACTION_SHOW_NOTIFICATION broadcast before any other receivers and that it modifies the broadcast to indicate that the notification should not be posted.

Right now you are sending your own personal private broadcast, but so far you only have one-way communication (Figure 28.3).

Figure 28.3  Regular broadcast intents

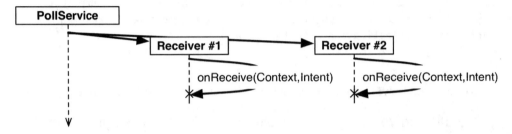

This is because a regular broadcast intent is conceptually received by everyone at the same time. In reality, because **onReceive(…)** is called on the main thread, your receivers are not actually executed concurrently. However, it is not possible to rely on them being executed in any particular order or to know when they have all completed execution. As a result, it is a hassle for the broadcast receivers to communicate with each other or for the sender of the intent to receive information from the receivers.

You can implement predictably ordered communication using an *ordered* broadcast intent (Figure 28.4). Ordered broadcasts allow a sequence of broadcast receivers to process a broadcast intent in order.

Figure 28.4  Ordered broadcast intents

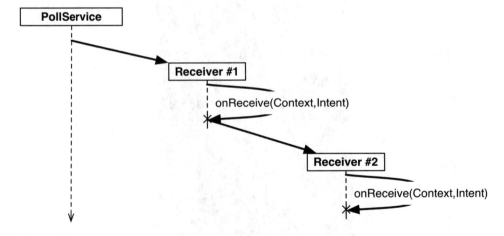

On the receiving side, this looks mostly the same as a regular broadcast. But you get an additional tool: a set of functions used to change the intent being passed along the chain. Here, you want to cancel the notification. This can be communicated by use of a simple integer result code by setting resultCode to Activity.RESULT_CANCELED.

Modify **VisibleFragment** to tell the sender of SHOW_NOTIFICATION whether the notification should be posted. This information will also be sent to any other broadcast receivers along the chain.

## Listing 28.10  Sending a simple result back (VisibleFragment.kt)

```
private const val TAG = "VisibleFragment"

abstract class VisibleFragment : Fragment() {

    private val onShowNotification = object : BroadcastReceiver() {
        override fun onReceive(context: Context, intent: Intent) {
            Toast.makeText(requireActivity(),
                "Got a broadcast:" + intent.getAction(),
                Toast.LENGTH_LONG)
                .show()
            // If we receive this, we're visible, so cancel
            // the notification
            Log.i(TAG, "canceling notification")
            resultCode = Activity.RESULT_CANCELED
        }
    }
    ...
}
```

Because all you need to do is signal yes or no here, you only need the result code. If you needed to pass more complicated data, you could set resultData or call **setResultExtras(Bundle?)**. And if you wanted to set all three values, you could call **setResult(Int, String?, Bundle?)**. Each subsequent receiver will be able to see or even modify these values.

For those functions to do anything useful, your broadcast needs to be ordered. Write a new function to send an ordered broadcast in **PollWorker**. This function will package up a **Notification** invocation and send it out as a broadcast. Update **doWork()** to call your new function and, in turn, send out an ordered broadcast instead of posting the notification directly to the **NotificationManager**.

## Listing 28.11  Sending an ordered broadcast (PollWorker.kt)

```kotlin
class PollWorker(val context: Context, workerParams: WorkerParameters) :
    Worker(context, workerParams) {

    override fun doWork(): Result {
        ...
        val resultId = items.first().id
        if (resultId == lastResultId) {
            Log.i(TAG, "Got an old result: $resultId")
        } else {
            ...
            val notification = NotificationCompat
                .Builder(context, NOTIFICATION_CHANNEL_ID)
                ...
                .build()

            val notificationManager = NotificationManagerCompat.from(context)
            notificationManager.notify(0, notification)

            context.sendBroadcast(Intent(ACTION_SHOW_NOTIFICATION), PERM_PRIVATE)

            showBackgroundNotification(0, notification)
        }

        return Result.success()
    }

    private fun showBackgroundNotification(
        requestCode: Int,
        notification: Notification
    ) {
        val intent = Intent(ACTION_SHOW_NOTIFICATION).apply {
            putExtra(REQUEST_CODE, requestCode)
            putExtra(NOTIFICATION, notification)
        }

        context.sendOrderedBroadcast(intent, PERM_PRIVATE)
    }

    companion object {
        const val ACTION_SHOW_NOTIFICATION =
            "com.bignerdranch.android.photogallery.SHOW_NOTIFICATION"
        const val PERM_PRIVATE = "com.bignerdranch.android.photogallery.PRIVATE"
        const val REQUEST_CODE = "REQUEST_CODE"
        const val NOTIFICATION = "NOTIFICATION"
    }
}
```

**Context.sendOrderedBroadcast(Intent, String?)** behaves much like **sendBroadcast(…)**, but it will guarantee that your broadcast is delivered to each receiver one at a time. The result code will be initially set to Activity.RESULT_OK when this ordered broadcast is sent.

Update **NotificationReceiver** so that it posts the notification to the user.

## Listing 28.12  Implementing your result receiver (NotificationReceiver.kt)

```
private const val TAG = "NotificationReceiver"

class NotificationReceiver : BroadcastReceiver() {

    override fun onReceive(context: Context, intent: Intent) {
        Log.i(TAG, "received broadcast: ${i.action} result: $resultCode")
        if (resultCode != Activity.RESULT_OK) {
            // A foreground activity canceled the broadcast
            return
        }

        val requestCode = intent.getIntExtra(PollWorker.REQUEST_CODE, 0)
        val notification: Notification =
            intent.getParcelableExtra(PollWorker.NOTIFICATION)

        val notificationManager = NotificationManagerCompat.from(context)
        notificationManager.notify(requestCode, notification)
    }
}
```

To ensure that **NotificationReceiver** receives the broadcast after your dynamically registered receiver (so it can check whether it should post the notification to **NotificationManager**), you need to set a low priority for **NotificationReceiver** in the manifest. Give it a priority of –999 so that it runs last. This is the lowest user-defined priority possible (–1000 and below are reserved).

## Listing 28.13  Prioritizing the notification receiver (manifests/AndroidManifest.xml)

```
<receiver ... >
    <intent-filter android:priority="-999">
        <action
            android:name="com.bignerdranch.android.photogallery.SHOW_NOTIFICATION" />
    </intent-filter>
</receiver>
```

Run PhotoGallery. You should see that notifications no longer appear when you have the app in the foreground. (You can toggle polling off and on to trigger your **PollWorker** to be run by **WorkManager**.)

# Receivers and Long-Running Tasks

So what do you do if you want a broadcast intent to kick off a longer-running task than the restrictions of the main run loop allow? You have two options.

The first is to put that work into a service instead and start the service in your broadcast receiver's small window of opportunity. A service can queue up multiple requests and run them in order or otherwise manage requests as it sees fit. This is the method we recommend. A service has a much longer window it can use to perform work, but it may still be stopped if it runs for long periods. (This threshold varies by OS version and device, but it is generally on the order of several minutes on newer devices.) You can also choose to run a service in the foreground to remove all limits on how long your work can run, which is ideal for tasks like backing up photos, playing music, or giving turn-by-turn navigation.

The second option is to use the **BroadcastReceiver.goAsync()** function. This function returns a **BroadcastReceiver.PendingResult** object, which can be used to provide a result at a later time. So you could give that **PendingResult** to an **AsyncTask** to perform some longer-running work and then respond to the broadcast by calling functions on **PendingResult**.

There is one downside to using the **goAsync()** function: It is less flexible. You still have to service the broadcast within 10 seconds or so, and you have fewer architectural options than you do with a service. Of course, **goAsync()** has one huge advantage: You can set results for ordered broadcasts with it. If you really need that, nothing else will do. Just make sure you do not take too long.

# For the More Curious: Local Events

Broadcast intents allow you to propagate information across the system in a global fashion. What if you want to broadcast the occurrence of an event within your app's process only? Using an event bus is a great alternative.

An *event bus* operates on the idea of having a shared bus, or stream of data, that components within your application can subscribe to. When an event is posted to the bus, subscribed components will be activated and have their callback code executed.

EventBus by greenrobot is a third-party event bus library we have used in some of our Android applications. You could also use Square's Otto, which is another event bus implementation, or RxJava **Subject**s and **Observable**.

Android does provide a way to send local broadcast intents, called **LocalBroadcastManager**. But we find that the third-party libraries mentioned here provide a more flexible and easier-to-use API for broadcasting local events.

## Using EventBus

To use EventBus in your application, you must add a library dependency to your project. Once the dependency is set up, you define a class representing an event (you can add fields to the event if you need to pass data along):

```
class NewFriendAddedEvent(val friendName: String)
```

You can post to the bus from just about anywhere in your app:

```
val eventBus: EventBus = EventBus.getDefault()
eventBus.post(NewFriendAddedEvent("Susie Q"))
```

Other parts of your app can subscribe to receive events by first registering to listen on the bus. Often you will register and unregister activities or fragments in corresponding lifecycle functions, such as **onStart(…)** and **onStop(…)**:

```
// In some fragment or activity...
private lateinit var eventBus: EventBus

public override fun onCreate(savedInstanceState: Bundle?) {
    super.onCreate(savedInstanceState)
    eventBus = EventBus.getDefault()
}

public override fun onStart() {
    super.onStart()
    eventBus.register(this)
}

public override fun onStop() {
    super.onStop()
    eventBus.unregister(this)
}
```

You specify how a subscriber should handle an event by implementing a function with the appropriate event type as input and adding the @Subscribe annotation to that function. Using the @Subscribe annotation with no parameters means the event will be processed on the same thread it was sent from. You could instead use @Subscribe(threadMode = ThreadMode.MAIN) to ensure that the event is processed on the main thread if it happens to be issued from a background thread.

```
// In some registered component, like a fragment or activity...
@Subscribe(threadMode = ThreadMode.MAIN)
fun onNewFriendAdded(event: NewFriendAddedEvent) {
    // Update the UI or do something in response to an event...
}
```

# Using RxJava

RxJava can also be used to implement an event broadcasting mechanism. RxJava is a library for writing "reactive"-style Java code. That "reactive" idea is broad and beyond the scope of what we can cover here. The short story is that it allows you to publish and subscribe to sequences of events and gives you a broad set of generic tools for manipulating these event sequences.

So you could create something called a **Subject**, which is an object you can publish events to as well as subscribe to events on:

```
val eventBus: Subject<Any, Any> =
        PublishSubject.create<Any>().toSerialized()
```

You can publish events to it:

```
val someNewFriend = "Susie Q"
val event = NewFriendAddedEvent(someNewFriend)
eventBus.onNext(event)
```

And subscribe to events on it:

```
eventBus.subscribe { event: Any ->
    if (event is NewFriendAddedEvent) {
        val friendName = event.friendName
        // Update the UI
    }
}
```

The advantage of RxJava's solution is that your eventBus is now also an **Observable**, RxJava's representation of a stream of events. That means that you get to use all of RxJava's various event manipulation tools. If that piques your interest, check out the wiki on RxJava's project page: github.com/ReactiveX/RxJava/wiki.

# For the More Curious: Limitations on Broadcast Receivers

As you saw earlier in this chapter, there are limitations on broadcast receivers declared in your Android manifest that may cause your receiver to not be called. This behavior does not apply to receivers that you register dynamically using `registerReceiver(…)` and is only applicable when your app runs on Android Oreo (API level 26) and newer versions of Android.

The limitations on standalone broadcast receivers were introduced with the goal of improving battery life and performance on users' devices. If a broadcast receiver is registered in your manifest and your app is not running, the system must spin up a new process whenever a broadcast needs to be delivered to this receiver. This act of spinning up processes is fairly unnoticeable if only one or two apps need to have their process started, but performance quickly deteriorates if many apps want to handle the same broadcast.

One example where this can directly harm user experience is if the user has apps that offer to automatically back up new photos taken by the camera. This would cause multiple processes to be started in the background whenever the user pressed the shutter button in the camera app, which would make the camera feel unresponsive to the user.

To alleviate this performance concern, new versions of Android beginning with Android Oreo no longer deliver implicit broadcasts to receivers declared in your manifest – with some exceptions. (Explicit broadcasts are not affected by these limitations, but recall that these kinds of broadcasts are only sent to one receiver and are rarely used.)

A number of system broadcasts are excluded from this rule. Broadcast receivers registered in your manifest for broadcasts including `BOOT_COMPLETE`, `TIMEZONE_CHANGED`, and `NEW_OUTGOING_CALL` will still receive those broadcasts. These and other broadcasts are exempt because they are either rarely sent or do not have an alternative way to perform functionality required by apps. You can find the full list of exemptions in the Android Developer documentation at `developer.android.com/guide/components/broadcast-exceptions`.

As you saw when working through this chapter, broadcasts sent with a signature-level permission are also exempt from this restriction. This allows you to keep using standalone broadcast receivers that are private to your app and any other apps that you build using the same signature. Because only apps from one developer have permission to send these broadcasts, it is unlikely that there will be performance issues in other parts of the system caused by these kinds of broadcasts.

# For the More Curious: Detecting the Visibility of Your Fragment

When you reflect on your PhotoGallery implementation, you may notice that you used the global broadcast mechanism to broadcast the `SHOW_NOTIFICATION` intent. However, you locked the receiving of that broadcast to items local to your app process by using custom permissions. You may find yourself asking, "Why am I using a global mechanism if I am just communicating with things in my own app? Why not a local mechanism instead?"

This is because you were specifically trying to solve the problem of knowing whether `PhotoGalleryFragment` was visible. The combination of ordered broadcasts, standalone receivers, and dynamically registered receivers you implemented gets the job done. There is not a more straightforward way to do this in Android.

More specifically, `LocalBroadcastManager` would not work for PhotoGallery's notification broadcast and visible fragment detection, for two main reasons.

First, `LocalBroadcastManager` does not support ordered broadcasts (though it does provide a blocking way to broadcast, namely `sendBroadcastSync(Intent)`). This will not work for PhotoGallery because you need to force `NotificationReceiver` to run last in the chain.

Second, `sendBroadcastSync(Intent)` does not support sending and receiving a broadcast on separate threads. In PhotoGallery, you need to send the broadcast from a background thread (in `PollWorker.doWork()`) and receive the intent on the main thread (by the dynamic receiver that is registered by `PhotoGalleryFragment` on the main thread in `onStart(…)`).

As of this writing, the semantics of `LocalBroadcastManager`'s thread delivery are not well documented or, in our experience, intuitive. For example, if you call `sendBroadcastSync(…)` from a background thread, all pending broadcasts will get flushed out on that background thread, even if they were posted from the main thread.

This is not to say `LocalBroadcastManager` is not useful. It is simply not the right tool for the problems you solved in this chapter.

# 29

# Browsing the Web and WebView

Each photo you get from Flickr has a page associated with it. In this chapter, you are going to update PhotoGallery so that users can press a photo to see its Flickr page. You will learn two different ways to integrate web content into your apps, shown in Figure 29.1. The first works with the device's browser app (left), and the second uses a **WebView** to display web content within PhotoGallery (right).

Figure 29.1 Web content: two different approaches

# One Last Bit of Flickr Data

No matter how you choose to open Flickr's photo page, you need to get its URL first. If you look at the JSON data you are currently receiving for each photo, you can see that the photo page is not part of those results.

```
{
    "photos": {
        ...,
        "photo": [
            {
                "id": "9452133594",
                "owner": "44494372@N05",
                "secret": "d6d20af93e",
                "server": "7365",
                "farm": 8,
                "title": "Low and Wisoff at Work",
                "ispublic": 1,
                "isfriend": 0,
                "isfamily": 0,
                "url_s":"https://farm8.staticflickr.com/7365/9452133594_d6d20af93e_m.jpg"
            }, ...
        ]
    },
    "stat": "ok"
}
```

(Recall that url_s is the URL for the small version of the photo, not the full-size photo.)

You might think that you are in for some more JSON request writing. Fortunately, that is not the case. If you look at the Web Page URLs section of Flickr's documentation at flickr.com/services/api/misc.urls.html, you will see that you can create the URL for an individual photo's page like so:

```
https://www.flickr.com/photos/user-id/photo-id
```

The photo-id in the URL is the same as the value of the id attribute from your JSON data. You are already stashing that in id in **GalleryItem**. What about user-id? If you poke around the documentation, you will find that the owner attribute in your JSON data is a user ID. So if you pull out the owner attribute, you should be able to build the URL from your photo JSON data:

```
https://www.flickr.com/photos/owner/id
```

Update **GalleryItem** to put this plan into action.

## Listing 29.1 Adding code for the photo page (GalleryItem.kt)

```
data class GalleryItem(
    var title: String = "",
    var id: String = "",
    @SerializedName("url_s") var url: String = "",
    @SerializedName("owner") var owner: String = ""
) {
    val photoPageUri: Uri
        get() {
            return Uri.parse("https://www.flickr.com/photos/")
                .buildUpon()
                .appendPath(owner)
                .appendPath(id)
                .build()
        }
}
```

To determine the photo URL, you create a new owner property and add a computed property called photoPageUri to generate photo page URLs as discussed above. Because Gson is translating your JSON responses into GalleryItems on your behalf, you can immediately start using the photoPageUri property without any other code changes.

# The Easy Way: Implicit Intents

You will browse to this URL first by using your old friend the implicit intent. This intent will start up the browser with your photo URL.

The first step is to make your app listen to presses on an item in the **RecyclerView**. Update **PhotoGalleryFragment**'s **PhotoHolder** to implement a click listener that will fire an implicit intent.

Listing 29.2  Firing an implicit intent when an item is pressed (PhotoGalleryFragment.kt)

```kotlin
class PhotoGalleryFragment : VisibleFragment() {
    ...
    private inner class PhotoHolder(private val itemImageView: ImageView)
        : RecyclerView.ViewHolder(itemImageView),
        View.OnClickListener {

        private lateinit var galleryItem: GalleryItem

        init {
            itemView.setOnClickListener(this)
        }

        val bindDrawable: (Drawable) -> Unit = itemImageView::setImageDrawable

        fun bindGalleryItem(item: GalleryItem) {
            galleryItem = item
        }

        override fun onClick(view: View) {
            val intent = Intent(Intent.ACTION_VIEW, galleryItem.photoPageUri)
            startActivity(intent)
        }
    }
    ...
}
```

Adding the `inner` keyword to the **PhotoHolder** allows you to access the outer class's properties and functions. In this case, you call **Fragment.startActivity(Intent)** from within **PhotoHolder**.

Next, bind the **PhotoHolder** to a **GalleryItem** in **PhotoAdapter.onBindViewHolder(…)**.

## Listing 29.3 Binding **GalleryItem** (PhotoGalleryFragment.kt)

```
class PhotoGalleryFragment : VisibleFragment() {
    ...
    private inner class PhotoAdapter(private val galleryItems: List<GalleryItem>) :
            RecyclerView.Adapter<PhotoHolder>() {
        ...
        override fun onBindViewHolder(holder: PhotoHolder, position: Int) {
            val galleryItem = galleryItems[position]
            holder.bindGalleryItem(galleryItem)
            val placeholder: Drawable = ContextCompat.getDrawable(
                requireContext(),
                R.drawable.bill_up_close
            ) ?: ColorDrawable()
            holder.bindDrawable(placeholder)
            thumbnailDownloader.queueThumbnail(holder, galleryItem.url)
        }
    }
    ...
}
```

That is it. Start up PhotoGallery and press on a photo. Your browser app should pop up and load the photo page for the item you pressed (similar to the image on the left in Figure 29.1).

# The Harder Way: WebView

Using an implicit intent to display the photo page is easy and effective. But what if you do not want your app to open the browser?

Often, you want to display web content within your own activities instead of heading off to the browser. You may want to display HTML that you generate yourself, or you may want to lock down the browser somehow. For apps that include help documentation, it is common to implement it as a web page so that it is easy to update. Opening a web browser to a help web page does not look professional, and it prevents you from customizing behavior or integrating that web page into your own UI.

When you want to present web content within your own UI, you use the **WebView** class. We are calling this the "harder" way here, but it is pretty darned easy. (Anything is hard compared to using implicit intents.)

The first step is to create a new activity and fragment to display the **WebView**. Start, as usual, by defining a layout file called res/layout/fragment_photo_page.xml. Make **ConstraintLayout** the top-level layout. In the Design view, drag a **WebView** into the **ConstraintLayout** as a child. (You will find **WebView** under the Widgets section.)

Once the **WebView** is added, add a constraint for every side to its parent. That gives you the following constraints:

- from the top of the **WebView** to the top of its parent

- from the bottom of the **WebView** to the bottom of its parent

- from the left of the **WebView** to the left of its parent

- from the right of the **WebView** to the right of its parent

Finally, change the height and width to Match Constraint and change all the margins to 0. Oh, and give your **WebView** an ID: web_view.

You may be thinking, "That **ConstraintLayout** is not useful." True enough – for the moment. You will fill it out later in the chapter with additional "chrome."

Next, get the rudiments of your fragment set up. Create **PhotoPageFragment** as a subclass of the **VisibleFragment** class you created in Chapter 28. You will need to inflate your layout file, extract your **WebView** from it, and forward along the URL to display as a fragment argument.

## Listing 29.4  Setting up your web browser fragment (PhotoPageFragment.kt)

```kotlin
private const val ARG_URI = "photo_page_url"

class PhotoPageFragment : VisibleFragment() {

    private lateinit var uri: Uri
    private lateinit var webView: WebView

    override fun onCreate(savedInstanceState: Bundle?) {
        super.onCreate(savedInstanceState)

        uri = arguments?.getParcelable(ARG_URI) ?: Uri.EMPTY
    }

    override fun onCreateView(
        inflater: LayoutInflater,
        container: ViewGroup?,
        savedInstanceState: Bundle?
    ): View? {
        val view = inflater.inflate(R.layout.fragment_photo_page, container, false)

        webView = view.findViewById(R.id.web_view)

        return view
    }

    companion object {
        fun newInstance(uri: Uri): PhotoPageFragment {
            return PhotoPageFragment().apply {
                arguments = Bundle().apply {
                    putParcelable(ARG_URI, uri)
                }
            }
        }
    }
}
```

For now, this is little more than a skeleton. You will fill it out a bit more in a moment. But first, create **PhotoPageActivity** to host your new **Fragment**.

## Listing 29.5  Creating a web activity (PhotoPageActivity.kt)

```kotlin
class PhotoPageActivity : AppCompatActivity() {

    override fun onCreate(savedInstanceState: Bundle?) {
        super.onCreate(savedInstanceState)
        setContentView(R.layout.activity_photo_page)

        val fm = supportFragmentManager
        val currentFragment = fm.findFragmentById(R.id.fragment_container)

        if (currentFragment == null) {
            val fragment = PhotoPageFragment.newInstance(intent.data)
            fm.beginTransaction()
                .add(R.id.fragment_container, fragment)
                .commit()
        }
    }

    companion object {
        fun newIntent(context: Context, photoPageUri: Uri): Intent {
            return Intent(context, PhotoPageActivity::class.java).apply {
                data = photoPageUri
            }
        }
    }
}
```

Create the missing res/layout/activity_photo_page.xml layout file and add a **FrameLayout** with an ID of fragment_container.

## Listing 29.6  Adding an activity layout (res/layout/activity_photo_page.xml)

```xml
<?xml version="1.0" encoding="utf-8"?>
<FrameLayout
        xmlns:android="http://schemas.android.com/apk/res/android"
        android:id="@+id/fragment_container"
        android:layout_width="match_parent"
        android:layout_height="match_parent"/>
```

Now, switch up your code in **PhotoGalleryFragment** to launch your new activity instead of the implicit intent.

### Listing 29.7 Switching to launch your activity (PhotoGalleryFragment.kt)

```
class PhotoGalleryFragment : VisibleFragment() {
    ...
    private inner class PhotoHolder(private val itemImageView: ImageView)
        : RecyclerView.ViewHolder(itemImageView),
            View.OnClickListener {
        ...
        override fun onClick(view: View) {
            val intent = Intent(Intent.ACTION_VIEW, galleryItem.photoPageUri)
            val intent = PhotoPageActivity
                .newIntent(requireContext(), galleryItem.photoPageUri)
            startActivity(intent)
        }
    }
    ...
}
```

And, finally, add your new activity to the manifest.

### Listing 29.8 Adding your activity to the manifest (manifests/AndroidManifest.xml)

```
<manifest ... >
    ...
    <application
        ... >
        <activity android:name=".PhotoGalleryActivity">
            ...
        </activity>
        <activity android:name=".PhotoPageActivity"/>
        <receiver android:name=".NotificationReceiver"
                ... >
            ...
        </receiver>
    </application>
</manifest>
```

Run PhotoGallery and press on a picture. You should see a new empty activity pop up.

OK, now to get to the meat and actually make your fragment do something. You need to do three things to make your **WebView** successfully display a Flickr photo page. The first one is straightforward – you need to tell it what URL to load.

The second thing you need to do is enable JavaScript. By default, JavaScript is off. You do not always need to have it on, but for Flickr, you do. (If you run Android Lint, it gives you a warning for doing this. It is worried about cross-site scripting attacks. You can suppress this Lint warning by annotating **onCreateView(…)** with @SuppressLint("SetJavaScriptEnabled").)

Finally, you need to provide a default implementation of a class called **WebViewClient**. **WebViewClient** is used to respond to rendering events on a **WebView**. We will discuss this class a bit more after you enter the code.

Make these changes in **PhotoPageFragment**.

## Listing 29.9  Loading the URL into **WebView** (PhotoPageFragment.kt)

```
class PhotoPageFragment : VisibleFragment() {
    ...
    @SuppressLint("SetJavaScriptEnabled")
    override fun onCreateView(
        inflater: LayoutInflater,
        container: ViewGroup?,
        savedInstanceState: Bundle?
    ): View? {
        val view = inflater.inflate(R.layout.fragment_photo_page, container, false)

        webView = view.findViewById(R.id.web_view)
        webView.settings.javaScriptEnabled = true
        webView.webViewClient = WebViewClient()
        webView.loadUrl(uri.toString())

        return view
    }
    ...
}
```

Loading the URL has to be done after configuring the **WebView**, so you do that last. Before that, you turn JavaScript on by accessing the settings property to get an instance of **WebSettings** and then setting WebSettings.javaScriptEnabled = true. **WebSettings** is the first of the three ways you can modify your **WebView**. It has various properties you can set, like the user agent string and text size.

After that, you add a **WebViewClient** to your **WebView**. To know why, let us first address what happens without a **WebViewClient**.

A new URL can be loaded in a couple of different ways: The page can tell you to go to another URL on its own (a redirect), or the user can click on a link. Without a **WebViewClient**, **WebView** will ask the activity manager to find an appropriate activity to load the new URL.

This is not what you want to have happen. Many sites (including Flickr's photo pages) immediately redirect to a mobile version of the same site when you load them from a phone browser. There is not much point to making your own view of the page if it is going to fire an implicit intent anyway when that happens.

If, on the other hand, you provide your own **WebViewClient** to your **WebView**, the process works differently. Instead of asking the activity manager what to do, it asks your **WebViewClient**. And in the default **WebViewClient** implementation, it says, "Go load the URL yourself!" So the page will appear in your **WebView**.

Run PhotoGallery, press an item, and you should see the item's photo page displayed in the **WebView** (like the image on the right in Figure 29.1).

# Using WebChromeClient to spruce things up

Since you are taking the time to create your own **WebView**, spruce it up a bit by adding a progress bar and updating the toolbar's subtitle with the title of the loaded page. These decorations and the UI outside of the **WebView** are referred to as *chrome* (not to be confused with the Google Chrome web browser). Crack open `fragment_photo_page.xml` once again.

In the Design view, drag in a **ProgressBar** as a second child for your **ConstraintLayout**. Use the ProgressBar (Horizontal) version of **ProgressBar**. Delete the **WebView**'s top constraint, and then set its height to Fixed so that you can easily work with its constraint handles.

With that done, create the following additional constraints:

- from the **ProgressBar** to the top, right, and left of its parent

- from the **WebView**'s top to the bottom of the **ProgressBar**

With that done, change the height of the **WebView** back to Match Constraint, change the **ProgressBar**'s height to wrap_content, and change the **ProgressBar**'s width to Match Constraint.

Finally, select the **ProgressBar** and move your attention to the attributes pane. Change the visibility to gone and change the tool visibility to visible. Rename its ID to progress_bar. Your result will look like Figure 29.2.

Figure 29.2  Adding a progress bar

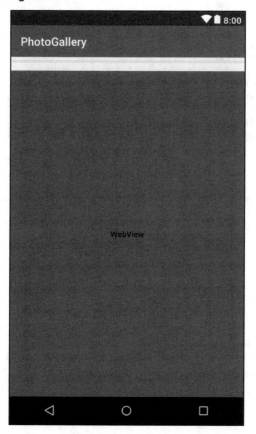

To hook up the **ProgressBar**, you will use the second callback on **WebView**, which is **WebChromeClient**. **WebViewClient** is an interface for responding to rendering events; **WebChromeClient** is an event interface for reacting to events that should change elements of chrome around the browser. This includes JavaScript alerts, favicons, and of course updates for loading progress and the title of the current page.

Hook it up in **onCreateView(…)**.

## Listing 29.10  Using **WebChromeClient** (PhotoPageFragment.kt)

```kotlin
class PhotoPageFragment : VisibleFragment() {

    private lateinit var uri: Uri
    private lateinit var webView: WebView
    private lateinit var progressBar: ProgressBar
    ...
    @SuppressLint("SetJavaScriptEnabled")
    override fun onCreateView(
        inflater: LayoutInflater,
        container: ViewGroup?,
        savedInstanceState: Bundle?
    ): View? {
        val view = inflater.inflate(R.layout.fragment_photo_page, container, false)

        progressBar = view.findViewById(R.id.progress_bar)
        progressBar.max = 100

        webView = view.findViewById(R.id.web_view)
        webView.settings.javaScriptEnabled = true
        webView.webChromeClient = object : WebChromeClient() {
            override fun onProgressChanged(webView: WebView, newProgress: Int) {
                if (newProgress == 100) {
                    progressBar.visibility = View.GONE
                } else {
                    progressBar.visibility = View.VISIBLE
                    progressBar.progress = newProgress
                }
            }

            override fun onReceivedTitle(view: WebView?, title: String?) {
                (activity as AppCompatActivity).supportActionBar?.subtitle = title
            }
        }
        webView.webViewClient = WebViewClient()
        webView.loadUrl(uri.toString())

        return view
    }
    ...
}
```

Progress updates and title updates each have their own callback function, **onProgressChanged(WebView, Int)** and **onReceivedTitle(WebView, String)**. The progress you receive from **onProgressChanged(WebView, Int)** is an integer from 0 to 100. If it is 100, you know that the page is done loading, so you hide the **ProgressBar** by setting its visibility to View.GONE.

Run PhotoGallery to test your changes. It should look like Figure 29.3.

Figure 29.3  Fancy **WebView**

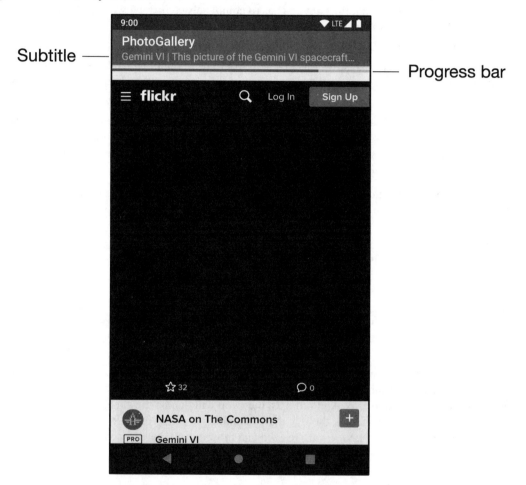

When you press on a photo, **PhotoPageActivity** pops up. A progress bar displays as the page loads, and a subtitle reflecting the title received in **onReceivedTitle(…)** appears in the toolbar. Once the page is loaded, the progress bar disappears.

# Proper Rotation with WebView

Make sure your emulator or device has auto-rotate turned on and try rotating your screen. While it does work correctly, you will notice that the `WebView` has to completely reload the web page. This is because `WebView` has too much data to save it all inside `onSaveInstanceState(…)`. It has to start from scratch each time it is re-created on rotation.

You may think the easiest way to resolve this problem would be to retain `PhotoPageFragment`. However, this would not work, because `WebView` is part of the view hierarchy and is thus still destroyed and re-created on rotation.

For some classes like this (`VideoView` is another one), the Android documentation recommends that you handle certain configuration changes, such as rotation, yourself. This means that instead of the activity being destroyed on rotation, its views will just be moved around to fit the new screen size. As a result, `WebView` does not have to reload all of its data.

To tell `PhotoPageActivity` that you will handle configuration changes, make the following tweak to `manifests/AndroidManifest.xml`.

### Listing 29.11  Handling configuration changes yourself (manifests/AndroidManifest.xml)

```
<manifest ... >
    ...
    <activity android:name=".PhotoPageActivity"
        android:configChanges="keyboardHidden|orientation|screenSize" />
    ...
</manifest>
```

This attribute says that if the configuration changes because the keyboard was opened or closed, due to an orientation change, or due to the screen size changing (which also happens when switching between portrait and landscape after Android 3.2), then you will handle the change inside the activity and it should not be destroyed. In fact, though, there is nothing special you need to do to handle the configuration change, because the views are resized and moved to fit the new screen automatically.

So that is it. Try rotating again and admire how smoothly the change is handled.

## Dangers of handling configuration changes

That is so easy and works so well that you are probably wondering why you do not do this all the time. It seems like it would make life so much easier. However, handling configuration changes on your own is a dangerous habit.

First, resource qualifier-based configuration changes no longer work automatically. You instead have to manually reload your view when a configuration change is detected. This can be more complicated than it sounds.

Second, and more important, this approach will likely cause you to not bother with overriding `Activity.onSavedInstanceState(…)` to stash transient UI states. Doing so is still necessary, even if the activity is retained across rotation, because you still have to worry about death and re-creation in low-memory situations. (Remember, the activity can be destroyed and stashed by the system at any time if it is not in the running state, as shown in Figure 4.9 on Page 92.)

# WebView vs a Custom UI

A UI built natively (without `WebView`) gives you full control over how your app looks and behaves. Also, it often feels more responsive and consistent to users. But there are a number of advantages to displaying web content instead of rolling out your own custom UI.

Displaying Flickr's site in a `WebView` lets you integrate a large feature much more quickly. You do not need to worry about fetching image descriptions, user account names, or other photo metadata to build out this UI. You can simply leverage what Flickr has already made available.

Another advantage to displaying web content is that the web content can change without you having to update your application. For example, if you need to display a privacy policy or terms of service in your app, you can choose to show a website instead of hardcoding the document into your application. That way, any changes can simply be pushed to a website instead of as an app update.

# For the More Curious: Injecting JavaScript Objects

In this chapter, you have seen how to use **WebViewClient** and **WebChromeClient** to respond to specific events that happen in your **WebView**. However, it is possible to do even more by injecting arbitrary JavaScript objects into the document contained in the **WebView** itself. Check out the documentation at developer.android.com/reference/android/webkit/WebView.html and scroll down to the **addJavascriptInterface(Object, String)** function. The documentation uses Java method signatures, but remember that **Object** is equivalent to **Any** in Kotlin. Using this, you can inject an arbitrary object into the document with a name you specify:

```
webView.addJavascriptInterface(object : Any() {
    @JavascriptInterface
    fun send(message: String) {
        Log.i(TAG, "Received message: $message")
    }
}, "androidObject")
```

And then invoke it like so:

```
<input type="button" value="In WebView!"
    onClick="sendToAndroid('In Android land')" />

<script type="text/javascript">
    function sendToAndroid(message) {
        androidObject.send(message);
    }
</script>
```

There are a couple of tricky parts about this. The first is that when you call **send(String)**, the Kotlin function is not called on the main thread. It is called on a thread owned by **WebView** instead. So if you want to update the Android UI, you will need to use a **Handler** to pass control back to the main thread.

The other part is that not many data types are supported. You have String, the core primitive types, and that is it. Anything more sophisticated must be marshalled through a String, usually by converting it to JSON before sending and then parsing it out when receiving.

Starting with API 17 (Jelly Bean 4.2) and up, only public functions annotated @JavascriptInterface are exported to JavaScript. Prior to that, all public functions in the object hierarchy were accessible.

Either way, this could be dangerous. You are letting some potentially strange web page fiddle with your program. So, to be safe, it is a good idea to make sure you own the HTML in question – either that, or be extremely conservative with the interface you expose.

# For the More Curious: WebView Updates

**WebView** is based on the Chromium open-source project. It shares the same rendering engine used by the Chrome for Android app, meaning pages should look and behave consistently across the two. (However, **WebView** does not have all the features Chrome for Android does. You can see a table comparing them at `developer.chrome.com/multidevice/webview/overview`.)

Being based on Chromium means that **WebView** stays up to date on web standards and JavaScript. From a development perspective, one of the most exciting features is the support for remote debugging of **WebView** using Chrome DevTools (which can be enabled by calling `WebView.setWebContentsDebuggingEnabled()`).

As of Lollipop (Android 5.0), the Chromium layer of **WebView** is updated automatically from the Google Play Store. Users no longer wait for new releases of Android to receive security updates (and new features). More recently, as of Nougat (Android 7.0), the Chromium layer for **WebView** comes directly from the Chrome APK file, lowering memory and resource usage. So you can rest easy, knowing that Google works to keep the **WebView** components up to date.

# For the More Curious: Chrome Custom Tabs (Another Easy Way)

You have already seen two ways to display web content: You can either launch the user's web browser or embed the content in your application. There is also a third option that is a hybrid of what you have seen so far.

Chrome Custom Tabs (`developer.chrome.com/multidevice/android/customtabs`) let you launch the Chrome web browser in a way that feels native to your application. You can configure its appearance to make it look like part of your app and feel like the user has never left your app. Figure 29.4 shows an example of a custom tab. You can see that the result looks like a mix of Google Chrome and your `PhotoPageActivity`.

Figure 29.4  A Chrome Custom Tab

When you use a custom tab, it behaves very similar to launching Chrome. The browser instance even has access to information like the user's saved passwords, browser cache, and cookies from the full Chrome browser. This means that if the user had logged into Flickr in Chrome, then they would also be logged into Flickr in every custom tab. With `WebView`, the user would have to log into Flickr in both Chrome and PhotoGallery.

The downside to using a custom tab instead of a `WebView` is that you do not have as much control over the content you are displaying. For example, you cannot choose to use custom tabs in only the top half of your screen or to add navigation buttons to the bottom of a custom tab.

To start using Chrome Custom Tabs, you add this dependency:

```
implementation 'androidx.browser:browser:1.0.0'
```

You can then launch a custom tab. For example, in PhotoGallery you could launch a custom tab instead of **PhotoPageActivity**:

```
class PhotoGalleryFragment : VisibleFragment() {
    ...
    private inner class PhotoHolder(private val itemImageView: ImageView)
        : RecyclerView.ViewHolder(itemImageView),
          View.OnClickListener {
        ...
        override fun onClick(view: View) {
            val intent = PhotoPageActivity
                .newIntent(requireContext(), galleryItem.photoPageUri)
            startActivity(intent)

            CustomTabsIntent.Builder()
                .setToolbarColor(ContextCompat.getColor(
                    requireContext(), R.color.colorPrimary))
                .setShowTitle(true)
                .build()
                .launchUrl(requireContext(), galleryItem.photoPageUri)
        }
    }
    ...
}
```

With this change, a user who clicks on a photo will see a custom tab like the one shown in Figure 29.4. (If the user did not have Chrome version 45 or higher installed, then PhotoGallery would fall back to using the system browser. The result would be just like when you used an implicit intent at the beginning of this chapter.)

# Challenge: Using the Back Button for Browser History

You may have noticed that you can follow other links within the **WebView** once you launch **PhotoPageActivity**. However, no matter how many links you follow, the Back button always brings you immediately back to **PhotoGalleryActivity**. What if you instead want the Back button to bring users through their browsing history within the **WebView**?

Implement this behavior by overriding the Back button function **Activity.onBackPressed()**. Within that function, use a combination of **WebView**'s browsing history functions (**WebView.canGoBack()** and **WebView.goBack()**) to do the right thing. If there are items in the **WebView**'s browsing history, go back to the previous item. Otherwise, allow the Back button to behave as normal by calling through to **super.onBackPressed()**.

# 30

# Custom Views and Touch Events

In this chapter, you will learn how to handle touch events by writing a custom subclass of **View** named **BoxDrawingView**. The **BoxDrawingView** class will be the star of a new project named DragAndDraw and will draw boxes in response to the user touching the screen and dragging. The finished product will look like Figure 30.1.

Figure 30.1 Boxes drawn in many shapes and sizes

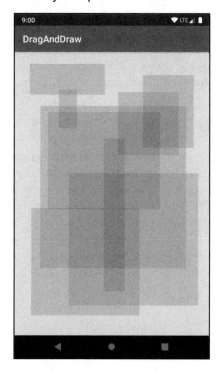

# Setting Up the DragAndDraw Project

Create a new project named DragAndDraw with API 21 as the minimum SDK and using AndroidX artifacts. Start the project without an activity, then create an empty launcher activity named **DragAndDrawActivity**.

**DragAndDrawActivity** will be a subclass of **AppCompatActivity** and will host a **BoxDrawingView**, the custom view that you are going to write. All of the drawing and touch-event handling will be implemented in **BoxDrawingView**.

# Creating a Custom View

Android provides many excellent standard views and widgets, but sometimes you need a custom view that presents visuals that are unique to your app.

While there are all kinds of custom views, you can shoehorn them into two broad categories:

*simple*          A simple view may be complicated inside; what makes it "simple" is that it has no child views. A simple view will almost always perform custom rendering.

*composite*       Composite views are composed of other view objects. Composite views typically manage child views but do not perform custom rendering. Instead, rendering is delegated to each child view.

There are three steps to follow when creating a custom view:

1. Pick a superclass. For a simple custom view, **View** is a blank canvas, so it is the most common choice. For a composite custom view, choose an appropriate layout class, such as **FrameLayout**.

2. Subclass this class and override the constructors from the superclass.

3. Override other key functions to customize behavior.

# Creating BoxDrawingView

**BoxDrawingView** will be a simple view and a direct subclass of **View**.

Create a new class named **BoxDrawingView** and make **View** its superclass. In BoxDrawingView.kt, add a constructor that takes in a **Context** object and a nullable **AttributeSet** with a default of null.

Listing 30.1  Initial implementation for **BoxDrawingView** (BoxDrawingView.kt)

```
class BoxDrawingView(context: Context, attrs: AttributeSet? = null) :
        View(context, attrs) {

}
```

Providing the null default value for the attribute set effectively provides two constructors for your view. Two constructors are needed, because your view could be instantiated in code or from a layout file. Views instantiated from a layout file receive an instance of **AttributeSet** containing the XML attributes that were specified in XML. Even if you do not plan on using both constructors, it is good practice to include them.

Next, update your res/layout/activity_drag_and_draw.xml layout file to use your new view.

Listing 30.2  Adding **BoxDrawingView** to the layout
(res/layout/activity_drag_and_draw.xml)

```
<androidx.constraintlayout.widget.ConstraintLayout
    xmlns:android="http://schemas.android.com/apk/res/android"
    xmlns:app="http://schemas.android.com/apk/res-auto"
    xmlns:tools="http://schemas.android.com/tools"
    android:layout_width="match_parent"
    android:layout_height="match_parent"
    tools:context="com.bignerdranch.android.draganddraw.DragAndDrawActivity">
</androidx.constraintlayout.widget.ConstraintLayout>
<com.bignerdranch.android.draganddraw.BoxDrawingView
    xmlns:android="http://schemas.android.com/apk/res/android"
    android:layout_width="match_parent"
    android:layout_height="match_parent" />
```

You must use **BoxDrawingView**'s fully qualified class name so that the layout inflater can find it. The inflater works through a layout file creating **View** instances. If the element name is an unqualified class name, then the inflater looks for a class with that name in the android.view and android.widget packages. If the class lives somewhere else, then the layout inflater will not find it, and your app will crash.

So, for custom classes and other classes that live outside of android.view and android.widget, you must always specify the fully qualified class name.

Run DragAndDraw to confirm that all the connections are correct. All you will see is an empty view (Figure 30.2).

Figure 30.2 **BoxDrawingView** with no boxes

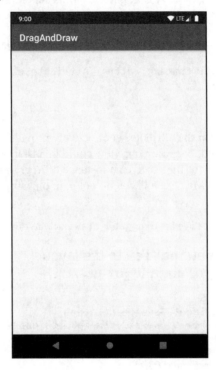

The next step is to get **BoxDrawingView** listening for touch events and using the information from them to draw boxes on the screen.

# Handling Touch Events

One way to listen for touch events is to set a touch event listener using the following **View** function:

```
fun setOnTouchListener(l: View.OnTouchListener)
```

This function works the same way as **setOnClickListener(View.OnClickListener)**. You provide an implementation of **View.OnTouchListener**, and your listener will be called every time a touch event happens.

However, because you are subclassing **View**, you can take a shortcut and override this **View** function instead:

```
override fun onTouchEvent(event: MotionEvent): Boolean
```

This function receives an instance of **MotionEvent**, a class that describes the touch event, including its location and its *action*. The action describes the stage of the event:

| Action constants | Description |
|---|---|
| ACTION_DOWN | user touches finger on the screen |
| ACTION_MOVE | user moves finger on the screen |
| ACTION_UP | user lifts finger off the screen |
| ACTION_CANCEL | a parent view has intercepted the touch event |

In your implementation of **onTouchEvent(MotionEvent)**, you can check the value of the action by calling the **MotionEvent** function:

```
final fun getAction(): Int
```

Let's get to it. In BoxDrawingView.kt, add a log tag and then an implementation of **onTouchEvent(MotionEvent)** that logs a message for each of the four actions.

## Listing 30.3 Implementing **BoxDrawingView** (BoxDrawingView.kt)

```
private const val TAG = "BoxDrawingView"

class BoxDrawingView(context: Context, attrs: AttributeSet? = null) :
        View(context, attrs) {

    override fun onTouchEvent(event: MotionEvent): Boolean {
        val current = PointF(event.x, event.y)
        var action = ""
        when (event.action) {
            MotionEvent.ACTION_DOWN -> {
                action = "ACTION_DOWN"
            }
            MotionEvent.ACTION_MOVE -> {
                action = "ACTION_MOVE"
            }
            MotionEvent.ACTION_UP -> {
                action = "ACTION_UP"
            }
            MotionEvent.ACTION_CANCEL -> {
                action = "ACTION_CANCEL"
            }
        }

        Log.i(TAG, "$action at x=${current.x}, y=${current.y}")

        return true
    }
}
```

Notice that you package your X and Y coordinates in a **PointF** object. You want to pass these two values together as you go through the rest of the chapter. **PointF** is a container class provided by Android that does this for you.

Run DragAndDraw and pull up Logcat. Touch the screen and drag your finger. (On the emulator, click and drag.) You should see a report of the X and Y coordinates of every touch action that **BoxDrawingView** receives.

## Tracking across motion events

**BoxDrawingView** is intended to draw boxes on the screen, not just log coordinates. There are a few problems to solve to get there.

First, to define a box, you need two points: the start point (where the finger was initially placed) and the end point (where the finger currently is).

To define a box, then, requires keeping track of data from more than one **MotionEvent**. You will store this data in a **Box** object.

Create a class named **Box** to represent the data that defines a single box.

### Listing 30.4  Adding **Box** (Box.kt)

```kotlin
class Box(val start: PointF) {

    var end: PointF = start

    val left: Float
        get() = Math.min(start.x, end.x)

    val right: Float
        get() = Math.max(start.x, end.x)

    val top: Float
        get() = Math.min(start.y, end.y)

    val bottom: Float
        get() = Math.max(start.y, end.y)

}
```

When the user touches **BoxDrawingView**, a new **Box** will be created and added to a list of existing boxes (Figure 30.3).

### Figure 30.3  Objects in DragAndDraw

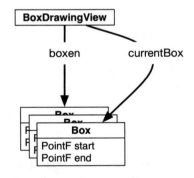

Back in **BoxDrawingView**, use your new **Box** object to track your drawing state.

## Listing 30.5 Adding drag lifecycle functions (BoxDrawingView.kt)

```kotlin
class BoxDrawingView(context: Context, attrs: AttributeSet? = null) :
        View(context, attrs) {

    private var currentBox: Box? = null
    private val boxen = mutableListOf<Box>()

    override fun onTouchEvent(event: MotionEvent): Boolean {
        val current = PointF(event.x, event.y)
        var action = ""
        when (event.action) {
            MotionEvent.ACTION_DOWN -> {
                action = "ACTION_DOWN"
                // Reset drawing state
                currentBox = Box(current).also {
                    boxen.add(it)
                }
            }
            MotionEvent.ACTION_MOVE -> {
                action = "ACTION_MOVE"
                updateCurrentBox(current)
            }
            MotionEvent.ACTION_UP -> {
                action = "ACTION_UP"
                updateCurrentBox(current)
                currentBox = null
            }
            MotionEvent.ACTION_CANCEL -> {
                action = "ACTION_CANCEL"
                currentBox = null
            }
        }

        Log.i(TAG, "$action at x=${current.x}, y=${current.y}")

        return true
    }

    private fun updateCurrentBox(current: PointF) {
        currentBox?.let {
            it.end = current
            invalidate()
        }
    }
}
```

Any time an ACTION_DOWN motion event is received, you set currentBox to be a new **Box** with its origin as the event's location. This new **Box** is added to the list of boxes. (In the next section, when you implement custom drawing, **BoxDrawingView** will draw every **Box** within this list to the screen.)

As the user's finger moves around the screen, you update currentBox.end. Then, when the touch is canceled or when the user's finger leaves the screen, you update the current box with the final reported location and null out currentBox to end your draw motion. The **Box** is complete; it is stored safely in the list but will no longer be updated about motion events.

Notice the call to **invalidate()** in the **updateCurrentBox()** function. This forces **BoxDrawingView** to redraw itself so that the user can see the box while dragging across the screen. Which brings you to the next step: drawing the boxes to the screen.

# Rendering Inside onDraw(Canvas)

When your application is launched, all of its views are *invalid*. This means that they have not drawn anything to the screen. To fix this situation, Android calls the top-level **View**'s **draw()** function. This causes that view to draw itself, which causes its children to draw themselves. Those children's children then draw themselves, and so on down the hierarchy. When all the views in the hierarchy have drawn themselves, the top-level **View** is no longer invalid.

You can also manually specify that a view is invalid, even if it is currently on the screen. This will cause the system to redraw the view with any necessary updates. You will mark the **BoxDrawingView** as invalid any time the user creates a new box or resizes a box by moving their finger. This will ensure that users can see what their boxes look like as they create them.

To hook into this drawing, you override the following **View** function:

```
protected fun onDraw(canvas: Canvas)
```

The call to **invalidate()** that you make in response to ACTION_MOVE in **onTouchEvent(MotionEvent)** makes the **BoxDrawingView** invalid again. This causes it to redraw itself and will cause **onDraw(Canvas)** to be called again.

Now let's consider the **Canvas** parameter. **Canvas** and **Paint** are the two main drawing classes in Android:

- The **Canvas** class has all the drawing operations you perform. The functions you call on **Canvas** determine where and what you draw – a line, a circle, a word, or a rectangle.

- The **Paint** class determines how these operations are done. The functions you call on **Paint** specify characteristics – whether shapes are filled, which font text is drawn in, and what color lines are.

In BoxDrawingView.kt, create two **Paint** objects when the **BoxDrawingView** is initialized.

## Listing 30.6  Creating your paint (BoxDrawingView.kt)

```
class BoxDrawingView(context: Context, attrs: AttributeSet? = null) :
        View(context, attrs) {

    private var currentBox: Box? = null
    private val boxen = mutableListOf<Box>()
    private val boxPaint = Paint().apply {
        color = 0x22ff0000.toInt()
    }
    private val backgroundPaint = Paint().apply {
        color = 0xfff8efe0.toInt()
    }
    ...
}
```

Armed with paint, you can now draw your boxes to the screen.

### Listing 30.7 Overriding **onDraw(Canvas)** (BoxDrawingView.kt)

```kotlin
class BoxDrawingView(context: Context, attrs: AttributeSet? = null) :
        View(context, attrs)
    ...
    override fun onDraw(canvas: Canvas) {
        // Fill the background
        canvas.drawPaint(backgroundPaint)

        boxen.forEach { box ->
            canvas.drawRect(box.left, box.top, box.right, box.bottom, boxPaint)
        }
    }
}
```

The first part of this code is straightforward: Using your off-white background paint, you fill the canvas with a backdrop for your boxes.

Then, for each box in your list of boxes, you determine what the left, right, top, and bottom of the box should be by looking at the two points for the box. The left and top values will be the minimum values, and the bottom and right values will be the maximum values.

After calculating these values, you call **Canvas.drawRect(…)** to draw a red rectangle onto the screen.

Run DragAndDraw and draw some red rectangles (Figure 30.4).

### Figure 30.4 An expression of programmerly emotion

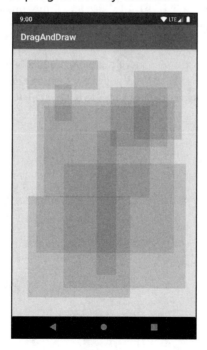

And that is it. You have now created a view that captures its own touch events and performs its own drawing.

# For the More Curious: GestureDetector

Another option for handling touch events is to use a **GestureDetector** object. Instead of adding logic to detect events like a swipe or a fling, the **GestureDetector** has listeners that do the heavy lifting and notify you when a particular event occurs. The **GestureDetector.OnGestureListener** implementation has functions for events such as long presses, flings, and scrolls. There is also a **GestureDetector.OnDoubleTapListener** that will fire when a double-press is detected. Many cases do not require the full control provided by overriding the **onTouch** function, so using the **GestureDetector** instead is a great choice.

# Challenge: Saving State

Figure out how to persist your boxes across orientation changes from within your **View**. This can be done with the following **View** functions:

```
protected fun onSaveInstanceState(): Parcelable
protected fun onRestoreInstanceState(state: Parcelable)
```

These functions do not work like **Activity** and **Fragment**'s **onSaveInstanceState(Bundle)**. First, they will only be called if your **View** has an ID. Second, instead of taking in a **Bundle**, they return and process an object that implements the **Parcelable** interface.

We recommend using a **Bundle** as the **Parcelable** instead of implementing a **Parcelable** class yourself. Kotlin has a @Parcelize annotation that makes it easier to create a **Parcelable** class, but the **Bundle** is a commonly used class in Android and most developers are very familiar with how it works.

Finally, you must also maintain the saved state of **BoxDrawingView**'s parent, the **View** class. Save the result of **super.onSaveInstanceState()** in your new **Bundle** and send that same result to the superclass when calling **super.onRestoreInstanceState(Parcelable)**.

# Challenge: Rotating Boxes

For a harder challenge, make it so that you can use a second finger to rotate your rectangles. To do this, you will need to handle multiple pointers in your **MotionEvent** handling code. You will also need to rotate your canvas.

When dealing with multiple touches, you need these extra ideas:

*pointer index*          tells you which pointer in the current set of pointers the event is for

*pointer ID*              gives you a unique ID for a specific finger in a gesture

The pointer index may change, but the pointer ID will not.

For more details, check out the documentation for the following **MotionEvent** functions:

```
final fun getActionMasked(): Int
final fun getActionIndex(): Int
final fun getPointerId(pointerIndex: Int): Int
final fun getX(pointerIndex: Int): Float
final fun getY(pointerIndex: Int): Float
```

Also look at the documentation for the ACTION_POINTER_UP and ACTION_POINTER_DOWN constants.

# Challenge: Accessibility Support

Built-in widgets provide support for accessibility options like TalkBack and Switch Access. Creating your own widgets places the responsibility on you as the developer to make sure your app is accessible. As a final challenge for this chapter, make your **BoxDrawingView** describable with TalkBack for low-vision users.

There are several ways you can approach this. You could provide an overall summary of the view and tell the user how much of the view is covered in boxes. Alternatively, you could also make each box an accessible element and have it describe its location on the screen to the user. Refer to Chapter 18 for more information on making your apps accessible.

# 31
# Property Animation

For an app to be functional, all you need to do is write your code correctly so that it does not crash. For an app to be a joy to use, though, you need to give it more love than that. You need to make it feel like a real, physical phenomenon playing out on a phone or tablet's screen.

Real things move. To make your UI move, you *animate* its elements into new positions.

In this chapter, you will write an app called Sunset that shows a scene of the sun in the sky. When you press on the scene, it will animate the sun down below the horizon, and the sky will change colors like a sunset.

## Building the Scene

The first step is to build the scene that will be animated. Create a new project called Sunset. Make sure that your minimum API level is set to 21, and use the empty activity template and AndroidX artifacts.

A sunset by the sea should be colorful, so it will help to start by naming a few colors. Open the colors.xml file in your res/values folder and add the following values to it.

Listing 31.1  Adding sunset colors (`res/values/colors.xml`)

```
<resources>
    <color name="colorPrimary">#008577</color>
    <color name="colorPrimaryDark">#00574B</color>
    <color name="colorAccent">#D81B60</color>

    <color name="bright_sun">#fcfcb7</color>
    <color name="blue_sky">#1e7ac7</color>
    <color name="sunset_sky">#ec8100</color>
    <color name="night_sky">#05192e</color>
    <color name="sea">#224869</color>
</resources>
```

Rectangular views will make for a fine impression of the sky and the sea. But, outside of Minecraft, people will not buy a rectangular sun, no matter how much you argue in favor of its technical simplicity. So, in the `res/drawable/` folder, add an oval shape drawable for a circular sun called `sun.xml`.

## Listing 31.2  Adding a sun XML drawable (res/drawable/sun.xml)

```xml
<shape xmlns:android="http://schemas.android.com/apk/res/android"
        android:shape="oval">
    <solid android:color="@color/bright_sun" />
</shape>
```

When you display this oval in a square view, you will get a circle. People will nod their heads in approval and then think about the real sun up in the sky.

Next, build the entire scene out in a layout file. Open `res/layout/activity_main.xml`, delete the current contents, and add the following.

## Listing 31.3  Setting up the layout (res/layout/activity_main.xml)

```xml
<LinearLayout xmlns:android="http://schemas.android.com/apk/res/android"
               android:id="@+id/scene"
               android:orientation="vertical"
               android:layout_width="match_parent"
               android:layout_height="match_parent">
    <FrameLayout
            android:id="@+id/sky"
            android:layout_width="match_parent"
            android:layout_height="0dp"
            android:layout_weight="0.61"
            android:background="@color/blue_sky">
        <ImageView
                android:id="@+id/sun"
                android:layout_width="100dp"
                android:layout_height="100dp"
                android:layout_gravity="center"
                android:src="@drawable/sun" />
    </FrameLayout>
    <View
            android:layout_width="match_parent"
            android:layout_height="0dp"
            android:layout_weight="0.39"
            android:background="@color/sea" />
</LinearLayout>
```

Check out the preview. You should see a daytime scene of the sun in a blue sky over a dark blue sea. Take a moment to run Sunset to make sure everything is hooked up correctly before moving on. It should look like Figure 31.1. Ahhh.

Figure 31.1  Before sunset

# Simple Property Animation

Now that you have the scene set up, it is time to make it do your bidding by moving parts of it around. You are going to animate the sun down below the horizon.

But before you start animating, you will want a few bits of information handy in your activity. Inside of `onCreate(…)`, pull out a couple of views into properties on **MainActivity**.

## Listing 31.4  Pulling out view references (MainActivity.kt)

```kotlin
class MainActivity : AppCompatActivity() {

    private lateinit var sceneView: View
    private lateinit var sunView: View
    private lateinit var skyView: View

    override fun onCreate(savedInstanceState: Bundle?) {
        super.onCreate(savedInstanceState)
        setContentView(R.layout.activity_main)

        sceneView = findViewById(R.id.scene)
        sunView = findViewById(R.id.sun)
        skyView = findViewById(R.id.sky)
    }
}
```

Now that you have those, you can write your code to animate the sun. Here is the plan: Smoothly move sunView so that its top is right at the edge of the bottom of the sky. Since the bottom of the sky and the top of the sea are the same, the sun will be hidden behind the sea view. You will do this by *translating* the location of the top of sunView to the bottom of its parent.

The reason the sun view moves behind the sea is not immediately apparent. This has to do with the draw order of the views. Views are drawn in the order they are declared in the layout. Views declared later in the layout are drawn on top of those further up. In this case, since the sun view is declared before the sea view, the sea view is on top of the sun view. When the sun animates past the sea, it will appear as though it goes behind it.

The first step is to find where the animation should start and end. Write this first step in a new function called **startAnimation()**.

## Listing 31.5  Getting tops of views (MainActivity.kt)

```kotlin
class MainActivity : AppCompatActivity() {
    ...
    override fun onCreate(savedInstanceState: Bundle?) {
        ...
    }

    private fun startAnimation() {
        val sunYStart = sunView.top.toFloat()
        val sunYEnd = skyView.height.toFloat()
    }
}
```

The top property is one of four properties on **View** that return the *local layout rect* for that view: top, bottom, right, and left. A rect (short for rectangle) is the rectangular bounding box for the view, which is specified by those four properties. A view's local layout rect specifies the position and size of that view in relation to its parent, as determined when the view was laid out.

It is possible to change the location of the view onscreen by modifying these values, but it is not recommended. They are reset every time a layout pass occurs, so they tend not to hold their value.

In any event, the animation will start with the top of the view at its current location. It needs to end with the top at the bottom of sunView's parent, skyView. To get it there, it should be as far down as skyView is tall, which you find by calling **height.toFloat()**. The height property's value is the same as bottom minus top.

Now that you know where the animation should start and end, create and run an **ObjectAnimator** to perform it.

### Listing 31.6  Creating a sun animator (MainActivity.kt)

```kotlin
private fun startAnimation() {
    val sunYStart = sunView.top.toFloat()
    val sunYEnd = skyView.height.toFloat()

    val heightAnimator = ObjectAnimator
        .ofFloat(sunView, "y", sunYStart, sunYEnd)
        .setDuration(3000)

    heightAnimator.start()
}
```

We will come back to how **ObjectAnimator** works in a moment. First, hook up **startAnimation()** so that it is called every time the user presses anywhere in the scene.

### Listing 31.7  Starting animation on press (MainActivity.kt)

```kotlin
override fun onCreate(savedInstanceState: Bundle?) {
    super.onCreate(savedInstanceState)
    setContentView(R.layout.activity_main)

    sceneView = findViewById(R.id.scene)
    sunView = findViewById(R.id.sun)
    skyView = findViewById(R.id.sky)

    sceneView.setOnClickListener {
        startAnimation()
    }
}
```

Run Sunset and press anywhere on the scene to run the animation (Figure 31.2).

## Figure 31.2  Setting sun

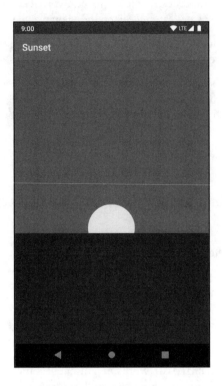

You should see the sun move below the horizon.

Here is how it works: **ObjectAnimator** is a *property animator*. Instead of knowing specifically about how to move a view around the screen, a property animator repeatedly calls property setter functions with different values.

You created an **ObjectAnimator** in the call to **ObjectAnimator.ofFloat(sunView, "y", 0, 1)**. When that **ObjectAnimator** is started, it then repeatedly calls **sunView.setY(Float)** with values starting at 0 and moving up. Like this:

```
sunView.setY(0)
sunView.setY(0.02)
sunView.setY(0.04)
sunView.setY(0.06)
sunView.setY(0.08)
...
```

… and so on, until it finally calls **sunView.setY(1)**. This process of finding values between a starting and ending point is called *interpolation*. Between each interpolated value, a little time will pass, which makes it look like the view is moving.

# View transformation properties

Property animators are great, but with them alone it would be impossible to animate a view as easily as you just did. Modern Android property animation works in concert with *transformation properties*.

We said earlier that your view has a local layout rect, which is the position and size it is assigned in the layout process. You can move the view around after that by setting additional properties on the view, called transformation properties. You have three properties to rotate the view (rotation, pivotX, and pivotY, shown in Figure 31.3), two properties to scale the view vertically and horizontally (scaleX and scaleY, shown in Figure 31.4), and two properties to move the view around the screen (translationX and translationY, shown in Figure 31.5).

## Figure 31.3  View rotation

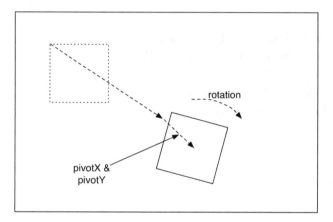

## Figure 31.4  View scaling

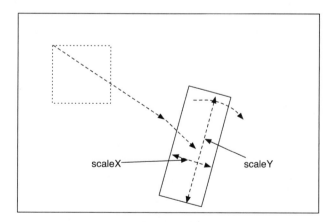

## Figure 31.5  View translation

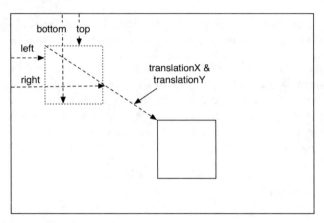

All of these properties can be fetched and modified. For example, if you wanted to know the current value of translationX, you would invoke view.translationX. If you wanted to set it, you would invoke view.translationX = Float.

So what does the y property do? The x and y properties are conveniences built on top of local layout coordinates and the transformation properties. They allow you to write code that simply says, "Put this view at this X coordinate and this Y coordinate." Under the hood, these properties will modify translationX or translationY to put the view where you want it to be. That means that setting sunView.y = 50 really means this:

```
sunView.translationY = 50 - sunView.top
```

# Using different interpolators

Your animation, while pretty, is abrupt. If the sun was really sitting there perfectly still in the sky, it would take a moment for it to accelerate into the animation you see. To add this sensation of acceleration, all you need to do is use a **TimeInterpolator**. **TimeInterpolator** has one role: to change the way your animation goes from point A to point B.

Use an **AccelerateInterpolator** in **startAnimation()** to make your sun speed up a bit at the beginning.

## Listing 31.8 Adding acceleration (`MainActivity.kt`)

```
private fun startAnimation() {
    val sunYStart = sunView.top.toFloat()
    val sunYEnd = skyView.height.toFloat()

    val heightAnimator = ObjectAnimator
        .ofFloat(sunView, "y", sunYStart, sunYEnd)
        .setDuration(3000)
    heightAnimator.interpolator = AccelerateInterpolator()

    heightAnimator.start()
}
```

Run Sunset one more time and press to see your animation. Your sun should now start moving slowly and accelerate to a quicker pace as it moves toward the horizon.

There are a lot of styles of motion you might want to use in your app, so there are a lot of different **TimeInterpolator**s. To see all the interpolators that ship with Android, look at the Known indirect subclasses section in the reference documentation for **TimeInterpolator**.

## Color evaluation

Now that your sun is animating down, let's animate the sky to a sunset-appropriate color. Pull out the colors you defined in colors.xml into properties using a lazy delegate.

### Listing 31.9  Pulling out sunset colors (MainActivity.kt)

```
class MainActivity : AppCompatActivity() {

    private lateinit var sceneView: View
    private lateinit var sunView: View
    private lateinit var skyView: View

    private val blueSkyColor: Int by lazy {
        ContextCompat.getColor(this, R.color.blue_sky)
    }
    private val sunsetSkyColor: Int by lazy {
        ContextCompat.getColor(this, R.color.sunset_sky)
    }
    private val nightSkyColor: Int by lazy {
        ContextCompat.getColor(this, R.color.night_sky)
    }
    ...
}
```

Now add an animation to **startAnimation()** to animate the sky from blueSkyColor to sunsetSkyColor.

### Listing 31.10  Animating sky colors (MainActivity.kt)

```
private fun startAnimation() {
    val sunYStart = sunView.top.toFloat()
    val sunYEnd = skyView.height.toFloat()

    val heightAnimator = ObjectAnimator
        .ofFloat(sunView, "y", sunYStart, sunYEnd)
        .setDuration(3000)
    heightAnimator.interpolator = AccelerateInterpolator()

    val sunsetSkyAnimator = ObjectAnimator
        .ofInt(skyView, "backgroundColor", blueSkyColor, sunsetSkyColor)
        .setDuration(3000)

    heightAnimator.start()
    sunsetSkyAnimator.start()
}
```

This seems like it is headed in the right direction, but if you run it you will see that something is amiss. Instead of moving smoothly from blue to orange, the colors will kaleidoscope wildly.

The reason this happens is that a color integer is not a simple number. It is four smaller numbers schlupped together into one Int. So for **ObjectAnimator** to properly evaluate which color is halfway between blue and orange, it needs to know how that works.

When **ObjectAnimator**'s normal understanding of how to find values between the start and end is insufficient, you can provide a subclass of **TypeEvaluator** to fix things. A **TypeEvaluator** is an object that tells **ObjectAnimator** what value is, say, a quarter of the way between a start value and end value. Android provides a subclass of **TypeEvaluator** called **ArgbEvaluator** that will do the trick here.

## Listing 31.11  Providing **ArgbEvaluator** (MainActivity.kt)

```kotlin
private fun startAnimation() {
    val sunYStart = sunView.top.toFloat()
    val sunYEnd = skyView.height.toFloat()

    val heightAnimator = ObjectAnimator
        .ofFloat(sunView, "y", sunYStart, sunYEnd)
        .setDuration(3000)
    heightAnimator.interpolator = AccelerateInterpolator()

    val sunsetSkyAnimator = ObjectAnimator
        .ofInt(skyView, "backgroundColor", blueSkyColor, sunsetSkyColor)
        .setDuration(3000)
    sunsetSkyAnimator.setEvaluator(ArgbEvaluator())

    heightAnimator.start()
    sunsetSkyAnimator.start()
}
```

(There are multiple versions of **ArgbEvaluator**; import the android.animation version.)

Run your animation once again, and you should see the sky fade to a beautiful orange color (Figure 31.6).

## Figure 31.6  Changing sunset color

# Playing Animators Together

If all you need to do is kick off a few animations at the same time, then your job is simple: Call **start()** on them all at the same time. They will all animate in sync with one another.

For more sophisticated animation choreography, this will not do the trick. For example, to complete the illusion of a sunset, it would be nice to show the sky turning from orange to a midnight blue after the sun goes down.

This can be done by using an **AnimatorListener**, which tells you when an animation completes. So you could write a listener that waits until the end of the first animation, at which time you can start the second night sky animation. But this is a huge hassle and requires a lot of listeners. It is much easier to use an **AnimatorSet**.

First, build out the night sky animation and delete your old animation start code.

Listing 31.12  Building night animation (`MainActivity.kt`)

```
private fun startAnimation() {
    val sunYStart = sunView.top.toFloat()
    val sunYEnd = skyView.height.toFloat()

    val heightAnimator = ObjectAnimator
        .ofFloat(sunView, "y", sunYStart, sunYEnd)
        .setDuration(3000)
    heightAnimator.interpolator = AccelerateInterpolator()

    val sunsetSkyAnimator = ObjectAnimator
        .ofInt(skyView, "backgroundColor", blueSkyColor, sunsetSkyColor)
        .setDuration(3000)
    sunsetSkyAnimator.setEvaluator(ArgbEvaluator())

    val nightSkyAnimator = ObjectAnimator
        .ofInt(skyView, "backgroundColor", sunsetSkyColor, nightSkyColor)
        .setDuration(1500)
    nightSkyAnimator.setEvaluator(ArgbEvaluator())

    heightAnimator.start()
    sunsetSkyAnimator.start()
}
```

And then build and run an **AnimatorSet**.

Listing 31.13  Building an animator set (`MainActivity.kt`)

```
private fun startAnimation() {
    ...
    val nightSkyAnimator = ObjectAnimator
        .ofInt(skyView, "backgroundColor", sunsetSkyColor, nightSkyColor)
        .setDuration(1500)
    nightSkyAnimator.setEvaluator(ArgbEvaluator())

    val animatorSet = AnimatorSet()
    animatorSet.play(heightAnimator)
        .with(sunsetSkyAnimator)
        .before(nightSkyAnimator)
    animatorSet.start()
}
```

An **AnimatorSet** is nothing more than a set of animations that can be played together. There are a few ways to build one, but the easiest way is to use the **play(Animator)** function you used above.

When you call **play(Animator)**, you get an **AnimatorSet.Builder**, which allows you to build a chain of instructions. The **Animator** passed into **play(Animator)** is the "subject" of the chain. So the chain of calls you wrote here could be described as, "Play heightAnimator with sunsetSkyAnimator; also, play heightAnimator before nightSkyAnimator." For complicated **AnimatorSet**s, you may find it necessary to call **play(Animator)** a few times, which is perfectly fine.

Run your app one more time and savor the soothing sunset you have created. Magic.

# For the More Curious: Other Animation APIs

While property animation is the most broadly useful tool in the animation toolbox, it is not the only one. Whether or not you are using them, it is a good idea to know about the other tools out there.

## Legacy animation tools

One set of tools is the classes living in the android.view.animation package. This should not be confused with the newer android.animation package, which was introduced in Honeycomb.

This is the legacy animation framework, which you should mainly know about so that you can ignore it. If you see the word "animaTION" in the class name instead of "animaTOR", that is a good sign that it is a legacy tool you should ignore.

## Transitions

Android 4.4 introduced a new transitions framework, which enables fancy transitions between view hierarchies. For example, you might define a transition that explodes a small view in one activity into a zoomed-in version of that view in another activity.

The basic idea of the transitions framework is that you can define scenes, which represent the state of a view hierarchy at some point, and transitions between those scenes. Scenes can be described in layout XML files, and transitions can be described in animation XML files.

When an activity is already running, as in this chapter, the transitions framework is not that useful. This is where the property animation framework shines. However, the property animation framework is not good at animating a layout as it is coming onto the screen.

Take CriminalIntent's crime pictures as an example. If you were to try to implement a "zoom" animation to the zoomed-in dialog of an image, you would have to figure out where the original image was and where the new image would be on the dialog. **ObjectAnimator** cannot achieve an effect like that without a lot of work. In that case, you would want to use the transitions framework instead.

# Challenges

For the first challenge, add the ability to *reverse* the sunset after it is completed, so your user can press for a sunset, and then press a second time to get a sunrise. You will need to build another **AnimatorSet** to do this – **AnimatorSet**s cannot be run in reverse.

For a second challenge, add a continuing animation to the sun. Make it pulsate with heat, or give it a spinning halo of rays. (You can use the **setRepeatCount(Int)** function on **ObjectAnimator** to make your animation repeat itself.)

Another good challenge would be to have a reflection of the sun in the water.

Your final challenge is to add the ability to press to reverse the sunset scene while it is still happening. So if your user presses the scene while the sun is halfway down, it will go right back up again seamlessly. Likewise, if your user presses the scene while transitioning to night, it will smoothly transition right back to a sunrise.

# 32

# Afterword

Congratulations! You are at the end of this guide. Not everyone has the discipline to do what you have done – and learn what you have learned. Take a moment to give yourself a pat on the back.

Your hard work has paid off: You are now an Android developer.

## The Final Challenge

We have one last challenge for you: Become a *good* Android developer. Good developers are each good in their own way, so you must find your own path from here on out.

Where might you start? Here are some places we recommend:

*Write code.* Now. You will quickly forget what you have learned here if you do not apply it. Contribute to a project or write a simple application of your own. Whatever you do, waste no time: Write code.

*Learn.* You have learned a little bit about a lot of things in this book. Did any of them spark your imagination? Write some code to play around with your favorite thing. Find and read more documentation about it – or an entire book, if there is one. Also, check out the Android Developers YouTube channel (`youtube.com/user/androiddevelopers`) and listen to the Android Developers Backstage podcast (`androidbackstage.blogspot.com`) for Android updates from Google.

*Meet people.* Local meetups are a good place to meet like-minded developers. Lots of top-notch Android developers are active on Twitter. Attend Android conferences to meet other Android developers (like us!).

*Explore the open-source community.* Android development is exploding on `github.com`. When you find a cool library, see what other projects its contributors are committing to. Share your own code, too – you never know who will find it useful or interesting. We find the Android Weekly mailing list (`androidweekly.net`) to be a great way to see what is happening in the Android community.

## Shameless Plugs

You can find all of us on Twitter. Kristin is `@kristinmars`, Brian is `@briangardnerdev`, Bill is `@billjings`, and Chris is `@cstew`.

If you enjoyed this book, check out the other Big Nerd Ranch Guides at `bignerdranch.com/books`. We also have a broad selection of weeklong courses for developers, where we can help you learn this amount of stuff in only a week. And, of course, if you just need someone to write great code, we do contract programming, too. For more information, go to our website at `bignerdranch.com`.

# Thank You

Without readers like you, our work would not exist. Thank you for buying and reading our book.

# Index

## Symbols

`.apk` file, 33, 438
9-patch images, 439
`<uses-feature>` tag, 327
`??` (null coalescing) operator, 389
`@+id`, 24
`@Before` annotation, 400
`@Bindable` annotation, 387
`@Dao` annotation (Room), 226
`@Database` annotation (Room), 224, 294
`@Entity` annotation (Room), 223
`@GET` annotation
    parameterless, 508
    with parameters, 475
`@Insert` annotation, 256
`@MainThread` annotation, 508
`@OnLifecycleEvent(Lifecycle.Event)`
annotation, 512
`@PrimaryKey` annotation (Room), 223
`@Query` annotation
    in Retrofit, 542
    in Room, 226
`@string/` syntax, 16
`@StringRes` annotation, 38
`@Test` annotation, 401
`@TypeConverter` annotation (Room), 225
`@TypeConverters` annotation (Room), 225
`@UiThread` annotation, 508
`@Update` annotation, 256
`@WorkerThread` annotation, 508
`@{}` (binding mustache) operator, 381, 384

## A

aapt2 (Android Asset Packing tool), 33
abstract classes, 224
accessibility
    (see also TalkBack)
    about, 345, 357
    accessibility focus, 349
    Accessibility Scanner, 359
    accessibility services, 346
    `android:contentDescription` attribute, 353
    `android:focusable` attribute, 356
    `android:labelFor` attribute, 364

Explore by Touch, 350
    `setContentDescription(…)`, 357
    ticker text, 565
    for touch targets, 362
Accessibility Scanner, 359
action views, 544
**ActionBar** class, 288
`ACTION_CALL` category, 309
`ACTION_DIAL` category, 309
`ACTION_IMAGE_CAPTURE` action (**MediaStore**), 319
`ACTION_PICK` category, 302
`ACTION_SEND` category, 298
activities
    (see also **Activity** class, fragments)
    about, 2
    adding to project, 5, 113-134
    as controllers, 40
    back stack, 134, 456
    base, 456
    child, 114, 127
    configuration changes and, 70-74, 604
    creating, 115
    declaring in manifest, 119
    finishing, 70
    fragment transactions and, 244
    hosting fragments, 150, 166, 167, 172
    keeping thin, 41
    label (display name), 451
    launcher, 131
    lifecycle, 61, 70
    lifecycle diagram, 92
    lifecycle, and hosted fragments, 172
    overriding functions in, 62, 64
    passing data between, 123-131
    process death and, 88
    record, 92
    rotation and, 70-74
    single activity architecture, 244
    stack, 132
    starting, defined, 114
    starting, in another application, 291
    starting, in current task, 456
    starting, in new task, 460
    starting, with `startActivity(Intent)`, 122
    states, 61, 92
    tasks and, 456
    UI flexibility and, 148
**Activity** class

about, 2
as **Context** subclass, 28
**getIntent()**, 126
lifecycle functions, 61-66
**onActivityResult(…)**, 129
**onCreate(Bundle?)**, 61
**onCreateOptionsMenu(Menu)**, 280
**onDestroy()**, 61
**onPause()**, 61
**onResume()**, 61
**onSaveInstanceState(Bundle)**, 88
**onStart()**, 61
**onStop()**, 61
overriding superclass functions, 64
**setContentView(…)**, 20
**setResult(…)**, 128
**startActivity(Intent)**, 122, 298
**startActivityForResult(…)**, 127
activity record, 92
**ActivityInfo** class (**ResolveInfo**), 454
**ActivityManager** class
back stack, 132, 134
starting activities, 122, 123, 129
**ActivityNotFoundException** class, 123
**Adapter** class
about, 185
**getItemCount()**, 186
**onBindViewHolder(…)**, 186
**onCreateViewHolder(…)**, 186
adb (Android Debug Bridge) driver, 54
**add(…)** function (**FragmentTransaction**), 169
**addFlags(Int)** function (**Intent**), 460
**addToBackStack(String)** function
(**FragmentTransaction**), 248
Android Asset Packing tool (aapt), 33
Android Asset Studio, 285
Android Debug Bridge (adb) driver, 54
Android developer documentation, 143, 144
Android firmware versions, 135
Android Lint
as code inspector, 38
as static analyzer, 107
compatibility and, 139-141
running, 107
suppressing warnings, 522
Android SDK Manager, xx
Android Studio
Android Asset Studio, 285

Android Lint code inspector, 38
**AppCompat** theme default, 417
assets (see assets)
build process, 33
build tool window, 8
code completion, 28, 160
creating activities, 115
creating classes, 38
creating layout files, 71
creating menu files, 278
creating packages, 224
creating projects, 3-7
creating values resource files, 330
debugger, 102, 104
(see also debugging)
devices view, 54
editor, 9
graphical layout tool, 197, 342
(see also layouts)
installing, xx
Instant Run, 4
Logcat, 32
(see also Logcat, logging)
9-patch editor, 443
plug-ins, 222
previewing layout decorations, 19
project tool window, 8
project window, 8
run configurations, 406
shortcut to override functions, 186
tool windows, 8
Translations Editor, 334
variables view, 105
Android versions (see SDK versions)
Android Virtual Device Manager, 29
Android Virtual Devices (AVDs), creating, 29
Android XML namespace, 15
**android.text.format.DateFormat** class, 220
**android.util.Log** class (see **Log** class)
android.view.animation package, 636
android:background attribute, 412
android:configChanges attribute, 604
android:contentDescription attribute, 58, 353
android:documentLaunchMode attribute, 468
android:drawableEnd attribute, 52
android:drawablePadding attribute, 52
android:focusable attribute, 356

`android:grantUriPermissions` attribute, 316, 321

`android:icon` attribute, 285

`android:id` attribute, 24

`android:labelFor` attribute, 364

`android:layout_gravity` attribute, 73

`android:layout_height` attribute, 16

`android:layout_margin` attribute, 218

`android:layout_width` attribute, 16

`android:name` attribute, 119

`android:orientation` attribute, 16

`android:padding` attribute, 218

`android:protectionLevel` attribute, 579

`android:text` attribute, 16

`AndroidManifest.xml` (see manifest)

AndroidX (see Jetpack libraries)

animation

    (see also transformation properties)

    about, 623-636

    `android.view.animation` package, 636

    draw order of views, 626

    interpolation, 628

    property animation vs transitions framework, 636

    running multiple animators, 634, 635

    simple property animation, 626-633

    transitions framework, 636

    translation, 626

`AnimatorListener` class, 634

`AnimatorSet` class

    about, 634

    `play(Animator)`, 634

API levels (see SDK versions)

`.apk` file, 33, 438

app bar

    about, 275

    action views in, 544

    `app:showAsAction` attribute, 278

    `colorPrimary` theme attribute and, 418

    default from `AppCompatActivity`, 276

    menu (see menus)

    previewing, 19

    terminology vs action bar, toolbar, 288

app features

    app bar, 275

    declaring in manifest, 327

app namespace, 279

`app/build.gradle` file, 78

`app/java` directory, 20

`app:showAsAction` attribute, 278

AppCompat foundation library

    about, 276

    app namespace, 279

    themes in, 417

`AppCompatActivity` class, 20

application architecture

    about, 368

    data binding and, 381

    Google Guide to App Architecture, 227

    Model-View-Controller (MVC), 40

    Model-View-View Model (MVVM), 368

    repository pattern, 227, 484

    single activity architecture, 244

    Single Responsibility Principle, 382

    with fragments, 173

`Application` class

    `onCreate()`, 228

    registering in manifest, 229

    subclassing, 228

application lifecycle, accessing, 228

`AppTheme` theme, 416

`Array.last(…)` function, 377

`AssetManager` class

    about, 376

    `list(String)`, 376

assets

    about, 373

    accessing, 394

    importing, 373-375

    managing, 376, 377

    presenting to user, 377-380

    vs resources, 373

attributes, 14

    (see also layout attributes, individual attribute names)

`AttributeSet` class, 613

auto-completion, 28

AVDs (Android Virtual Devices), creating, 29

## B

Back button, 70, 456, 610

back stack, 132

background threads

    about, 235

    `@WorkerThread` annotation, 508

**Call.enqueue(…)** (Retrofit) and, 479
communication with main thread, 516
dedicated, 509
**doWork()** and, 556
**Executor** and, 257
for asynchronous network requests, 479
for long-running tasks, 235
**HandlerThread** and, 510
lifecycle aware, 511
**LiveData** and, 236
scheduling work on, 557
scheduling work on main thread from, 524
**Worker** and, 555
**BaseObservable** class, 386
@Before annotation, 400
**beginTransaction()** function
(**FragmentManager**), 169
@Bindable annotation, 387
**Bitmap** class, 322
**BitmapFactory** class
**decodeFile(photoFile.getPath())**, 322
**decodeStream(InputStream)**, 508
bitmaps
caching, 537
downloading, 508
resizing, 322
scaling and displaying, 322-326
**bottom** property (**View**), 627
breakpoints, setting, 102-106
(see also debugging)
broadcast intents
about, 573
ordered, 582-585
permissions and, 577
registered in code, 580, 581
regular intents vs, 573
sending, 575
broadcast receivers
about, 573
dynamic, 580, 581
implementing, 576-581
intent filters and, 574
limitations, 589
long-running tasks and, 586
permissions and, 577-579
standalone, 575
broadcasts, system vs custom, 573
build errors, 25, 111

(see also debugging)
build process, 33
build tool window (Android Studio), 8
**build.gradle**, 137
**Build.VERSION.SDK_INT**, 140
**Bundle** class
in **onCreate(Bundle?)**, 88
in **onSaveInstanceState(Bundle)**, 88
**putCharSequence(…)**, 249
**putInt(…)**, 249
**putSerializable(…)**, 249
**Button** class
example, 12
vs **ImageButton**, 57
inheritance, 58
buttons
(see also **Button** class, **ImageButton** class)
adding icons, 52
adding IDs, 24
drawables for, 429
modifying attributes, 423-426
9-patch images for, 439
by **lazy**, 86

## C

caching
about, 537
LRU (least recently used) strategy, 537
**Calendar** class, 270
**Call** class (Retrofit), 475
callback interfaces, in fragments, 244-246
camera
about, 311-328
firing intent, 319
taking pictures with intents, 318-321
**Canvas** class, 618
**Channel** class, 563
**CheckBox** class, 156
choosers, creating, 300
Chrome Custom Tabs, 608
**Class** class, explicit intents and, 122
classes
(see also singletons)
abstract classes, 224
dependencies, 500
importing, 25
inner classes, 523

code completion, 28
codenames, version, 135
color
    colorAccent theme attribute, 419
    colorPrimary theme attribute, 418
    colorPrimaryDark theme attribute, 418
    for animation, 632
    res/values/colors.xml, 412
    resources, 412
    themes and, 418
companion objects, 125
compatibility
    Android Lint and, 139-141
    fragments and, 159
    importance, 136
    issues, 136
    Jetpack libraries and, 159
    minimum SDK version and, 138
    using conditional code for, 140
    wrapping code for, 139-142
compile SDK version, 138
compileSdkVersion, 137
ComponentName class, 455
components, 122
concurrent documents, 467
configuration changes
    activity/fragment lifecycles and, 163
    android:configChanges attribute and, 604
    effect on activities, 70
    effect on fragments, 531
configuration qualifiers
    about, 72
    for language, 330
    listed, 337
    multiple, 340-342
    order of precedence, 338-342
    for screen density, 49, 333
    for screen orientation, 72
    for screen size, 343
ConstraintLayout class
    about, 196
    converting layout to use, 198
    Guideline, 219
    MotionLayout, 219
constraints
    about, 196
    adding in graphical layout editor, 205
    in XML, 208

removing, 201
    warnings when insufficient, 201
Constraints class, and WorkRequest, 558
contacts
    getting data from, 304
    permissions for, 306
container views
    about, 166
    IDs, 169
ContentProvider class, 304, 316
    (see also FileProvider convenience class)
ContentResolver class, 304
Context class
    AssetManager, 376
    explicit intents and, 122
    functions for private files and directories, 315
    resource IDs and, 28
    revokeUriPermission(…), 325
Context.MODE_WORLD_READABLE, 315
controller objects, 40
conventions (see naming conventions)
Converter.Factory class (Retrofit), 477
converters
    about, 476
    converter factories, 477
    scalars converter, 476
createChooser(…) function (Intent), 300

D

d(String, String, Throwable) function (Log), 101
@Dao annotation (Room), 226
data access objects (DAOs), 226
data binding
    about, 370
    @{} (binding mustache) operator, 381, 384, 387, 389
    application architecture and, 381
    binding adapters, 390
    binding classes, 370
    declaring objects in layout files, 381
    enabling, 370
    lambda expressions, 389
    layout files and, 370
    null handling in, 389
    observable data, 386
    view models and, 382, 384, 385

Data Binding architecture component library (see data binding)

data classes, 38

data persistence
    using databases, 221
    using fragment arguments, 259
    using saved instance state, 88
    using **SharedPreferences**, 549
    using **ViewModel**, 81

data/data directory, 231

@Database annotation (Room), 224, 294

databases
    (see also Room architecture component library)
    accessing, 227
    accessing on a background thread, 235
    data access objects (DAOs), 226
    database classes, 224
    entities, 223
    for storing app data, 221
    primary keys, 223
    repository pattern, 227
    schemas, 241
    Structured Query Language (SQL), 226
    type conversion, 225

**Date** class, 270

**DateFormat** class, 220

**DatePickerDialog** class
    about, 263
    wrapping in **DialogFragment**, 264

debug key, 33

debugging
    (see also Android Lint, Android Studio)
    about, 97
    build errors, 111
    crashes, 99
    crashes on unconnected device, 100
    issues with **R** class, 111
    logging stack traces vs setting breakpoints, 106
    misbehaviors, 100
    online help for, 111
    running app with debugger, 103
    stopping debugger, 106
    using breakpoints, 102-106

DEFAULT category (**Intent**), 462

default resources, 333

density-independent pixel, 53

dependencies, adding, 78

dependency injection (DI) design pattern
    about, 501
    injectors, 242

developer documentation, 143, 144

devices
    configurations, 71
        (see also configuration qualifiers)
    configuring language settings, 330
    enabling developer options, 90
    hardware, 29
    testing configurations, 342
    virtual, 29

devices view (Android Studio), 54

**Dialog** class, 263

**DialogFragment** class
    about, 264
    **onCreateDialog(Bundle?)**, 265
    **show(…)**, 266

dialogs, 263-267

dip (density-independent pixel), 53

documentation, 143

dp (density-independent pixel), 53

**draw()** function (**View**), 618

drawables
    about, 429
    directories, 49
    layer list, 435
    9-patch images, 439
    referencing, 52
    screen density and, 49
    shape, 431
    state list, 433
    XML drawables, 429

drawing
    **Canvas**, 618
    in **onDraw(Canvas)**, 618
    **Paint**, 618

## E

editor (Android Studio), 9

**EditText** class, 156

emulator
    creating a virtual device for, 29
    enabling developer options, 90
    installing, xx
    Quick Settings, 60

rotating, 52, 59
running on, 29
search queries on, 548
simulating network types, 558
enqueue(…) function (Retrofit), 478
@Entity annotation (Room), 223
errors
    (see also debugging, exceptions)
    Android Studio indicators, 25
    avoiding using StrictMode, 536
    ERROR log level, 76
escape sequence (in string), 44
event buses, 587
event driven applications, 26
Exception class, 101
exceptions
    (see also debugging, errors)
    about, 101
    ActivityNotFoundException, 123
    creating, 101
    IllegalStateException, 84, 228, 267
    in Logcat, 32, 99
    java.lang exceptions in Kotlin code, 99
    kotlin.RuntimeException, 99
    logging, 76
    NetworkOnMainThreadException, 479
    Resources.NotFoundException, 333
    StrictMode and, 536
    type-aliasing and, 99
    UninitializedPropertyAccessException,
    99, 492
execute function (Executor), 257
executePendingBindings() function
(ViewDataBinding), 385
Executor class
    about, 257
    and Executors.newSingleThreadExecutor(),
    257
    execute, 257
explicit intents
    about, 123, 291
    creating, 122
    creating at runtime, 455
    implicit intents vs, 291
Explore by Touch, 350
extras
    about, 124
    as key-value pairs, 124

naming, 124
putting, 124, 125
retrieving, 125
structure, 124

**F**

File class
    getCacheDir(), 315
    getDir(…), 315
    getFilesDir(), 315
file storage
    authorities, 316
    granting write permission, 316, 321
    private, 315
    revoking write permission, 325
    shared between apps, 315
FileDescriptor class, 394
FileInputStream.openFileInput(…), 315
fileList(…) function (String), 315
FileOutputStream.openFileOutput(…), 315
FileProvider convenience class, 316
Flickr
    API, 485
    searching in, 540-543
fluent interface, 169
format strings, 294
fragment arguments, 249-251, 259, 269
Fragment class
    getArguments(…), 251
    getTargetFragment(), 271
    getTargetRequestCode(), 271
    newInstance(…), 250
    onActivityCreated(Bundle?), 172
    onActivityResult(…), 268
    onAttach(Context?), 172
    onCreate(Bundle?), 161, 172
    onCreateOptionsMenu(…), 280
    onCreateView(…), 161, 172
    onDestroy(), 172
    onDestroyView(), 172
    onDetach(), 172
    onOptionsItemSelected(MenuItem), 280,
    283
    onPause(), 172
    onResume(), 172
    onSaveInstanceState(Bundle), 161
    onStart(), 172

**onStop()**, 172
**onViewCreated(…)**, 172
**setArguments(…)**, 250
**setHasOptionsMenu(Boolean)**, 280
**setTargetFragment(…)**, 271
**startActivity(Intent)**, 299
versions, 159
fragment transactions
(see also **FragmentTransaction** class)
about, 168-170
activities and, 244
adding a fragment to an activity, 169
adding to back stack, 248
replacing a fragment in an activity, 247
**FragmentManager** class
adding fragments, 169, 170
**beginTransaction()**, 169
responsibilities, 168
role in rotation, 531
fragments
(see also **Fragment** class, fragment
transactions, **FragmentManager** class)
about, 149
activities vs, 148
activity lifecycle and, 172
adding to **FragmentManager**, 168-173
application architecture with, 173
arguments bundle, 249-251
as composable units, 148, 244
checking for existing, 170, 472
compatibility and, 159
container view IDs, 169
container views for, 166
creating, 156
defining a callback interface, 244-246
delegating functionality to activity, 244
effect of configuration changes on, 531
fragment transactions, 169
hosting, 150, 166, 167
implementing lifecycle functions, 160, 161
in single activity architecture, 244
inflating layouts for, 161
Jetpack libraries and, 159
lifecycle, 160, 172
lifecycle diagram, 533
lifecycle functions, 172
maintaining independence, 244
passing data between (same activity), 268

passing data with fragment arguments, 269
perceived lifetime, 511
reasons for, 148, 174
reasons not to retain, 534
retaining, 531-534
setting listeners in, 162
target fragments, 271
UI flexibility and, 148
using Jetpack (**androidx**) version, 159
widgets and, 162
**FragmentTransaction** class
**add(…)**, 169
**addToBackStack(String)**, 248
**replace(…)**, 247
**FrameLayout** class
about, 73
as container view for fragments, 166

**G**

**GestureDetector** class, 620
**@GET** annotation
parameterless, 508
with parameters, 475
**getAction()** function (**MotionEvent**), 615
**getArguments(…)** function (**Fragment**), 251
**getBooleanExtra(…)** function (**Intent**), 125
**getCacheDir()** function (**File**), 315
**getDir(…)** function (**File**), 315
**getFilesDir()** function (**File**), 315
**getIntent()** function (**Activity**), 126
**getTargetFragment()** function (**Fragment**), 271
**getTargetRequestCode()** function (**Fragment**), 271
Google Drive, 468
graphical layout tool (Android Studio), 197, 342
**GridLayoutManager** class, 472, 505
**GridView** class, 193
Gson library, 489
**Guideline** class, 219

**H**

**Handler** class
as target of **Message**, 518
for communication between threads, 517
**Looper** and, 524
**post(Runnable)**, 525
handlers, 518-531

**HandlerThread** class
    background threads and, 510
    **Looper** and, 517
hardware devices, 29
-hdpi suffix, 49
height property (**View**), 627
Home button, 66
HOME category (**Intent**), 462
Home screen, 462, 463
HTTP networking (see networking)

# I

icons, 285-287
**IllegalStateException** class, 84, 228, 267
**ImageButton** class, 57
images, layouts for, 312-314
implicit intents
    about, 123, 291
    action, 296, 449
    ACTION_CALL category, 309
    ACTION_DIAL category, 309
    ACTION_IMAGE_CAPTURE action, 318
    ACTION_PICK category, 302
    ACTION_SEND category, 298
    benefits of using, 291
    categories, 296, 449
    CATEGORY_DEFAULT flag, 451
    data, 296
    DEFAULT category, 462
    explicit intents vs, 291, 296
    extras, 297
    EXTRA_OUTPUT extra, 319
    FLAG_ACTIVITY_NEW_DOCUMENT flag, 468
    FLAG_GRANT_READ_URI_PERMISSION flag, 306
    FLAG_GRANT_WRITE_URI_PERMISSION flag, 321
    for browsing web content, 594
    HOME category, 462
    LAUNCHER category, 131, 451
    MAIN category, 131, 451
    parts of, 296
    taking pictures with, 318-321
inflating layouts, 20, 161
inheritance, 414, 427
inner classes, and memory leaks, 523
inner keyword, 506
@Insert annotation, 256
integration testing

about, 408
Espresso tool, 408
mock objects, 409
vs unit testing, 399
**Intent** class
    about, 296
    **addFlags(Int)**, 460
    constructors, 122, 298
    **createChooser(…)**, 300
    **getBooleanExtra(…)**, 125
    **putExtra(…)**, 124
    **setClassName(…)**, 455
intent filters
    about, 131
    explained, 297
    SHOW_NOTIFICATION, 580
Intent.FLAG_ACTIVITY_NEW_DOCUMENT flag, 468
Intent.FLAG_GRANT_READ_URI_PERMISSION flag, 306
Intent.FLAG_GRANT_WRITE_URI_PERMISSION flag, 321
intents
    (see also broadcast intents, explicit intents, extras, implicit intents, **Intent** class)
    about, 122
    checking for responding activities, 307
    communicating with, 122, 123
    and companion objects, 125
    extras, 124
    implicit vs explicit, 123, 291
    permissions and, 306
    regular vs broadcast, 573
    setting results, 128
    taking pictures with, 318-321
interceptors, 540
interfaces, with a single abstract method (SAMs), 26
interpolators, 631
**invalidate()** function (**View**), 618

# J

JavaScript
    enabling, 599
    injecting objects, 606
JavaScript Object Notation (JSON) (see JSON (JavaScript Object Notation))
javaScriptEnabled property (**WebSettings**), 600

Jetpack component libraries
    about, 6, 95
    Android KTX foundation library, 553
    androidx.lifecycle package, 78
    **AppCompat** theme, 417
    enabling, 5
    for backward compatibility, 142
    lifecycle-extensions architecture
    component library (**ViewModel**), 78
    Navigation architecture component library,
    260
Jetpack libraries
    (see also AppCompat foundation library,
    Room architecture component library,
    WorkManager architecture component library)
    Data Binding architecture component library
    (see data binding)
JSON (JavaScript Object Notation)
    about, 485
    arrays, 489
    deserializing, 489
    Gson library, 489
    Moshi library, 498
    objects, 489
**jumpDrawablesToCurrentState()** function
(**View**), 255

## K

Kotlin
    enabling in an Android Studio project, 6
    exceptions, compiled to java.lang exceptions,
    99
    extensions in Android KTX, 553
    functions public by default, 161
    Kotlin annotation processor tool (kotlin-
    kapt), 222
    Kotlin files in java directory, 20
    Mockito library and, 397
    single abstract method interfaces (SAMs) and,
    26
**kotlin.RuntimeException** class, 99

## L

lambda expressions, 389
-land qualifier, 72
language qualifiers, 330
language settings, device, 330
language-region qualifiers, 335
**last(...)** function (Array), 377
launcher activities, 131
LAUNCHER category (**Intent**), 131, 451
layer list drawables, 435
layout attributes
    android:background, 412
    android:drawableEnd, 52
    android:drawablePadding, 52
    android:icon, 285
    android:id, 24
    android:layout_gravity, 73
    android:layout_height, 16
    android:layout_margin, 218
    android:layout_width, 16
    android:orientation, 16
    android:padding, 218
    android:text, 16
    colorAccent, 419
    colorPrimary, 418
    colorPrimaryDark, 418
layout constraints (see constraints)
layout parameters, 208
**LayoutInflater** class, 33, 161
**LayoutManager** class, 181
layouts
    (see also constraints, graphical layout tool
    (Android Studio), layout attributes)
    about, 2
    alternative, 71-74
    animating, 219
    creating layout files, 71
    defining in XML, 13-16
    design guidelines, 210
    for images, 312-314
    inflating, 20, 161
    landscape, 71-74
    naming, 10
    nested vs flat, 196
    previewing, 18, 118, 342
    for property animation, 624
    root element, 15
    testing, 342
    using guidelines, 219
    view groups and, 11
    view hierarchy and, 15
lazy initialization, 86
-ldpi suffix, 49

left property (**View**), 627
libraries, 78
lifecycle awareness
   `@OnLifecycleEvent(Lifecycle.Event)` annotation, 512
   ending lifecycle observation, 513
   lifecycle observers and lifecycle owners, 511
lifecycle callbacks, 62
lifecycle owners, 239
lifecycle-aware components, 79, 239
`lifecycle-extensions` architecture component library (`androidx.lifecycle`), 78
**LifecycleObserver** interface, 511
**LifecycleOwner** interface
   about, 511
   `lifecycle` property, 513
**LinearLayout** class, 12, 15
Lint (see Android Lint)
**list(String)** function (**AssetManager**), 376
list-detail interfaces, 147
listeners
   about, 26
   as interfaces, 26
   setting in fragments, 162
   setting up, 26-28
lists
   displaying, 175
   getting item data, 185
**ListView** class, 193
live data transformations, 253
**LiveData** class
   about, 236
   and **LifecycleOwner**, 238
   **observe()**, 238
   **Observer** and, 238
   threading and, 236
   **Transformation** and, 253
**load(…)** function (**SoundPool**), 395
**loadLabel(PackageManager)** function (**ResolveInfo**), 451
local files, 231
local layout rect, 627
**LocalBroadcastManager** class, 587, 590
localization
   about, 329
   creating values resource files, 330
   default resources and, 333
   language qualifiers, 330

language-region qualifiers, 335
   and other configuration qualifiers, 338
   resource selection and Android versions, 335
   testing, 342
   Translations Editor, 334
**Log** class
   **d(String, String, Throwable)**, 101
   levels, 76
   logging messages, 63
Logcat
   (see also logging)
   about, 65, 66
   filtering, 32, 65, 82
   logging messages, 63
   setting log level, 99
   wrapping output, 487
logging
   exceptions, 101
   messages, 63
   stack traces, 101
   TAG constant, 63
**Looper** class
   as message loop manager, 516
   **Handler** and, 524
   **Handler**, **Message**, and, 518
LRU (least recently used) caching strategy, 537
**LRUCache** class, 537

# M

MAIN category (**Intent**), 131, 451
main thread
   about, 234
   @MainThread annotation, 508
   application not responding (ANR) error and, 235
   as message loop, 517
   communication with background threads, 516
   for UI updates, 235
   **IllegalStateException** and, 234
   **NetworkOnMainThreadException** and, 479
   UI and, 234
   UI responsiveness and, 235
@MainThread annotation, 508
**makeText(…)** function (**Toast**), 28
manifest
   about, 119
   adding network permissions, 480

adding uses-permission, 480
Android versions in, 137
build process and, 33
declaring **Activity** in, 119
margins, 218
master-detail interfaces, 147
matchers, for testing, 397
match_parent, 16
-mdpi suffix, 49
**MediaStore** class
about, 318
ACTION_IMAGE_CAPTURE action, 318
EXTRA_OUTPUT extra, 319
memory leaks, 84
**MenuItem** class, 283
menus
(see also app bar)
about, 277
app:showAsAction attribute, 278
creating, 280
creating XML file for, 278
defining in XML, 278
determining selected item, 283
overflow menu, 278
populating with items, 280
as resources, 278
responding to selections, 283
**Message** class
about, 518
**Handler** and, 517
messages
about, 518-531
message handlers, 518-531
message loop, 516
message queue, 516
**Migration** class (Room), 293
minimum required SDK, 137
minSdkVersion, 137
mipmap images, 438
mock objects, for testing, 397, 403, 409
model classes, using data keyword, 38
model layer, 40
model objects, 40
Model-View-Controller (MVC)
about, 40
benefits, 41
drawbacks, 368
flow of control, 41

when not to use, 41
Model-View-View Model (MVVM), 368, 382
Moshi library, 498
motion events, handling, 614-618
**MotionEvent** class
about, 615
actions, 615
**getAction()**, 615
**MotionLayout** class, 219
multi-window (split screen) mode
activity states and, 75
entering and exiting, 69
multi-resume support, 75
MVC (see Model-View-Controller)
MVVM (Model-View-View Model), 368, 382

**N**

namespaces
android, 420
Android resource XML, 15
app, 279
tools, 42
naming conventions
for classes, 9
for extras, 124
for layouts, 10
for menu files, 278
for packages, 6
for unused parameters, 273
for style inheritance, 414
Navigation architecture component library, 260
networking
about, 470
background threads and, 508
canceling requests, 499
configuration changes and, 493
limiting by network type, 558
permissions, 480
providing user control, 568
scheduling, 557
**StrictMode** and, 536
**NetworkOnMainThreadException** class, 479
**newInstance(…)** function (**Fragment**), 250
**newSingleThreadExecutor()** function
(**Executors**), 257
9-patch images, 439
nonexistent activity state, 62

**Notification** class
  (see also notifications)
  about, 565
  **NotificationManager** and, 565
**NotificationCompat** class, 566
**NotificationManager** class
  **Notification** and, 565
  **notify(…)**, 565
notifications
  about, 563-567
  configuring, 566
  filtering from app in the foreground, 574
  notification channels, 563
**notify(…)** function (**NotificationManager**), 565
null coalescing (??) operator, 389

## O

**ObjectAnimator** class, 627
**Observable** interface, 386
**observe()** function (**LiveData**), 238
**onActivityCreated(Bundle?)** function
(**Fragment**), 172
**onActivityResult(…)** function (**Activity**), 129
**onActivityResult(…)** function (**Fragment**), 268
**onAttach(Context?)** function (**Fragment**), 172
**OnCheckedChangeListener** interface, 165
**onCleared()** function (**ViewModel**), 79
**OnClickListener** interface, 26
**onCreate()** function (**Application**), overriding,
228
**onCreate(Bundle?)** function (**Activity**), 61
**onCreate(Bundle?)** function (**Fragment**), 161,
172
**onCreateDialog(Bundle?)** function
(**DialogFragment**), 265
**onCreateOptionsMenu(Menu)** function
(**Activity**), 280
**onCreateOptionsMenu(…)** function (**Fragment**),
280
**onCreateView(…)** function (**Fragment**), 161, 172
**onDestroy()** function (**Activity**), 61
**onDestroy()** function (**Fragment**), 172
**onDestroyView()** function (**Fragment**), 172
**onDetach()** function (**Fragment**), 172
**onDraw(Canvas)** function (**View**), 618
**OneTimeWorkRequest** class (**WorkRequest**), 557

@OnLifecycleEvent(Lifecycle.Event)
annotation, 512
**onOptionsItemSelected(MenuItem)** function
(**Fragment**), 280, 283
**onPause()** function (**Activity**), 61
**onPause()** function (**Fragment**), 172
**onProgressChanged(…)** function
(**WebChromeClient**), 602
**OnQueryTextListener(…)** interface
(**SearchView**), 546
**onReceivedTitle(…)** function
(**WebChromeClient**), 602
**onRestoreInstanceState(Parcelable)** function
(**View**), 620
**onResume()** function (**Activity**), 61
**onResume()** function (**Fragment**), 172
**onSaveInstanceState()** function (**View**), 620
**onSaveInstanceState(Bundle)** function
(**Activity**), 88
**onSaveInstanceState(Bundle)** function
(**Fragment**), 161
**onStart()** function (**Activity**), 61
**onStart()** function (**Fragment**), 172
**onStop()** function (**Activity**), 61
**onStop()** function (**Fragment**), 172
**onTextChanged(…)** function (**TextWatcher**), 163
**onTouchEvent(MotionEvent)** function (**View**),
614
**OnTouchListener** interface (**View**), 614
**onViewCreated(…)** function (**Fragment**), 172
**openFileInput(…)** function (**FileInputStream**),
315
**openFileOutput(…)** function
(**FileInputStream**), 315
overflow menu, 278
override keyword, 64
overriding functions, Android Studio shortcut,
160
overview screen, 67, 457

## P

**PackageManager** class
  about, 307
  querying, 320
  **resolveActivity(…)**, 307
packages, naming, 6
padding, 218

**Paint** class, 618
parameters, _ to denote unused, 273
**Parcelable** interface, 620
paused activity state, 62, 75
perceived lifetime of a fragment, 511
**PeriodicWorkRequest** class (**WorkRequest**), 557
permissions
    adding to manifest, 480
    android:grantUriPermissions attribute, 316, 321
    for broadcast receivers, 577
    for contacts database, 306
    Intent.FLAG_GRANT_READ_URI_PERMISSION flag, 306
    Intent.FLAG_GRANT_WRITE_URI_PERMISSION flag, 321
    INTERNET, 480
    normal, 480
    private, 577
    protection levels, 579
    Request App Permissions guide, 309
    revoking, 325
    runtime, 309
photos
    capturing full resolution, 319
    capturing thumbnails, 319
    designating file location for, 317
    scaling and displaying bitmaps, 322-326
    taking with intents, 318-321
**PhotoView** class, 323
placeholders (in format strings), 294
**play(Animator)** function (**AnimatorSet**), 634
**play(…)** function (**SoundPool**), 396
**PointF** class, 615
**post(Runnable)** function (**Handler**), 525
preloading, 537
presses (see touch events)
@PrimaryKey annotation (Room), 223
processes
    about, 464
    death, 88
    "task killer" apps and, 466
progress indicator, hiding, 602
project tool window (Android Studio), 8
project window (Android Studio), 8
projects
    adding dependencies, 78
    adding resources, 50

app/java directory, 20
    configuring, 5
    creating, 3-7
    layout, 10
    res/layout directory, 21
    res/menu directory, 278
    res/values directory, 21
    setting package name, 5
    setting project name, 5
property animation (see animation)
protection level values, 579
**putCharSequence(…)** function (**Bundle**), 249
**putInt(…)** function (**Bundle**), 249
**putSerializable(…)** function (**Bundle**), 249

## Q

@Query annotation
    in Retrofit, 542
    in Room, 226

## R

**randomUUID()** function (**UUID**), 155
Recents button, 67
**RecyclerView** class
    about, 180-188
    as a **ViewGroup**, 182
    creating views, 190
    for displaying a grid, 472
    for downloading on demand, 509
    item views, 182
    **LayoutManager** and, 181
    **setOnItemClickListener(…)**, 594
    **ViewHolder** and, 183
    vs **ListView** and **GridView**, 193
release key, 33
**release()** function (**SoundPool**), 407
**replace(…)** function (**FragmentTransaction**), 247
**replace(…)** function (String), 377
repositories, 227, 484
repository pattern for app architecture, 227, 484
request code (**Activity**), 127
res/layout directory, 21
res/menu directory, 278
res/values directory, 17, 21
res/values/colors.xml file, 412
res/values/styles.xml file, 412

**resolveActivity(…)** function
(**PackageManager**), 307
**ResolveInfo** class
    about, 451
    **ActivityInfo** and, 454
    **loadLabel(PackageManager)**, 451
resource IDs
    about, 21-24
    + prefix in, 24
resources
    (see also configuration qualifiers, drawables,
    layouts, menus, string resources)
    about, 21
    adding, 50
    alternative, 338-342
    vs assets, 373
    default, 333
    localizing, 329-332
    location, 21
    referencing in XML, 52
    string, 16, 17
**Resources.NotFoundException** class, 333
result code (**Activity**), 128
resumed activity state, 62, 75
retainInstance property (**Fragment**), 532
Retrofit library
    about, 474-484
    **Call** class, 475
    **Converter.Factory** class, 477
    defining an API interface, 475
    **enqueue(…)**, 478
    **Retrofit.Builder()** class, 476
**Retrofit.Builder()** class (Retrofit), 476
**revokeUriPermission(…)** function (**Context**),
325
right property (**View**), 627
Room architecture component library
    @Dao annotation, 226
    @Database annotation, 224, 294
    @Entity annotation, 223
    @Insert annotation, 256
    @PrimaryKey annotation, 223
    @Query annotation, 226
    @TypeConverter annotation, 225
    @TypeConverters annotation, 225
    @Update annotation, 256
    accessing a database, 227
    adding database properties, 293, 294

defining a data access object (DAO), 226
defining a database class, 224
defining database entities, 223
defining database primary key, 223
instantiating a database, 229
**LiveData** and, 236
**Migration** class, 293
**Room.databaseBuilder()**, 229
setting up a database, 222-225
specifying type converters, 225
SQL commands, 226
SQLite in, 224
updating database version, 293, 294
rotation
    activity lifecycle and, 70-74, 163
    fragment lifecycle and, 163
run configurations (Android Studio), 406
running on device, 54, 55
RxJava, 588

## S

SAMs (single abstract method interfaces), 26
sandbox, 231
saved instance state
    about, 88
    strengths and weaknesses, 93
    vs **ViewModel** class, 93
scale-independent pixel, 53
scope, 81
screen orientation, 72
screen pixel density, 49, 52, 333
screen size, determining, 343
SDK versions
    (see also compatibility)
    about, 138
    codenames, 135
    compatibility, 136
    installing, xx
    listed, 135
    minimum required, 137
    target, 137
    updating, xxi
search
    about, 539-552
    in Flickr, 540-543
    integrating into app, 539
    user-initiated, 544-548

**SearchView** class
about, 544-548
bug, 548
**OnQueryTextListener(…)**, 546
responding to user interactions, 546
**setArguments(…)** function (**Fragment**), 250
**setClassName(…)** function (**Intent**), 455
**setContentView(…)** function (**Activity**), 20
**setHasOptionsMenu(Boolean)** function
(**Fragment**), 280
**setOnClickListener(OnClickListener)**
function (**View**), 26
**setOnItemClickListener(…)** function
(**RecyclerView**), 594
**setOnTouchListener(…)** function (**View**), 614
**setResult(…)** function (**Activity**), 128
**setTargetFragment(…)** function (**Fragment**), 271
**setText(Int)** function (**TextView**), 126
shape drawables, 431
**ShapeDrawable** class, 431
**SharedPreferences** class, 549
**shouldOverrideUrlLoading(…)** function
(**WebViewClient**), 600
**show()** function (**Toast**), 28
**show(…)** function (**DialogFragment**), 266
simulator (see emulator)
single abstract method interfaces (SAMs), 26
single activity architecture, 244
Single Responsibility Principle, 382
singletons
about, 228
activity/fragment lifecycles and, 228
benefits and drawbacks, 242
solutions file, 49
**SoundPool** class
about, 393, 394
audio playback, 396-407
creating, 393
**load(…)**, 395
loading sounds, 394
**play(…)**, 396
**release()**, 407
unloading sounds, 407
sp (scale-independent pixel), 53
**split(…)** function (**String**), 377
stack traces
in Logcat, 99
logging, 101

**startActivity(Intent)** function (**Activity**),
122, 298
**startActivity(Intent)** function (**Fragment**),
299
**startActivityForResult(…)** function
(**Activity**), 127
stashed activity state, 92
state list drawables, 433
stopped activity state, 62
**StrictMode** class, 536
@string/ syntax, 16
string resources
about, 16
creating, 17
referencing, 52
res/values/strings.xml, 17
strings file, 16
String type
**fileList(…)**, 315
**replace(…)**, 377
**split(…)**, 377
@StringRes annotation, 38
strings, format, 294
Structured Query Language (SQL), 226
styles
about, 217, 412-415
inheritance, 414, 427
modifying widget attributes, 423-426
res/values/styles.xml file, 412
themes and, 217
system icons, 285-287

**T**

TAG constant, 63
TalkBack
about, 346
Android widgets' inherent support, 350
enabling, 347
linear navigation by swiping, 351
non-text elements and, 353-356
target fragments, 271
target SDK version, 137, 138
targetSdkVersion, 137
tasks
about, 456
Back button and, 456
vs processes, 464, 466

starting new, 458-461
switching between, 457
@Test annotation, 401
**TextView** class
    example, 12
    inheritance, 58
    **setText(Int)**, 126
    tools:text and, 42
**TextWatcher** interface, **onTextChanged(…)**, 163
theme attribute, 416
themes
    about, 416-422
    accessing attributes, 428
    adding colors, 418
    attributes, 418
    modifying, 416
    overriding attributes, 419-422
    styles and, 217
threads
    (see also background threads, main thread)
    @MainThread annotation, 508
    @UiThread annotation, 508
    @WorkerThread annotation, 508
    communication between main and background threads, 516-526
    **Handler** and, 517
    main vs background, 479
    message queue, 516
    processes and, 464
    as sequences of execution, 234
    UI, 234
ticker text, 565
**TimeInterpolator** class, 631
tinting, widgets, 419
**Toast** class
    **makeText(…)**, 28
    **show()**, 28
toasts, 27, 28
tool windows (Android Studio), 8
**Toolbar** class, 288
tools:text attribute, 42
top property (**View**), 627
touch events
    action constants, 615
    handling, 192, 614-618
    handling with **GestureDetector**, 620
    **MotionEvent** and, 615

recommended minimum size for touch targets, 362
transformation properties
    pivotX, 629
    pivotY, 629
    rotation, 629
    scaleX, 629
    scaleY, 629
    translationX, 629
    translationY, 629
transitions framework, for animation, 636
Translations Editor, 334
-tvdpi suffix, 49
@TypeConverter annotation (Room), 225
@TypeConverters annotation (Room), 225
**TypeEvaluator** class, 633

## U

UI fragments (see fragments)
UI thread (see main thread)
@UiThread annotation, 508
**UninitializedPropertyAccessException** class, 99, 492
unit testing
    about, 393
    @Before annotation, 400, 401
    Hamcrest tool, 397
    vs integration testing, 399
    JUnit testing framework, 398
    matchers, 397
    mock objects, 397, 403, 409
    Mockito tool, 397
    naming conventions for, 400
    testing frameworks, 398
    testing object interactions, 402
@Update annotation, 256
**Uri** class, 319
user interfaces
    activities vs fragments in, 148
    defined by layout, 2
    flexibility in, 148
    laying out, 10-18
    UI fragments and, 149
<uses-feature> tag, 327
**UUID.randomUUID()** function, 155

# V

variables view (Android Studio), 105
versions (Android SDK) (see SDK versions)
versions (firmware), 135
**View** class
  (see also views, widgets)
  bottom, 627
  **draw()**, 618
  height, 627
  **invalidate()**, 618
  **jumpDrawablesToCurrentState()**, 255
  left, 627
  **OnClickListener** interface, 26
  **onDraw(Canvas)**, 618
  **onRestoreInstanceState(Parcelable)**, 620
  **onSaveInstanceState()**, 620
  **onTouchEvent(MotionEvent)**, 614
  **OnTouchListener**, 614
  right, 627
  **setOnClickListener(OnClickListener)**, 26
  **setOnTouchListener(…)**, 614
  subclasses, 11, 58
  top, 627
view models (in MVVM), 382
**ViewDataBinding.executePendingBindings()**, 385
**ViewGroup** class, 11, 15, 73
**ViewHolder** class, as **OnClickListener**, 192
**ViewModel** class
  about, 79-94
  activity lifecycle and, 81
  fragment lifecycle and, 178, 493
  **onCleared()**, 79
  for storage, 177
  strengths and weaknesses, 93
  vs saved instance state, 93
**ViewModelProvider** class, 80
**ViewModelProviders** class, 80
views
  about, 11
  action, 544
  adding in graphical layout editor, 204
  creating custom views, 612
  creation by **RecyclerView**, 190
  custom, 612-614
  draw order, 626
  hierarchy, 15

invalid, 618
persisting, 620
simple vs composite, 612
size settings, 202
touch events and, 614-618
using fully qualified name in layout, 613
view groups, 11
view layer, 40
view objects, 40
widgets, 11
**ViewTreeObserver** class, 328
virtual devices (see emulator)

# W

web content
  browsing via implicit intent, 594
  converting web response data, 476
  displaying within an activity, 596
  enabling JavaScript, 599
  in Chrome Custom Tabs, 608
web rendering events, responding to, 600
**WebChromeClient** interface
  about, 602
  for enhancing appearance of **WebView**, 601
  **onProgressChanged(…)**, 602
  **onReceivedTitle(…)**, 602
**WebSettings** class, 600
**WebView** class
  for presenting web content, 596
  handling rotation, 604
  vs custom UI, 605
**WebViewClient** class
  about, 600
  **shouldOverrideUrlLoading(…)**, 600
widgets
  about, 11
  adding in graphical layout editor, 204
  attributes, 14
  **Button**, 12, 57
  **CheckBox**, 156
  defining in XML, 13-16
  **EditText**, 156
  **FrameLayout**, 73
  **ImageButton**, 57
  **LinearLayout**, 12, 15
  margins, 218
  modifying attributes, 423-426

padding, 218
references, 25
styles and, 412
and TalkBack, 350-356
**TextView**, 12, 42
in view hierarchy, 15
as view layer, 40
wiring up, 25
wiring up in fragments, 162
work requests
about, 557
constraints for, 558
**Worker** class
about, 555
**doWork()**, 556
enabling and disabling, 568
performing synchronous tasks, 560
scheduling with **WorkRequest**, 557
@WorkerThread annotation, 508
WorkManager architecture component library
(see also individual class names)
about, 555
**Constraints**, 558
**Worker**, 555
**WorkRequest**, 555
**WorkRequest** class
about, 555
**Constraints** and, 558
scheduling a **Worker**, 557
subclasses, 557
wrap_content, 16

## X

–xhdpi, –xxhdpi, –xxxhdpi suffixes, 49
XML
Android namespace, 15
referencing resources in, 52
XML drawables (see drawables)

# BIG NERD RANCH
# CODING BOOTCAMPS

Looking for additional support? Look into one of our coding bootcamps. Students learn from authors and full-time consultants who work on projects every day. Don't take our word for it; hear from our alumni:

*LIFE CHANGING. The Big Nerd Ranch changed my life. I was working as a lawyer and writing software on the side. I wanted to transition to writing software full-time, but I didn't have the confidence to make the switch. I heard about the Big Nerd Ranch from a friend and I decided to attend a seven-day bootcamp in Atlanta. I was very nervous because I wasn't a professional software developer and I didn't have a computer science degree. The first morning, my instructor made me feel at ease. As we worked through the materials and the examples, I noticed that I knew as much or more than my peers. I took advantage of the lunch and dinner time to speak with my instructors and peers and my confidence continued to grow. I got home and, with my Big Nerd Ranch certification in hand, I applied to several software development jobs. After several offers, I closed up my law firm and started my new career as a software developer. I still work as a software developer. I even write software for some of my lawyer friends. All thanks to The Big Nerd Ranch.*

—Larry Staton, Jr., Alumnus

**We offer classes in Android, Kotlin, Front End, iOS, Swift, design, and more. Take $100 off your bootcamp tuition by using code BNRGUIDE100 when you register.**

Alumni gain access to an exclusive developer community to network and nurture their career growth.

**www.bignerdranch.com**